New Waves in Innovation Management Research

Edited by

Marcus Tynnhammar

ISPIM, United Kingdom

Luleå University of Technology, Sweden

Series in Innovation Studies

 VERNON PRESS

www.vernonpress.com

In the Americas:
Vernon Press
1000 N West Street,
Suite 1200, Wilmington,
Delaware 19801
United States

In the rest of the world:
Vernon Press
C/Sancti Espiritu 17,
Malaga, 29006
Spain

Series in Innovation Studies

Library of Congress Control Number: 2018948070

ISBN: 978-1-62273-530-3

Also available:

ISBN: 978-1-62273-434-4 (Hardback)

Cover design by Vernon Press.

Cover image: designed by starline / Freepik.

Table of contents

List of Figures   *vii*

List of Tables   *ix*

Introduction   *xi*
Marcus Tynnhammar

Chapter 1   **The Resilient Innovation Team:**
             a Study of Teams Coping with Critical
             Incidents during Innovation Projects   1

             Peter R.A. Oeij

Chapter 2   **The Benefits of Trusted Bridging Chains**
             for Open Innovation   19

             Margarethe Lombard

Chapter 3   **An Analytical Approach to Assess**
             the Matching Quality of Academic Partners
             for Open Innovation in the Form
             of University-Industry Collaboration   37

             Nisit Manotungvorapun*, Nathasit Gerdsri

Chapter 4   **Exploring Inter-Organizational Collaboration**
             for Innovation in a Regional Ecosystem   55

             Agnieszka Radziwon*

Chapter 5   **The Contribution of Socially Driven**
             Businesses and Innovations
             to Social Sustainability   69

             Rakhshanda Khan*

Chapter 6   **Awakening Employee Creativity**
             in Organizations   97

             Wenjing Cai*

Chapter 7   **Building Higher-Order Capabilities: Insights**
             from Resource-Scarce Environments   115

Dr. Pavan Soni

Chapter 8   **Investigating Innovation Champions
              in the Nonprofit Sector**   129
              Courtney Molloy*

Chapter 9   **Design and Evaluation of a Process Model
              for the Early Stages of Product Innovation**   149
              Patrick Brandtner*

Chapter 10   **Firm Responses to Disruptive Innovations**   163
              Amber Geurts*

Chapter 11   **A Framework for Accelerated Product
              Innovation in a Big Data Environment**   175
              Yuanzhu Zhan*

Chapter 12   **A Framework to Evaluate the Impact of ICT
              Usage on Collaborative Product Development
              Performance in Manufacturing Firms**   191
              C. W. Chathurani Silva*

Chapter 13   **The Effects of Procedural Knowledge
              Transparency on Adoption in Corporate
              Social Networks**   205
              Bjørn J. M. Jensen*

Chapter 14   **Technology Planning for Aligning Emerging
              Business Models and Regulatory Structures -
              the Case of Electric Vehicle Charging and the
              Smart Grid**   219
              Kelly R. Cowan

Chapter 15   **From Gamestorming to Mobile Learning:
              a Conceptual Framework and a Gaming
              Proposition to Explore the Design
              of Flourishing Business Models**   235
              Albert Lejeune*

Chapter 16   **Chinese Multinational Enterprises'
R&D "Going out": a Prelude
to Inclusive Globalization**   249

Sheng Wu*

Chapter 17   **The Impact of Strategic Alliances and Internal
Knowledge Sources on the Manufacturing
Firms' Innovation and on Their Financial
Performance: a Comparison between
Brazil and Europe**   273

Fábio O. Paula*

Chapter 18   **Reverse Innovation: Towards a New Global
Innovation Model for Multinationals**   287

Marine Hadengue*

Chapter 19   **Never Venture, Never Win! The Chinese Rush
to Innovation and Regional Development**   303

Antonio Crupi*

Chapter 20   **Innovation Management Systems: Systematic
Structuration, Semantic Interoperability
and Multi-Dimensional Measurement
for Continuous Performance Improvement**   323

Lamyaa EL BASSITI*

Chapter 21   **First Things First - Think before You Decide
the How, What and Who of Idea Screening**   349

Johan Netz*

Chapter 22   **Consumer Resistance to Innovations -
Essays on Antecedents, Manifestations
and Ways of Overcoming It**   365

Nadine Hietschold*

Chapter 23   **Entrepreneurial Opportunity Perception:
Analysing the Effect of the Learning Style**   379

Alexandros Kakouris*

Chapter 24   **Antecedents and Consequences
of Exploration and Exploitation Decisions:**

Evidence from Corporate Venture
Capital Investing   391

Eui Ju Jeon*

Chapter 25   A Journey through University Technology
              Transfer, Organizational Learning
              and the Search for Innovation   403

Roberta Pellegrino

Chapter 26   Processes and Ecosystems of Innovation with
              a Multi-KET Approach to Foster Technology
              Transfer and Commercialization of
              Nanotechnologies in the Field of Healthcare   417

Cristina Páez-Avilés*

Chapter 27   Innovation Hubs in Africa: Assemblers
              of Technology Entrepreneurs   435

Nicolas Friederici*

Chapter 28   Exploring Knowledge Intensity
              in Entrepreneurship: A Quantitative Study
              of Knowledge, Innovation and Performance
              in Entrepreneurial Firms   455

Ethan A. Gifford*

Acronyms   *467*

Index   *469*

List of Figures

Figure 1.1 Framework of the research.   6

Figure 2.1 Direct relationships versus searching through
trusted bridging chains.   22

Figure 3.1 Research methodology   43

Figure 3.2 The Complementarity vs. Compatibility Matrix   45

Figure 3.3 The matching quality radar charts of university A   46

Figure 3.4 Three conditions of the matching quality translated
from the matching quality radar   47

Figure 4.1 Key characteristics of the ecosystem and its members Source:
Radziwon (2017)   60

Figure 6.1 An organizing framework for studies in the dissertation.   103

Figure 7.1 Research model depicting the task environment,
managerial activities, and the creation of capabilities   120

Figure 8.1 Conceptual framework – championing and context   132

Figure 9.1 Summary of the research approach   154

Figure 9.2 Structural overview of the develop process model   156

Figure 11.1 Framework for accelerated product innovation
in a big data environment   181

Figure 12.1 Finalized framework for evaluating the impact of ICT usage
on CPD performance   197

Figure 13.1 Theoretical Model   210

Figure 14.1 Key Elements and Drivers Contributing to Smart Grid   222

Figure 14.2 Balancing Planning Perspectives in Regulated Industries   224

Figure 14.3 Summary of Research Gaps, Goals, and Questions   226

Figure 14.4 Research Outline   226

Figure 15.1 From Cube 1: Three Challenges
from the Physical Environment   243

Figure 16.1 Number of overseas R&D subsidiaries   251

Figure 16.2 Regional distribution of parent firms   251

Figure 16.3 Global distribution of overseas R&D subsidiaries   252

Figure 16.4 Industrial distribution of overseas R&D subsidiaries   252

Figure 16.5 Nature of Overseas R&D theory system   255

Figure 16.6 Research roadmap   258

Figure 16.7 Theoretical framework on location determinants
of Chinese firms' overseas R&D subsidiaries   259

Figure 16.8 Huawei's global R&D network   261

Figure 16.9 Evolution of Huawei's global R&D network   262

Figure 16.10 betweenness centrality and influencer   265
Figure 16.11 entry of actors into the network   266
Figure 16.12 Huawei's strategic route for production
    internationalization and R&D globalization   266
Figure 16.13 Global R&D organizational configurations system
    and adoption mechanism   267
Figure 16.14 Adoption of global R&D organizational
    configurations modes   268
Figure 17.1 Theoretical model   277
Figure 20.1 GenID Main Activities Model   336
Figure 20.2 GenID Lifecycle Model   337
Figure 20.3 GenID Learning Engine   338
Figure 20.4 GenID Ontology Main Concepts   339
Figure 20.5 GenID Actor Sub-Ontology Knowledge View   340
Figure 20.6 GenID Core-Idea Sub-Ontology Knowledge View   341
Figure 20.7 Innovation Context Sub-Ontology Knowledge View   342
Figure 21.1 Connections between projects, papers
    and research questions.   354
Figure 23.1 Shane's (2000) model for the effect of prior knowledge
    on opportunity recognition.   382
Figure 26.1 Summary of methodology used in the empirical study.   423
Figure 26.2 MCA for each categorical variable. Ellipses plot. Variables:
    (a) level of cross-fertilization, (b) technological distance,
    (c) technological effort, (d) access to information,
    (e) previous collaboration, (f) type of collaboration,
    (g) market orientation, (h) customer prioritization,
    and (i) experience in TRLs.   425

List of Tables

Table 1.1 Learnings from HROs for innovation teams   11

Table 2.1 Configurations for good and bad solutions   27

Table 3.1 Examples of studies on matching approaches for UICs   41

Table 3.2 The numeric results   44

Table 3.3 The matching quality gap bar charts of university A   47

Table 7.1 General model of capability creation   124

Table 7.2 Summary of how sequence/salience varies
with external environment   125

Table 7.3 Elucidation of four environment-agnostic steps
to capability creation across the six cases   126

Table 9.1 Summary of identified literature gaps and goals of the thesis   152

Table 10.1 Market size and the market share (turnover) of digital music   168

Table 13.1 Parameter Estimates Found Significant
for Key Predictor Variables   213

Table 13.2 Confirmatory Answers (x) to RQs   214

Table 16.1 Variables, indicators and data source   259

Table 16.2 Regression results: Determinants of location choice
of Chinese MNEs' overseas R&D   263

Table 17.1 Model's hypotheses   277

Table 17.2 Model's variables – Brazil and Europe   278

Table 17.3 Results of SEM – Brazilian firms   281

Table 17.4 Results of SEM – European firms   281

Table 18.1 Summary of the research organization   292

Table 18.2 Summary of methodologies used in the dissertation
(by article)   293

Table 19.1 list of variables model 1   309

Table 19.2 list of variables model 2   310

Table 19.3 list of variables model 3   312

Table 19.4 results model 1   313

Table 19.5 results model 2   315

Table 19.6 results model 3 – first least square   316

Table 19.7 results model 3 – second least square   317

Table 20.1 Innovation Management Process Models Comparison
(El Bassiti et al., 2017)   327

Table 20.2 Innovation Ontologies Evaluation (El Bassiti, 2017)   329

Table 20.3 Innovation Performance Models Review
(El Bassiti a Ajhoun, 2016)   330

Table 22.1 Future research agenda 376
Table 22.2 Strategies for decision-makers 377
Table 25.1 Variables and Definitions 408
Table 25.2 Results 409
Table 27.1 Theoretical framework based on incubator/incubation
literature 440
Table 27.2 Differences between broker-type intermediaries,
incubators, and hubs 444
Table 28.1 Sectors included in the samples 460

Introduction

Marcus Tynnhammar

ISPIM, United Kingdom

Luleå University of Technology, Sweden

E-mail: marcus.tynnhammar@ltu.se

The ISPIM Dissertation Award was launched in 2011 to recognize the prolific contribution that PhD dissertations make to the field of Innovation Management. With the generous support of Innovation Leaders (*a global research programme that identifies the world's most effective innovators*), three winners are selected from the 100+ entries every year and receive their award at the annual ISPIM Innovation Conference.

Through this publication, the 2018 ISPIM Dissertation Award casts its spotlight beyond the top three dissertations and onto a much greater number of top submissions that cover a broad range of topics. It illustrates the depth and breadth of the coming wave in innovation management research.

Articles in the first section explore the theme of **Collaboration**. "The Resilient Innovation Team" suggests how a team might handle "critical incidents" during their projects. Next "The Benefits of Trusted Bridging Chains for Open Innovation," illustrates how trust in the form of social capital plays a big part in shaping Open Innovation relationships. Continuing with the theme of Open Innovation, "An Analytical Approach to Assess the Matching Quality of Academic Partners for Open Innovation in the Form of University-Industry Collaboration" showcases how partners can be selected, in particular when the perfect match between academia and industry is rare. "Exploring inter-organizational collaboration for innovation in a regional ecosystem" is the fourth contribution and it also deals with inter-organizational collaboration but moves the lens to understand how SMEs might work together in regional ecosystems. The final article in the section: "The Contribution of Socially Driven Businesses and Innovations to Social Sustainability," puts collaboration in a social setting by examining the importance of socially-driven businesses for sustainable development.

The second section is on **Creativity**, and starts with "Awakening employee creativity in organizations," which shows the different ways to increase employee creativity, from both the employee and employer perspectives. Next, "Building Higher-Order Capabilities" shows that creativity is a crucial ingredient when pursuing big endeavors with limited resources. Another way to study creativity is to look at how innovation champions promote innovations within their organizations, and this is the focus of the third article in this section: "Investigating innovation champions in the non-profit sector." Next, "Design and Evaluation of a Process Model for the Early Stages of Product Innovation" shows how the early creative phase of development can be structured. The final contribution to the section, "Firm Responses to Disruptive Innovations," leads into the following section on Digitalization by looking at how firms need to be creative in their response to digital disruption.

Digitalization has really become a popular topic in Innovation Management. "A Framework for Accelerated Product Innovation in a Big Data Environment" deals with Big Data and its effect on new product development. "A Framework to Evaluate the Impact of ICT Usage on Collaborative Product Development Performance in Manufacturing Firms" refines the focus to the effects of Big Data on collaboration. One way to collaborate is through social media, and the contribution "The Effects of Procedural Knowledge Transparency on Adoption in Corporate Social Networks" shows how this can have an effect on knowledge sharing. Another new disruptive technology is electric cars, and the article "Technology Planning for Aligning Emerging Business Models and Regulatory Structures" shows how companies can adapt to fit within these types of disruptions. The section closes with "From gamestorming to mobile learning," which shows how business models are changing to fit with digitalization.

Globalization is a well-examined topic and the next section has examples from all over the world on how countries adapt and try to be competitive in the global arena. "Chinese Multinational Enterprises' R&D" explains how China is reaching out to the global market. Next, "The Impact of Strategic Alliances and Internal Knowledge Sources on the Manufacturing Firms' Innovation and on Their Financial Performance" continues the globalization theme by comparing Brazil and Europe in terms of financial performance. The contribution of "Reverse Innovation" is to look at globalization from the perspective of how multinationals might need a new innovation model to succeed globally. And finally, "Never venture, never win! The Chinese rush to innovation and regional development" brings us back to China for a look at how regional development is being encouraged as a path to innovation.

The **Management** section starts with "Innovation Management Systems," on how to manage for continuous performance improvements. A crucial part of idea management is the ability to think before you decide, which is dealt with in "First things first - think before you decide." Besides managing operations and similar aspects, there is also a need to handle consumer resistance, which is explained in "Consumer Resistance to Innovations," which suggests how to overcome such resistance. Next, "Entrepreneurial opportunity perception" discusses the learning styles of entrepreneurs. The final section looks at management through a financial lens: "Antecedents and Consequences of Exploration and Exploitation Decisions" deals with venture capital investments and innovation.

The final section in this book has four contributions on **Technology Transfer**. It starts with "A Journey through University Technology Transfer," on how academia affects innovation beyond the academic sphere. "Processes and Ecosystems of Innovation" is next and sheds light on effective ecosystems and the application of nanotechnology. Another common area for technology transfer is Innovation Hubs, and in the second to last article, "Innovation Hubs in Africa," we learn more about how these hubs assist in helping entrepreneurs. The final contribution, "Exploring knowledge intensity in entrepreneurship," also deals with entrepreneurs by looking at the role of knowledge intensity.

This publication provides both a showcase of what the latest generation of scholars are contributing to innovation management's body of knowledge as well as an insight into what they find significant and what might become important for the field as a whole over time. Scholars from 20 countries from Europe, Asia, North America and Africa are represented.

Chapter 1

The Resilient Innovation Team: a Study of Teams Coping with Critical Incidents during Innovation Projects

Peter R.A. Oeij

E-mail: peter.oeij@tno.nl

Abstract: Organising in a mindful way is key to helping innovation teams become more resilient and thereby increase the chances of innovation success. Organising in a mindful way, called 'mindful infrastructure,' implies creating the right conditions for teams to excel. To this end, four elements are crucial. When teams are 1) feeling psychologically safe, 2) experience a learning environment, 3) have a say in decision-making, and 4) see that leadership creates synergy, the foundation is laid for resilient team behavior. In turn, this 'team innovation resilience behavior' enables teams to successfully deal with critical incidents, which, otherwise, could lead to innovation failure. Resilient innovation teams are extremely alert to small things that can become big problems, hate to jump to conclusions, link management goals with operational practice, value expertise stronger than rank, and can radically change course if required. This helps them keep their innovation projects on track and thus improve the chances of innovation success. This study has sought to investigate the scientific underpinnings of mindful infrastructure and team innovation resilience behavior. In addition, it provides practical guidelines for building a Resilient Innovation Team.

Keywords: Innovation; teams; project management; resilience; mindfulness; HRO.

1. Introduction

The study *The resilient innovation team: a study of teams coping with critical incidents during innovation projects* (Oeij 2017a) is rooted in the author's fascination about why so many innovations seem to fail (Sauser, Reilly and Shenhar, 2009). Innovations, in this study, are understood as new products, new services, new processes, or new working methods that are being developed in projects. Unlike other studies that explain reasons for innovation failure due to the role of markets, finance, technology, consumer demands and organizational developments, this study focuses on team behavior as a reason for innovation failure (Azim et al., 2010). The researcher's curiosity was driven by initial questions such as: do innovation projects fail because such projects are complex? (Cicmil and Marshall, 2005). Do they fail because people in teams become defensive when there is tension, uncertainty and fear (Argyris, 2010) and become risk avoidant (Andriopoulos, Gotsi, Lewis and Ingram 2017)? Somewhere, outside the world of innovation management, there are teams that hardly ever fail. These are teams working in high-risk situations, namely teams in nuclear plants, on aircraft-carriers, in operating rooms, and in fire-brigades (Weick and Sutcliffe, 2007). Such teams are called HRO-teams after the High Reliability Organizations (HROs) that they are part of. HROs are studied in fields of safety and crisis management. Why do such teams hardly ever fail? Moreover, can innovation teams learn from HRO-teams? These questions led to the assumptions behind this study, namely, that knowledge from the field of safety and crisis management and their HRO-principles could be applied to the field of innovation management.

HRO-teams are characterized by the following: they are embedded in an organizational context that nourishes trust, learning, commitment and supportive leadership: a mindful infrastructure. Due to that context, particular team behavior is enabled that minimizes making mistakes and gets a team back on track should a mistake or accident occur. That type of team behavior is based on five HRO-principles (Weick and Sutcliffe, 2007), explained in Section 2. We mapped this team behavior to innovation teams and called it *innovation resilience behavior*. HRO-teams can minimize accidents and contain their escalation should they nonetheless occur: they have excellent team results. However, team results of innovation teams are different, namely achieving progress and positive results instead of the failure of innovations. Therefore, the research is directed at the applicability of HRO-principles in the context of innovation (management).

There are many reasons why projects and innovations fail or succeed, and there are several overviews of possible factors (Cooke-Davies, 2002; Han and Lorenz, 2015; Sauser, Reilly and Shenhar, 2009). Shenhar and Dvir (2007) argue that most people believe projects fail due to poor planning, a lack of communication, or inadequate resources, but the evidence suggests that failure is often found even in well-managed projects run by experienced managers and supported by highly regarded organizations. Projects are strongly affected by the dynamics of the environment, technology, or markets. That is why 'one size does not fit all,' and project success demands an adaptive approach to adjust the project to the environment, the task, and the goal (Shenhar and Dvir, 2007). Being able to adjust a project requires a shift of attention from only the 'hard factors' to including the 'soft factors.' Hard factors, such as the project management's iron triangle - the triple constraint of the criteria to complete the project on time, within budget and within performance goals or requirements - remain important, but soft factors, such as behavior, leadership, skills, communication, and organizational culture, should not be ignored. The complexity of projects, where the small details of projects are inherently unpredictable, which can have serious consequences, is more often caused by people, than by a product or process, according to project managers (Azim, et al., 2010). Team behavior and the environment of teams, therefore, contain crucial leverage factors for both failure and success. This study has chosen specific aspects of team dynamics as its research topic to address the following theoretical gap and practitioner problem:

> theoretical lacuna: this study applies insights from crisis and safety management within the field of innovations and their teams, which is somewhat novel. The gap is the absence of discussion about effective teamwork as developed within crisis and safety management in the innovation management literature; practitioner problems: although it is unclear how many innovations really 'fail' - definitions of failure vary - the reported average of 40% of product innovations is significant (Castellion and Markham, 2013). It seems clear that organizations have much to gain by improving the process of innovation in teams, acquiring a more profitable return on investments (ROI). This study intends to create knowledge that can help to reduce the percentage of failing innovation projects. Its main contribution is to develop a team context ('mindful infrastructure') and team behavior ('innovation resilience behavior') that foster intrapreneurship - acting like an entrepreneur within the organization - and risk taking, instead of playing safe and avoiding risky experiments which are so crucial for innovation.

2. Background and theory

Why should innovation teams act as mindful and innovation resilient?

There are four reasons why project teams in innovation should become capable of innovation resilience behavior and these reasons are interrelated. The first reason is that many projects and innovations are not successful (Castellion and Markham, 2013) and that greater success improves the competitiveness of organizations. The second reason is that higher alertness and resilience make teams more effective and efficient, analogous to HROs which make almost no mistakes (Alliger et al., 2015), and enable teams to recover from disappointing events such as project terminations (Todt, Weiss and Hoegl, 2017). The third reason is that organizations could make a challenging business case for higher success rates of innovation processes because it would not only save costs but improve their returns on investments more often, and faster (Castellion, 2013). The fourth reason is that there is suggestive evidence that organizational mindfulness is associated with a greater number of patents, as an indicator of innovation (Vogus and Welbourne, 2003). These reasons suggest a sense of urgency for agents in the innovation management domain to act.

HROs invest in mindful working because it makes them more reliable; to them safety is more important than economic goals. Investing in HRO-principles is also beneficial for non-HROs, however. For non-HRO's striving for innovation thru organizational learning is a key factor, as safety is for HROs. These non-HROs do not invest in safety, but in organizational learning. Weick, Sutcliffe and Obtsfeld (1999) plausibly suggest that learning capabilities enhance innovative capabilities, trust, motivation, collaboration and communication, and thus favor non-HROs. Teams nowadays are ubiquitous in the working world; many teams face challenges that can drain resources, adversely affect performance, and diminish team cohesion and team member well-being (Alliger et al., 2015).

The relevance of the crisis management and safety literature for innovation management

High-Reliability Organizations include power grid dispatching centers, air traffic control systems, nuclear aircraft carriers, nuclear power generating plants, hospital emergency departments, wildland firefighting crews, aircraft operators, and accident investigation teams. They operate "under very trying conditions all the time and yet manage to have fewer than their fair share of accidents" (Weick and Sutcliffe, 2007: pp. 17-18). According to Weick and colleagues (1999; 2007), the reason for this reliability is that these organizations have the characteristics of "mindful organizations." Five characteristics of mindful organization constitute a collective state of mindfulness. The attractiveness of HROs as a model or ideal type is that any organization can be measured against them (Hopkins, 2014). Despite some very good examples of HROs, there is no authoritative, systematic, representative and quantitative evaluation of HROs that provides compelling scientific evidence why HROs operate safely and how they manage to do so (Lekka, 2011). The best evidence of HROs to minimize accidents and mistakes comes from the many but scattered studied cases. Weick and colleagues (1999) analyzed these studies and drew general conclusions about HROs that count as an authoritative analysis (Hopkins, 2014).

The five HRO-principles

The HRO-principles have a psychological basis in the motivation to pursue cognitive effort in order to detect errors and act upon them, adapting the situation to effectively deal with (possible) errors. In this sense reliability refers to the stability of cognitive processes. The motivation to continually be aware of unforeseen situations leads to stable cognitive processes with which to detect possible errors, and to a variable pattern of activities to adapt to events which require revision. This stability of cognitive processes ensures continuous learning from events that unfold in slightly different ways each time, and that eventually results in reliability (Weick et al., 1999: pp. 86-88).

Weick and colleagues then relate stable cognitive processes to effective error detection in five areas of concern. These five concerns are tied together by their joint ability to induce a rich awareness of discriminatory detail and a capacity for action, which the authors call 'mindfulness' (Weick et al., 1999: pp. 88-90). A successful HRO is an organization characterized by the absence of failures and errors through maximizing its reliability, by applying these five principles.

1. Preoccupation with failure involves learning from events that seldom occur and to converting them into grounds for improvement (being alert to weak signals).

2. Reluctance to simplify involves restricting simplification in interpretations to increase the number of precautions and minimize surprises.

3. Sensitivity to operations involves perceiving the integrated big picture of operations in the moment, at a higher level than operational level, and comprising the collective mind beyond the individual operator. There must be an unambiguous relationship and alignment between the actions at shop floor level and management level.

4. Commitment to resilience involves anticipation and resilience. Anticipation is the prediction and prevention of potential dangers before damage is done, whereas resilience is the capacity to cope with unanticipated dangers after they have become manifest and learning to bounce back. Resilience is the ability to not only bounce back from errors, but also to cope with surprises in the moment, and to respond as they occur.

5. Under-specification of structures refers to loosening the designation of the 'important' decision maker in order to allow decision making to migrate with problems. Weick and Sutcliffe (2007) later renamed this as 'deference to expertise': it is not the highest rank that makes decisions, but the person who is most expert.

Scientific evidence or entrepreneurial gut?

It was noted above that projects and product innovations have a substantial failure rate (Castellion and Markham, 2013). Castellion and Markham argue that the failure rate of new products can be whatever management tolerates, therefore the urgency to prevent failure is a business case: for HROs it is being reliable and safe; for businesses it is being profitable and competitive. Thus, there is the issue of whether HRO-thinking is suitable for non-HROs, which has not been much researched in the context of innovation and team dynamics. The evidence of HRO-principles in organizational performance is limited and context-specific. Paradoxically, the delivery of energy and electricity from a nuclear power plant, for example, is its primary production goal, and can at times be made subordinate to the safety of lives and the environment. Maximising reliability to maximize safety comes with an investment in mindful organizing, such as investing in training and facilitating the five key principles. For HROs, making the trade-off between investing in these resources and running the risk of failure is clear-cut: safety pays off.

For non-HROs, the trade-offs may be not as clear when the investments are high (Rousseau, 1989). The development of the five HRO-principles requires high investment in the selection and training of staff competences, and in organizational 'slack' to create space for maneuvering, all for the sake of safety. Not only are they a huge investment, but the evidence that HRO-principles are working is also merely suggestive, and the literature lacks convincing direct tests of whether, and through which mechanisms, genuine and emulating (i.e., hospitals) HROs enhance reliability (Lekka, 2011; Vogus and Iacobucci, 2016). Investing in HRO-principles remains a management choice, presumably based more on entrepreneurial guts than scientific fact. Weick and Sutcliffe (2007), are of the opinion that HRO-principles require a sense of urgency for non-HROs as well, not to invest in safety, but in (organizational) learning. Having said that, HRO-principles are thus far not investigated in relation to team behavior in innovation projects. To connect HRO-thinking about safety- and crisis management to innovation management and project teams, we developed a conceptual model that explains how innovation resilience behavior - a transfer of HRO-principles to the context of innovation - can emerge. Mindful infrastructure must be present to enable Team IRB. Figure 1.1 depicts the model in a simple format.

Figure 1.1 Framework of the research.

The **central question** of the study is: *How do project teams deal with critical incidents during their innovation projects?*

A critical incident is an event or situation that could cause a project to fail. What do these teams do in their projects when they encounter such critical incidents? And what characteristics do such teams have? Are these teams embedded in a mindful infrastructure (Vogus and Sutcliffe, 2012)? To investigate this, the study considers the presence of team psychological safety, team learning behavior (Edmondson, 1999), team voice (LePine and Van Dyne, 2001) and complexity leadership (Lawrence, Lenk and Quinn, 2009) that together constitute mindful infrastructure. These are the research variables mapping on the above-mentioned concepts of trust, learning, commitment and supportive leadership. Do teams exhibit innovation resilience behavior (Team IRB)? To investigate this, the study assesses the presence of the five HRO-principles that were modified by team behavior in innovation teams.

The **overall hypothesis** of the PhD thesis is that mindful infrastructure enables Team IRB, and that Team IRB has positive effects on project outcomes. The main question is divided into seven research questions:

1. What is mindful infrastructure and what is Team IRB? What is their relationship?

2. Does IRB affect perceived project results and perceived project progress?

3. Do teams have different configurations of mindful infrastructure?

4. Is IRB associated with defensive behaviors?

5. How do project leaders manage innovation projects?

6. How do teams respond to critical incidents during innovation projects?

7. What can innovation management teams learn from HRO teams?

3. Research design

The research took place among eleven Netherlands-based organizations, some of them are multi-nationals. These organizations are selected from the manufacturing sector, services and education; some are profit organizations, others are non-profit organizations. In these eleven organizations, eighteen teams and their innovation projects are studied as cases studies, and additionally team members working in similar projects in those companies participated in a survey. A pilot study preceding the main study was executed in a Dutch research and technology organization. The study combines survey data, in-depth face-to-face interviews, and the observation of project teams.

The thesis consists of six studies. Study 1 is a pilot study of a single case, namely an innovation programme in a research and technology organization. Based on this study, the framework model above was developed. The study combines survey data, in-depth face-to-face interviews, and the observation of a project team, and concludes that there are positive associations between team mindfulness, team psychological safety, and team learning behavior. To the degree that more team mindfulness, team psychological safety, and team learning behavior are present, there are better project results, in terms of more team innovativeness, and team external and team internal effectiveness. A relation with the type of project (innovation project or regular, non-innovative project) and project complexity was not found.

Study 2 explores the main relations of the model based on survey data from innovation teams from eleven companies where project teams are working on innovations (study 2 addresses questions 1 and 2). The elements of mindful infrastructure - team psychological safety, team learning behavior, team voice and the leadership style control - were associated with Team IRB. Similar to study 1, this study found that perceived project complexity did not influence Team IRB. Further, mindful infrastructure was positively associated with project outcomes (perceived project success and perceived project progress), but this relation was significantly stronger when Team IRB was present at the same time. Team IRB mediated the relationship between mindful infrastructure and project outcomes.

Study 3 investigates patterns of mindful infrastructure, that is, the presence in teams of combinations of (seven) variables of mindful infrastructure, so-called 'configurations' (this study addressed question 3). Based on 18 cases of innovation projects of just as many teams, there were eight different combinations of mindful infrastructure variables discovered that have a similar result, as it happens to be that each of those patterns was related to the presence of Team IRB in these teams. This implies that teams can have a different design of mindful infrastructure to achieve Team IRB. However, the eight patterns found suggest that those combinations have a better chance to enable Team IRB than other combinations. With a certain probability it is concluded one should realize that seven variables can lead to 128 possible configurations, thus 120 configurations are not "true."

Study 4 investigates defensiveness in teams (and addressed question 4). Indications were found that teams that were less capable of Team IRB were more inclined to show defensive behavior, which means these teams were more conducive to try to be in control, to prevent losing control and to avoid feelings of embarrassment. It seems that teams less capable of Team IRB were more risk-avoiding. The study seems to point out that teams capable of Team IRB have more project success. The research also led to the development of an instrument to measure certain defensive behaviors when analyzing conversations.

Study 5 researches how project leaders manage their innovation projects (research question 5). Some project leaders implicitly applied a rigorous research methodology when they have to deal with critical incidents. They followed specific steps: recognize the problem, investigate the problem, develop alternative solutions, test their validity, try out and experiment solutions, select and apply one solution, and evaluate the completed process. Surprisingly these project leaders applied the model of the 'reflective practitioner' developed by Schön (1983), who contended that experienced professionals use that model tacitly, without being aware of it. Theorising on what we observed, in a subsequent conceptual step, we linked the reflective practitioner model to the control cycle that is part of the organizational learning model (Argyris and Schön, 1996), which integrates single, double and triple loop learning. By making the combined model explicit, assistance was provided for developing ways to train project leaders in becoming more rigorous whilst learning in leading their innovation projects, and thus reducing the chance of project failure.

Study 6 explored how teams deal with critical incidents during innovation projects (research question 6). Focusing on the twelve out of eighteen teams that were capable of performing Team IRB, the main finding was that these twelve teams were better at managing and mending critical incidents than in minimizing critical incidents. One can say that, unlike HRO teams, who excel in preventing incidents from escalating, the innovation teams capable of Team IRB were more responsive than pro-active, except for those teams embedded in an R&D environment. In these R&D-embedded teams specific project management tools were present, which might explain a more pro-active position and attention toward risk management.

4. Conclusion

In the concluding chapter, the question of what innovation management teams can learn from HRO teams is addressed (question 7). The answer is found in the HROs' emphasis on the psychology of mindful acting and the organizational discipline to systematically embed organizational routines such as dedicated briefings and debriefings. HROs excel in creating space for learning and speaking up, and to meticulously improve the work process wherever possible, and in so doing test and redesign their routines; their routines never stay the same for long, as they continuously evolve. Paradoxically,

HROs are capable of balancing between required rule-based routines and the emerging need to adapt those routines. HROs inform innovation management with its attention toward the psychology of avoiding mistakes and putting effort in unnatural human behavior. The psychological concepts of reliability and mindfulness, underlying the five HRO-principles, explain the motivation to continuously be aware of unforeseen situations, and ensure continuous learning from events that each time unfold in slightly different ways. Applying these insights can support the signaling of weak signals of failure by innovation team members and suppress defensive, risk-avoiding behavior, and therefore ultimately enhance the chance of innovation success.

The main conclusion of the study is that, indeed, mindful infrastructure and Team IRB are concepts that can be applied to innovation management and project teams working on innovation. Innovation teams that do apply these insights seem to be less defensive and report positive project outcomes more often. While this insight is instructive to innovation management as a field, the findings also add to the knowledge of safety and crisis management, in the sense that mindful infrastructure consists of the elements of team psychological safety, team learning behavior, team voice and complexity leadership. These are building blocks for the HRO-principles already applied.

The study revealed that mindful infrastructure was positively associated with project outcomes (perceived project success and perceived project progress), but this relation was significantly stronger when Team IRB was present at the same time. Team IRB mediated the relationship between mindful infrastructure and project outcomes. However, teams can have a different design of mindful infrastructure to achieve Team IRB. Further, perceived project complexity did not influence the outcomes.

What can innovation teams learn from HRO teams?

This study focuses on specific parts of team dynamics, such as psychological safety, learning, leadership, and voice. Innovation teams can learn the psychology of mindful acting and organizational discipline from HRO teams, in order to embed systematic organizational routines such as dedicated briefings and debriefings. The underlying argument throughout this study was that complex projects may lead to risk-avoidance, and ultimately project failure, if defensive behavior is not countervailed or prevented by Team IRB. The HRO-literature is relevant to innovation management in its attention to the psychology of avoiding mistakes and the need to put much effort in unnatural human behavior. Reliability refers to the stability of cognitive processes to detect possible errors, and to adapt to events which require revision (Weick et al., 1999). Mindfulness in HROs is the willingness to both see and act, and this continually expands the ability to discover and manage unexpected events; the buildup of shared cognitive awareness and the varying ability to act. Variation in action patterns thus becomes a 'collective mindfulness' throughout the organization. In contrast to this kind of organizational learning, if people are blocked from acting on hazards and from detecting weak signals of hazards, these hazards will be ignored and denied, and errors will accumulate unnoticed. Mindlessness, risk-avoidance and defensiveness will reign, characterized by a reliance on past categories, acting on 'automatic pilot,' complacency, and fixation on a single perspective without awareness that things could be otherwise. HROs actively strive to suppress this inertia or mindlessness.

5. Implications and future research

Table 1.1 summarises what innovation teams can learn from HROs. HROs excel in that they have the HRO-principles, mindful infrastructure and non-defensiveness by acting according to espoused values (mainly safety and preventing accidents), at their disposal. HROs understand better than markets and other non-profit organizations the importance of cognitive and social psychological qualities and competencies. They have no 'invisible hand' or 'market forces' that implicitly guide their actions. Setting goals may perhaps be easier for them because their sense of urgency is fuelled by a strong and clear-cut public interest. Defining the required competencies is therefore also easier for them (Column 2). Translating these competencies into learning for innovation teams who are working on projects, results in a list of topics that could be applied within the innovation management domain (Column 3).

Table 1.1 Learnings from HROs for innovation teams

HRO-principles, infrastructure and espoused theory	Competencies of HRO-teams	Lessons for innovation teams performing in projects
Management philosophy and main driver	Act safely; be able to prevent accidents or to contain them	Act to learn; be able to anticipate critical incidents and to operate with several outcome scenarios
Preoccupation with failure	Able to act mindfully	Inventory of thinkable errors related to inputs, throughputs and outputs; risk and consequence management
Resistance of oversimplification	Able to resist confirmation bias	Check important team/project decisions against central project goals; seek alternative solutions before deciding

Sensitivity to operations	Arrange that the top (senior management) understands shop floor events; situational awareness at every level about other levels	The project goals are related to the overarching organization goals or pro-gramme goals; there is aware-ness of how the two levels interact and there is sensitivi-ty about the outcomes
Commitment to resilience	Train to be resilient; organizes 'slack'	Back and forth thinking about wanted and unwanted outcomes and assessing how to act, including external effects on the project
Deference to expertise	Hierarchy is flexible to judg-ment from experts and to knowledge flows	Peer review and inter-vision; absorption of external exper-tise; feedback from end-users
Mindful infrastructure	• Fosters learning, just cultures and 'mindful' leadership • Briefings, debriefings, monitoring, research, in-cident reports	• Psychological safety, learning, leadership, voice • (Self-developed) project management tools that are simple but not simplistic and easily applied; applica-tion automates behavior
Organizational non-defensiveness	• Seeks valid and testable information • Creates informed choice • Monitors for errors vigi-lantly	• Create 'slack' • Make ambiguity and mixed messaging discussable • Celebrate constructive reporting of critical incidents

This study has shown that innovation resilience behavior is a promising con-cept. Weick et al. unveiled its usefulness for HROs. The thesis supported the suggestion that it is applicable in innovation management environment as well, because when we observed that mindful infrastructure was positively associated with project outcomes (perceived project success and perceived project progress), this relation proved to be significantly stronger when Team IRB was present at the same time.

Practical implication: The IRB Tool

Recommendations to develop 'The Resilient Innovation Team' are formulated in the chapter about practical implementation (so-called valorization). The re-search suggests that mindful infrastructures that support openness and trust, enable teams to perform Team IRB and be less defensive, are all helpful in making complex issues and uncertainties discussable. Instead of becoming risk-averse such teams are solving the project's risks and critical incidents with openness and effectiveness. Some innovation teams are better at preventing and minimizing critical incidents than other teams. HRO-teams are still even better at minimizing incidents and accidents, which means that for innovation teams much is to be won in this regard. Practical guidelines and a tool are provided to develop both mindful infrastructure and Team IRB, and to combat defensive behavior. The IRB tool is an instrument to improve Team IRB and can be used by teams themselves (Oeij 2017b). The IRB tool is in the first place a diagnostic tool to assess the present situation as regards three aspects:

1. the presence of defensiveness, and thus insight into possible causes for risk avoidance;

2. the presence of mindful infrastructure, in other words, characteristics that facilitate innovation resilience behavior;

3. the presence of innovation resilience behavior, in other words, the behaviors and competences to keep an innovation team on track and to get it back on track.

The IRB tool is also a guide for developing simple and applicable team meeting tools. The IRB tool manual will guide users through these steps, during which six exercises are carried out. A team can do this in one day or in two separate day-shifts. One example of such an exercise is to 'Develop your own tools'. HRO-teams try to automate unnatural behavior or organizational learning by creating procedures such as briefing and debriefing, and continuously improving processes and behaviors. Teams working on innovation could also do this and develop their own briefing and debriefing tools. Think, for example, of processing a checklist of project management issues at the beginning of a project and evaluating the project afterwards with the intention of improving the checklist. It is possible to break the innovation process of a project into phases or steps, and scrutinize the requirements of each step, and make an inventory of them. Another way is to look at the relevant aspects of a project, such as project decision making, stakeholder management, requirements of the end-result, future market opportunities, and the development of a pilot to test the result. For each of these aspects a two-item question could be answered: what proactive team behavior would this require from the perspective of each HRO-principle to prevent a critical incident to emerge (weak signals, oversimplification, sensitivity and so on); and, what resilient team behavior would this require once a critical incident had occurred after all? The tools that the teams develop for themselves are made and owned by the teams, which enhances the likelihood of their application and team commitment; simple but not simplistic tools. To make tools so simple that they will be used and that it improves the work and an individual's competences and skills the more they use them, means that their application is a task that becomes automated organizational learning. For example, if the team sums up the decisions that have been taken during their meeting, they could apply a checklist from the clients' perspective to assess the quality of every major decision:

Alertness: Are we aware of the wishes of our clients, and could this decision harm their interests?

Simplification: Did we consider all possible alternatives and is our decision based on facts?

Sensitivity: Have we checked the effect of the decision on the rest of the organization, other teams, other aspects of the innovation, other projects for the same client?

Resilience: Do we know all consequences of our decision and do we have alternative/restoring actions in place?

Expertise: Do we know who to turn to in the case of every thinkable unwanted effect, and is this person/expertise available when we need it?

If project teams apply this during meetings, the checklist eventually becomes automated behavior that requires neither much time nor separate learning. The advantages of such tools are their low thresholds for creating a mindful organizational culture with limited effort.

Future research

Firstly, innovation resilience behavior is conceptualized as a set of team behaviors rooted in the five HRO-principles to manage critical incidents and to enact critical recoveries. The concept could be tested further among representative samples of the populations of project teams in innovation. Team IRB functions as a mediator between mindful infrastructure variables and project outcomes. The exact nature of the relationships between mindful infrastructure variables, the five Team IRB behaviors and the project outcomes are still unclear and require further scrutiny. Secondly, mindful infrastructure is conceptualized as team psychological safety, team learning, complexity leadership and team voice, but how these factors relate to each other and the exact mechanism by which it enables Team IRB, involves several unanswered questions. The research established the presence of eight combinations associated with Team IRB, but this is just the start of investigating its working mechanisms. Larger samples of cases will undoubtedly reveal the presence of other paths as well, and this would help to see whether certain paths are significantly more commonly chosen than others. Thirdly, defensive behavior has been studied through observation, oral interviews and discourse analysis. In different ways, and to a different extent, there were indications that defensive behaviors might be associated with risk-averse behaviors. Research is encouraged to more firmly establish the relationships of defensive behaviors and risk-averse behaviors with project outcomes. This would demonstrate the importance of mindful infrastructure and Team IRB so as to suppress defensive behaviors and to reduce negative effects on project outcomes and innovation. Finally, the IRB Tool suggests developing one's own 'project management tools,' which can be used and learned on the job so that those tools become automated behavior and can be developed by teams so that ownership guarantees the motivation to apply them. Experimental research, comparing teams that do and do not develop such tools, could evaluate the effect of these tools as interventions with a pre-test and post-test design. Variables that must be considered for integration into the study design are mindful infrastructure, Team IRB and project outcomes.

References

Alliger, G.M., Cerasoli, C.P., Tannenbaum, S.I. and Vessey, W.B., (2015). 'Team resilience: How teams flourish under pressure'. *Organizational Dynamics,* 44(3), pp. 176-184.

Andriopoulos, C., Gotsi, M., Lewis, M.W. and Ingram, A.E., (2017). 'Turning the Sword: How NPD Teams Cope with Front-End Tensions'. *Journal of Product Innovation Management.* DOI: 10.1111/jpim.12423.

Argyris, C., (2010). *Organizational traps. Leadership, culture, organizational design.* Oxford: Oxford University Press.

Argyris, C. and Schön, D.A., (1996). *Organizational learning II. Theory, method, and practice.* 2nd ed. (1st ed. 1978) Reading (MA), etc.: Addison-Wesley.

Azim, S., Gale, A., Lawlor-Wright, T., Kirkham, R., Khan, A. and Alam, M., (2010). 'The importance of soft skills in complex projects'. *International Journal of Managing Projects in Business,* 3(3), pp. 387-401.

Castellion, G. (2013). *Is the 80% product failure rate statistic actually true?* [online] Available at: <https://www.quora.com/Is-the-80-product-failure-rate-statistic-actually-true> [Accessed, 28 June 2016].

Castellion, G. and Markham, S.K., (2013). 'Perspective: New product failure rates: Influence of argumentum ad populum and self-interest'. *Journal of Product Innovation Management,* 30(5), pp. 976–979.

Cicmil, S. and Marshall, D., (2005). 'Insights into collaboration at the project level: Complexity, social interaction and procurement mechanisms'. *Building Research & Information,* 33(6), pp. 523-535.

Cooke-Davies, T., (2002). 'The "real" success factors on projects'. *International journal of project management,* 20(3), pp. 185-190.

Edmondson, A., (1999). 'Psychological safety and learning behavior in work teams'. *Administrative Science Quarterly,* 44(2), pp. 350-383.

Han, Z. & Lorenz, R., (2015). 'Insights into success factors of innovation projects'. *International Journal of Entrepreneurship and Innovation Management,* 19(3-4), pp. 163-193.

Hopkins, A., (2014). 'Issues in safety science'. *Safety Science,* 67, pp. 6-14.

Lawrence, K.A., Lenk, P. and Quinn, R.E., (2009). 'Behavioral complexity in leadership: The psychometric properties of a new instrument to measure behavioral repertoire'. *The Leadership Quarterly,* 20(2), pp. 87-102.

Lekka, C., (2011). *High reliability organisations: A review of the literature.* Research Report RR899. Bootle, UK: Health and Safety Executive.

LePine, J.A. and Van Dyne, L., (2001). 'Voice and cooperative behavior as contrasting forms of contextual performance: Evidence of differential relationships with Big Five personality characteristics and cognitive ability'. *Journal of Applied Psychology,* 86(2), pp. 326-336.

Oeij, P.R.A. (2017a). *The resilient innovation team: a study of teams coping with critical incidents during innovation projects.* PhD Dissertation Open University of The Netherlands. http://publications.tno.nl/publication/34622536/QA3j9S/oeij-2017-resilient.pdf

Oeij, P.R.A. (2017b). 'From automated defensive behaviour to innovation resilience behaviour: A tool for resilient teamwork as an example of workplace innovation'. In: P.R.A. Oeij, D. Rus & F.D. Pot (Eds). *Workplace Innovation: Theory, Research and Practice,* Volume in 'Aligning Perspectives on Health, Safety and Well-Being' series (pp. 375-396). Berlin etc.; Springer.

Rousseau, D.M., (1989). 'The price of success? Security-oriented cultures and high reliability organizations'. *Organization & Environment* (previously: *Industrial Crisis Quarterly),* 3(4), pp. 285-302.

Sauser, B.J., Reilly, R.R. and Shenhar, A.J., (2009). ,Why projects fail? How contingency theory can provide new insights - A comparative analysis of NASAs Mars Climate Orbiter loss'. *International Journal of Project Management,* 27(7), pp. 665-679.

Schön, D.A., (1983). *The reflective practitioner: How professionals think in action.* New York: Basic Books.

Shenhar, A.J. and Dvir, D., (2007). *Reinventing project management. The diamond approach to successful growth and innovation.* Boston, MA: Harvard Business School Press, pp. 9-10.

Todt, G., Weiss, M. and Hoegl, M., (2017). 'Mitigating Negative Side Effects of Innovation Project Terminations: The Role of Resilience and Social Support'. *Journal of Product Innovation Management.* Doi:10.1111/jpim.12426

Vogus, T. and Iacobucci, D., (2016). 'Creating highly reliable health care: How reliability-enhancing work practices affect patient safety in hospitals'. *Industrial and Labor Relations Review / ILR Review,* 69(4), pp. 911-938.

Vogus, T.J. and Sutcliffe, K.M., (2012). 'Organizational mindfulness and mindful organizing: A reconciliation and path forward'. *Academy of Management Learning & Education,* 11(4), pp. 722-735.

Vogus, T.J. and Welbourne, T.M., (2003). 'Structuring for high reliability: HR practices and mindful processes in reliability-seeking organizations'. *Journal of Organizational Behavior,* 24(7), pp. 877-903.

Weick, K.E. and Sutcliffe, K M., (2007). *Managing the unexpected. Resilient performance in an age of uncertainty.* 2nd ed. (1st ed. 2001). San Francisco: Jossey-Bass.

Weick, K.E., Sutcliffe, K.M. and Obstfeld, D., (1999). 'Organizing for high reliability: Processes of collective mindfulness'. In: R.S. Sutton and B.M. Staw, eds. 1999. *Research in Organizational Behavior, 1.* Stanford: Jai Press. pp. 81-123.

Chapter 2

The Benefits of Trusted Bridging Chains for Open Innovation

Margarethe Lombard

E-mail: maggie@polynate.co.za

Abstract: Innovation search typically involves one-to-many relationships of a focal organization, even though searching too broadly for innovative solutions is costly and ineffective. Because indirect relationships can generate new information, deliberately deepening rather than widening the search for innovative solutions across a chain of interpersonal relationships is suggested. This meets the documented need to balance support (trust and closeness) with bridging (diversity). A quasi-experiment was developed in which members of a starter group were asked to solve a complex technical problem by approaching individuals from their social networks who could, in turn, tap their respective networks. Using fuzzy set qualitative comparative analysis, quality solutions were shown to result from interpersonal relationships indirect to an organization, facilitated by a bridging chain stretching across network horizons. Although too much diversity undermines innovation (knowledge diversity and geographical distance revealed a substitutive relationship), supporting features of social capital like trust are peripheral to the quality of solutions.

Keywords: trusted bridging chains; social capital; indirect relationships; innovation; open innovation; supporting features; bridging features; chains.

1. Introduction

It is a truism that organizations are compelled to innovate and to transform innovation processes, in order to stay ahead of the competition or to make inroads into new markets. However, although incremental innovations are ubiquitous, innovation seems to be less than radical in nature (Leitner, Warnke and Rhomberg, 2016). Existing innovation strategies, therefore, require drastic transformation in order to remain key enablers of competitiveness. Merely investing in internal research and development (R&D) functions, and/or resources for innovation purposes may be insufficient.

Firms are increasingly looking outwards to innovate through inter alia alliances, partnerships and in-licensing – a paradigm also known as "open innovation" (Chesbrough, 2003). Open innovation suggests that firms need not internalize all the resources needed to innovate. Firms generally forge relationships with innovators through alliances (Lambe and Spekman, 1997; Narula and Hagedoorn, 1999), joint ventures (Bingham and Spradlin, 2011; Peck, 1986) or technology sourcing and acquisition (Arora, Fosfuri and Gambardella, 2001; Nicholls-Nixon and Woo, 2003; Veugelers, 1997). This process mostly involves one-to-one or one-to-many direct relationships with innovators or groups of people (Howe, 2008).

However, studies have shown that searching too widely for external innovations can be expensive and ineffective (Katila and Ahuja, 2002; Laursen and Salter, 2004; Laursen and Salter, 2006; Vanhaverbeke, Duysters and Beerkens, 2002) and can actually slow down the innovation process (Leitner, Warnke and Rhomberg, 2016). Given the substantial evidence about the need for a relatively narrowly focused search strategy, the question has to be asked whether firms can benefit from a deepening rather than widening of their search. Yet, in extant theory, "depth" implies searching only existing external sources extensively (Katila and Ahuja, 2002).

Although some studies have shown that indirect interpersonal relationships can generate new information, this is seen to occur more through chance than design (Ahuja, 2000; Almeida and Kogut, 1999; Burt, 1997; Burt, 2010; Jaffe, Trajtenberg and Henderson, 1993). How might OI processes benefit from sourcing innovative solutions across network horizons?

Little if any attention has been given to the search for innovative solutions via a chain of interpersonal relationships across network horizons. Hence the aim of this study: to identify the conditions under which bridging chains of interpersonal relationships that potentially span firms, industries and even countries can yield useful innovative solutions. The evidence helps reframe the notion of "searching", suggesting that search can be conceptualized not only in terms of breadth but also depth. Thus, the conditions are explored under which a chain with two or more agents connected across deeper network horizons can realize positive innovation outcomes.

Some studies have explored network ties that bridge organizational boundaries (Leenders and Dolfsma, 2016), while additional research has focused on the bridging and bonding aspects of social capital (Lin, 2005; Portes, 1998; Putnam, 2000). Yet, studies that bridge organizational boundaries are scarce (Leenders and Dolfsma, 2016). This study refines ideas about network structure and diversity and how these could contribute to the success of OI. It shows that social capital is based on supporting elements (such as trust) as well as bridging elements (such as weak ties and structural holes) and that it can consequently be defined in terms of a combination of bridging and bonding.

There are methodological challenges for studies in collecting referral data (across fields) due to the limit to horizons of observability regarding indirect ties (Friedkin, 1982), which this study circumvented by means of the development and deployment of software that drove the data collection process across chains of referrals. The study also has many other practical implications to leverage indirect social capital for innovation (and across other domains) and not merely by chance.

Research on social capital is explored to build the argument. It has long been recognized that social capital has both bonding (Coleman, 1988) and bridging (Burt, 1997) features. Various scholars have documented benefits in the co-occurrence of bonding and bridging features (Levin and Cross, 2004; Levin, Walter, Appleyard and Cross, 2015). It is argued that effective search depth can be obtained when referral chains have both bonding features (e.g., trust), and bridging features such as diversity in knowledge or geography.

The study is situated in South Africa, a country behind the technological frontier and geographically quite far away from the technological leaders of the world. Local pockets of excellence exist (e.g., Barnard, Bromfield and Cantwell, 2009), but overall, the local knowledge base lags that of the industrial leaders. Thus, OI sourcing is an attractive strategy in developing countries where firms' ability to secure in-house innovation resources is often limited (Gaur, Kumar and Singh, 2014). Moreover, the differences between the local and global knowledge base help make more salient differences in outcome between searches that bridge to industrialized economies and those that remain local.

To summarise: the research problem focuses on the benefits of searching more deeply for OI return, through trusted, external bridging chains which benefit the organization and exploring the extent to which such chains have a positive effect on OI.

2. Background

The use of external networks for innovation, referred to as "network-centric innovation" (Nambisan and Sawhney, 2011) has been receiving increasing attention. In spite of significant research on the effect of inter-organizational networks on innovation (Nambisan and Sawhney, 2011; Narula and Hagedoorn; 1999; Lew and Sinkovics, 2013; Powell, Koput, Smith-Doerr and Owen-Smith, 1999), very little work has been done on individual boundary spanning network ties (Leenders and Dolfsma, 2016), while even less work has been done on searching for innovative solutions through indirect interpersonal relationships.

Indirect interpersonal relationships, those involving "a friend of a friend," have been found to be of value in other contexts, notably Granovetter's (1973) work on job seekers. It, therefore, seems possible that similar trusted bridging chains could be of value in innovation.

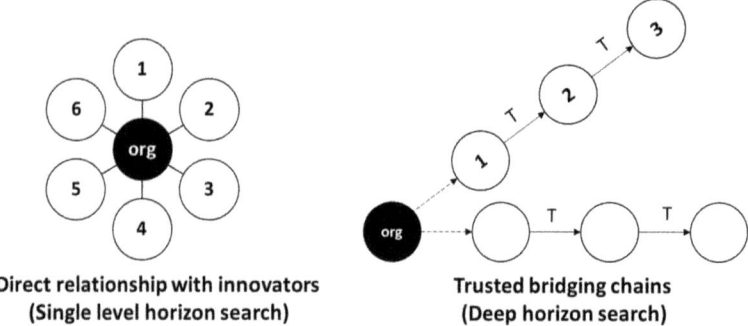

Figure 2.1 Direct relationships versus searching through trusted bridging chains.

Figure 2.1 demonstrates how such a deep horizon search, consisting of referral chains, differs from the more conventional way in which (especially open) innovation search is conceptualized. By challenging the limitations of a single level search horizon, a referral chain can be leveraged to solve innovation problems for an organization by harnessing the power of interpersonal relationships outside its boundary.

Search breadth versus search depth

Collaboration with different types of partners has been shown to enable novelty and innovation (Amara and Landry, 2005; Nieto and Santamaria, 2007) although too much openness has shown to be detrimental to innovation performance (Ahuja, 2000; Ahuja and Katila, 2004; Laursen and Salter, 2004; Laursen and Salter, 2006).

Some studies have indicated that indirect interpersonal relationships can generate new information, but this has seemed to occur more through chance than design (Ahuja, 2000; Almeida and Kogut, 1999; Burt, 1997; 2010; Jaffe, Trajtenberg and Henderson, 1993). In most cases, referral chains have been studied retrospectively, e.g. in job referral studies (Bian, 1997; Granovetter, 1973; Lin, 1999; Lin, 2005), and in small world studies (Newman, 2003; Uzzi and Spiro, 2005; Watts, 1999; Watts and Strogatz, 1998), with the latter mostly based on algorithmic problems rather than practical, "real world" challenges (Schnettler, 2009). Finally, pyramiding search, aimed at finding experts through a referral approach (von Hippel, Franke and Prugl, 2009), is more reliant on the researcher's or organizational team's own motivations (Poetz and Prügl, 2010) than the motivations of the referrer.

It is argued that an understanding of social capital, and in particular how its "bridging" and "bonding" features work together, can help predict under which conditions a conscious strategy of deep search will yield useful innovation outcomes.

Social capital

Social capital can be defined as the returns that can be gained through social networks with innate structural and relational characteristics (Coleman, 1988). Nahapiet and Ghoshal define social capital not in terms of returns, but in terms of resources: "the sum of the actual and potential resources embedded within, available through, and derived from the network of relationships possessed by an individual or social unit" (1988, p. 243).

What the various definitions have in common is that social capital is enabled through relationships and that relationships may have vastly different origins, such as through personal or professional, individual or organizational contacts. To enable innovation, it follows that social capital would have to yield novel and diverse outcomes. For this reason, it is important to establish the functioning of social capital characterized by access to novelty by means of bridging relations.

Bridging features of social capital

For Burt (1997; 2000), structural holes are the key characteristic of social networks. Burt maintained that social capital could be gained through a person's relationships with "friends, colleagues, and more general contact through whom you receive opportunities to use for your financial and human capital" and that social capital is a function of "the brokerage opportunities in a network" (Burt, 1997, p. 340). In other words, the most valuable dimension of social capital lies not in the closeness of relationships, but in opportunities to bridge between otherwise disconnected worlds.

Bridging features of social capital are evident in relationships with others through ties that bridge diverse information sources. Granovetter's (1973) work on job seeking suggested the power of "weak" ties as sources of novel information. However, subsequent research has found evidence that strong ties can also act as sources of novel information, provided they are able to connect (people from) different networks (Levin and Cross, 2004).

The arguably best-recognized sources of difference in networks are differences in knowledge bases (Ahuja and Katila, 2004; Becker and Dietz, 2004; Miller, Fern and Cardinal, 2007) and geographic distance (Lahiri, 2010; Letaifa and Rabeau, 2013; Levin and Barnard, 2013; Whittington, Owen-Smith and Powell, 2009).

In terms of geographic diversity, it has been shown that better global positions, foreign partners or distant alliances are important conduits for new information when access to local diversity is low (Beers and Zand, 2014; Capaldo and Petruzzelli, 2014; Levin and Barnard, 2013; Whittington, Owen-Smith and Powell, 2009). A deeper search that reaches into different regions or even countries is thus likely to result in improved innovation outcomes.

Bonding features of social capital

Much as bridging enables access to novelty in social networks, balance is important. It has been shown that too much diversity can hamper mutual understanding (Nooteboom, 1992; Nooteboom, 1999; Nooteboom, Van Haverbeke, Duysters, Gilsing and Van den Oord, 2007) while a surfeit of sup-porting relations results in a closed network with limited novelty (Fleming, Mingo and Chen, 2007; Uzzi and Spiro, 2005). Indeed, studies of social capital and innovation are characterized by evidence of not only bridging relation-ships, but also the persistent importance of bonding features such as trust, obligations, expectations, reciprocity, norms and values (Coleman, 1988).

Three types of bonding features can be identified: closeness, frequent communication and trust. Both closeness and frequent communication have their origins in the work of Granovetter (1973), who measured the strength of ties in terms of the frequency of communication. Later work (Marsden and Campbell, 1984; Marsden and Campbell, 2012; Wellman and Wortley, 1990) found that closeness was a better indication of the strength of ties. Intimacy (closeness) and activity (here conceptualized as the frequency of communica-tion) both contribute to bonding in a social network and, it is argued, to the likelihood of an effective deepening of the search horizon.

Trust facilitates obligations, expectations and reciprocity (Coleman, 1988) as well as learning (Nielsen and Nielsen, 2009). The role of trust in increasing the number of sources of information on which firms can profitably draw in the innovation process has been repeatedly noted (Vanhaverbeke, 2006; Westergren and Holmström, 2012). Relationships based on trust lead to better knowledge ex-change (Inkpen and Tsang, 2005; Levin and Cross, 2004; Levin, Walter, Appleyard and Cross, 2015). Trustworthiness has been positively associated with resource exchange, which, in turn, positively affects innovation (Tsai and Ghoshal, 1998). Trust is also seen as important for the generation of new ideas and products (Clegg, Unsworth, Epitropaki and Parker, 2002; Lee and Choi 2003).

3. Research design

Research questions and hypotheses

The overarching research question probes the benefits of trusted bridging chains for open innovation:

Do trusted bridging chains have a positive effect on open innovation?

In order to answer the research question, the following research hypotheses were proposed:

Hypothesis 1: Trust is positively correlated with the depth of search

Hypothesis 2: Trust is positively associated with the quality of OI solutions

Hypothesis 3: Diversity in knowledge bases is associated with the quality of OI solutions

Hypothesis 4: Geographic diversity is associated with the quality of OI solutions

Hypothesis 5: Depth of search is associated with the quality of OI solutions

Hypothesis 6: Weak chains, more so than strong chains, are associated with the discovery of OI solutions, regardless of the quality of the solutions.

Research setting

As is typical in open innovation research (see West and Bogers, 2014), the research design is anchored on a problem for which a solution was sought from a wider community of managers and specialists. In this case, a South African gold processing facility wished to reduce a copper cyanide build-up in the process water circuits that was increasing cyanide consumption and negatively impacting the electrowinning of gold.

Previous studies of the search depth of job seekers (except for the founding work on "six degrees of separation" by Milgram, 1967) have relied on post-hoc data gathering. However, this approach carries the risk of memory bias and undercounting incomplete chains. For this reason, a quasi-experimental design was used. The participants in the study were asked to solve the problem either themselves or by tapping into their social networks and referring the challenge to someone else who could do so. Referred individuals, in turn, could tap into their respective networks to seek a solution. The research design was therefore based on a survey integrated within the referral process: the referrer was required to answer various survey questions as he/she referred another person. Functionality also existed for an innovator to submit an innovative solution.

A software platform was developed to simultaneously facilitate and capture referrals and the submission of solutions. Members of two professional associations were contacted, one local, the Southern African Institute of Mining and Metallurgy

(SAIMM) and one international, the International Association of Innovation Professionals (IAOIP). A survey instrument of close-ended questions was posed during the referral process. The population for the study, an opted-in starter group of 121 individuals, was asked to solve a complex technical problem themselves or tap into their social networks and source someone else who could do so. They, in turn, could tap into their own respective networks to seek a solution.

The problem for the final study was "open" for just over two months to allow for the referral of individuals as well as the subsequent submission of solutions. An individual was not able to refer a person who was already referred. This proved to be a limitation, as referrals by different individuals may have helped identify key innovators. The starter group made 44 referrals which resulted in 75 valid referrals and 60 referral chains. A total of nine solutions were submitted; six generated through chains, and three submitted by the starter population directly. The unit of analysis was, therefore, the referral chain, which comprised two components: referrals and solutions.

Analytic approach

Individuals could search for innovative solutions in many different ways, along different search routes. For this reason, the fuzzy set Qualitative Comparative Analysis (fsQCA) method was used to uncover the causal conditions in finding both good and bad solutions. fsQCA is an analysis of set relations, whereby the effect of a combination of conditions on the outcome is more important than the evaluation of the effect of the independent variables on the dependent variable (quantitative analysis) alone. Fuzzy sets make it possible to analyze fine gradations in the degree of membership to sets, or groups of things (Ragin, 2008). Unlike normal regression analysis, necessary and sufficient conditions are causally asymmetric. Therefore, the set of causal conditions necessary and sufficient for the outcome might be very different for the absence of the causal condition (Fiss, 2011). The fsQCA analytical method provides a configurational perspective to the research, which is largely absent in OI research. Furthermore, fsQCA was also used because of the small number of cases not requiring statistical power for analysis. The data was presented according to Fiss (2011), who introduced the concept of core and peripheral conditions as dual concepts for the understanding of typologies. Coreness relates to elements which can be causally connected to specific outcomes. Coreness can also be defined as "those causal conditions for which the evidence indicates a strong causal relationship with the outcome of interest," while peripheral elements are "those for which the evidence for a causal relationship with the outcome is weaker" (Fiss, 2011, p. 398).

A quantitative method was added for regression analysis for finding solutions *per se* and not necessarily the quality of solutions. Apart from reliability analysis, logistic regressions were mainly used in the quantitative analysis.

4. Conclusion

OI studies have focused extensively on the role of search strategies in sourcing innovations and ideas. However, it has been demonstrated that searching too widely can be expensive, ineffective and debilitating. Research into networked innovation has shown that trust is embedded in the supporting features of social capital, while diversity is intrinsic to bridging features. This study envisaged that a trusted bridging chain, driven by trust and imbued with diversity, could reach across deeper horizons in search of innovative solutions, and offer an alternative to searching widely for innovative solutions. It was also proposed that a trusted bridging chain could be assembled via trusted interpersonal relationship referrals to unlock social capital. The results, based on Fiss' (2011) analytical presentation, was presented in Table 2.1 below.

Table 2.1 Configurations for good and bad solutions

Configuration	Solutions				
	Outcome (good solutions)			Negated outcome (bad solutions)	
	1a	1b	1c	2a	2b
Diversity					
Geographic distance	●	⊗	⊗	●	●
Knowledge diversity	⊗	●	●	●	●
Trust					
Competence-based trust	●	●	●	●	●
Benevolence-based trust	⊗	⊗	●	⊗	●
Strength of ties	⊗	⊗	⊗	⊗	●
Communication	⊗	⊗	●	⊗	⊗
Consistency	0.987	1.000	1.000	0.988	0.980
Raw coverage	0.344	0.196	0.146	0.434	0.233
Unique coverage	0.308	0.131	0.102	0.398	0.197
Overall solution consistency	0.992			0.991	
Overall solution coverage	0.605			0.630	

Table 2.1 shows the configurations for good and bad solutions. A solid black circle "●" was used to show the necessary presence of a condition, and a circle that was crossed out "⊗" was used to represent the necessary absence of a condition, similar to the presentation used in Fiss (2011). Larger circles represented core causal conditions and smaller circles represented peripheral conditions.

In reference to Table 2.1, the results indicated that chains of referrals, inhering trust and diversity, enabled the unlocking of social capital for OI returns. Although it was revealed that competence-based trust (supporting feature of social capital), particularly enabled the formation of chains that facilitated depth of search, it was found that trust did not contribute to the quality of solutions found, as it was a necessary condition for good and bad solutions in Table 1. However, benevolence-based trust was not significant in this regard.

Moreover, although weak ties proved to be instrumental in finding solutions, they did not determine the quality of these solutions (necessary condition for good and bad solutions in Table 2.1). It is increasingly understood that weak ties are not necessarily an indicator of novelty (Levin and Barnard, 2013; Levin and Cross, 2004). Rather, the study revealed the importance of knowledge diversity and geographical distance as two sources of novelty. Moreover, it showed a substitutive relationship between knowledge diversity and geographical distance, suggesting that too much diversity led to bad solutions. This finding is also consistent with what has been previously found (e.g., Lahiri, 2010). The study also showed the minimal role of frequent communication.

The quantitative results indicated that solutions were discovered through predominantly weak chains, although the strength of chains did not have an effect on the quality of solutions, as seen in Table 2.1. It was also found that greater numbers of referrals diminished the likelihood of finding solutions.

Finally, the research showed that trusted bridging chains did not specifically influence the quality of solutions, as chains constituting mainly of weak links generated good and bad solutions. However, trusted bridging chains proved to be a viable alternative to searching too widely, and therefore this study opens the door for further research on the benefits of trusted bridging chains for OI.

The evidence helps to reframe the notion of "searching," suggesting that search can be conceptualized not only in terms of breadth but also depth. Benefits can indeed be derived from indirect interpersonal relationships, where organizations search for innovative solutions through external bridging chains of referrals. Diversity in the knowledge base between the referrer and the referee is a core element of successful innovative solutions. This diversity can be either geographic, i.e., advice giving by a person who is physically far away from the referrer, or in terms of differences in the knowledge bases of the involved parties, although the innovativeness of solutions suffers when both knowledge and geographic diversity are present. In all cases, trust, and in particular competence-based trust, is a peripheral underpinning element of bridging chains.

5. Implications and future research

Theoretical Implications

This study suggests that it is possible to facilitate a deeper, rather than broader, search horizon for OI. But even though every attempt was made to focus and deepen the search process, the disadvantages of what can perhaps be seen as a "shotgun" approach are apparent: Extensive referrals seem to reduce the probability of finding solutions. This suggests that OI will be more powerful to the extent that it can access diverse views, but in a targeted way.

Trust plays an important supporting role in enabling referrals. The supporting role played by trust is complex: it is competence-based trust, rather than benevolence-based trust, that enables referrals. Thus, people are likely to refer the challenge to people whom they trust to be competent (rather than people they "like"). However, even competence-based trust does not predict the quality of innovation solutions identified.

Instead, the quality of solutions can be explained by diversity, by what is termed "bridging." Both knowledge diversity and geographical distance prove to be core conditions, and quality solutions have either one or the other. But it is important to note that the relationship is substitutive. Too much diversity weakens solutions – in this case, knowledge diversity combined with geographical distance. This is consistent with prior research (Lahiri, 2010).

Theoretically, this study, therefore, demonstrates the benefits of the co-occurrence of bonding and bridging features of social capital, especially across organizational boundaries. Through the activation of trusted bridging chains, OI solutions are generated that rely on existing ties, yet generate novel knowledge.

This study also demonstrates the usefulness of making a distinction between direct social capital and indirect social capital, where people consciously activate more distant connections. Finally, given the challenges in conceptualizing social capital (Patulny and Svendsen, 2007; Payne, Moore, Griffis and Autry, 2011), this study builds on existing theory to define and describe two levels of social capital: direct and indirect. It is proposed that a distinction between direct and indirect social capital is useful. Current conceptualizations of social capital refer to all value that can be garnered through relationships, whether they are direct personal relationships or "contacts of contacts" (Burt, 1997; Burt, 2010; Granovetter, 1973). The evidence in this thesis suggests that a conceptual distinction between direct and indirect social capital can and should be made.

Studies on ties that bridge organizational boundaries are scarce and therefore this study may become the basis for future network studies focusing on bridging organizational boundaries. In addition to this, the study refines many ideas about network structure and diversity and how these would contribute to the success of OI, which future studies could expand on. Future research could also further investigate the role of trust when spanning boundaries, taking into account the fact that competence-based trust drove the referral process, but benevolence-based trust was low, except when communication was frequent, or ties were strong.

Finally, future studies could also focus on the analysis of chain patterns, with regards to diversity and trust across the chains (especially for longer chains), instead of using variable averages across the chain. As such, measurement of the type of networks that are bridged by different types of chains might highlight well-known combinations of the trust and diversity across these chains.

Practical Implications

The research proposes a practical new way of expanding the population of participants who contribute to the generation of OI solutions. Relying on the contacts of contacts, a firm can deepen its search, and with a smaller initial search horizon, obtain arguably at least the same quality solution, if not better. For example, for beneficiaries where there are few or suboptimal alternative knowledge sources, for example, firms in developing countries encountering technical challenges, it is exciting that a bridge of referrals can result in useful open innovation solutions. Interpersonal relationships can be used to mitigate some of the systemic and institutional weaknesses in a developing country, either when the knowledge is sought from geographically proximate entities with a different knowledge base, or from distant entities with a similar knowledge base.

Searching through deeper horizons across social relations is not a current practice when seeking OI solutions. Most OI searches for innovative solutions operate through direct links with diverse partners (eco-network search), or through an intermediary with such links. Organizations sometimes leverage informal spillages through social integration, but rarely purposively. This research demonstrates the value of purposively using the interpersonal social relationships outside of the organization.

Moreover, evidence about the substitutive relationship between knowledge and geographic distance suggests how firms can most effectively design their deep searches. For example, organizations can tap networks within the same industry (knowledge similarity) but request chain participants to seek out global reach (geographic distance). This purposive request for distant referrals could allow access to otherwise hard-to-obtain knowledge from foreign partners.

Furthermore, effective deep search strategies are possible to the extent that contacts outside of the firm can be effectively reached. This thesis also demonstrates the technological feasibility of creating trusted bridging chains.

Methodological Implications

The study makes a methodological contribution considering that software was developed that allows not only for referrals and their real-time tracking, but also for the simultaneous gathering of data, minimizing data recall which often plagues scholarship on networks. This methodological approach creates opportunities for practical application as well as research unrelated to OI. Hence, the developed process can also be used in practice across fields, such as for head hunting and marketing processes. The fsCQA analysis used for this research provided a configurational perspective which is largely absent in OI research. Applying this analytical method in future OI research studies may create more insight around the complementarity and equifinality of OI processes.

Conclusion

The evidence about the effectiveness of search depth suggests that scholars of innovation more generally may benefit if they can complement the current emphasis on search breadth with a much more considered examination of how search depth can shape innovation.

The question is also, whether social capital belongs to an individual or the firm employing him or her. Firms have long had standard agreements in which individuals sign over the intellectual property of the work they do in the service of that firm, but there is no common understanding of how much claim the firm can lay on the interpersonal ties of an individual. Of course, it has long been the case that people were employed not only for their capabilities but also for their "contacts" – their social capital. The evidence that firms can potentially access effective solutions through the systematic exploration and exploitation of the social capital of their employees, beyond the boundaries of the organization, makes it important to clarify the ownership of social capital.

References

Ahuja, G. (2000). 'Collaboration networks, structural holes, and innovation: A longitudinal study'. *Administrative science quarterly,* 45(3), pp. 425-455.

Ahuja, G. and Katila, R. (2004). 'Where do resources come from? The role of idiosyncratic situations'. *Strategic Management Journal,* 25 (8–9), pp. 887–907.

Almeida, P., and Kogut, B. (1999). 'Localization of knowledge and the mobility of engineers in regional networks'. *Management science,* 45(7), pp. 905-917.

Amara, N. and Landry, R. (2005). 'Sources of information as determinants of novelty of innovation in manufacturing firms: evidence from the 1999 statistics Canada innovation survey'. *Technovation,* 25(3), pp. 245-259.

Arora, A., Fosfuri, A. and Gambardella, A. (2001). 'Markets for technology and their implications for corporate strategy'. *Industrial and corporate change,* 10(2), pp. 419-451.

Barnard, H., Bromfield, T., Cantwell, J. (2009). 'The role of indigenous firms in innovation systems in developing countries: the developmental implications of national champion firms' response to underdeveloped national innovation systems'. In: Lundvall, B.-A., Joseph, K., Vang, J., Chaminade, C. (Eds.), *Handbook of Innovation Systems and Developing Countries.* Edward Elgar, UK: Cheltenham, pp. 249–279.

Becker, W. and Dietz, J. R. (2004). 'R&D cooperation and innovation activities of firms: evidence for the German manufacturing industry'. *Research Policy,* 33(2), pp. 209.

Beers, C. and Zand, F. (2014). 'R&D cooperation, partner diversity, and innovation performance: an empirical analysi's. *Journal of Product Innovation Management,* 31(2), pp. 292-312.

Bian, Y. (1997). 'Bringing strong ties back in: Indirect ties, network bridges, and job searches in China'. *American sociological review,* pp. 366-385.

Bingham, A. and Spradlin, D. (2011). *The open innovation marketplace: creating value in the challenge driven enterprise.* New Jersey, FT press.

Burt, R. S. (2010). *Neighbor networks: Competitive advantage local and personal.* Oxford University Press.

Burt, R. S. (1997). 'A note on social capital and network content'. *Social networks,* 19(4), pp. 355-373.

Burt, R. S. (2000). 'The network structure of social capital'. *Research in organizational behavior,* 22, pp. 345-423.

Capaldo, A. and Petruzzelli, A. M. (2014). 'Partner Geographic and Organizational Proximity and the Innovative Performance of Knowledge-Creating Alliances'. *European Management Review,* 11(1), pp. 63-84.

Chesbrough, H. W. (2003). *Open innovation: The new imperative for creating and profiting from technology.* Boston: Harvard Business Press.

Clegg, C., Unsworth, K., Epitropaki, O. and Parker, G. (2002). 'Implicating trust in the innovation process'. *Journal of Occupational and Organizational Psychology,* 75(4), pp. 409-422.

Coleman, J. S. (1988). 'Social capital in the creation of human capita'l. *American journal of sociology,* S95-S120.

Fiss, P. C. (2011). 'Building better causal theories: A fuzzy set approach to typologies in organization research'. *Academy of Management Journal,* 54(2), pp. 393-420.

Fleming, L., Mingo, S. and Chen, D. (2007). 'Collaborative brokerage, generative creativity, and creative success'. *Administrative science quarterly,* 52(3), pp. 443-475.

Friedkin, N. E. (1982). 'Information flow through strong and weak ties in intraorganizational social networks'. *Social networks*, 3(4), pp. 273-285.

Gaur, A. S., Kumar, V. and Singh, D. (2014). 'Institutions, resources, and internationalization of emerging economy firms'. *Journal of World Business*, 49(1), pp. 12-20.

Granovetter, M. S. (1973). 'The strength of weak ties'. *American journal of sociology*, pp. 1360- 1380.

Howe, J. (2008). Crowdsourcing: *How the power of the crowd is driving the future of business.* New York: Random House.

Inkpen, A. C. and Tsang, E. W. (2005). 'Social capital, networks, and knowledge transfer'. *Academy of management review*, 30(1), pp.146-165.

Jaffe, A. B., Trajtenberg, M. and Henderson, R. (1993). 'Geographic localization of knowledge spillovers as evidenced by patent citations'. *The Quarterly journal of Economics*, pp. 577-598.

Katila, R. and Ahuja, G. (2002). 'Something old, something new: A longitudinal study of search behavior and new product introduction'. *Academy of management journal*, 45(6), pp. 1183-1194.

Lahiri, N. (2010). 'Geographic distribution of R&D activity: how does it affect innovation quality?' *Academy of Management Journal*, 53(5), pp. 1194-1209.

Lambe, C. J. and Spekman, R. E. (1997). 'Alliances, external technology acquisition, and discontinuous technological change'. *Journal of product innovation management*, 14(2), pp. 102-116.

Laursen, K. and Salter, A. (2004). 'Searching high and low: what types of firms use universities as a source of innovation?'. *Research Policy*, 33(8), pp. 1201-1215.

Laursen, K. and Salter, A. (2006). 'Open for innovation: the role of openness in explaining innovation performance among UK manufacturing firms'. *Strategic management journal*, 27(2), pp. 131-150.

Lee, H. and Choi, B. (2003). 'Knowledge management enablers, processes, and organizational performance: An integrative view and empirical examination'. *Journal of management information systems*, 20(1), pp. 179-228.

Leenders, R. T. and Dolfsma, W. A. (2016). 'Social networks for innovation and new product development'. *Journal of Product Innovation Management*, 33(2), pp. 123-131.

Leitner, K. H., Warnke, P. and Rhomberg, W. (2016). 'New forms of innovation: critical issues for future pathways'. *foresight*, 18(3).

Letaifa, S. B. and Rabeau, Y. (2013). 'Too close to collaborate? How geographic proximity could impede entrepreneurship and innovation'. *Journal of Business Research*, 66(10), pp. 2071-2078.

Levin, D. Z. and Barnard, H. (2013). 'Connections to distant knowledge: Interpersonal ties between more-and less-developed countries'. *Journal of International Business Studies*, 44(7), pp. 676-698.

Levin, D. Z. and Cross, R. (2004). 'The strength of weak ties you can trust: The mediating role of trust in effective knowledge transfer'. *Management science*, 50(11), pp. 1477-1490.

Levin, D. Z., Walter, J., Appleyard, M. M. and Cross, R. (2015). 'Relational Enhancement How the Relational Dimension of Social Capital Unlocks the

Value of Network-Bridging Ties'. *Group & Organization Management,* 1059601115574429.

Lew, Y.K. and Sinkovics, R.R., (2013). 'Crossing borders and industry sectors: behavioral governance in strategic alliances and product innovation for competitive advantage'. *Long Range Planning,* 46(1), pp. 13-38.

Lin, N. (1999). 'Building a network theory of social capital'. *Connections,* 22(1), pp. 28-51.

Lin, N. (2005). 'Social Capital', in: Castiglione, D., van Deth, J.W. & Wolleb, G. (Eds.). (2008). The handbook of social capital. Oxford University Press.

Marsden, P. V. and Campbell, K. E. (1984). 'Measuring tie strength'. *Social forces,* 63(2), pp.482-501.

Marsden, P. V. and Campbell, K. E. (2012). 'Reflections on conceptualizing and measuring tie strength'. *Social forces,* 91(1), pp. 17-23.

Milgram, S. (1967). 'The small world problem'. *Psychology today,* 2(1), pp. 60-67.

Miller, D.J., Fern, M.J. and Cardinal, L.B. (2007). 'The use of knowledge for technological innovation within diversified firms'. *Academy of Management Journal,* 50(2), pp. 307-325.

Nahapiet, J. and Ghoshal, S. (1998). 'Social capital, intellectual capital, and the organizational advantage'. *Academy of management review,* 23(2), pp. 242-266.

Nambisan, S. and Sawhney, M. (2011). 'Orchestration processes in network-centric innovation: Evidence from the field'. *The Academy of Management Perspectives,* 25(3), pp. 40-57.

Narula, R. and Hagedoorn, J. (1999). 'Innovating through strategic alliances: moving towards international partnerships and contractual agreements'. *Technovation,* 19(5), pp. 283-294.

Newman, M. E. (2003). 'The structure and function of complex networks'. *SIAM review,* 45(2), pp. 167-256.

Nicholls-Nixon, C. L. and Woo, C. Y. (2003). 'Technology sourcing and output of established firms in a regime of encompassing technological change'. *Strategic Management Journal,* 24(7), pp. 651-666.

Nielsen, B. B. and Nielsen, S. (2009). 'Learning and innovation in international strategic alliances: An empirical test of the role of trust and tacitness'. *Journal of Management Studies,* 46(6), pp. 1031-1056.

Nieto, M. J. and Santamaría, L. (2007). 'The importance of diverse collaborative networks for the novelty of product innovation'. *Technovation,* 27(6), pp. 367-377.

Nooteboom, B. (1992). 'Towards a dynamic theory of transactions'. *Journal of evolutionary economics,* 2(4), pp. 281-299.

Nooteboom, B. (1999). 'Innovation, learning and industrial organisation'. *Cambridge Journal of economics,* 23(2), pp. 127-150.

Nooteboom, B., Van Haverbeke, W., Duysters, G., Gilsing, V. and Van den Oord, A. (2007). 'Optimal cognitive distance and absorptive capacity'. *Research policy,* 36(7), pp. 1016-1034.

Patulny, R. V. and Svendsen, G. L. H. (2007). 'Exploring the social capital grid: bonding, bridging, qualitative, quantitative'. *International Journal of Sociology and Social Policy,* 27(1/2), pp. 32-51.

Payne, G. T., Moore, C. B., Griffis, S. E. and Autry, C. W. (2011). 'Multilevel challenges and opportunities in social capital research'. *Journal of Management,* 37(2), pp. 491-520.

Peck, M. J. (1986). 'Joint R&D: The case of microelectronics and computer technology corporation'. *Research Policy,* 15(5), pp. 219-231.

Poetz, M. K. and Prügl, R. (2010). 'Crossing domain-specific boundaries in search of innovation: exploring the potential of pyramiding'. *Journal of Product Innovation Management,* 27(6), pp. 897-914.

Portes, A. (1998). 'Social capital: Its origins and applications in modern sociology'. *Annual Review of Sociology,* 24, pp. 1-24.

Powell, W. W., Koput, K. W., Smith-Doerr, L. and Owen-Smith, J. (1999). 'Network position and firm performance: Organizational returns to collaboration in the biotechnology industry'. *Research in the Sociology of Organizations,* 16(1), pp. 129-159.

Putnam, R. D. (2000). 'Bowling alone: America's declining social capital'. *In Culture and Politics.* US: Palgrave Macmillan. pp. 23-234.

Ragin, C. C. (2008). *Redesigning social inquiry: Fuzzy sets and beyond* (Vol. 240). Chicago: University of Chicago Press.

Schnettler, S. (2009). 'A structured overview of 50 years of small-world research'. *Social Networks,* 31(3), pp. 165-178.

Tsai, W. & Ghoshal, S. (1998). 'Social capital and value creation: The role of intrafirm networks'. *Academy of Management Journal,* 41(4), pp. 464–476.

Uzzi, B. and Spiro, J. (2005). 'Collaboration and Creativity: The Small World Problem1'. *American journal of sociology,* 111(2), pp. 447-504.

Vanhaverbeke, W. (2006). 'The interorganizational context of open innovation'. Open innovation: *Researching a new paradigm,* pp. 205-219.

Vanhaverbeke, W., Duysters, G. and Beerkens, B. (2002). 'Technological capability building through networking strategies within high-tech industries'. *Academy of Management Proceedings,* 2002 (1), pp. F1-F6.

Veugelers, R. (1997). 'Internal R & D expenditures and external technology sourcing'. *Research policy,* 26(3), pp. 303-315.

Von Hippel, E., Franke, N. and Prügl, R. (2009). 'Pyramiding: Efficient search for rare subjects'. *Research Policy,* 38(9), pp. 1397-1406.

Watts, D. J. (1999). 'Networks, dynamics, and the small-world phenomenon 1'. *American Journal of Sociology,* 105(2), pp. 493-527.

Watts, D. J. and Strogatz, S. H. (1998). 'Collective dynamics of 'small-world'networks'. *nature,* 393(6684), pp. 440-442.

Wellman, B. and Wortley, S. (1990). 'Different strokes from different folks: Community ties and social support'. *American journal of Sociology,* pp. 558-588.

West, J. and Bogers, M. (2014). 'Leveraging external sources of innovation: a review of research on open innovation'. *Journal of Product Innovation Management,* 31(4), pp. 814-831.

Westergren, U. H. and Holmström, J. (2012). 'Exploring preconditions for open innovation: Value networks in industrial firms'. *Information and Organization,* 22(4), pp. 209-226.

Whittington, K. B., Owen-Smith, J. and Powell, W. W. (2009). 'Networks, pro-
pinquity, and innovation in knowledge-intensive industries'. *Administrative Science Quarterly,* 54(1), pp. 90-122.

Chapter 3

An Analytical Approach to Assess the Matching Quality of Academic Partners for Open Innovation in the Form of University-Industry Collaboration

Nisit Manotungvorapun*, Nathasit Gerdsri

E-mail: nisit.m@gmail.com, nathasit.ger@mahidol.ac.th

Abstract: While firms adopt an open innovation concept in the form of university-industry collaboration (UIC), unproductive performances and unsmooth interactions are commonly found due to various gaps in characteristics between industries and academia, e.g., gaps in common knowledge base, gaps in agreements on intellectual property management policy, or gaps in organizational culture, etc. Managers should be able to identify how well academic partners match with the firm and what are the gaps between the two parties in order to reduce the risk of ineffective collaboration. Hence, this dissertation proposes an analytical approach to assessing the matching quality of academic partners. With a series of interviews and a comprehensive literature review, the major finding is the systematic approach which contains the specific criteria set for assessing the appropriateness of academic partners and the matching quality assessment model for identifying potential gaps between industries and academia.

Keywords: Open Innovation; University-Industry Collaboration; Matching Quality; Complementarity, Compatibility, Hierarchical Decision Modeling; Partnership; Collaboration Capability; Absorptive Capacity; Appropriability; Transformational Leadership.

1. Introduction

Innovating in-house with limited resources and capabilities might be an inappropriate strategy to survive in today's market which is full of challenges, including shortened technology life cycles, greater complexity of interdisciplinary knowledge, intense and fast-changing competition, and increasingly mobile talent. Consequently, firms increasingly interact with external partners in order to explore missing technology and exploit their unused technology. This phenomenon has been captured by Henry Chesbrough who first introduced 'open innovation' in 2003. Open innovation refers to 'the use of purposive inflows and outflows of knowledge to accelerate internal innovation, and expand the markets for external use of innovation, respectively' (Chesbrough, 2003c, Chesbrough, 2003b). His open innovation concept promises effective innovation performance with the notion of technology exploration and technology exploitation outside the firm's boundary (Lichtenthaler, 2008). Additionally, he and his colleague provide evidence of firms who achieve better innovation results by adopting open innovation, e.g., Procter and Gamble, General Mills, Volvo, Zerox etc. (Chesbrough, 2017, Huston and Sakkab, 2006, Ades et al., 2013, Chesbrough, 2003a, Chesbrough, 2003b).

The popularity of open innovation alongside driving technological and social factors has shifted managerial focus from innovation development as knowledge production into knowledge capture and flow. Open innovation has changed the landscape of technological competition from a battle of individual firms to a battle of networks. In other words, the wave of technology management from 'standalone' to 'alliances' confirms the significance of collaboration in the value chain (Gassmann et al., 2010). Therefore, partnerships are regarded as having central roles in open innovation and external alliances are the key sources of new knowledge and technological capabilities that firms can access, absorb and integrate with internal competencies (Cohen and Levinthal, 1989). One of the key success factors of open innovation is working with well-matched partners (Mitsuhashi and Greve, 2009, Barnes et al., 2002, Spekman et al., 1996) but identifying appropriate ones is also a critical challenge. There are technology brokers (e.g., Innocentive, Yet2.com and NineSigma, etc.) who match qualified professionals with client firms who post R&D challenges and offer rewards for talents who provide practical solutions (Lichtenthaler, 2013). However, these brokers only search for experts and their technology intelligence that relates to a client's strategic objectives. They do not cover whether and how these external capabilities can be integrated with a client's technology transfer management schema (Park and Yoon, 2013). Lichtenthaler (Lichtenthaler, 2013, Lichtenthaler and Lichtenthaler, 2009) highlights that the management of technology exchange requires absorptive, integrative and desorptive capacity.

While some firms employ the services of technology brokers, self-formation of partnerships is another approach. Among various types of partnering firms in a technology market, many firms co-innovate with universities in various forms of university-industry collaboration (UIC) (Laursen and Salter, 2004). However, the university-industry relationship is shaped in an idiosyncratic manner and characteristics (e.g., the missions of commercialization of the research and free-revealed publications, academic working styles, etc.) and such relations are often mediated by university's commercialization units (e.g., Technology Transfer Office (TTO), Intellectual Property Office (IPO) and Research Innovation Office (RIO), etc.).

UIC has been studied in various ways. While some scholars concentrate on how to manage the partnership (Almirall and Wareham, 2008, Perkmann and Salter, 2012, Edmondson et al., 2012, Bianchi et al., 2011, Casper and Miozzo, 2013), many researchers investigate causes of ineffective collaboration e.g. academia's research competence (Mindruta, 2013, Hemmert et al., 2014, Salom, 2013), the common knowledge distance between industry and university (Benner and Waldfogel, 2008, Cummings and Teng, 2003, Svetlik et al., 2007, Lakemond et al.), the incongruence of strategic objectives (Stern, 2004, Boudreau and Lakhani, 2012, Antikainen et al., 2010, Ankrah and Omar, 2015) and the incompatible working culture (Mindruta, 2013, Ades et al., 2013, Hall et al., 2003, Philbin, 2008). Thus, how to systematically identify the appropriateness of academic partners is a significant issue, but open innovation researchers acknowledge the lack of systematization in an open innovation practice (Gassmann et al., 2010, West et al., 2014, Grönlund, 2010). Moreover, existing studies on matching models of UIC show the different typology of criteria (Wu and Barnes, 2011, Chatenier et al., 2010) and some use complex academic publication analysis and advanced mathematic techniques (Banal-Estañol et al., 2013, Mindruta, 2013), which limit the communication process and the accessibility for practicing firms.

This dissertation addresses the ineffectiveness of collaboration caused by gaps between the host firm and its academic partners. The identification of how well academic partners match with the firm and which gaps need to be bridged are essential for the preparation and delivery of solutions that lead to effective collaboration. This study proposes a systematic approach tailored to firms who practice UIC under an open innovation strategy and want to identify the matching quality of their academic partners. With an exploratory research methodology, the systematic approach was designed and the assessment model was developed to provide a clear classification of criteria and the avoidance of complexity in use. The output is a specific set of criteria for determining the appropriateness of academic partners. In addition, the matching quality and the matching quality gaps between the host firm and an academic partner are identified and presented in three graphical forms: 1.) the complementarity vs. compatibility matrix, 2.) the matching quality radar chart and 3.) the matching quality gap bar chart. These feedback mechanisms enable managers to identify the matching quality of their academic partners as well as the matching quality gaps that need to be managed for effective collaboration.

2. Background

A few studies have analyzed open innovation in the form of UICs as private-public partnerships (West et al., 2014) and some scholars have addressed the systematic practice of UICs. For instance, Du et al. (Du et al., 2014a) claim a dearth of research on university-industry relations at the level of R&D projects. Perkmann and Walsh (Perkmann and Walsh, 2007) address the search and matching of academic partners for open innovation projects. West et al. (West et al., 2014) highlight that the systematic application of university-industry collaboration when under an open innovation strategy is a research focus in its own right. Philbin (Philbin, 2008) conducted an empirical study and found that R&D collaborations still lack integrative frameworks for management. Caetano and Amaral (Caetano and Amaral, 2011) address the absence of systems for identifying and selecting various types of partners (including universities) in technology road mapping.

While the systemization of UIC has been addressed, the effectiveness of UIC relies on how well academic partners match with the firm (Gulati, 1998). Some researchers concentrate on particular criteria that managers use to determine the fit of academia and propose their matching approaches to identify how well an academic partner matches the firm. For instance, Carayol N. (Carayol, 2003) tests the correlation between the characteristics of academics' and firms' research agendas (the basis of the research and the level of research excellence) and the degree of risk of research itself and the impracticability of research results. They confirm the "assortative" matching hypothesis that the likelihood of a matching process leading firms and academics to collaborate is positively affected by the degree of research excellence of the affiliated institution, the research's its basic degree and the degree of tolerance of project risk. Banal-Estañol et al. (Banal-Estañol et al., 2013) construct a two-sided matching model by considering characteristics associated with the preferences for a type of research and those related to the capacity to produce high-quality research outputs. Their empirical results show that the possibility of collaboration increases with the type and the capacity of academics in the project, i.e. academics that prefer applied research and can produce high-quality research results are more likely to work with industry. Mindruta (Mindruta, 2013) develop a matching model of firm-scientist research collaboration that estimates how three attributes, including knowledge type (breadth and depth), research quality and technological capabilities, complement or substitute each other in knowledge creation. Her model has two important findings: 1.) collaboration tends to occur when scientists with higher research quality connect with firms with lower technological capabilities and 2.) the greatest value of scientist-firm collaboration is created by a combination of complementarity in scientific capabilities and substitutability in knowledge type and technological skills. Table 3.1 below shows the list of example studies on matching models for UICs.

Table 3.1 Examples of studies on matching approaches for UICs

Authors	Criteria	Findings
Carayol N. (Carayol, 2003)	knowledge type)breadth and depth(, research quality and technological capabilities	The propensity of matching occurs when scientists whose higher research quality connect with firms with lower technological capabilities.
Banal-Estañol et al. (Banal-Estañol et al., 2013)	1. The types of research)basic vs. applied research(2. Scientific ability	The tendency of effective collaboration takes place when *the most able and the most applied academic researchers* match with *the most able and the most basic firms.*
Mindutra (Mindruta, 2013)	1. Expertise and productivity of scientists 2. Capacity to complete projects 3. Experience in managing projects 4. Time commitment	Effective collaborations with complementarity occur when one party possess knowledge breath)diversification(and another has knowledge depth)expertise(. However, his model does not concern search costs, the adverse selection and market frictions)e.g., institutional policies, geographical location(.
Yamada et al. (Yamada et al., 2013)	The relevance of patents and scientific papers	The authors propose a matching system for companies and researchers using patents and scientific papers. Their information retrieval system provides a list of patents and published papers based on the query for an abstract and each characteristic word. However, the focus of outputs is the quantity of potential university researchers not the appropriateness of found ones.
Ning and Xue-wei (Ning and Xue-wei, 2006)	1. Firm status 2. Cooperation relationship 3. Cooperation record	Authors apply Interpretive structural modeling)ISM(to transform the partner selection evaluation system into the matrix model. And Analytic Network Process)ANP(method is applied to analyze the interrelationships between one criteria and another.

Besides the different typology of criteria, matching approaches as shown above measure the research excellence of universities through patent citations and publications using advanced mathematical techniques. This type of technical analysis contains technical language which might delay the communication of results across functional units in a firm and also potentially lead to misunderstandings and ambiguities. Also, these matching approaches involve specialized units (e.g., technology scouting team) which are more prevalent in firms with high R&D intensity or with a strong appropriability regime. As mentioned, the antecedents of effective university-industry collaboration include not only the complementary research-oriented characteristics but also compatible relationship-oriented ones. Mitsuhashi and Greve (Mitsuhashi and Greve, 2009) state that the matching quality in alliances is comprised of two dimensions: complementarity and compatibility. Therefore, the concrete set of criteria must capture the roles of complementarity and compatibility dimensions.

3. Research design

To meet the need for identification of the academic partner's appropriateness, this dissertation employs prescriptive research by developing and testing artefacts (Ahlemann et al., 2013). The combination of an inductive and deductive approach is used to analyze the linkages between research findings and existing relevant literature (Thomas, 2006, Hyde, 2000). The data collection involves in-depth interviews and workshops with R&D personnel of the host firm, integrating with a review of relevant literature and documents (e.g., meeting agendas and archives). This dissertation designs the analytical approach which consists of four phases; I.) Exploration of managerial requirements, II.) Construction of the matching quality assessment model for matching quality, III.) Operation of the assessment model, and IV.) Analysis and feedback on the matching quality. These four phases branch out into ten steps as shown in Figure 3.1 below.

This dissertation employs an inductive approach to explore in-depth issues that are not well defined (Eisenhardt, 1989, Thomas, 2006), e.g., the specific set of criteria that managers use to determine the appropriateness of academic partners. On the other hand, a deductive approach is used to ensure that insights from literature are applicable for specific real instances (Hyde, 2000). This study also contains initial exploratory research with an interview-based case study method and incorporates derived quotations from relevant literature in order to understand the complexity of UIC under an open innovation strategy.

This research targeted domestic firms who engage in UIC with domestic or foreign universities. Two case companies agreed to participate in semi-structured interviews and workshops for this research including **Company X** (the leading integrated petrochemical and refining manufacturer with over3,500 employees and 105 R&D personnel) and ***Company Y*** (the top manufacturer of canned seafood with about 1,028 employees and 4 R&D employees).

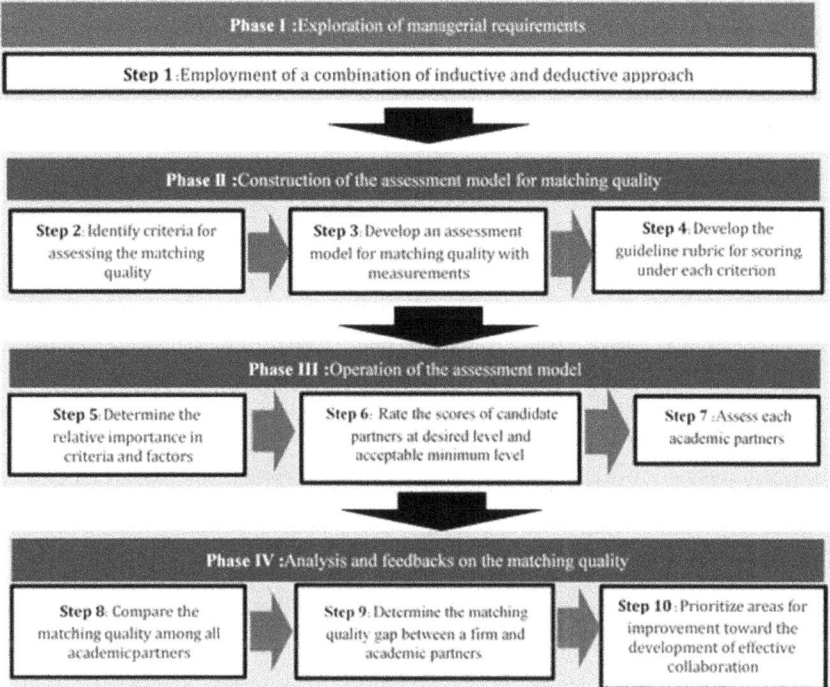

Figure 3.1 Research methodology

During Phase I of the research, managers of both case companies were asked to recall one past UIC project which would be used as the reference for this study. Themes of questions included the characteristics of their academic partners, the process of determining academic partners, the list of candidate universities (without revealing the selected one) as well as the performance and obstacles in the project. During Phase II, the interview outputs were incorporated with the relevant literature to construct the assessment model. This dissertation concentrates literature on the three particular areas of open innovation, university-industry collaboration and the matching quality. The assessment model consists of the criteria set for determining the matching quality of academic partners, the measurement items and the guideline rubrics. Next, the workshops were held to test the operation of the model in Phase III. In this phase, managers of the host firm were asked to determine the weight, the desirable level and the acceptable minimum level for each criterion while R&D members of the host firm were asked to assess each of the academic partners. Then, the outputs from the operation were analyzed and presented in three forms of graphical feedback during Phase IV. The first graphical feedback is the **Complementarity vs. Compatibility matrix** which compares the positions of assessed academic partners. The second feedback of **the Matching Quality Radar Chart** reveals the gaps between individual academic partner and the host firm while the third one of **the Matching Quality Gap Bar Chart** prioritizes areas for improvement in the development of effective collaboration.

4. Conclusion

The project goal of Company X was to develop biochemistry technology for Company X while for Company Y it was to encapsulate fish oil from production waste. At that time, Company X had four candidate universities while Company Y had three. Both companies determined three categories of partner characteristics including _1. Complementarity of research capability, 2. Compatibility of business mindset and 3. Compatibility of relationship._ From these three categories, both companies commonly determined nine associating characteristics including _1. Competency of research excellence (CE) 2. Capability of commercialization (CC) 3. Capacity of common knowledge base (CK) 4. Contribution of research resource (CR) 5. Adaptability with project goals (AG) 6. Adaptability with agreements on IP management policy (AP) 7. Adaptability with changes impacting the project (AC) 8. Ability to orchestrate with project team(AO) 9. Anecdotes of relationship (AR)._

In Phase II, three broad categories and nine characteristics were used as criteria and factors for the construction of the assessment model. In Phase III, the assessment model was operated by Company X and the numerical results were derived and computed as shown in Table 3.2 below.

Table 3.2 The numeric results

Dimension/ Factors	Relative importance of factor (Wij)	Full score	Desired level (Dij)	Acceptable minimum level (Mij)	Assessment score of candidate university (Sij)			
					A	B	C	D
CE	0.34	5	4	3	3.50	3.50	3.25	3.25
CC	0.15	5	5	4	3.00	2.83	2.83	3.00
CK	0.11	5	4	3	3.00	3.00	3.00	2.80
CR	0.04	5	4	3	4.00	4.00	4.00	3.60

Complementarity score	0.64	3.20	2.71	2.07	2.13	2.11	2.02	2.01
Proportion of complementarity dimension (%)			84.69	64.69	66.62	65.84	63.17	62.76
AG	0.11	5	4	3	3.83	3.83	3.83	3.83
AP	0.05	5	5	3	3.67	3.67	3.67	3.67
AC	0.10	5	5	3	2.80	3.00	3.00	2.60
AO	0.07	5	5	4	4.33	4.33	4.33	4.33
AR	0.03	5	3	2	3.50	3.50	3.25	3.50
Compatibility score	0.36	1.80	1.63	1.11	1.29	1.31	1.30	1.27
Proportion of compatibility dimension (%)			90.38	61.81	71.50	72.64	72.19	70.36

In phase IV, the results in Table 3.2 were drawn for the analysis and the provision of three graphics. Firstly, ***the complementarity vs. compatibility matrix*** was developed to compare the matching quality among all candidate universities as shown in Figure 3.2 below. In light of the complementarity, candidate university A and B perform higher than the acceptable minimum level while candidate universities C and D fare less well. As for the compatibility, all candidates perform above the acceptable minimum level.

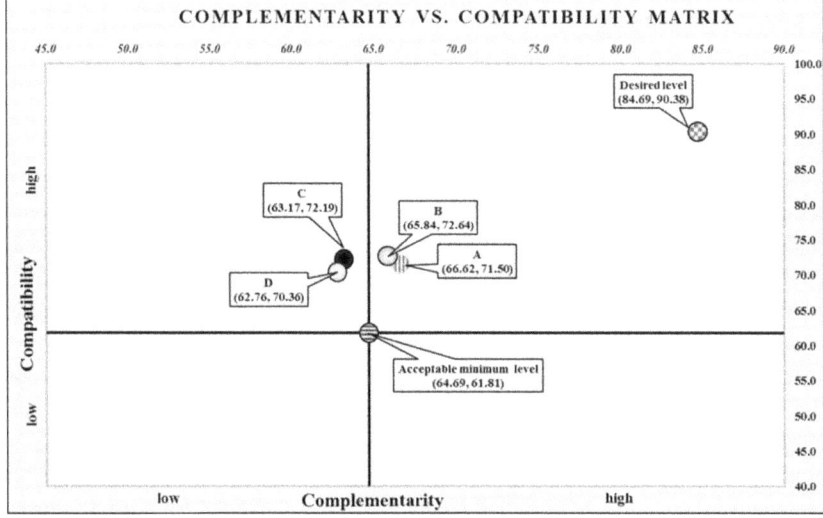

Figure 3.2 The Complementarity vs. Compatibility Matrix

Secondly, the values of desired levels, acceptable minimum levels and average actual scores of individual candidate universities are presented in t*he Matching Quality Radar Chart* as shown in Figure 3.3 below.

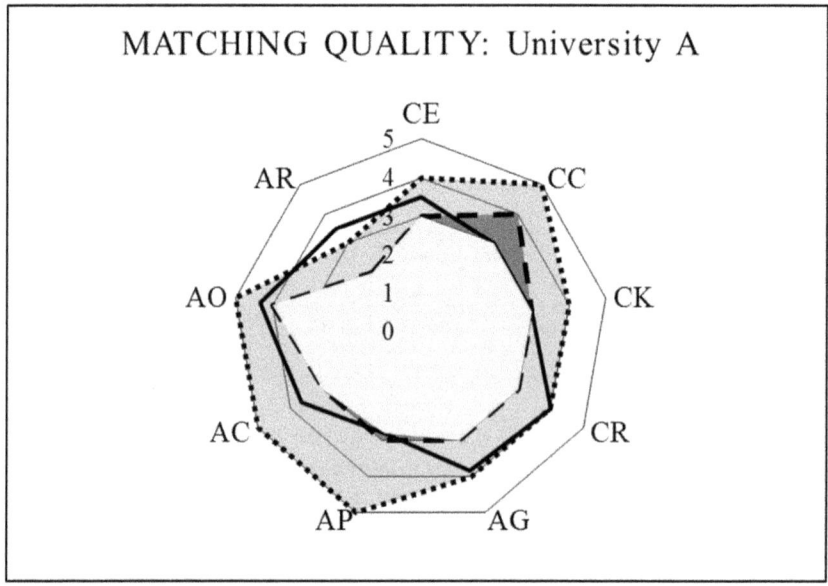

Figure 3.3 The matching quality radar charts of university A

———————   Assessment score

———————   Acceptable minimum level

— — —   Desired level

Three lines drawn in the radar chart create gaps that are used to determine the matching quality between a firm and an academic partner. Gaps can be differentiated in three conditions of 1.) the critical zone, 2.) the tolerance zone, and 3.) the preferable zone as depicted in Fig 3.4 below. When the assessment score (a dense line) lies below the acceptable minimum level (a dash line), the critical zone occurs (see condition A in Figure 3.4). The critical zone signals the serious mismatch between the host firm and an academic partner and it requires an immediate attention to be bridged. When the assessment score (a dense line) lies in between the desired level (a dot line) and the acceptable minimum level (a dash line), the tolerance zone occurs (see condition B in Fig 3.4). The tolerance zone signals potential difficulties associated with that particular factor and waits to be mitigated. And when the assessment score (a dense line) lies above the desired level (a dot line), the preferable zone occurs (see condition C in Fig 3.4). The preferable zone signals a condition where an academic partner is above the host firm's desirable level. Potential benefits associated with that particular factor wait to be utilized.

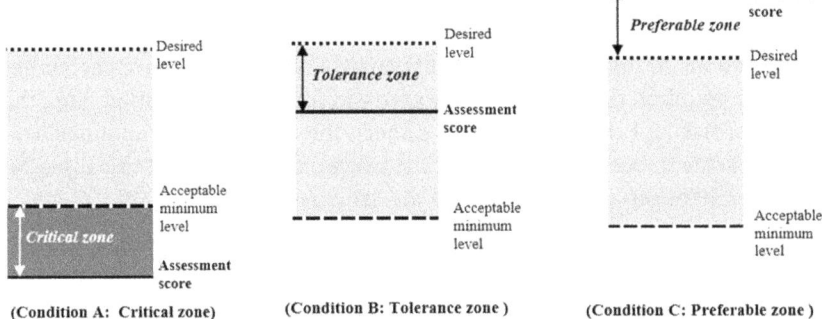

(Condition A: Critical zone)   (Condition B: Tolerance zone)   (Condition C: Preferable zone)

Figure 3.4 Three conditions of the matching quality translated from the matching quality radar

Thirdly, the values of critical and tolerance zones are visualized in ***the Matching Quality Gap Bar Chart*** as shown in Table 3.3 below. This gap bar chart enables managers to prioritize the matching quality gaps of individual academic partners at the factor level.

Table 3.3 The matching quality gap bar charts of university A

Criterion	Factor	Candidate University A	
		The critical zone	The tolerance zone
C1: complementarity of research capability	CE		-0.17
	CC	-0.25	-0.50
	CK		-0.33
	CR		
C2: compatibility of business minset	AG		-0.06
	AP		-0.33
	AC	-0.05	-0.55
C3: compatibility of relations	AO		-0.17
	AR		

5. Implications and future research

This dissertation offers an approach to determining the matching quality of external academic partners for the firms who practice open innovation with UICs. While the institutionalization of the proposed 10-step approach among firms who adopt open innovation for R&D collaboration is possible, some modifications to the approach (e.g., the criteria set, the weights of each criterion) are required depending on the scenario for the collaboration (e.g., the degree of risk and complexity of the project, the availability of potential academic partners, business conditions). However, the findings of this dissertation offer managerial implications for the firms as follows.

First, the proposed approach advances the partner knowledge management in two ways: documenting and communicating partner profiles. For the first aspect of documenting partner profiles, our proposed approach serves as a systematic way to document profiles in a holistic manner for managers. This study points out that some managers use their subjective judgements to determine the appropriateness of academic partners due to the diversity of criteria (Wu and Barnes, 2011, Chatenier et al., 2010) and the complexity of patent- and publication-based partner search tools (Park and Yoon, 2013, Yoon and Song, 2014, Lee et al., 2016, Yamada et al., 2013). To manage the diversity of the criteria, the term "matching quality" is contextualized and used to explain the appropriateness of academic partners. To avoid the complex use of patent citation and publication databases, this study codifies managers' expectations and internal R&D team members' perceptions of the characteristics of academic partners as a way to assess the matching quality between a firm and academic partner.

For the second aspect, communicating partner profiles, Manotungvorapun and Gerdsri (Manotungvorapun and Gerdsri, 2015) proposed earlier a systematic approach to codify the characteristics of partners and communicate them in a radar chart that supports matching partners for open innovation practice. We build on this work by proposing how to identify how well a university partner matches with the firm. As a result, feedback of the assessment model can be used as the learning material for knowledge mobility, i.e. a manager can explicitly communicate and transmit the academic partner profile to other managers who will lead future UIC projects. This reinforcement of knowledge mobility supports organizational learning processes and boosts the alliance capability of the firm (Draulans et al., 2003). Kale et al. (Kale et al., 2002) define the alliance capability as *'specific systems to capture, codify, communicate and create alliance management lessons and insights associated with their alliance experience'* (referred from the work of Blomqvist and Levy (2006) (Kale et al., 2002). By connecting with their definition, our proposed approach offers a systematic way to capture and codify managers' expectations and R&D members' perceptions of the characteristics of academic partners. During the operation of our proposed model, managers' expectation is codified and computed within a desirable range (i.e., the difference between the target level and the acceptable minimum level in our assessment model) while internal R&D team members' perceptions are codified during the assessment. The involvement of both managers and internal R&D personnel during the operation of the model opens a channel for sharing lessons and experiences in collaborating with academic partners. Often, decisions to develop and commercialize a product or process innovation are made and approved by the committee consisting of managers from various departments to evaluate the viability of the projects at the macro level (e.g., finance, marketing, manufacturing, and human resources, etc.). Therefore, the outputs of the assessment model act as the translator of matching quality from elusive, technical language into quantitative, management-friendly and easy-to-communicate language for managers from various departments. Feedback from the model functions as artefacts which renders implicit partner knowledge explicit and facilitates knowledge transfer within the firm.

Second, the proposed approach supports the design of strategic modification by providing strategic guidelines on how to improve the matching quality between a firm and an academic partner. As previously demonstrated, the complementarity versus compatibility matrix presents the positions of candidate universities as well as the distances between them. By connecting with the firm's purpose, this matrix guides what dimension (and how far) the host firm has to go to achieve effective collaboration. If the firm aims to accomplish research-based performance, but the complementarity positions of candidate universities are below the desired level, the firm should initiate solutions to boost academics' research competence e.g. providing milestone completion-based rewards to motivate academic partners to improve their professionalization level (Borrell-Damian et al., 2014), mutually developing and using the knowledge portal to integrate the knowledge base (McAdam et al., 2008). Meanwhile, the firm that experiences a compatible collaboration situation should implement orchestration strategies such as using a liaison to mediate the connection between the different objectives of both parties (Bloedon and Stokes, 1994), create an open and informal atmosphere to foster closer relationships (Du et al., 2014b), etc.

While the complementarity vs. compatibility matrix initially suggests what dimension (and how far) the firm has to go; the matching quality radar chart specifies how well the candidate university matches with the host firm and which gaps should be bridged. Thus, the radar chart serves as a basis for a manager's to initiate precise strategies. The matching quality gap bar chart depicts the degree of matching quality gap and a manager can use this bar chart as a reference for deciding on the priority of strategic modification. Therefore, our proposed approach produces feedback to help the firm to reduce the risk of collaboration by encouraging the preparation of solutions and supporting the decision in the design of strategic modification.

However, this dissertation has some limitations and provides suggestions for future development as follows.

Firstly, the matching quality assessment model needs more internal validity and generalizability. Since this study concerns the various activities of open innovation and the different typology of criteria, the scope of this study is narrowed by focusing on UIC at a dual level between a large firm in the chemicals industry and its university partner. Therefore, future research should modify the model for other different scenarios such as other forms of open innovation activities (e.g., R&D contracts, in-licensing, out-licensing), other types of partners (e.g., suppliers, lead customers, government), and other domains (e.g., consumer products, computer software, automobiles, telecommunication).

Secondly, the matching quality assessment model was tested in the setting of a bilateral relationship between one host firm and one university partner. However, most firms today encounter increases in the size and complexity of the partner portfolios (Hoffmann, 2005). Another challenge is how a firm strategically manages the collaboration project engaged in by multiple partners for a mutual goal (Medcof, 1997). Therefore, the scenario where there are multiple partner universities should be further developed.

Thirdly, the proposed model was tested with the past project. But the advancement of the project when adopting recommended strategies in parallel with the routine jobs should be also monitored and assessed throughout the course of the project. As such, action research and longitudinal research methodologies are required to investigate changes in the performance of the project and the capabilities of all involved parties. To achieve this, the matching quality should be assessed at before, during and after the project. Also, some other output indicators should be added, e.g., financial performance of collaboration, the accomplishment of project goals, and the degrees of openness and relationship.

Fourthly, criteria and numerical inputs contained in the matching quality assessment model were derived from the standpoint of the host firm. Draulans et al. (Draulans et al., 2003) state that managers should not only determine the appropriateness of partners but also the partnership management capability of the partners. Therefore, the study of how to develop an integrated matching quality assessment model which regards the standpoints of both the host firm and its external partners should be conducted.

References

Ades, C., Figlioli, A., Sbragia, R., Porto, G., Plonski, G. A. & Celadon, K. (2013). 'Implementing Open Innovation: The Case of Natura, IBM and Siemens'. *Journal of Technology Management & Innovation, 8*, 12-25.

Ahlemann, F., el Arbi, F., Kaiser, M. G. & Heck, A. (2013). 'A process framework for theoretically grounded prescriptive research in the project management field'. *International Journal of Project Management, 31*, 43-56.

Almirall, E. & Wareham, J. (2008). 'Living Labs and open innovation: roles and applicability'. *The Electronic Journal for Virtual Organizations and Networks, 10*, 21-46.

Ankrah, S. & Omar, A.-T. (2015). 'Universities–industry collaboration: A systematic review'. *Scandinavian Journal of Management.*

Antikainen, M., Mäkipää, M. & Ahonen, M. (2010). 'Motivating and supporting collaboration in open innovation'. *European Journal of Innovation Management, 13*, 100-119.

Banal-Estañol, A., Macho-Stadler, I. & Pérez castrillo, D. (2013). Endogeneous matching in university-industry collaboration: Theory and empirical evidence from the UK.

Barnes, T., Pashby, I. & Gibbons, A. (2002). 'Effective University–Industry Interaction:: A Multi-case Evaluation of Collaborative R&D Projects'. *European Management Journal, 20*, 272-285.

Benner, M. & Waldfogel, J. (2008). 'Close to you? Bias and precision in patent-based measures of technological proximity'. *Research Policy, 37*, 1556-1567.

Bianchi, M., Cavaliere, A., Chiaroni, D., Frattini, F. & Chiesa, V. (2011). 'Organisational modes for Open Innovation in the bio-pharmaceutical industry: An exploratory analysis'. *Technovation, 31*, 22-33.

Bloedon, R. V. & Stokes, D. R. (1994). 'Making university/industry collaborative research succeed'. *Research Technology Management, 37*, 44.

Borrell-Damian, L., Morais, R. & Smith, J. H. (2014). University-business Collaborative Research: goals, outcomes and new assessment tools The EUIMA Collaborative Research Project Report. EUA Publications.

Boudreau, K. J. & Lakhani, K. R. (2012). 'How to manage outside innovation'. *Image.*

Caetano, M. & Amaral, D. C. (2011). 'Roadmapping for technology push and partnership: A contribution for open innovation environments'. *Technovation, 31*, 320-335.

CarayoL, N. (2003). 'Objectives, agreements and matching in science–industry collaborations: reassembling the pieces of the puzzle'. *Research policy, 32*, 887-908.

Casper, S. & Miozzo, M. (2013). Open innovation and governance: Innovation partnerships between industry and university in science-based sectors. 35th DRUID Celebration Conference, Barcelona, Spain, 17-19.

Chatenier, E. D., Verstegen, J. A., Biemans, H. J., Mulder, M. & Omta, O. S. (2010). 'Identification of competencies for professionals in open innovation teams'. *R&D Management, 40*, 271-280.

Chesbrough, H. (2003a). 'The governance and performance of Xerox's technology spin-off companies'. *Research Policy, 32*, 403-421.

Chesbrough, H. (2017). 'The Future of Open Innovation'. *Research-Technology Management,* 60, 35-38.

Chesbrough, H. W. (2003b). 'The era of open innovation'. *MIT Sloan Management Review,* 44, 35-41.

Chesbrough, H. W. (2003c). *Open innovation: The new imperative for creating and profiting from technology,* Harvard Business Press.

Cohen, W. M. & Levinthal, D. A. (1989). 'Innovation and learning: the two faces of R&D'. *The economic journal,* 99, 569-596.

Cummings, J. L. & Teng, B.-S. (2003). 'Transferring R&D knowledge: the key factors affecting knowledge transfer succes's. *Journal of Engineering and technology management,* 20, 39-68.

Draulans, J., Deman, A.-P. & Volberda, H. W. (2003). 'Building Alliance Capability:: Management Techniques for Superior Alliance Performance'. *Long Range Planning,* 36, 151-166.

Du, J., Leten, B. & Vanhaverbeke, W. (2014a). 'Managing open innovation projects with science-based and market-based partners'. *Research Policy,* 43, 828-840.

Du, J., Leten, B. & Vanhaverbeke, W. (2014b). 'Managing open innovation projects with science-based and market-based partners'. *Research Policy.*

Edmondson, G., Valigra, L., Kenward, M., Hudson, R. & Belfield, H. (2012).' Making industry-university partnerships work: Lessons from successful collaboration's. *Science Business Innovation Board AISBL.*

EisenhardT, K. M. (1989). 'Building theories from case study research'. *Academy of Management Review,* 14, 532-550.

Gassmann, O., Enkel, E. & Chesbrough, H. (2010). 'The future of open innovation'. *R&D Management,* 40, 213-221.

Grönlund, J. (2010). *Open innovation and the Stage-Gate process: a revised model for new product development.*

Gulati, R. (1998). 'Alliances and network's. *Strategic management journal,* 19, 293-317.

Hall, B. H., Link, A. N. & Scott, J. T. 2003. 'Universities as research partners'. *Review of Economics and Statistics,* 85, 485-491.

Hemmert, M., Bstieler, L. & Okamuro, H. (2014). 'Bridging the cultural divide: Trust formation in university–industry research collaborations in the US, Japan, and South Korea'. *Technovation,* 34, 605-616.

Hoffmann, W. H. (2005). 'How to manage a portfolio of alliances'. *Long Range Planning,* 38, 121-143.

Huston, L. & Sakkab, N. (2006). 'Connect and develop'. *Harvard business review,* 84, 58-66.

Hyde, K. F. (2000). 'Recognising deductive processes in qualitative research'. *Qualitative market research: An international journal,* 3, 82-90.

Kale, P., Dyer, J. H. & Singh, H. (2002). 'Alliance capability, stock market response, and long-term alliance success: the role of the alliance function'. *Strategic Management Journal,* 23, 747-767.

Lakemond, N., Bengtsson, L., Laursen, K. & Tell, F. *Match & Manage: The use of knowledge matching and project management to integrate knowledge in collaborative inbound open innovation.*

Laursen, K. & Salter, A. (2004). 'Searching high and low: what types of firms use universities as a source of innovation?' *Research Policy*, 33, 1201-1215.

Lee, K., Park, I. & Yoon, B. (2016). 'An Approach for R&D Partner Selection in Alliances between Large Companies, and Small and Medium Enterprises (SMEs): Application of Bayesian Network and Patent Analysis'. *Sustainability*, 8, 117.

Lichtenthaler, U. (2008). 'Open innovation in practice: an analysis of strategic approaches to technology transactions'. *Engineering Management, IEEE Transactions on*, 55, 148-157.

Lichtenthaler, U. (2013). 'The Collaboration of Innovation Intermediaries and Manufacturing Firms in the Markets for Technology'. *Journal of Product Innovation Management*, 30, 142-158.

Lichtenthaler, U. & Lichtenthaler, E. (2009). 'A Capability-Based Framework for Open Innovation: Complementing Absorptive Capacity'. *Journal of Management Studies*, 46, 1315-1338.

Manotungvorapun, N. & Gerdsri, N. (2015) Matching partners for Open Innovation practice. 2015 Portland International Conference on Management of Engineering and Technology (PICMET), IEEE, 718-727.

Mcadam, R., O'Hare, T. & Moffett, S. (2008). 'Collaborative knowledge sharing in Composite New Product Development: An aerospace study'. *Technovation*, 28, 245-256.

Medcof, J. W. (1997). 'Why too many alliances end in divorce'. *Long Range Planning*, 30, 718-732.

Mindruta, D. (2013). 'Value creation in university-firm research collaborations: A matching approach'. *Strategic management journal*, 34, 644-665.

Mitsuhashi, H. & Greve, H. R. (2009). 'A matching theory of alliance formation and organizational success: Complementarity and compatibility'. *Academy of Management Journal*, 52, 975-995.

Ning, M. & Xue-Wei, L. (2006). University-Industry Alliance Partner Selection Method Based on ISM and ANP. 2006 International Conference on Management Science and Engineering, 5-7 Oct 2006. 981-985.

Park, I. & Yoon, B. (2013). 'Identifying Potential Parntership for Open Innovation by using Bibliographic Coupling and Keyword Vector Mapping'. *World Academy of Science, Engineering and Technology*, 7, 375-380.

Perkmann, M. & Salter, A. (2012). 'How to create productive partnerships with universities'. *MIT Sloan Management Review*, 53, 79-105.

Perkmann, M. & Walsh, K. (2007). 'University–industry relationships and open innovation: Towards a research agenda'. *International Journal of Management Reviews*, 9, 259-280.

Philbin, S. (2008). 'Process model for university-industry research collaboration'. *European Journal of Innovation Management*, 11, 488-521.

Salom, M. D. (2013). 'Research capability of the faculty members of dmmmsu mid la union campus'. *INternational Scientific Research Journal*, 5, 45-55.

Spekman, R. E., Isabella, L. A., Macavoy, T. C. & Forbes, T. (1996). 'Creating strategic alliances which endure'. *Long range planning*, 29, 346-357.

Stern, S. (2004). 'Do scientists pay to be scientists?' *Management science*, 50, 835-853.

Svetlik, I., Stavrou-Costea, E. & Lin, H.-F. (2007). 'Knowledge sharing and firm innovation capability: an empirical study'. *International Journal of manpower,* 28, 315-332.

Thomas, D. R. (2006). 'A general inductive approach for analyzing qualitative evaluation data'. *American journal of evaluation,* 27, 237-246.

West, J., Salter, A., Vanhaverbeke, W. & Chesbrough, H. (2014). 'Open innovation: The next decade'. *Research Policy,* 43, 805-811.

Wu, C. & Barnes, D. (2011). 'A literature review of decision-making models and approaches for partner selection in agile supply chains'. *Journal of Purchasing and Supply Management,* 17, 256-274.

Yamada, Y., Tansho, T. & Hirokawa, S. (2013). Proposal of a Matching System for Companies and Researchers Using Patents and Scientific Papers. 2013 Second IIAI International Conference on Advanced Applied Informatics, Aug. 31 2013-Sept. 4 2013. 397-398.

Yoon, B. & Song, B. (2014). 'A systematic approach of partner selection for open innovation'. *Industrial Management & Data Systems,* 114.

Chapter 4

Exploring Inter-Organizational Collaboration for Innovation in a Regional Ecosystem

Agnieszka Radziwon*

E-mail: agra@btech.au.dk

Abstract: Communities, networks, ecosystems, alliances, and other coupled forms of open innovation have increased their prevalence and impact on an organization's development. Still relatively few studies address the challenges of open innovation from the small and medium sized enterprises (SMEs) perspective, especially at the level of business ecosystems. Therefore, this research fills this gap by providing a study immersed in an open innovation context with a particular focus on the ways how SMEs contribute to the development of the ecosystem they are embedded in. A central point of attention is inter-organizational collaboration between SMEs and other stakeholders co-evolving in a regional business ecosystem. The empirical work is based on a qualitative inquiry combined with grounded theory and action research elements. The main findings offer insights into the mutual knowledge flows across organizational boundaries, resource recombination in inter-organizational collaboration as well as value creation and capturing processes.

Keywords: open innovation; SMEs, ecosystem, inter-organizational collaboration.

1. Introduction

An increasing number of small and medium enterprises (SMEs) embrace open innovation practices to gain competitive advantage. These are an important part of the economy and despite constituting, the majority of firms in the European industrial setup, these generate only three-fifths of the EU value added (Muller, Caliandro, Peycheva, et al. 2016). Due to their agility to respond to opportunities, fast-decision making process and flexibility SMEs occupy a special place in the innovation landscape (Mitra 2017), but their innovation potential is not fully explored yet. It is partially because SMEs do not benefit from open innovation in the same way as large firms (Vanhaverbeke 2017) so we cannot extrapolate the successful open innovation examples from multinational corporations to small firms. A more detailed understanding of the conditions under which SMEs can implement an open approach to innovation it thus still lacking.

Forming inter-organizational partnerships and engaging in formal and informal collaboration arrangements, has proven to be important for a firms' growth, and their market survival (Deschryvere 2014). Due to resource shortages, SMEs do not have extensive project portfolios and special departments responsible for innovation (Vanhaverbeke 2017). That is why for SMEs inter-organizational collaboration can be a crucial driver for improving innovation performance (Powell, Koput and Smith-Doerr 1996). Nevertheless, in order to benefit from innovation focused inter-organizational collaboration, SMEs have to consider how to successfully organize and manage the inter-organizational knowledge flows.

Despite both researchers' and practitioners' interest in further exploration of ecosystems, only relatively few studies that focused on open innovation in business ecosystems (Ritala, Agouridas, Assimakopoulos, et al. 2013; Radziwon, Bogers and Bilberg 2017; Van Der Borgh, Cloodt and Romme 2012) analyze business ecosystems from the SMEs' perspective. Close geographical and cognitive proximity, strong interdependences and co-evolution could provide a very fruitful ground for improvement of innovation performance of entire ecosystems, but also of SMEs that constitute it. That is why this research project intended to shed some light on the ways how an inter-organizational collaboration between SMEs and other ecosystem stakeholders contributes to the development of a regional business ecosystem (Radziwon 2017). In order to operationalize the research and to ensure the depth of the investigation, the overall research question was narrowed to four sub-questions each with a focus on a specific issue of: ecosystem conceptualization (Scaringella and Radziwon 2018); mutual knowledge flows across organizational boundaries (Radziwon and Bogers 2018a); inter-organizational collaboration (Radziwon and Bogers 2018b) ;and value creation and capture processes (Radziwon, Bogers and Bilberg 2017).

The overall motivation to pursue this study could be summarized in a form of four interest pillars. These are:

1.   the research gaps related to the organizational boundaries, inter-organizational collaboration as well as value creation and capture processes;

2.   call for more practically oriented research methods, which application could increase the understanding of the organizational change and all underlying processes;

3. the interest in tackling a practical problem of organizing and managing inter-organizational collaboration in the way that it could maximize the added value to the ecosystem;

4. strong interest in exploring the ways how SMEs (in particular) could contribute to the development of an ecosystem that they are embedded in.

This manuscript is organized as follows. It starts with the demarcation of the literature background along with key theoretical perspectives. Then it offers the overview of the applied methodology and particular methods used in order to collect and analyze the empirical evidence. As the overall research is based on four studies this manuscript offers a holistic approach, and the key concepts discussed in the findings section do not reflect the exact findings from solely one study, but instead, embrace their related elements as well offer their further conceptualization. Last, but not least as a summary this manuscript offers, conclusion, limitations, further research outlook and insights into both theoretical and practical contributions.

2. Background

This section encompasses the overview of the context, the phenomenon as well as the theoretical perspectives, which serve as a base for further investigation.

The context: open innovation in SMEs

The past decade has witnessed a shift from a closed to an open innovation model, where firms complement their own resources with external resources and competencies. Nevertheless, many aspects of open innovation are not yet well explored (Bogers, Zobel, Afuah, et al. 2017). Even though recently one can observe and increasing number of studies related to open innovation and in particular open innovation in SMEs (e.g. (Vanhaverbeke, Frattini, Roijakkers, et al. 2018)) at the beginning of this research project the research in this area was rather scant. We had some evidence offering insights into the trends, motives and management challenges (Van de Vrande, De Jong, Vanhaverbeke, et al. 2009), and intermediation and its role in facilitating innovation in SMEs (Lee, Park, Yoon, et al. 2010; Spithoven, Clarysse and Knockaert 2011). That is why, a better understanding of open innovation processes within SMEs was necessary, especially in order to enhance the understanding of the drivers and challenges for establishing successful partnerships (Brunswicker and Van de Vrande 2014).

Although studies have predominantly been on the company level of analysis, other units of analysis need to be researched to get a complete picture of the relevant processes and contingencies (West, Salter, Vanhaverbeke, et al. 2014). One such level of analysis that relates to the constellation of innovation actors is the business ecosystem ((Rohrbeck, Hoelzle and Gemünden 2009; Adner and Kapoor 2010). What is more within the very few studies focusing on open innovation in business ecosystems (Van Der Borgh et al., 2012), the attention to SMEs and their potential contribution is (still) very limited. That is why, through this research, the author would like to contribute both to business ecosystems and open innovation literature by developing a better understanding of the SMEs' potential contribution to ecosystem development through the application of open innovation practices.

The phenomenon: ecosystem development

One of the areas that have recently received increased interest is the notion of the ecosystem (Oh et al., 2016; Ritala and Almpanopoulou, 2017). The original concept constitutes a biological parallel to an ecosystem where various spe-cies interact and co-evolve in a particular geographic location. The adapted ecosystem conceptualization defines an ecosystem as:

> *"interconnected and interdependent stakeholders located at a particular territory, which is not necessarily limited to a region"* (Radziwon 2017)

Previous empirical research explored ecosystems from a firm's strategy per-spective and focused on life cycle and technology substitution (Rong, Hu, Hou, et al. 2013) and the industry convergence (Rong, Shi and Yu 2013). Therefore, Lu et al. (2014) highlight the importance of analyzing the evolution and development of the business ecosystem. Moore (1993, 1993) distin-guishes four distinct development stages which constitute an ecosystem life cycle: birth, expansion, leadership, and self-renewal or death. These were further developed by Lu, Rong, You et al. (2014) who proposed six phases: emerging, initiating, diversifying, converging, consolidating and renewing. According to Hu, Rong, Shi, et al. (2014) these phases belong to an ecosystem Context. Moreover, next to the Context they distinguish two additional di-mensions Configuration and Cooperation. Nevertheless, the collective eco-system development is relatively understudied and its study may provide important insights into the understanding of the value creation process in ecosystems (Van Der Borgh et al., 2012). As the ecosystem development is dependent on value creation and the value capture process on an inter-organizational level, a purposive management of knowledge flows across organizational boundaries of both the ecosystem and its members can have a strong impact on its innovation performance.

In this research, the development of an ecosystem is conceptualized as 'a sum of developments' of its members, which implicitly implies that it can take place either on an organizational or inter-organizational level. Whenever ecosystem members generate value added this 'counts' as a contribution to ecosystem development. Therefore, the contribution to ecosystem development encompasses all contributions of all members. The collaboration is perceived as deliberate activities conducted both formally and informally between at least two organizations (these do not need to be firms) out of which at least one is an ecosystem member.

The key theoretical perspectives

Establishing new ties and creating interdependencies between ecosystem members both through knowledge sourcing or resource sharing is one of the ways to enhance value creation and capture for the entire ecosystem and thus contribute to the ecosystem development. The key theoretical perspectives that this research project builds upon include system theory, the theory of the firm, the resource-based theories and the strategic management theories. The theoretical affiliation of business ecosystem to the complex evolutionary system theory (Mitleton-Kelly 2003) helps in the understanding of the key ecosystem conceptualizations along with identification of the key invariants between ecosystems and its archetypes grounded in the territorial innovation models (Moulaert and Sekia 2003). The theory of the firm focused on the Santos and Eisenhardt (2005) organizational boundaries, which are an innovation frontier facilitate mutual knowledge flows. The resource-based theories, represented by transaction cost theory (TCE) (Williamson 1981) and resource-based view (RBV) (Barney 1991), explain the inter-organizational collaboration mechanisms. Last, but not least the strategic management's theory view on business models (Casadesus-Masanell and Ricart 2010) guides the modeling process of value creation and capture on the inter-organizational level.

3. Research design

The overall research design had an exploratory nature and covered a combination of systematic literature review (Tranfield, Denyer and Smart 2003), a case study (Yin 2009) and an action research study (Coughlan and Coghlan 2009). This research addresses the 'how', and 'what' questions (Yin 2009; Eisenhardt and Graebner 2007), which, based on its qualitative nature guide, the process of understanding the world from the informants and research participants' perspective as well as for examining and articulating the observed processes. The chosen research design helped the author in becoming first an observant and then an active participant in the day-to-day business reality of over 50 SMEs.

The research setting

The overall research is deeply embedded in a regional business ecosystem (located in the area of Southern Denmark), which is characterized by close geographical proximity, strong interdependencies between ecosystem stakeholders developed in the process of joined co-evolution and collaboration history as well as the presence of a (potential) orchestrator (Radziwon and Bogers 2018b). **Figure 4.1** outlines the overall characteristics of the ecosystem and its key members.

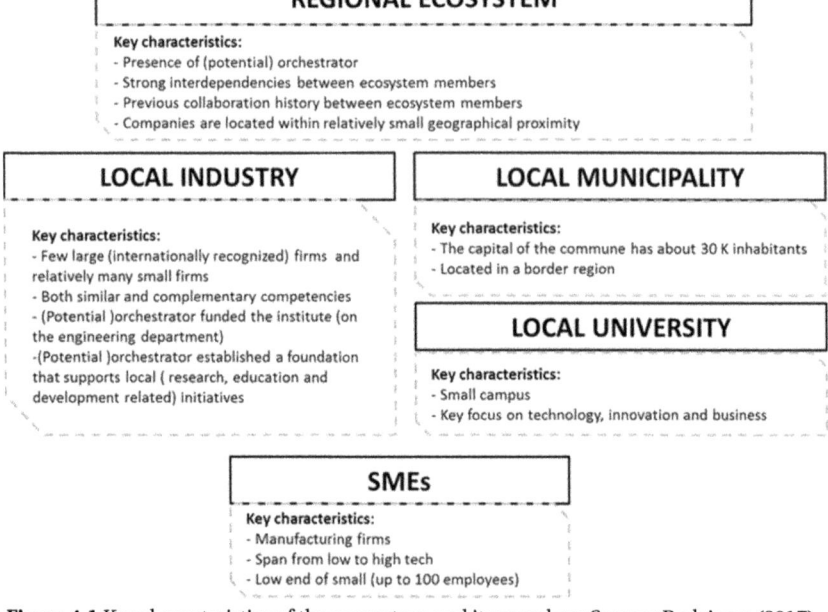

Figure 4.1 Key characteristics of the ecosystem and its members Source: Radziwon (2017)

Data analysis

The data analysis was based on a critical revision of the context of the study. The next step focused on finding out what the informants said by developing (first-order codes, provisional codes). The following step was the identification of the emerged themes and their comparison across the cases (Yin 2009). These themes were grouped into categories (selective coding) which served as a base to build a story that connects them. This 'connecting process' involved the theory enfolding through literature study in order to develop (second-order codes, axial coding).

4. Conclusion

As an outcome of this research project, the author began with clarifying the key ecosystem conceptualizations, which cover four main types of ecosystems, namely business, innovation, entrepreneurial/entrepreneurship and knowledge ecosystems, which are outlined along with the research phenomenon. As a part of this clarification process, the author offers insights into the invariants of the business ecosystem (which is the fundamental ecosystem concept) as well as clusters and regional innovation systems, which are found to belong to the ecosystem archetypes due to common roots in the complex evolution system theory.

The purposefully managed mutual knowledge flows (Chesbrough and Bogers 2014) were investigated through an organizational boundaries perspective (Santos and Eisenhardt 2005) and based on the combination of empirical analysis grounded in the theory that the author proposed an Inter-organizational Knowledge-Based View (Radziwon 2017). This view offers insights into the key elements that shape the boundaries of ecosystem, inter-organizational and organizational level in a way that maximizes the value of purposefully sourced and managed mutual knowledge flows. This concept extends the Knowledge-Based View (Nickerson and Zenger 2004), which has its key focus only on the firm level of analysis.

Resource recombination through maximizing the value of existing resources as well co-evolving the overall resource configurations was investigated through a combination of the empirical analysis grounded in the theory. The particular theoretical grounding consists of Inter-organizational Knowledge-Based View as well as the Resource-Based Theories (TCE (Williamson 1981) and RBV (Barney 1991)), based on which the author proposes the Ecosystem Safe Net Concept (Radziwon 2017). Ecosystem Safe Net offers insights into the key elements that facilitate the process of maximizing the value of existing resources as well co-evolving the overall resource configurations across organizational boundaries within an ecosystem. Its central point is ecosystem members that may be the experiencing the biggest resource-related constraints.

In order to structure the knowledge related to the value creation and capture processes in inter-organizational collaboration within an ecosystem, the author adds to the conversation about value creation and capture process within an ecosystem (Ritala, Agouridas, Assimakopoulos, et al. 2013). In particular, it proposes the Value Creation and Capture Model (Radziwon 2017) that outlines the key elements influencing a successful ecosystem development. The organizational level element that supports value creation process is balance between the core and side activities; elements that are conditional for value capture process are: presence and recognition of potential gain (Dodgson 1993) as well as long-run contribution potential; and in order to facilitate both value creation and capture process elements like: commitment to join and motivation to remain active, internal financial resources (which help to avoid crowding out effect (Osterloh and Frey 2000) and drive to collaborate are very important. On the inter-organizational elements that support value creation process are: trust and familiarity (Gulati 1995) as well as shared business objectives; successful value capture process stand in need for a similar cognitive frame; an element that is conditional for both value creation and capture process is power balance between partners. Last, but not least there are two important elements that support both value creation and capture process and may be located on the ecosystem level, these are external financial support and management, coordination as well as facilitation of the joined activities.

Finally, based on the overall research findings the author proposes three Ecosystem Fostering Mechanisms: Constant Renewal, Resource Sharing, Connection-through-Innovation (Radziwon 2017). These mechanisms primarily complement Mitleton-Kelly (2003) ten generic complex evolutionary system characteristics; however, these also encompass the overall conceptual framing of the study. Constant Renewal considers vulnerability or ecosystem members and assures the diversification of input to the ecosystem as well as the continuation of the overall ecosystem development. Resource Sharing covers all types of tangible and intangible resources as well as the overall process of its recombination. Last, but not least Connection-through-Innovation mechanism acts as a trigger to establish new initiatives among ecosystem members based on knowledge flows and resource recombination in the process of value creation and capture.

The research concludes that both maximizations of benefits from purposive knowledge flow across organizational boundaries as well as resource recombination and co-evolution, in the process of value creation can lead to value capture not only for a single ecosystem member but also for the ecosystem as a whole. Furthermore, the process of value appropriation is exposed to ecosystem fostering mechanisms. In particular, it increases or decreased 'the pool' resources which could be always a subject of sharing; triggers the renewal (in positive or negative sense for the organization), and finally incentivize ecosystem members to establish new connections and leverage them in order to achieve new (incremental or radical innovations).

SMEs may play many different roles starting with the customer, supplier, competitor or just a partner. Nevertheless, various interdependencies between ecosystem members make them very important contributors to the process of value creation and capture within the ecosystem. Open innovation practices that take place on the cross sections of organizational boundaries may constitute good ground for recombining and exchanging various types or resources as well as form new collaborative initiatives in a low transaction and coordination cost environment. As SMEs maybe face significant resource-related constraints and to a large extent dependent on external partners in this respect, their embeddedness in a regional ecosystem could help them to leverage low transactional cost advantages by opening up for external sources of knowledge.

5. Implications, contribution and future research

On the theoretical side, this research increases the understanding of the notion of an ecosystem as well as the ways how SMEs can contribute to the development of regional ecosystems through inter-organizational collaboration. Thus, it adds to the ecosystem and open innovation literature with a special focus on SMEs, specifically the discussions related to open innovation practices applied and observed in SMEs as well as the importance and benefits of opening up for external knowledge in regional ecosystems (Van Der Borgh et al., 2012; Vanhaverbeke, 2017). The findings contribute to the discussion about ecosystems (Ritala and Almpanopoulou 2017; Oh, Phillips, Park, et al. 2016) and extends the current understanding of the value creation and capture process in an ecosystem (Ritala et al., 2013) by outlining the elements that contribute to the process of value generation on multiple levels of analysis. Moreover, this study bridges the ecosystem research with its archetypes grounded in the territorial innovation models (Moulaert and Sekia, 2003).

Moreover, this research increases the understanding of the notion of organizational boundaries in the context of open innovation (Chesbrough and Bogers 2014) and broadens the Knowledge-Based View (Nickerson and Zenger, 2004), by focusing only on the firm level of analysis by providing its inter-organizational level extension. Furthermore, the author offers a fresh perspective of resource co-evolution and recombination under ecosystem embeddedness based Safe Net, which provides insights into the resource-based aspects of inter-organizational collaboration. This research extends Mitleton-Kelly's (2003) ten generic complex evolutionary system characteristics, by three complementary ecosystem fostering mechanisms.

Despite the academic focus, this research offers considerable attention to practitioners. In particular, it tries to increase the understanding of the key drivers and mechanisms of inter-organizational collaboration that could help in the further development of 'their' ecosystem. Furthermore, the overall research findings and theoretical concepts get 'translated' into very specific, practical recommendations to take into account by managers. These among the others include Knowledge Transfer guidelines among ecosystem members; Resource Recombination both and without financial benefits; Safe ecosystem Environment and its key highlights; Sustainable Financing and its implications for intrinsic and extrinsic motivation; Gain Potential and its alignment between collaboration partners as well as Considerable Attention implied by ecosystem embeddedness.

Finally, from a methodological point of view, this research advances the application of action research in the open innovation studies particularly by applying this method with the active participation of over 50 SMEs.

Further research

One of the potential areas of further investigation could be a comparative study of two or three ecosystems either from the same or different countries. This could be especially interesting in the context of regional business ecosystems. The additional dimension of a comparative study could take into consideration various strategic profiles of the companies, which could be a mix of high-tech and low-tech companies with service-oriented enterprises. The empirical data collection and analysis sourced from other ecosystems would allow them to challenge (or confirm) the current findings and their interpretations.

Another natural research follow up would be a quantitative study that could include the key elements of value creation and capturing model and try to measure their influence on the ecosystem (open) innovation performance. These could, in particular, be used as measures of success of OI projects conducted by ecosystem members thus answer the call for research on the inter-organizational level of analysis (Bogers et al. 2017).

Furthermore, it would also be very interesting to explore the relationships and the role that both small and large firms play together in the process of development of both business ecosystems and innovation ecosystems. Further research could also explore the role of entrepreneurial universities (Etzkowitz 2003) not only in the context of start-ups and research projects (Hayter 2016; Brem and Radziwon 2017) but also SMEs.

Another interesting area of potential investigation could cover a range of quantitative studies that would take into consideration ecosystem evolution and growth. This could be measured by longitudinal studies, ideally comprising mixed method techniques, which could consider important events and observe the development of the ecosystem members and also collect both numerical growth indicators as well as survey data that could test the importance and influence of all discussed ecosystem characteristics on its growth.

References

Adner, R. and Kapoor, R. (2010). 'Value creation in innovation ecosystems: how the structure of technological interdependence affects firm performance in new technology generations'. *Strategic Management Journal.* 31 (3), 306–333.

Barney, J. (1991). 'Firm resources and sustained competitive advantage'. *Journal of Management.* 17 (1), 99–120.

Bogers, M., Zobel, A.-K., Afuah, A., Almirall, E., et al. (2017) 'The open innovation research landscape: established perspectives and emerging themes across different levels of analysis'. *Industry and Innovation.* 24 (1), 8–40.

Brem, A. and Radziwon, A. (2017). 'Efficient Triple-Helix collaboration fostering local niche innovation projects: A case from Denmark'. *Technological Forecasting and Social Change.* 123130–141.

Brunswicker, S. and Van de Vrande, V. (2014). 'Exploring Open Innovation in Small and Medium-Sized Enterprises'. In: Chesbrough, H., Vanhaverbeke, W. & West, J. (ed.). *New Frontiers in Open Innovation.* Oxford: Oxford University Press. pp. 135–156.

Casadesus-Masanell, R. and Ricart, J.E. (2010). 'From strategy to business models and onto tactics'. *Long Range Planning.* 43 (2), 195–215.

Chesbrough, H. and Bogers, M. (2014).' Explicating Open Innovation: Clarifying an Emerging Paradigm for Understanding Innovation'. In: H. Chesbrough, W. Vanhaverbeke & J. West (ed.). *New Frontiers in Open Innovation.* Oxford: Oxford University Press. pp. 3–28.

Coughlan, P. and Coghlan, D. (2009). 'Action Research'. In: C. Karlsson (ed.). *Researching Operations Management.* New York: Routledge.

Deschryvere, M. (2014). 'R&D, firm growth and the role of innovation persistence: An analysis of Finnish SMEs and large firms'. *Small Business Economics.* 1–19.

Dodgson, M. (1993). 'Learning, trust, and technological collaboration'. *Human Relations.* 46 (1), 77–95.

Eisenhardt, K.M. and Graebner, M.E. (2007). Theory building from cases: opportunities and challenges. *Academy of Management Journal.* 50 (1), 25–32.

Etzkowitz, H. (2003). 'Innovation in Innovation: The Triple Helix of University-Industry-Government Relations'. *Social Science Information.* 42 (3), 293–337.

Gulati, R. (1995). 'Social structure and alliance formation patterns: A longitudinal analysis'. *Administrative science quarterly.* 619–652.

Hayter, C.S. (2016). 'A trajectory of early-stage spinoff success: the role of knowledge intermediaries within an entrepreneurial university ecosystem'. *Small Business Economics.* 47 (3), 633–656.

Hu, G., Rong, K., Shi, Y. and Yu, J. (2014). 'Sustaining the emerging carbon trading industry development: A business ecosystem approach of carbon traders'. *Energy Policy.* 73587–597.

Lee, Park, Yoon and Park (2010). 'Open innovation in SMEs—An intermediated network model'. *Research Policy.* 39 (2), 290–300.

Lu, C., Rong, K., You, J. and Shi, Y. (2014). 'Business ecosystem and stakeholders' role transformation: Evidence from Chinese emerging electric vehicle industry'. *Expert Systems with Application.* 41 (10), 4579–4595.

Mitleton-Kelly, E. (2003). *Complex systems and evolutionary perspectives on organisations: the application of complexity theory to organisations.* Elsevier Science Ltd.

Mitra, J. (2017). *The Business of Innovation.* Sage.

Moore, J.F. (1993). 'Predators and prey: A new ecology of competition'. *Harvard Business Review*. 71 (3), 75–86.

Moulaert, F. and Sekia, F. (2003). 'Territorial innovation models: a critical survey'. *Regional Studies*. 37 (3), 289–302.

Muller, P., Caliandro, C., Peycheva, V., Gagliardi, D., et al. (2016). *Annual Report on European SMEs 2015/2016*.

Nickerson, J.A. and Zenger, T.R. (2004). A knowledge-based theory of the firm—The problem-solving perspective. *Organization Science*. 15 (6), 617–632.

Oh, D.-S., Phillips, F., Park, S. and Lee, E. (2016). 'Innovation ecosystems: A critical examination'. *Technovation*. 541–6.

Osterloh, M. and Frey, B.S. (2000). 'Motivation, knowledge transfer, and organizational forms'. *Organization Science*. 11 (5), 538–550.

Powell, W.W., Koput, K.W. and Smith-Doerr, L. (1996). 'Interorganizational collaboration and the locus of innovation: Networks of learning in biotechnology'. *Administrative Science Quarterly*. 41 (4), 116–145.

Radziwon, A. (2017). *Exploring inter-organizational collaboration for innovation in a regional ecosystem*.

Radziwon, A. and Bogers, M. (2018a). 'Managing SMEs' Collaboration Across Organizational Boundaries Within a Regional Business Ecosystem'. In: Vanhaverbeke, W. and Frattini, F. and Roijakkers, N. and Usman, M. (ed.). *Researching Open Innovation in SMEs*. pp. 213–248.

Radziwon, A. and Bogers, M. (2018b). 'Open innovation in SMEs: Exploring inter-organizational relationships in an ecosystem'. *Technological Forecasting and Social Change*.

Radziwon, A., Bogers, M. and Bilberg, A. (2017). 'Creating and Capturing Value in a Regional Innovation Ecosystem: A Study of How Manufacturing SMEs Develop Collaborative Solutions'. *International Journal of Technology Management*. 75 (1-4), 73–96.

Ritala, P., Agouridas, V., Assimakopoulos, D. and Gies, O. (2013). 'Value creation and capture mechanisms in innovation ecosystems: A comparative case study'. *International Journal of Technology Management*. 63 (3), 244–267.

Ritala, P. and Almpanopoulou, A. (2017). 'In defense of "eco" in innovation ecosystem'. *Technovation*. 60-61 (39-42).

Rohrbeck, R., Hoelzle, K. and Gemünden, H.G. (2009). 'Opening up for competitive advantage - How Deutsche Telekom creates an open innovation ecosystem'. *R&D Management*. 39 (4), 420–430.

Rong, K., Hu, G., Hou, J., Ma, R., et al. (2013). 'Business ecosystem extension: facilitating the technology substitution'. *International Journal of Technology Management*. 63 (3-4), 268–294.

Rong, K., Shi, Y. and Yu, J. (2013). 'Nurturing business ecosystems to deal with industry uncertainties'. *Industrial Management & Data systems*. 113 (3), 385–402.

Santos, F.M. and Eisenhardt, K.M. (2005). 'Organizational boundaries and theories of organization'. *Organization Science*. 16 (5), 491–508.

Scaringella, L. and Radziwon, A. (2018). 'Innovation, entrepreneurial, knowledge, and business ecosystems: Old wine'. *Technological Forecasting and Social Change*. forthcoming.

Spithoven, A., Clarysse, B. and Knockaert, M. (2011). 'Building absorptive capacity to organise inbound open innovation in traditional industries'. *Technovation*. 31 (1), 10–21.

Tranfield, D.R., Denyer, D. and Smart, P. (2003). 'Towards a methodology for developing evidence-informed management knowledge by means of systematic review'. *British Journal of Management*. 14207–222.

Van Der Borgh, M., Cloodt, M. and Romme, A. (2012). 'Value creation by knowledge-based ecosystems: Evidence from a field study'. *R&D Management*. 42 (2), 150–169.

Vanhaverbeke, W. (2017). *Managing open innovation in SMEs*. Cambridge University Press .

Vanhaverbeke, W., Frattini, F., Roijakkers, N. and Usman, M. (2018). *Researching Open Innovation in SMEs*. World Scientific Publishing Co. Pte. Ltd.

Van de Vrande, V., De Jong, J.P., Vanhaverbeke, W. and De Rochemont, M. (2009). 'Open innovation in SMEs: Trends, motives and management challenges'. *Technovation*. 29 (6), 423–437.

West, J., Salter, A., Vanhaverbeke, W. and Chesbrough, H. (2014.) 'Open innovation: The next decade'. *Research Policy*. 43 (5), 805–811.

Williamson, O.E. (1981). 'The economics of organization: The transaction cost approach'. *American Journal of Sociology*. 548–577.

Yin, R.K. (2009). *Case study research: Design and methods*. Thousand Oaks, CA: Sage.

Chapter 5

The Contribution of Socially Driven Businesses and Innovations to Social Sustainability

Rakhshanda Khan*

E-mail: rakhshanda.khan@lut.fi

Abstract: Social sustainability is considered a fundamental component of sustainable development. A multifaceted concept, social sustainability has been studied through the lenses of disparate disciplines and theoretical perspectives. Businesses, provided that they are socially driven, have the power to play a crucial role in social sustainability. This study seeks to understand the contribution of these socially driven businesses – particularly micro and small enterprises – and socially driven innovations to achieving and ensuring social sustainability. The focus of this study is to tackle the intangible concept of social sustainability at a practical level, by presenting how socially driven businesses and innovations have the potential to address pressing societal needs and contribute to realizing social sustainability.

This dissertation is primarily qualitative in nature and makes use of a wide range of evidence: documents, semi-structured interviews, field observations, literature review and questionnaires. It makes three main contributions. Firstly, it provides empirical evidence about the connection between social sustainability and socially driven businesses and innovations. Secondly, it provides an opportunity to view sustainable businesses specifically from the vantage point of social sustainability. Thirdly, it clarifies how frugal innovation can be viewed as a practical approach to boosting social sustainability.

Keywords: social sustainability; socially driven business; socially driven innovation; frugal innovation; social enterprises; social innovation; sustainable business; sustainable development; sustainability.

1. Introduction

Almost three decades have passed since the Brundtland Commission defined sustainable development as 'development that meets the needs of present generations without compromising the ability of future generations to meet their own needs.' In doing so, the Commission pointed towards a concern for development considered fully from social, economic and environmental dimensions (United Nation's World Commission on Environment and Development, 1987:

p. 43). In order to comprehend this elusive concept of sustainable development, numerous attempts have been made to connect its three fundamental pillars: environmental, economic and social sustainability (Lozano, 2008; Vallance, Perkins and Dixon, 2011). Scholars are of the opinion that the relationships between these three dimensions remain unclear, and the social pillar is the least studied (Assefa and Frostell, 2007; Colantonio, 2011; Missimer, Robert, Broman and Sverdrup, 2010; Vifell and Soneryd, 2012). Nevertheless, there is a consensus that the social pillar is critical to sustainability discourse, and the other two pillars are intertwined with it (Colantonio, 2011; Murphy, 2012; Spangenberg and Omann, 2006). The social pillar of sustainability facilitates environmental and economic sustainability (Thomsen and King, 2009).

Businesses are embedded in society and thus have the power to play a crucial role in sustainable development (DeSimone and Popoff, 2000; Porritt, 2005). This role can be negative or positive, depending largely on the way a business is operated. On the one hand, the business world is viewed as largely negative, due to its detrimental impacts on society (see for example, Klein, 2000; Korten, 2000). On the other hand, researchers have argued that businesses do not set out with the intention to harm people or the environment and that the unintentional, unavoidable harm they cause stakeholders can be avoided by employing strategies that can turn the business, its stakeholders, and the environment into winners (Elkington, 1994).

For some time now, businesses have been involved in improving eco-efficiency (Flammer, 2013) and environmental corporate social responsibility (CSR) (Ambec and Lanoie, 2008; Lindgreen and Swaen, 2010), as there is constant pressure to address a sustainable vision (Gupta, 2010). Firms have had dedicated departments dealing with CSR while their business strategies remained unaffected. Today, sustainability can no longer be an adjunct corporate function; it has to be embedded in the heart of a business so that the variety of social challenges that are barriers to achieving sustainability can be addressed holistically (Fisk, 2010). This dissertation seeks to explore the role of socially driven businesses, particularly micro and small enterprises, and socially driven innovations that benefit society and help achieve and ensure social sustainability at an intrinsic, practical level.

This dissertation explores the concept of social sustainability from the perspective of socially driven businesses and innovations. The main objective of this study is to understand how socially driven businesses and innovations contribute to social sustainability. The main research question and sub questions are:

How do socially driven businesses and innovations contribute to social sustainability?

a) How can socially driven businesses be sustainable and contribute to social sustainability?

b) How can socially driven innovation benefit society?

c) How does frugal innovation support social sustainability?

This dissertation tackles the intangible concept of social sustainability at a practical level by presenting how socially driven businesses and innovations have
the potential to address pressing societal needs, thus realizing social sustainability in part. The focus is on social sustainability, which is defined in this study as
'both a) the processes that generate social health and well-being now and in the
future and (b) those social institutions that facilitate environmental and economic sustainability now and for the future' (Thomsen and King, 2009: p. 203).

This research is cross-disciplinary, and the literature is derived from the
fields of social sustainability and business. Social sustainability has been
studied from various disciplinary perspectives; understanding of the concept
has been limited by disciplinary-dependent definitions (Colantonio, 2009). In
recent years, urban sustainability and delivery of sustainable cities have been
the main focal areas of social sustainability research. The focus of this study is
not urban sustainability, urban regeneration, housing, sustainable cities or
the policy discourse surrounding these topics. Nor does this study focus on
social sustainability assessment methodologies, measurement tools and
frameworks as viewed from any specific field of research. Instead, the focus is
on social sustainability in practice.

Similarly, this dissertation does not focus on CSR or the role MNCs and big
businesses play in sustainability. Instead, the aim is to better understand the
contribution of micro and small socially driven businesses and innovations to
achieving social sustainability in both emerging markets and developed
economies. The researcher has chosen cases from India and Finland and has
conducted research in these two countries.

2. Background

In order to understand the role socially driven businesses and innovations
play in social sustainability, this dissertation draws on literature from the
fields of social sustainability, social enterprise, sustainable business, social
innovation and frugal innovation.

The literature on social sustainability is rather fragmented. Much social sustainability literature has emerged from the field of urban studies, from both
academic and policy perspectives (e.g. Polese and Stren, 2000; Chiu, 2003;

Cuthill, 2009; Colantonio, 2007; Colantonio, 2011; Dempsey Bramley, Power and Brown 2011; Mak and Peacock, 2011; Landorff, 2011; Ghahramanpouri, Lamit and Sedaghatnia, 2013). For the purposes of this dissertation, definitions, meanings and concepts of social sustainability have been derived from this tradition, even though this dissertation does not focus on urban development per se. Another substantial volume of literature that broadens understandings of the concept of social sustainability has been written from various other non-business-centred perspectives (e.g. Sach, 1999; Koning, 2001; McKenzie, 2004; Littig and Griessler, 2005; Spangenberg and Omann, 2006; Vavik and Keitsch, 2010; Vallance et al. 2011; Boström, 2012; Vifell and Soneryd, 2012; Murphy, 2012). This literature describes the importance of social sustainability and how it fits into the overall concept of sustainable development without discussing any link to business.

There have also been discussions on how businesses could be more socially responsible. Scholars have extensively discussed CSR (see e.g. McGuire, 1963; Walton, 1967; Davis, 1973; Elkington, 1998; Carroll, 1999; McWilliams and Siegel, 2001; Bansal, 2005; Werther Jr. and Chandler, 2005; Dahlsrud, 2008; Fernando, 2010; Carroll and Buchholtz, 2009; Freundlieb and Tenteberg, 2013; Aagaard, 2016) and role of multinational corporations (MNCs) in sustainable development. However, small and medium sized enterprises (SMEs) have been relatively marginalized in the sustainability debate and ignored in academic research (Sanders and Wood, 2015). Current approaches have not focused on micro and small firms, and empirical research has not produced enough evidence about how such businesses can help in achieving social sustainability.

Furthermore, the notion of green and sustainable business has been widely discussed over the last decade, as in the work of DeSimone and Popoff, 2000; Fisk, 2010; Tueth, 2010; Weybrecht, 2010; and Soyka, 2012. This literature describes the link between business and sustainable development, but it does not explore the connection between business and social sustainability specifically. In most cases, this literature focuses on transforming a business into a 'green' business and effects on profitability or incorporating sustainability principles into a firm's everyday practices. One study that tries to bring social sustainability and sustainable businesses together was conducted by Thomsen and King (2009), who explored the impact of sustainable businesses on fostering social sustainability. The focus of their research, however, was limited to discovering business owners' conceptions of social sustainability and actions that might be considered to foster social sustainability. One can state, then, that there is a lack of evidence about the roles socially driven micro and small businesses play in achieving social sustainability.

The notion of social enterprises has been discussed widely in the last decade, which is reflected in the work of Kerlin (2006), Mair and Martí (2006),

Young (2008), Huybrechts and Nicholls (2013) and many others. This literature emphasizes the contribution of social enterprises to society; however, it
is also important to understand how social enterprises relate to social sustainability. Likewise, the literature on social innovation has been written from
various perspectives (see for example, Phills, Deiglmeier and Miller, 2008;
Manzini, 2014; Poll and Ville, 2009; Mulgan, Tucker, Ali, and Sanders, 2007;
Hämäläinen and Heiskala, 2007; Howaldt and Schwarz, 2010). However, there
is a need to understand how sustainability thinking and social innovation are
linked, and this link has not been comprehensively addressed in the literature
(Pisano, Lange and Berger, 2015) despite the fact that social innovation could
be an important success factor in achieving social sustainability. Lastly, frugal
innovation, considered by many as the future of innovation management
(Zeschky, Winterhalter and Gassmann, 2014), has been a topic of discussion
in innovation literature over the last decade. This is reflected in the work of
numerous scholars (see for example, Tiwari and Herstatt, 2012a; Zeschky,
Widenmayer and Gassmann, 2011; Zeschky, Winterhalter and Gassmann,
2014; Rajdou and Prabhu, 2014; Immelt, Govindarajan and Trimble, 2009;
Bhatti and Ventresca, 2016; Radjou, Prabhu, and Ahuja, 2012; Govindarajan
and Ramamurti, 2011; Prahalad, and Hart, 2002; Basu, Banerjee and Sweeny,
2013; Rao, 2013) who have studied various related concepts, such as reverse
innovation, jugaad innovation, grassroot innovation, bottom of the pyramid
(BoP) innovation, and so on. Most of this literature has not established any
connection with sustainable development, despite the analysis this relationship deserves. Some work on this has been done recently (see for example,
Levänen et al., 2016; Pansera and Sarkar, 2016; Hyvärinen, Keskinen and Varis,
2016; Shan and Khan, 2016), but there is still a need to understand more fully
how social sustainability, in particular, is related to frugal innovation.

This survey of the existing literature makes plain that current approaches have
not sufficed to provide much information on the contribution of micro and
small-scale socially driven businesses and social and frugal innovations to social
sustainability. This dissertation attempts to address this gap in the literature.

3. Research design

The strategy used in this dissertation is a case study, a relevant choice for many
reasons. Firstly, this dissertation deals with answering the research question,
'How do socially driven businesses and innovations contribute to social sustainability?', which requires extensive, in-depth descriptions of the contribution of
these socially driven businesses and innovations to the complex, multidisciplinary phenomenon of social sustainability. Secondly, this dissertation attempts
to understand relatively new phenomena on which a limited amount of
knowledge is available: the social aspects of sustainability, for example, have

received less attention as a research area than other aspects of sustainability (Thomsen and King, 2009). Thirdly, this study attempts to explain a link between socially driven businesses and innovations and social sustainability, and this link is far too complex to be able to grasp using experimental or deductive survey strategies alone. Lastly, this study has employed a full range of evidence – documents, semi-structured interviews, field observations, literature review and questionnaires – which is a unique strength of case study research. The research question is answered through multiple case studies that approach it from various perspectives. These carefully selected cases are distinct in approach, context and level of analysis, yet they all answer the main research question and, taken together, form a meaningful whole.

Case selection and research context

This dissertation starts from the premise that socially driven businesses and innovations contribute to social sustainability; all four cases and five substudies attempt to show this link. Each case study has been carefully chosen to highlight one or more distinct dimensions of this link and to work together to provide an overall understanding of it within the research context. These distinct dimensions form the basis of evaluation in each case of socially driven businesses or innovations.

The case studies were selected according to the following criteria. Firstly, the cases were chosen based on their relevance in terms of sustainability, whether environmental, economic or social. Some cases focus on environmental friendliness, others on economic or social sustainability, and some on combinations with varying degrees of these dimensions. However, all displayed a strong sustainability dimension. Secondly, they represent different fields of business. For example, Case I is a construction material-related business; Case II is green-energy technology business; Case III represents an interesting mix of organizations that are either work integration social enterprises or have earned a social enterprise mark; and Case IV represents organizations ranging from health organizations and energy technologies to mobile money transfer services. Thirdly, most of the organizations are so small they fall into the micro category, while a few are considered small. Case IV is an exception: some of the frugal innovation cases come from larger organizations. Lastly, the cases are a combination of individual businesses or innovations and clusters. For instance, Case I and many business case examples from Case IV represent individual businesses, while Case III represents a cluster of Finnish social enterprises and Case II deals with India's small hydropower (SHP) industry as a whole.

Case I was selected because cellulose insulation technology is considered to be an eco-friendly technology and its business in Finland has been quite successful. Its applicability to Srinagar, India was investigated, as it was seen as a solution to the problem of uncomfortable housing in Srinagar, especially during winters. Various social, economic and environmental sustainability dimensions of the technology's potential adoption were studied, with social sustainability being the most important. This research was conducted in Srinagar, the capital of Jammu and Kashmir, India's northernmost state. The climate there is considered humid continental, with warm summers and cold winters; the lowest temperature recorded is -14 °C. The researcher selected Srinagar as a research area, as the harsh winters and lack of comfortable housing make it a suitable research target for cellulose insulation technology.

Case II was selected because SHP is a green-energy technology considered a lucrative business in India. The renewable energy business in India has generated increased social sustainability in the areas where SHP units are constructed. The purpose was to analyze the contribution of SHP to social sustainability (Sub-study II) as well as economic and environmental sustainability (Sub-study IV). This research was conducted in four states: New Delhi, Himachal Pradesh, Uttaranchal and Jammu and Kashmir. India is an emerging market known for its tremendous SHP potential, and the selected areas are located in mountainous regions with good water reserves and sites suitable for generating power. These regions offer the most potential for SHP in India.

Case III deals with micro and small social enterprises in Finland. The purpose of this research was to analyze their contributions to social sustainability. This research was conducted in Finland, primarily through a survey sent to the social enterprises found in the Finnish register of social enterprises. Social enterprises are challenging targets due to definitional problems; Finnish society and its records were assessed as being a sufficiently reliable avenue for conducting this research.

Case IV was selected because the concepts of frugal innovation and sustainability are closely linked. The purpose of this study was to find connections between the practical case of frugal innovation and the more nebulous social sustainability and to analyze how frugal innovation promotes social sustainability. India and other BoP markets, like Kenya and China, were the sources of information on frugal innovations.

4. Conclusion

The contribution of socially driven businesses to social sustainability

Sub-question (a), *How can socially driven businesses be sustainable and contribute to social sustainability?* is answered in Sub-studies II, III and IV. The summarised results of these sub-studies are presented below.

*Sub-study II: 'Towards realizing social sustainability in the small
hydropower sector in India: opportunities for social innovations'*

Background and objectives

The goal of sustainable development is to create a system that provides for
quality of life by integrating social, economic and environmental sustainability (Kleef and Roome, 2007). Social sustainability is, thus, a fundamental element of sustainable development that cannot be ignored (Magis and Shin,
2009). In a similar vein, the social innovations that prioritize human welfare
are inherently linked to sustainable development, as changes in the behavior
of individuals and institutions are considered critical to sustainable development (Dobson, 2007) and these changes are key concerns in generating social
innovations. This study investigates a green-energy business in India: small
hydropower, or SHP. SHP is promoted as one of the most cost-effective energy
technologies for generating power in the rural areas of developing countries
(Paish, 2002). Green-energy technologies have been a topic of research interest for years, yet the social sustainability and social innovations carried out
due to green-energy businesses have not been subjected to empirical analysis. This study focuses on the SHP industry to understand its role in and any
contributions to social sustainability in surrounding communities. The sub-
study includes a description of India's SHP industry, with a special focus on
challenges faced by the industry. These barriers are then studied as opportunities for social innovations. Furthermore, this study also suggests steps for
making SHP more socially sustainable.

   This study answers the following research questions: How is social sustainability achieved through the development of the SHP sector in India? Are
there any possibilities for the generation of social innovations?

Findings

The results of this study indicate that the development of SHP units has contributed to the larger goal of social sustainability in the surrounding communities. Generally speaking, the remote areas where the SHP plants are established become more socially sustainable. The villages not only get electrified,
but the SHP units also generate employment, support small-scale industry
and improve infrastructure. Other benefits include reduced migration of local
people from the area and the establishment of local schools, parks, hospitals,
temples, and so on. On the other hand, the SHP industry also faces challenges, such as getting statutory clearances, resistance from local communities,
construction difficulties, unskilled labor, ambiguous government policies,

high interest rates and management problems. Efforts have to be made to characterize SHP as 'socially sustainable.' In order to be fully socially sustainable, the SHP sector needs to continue to promote human well-being, improve working conditions for workers, encourage equal participation in local communities and governments, and strengthen stakeholder relationships. This study explores these challenges as opportunities for social innovation and proposes some suggestions for the successful implementation of SHP projects. First of all, the government should assign these projects to independent power producers only after getting all the clearances from different departments. Second, training should be provided to those who create SHP policies at the national level as well as to the local employees who operate and manage these SHP plants. Third, infrastructure problems need to be addressed by building roads, bridges and transmission lines. Lastly, the independent power producers should search for foreign funding in order to lower their interest rates and get better returns on their investments.

Sub-study III: 'How Social Enterprises Support Social Sustainability'

Background and objectives

In order to tackle the concept of sustainable development and achieve ambitious sustainability goals for current and future generations, much interdisciplinary work needs to be dedicated to dealing with pressing societal problems (Turvey, 2015). In the past, ecological concerns have taken precedence over societal concerns in the sustainability debate (Ratamäki, 2013). However, it is clear that new mechanisms need to be developed, ones that would also address social sustainability. Social enterprises, organizations focused on addressing social issues (Borzaga and Defourny, 2001) could be viewed as a small step towards realizing social sustainability. The link between social enterprises and social sustainability has not been much discussed in the literature. This study investigates whether social enterprises in Finland are socially sustainable and support social sustainability. It sheds light on the link between the concepts of social sustainability and social enterprises and recognizes the possibility of realizing social sustainability through the development of social enterprises.

Findings

Social sustainability indicators were developed to assess the social dimensions of sustainability in the social enterprises being studied. These indicators were classified into three main categories: employee relations, community relations and customer relations. The analysis showed that, among the social enterprises, employee participation was highly valued and employees were given equal opportunities. However, the social enterprises needed improvement in terms of workplace practices. Most lacked systematic approaches to evaluating employee performance. They collaborated with businesses, NGOs and public sector organizations but exhibited little collaboration with universities or research organizations. They engaged customers, but lacked a systematic approach to gathering development ideas from them. The role of social enterprises is still unstable and developing. Their most important role is employment generation, which has had a positive social impact. Social enterprises empower the long-term unemployed and those on the margins of society by providing them with a stepping-stone to working life. The biggest challenges faced by these social enterprises are lack of resources and inadequate funding. In short, social enterprises fulfill basic social sustainability criteria; however, improvements are needed in certain areas as measured by the indicators.

Sub-study IV: 'Small hydropower in India: Is it a sustainable business?'

Background and objectives

Business plays a critical role in sustainable development (Porritt, 2005), and the development of green businesses is critical to achieving long-term sustainability, as it encompasses economic and social concerns alongside environmental ones (Tueth, 2010). In this context, green-energy businesses have garnered a lot of attention in that, unlike the non-renewable energy sources, they generate clean energy and minimize the release of greenhouse gases. This study investigates one source of green energy: small hydropower, or SHP. SHP plants are green-energy generation sources that are economically viable and require little time to implement (Ghosh, 2012). In India, SHP refers to hydropower units that possess a generation capacity of less than 25MW. This study investigates the sustainable nature of SHP in India. This objective was realized by taking into account the complex network of SHP stakeholders, each of whom has a variety of interests. The study increases understanding of the three interconnected dimensions of sustainability – social, economic and environmental – in relation to India's SHP industry.

This study answers the following questions: Is the SHP business in India a sustainable business? Does it realize all three dimensions of sustainability?

Findings

Sustainable development concerns three interconnected dimensions: economic, environmental and social sustainability. A business that attempts to strike a balance between these dimensions in business decision making is a sustainable business. India's SHP industry was studied with this definition in mind, and the results indicate that the SHP industry has both strengths and weaknesses. With regard to economic sustainability, it was noted that most SHP projects are economically viable, yet viability depends on many factors, including site, conditions and size of SHP project. Long gestation periods and high interest rates prolong the payback period. Delays in acquiring government clearances, inadequate evacuation and transmission facilities, high upfront costs, and poor grid connectivity are some of the obstacles that can impact project profitability. Changes like alternate funding options and a formalized clearance procedure could make SHP more economically viable. Secondly, environmental sustainability has not been yet fully achieved, and significant continuing efforts need to be expended to make SHP plants truly environmentally friendly. All SHP plants impact the environment to a certain extent, by altering river ecosystems. However, this impact is minimal as compared to other energy-generation sources. On a positive note, SHP is a renewable, clean and non-polluting energy source that generates no waste and offers significant carbon emission reduction. Nevertheless, it is possible to build environmentally friendly SHP plants sustainably or less sustainably. In India, environmental awareness has to be improved, and investments in technological research should be made to make this sector more sustainable. Lastly, with regard to social sustainability, numerous benefits, like village electrification, employment generation and promotion of small-scale industry have resulted from SHP development. Nevertheless, many social challenges continue to exist. In short, all three pillars of sustainability are being realized to a certain extent. However, to be considered a truly sustainable industry, a considerable amount of hard work needs to be dedicated to addressing the factors mentioned above.

The contribution of socially driven innovations to social sustainability

Sub-question (b), *How can a socially driven innovation benefit a society?* is answered in Sub-studies I and V, while sub-question (c), *How does frugal innovation support social sustainability?* is answered in Sub-study V. The results of these studies are summarised below.

Sub-study I: 'An Environmentally Friendly Cellulose Insulation Technology for Srinagar, India: A Sustainable Business and Social Innovation'

Background and objectives

Social innovation originates from various sources and can be applied to various disciplines. It has no fixed boundaries and cuts across all sectors (BEPA, 2010). Social innovation has the potential to act as an instrument of change and overcome societal challenges. It has many definitions; one definition that is suitable in the context of this study is that social innovation can be seen as new application of an old idea or the transfer of an idea from one part of the world to another in a way that effectively meets social needs (Mulgan et al., 2012).

This study focuses on Srinagar, which is a northern Indian city that faces harsh winters. Buildings in Srinagar are not insulated, which makes it very hard for people to survive the cold. Lack of electricity and heating facilities result in poor quality of life. In this study, a sustainable cellulose insulation technological solution – an idea borrowed from Finland – is proposed for Srinagar. It can be seen as a social innovation, since the transfer of this technology and the adoption of the cellulose insulation business could positively benefit society in Srinagar. It can also be seen as a sustainable business, as it has the potential to holistically address economic, social and environmental challenges (Tueth, 2010). This study explores the applicability of a sustainable cellulose insulation business in the context of Srinagar. The main research aims are to discover the demand for cellulose insulation in Srinagar and whether it could be seen as a socially driven innovation and a sustainable business option for Srinagar. This study also aims to identify the main challenges and opportunities associated with bringing this business to Srinagar.

Findings

The cellulose insulation business in Srinagar could be seen as a sustainable business solution that has the potential to benefit society. It is a sustainable business that will not only save energy by reducing the electricity bills of the inhabitants and assist in waste management, but it will also produce economic benefits for the region. The research establishes that there is potential for a cellulose insulation business in Srinagar, as there is hardly any competition in this sector. Lack of availability of insulation materials in the valley was the main cause of its unusability. The government offers attractive incentive packages for industries that plan to set up ventures in Srinagar. Some threats to the business are also identified, including political disturbances in the valley, corruption and weak IPR protection. This study also proposes some recommendations for investors interested in pursuing the cellulose business in Srinagar.

The main objective of this sub-study was to identify the relevance of the cellulose insulation technology for Srinagar, and much of the information presented in it is critical to justifying that perspective. This sub-study shows how cellulose insulation technology could act as a socially driven innovation and contribute positively to the surrounding society. Not only could it generate economic benefits, solve waste management problems and produce energy efficiency, but the social sustainability of Srinagar could also positively be improved by protecting its residents from cold and illnesses and providing them with comfortable lives during harsh winters. The quality of life of the city's residents will be improved once they get access to the basic need of comfortable shelter. The adoption of cellulose insulation in Srinagar could help realize some important features of social sustainability: 'human well-being' (Boström, 2012, Colantonio, 2011, Chiu 2003, Magis and Shinn, 2009), 'basic needs and quality of life' (Littig and Griessler, 2005, McKenzie, 2004, Polese and Stren, 2000, Spangenberg and Omman, 2006), 'broad concept of equity' (Cuthill, 2009, Dempsey et al. 2011, Murphy, 2012) and 'improved living conditions' (Holden, 2012).

Sub-study V: 'How frugal innovation promotes social sustainability'

Background and objectives

In sustainability discourse, environmental protection, economic prosperity and social equity are intertwined. According to Torjman (2000), it is impossible to sustain human well-being in the absence of a healthy environment and a vibrant economy. Social sustainability has to be understood in relation to both economic and environmental sustainability. Keeping this principle in mind, this study highlights how social sustainability is linked to frugal innovation. Frugal innovation has had a positive impact on societies, as it has aimed to solve pressing societal problems while creating more business and minimizing the use of resources (Radjou and Prabhu, 2014). It has been argued that frugal innovation can improve the sustainability performance of a business (Brem and Ivens, 2013). However, the link between frugal innovation and social sustainability specifically has not received much attention. The researcher argues that it is important to study the role of frugal innovation in sustainable development, devise better tools to study this relationship and establish a strong link between the two concepts. The objective of this sub-study is, through reviewing the existing literature concerning both fields, to find the connections between social sustainability and frugal innovation; this literature shows how frugal innovation promotes social sustainability by identifying essential themes of social sustainability and exploring them through existing frugal innovations. Frugal innovation could be viewed as an approach to realizing social sustainability and fulfilling the United Nations' Sustainable Development Goals (SDGs).

Findings

The literature review on social sustainability and frugal innovation revealed a strong connection between the two concepts. Social sustainability was studied to identify critical themes, and eight cases of frugal innovation were analyzed in light of these themes. In nearly all cases, it was discovered that the most important themes of social sustainability – human well-being, basic needs, quality of life, social justice, social inclusion, poverty reduction and so on – are being addressed in frugal innovations. All cases of frugal innovation studied offered solutions to existing problems. Frugal innovation was determined to be one way of solving the challenges of social inclusion in BoP markets. In addition, in BoP markets, even the poorest segments of society gain access to essential services through frugal innovation. Frugal innovation plays an important role in fulfilling social sustainability, promotes SDGs and contributes towards the larger goal of sustainable development. The most common SDGs promoted by frugal innovation cases include SDGs 1 (no poverty), 3 (good health and well-being), 4 (quality education), 7 (affordable and clean energy), 8 (decent work and economic growth), 9 (industry innovation and infrastructure), 10 (reduced inequalities), 12 (responsible consumption and production) and 16 (peace, justice and strong institutions).

5. Implications and future research

Theoretical implications

First of all, this dissertation contributes to the scientific discussion by establishing a sturdy link between socially driven businesses and innovations and social sustainability, integrating the two sectors of study. Most literature on social sustainability has come from the field of urban development, and this dissertation expands on it by engaging in a cross-disciplinary exploration of social sustainability, studying it from the perspective of sustainable businesses, social and frugal innovations and social enterprises, with real-world cases complementing the theoretical exploration. A strong connection between business and sustainable development has been recognized for years (DeSimone and Popoff, 2000; Fisk, 2010; Tueth, 2010). This dissertation furthers this existing research, which has primarily focused on the contributions of large firms to sustainability, by highlighting micro and small firms and their contributions to social sustainability.

Secondly, this study indicates that micro and small-scale socially driven businesses and socially driven innovations can be viewed as vehicles for achieving greater social sustainability in a given community. At present, sustainability studies suffer from lack of a framework for improving social sustainability through socially driven businesses (such as social enterprises) or socially driven innovations (such as social and frugal innovation). Through numerous case examples, this dissertation shows how socially driven businesses and innovations address various social sustainability themes that jointly promote sustainable development. The results can act as a stepping-stone for future studies on practical approaches to achieving social sustainability.

Thirdly, viewing research on green and sustainable businesses through the specific lens of social sustainability brings new findings to the surface. It not only recognizes profitability and sustainability from the perspective of the businesses, but also identifies their promotion of social sustainability. This applicability of sustainable businesses and technologies could be seen as a tool that has the potential to bring about positive social changes in a society, improving its social sustainability. The results from this research contribute to social sustainability by providing evidence for how sustainable businesses can generate value for a given society by addressing social challenges plaguing that society.

Lastly, this research emphasizes how the existence of social enterprises relates to social sustainability. It suggests ways of assessing and improving the sustainability of social enterprises, while showing the contribution of social enterprises to social sustainability. Similarly, with regards to frugal innovation, this dissertation has positively contributed by highlighting its link to sustainability, which has been previously ignored in the literature.

Managerial implications

This dissertation explores the role of micro and small-scale businesses in generating social sustainability through case studies that focus on several unique, socially driven businesses and technologies. The cases offer evidence about the connection between socially driven micro and small businesses and technologies and social sustainability and indicate that socially driven businesses have the potential to have a strong impact on social sustainability.

The evidence presented in the cases can act as a foundation for socially driven businesses to direct their efforts towards further improving sustainability, and indeed most of the cases offer the stakeholders involved novel viewpoints, lessons learned, and numerous suggestions for better gauging and operationalising sustainability, thereby boosting their social sustainability impact (see for example, Sub-studies I, II, III and IV). These new insights this dissertation provides the managers of socially driven businesses can be considered a contribution to practice.

Socially driven innovations have been instrumental in solving wicked societal problems. This dissertation highlights the contribution of these innovations to social sustainability and the overarching goal of sustainable development. Reciprocally, the insights this dissertation provides could be used by these innovators when marketing and promoting their products and services, by showing the impact of these products from a larger perspective and highlighting the sturdy link that exists between these innovations and sustainable development.

Future research

This dissertation explored social sustainability from a rather novel approach: micro-level business cases, which were studied in depth and then analyzed in terms of links to the macro concept of social sustainability. This enigmatic concept of social sustainability was studied through practical business cases, like cellulose insulation or small hydropower, social enterprises and numerous frugal innovations, enhancing understanding of how these micro and small businesses or innovations can be instrumental in promoting social sustainability. Even small steps have the potential to make marked contributions to the overarching goal of social sustainability.

The findings generated some interesting possible opportunities for future research. First of all, this dissertation either focussed on the application of Finnish technologies in an Indian context or the study of Finnish and Indian micro and/or small businesses and their role in generating social sustainability. Future studies could focus on contexts other than Finland and India. One particularly fruitful avenue would be to study the role of social enterprises in social sustainability in other countries and then compare the results to Finnish social enterprises (Case III). Comparing and contrasting findings from different parts of the world would make it possible to achieve a holistic perspective and gain an enriched understanding of this concept.

This study was challenging in that the topic has not received much attention, and existing indicators for measuring the social sustainability of micro and small-scale businesses or innovations were limited. Measuring social sustainability was difficult: for the most part, the researcher devised new indicators based on the three pillars of sustainability. In future studies, it could be interesting to study this relationship using different indicators and instruments. According to recent research, impact assessment tools (Best and Harji, 2016; So and Staskevicius 2016) have proven quite useful in assessing the social impact of business models and projects, making them an attractive and intriguing alternative for future study.

In this dissertation, the researcher relied primarily on qualitative methods; future research could be conducted on a much larger scale by employing quantitative methods. This may be useful when attempting to generalize findings and conducting research in a value-free way where the researcher is independent of the data, which may lead to more objective results (Saunders et al. 2009). The present study explored the topic through in-depth cases, which was important to understanding the relationship of this little-researched field. However, it did not approach the whole population or even a considerable sample of the micro and small businesses in India or Finland. Future studies could target a bigger sample through quantitative methods.

Lastly, it would be interesting to study the contribution of multinational companies to social sustainability specifically.

References

American Psychological Association. (2009). *Publication manual of the American Psychological Association.* Washington, DC: American Psychological Association, 272.

Bagnold, R. A. (1941). *The physics of blown sand and desert dunes.* William Morrow & Co.

Basu, P. (2006). *Combustion and gasification in fluidized beds.* Boca Raton, FL: CRC Press.

Cuthill, M. (2009). Strengthening the 'social' in sustainable development: Developing a conceptual framework for social sustainability in a rapid urban growth region in Australia. Sust. Dev., 18: 362-373. doi:10.1002/sd.397

King, D. (1992). "Fluidized catalytic crackers: an engineering review." Leikannut O.E. Potter ja D.J. Nicklin. *Proceedings of the Seventh Engineering Conference on Fluidization.* New York: Engineering Foundation,15-26.

Lappeenranta University of Technology. (2010) *Recommendations by the LUT dissertation committee.* 2010. http://www.lut.fi/fi/lut/studies/postgraduate/instructions/Documents/RE COMMENDATIONS%20BY%20THE%20LUT%20DISSERTATION%20COMM ITTEE.pdf (haettu 26. 3).

van Wachem, Berend, ja Srdjan Sasic, (2008) "Derivation, simulation and validation of a cohesive particle flow CFD model." *AIChE Journal* ({JOHN WILEY \& SONS INC}) 54, nro 1: 9-19.

Dahlsrud, A. (2008). 'How corporate social responsibility is defined: an analysis of 37 definitions'. *Corporate Social Responsibility and Environmental Management,* 15(1), pp. 1-13.

Dart, R. (2004). 'The legitimacy of social enterprise', *Nonprofit Management & Leadership,* Vol. 14 No. 4, pp. 411-424.

Davidson, M. (2009).' Social sustainability: A potential for politics?' *Local Environment, 14*(7), 607–619.

Davis, K. (1973). 'The Case For and Against Business Assumption of Social Responsibilities', *Academy of Management Journal,* 1, pp. 312-322.

Defourny, J., and Nyssens, M. (2006). 'Defining social enterpris'e. In M. Nyssens (Ed.), *Social enterprise: At the crossroads of market, public policies and civil society* (pp. 3–26). Abingdon: Routledge.

Defourny, J., and Nyssens, M. (2012). 'Conceptions of Social Enterprises in Europe: A Comparative Perspective with the United States'. In Gidron B, Hasenfeld Y (eds) *Social Enterprises. An Organizational Perspective.* Basingstoke: Palgrave Macmillan, 71-90.

Dempsey, N., Bramley, G., Power, S. and Brown, C. (2011). 'The social dimension of sustainable development: Defining urban social sustainability', *Sustainable Development,* 19(5), pp.289–300.

Denzin, N. and Lincoln, Y. (2008). *Collecting and Interpreting Qualitative Material,* 3rd Edition. London: Sage.

DeSimone, L. D., and Popoff, F. (2000). *Eco-efficiency: The business link to sustainable development.* USA: Massachusetts Institute of Technology.

Doane D, MacGillivray A. (2001). Economic sustainability: the business of staying in business, sigma project. New Economics Foundation.

Dobson, A. (2007). 'Environmental citizenship: towards sustainable develop-men't, *Sustainable Development,* 15, pp. 276–285.

Doranova, A., Griniece, E., Miedzinski, M. and Reid, A. (2012). Connecting smart and sustainable growth through smart specialization. A practical guide for ERDF managing authorities. Brussels: European Commission.

Du, S., Bhattacharya, C.B. and Sen, S. (2010). 'Maximizing Business Returns to Corporate Social Responsibility (CSR): The Role of CSR Communication'. *International Journal of Management Reviews,* 12, pp. 8–19

Dyllick, T. and Hockerts, K. (2002). 'Beyond the business case for corporate sustainability'. *Business Strategy and the Environment.* 11(2), pp. 130-141.

Ehrgott, Matthias, Felix Reimann, Lutz Kaufmann, and Craig R. Carter (2011). 'Social Sustainability in Selecting Emerging Economy Supplier's, *Journal of Business Ethics,* 98, pp. 99-119.

Eisenhardt, K. (1989). 'Building theories from case study research'. *The Academy of Management Review,* 14(4), 532–550.

Elkington, J. (1994). 'Towards the sustainable corporation: Win-win-win business strategies for sustainable development'. *California Management Review,* 36(2), pp. 90–100.

Elkington, J. (1998). 'Partnerships from cannibals with forks: the triple bottom line of 21st century business'. *Environmental Quality Management.* 8(1), pp. 37–51.

EU. (2012). Work Programme 2013. Cooperation: Theme 8, socio-economic sciences and humanities. European Commission C 4536 of 09 July 2012. [Retrieved August 7, 2016],url:http://ec.europa.eu/research/participants/data/ref/fp7/132141/h-wp-201301_en.pdf

EU. (2016). Growth: Internal Market, Industry, Entrepreneurship and SMEs. What is an SME? [Retrieved May 7, 2016] url: http://ec.europa.eu/growth/smes/business-friendly-environment/sme-definition/

Fernando, M. (2010). Corporate social responsibility in the wake of the Asian tsunami: Effect of time on the genuineness of CSR initiatives. *European Management Journal,* 28(1), pp. 68–79.

Fisk P. (2010). *People, planet, profit: how to embrace sustainability for innovation and business growth.* London, UK: Kogan Page Limited.

Finnish Ministry of Employment and the Economy (2011). Development of social enterprise model. Ministry of Employment and the Economy. [Retrieved June 30, 2016], url: https://www.tem.fi/yritykset/sosiaalinen_yritys

Flammer, C. (2013). 'Corporate Social Responsibility and Shareholder Reaction: The Environmental Awareness of Investor's. *Academy of Management Journal,* 56(3), pp. 758–781.

Frederick, W.C. (1994). From CSR1 to CSR2: The Maturing of Business-and-Society Thought, Business and Society, 33(2), pp. 150–164.

Freundlieb, M and Teuteberg, F. (2013). 'Corporate social responsibility reporting – a transnational analysis of online corporate social responsibility
reports by market-listed companies: contents and their evolution'. *International Journal of Innovation and Sustainable Development*, 7(1), pp. 1–26.

Funk, K. Sustainability and Performance. (2003). *MIT Sloan Management
Review*, 44, pp. 65–70.

Gadamer, Hans-G. (1976). *Philosophical Hermeneutics*. Berkeley: University of
California Press.

Galuppo, L., Gorli, M., Scaratti, G. and Kaneklin, C. (2014). 'Building social
sustainability: Multi-stakeholder processes and confiict management'. *Social Responsibility Journal*, 10, pp. 685–701.

Geibler, J.; Liedtke, C.; Wallbaum, H.; Schaller, S. (2006). 'Accounting for the
Social Dimension of Sustainability: Experiences from the Biotechnology Industry'. *Business Strategy and the Environment*, 15, pp. 334–346.

George, G., McGahan, A.M., Prabhu, J. and Macgahan, A. (2012). 'Innovation
for inclusive growth: Towards a theoretical framework and a research agenda'. *Journal of Management Studies*, 49, pp. 662–683.

Ghahramanpouri, A., Lamit, H. and Sedaghatnia, S. (2013). 'Urban Social Sustainability Trends in Research Literature'. *Asian Social Science*, 9, 185–193.

Ghosh, A., Majumdar, S. and Kaur, A. (2012). A steady growth in small hydro
power in India. New Delhi: ICRA Rating Feature. [Retrieved online June 3,
2016] url: http://www.icra.in/Files/ticker/SHP%20note-.pdf

Gladwin T, Kennelly J, Krause TS. (1995). 'Beyond eco-efficiency: towards
socially sustainable business'. *Sustainable Development* 3, pp. 35–43.

Godfrey-Smith, P. (2003). *Theory and reality: An introduction to philosophy of
science*. London: University of Chicago Press.

Goldenberg, M. (2010). 'Reflections on Social Innovation', *The Philanthropist*,
23 (3), pp. 207–220.

Gould, S. (2006). *Social Enterprise and Business Structures in Canada*, Fraser
Valley Centre for Social Enterprise. [Retrieved online June 30, 2016], url:
http://www.fvcse.stirsite.com/F/SEandBusinessStructures.doc

Govindarajan, V. and Ramamurti, R. (2011). 'Reverse innovation, emerging
markets, and global Strategy'. *Global Strategy Journal*, 1, pp. 191–205.

Gray, D. (2014). *Doing Research in the Real World*. 3rd Edition. London: Sage.

Gummesson, E. (2000). *Qualitative Methods in Management Research*, 2nd
edition. Newbury Park: Sage.

Gupta, A. (2012). 'Innovations for the poor by the poor'. *Int. J. Technological
Learning, Innovation and Development*, 5(1/2), pp. 28–39.

Gupta, A. D. (Ed.). (2010). *Ethics, Business and Society: Managing Responsibly*.
SAGE Publications India.

Gupta, A.K. 'Grassroot Green Innovations for Inclusive, Sustainable Develop-
ment'. (2010). In *The Innovation for Development Report 2009–2010:
Strengthening Innovation for the Prosperity of Nations*; López-Carlos, A., Ed.;
Palgrave Macmillan: Hampshire, UK, pp. 137–146.

Hall, J.; Matos, S.; Sheehan, L.; Silvestre, B. (2012). 'Entrepreneurship and Innovation at the Base of the Pyramid: A Recipe for Inclusive Growth or Social Exclusion'? *J. Manag. Stud., 49,* pp. 785–812.

Hämäläinen, T.J. and Heiskala, R. (eds) (2007). *Social Innovations, Institutional Change and Economic Performance: Making Sense of Cultural Adjustment Processes in Industrial Sectors, Regions and Societies,* SITRA: Edward Elgar.

Hart SL. (1997).' Beyond greening: strategies for a sustainable world'. *Harvard Business Review,* 75: pp. 66–76.

Hart, S. and Christensen, C.M. (2002). 'The great leap. Driving innovation from the Base of the Pyramid'. *MIT Sloan Management Review, 44,* pp. 51–56.

Haywood LK, Brent AC, Trotter DH, Wise R. (2010). 'Corporate sustainability: a social ecological research agenda for South African business'. *Journal of Contemporary Management,* 7, pp. 325–45.

Heckl E, Pecher I, Aaltonen S, Stenholm P. (2007). Study on Practices and Policies in the Social Enterprise Sector in Europe. Final Report. KMU Forschnung Austria.

Henriques, A. and Richardson, J. (2004). 'Introduction: Triple Bottom Line – Does it All Add Up?' In: Henriques, A. & Richardson, J., eds, *The Triple Bottom Line: Does It All Add Up? Assessing the Sustainability of Business and CSR.* London: Earthscan.

Hitchcock D. and Willard, M. (2009). *The Business Guide to Sustainability: Practical Strategies and Tools for Organisations.* 2nd Edition, London, UK: Earthscan.

Holden, M. (2012). 'Urban Policy Engagement with Social Sustainability in Metro Vancouver'. *Urban Studies,* 49, pp. 527–542.

Holliday, C.O., Schmidheiny, S. and Watts, P. (2002). *Walking the Talk: The Business Case for Sustainable Development,* Sheffield, UK: Greenleaf Publishing.

Howaldt, J. and Schwarz, M. (2010). Social Innovation: Concepts, research fields and international trends, [Retrieved Aug. 27, 2016], url

http://www.asprea.org/imagenes/IMO%20Trendstudie_Howaldt_englisch_Final%20ds.pdf

Hubert, A. 2010. *Empowering people, driving change: social innovation in the European Union. Bureau of European Policy Advisors.* Publications Office of the European Union,

Luxembourg City, Luxembourg. [Retrived August 8, 2016] url: http://ec.europa.eu/DocsRoom/documents/13402/attachments/1/translations/en/renditions/pdf

Huq, F.A., Stevenson, M. and Zorzini, M. (2014). Social sustainability in developing country suppliers. *Int. J. Oper. Prod. Manag., 34,* pp. 610–638.

Hutchins, M.J.and Sutherland, J.W (2008). 'An exploration of measures of social sustainability and their application to supply chain decisions'. *Journal of Cleaner Production,* 16, pp.1688–1698.

Huybrechts, B., and Nicholls, A. (2013). 'The role of legitimacy in social enterprise-corporate collaboration'. *Social Enterprise Journal,* 9(2), pp. 130–146.

Hyvärinen, A., Keskinen, M. and Varis, O. (2016). 'Potential and Pitfalls of Frugal Innovation in the Water Sector: Insights from Tanzania to Global Value Chains'. *Sustainability,* 8, 888.

Immelt, J.R., Govindarajan, V. and Trimble, C. (2009). 'How GE is disrupting itself', *Harvard Business Review*, 87, pp. 56–65.

Karnani, A. (2007). 'Misfortune at the Bottom of the Pyramid'. *Greener Management International*, 51, pp. 99–110.

Karnani, A. (2011). 'Doing Well by Doing Good: The Grand Illusion'. *California Management Review*, *53*, pp. 69–86.

Kerlin, J.A., (2006). *A comparative analysis of the global emergence of social enterprise.* Georgia: Georgia State University.

Khan, R., Pekkarinen, S., Konsti-Laakso, S.and Melkas, H. (2015). 'How the Social Enterprises Support Social Sustainability'. *International Journal of Information Systems and Social Change*, 6(4), pp. 33–51.

Kira, M and van Eijnatten, F.M. (2008). 'Socially sustainable work organizations: a chaordic systems approach'. *Systems Research and Behavioural Science*, 27(6), pp. 713–721

Kleef, J and Roome, N. (2007). 'Developing capabilities and competence for sustainable business management as innovation: a research agenda'. *Journal of Cleaner Production*, 15, pp.38-51.

Klein, N. (2000). *No Logo No substance.* London, UK: HarperCollins Publishers.

Kolk, A. (2010). 'Trajectories of sustainability reporting by MNC's, *Journal of World Business*, 45(4), pp. 367–374.

Kolk, A., Rivera-Santos, M. and Rufin, C. (2013). 'Reviewing a Decade of Research on the "Base/Bottom of the Pyramid"' (BOP) Concept. *Bus. Soc.*, *20*, pp. 1–40.

Koning, J. (2001). Social sustainability in a globalizing world context, theory and methodology explored. In Proceedings of the UNESCO/MOST Meeting, The Hague, The Netherlands, 22–23 November.

Kopnina, H. and Blewitt, J. (2015). *Sustainable business: Key issues.* New York: Routledge.

Korten, D.C. (2000). *The post-corporate world.* San Francisco, CA: Berrett-Koehler.

Krishnan, R. (2010). *From Jugaad to Systematic Innovation: The Challenge for India*; Utpreraka Foundation: Bangalore, India.

Labuschagne, C. and Brent, A.C. (2006). 'Social Indicators for Sustainable Project and Technology Life Cycle Management in the Process Industry'. *International Journal of Life Cycle Assessment*, 11, 3–15.

Labuschagne, C., Brent, A.C. and van Erck, R.P.G. (2005). 'Assessing the sustainability performances of industries'. *Journal of Cleaner Production*, 13, pp. 373–385.

Landorf, C. (2011). 'Evaluating social sustainability in historic urban environments'. *International Journal of Heritage Studies*, 17, pp. 463–477.

Larsen, G. (2009). 'An inquiry into the theoretical basis of sustainability: Ten proposition's. In J. Dillard, V. Dujon, & M. C. King (Eds.), *Understanding the social dimension of sustainability* (pp. 45–83). New York: Routledge.

Levänen, J., Hossain, M., Lyytinen, T., Hyvärinen, A., Numminen, S. and Halme, M. (2016). 'Implications of Frugal Innovations on Sustainable Development: Evaluating Water and Energy Innovations'. *Sustainability*, 8, 4.

Lim, C., Han, S. and Ito, H. (2013). 'Capability building through innovation for unserved lower end mega markets'. *Technovation*, 3, pp. 391–404.

Lindgreen, A., Antioco, M., Harness, D. and van Sloot, R. (2009). 'Purchasing and Marketing of Social and Environmental Sustainability for High-Tech Medical Equipment'. *Journal of Business Ethics*, 85, pp. 445–462.

Lindgreen, A. and Swaen, V. (2010). 'Corporate Social Responsibility'. *International Journal of Management Reviews*, 12(1), pp. 1-7.

Littig, B., and Griessler, E. (2005). 'Social sustainability: A catchword between political pragmatism and social theory'. *International Journal of Sustainable Development*, 8(1–2), pp. 65–79.

London, T. (2009). 'Making Better Investments at the Base of the Pyramid'. *Harvard Business Review*, 87, pp. 106–113.

London, T. and Hart, S.T. (2004). 'Reinventing strategies for emerging markets: Beyond the Transnational Model'. *Journal of Int. Business Studies*, 35, pp. 350–370.

Lozano, R. (2008). 'Envisioning sustainability three-dimensionally'. *Journal of Cleaner Production*, 16, pp. 1838–1846.

Magee, L., Scerri, A., James, P., Thom, J.A., Padgham, L., Hickmott, S., Deng, H. and Cahill, F. (2013). 'Reframing social sustainability reporting: Towards an engaged approach'. *Environ. Dev. Sustain.*, 15, pp. 225–243.

Magis, K., and Shinn, C. (2009). 'Emergent principles of social sustainabilit'y. In J. Dillard, V. Dujon, & M. C. King (Eds.), *Understanding the social dimension of sustainability* (pp. 15–44). New York, USA: Routledge.

Mahajan, V. (2009). *Africa Rising: How 900 Million African Consumers Offer more than You Think*; Upper Saddle River, NJ, USA: Wharton School Publishing.

Mahajan, V., Banga, K. and Gunther, R. (2006). *The 86 Percent Solution: How to Succeed in the Biggest Market Opportunity of the Next 50 Years*; Wharton School Publishing: Upper Saddle River, NJ, USA.

Maignan, I. and Ferrell, O. C. (2004). 'Corporate Social Responsibility and Marketing: An Integrative Framework'. In: *Journal of the Academy of Marketing Science*, 32(1), pp. 3–19.

Mair, J., and Martí, I. (2006). 'Social entrepreneurship research: A source of explanation, prediction and delight'. *Journal of World Business*, 41(1), pp. 36–44.

Mair, J., Marti, I. and Ventresca, M.J. (2012). 'Building Inclusive Markets in Rural Bangladesh: How Intermediaries Work Institutional voids'. *Academy of Management Journal*, 55, 819–850.

Mak, M. Y., and Peacock, C. J. (2011). *Social sustainability: A comparison of case studies in UK, USA and Australia.* Paper presented at the 17th Pacific Rim Real Estate Society Conference, Gold Coast. [Retrieved May 28, 2016], url: http://www.prres.net/papers/Mak_Peacock_Social_Sustainability.pdf

Manzini, E. (2014). 'Making Things Happen: Social Innovation and Design'. *Massachusetts Institute of Technology Design Issues*, 30 (1), pp. 57-66.

Marcy, R. T. and Mumford, M. D. (2007). 'Social Innovation: Enhancing Creative Performance Through Causal Analysis'. *Creativity Research Journal*, 19(2), pp. 123-140.

Maylor, H and Blackmon, K. (2005). *Researching Business and Management*. New York: Palgrave Macmillan.

McElroy, M.W., Jorna, R.J. and van Engelen, J. (2008). 'Sustainability Quotients and the Social Footprint'. *Corp. Soc. Responsib. Environ. Management*, 15, pp. 223–234.

McGuire, J. W. (1963). *Business and Society*. New York: Mc Graw-Hill.

McKenzie, S. (2004). *Social Sustainability: Towards Some Definitions*; Working Paper No. 27; Hawk Research Institute, University of South Australia: Magill, Australia, 2004.

McWilliams, A. and Siegel, D. (2001). 'Corporate social responsibility: A theory of the firm perspective'. *Academy of Management Review*, 26, pp. 117-127.

Michaelis, L. (2003). 'The role of business in sustainable consumption'. *Journal of Cleaner Production*, 11, pp. 915-921.

Mirvis, P. (2010). 'Employee engagement and CSR: Transactional, relational and developmental approaches'. *California Management Review*, 54(4) pp. 93-117.

Missimer, M., Robèrt, K.-H. and Broman, G. A. (2016). 'Strategic Approach to Social Sustainability—Part 1: Exploring the Social System'. *Journal of Cleaner Production*, in press.

Missimer, M., Robert, K.H., Broman, G. and Sverdrup, H. (2010). 'Exploring the possibility of a systematic and generic approach to social sustainability'. *Journal of Cleaner Production*, 18, pp. 1107–1112.

Mulgan, G. (2006). 'The process of social innovation'. *Innovations*, 1, pp. 145–162.

Murphy, K. (2012). 'The Social Pillar of Sustainable Development: A Literature Review and Framework for Policy Analysis'. *Sustainability Science Practice and Policy*, 8, pp. 15–29.

Mulgan, G., Murray, R. and Grice, J.C. (2010). *The Open Book of Social Innovations* [Retrieved July 7, 2016], url: http://www.nesta.org.uk/library/documents/Social_Innovator_020310.pdf.

Mulgan, G., Tucker, S., Ali, R. and Sanders, B. (2007), *Social Innovation: what it is, why it matters, how it can be accelerated*, Young Foundation, e-document [Retrieved July 1, 2016], url: http://www.youngfoundation.org/files/images/03_07_What_it_is__SAID_.pdf.

Nunes, M.F. and Park, C.L. (2016). 'Self-claimed sustainability: Building social and environmental reputations with words'. *Sustainable Production and Consumption*. in press.

Osburg, T and Schmidpeter, R (Eds.) (2013). *Social Innovation: Solutions for a Sustainable Future*. Heidelberg: Springer.

Pansera, M.and Sarkar, S. (2016). 'Crafting Sustainable Development Solutions: Frugal Innovations of Grassroots Entrepreneurs'. *Sustainability*, 8, 51.

Paish, O. (2002). 'Small hydro power: technology and current status'. *Renewable and Sustainable Energy Reviews*, 6, pp.537-556.

Paton, B. and Halme, M. (2007). 'Bringing the needs of the poor into the BOP debate'. *Bus. Strategy Environ.*, *16*, pp. 585–586.

Patton, M.Q. (2002). *Qualitative research and evaluation methods*. 3rd edition. Thousand Oaks, CA: Sage.

Pervez, T, Maritz, A and De Waal, A. (2013). 'Innovation and social entrepreneurship at the bottom of the pyramid - A conceptual framework'. *South African Journal of Economic and Management Sciences*, 16(5), pp. 54–66.

Pfeffer, J. (2010). 'Building Sustainable Organizations: The Human Factor'. *Acad. Manag. Perspect. 24*, pp. 34–45.

Phills Jr., J.A., Deiglmeier, K. and Miller, D.T. (2008) *Rediscovering Social Innovation, Stanford Centre for Social Innovation Review*, [Retrieved April 14, 2016], url: http://www.ssireview.org/articles/entry/ rediscovering_social_innovation

Piercy, N. and Rich, N. (2015) 'The relationship between lean operations and sustainable operations'. *International Journal of Operations and Production Management*, 35(2), pp. 282-315.

Pisano, U, Lange, L and Berger, G. (2015). 'Social Innovation in Europe: An overview of the concept of social innovation in the context of European initiatives and practices'. *ESDN Quarterly Report* No. 36; ESDN: Vienna, Austria. [Retrieved June 28, 2016], url:

http://www.sd-network.eu/quarterly%20reports/report%20files/pdf/2015-April-Social_Innovation_in_Europe.pdf

Pitta, D.A., Guesalaga, R. and Marshall, P. (2008). 'The quest for the fortune at the bottom of the pyramid: Potential and challenges'. *J. Consum. Mark., 25*, pp. 393–401.

Pol, E. and Ville, S. (2009) 'Social innovation: buzz word or enduring term', *The Journal of Socio-Economics*, Vol. 38, No. 6, pp.878–885.

Polese, M., and Stren, R. (Eds.). (2000). *The social sustainability of cities: Diversity and the management of change, emergence of social enterprise*. Toronto: University of Toronto Press.

Porritt, J. (2005). *Capitalism as if the World Matters*, Sterling, VA, USA: Earthscan.

Pot, F and Vaas, F. (2008), 'Social Innovation, the New Challenge for Europe', *International Journal of Productivity and Performance Management*, 57 (6), pp. 468-473.

Prahalad, C.K. (2010). *The Fortune at the Bottom of the Pyramid: Eradicating Poverty through Profits*, 2nd ed. Upper Saddle River, NJ, USA: Pearson Education.

Prahalad, C.K. (2012). 'Bottom of the Pyramid as a Source of Breakthrough Innovations'. *Journal of Product Innovation Management*, 29, pp. 6–12.

Prahalad, C.K. The innovation sandbox. *Strategy+Business*, 2006. [Retrieved February 10, 2016], url: http://www.strategy-business.com/media/file/sb44_06306.pdf

Prahalad, C.K.; Hart, S.L. (2002). The Fortune at the Bottom of the Pyramid. Strategy+Business, [Retrieved April 15, 2016], url: http://www.cs.berkeley.edu/~brewer/ict4b/Fortune-BoP.pdf

Prathap, G. (2014). 'The myth of frugal innovation in India'. *Current Science, 106*, pp. 374–377.

Radjou, N. and Prabhu, J. (2014). *Frugal Innovation: How to Do More with Less*, 1st ed.; London, UK: Profile Books Ltd.

Radjou, N.; Prabhu, J. and Ahuja, S. (2012). *Jugaad Innovation: Think Frugal, Be Flexible, Generate Breakthrough Growth*, San Francisco, CA, USA: Jossey-Bass.

Rao, B.C. (2013).' How disruptive is frugal?' *Technology in Society*. 35, pp. 65–73.

Ratamäki, O. (2013). 'From ecological concerns toward solving societal problems: A case study of the development of Finland's Wolf Policy'. *International Journal of Information Systems and Social Change*, 4(2), pp. 42-58.

Rinkinen, S, Oikarinen, T and Melkas, H. (2016). 'Social enterprises in regional innovation systems: a review of Finnish regional strategies'. *European Planning Studies*, 24(4), pp. 723-741.

Robinson, J. (2004). 'Squaring the circle? Some thoughts on the idea of sustainable development'. *Ecological Economics* 48, pp. 369–384.

Robson, C. (2002). *Real World Research: A Resource for Social Scientists and Practitioner Researchers*. 2nd Edition. Oxford: Blackwell Publishers.

Rosing MV, Hove M, Scheel HV. (2012). Initial thoughts on a sustainability framework:

detailing business and IT requirements to a holistic Sustainability Framework, [Retrieved June 30, 2016], url:

http://www.valueteam.biz/wordpress/wp-content/uploads/2012/12/von-Rosing-M-Hove-M-Scheel-H-Initial-thoughts-on-a-Sustainability-Framework_2012.pdf

Rusinko, C. A. (2007). 'Green manufacturing: an evaluation of environmentally sustainable manufacturing practices and their impact on competitive outcomes'. *IEEE Transactions on Engineering Management*, 54(3), pp. 445-454.

Sachs, I. (1999). 'Social Sustainability and Whole Development: Exploring the Dimensions of Sustainable Development'. In *Sustainability and the Social Sciences: A Cross-Disciplinary Approach to Integrating Environmental Considerations into Theoretical Reorientation*; Egon, B., Thomas, J., Eds.; London, UK: Zed Books.

Sanders, N.R. and Wood, J.D. (2015). *Foundations of Sustainable Business: Theory, Function, and Strategy*. USA: John Wiley and Sons.

Saunders, M., Lewis, P. and Thornhill, A. (2009). *Research Methods for Business Students*, 5th edition, Prentice Hall, Harlow.

Schuh, G., Lenders, M. and Hieber, S. (2011). 'Lean Innovation: Introducing value systems to product development'. *International Journal of Innovation and Technology Management*, 8 (1), pp. 41-54.

Shan, J. and Khan, M.A. (2016). 'Implications of Reverse Innovation for Socio-Economic Sustainability: A Case Study of Philips China'. *Sustainability*, 8, 530.

Sharma, A. and Iyer, G.R. (2012). 'Resource-constrained product development: Implications for green marketing and green supply chains'. *Ind. Mark. Manag.* 41, pp. 599–608.

Shaw, E. and Carter, S. (2007). 'Social entrepreneurship. Theoretical antecedents and empirical analysis of entrepreneurial processes and outcomes'. *Journal of Small Business and Enterprise Development*, 14(3), pp. 418-434.

Silverman, D. (2005). *Doing Qualitative Research*. Los Angeles: Sage.

Simula, H., Hossain, M. and Halme, M. (2015). 'Frugal and Reverse Innovations—Quo Vadis?' *Current Science, 109*, pp. 1–6.

Singh, R., Gupta, V. and Mondal, A. (2012). 'Jugaad—From 'Making Do' and 'Quick Fix' to an Innovative, Sustainable and Low-Cost Survival Strategy at the Bottom of the Pyramid'. *Int. J. Rural. Manag., 8*, 87–105.

Smith, A., Fressoli, M.and Thomas, H. (2014). 'Grassroots innovation movements: Challenges and contributions'. *Journal of Cleaner Production. 63*, pp.114–124.

So, I.; Staskevicius, A. *Measuring the Impact in Impact Investing.* [Retrieved Sep. 27, 2016], url: http://www.hbs.edu/socialenterprise/Documents/MeasuringImpact.pdf

Soyka, P. A. (2012). *Creating a sustainable organization: approaches for enhancing corporate value through sustainability.* New Jersey, USA: Pearson Education.

Spangenberg, J.H. and Omann, I. (2006). 'Assessing social sustainability: Social sustainability and its multicriteria assessment in a sustainability scenario for Germany'. *International Journal of Innovation and Sustainable Development.* 1, pp.318–348.

Stake, R. E. (2005). 'Qualitative case studies'. In N. K. Denzin & Y. S. Lincoln (Eds.), *The Sage handbook of qualitative research* (3rd ed., pp. 443-466). Thousand Oaks, CA: Sage.

Steurer, R., Langer, M. E., Konrad, A., and Martinuzzi, A. (2005). 'Corporations, stakeholders and sustainable development: A theoretical exploration of business-society relations'. *Journal of Business Ethics*, 61, pp. 263-281.

Stokes, P. (2011). *Key Concepts in business and management research methods.* UK: Palgrave Macmillan.

Strauss A, Corbin, J (1998). *Basics of Qualitative Research: Techniques and Procedures for developing Grounded Theory.* Thousand Oaks, CA: Sage.

Stubbs, W. and Cocklin, C. (2008). 'Conceptualizing a "Sustainability Business Model"'. *Organization and Environment*, 21(2), pp. 103-127.

Suopajärvi, L, Poelzer, G. A. Ejdemo, T. Klyuchnikova, E. (2016). 'Social sustainability in northern mining communities: A study of the European North and Northwest Russia'. *Resources policy*, Vol. 47, pp. 61-68.

Tashakkori, A and Teddlie, C (1998). *Mixed Methodology: Combining Qualitative and Quantitative Approaches*, Thousand Oaks, CA: Sage.

Taylor, S.J and Bogdan, R. (1998*). Introduction to Qualitative Research Methods: A Guidebook and Resource.* 3rd edition, New York: John Wiley and Sons.

Thomsen, G. K., and King, M. C. (2009). 'Working out Social Sustainability on the Ground'. In J. Dillard, V. Dujon, & M. C. King (Eds.), *Understanding the social dimension of sustainability* (pp. 199–210). New York: Routledge.

Tidd, J., Bessant, J. and Pavitt, K. (2005), *Managing innovation: Integrating technological, market and organizational change*, Third edition, Chichester, John Wiley and Sons.

Tiwari, R.; Herstatt, C. (2012a). *India—A Lead Market for Frugal Innovations? Extending the Lead Market Theory to Emerging Economies*; Working Paper No. 67; Institute for Technology and Innovation Management, Hamburg University of Technology: Hamburg, Germany.

Tiwari, R. and Herstatt, C. (2012b). 'Frugal Innovation: A Global Networks' Perspective in Die Unternehmung'. *Swiss Journal of Business Research and Practice*, 66, pp. 245–274.

Torjman, S. (2000). The social dimension of sustainable development, A paper prepared for Commissioner of Environment and Sustainable Development; Caledon Institute of Social Policy, Ottawa, Canada.

Travers, M. (2001). *Qualitative Research through Case Studies.* London: Sage.

Tseng, M.L., Chiu, S.F., Tan, R.R., Siriban-Manalang, A. (2013). 'Sustainable consumption and production for Asia: sustainability through green design and practice'. *Journal of Cleaner Production*, 40, pp.1-5.

Tueth M. (2010). *Fundamentals of sustainable business: a guide to the next 100 years*. Hackensack, NJ, USA: World Scientific.

Turvey, R.A. (2015). 'Interdisciplinarity in sustainability science: challenge or opportunity?' *International Journal of Information Systems and Social Change*, 6(1), pp.41-58.

United Nations World Commission on Environment and Development (1987). Our Common Future. Oxford: Oxford University Press.

Vachon, S. and Mao, Z. (2008). 'Linking supply chain strength to sustainable development: A country-level analysis'. *Journal of Cleaner Production*, 16 (15), pp. 1552-1560.

Valdes-Vasquez, R. and Klotz, L. (2013). 'Social Sustainability Considerations during Planning and Design: Framework of Processes for Construction Projects'. *Journal of Construction Engineering and Management*, 10, pp. 80-89.

Vallance, S., Perkins, H.C. and Dixon, J.E. (2011). 'What is social sustainability? A clarification of concepts'. *Geoforum*, 42, pp. 342–348.

Vavik, T., and Keitsch, M. (2001). 'Exploring relationships between universal design and social sustainable development: Some methodological aspects to the debate on the sciences of sustainability'. *Sustainable Development*, 18(5), pp. 295–305.

Vifell, C. Å., and Soneryd, L. (2012). 'Organizing matters: How the 'social dimension' gets lost in sustainability project's. *Sustainable Development*, 20(1), pp. 18–27.

Visser, W. and Sunter, C. (2002). *Beyond Reasonable Greed: Why Sustainable Business Is a Much Better Idea*. Cape Town: Human and Rousseau Tafelberg.

Walker, H, Sisto, L.D. and McBain, D. (2008). 'Drivers and barriers to environmental supply chain management practices: Lessons from the public and private sectors'. *Journal of Purchasing and Supply Management* 14(1), pp. 69-85.

Walton, C C. (1967). *Corporate Social Responsibilities*. Belmont, CA: Wadsworth.

Walton, D. (2005). *Abductive Reasoning*. Alabama, USA: University of Alabama Press.

Weingaertner, C. and Moberg, Å. (2014). 'Exploring social sustainability: Learning from perspectives on urban development and companies and products'. *Sustainable Development*, 22, pp. 122–133.

Wells, P. (2013). 'Sustainable business models and the automotive industry: A commentary'. *IIMB Management Review*, 25(4), pp. 228-239.

Werther Jr.,W.B. and Chandler, D. (2005). 'Strategic corporate social responsibility as global brand insurance'. *Business*, 48, pp. 317-324.

Westley, F. and Antadze, N., (2010). 'Making a difference: strategies for scaling social innovation for greater impact'. *The Innovation Journal: The Public Sector Innovation Journal*, 15(2), pp. 1-15.

Weybrecht, G. (2010). *The Sustainable MBA: The manager's guide to green business*. West Sussex: John Wiley and Sons.

Willis, J.W. (2007). *Foundations of Qualitative Research: Interpretive and critical approaches.* Thousand Oaks, CA: Sage.

Woodside, A.G. and Wilson, E. J. (2003),'Case study research methods for theory building', *Journal of Business & Industrial Marketing,* 18(6/7), pp. 493-508.

Woolridge, A. The World Turned Upside down. *The Economist,* 2010. [Retrieved March 20, 2016], url: http://www.economist.com/node/15879369

Yin, R.K. (2003). *Applications of Case Study Research.* 2nd edition. Thousand Oaks, CA: Sage.

Yin, R.K. (2009). *Case study research: design and methods.* 4th edition. Los Angeles, CA: Sage.

Young, D. (2008). 'Alternative perspective on social enterpris'e. In J. J. Cordes & E. C. Steuerle (Eds.), *Nonprofits business.* Washington, DC: The Urban Institute.

Yunus, M. (2011). *Building social business: The new kind of capitalism that serves humanity's most pressing needs.* NY, USA: PublicAffairs.

Zeschky, M., Widenmayer, B. and Gassmann, O. (2011). 'Frugal Innovation in Emerging Markets: The Case of Mettler Toledo'. *Research Technology Management,* 54, pp. 38–45.

Zeschky, M.B., Winterhalter, S. and Gassmann, O. (2014). 'From Cost to Frugal and Reverse Innovation: Mapping the Field and Implications for Global Competitiveness'. *Research Technology Management,* 57, pp. 20–27.

Chapter 6

Awakening Employee Creativity in Organizations

Wenjing Cai*

E-mail: w.cai@vu.nl

Abstract: Employee creativity is a critical determinant of organizational innovation, performance, success, and long-term survival in the dynamically changing world. Researchers have investigated different predictors to facilitate employee creativity. However, existing knowledge about how these predictors from multiple aspects can be aligned to awaken employee creativity remains incomplete. To address this limitation, this dissertation explores through what explanatory mechanisms and under what boundary conditions the various factors from both organizational and individual aspects can simultaneously trigger employee creativity. The results suggest that organizational human resource management (HRM) practices should be bundled to manage employee creativity. Based on empirical studies, both entrepreneurial leadership and servant leadership promote workplace creativity by fostering individual psychological attributes. The findings further reveal that job characteristics and supervisor support represent key boundary conditions that strengthen the effects of predictors on higher levels of creativity.

Keywords: Employee creativity; innovative work behavior; HRM practices; leadership and supervisory behaviors; psychological attributes; job characteristics; team creativity.

1. Introduction

In the dynamically changing world, organizations are pursuing innovation to maintain competitive advantages. Faced with competition and unpredictable technological change, they are realizing the essential and fundamental role of employee creativity. Since creativity is the first step of innovation (e.g., Shalley et al., 2004), by promoting employees to generate creative ideas and products for the market, organizations can achieve innovation goals (e.g., Liu et al., 2017; Sawyer, 2011; Zhou and Shalley, 2008). Considering the critical importance of creativity, practitioners are searching for means to facilitate employees' creative performance. For example, organizations build sound working conditions and provide support and encouragement to stimulate employees to develop creative ideas.

Given the critical role of employee creativity and innovation, researchers have investigated creativity predictors based on organizational and individual aspects

(Anderson et al., 2014). Specifically, there is a stream of research efforts focused primarily on the importance of individual differences for the creative process and the production of creative products, such as traits, values, and psychological states (e.g., Raja and Johns, 2010; Shin and Zhou, 2003; Sweetman et al., 2011). The other line of research lies in examining the effects on creativity of those contextual factors that comprise the employee's environment, such as leadership and supervision, social networks, and job characteristics (e.g., Baer, 2010; Liu et al., 2012; Shalley et al., 2009; Zhang and Bartol, 2010). As employees produce creativity in the working context, creativity is a result of the combined influences of individual and contextual factors (e.g., Zhou and Hoever, 2014). Thus, scholars are investigating the co-determinants of these predictors considering employees and organizations in the creativity literature.

Problem statement

Although researchers suggest that creativity results from the integration of organizational and individual predictors, our knowledge of *how a broader range of predictors could be well aligned to engender creative and innovative results* is still incomplete. To help organizations effectively manage employees' creativity, this dissertation aims to elucidate what predictors within organizations and employees can align to engender creative results.

Considering the rapid changes in the knowledge economy, our managerial ideas are correspondingly developing to effectively promote employee creativity and innovation. For example, as the young generation grows in the workforce, their distinctive personal attributes, compared with those of the traditional generation, should be highly considered and effectively utilized to encourage creative and innovative achievements. However, our knowledge in this regard is far from complete because extant studies fail to explore the potential factors (e.g., creative leadership styles and building employees' perception of meaningful work) that can effectively promote employee creativity.

Moreover, although the interactional approach in creativity research (e.g., Zhou and Hoever, 2014) suggests that the interactions between contextual factors and employee characteristics promote creativity, the results to date fail to indicate the extent to which the complex interplay may effectively boost creativity. For example, early research has suggested that rewards are detrimental to creativity, yet Baer and coauthors (2003) found that when employees with adaptive cognition work in simple jobs, rewards may facilitate their ability to exhibit higher creativity. Thus, employee creative potential is not uniform and can be stimulated by considering different combinations of contextual and personal predictors.

Finally, based on the componential model (Amabile, 1996; Amabile and Pratt, 2016), scholars have shown the psychological mechanism (e.g., intrinsic motivation) through which contextual predictors (e.g., leadership styles) promote creativity. However, burgeoning research has questioned the role of intrinsic motivation and proposed some other important mediators (e.g., self-efficacy and meaningful work) (e.g., Gong et al., 2009). Given the limited empirical evidence in this regard, further examination is encouraged to establish these psychological mechanisms. Additionally, considering the changes in work environments and employees' personal growth, researchers are calling for a broader exploration of the diversity of creativity predictors (Anderson et al., 2014). For example, although team-based working characteristics are widely designed in contemporary organizations, whether team context shapes employee creativity remains underexplored.

Purpose of the dissertation

The purpose of this dissertation is to fill in the research gaps described above to extend our understanding of how to effectively manage employee creativity in organizations. Therefore, this dissertation targets identifying factors from both organizations and employees that simultaneously trigger employee creativity. Specifically, I propose five main topics that are relevant for explaining the complex influences on employee creativity:

1. How can human resources (HR) awaken employee creativity?

2. How can employees awaken their own creativity?

3. How can leaders awaken employee creativity?

4. How can job design awaken employee creativity?

5. How can employee creativity be awakened in teams?

For each research topic, I not only aim to reflect on each main aspect of awakened initiatives from organizations and employees but also to illuminate the interdependence of this aspect with other initiatives.

2. Background

Throughout my dissertation, I use the widely accepted definition of employee creativity—i.e., individuals generating novel and useful ideas, products, and processes (e.g., Amabile, 1996; Anderson et al., 2014; Woodman et al., 1993)— and employee innovative work behaviors (IWB), i.e., a series of individual activities for the generation, promotion, and realization of ideas for new technologies, processes, techniques, or products (Janssen, 2000; Janssen and Van Yperen, 2004; Yuan and Woodman, 2010).

Awakening employee creativity from an HR perspective

Given that employees are the major assets supporting organizational innovation, scholars have recently suggested that human resource management (HRM) can facilitate creativity (Agarwal and Farndale, 2017; Chang et al., 2014). Although existing theoretical arguments suggest a strong connection between HRM and employ creativity, few studies in the creativity research field have investigated the role of HRM (Jiang et al., 2012a). To address this important yet relatively limited research issue, I draw on ability-motivation-opportunity (AMO) theory—a basic HRM theory—to address the narrow view of interactions in the existing creativity literature. Specifically, creativity predictors can be categorized into HR practices within AMO theory—that is, creativity antecedents represent the implementation of *ability-, motivation-,* and *opportunity-enhancing HRM practices* (Appelbaum, 2000; Boselie et al., 2005; Jiang et al., 2012b; Paauwe, 2009). Moreover, the basic models in the AMO theory in the HRM literature can explain the interactions in creative processes—that is, the bundles of HR practices from the above three dimensions exert complementary or synergistic influences on employee performance (Subramony, 2009). This assumption aligns with the interactionist model in the creativity literature (Farr and Tran, 2008).

Employees awakening their own creativity

The aforementioned arguments have shown the research on personal characteristics facilitating employee creativity. However, existing research has integrated only the role of personal psychological attributes to a limited extent: 1) although scholars acknowledge the potential benefits of positive psychology on creative outcomes (e.g., Sweetman et al., 2011), surprisingly little is known about how to maximize the effects of PsyCap—a typical positive psychological factor for creativity (Rego et al., 2012). 2) Despite the positive impacts of creative self-efficacy—an important aspect of PsyCap—on employee creative performance (e.g., Tierney and Farmer, 2002; 2011), the mixed results regarding whether creative self-efficacy transfers the influence of the context (e.g., leadership) to creativity calls for deeper examination of creative self-efficacy as a mediator (Liu et al., 2016). 3) Similarly, the inconsistent results regarding traditional psychological factors (e.g., intrinsic motivation) in creativity research call for further explorations of other motivational mechanisms that link the context to creativity (Amabile and Pratt, 2016; Liu et al., 2011). Thus, I follow two main theoretical frameworks in the creativity literature to address these research gaps by illustrating the influences of various personal psychology (i.e., *PsyCap, creative self-efficacy,* and *meaningful work*) and organizational factors simultaneously.

Leaders awakening employee creativity

As proximal contextual factors, leadership or supervisory factors, such as transformational leadership, authentic leadership, and supervisor behavior (e.g., Gong et al., 2009; Rego et al., 2012), have been fundamentally and significantly indicated in many studies to influence creativity (Anderson et al., 2014; Shalley and Gilson, 2004). However, the evidence thus far indicates that traditional leadership styles offer a weak explanation for creativity in the literature. For example, the influence of transformational leadership—a typical traditional leadership style—on creativity is mixed in existing research (Hammond et al., 2011; Rosing et al., 2011), and it is empirically redundant (Van Knippenberg and Sitkin, 2013). Thus, this major problem regarding the incompatibility of leadership and creativity engenders an emergent research topic: how creativity-oriented leadership or supervisory behavior, specifically, influences creativity (Anderson et al., 2014; Mainemelis et al., 2015). To address this research gap, scholars have called for research addressing a broad range of different leadership styles or supervisory behaviors. Therefore, I follow previous research suggestions and propose three important leadership and supervisory factors—*entrepreneurial leadership, servant leadership,* and *supervisor support for creativity*—to explain their influences on the creativity research field. The theory claims that all these factors contribute to creativity, but little empirical research has examined them in detail.

Awakening employee creativity through job design

Research suggests that well-designed tasks—which are significant and identifiable and provide autonomy, feedback, and opportunities to use employees' skills (Hackman and Oldham, 1976)—stimulate employees' "excitement about their work activities and their interest in completing these activities, and this excitement should foster creativity" (Shalley et al., 2004). Recent studies have treated job characteristics as a boundary condition through which creativity can be enhanced given certain predictors (e.g., Shalley et al., 2009) since variations in creativity are mainly dependent on whether employees' tasks have a creativity requirement (Shalley et al., 2000). However, the scant number of empirical examinations in this line of research limits our comprehensive understanding of the influence of job design on creativity. Consequently, following the reasoning above, I primarily provide a comprehensive picture on the moderating effects of *job characteristics* (i.e., *task sig-*

nificance, skill variety, task identification, feedback, and *job autonomy)* on the relation between various factors and employee creative or innovative results.

Awakening employee creativity in teams

Organizations are turning to design team-based work systems to allow more employees to work together towards creative achievements (Pirola-Merlo and Mann, 2004). Given that creativity cannot occur in isolation, teams act as a major component of the working context that influences employees' creative endeavors (Hirst et al., 2009; Hirst et al., 2011). Specifically, team characteristics (e.g., team learning behaviors, team diversity, and team goal orientation) shape employee creativity in teams, since the interactions within teams potentially affect team members' cognitive resources for identifying problems, processing information, and devising creative solutions (Gong et al., 2013). However, empirical studies regarding the potential benefits of teams for creativity remain limited (Chen et al., 2013; Taggar, 2002). The deep knowledge about how team characteristics trigger employee creativity has significant implications for organizations' ability to manage teams and employee creativity (Zhou and Shalley, 2008). Therefore, I aim to enrich this line of research by investigating the influences of *team creative efficacy* belief on employee creativity.

3. Research design

Structure of the dissertation

This dissertation explores the complex combinations of organizational and individual factors supporting employee creativity and innovation. It consists of an introductory chapter, four independent conceptual and empirical studies, and a concluding chapter, which altogether address the research problems stated above. Figure 6.1 shows an organizing framework that contains the research variables from all of the studies.

Specifically, the Introduction introduces and provides an overview of the research that I have undertaken. Regarding the first research topic, in Study 1, I draw on the HRM perspective and utilize AMO theory to provide a typology of interactions to understand the interactions discussed in the creativity literature. By reviewing relevant empirical studies, this conceptual article provides a combination model and a multiplicative model to theoretically explain how the various interactions of creativity predictors may predict a high, higher, or the highest level of employee creativity. The results of this complex interplay are empirically supported in Study 1, in which the highest level of creativity is found to exist when PayCap and two distinct contextual drivers (i.e., supervisor support for creativity and job characteristics) are both high. The second topic is addressed in Studies 2, 3, and 4. These three studies examine the influence of employee psychological characteristics on creativity (PsyCap in Study 2, creative self-efficacy in Study 3, and meaningful work in Study 4). To address the topic of leadership issues, I examine the ability of supervisor support for creativity (Study 2), entrepreneurial leadership (Study 3), and servant leadership (Study 4) to nurture employee creativity and innovation. Studies 2 and 4 mainly address the fourth topic by examining the moderating effects of job design. Finally, Study 3 tests whether team factors (i.e., creative team efficacy) contribute to employee creativity, which provides evidence to address the last topic.

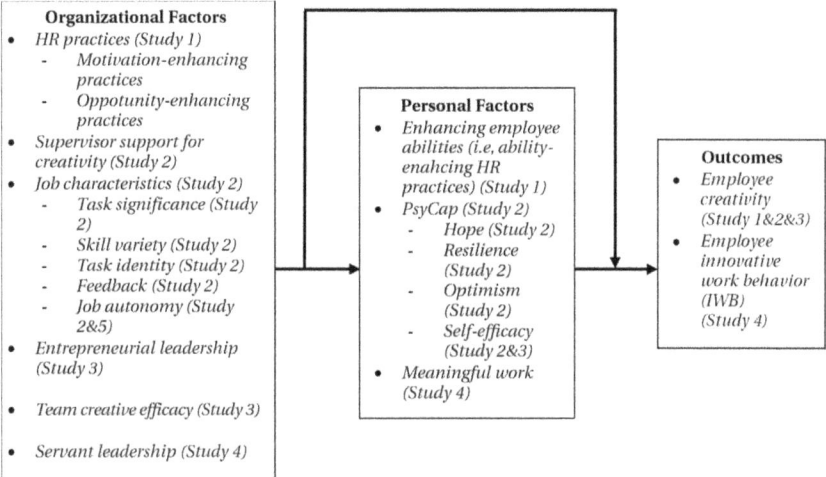

Figure 6.1 An organizing framework for studies in the dissertation.

Note: Italicized factors are studied in each of the separate studies

Methodology of the dissertation

In this dissertation, I used a mixed method—an integration of qualitative (Study 1) and quantitative (Studies 2, 3, and 4) studies. There are two main reasons for the methodological choices. First, despite this high level of scholarly interest, the study of creativity with regard to the alignment of predictors has arguably lacked coherence due to the absence of an overarching theoretical model to guide research. This lack, in turn, may hinder researchers' ability to develop our understanding of how to enhance employee creativity by conducting empirical examinations. Therefore, I performed a conceptual study to provide theoretical signals for the following three empirical studies. In doing so, I developed a comprehensive picture to illustrate how various predictors co-determine employee creative and innovative outputs. Second, in the three quantitative studies, I collected data from various industries in China to provide support for the external validity of the creativity results. The various sources of samples in this dissertation permit a more complete and synergistic utilization of data to provide insights into awakening employee creativity in organizations. Furthermore, since the models and theories of creativity are located and widely tested in Western countries, it is questioned whether they can be applied to other cultural contexts (e.g., China). The cross-cultural creativity studies in this dissertation extend the creativity literature to the international context. Relatedly, to increase generalizability, the samples of these studies are not specific to a single industry or company.

4. Conclusion

Across the four independent studies, this dissertation highlights how the various factors from organizations and employees can together promote employee creativity and innovation in organizations. Some main findings are illustrated in the following subsections, corresponding to each of the research topics.

HR practices focused on creativity management

Given the ongoing scholarly attention on how to advance existing knowledge on the complex interactionist approach in the creativity literature, I draw on domain theory in the HRM literature—the AMO theory—to provide a new lens to understand creativity research in depth, especially with respect to the interactional perspective. That is, the results provide a refined categorization of creativity predictors in AMO theory, and based on this, the study moved further to frame two distinct models that explain employee creativity in terms of bundles of HR practices within AMO theory. Specifically, the combination model (in which motivation- and opportunity-enhancing practices are interacted with ability-enhancing practices) delivers a higher level of creativity than the main effects of ability predictors on creativity; moreover, the multiplicative model (in which motivation- and opportunity-enhancing practices are simultaneously interacted with ability-enhancing practices) exhibits the highest level of creativity. In addition, these conceptual results are empirically examined in Study 2 (i.e., the interactions of PsyCap, supervisor support for creativity, and job characteristics with respect to creativity).

The psychological role of employee themselves

The significant conclusions in this thesis highlight that individuals' psychological attributes, which are specified as PsyCap (Study 2), creative efficacy beliefs (Study 3), and meaningful work (Study 4), are important for their creative outcomes. These psychological states indicate whether employees are psychologically capable of doing creative and innovative work. Specifically, in terms of main effects, PsyCap, a high-order construct, captures the main meaning of positive psychology to trigger employee creativity. This empirical explanation of the moderators of favorable contextual predictors (e.g., supervisor support for creativity and job characteristics) also indicates that the advantages of followers' positive psychology on creativity can be strengthened by the joint interactions of multiple contextual facilitators. Moreover, in line with the motivation mechanisms in the creativity literature, Studies 3 and 4 highlighted the mediating role of creative self-efficacy and meaningful work in bridging the positive effects of desirable leadership styles on employee creative and innovative outcomes.

The leadership approach in creativity research

In line with the acknowledgement that leadership or supervisory behavior affects employee creativity (Tierney, 2008), I extend the limited area addressing how leaders influence creativity and innovation by answering scholars' calls to investigate a broad range of leadership styles (Amabile, 1996; Mainemelis et al., 2015; Shalley and Gilson, 2004). Basically, because of the uncertainty and risk taking during the process of generating and implementing ideas, consideration of the potential advantages of leaders indicates that leaders should have a strong creativity and innovation orientation and exhibit behaviors and attitudes in favor of fostering employees' creativity (Mainemelis et al., 2015; Mumford et al., 2002). In particular, Study 1 generalizes the basic role of leaders—motivating employees to devise creative ideas. Consistently, Study 2 provides empirical evidence showing that supervisor support for creativity activates a process through which employees utilize PsyCap for creative performance, which responds to the scholarly debate about the benefits of leader support for creativity (Baer and Oldham, 2006). Furthermore, to have a comprehensive understanding of how leadership or supervisor behaviors exactly result in creative and innovative outcomes, Studies 3 and 4 contextualize entrepreneurial leadership and servant leadership, respectively, to provide consistent support for the argument that creativity-specific leadership styles indeed play an important role in promoting creativity and IWB. The abovementioned results highlight that creativity- and innovation-oriented leadership or supervisory behavior not only lead to creativity and IWB at the individual level but also act as a crucial contingency factor that facilitates a higher level of creativity from employees' positive psychology.

Well-designed jobs as a strengthening factor

The consideration of job characteristics is consistent with the applications of the person-in situation theory in the creativity literature. The results indicate that organizations that enhance employee tasks along five dimensions (i.e., variety, identity, significance, autonomy, and feedback) may create a positive context to moderate the influences of personal psychological attributes on creative results. Specifically, in Study 1, the conceptual results indicate that job characteristics that potentially provide opportunities for employees may interact with motivation-enhancing practices (e.g., leadership) in positively influencing the psychology-creativity relationship to the greatest extent. Empirically, Study 2 considers this entire construct and teases out the combined effects of job characteristics, supervisor support for creativity, and PsyCap with respect to the highest level of creativity. Further understanding of the boundary conditions of job characteristics lies in extending the situational leadership theory in creativity and innovation studies. Study 4 advances the understanding of this line of theoretical arguments by specifically identifying that higher job autonomy, rather than lower job autonomy, significantly accentuates the indirect influences of servant leadership on IWB via meaningful work.

Creativity in a team environment

Consistent with the theoretical arguments that the team context generates a strong influence on employee creativity, putting employee creativity into a team context deepens scholars' understanding of how to make team members more creative. In Study 3, the delineation of the top-down influences of team-level creative efficacy beliefs on individual-level employee creativity goes beyond the extant research by considering the effects of creative self- and team efficacy simultaneously. That is, the results indicate the similar positive motivational effects of creative efficacy beliefs on employee creative results, especially the cross-level effect of team efficacy. Moreover, specific to the empirical study context (i.e., Chinese organizations), the results of the positive role of team efficacy belief consistently provide evidence-based insights into the arguments that team properties (e.g., team creative efficacy) significantly benefit employee (creative) outcomes in a collectivistic culture (e.g., China) (Schaubroeck et al., 2000; Shin and Zhou, 2007).

5. Implications and future research

Theoretical implications

In addressing these research topics, I make several important contributions to the existing creativity research. First, by discovering new contextual and personal factors (e.g., entrepreneurial leadership and meaningful work) and showing their contributions to creative outcomes, I integrate theories related to these factors with creativity theory to provide a comprehensive picture of various predictors of creativity. Such an investigation answers scholars' call for research analyzing a broad range of unexplored creativity predictors. In addition, by re-examining the effects of several factors (e.g., creative self-efficacy and supervisor support for creativity) under continued debate in creativity research, this thesis provides new evidence to establish their influence on creativity. Hence, I add more consistent findings to creativity research. Overall, this thesis then refines the scholarly understanding of the role of various contextual and individual predictors of creativity.

Second, this thesis helps enrich the paucity of studies investigating the mechanisms by which the context boosts employee creativity. Based on the newly identified and re-examined variables above, I test the influences of leadership styles (i.e., entrepreneurial leadership and servant leadership) on creativity from a mediator-based perspective. Relying on motivational mechanisms, I specifically open the black box of leadership-creativity associations by establishing key employee psychological characteristics (i.e., creative self-efficacy and meaningful work) to extend the incomplete understanding of the motivational processes that link leadership and creativity. Furthermore, by considering the multilevel nature of the mechanisms, I add empirical evidence to the limited stream of studies by testing whether a motivational factor at the team level (i.e., team creative efficacy) may transfer the effect of leadership to creativity in the workplace. In this way, this thesis offers significant insights into multilevel phenomenon in the creativity literature—advancing a more complete account of drivers of creativity across levels.

Finally, from an interactional perspective, I provide a new lens that allows in-depth understanding of the complex interplay between the personal and contextual factors driving creativity with two different studies. Specifically, a conceptual framework analyzes different interactions in which various contextual factors may separately or jointly accentuate the positive effects of personal factors on creativity and is fully supported by an empirical study. Moreover, this thesis goes beyond the mediation and moderation effects in creativity research by studying the conditional indirect effects, thereby extending theoretical arguments regarding whether task characteristics determine the effect of leadership styles on follower outcomes.

Practical implications

The findings presented in this dissertation have important practical implications for organizations in terms of fostering workplace creativity and innovation. First, as Study 1 generally conceptualizes the importance of enhancing abilities, organizations should highly focus on selecting and training leaders and employees to have or develop characteristics such as creative efficacy and on providing support for creativity. Second, given the direct influence of personal psychology on creative and innovative results, organizations should create an environment where employees can develop their psychological attributes. Third, since job characteristics determine how leaders influence followers' psychology and creativity, organizations should design employees' tasks in an effective way. Furthermore, considering the results showing that team properties foster employee creative achievements, organizations should organize efficacious teams. In addition, the combined effects of leaders, psychological attributes, and job design should encourage organizations to implement a bundle of practices to facilitate workplace creativity and innovation to the greatest extent. Finally, the Chinese research context generates special implications for developing effective creativity and innovation management and practices for Chinese employees.

Future research directions

Employee creativity is a developing research area that requires further progress. Based on the evidence presented in this dissertation, some exciting possibilities for future research directions can be proposed. First, given the conceptual confirmation of the connections between HRM and creativity, future research is highly encouraged to ensure that these findings apply broadly—for example, as AMO theory is developing with regard to the argument that the three dimensions of HR practices may exert indirect influences on employee outcomes (e.g., Jiang et al., 2012a), it would be promising to investigate the mechanisms through which these interactions affect creativity.

Second, although these studies attempt to identify the positive relationship between employee psychology and creativity, future research is encouraged to broaden this concept of psychology in the creativity and innovation literature by exploring other types, such as prosocial motivations. For example, as creativity requires both novelty and usefulness, employees' preferences in taking others' opinions are highly critical for creativity (Grant and Berry, 2011). That is, prosocial motivation may direct employees' thinking in other ways (Hoever et al., 2012) and foster generous actions (Carmeli et al., 2014), which in turn internally motivates employees to produce creative outcomes (Bai et al., 2016). The result that prosocial motivation mediates the context-creativity relationship in the meta-analysis of Liu et al. (2016) also indicates that future research should consider how leaders nurture employees' prosocial motivation through a role-model process that facilitates employees' creative achievements.

Third, given the significance of leaders, studies in the future are needed to examine how supervisory behavior fits together with other contextual factors, especially opportunity-enhancing predictors, to generate the highest level of creativity and innovation, such as whether supervisor (supportive) behaviors and participative management practices (e.g., organizational structures) jointly accentuate the psychological characteristics-creativity relationship. Moreover, to further develop the arguments that leadership approaches address the underpinnings of creativity, research in the future may explore whether other undeveloped leadership styles that potentially motivate employees' creative engagement, such as participative leadership and visionary leadership, could predict creativity and IWB.

Furthermore, to fully examine the strength of task characteristics, further clarification regarding whether other facets of jobs, such as time pressure, task challenges, and job demand and resources, may substitute for, neutralize, or enhance the influences of leadership issues on creativity and innovation is required. In addition, considering that job characteristics have multiple dimensions, more research distinguishing between these dimensions may generate a clear understanding of their similar or different effects in creativity research.

Finally, the studies in this thesis include only one aspect of the team context that influences employee creativity directly; therefore, further investigations should focus on how team properties may interact with other creativity predictors in fostering employee creative performance. For example, given that team-level factors may influence the development of individual-level psychological variables through complex interactional and reciprocal effects on individuals' motivations, beliefs and orientations (Gully et al., 2002), team creative efficacy may activate the potential benefits of employee psychological states (e.g., learning orientation) on creativity. Moreover, since team creativity is not an aggregation of employee creativity (Pirola-Merlo and Mann, 2004), to enrich the incomplete phenomenon of creativity and innovation at multiple levels, more studies are needed to investigate how creativity predictors from various levels may simultaneously boost team and employee creativity.

References

Agarwal, P. & Farndale, E. (2017). 'High-performance work systems and creativity implementation: the role of psychological capital and psychological safety'. *Human Resource Management Journal.* 27(3), 440-458.

Amabile, T. M. (1996). *Creativity in context: Update to" the social psychology of creativity.".* Westview press.

Amabile, T. M. & Pratt, M. G. (2016.) 'The dynamic componential model of creativity and innovation in organizations: Making progress, making meaning'. *Research in Organizational Behavior*, 36, 157-183.

Anderson, N., Potočnik, K. & Zhou, J. (2014). 'Innovation and Creativity in Organizations A State-of-the-Science Review, Prospective Commentary, and Guiding Framework'. *Journal of Management*, 40(5), 1297-1333.

Appelbaum, E. (2000). *Manufacturing advantage: Why high-performance work systems pay off.* Cornell University Press.

Baer, M. (2010). 'The strength-of-weak-ties perspective on creativity: a comprehensive examination and extension'. *Journal of Applied Psychology*, 95(3), 592-601.

Baer, M. & Oldham, G. R. (2006). 'The curvilinear relation between experienced creative time pressure and creativity: moderating effects of openness to experience and support for creativity'. *Journal of Applied Psychology*, 91(4), 963-970.

Baer, M., Oldham, G. R. & Cummings, A. (2003). 'Rewarding creativity: When does it really matter?'. *The Leadership Quarterly*, 14(4-5), 569-586.

Bai, X., Li, Y. & Lin, L. (2016). 'Caring for others matters: Flexibility and persistence as the dual pathways whereby intrinsic and prosocial motivations enhance creativity'. *International Journal of Psychology*, 51, 745.

Boselie, P., Dietz, G. & Boon, C. (2005). 'Commonalities and contradictions in HRM and performance research'. *Human Resource Management Journal*, 15(3), 67-94.

Carmeli, A., McKay, A. S. & Kaufman, J. C. (2014). 'Emotional intelligence and creativity: The mediating role of generosity and vigor'. *The Journal of Creative Behavior*, 48(4), 290-309.

Chang, S., Jia, L., Takeuchi, R. & Cai, Y. (2014.) *Do High-Commitment Work Systems Affect Creativity? A Multilevel Combinational Approach to Employee Creativity.*

Chen, G., Farh, J.-L., Campbell-Bush, E. M., Wu, Z. & Wu, X. (2013). 'Teams as innovative systems: Multilevel motivational antecedents of innovation in R&D team's. *Journal of Applied Psychology*, 98(6), 1018-1027.

Farr, J. L. & Tran, V. (2008). 'Linking innovation and creativity with human resources strategies and practices: A matter of fit or flexibility?' *Research in Multi Level Issues*, 7, 377-392.

Gong, Y., Huang, J.-C. & Farh, J.-L. (2009). 'Employee learning orientation, transformational leadership, and employee creativity: The mediating role of employee creative self-efficacy'. *Academy of Management Journal*, 52(4), 765-778.

Gong, Y., Kim, T.-Y., Lee, D.-R. & Zhu, J. (2013). 'A multilevel model of team goal orientation, information exchange, and creativity'. *Academy of Management Journal*, 56(3), 827-851.

Grant, A. M. & Berry, J. W. (2011). 'The necessity of others is the mother of invention: Intrinsic and prosocial motivations, perspective taking, and creativity'. *Academy of Management Journal*, 54(1), 73-96.

Gully, S. M., Incalcaterra, K. A., Joshi, A. & Beaubien, J. M. (2002). 'A meta-analysis of team-efficacy, potency, and performance: interdependence and level of analysis as moderators of observed relationships'. *Journal of applied psychology*, 87(5), 819-832.

Hackman, J. R. & Oldham, G. R. (1976). 'Motivation through the design of work: Test of a theory'. *Organizational Behavior and Human Performance*, 16(2), 250-279.

Hammond, M. M., Neff, N. L., Farr, J. L., Schwall, A. R. & Zhao, X. (2011). 'Predictors of individual-level innovation at work: A meta-analysis'. *Psychology of Aesthetics, Creativity, and the Arts*, 5(1), 90-105.

Hirst, G., Van Dick, R. & Van Knippenberg, D. (2009). 'A social identity perspective on leadership and employee creativity'. *Journal of Organizational Behavior*, 30(7), 963-982.

Hirst, G., Van Knippenberg, D., Chen, C.-h. & Sacramento, C. A. (2011). 'How does bureaucracy impact individual creativity? A cross-level investigation of team contextual influences on goal orientation–creativity relationships'. *Academy of Management Journal*, 54(3), 624-641.

Hoever, I. J., Van Knippenberg, D., Van Ginkel, W. P. & Barkema, H. G. (2012). 'Fostering team creativity: perspective taking as key to unlocking diversity's potential'. *Journal of Applied Psychology*, 97(5), 982-996.

Janssen, O. (2000). 'Job demands, perceptions of effort-reward fairness and innovative work behaviour'. *Journal of Occupational and Organizational Psychology*, 73(3), 287-302.

Janssen, O. & Van Yperen, N. W. (2004). 'Employees' goal orientations, the quality of leader-member exchange, and the outcomes of job performance and job satisfaction'. *Academy of Management Journal*, 47(3), 368-384.

Jiang, J., Wang, S. & Zhao, S. (2012a). 'Does HRM facilitate employee creativity and organizational innovation? A study of Chinese firms'. *The International Journal of Human Resource Management*, 23(19), 4025-4047.

Jiang, K., Lepak, D. P., Hu, J. & Baer, J. C. (2012b). 'How does human resource management influence organizational outcomes? A meta-analytic investigation of mediating mechanisms'. *Academy of Management Journal*, 55(6), 1264-1294.

Liu, D., Chen, X.-P. & Yao, X. (2011). 'From autonomy to creativity: a multilevel investigation of the mediating role of harmonious passion'. *Journal of Applied Psychology*, 96(2), 294-309.

Liu, D., Gong, Y., Zhou, J. & Huang, J.-C. (2017). 'Human resource systems, employee creativity, and firm innovation: The moderating role of firm ownership'. *Academy of Management Journal*, 60(3), 1164-1188.

Liu, D., Jiang, K., Shalley, C. E., Keem, S. & Zhou, J. (2016). 'Motivational mechanisms of employee creativity: A meta-analytic examination and theoretical extension of the creativity literature'. *Organizational Behavior and Human Decision Processes*, 137, 236-263.

Liu, D., Liao, H. & Loi, R. (2012). 'The dark side of leadership: A three-level investigation of the cascading effect of abusive supervision on employee creativity'. *Academy of Management Journal*, 55(5), 1187-1212.

Mainemelis, C., Kark, R. & Epitropaki, O. (2015). 'Creative leadership: A multi-context conceptualization'. *The Academy of Management Annals*, 9(1), 393-482.

Mumford, M. D., Scott, G. M., Gaddis, B. & Strange, J. M. (2002). 'Leading creative people: Orchestrating expertise and relationships'. *The Leadership Quarterly*, 13(6), 705-750.

Paauwe, J. (2009). 'HRM and performance: Achievements, methodological issues and prospects'. *Journal of Management Studies*, 46(1), 129-142.

Pirola-Merlo, A. & Mann, L. (2004). 'The relationship between individual creativity and team creativity: Aggregating across people and time'. *Journal of Organizational Behavior*, 25(2), 235-257.

Raja, U. & Johns, G. (2010). 'The joint effects of personality and job scope on in-role performance, citizenship behaviors, and creativity'. *Human Relations*, 63(7), 981-1005.

Rego, A., Sousa, F. & Marques, C. (2012). 'Authentic leadership promoting employees' psychological capital and creativity'. *Journal of Business Research*, 65(3), 429-437.

Rosing, K., Frese, M. & Bausch, A. (2011). 'Explaining the heterogeneity of the leadership-innovation relationship: Ambidextrous leadership'. *The Leadership Quarterly*, 22(5), 956-974.

Sawyer, R. K. (2011). *Explaining creativity: The science of human innovation.* Oxford University Press.

Schaubroeck, J., Lam, S. S. & Xie, J. L. (2000). 'Collective efficacy versus self-efficacy in coping responses to stressors and control: a cross-cultural study'. *Journal of Applied Psychology*, 85(4), 512-525.

Shalley, C. E. & Gilson, L. L. (2004). 'What leaders need to know: A review of social and contextual factors that can foster or hinder creativity'. *The Leadership Quarterly*, 15(1), 33-53.

Shalley, C. E., Gilson, L. L. & Blum, T. C. (2000). 'Matching creativity requirements and the work environment: Effects on satisfaction and intentions to leave'. *Academy of Management Journal*, 43(2), 215-223.

Shalley, C. E., Gilson, L. L. & Blum, T. C. (2009). 'Interactive effects of growth need strength, work context, and job complexity on self-reported creative performance'. *Academy of Management Journal*, 52(3), 489-505.

Shalley, C. E., Zhou, J. & Oldham, G. R. (2004). 'The effects of personal and contextual characteristics on creativity: Where should we from here?' *Journal of Management*, 30(6), 933-958.

Shin, S. J. & Zhou, J. (2007). 'When is educational specialization heterogeneity related to creativity in research and development teams? Transformational leadership as a moderator'. *Journal of Applied Psychology*, 92(6), 1709-1721.

Shin, S. J. & Zhou, J. (2003). 'Transformational leadership, conservation, and creativity: Evidence from Korea'. *Academy of Management Journal*, 46(6), 703-714.

Subramony, M. (2009). 'A meta-analytic investigation of the relationship between hrm bundles and firm performance'. *Human Resource Management*, 48(5), 745-768.

Sweetman, D., Luthans, F., Avey, J. B. & Luthans, B. C. (2011). 'Relationship between positive psychological capital and creative performance'. *Canadian Journal of Administrative Sciences/Revue Canadienne des Sciences de l'Administration*, 28(1), 4-13.

Taggar, S. (2002). 'Individual creativity and group ability to utilize individual creative resources: A multilevel model'. *Academy of Management Journal*, 45(2), 315-330.

Tierney, P. (2008). 'Leadership and employee creativity'. *Handbook of organizational creativity*, 95-123.

Tierney, P. & Farmer, S. M. (2002). 'Creative self-efficacy: Its potential antecedents and relationship to creative performance'. *Academy of Management Journal*, 45(6), 1137-1148.

Tierney, P. & Farmer, S. M. (2011). 'Creative self-efficacy development and creative performance over time'. *Journal of Applied Psychology*, 96(2), 277-293.

Van Knippenberg, D. & Sitkin, S. B. (2013). 'A Critical Assessment of CharismaticTransformational Leadership Research: Back to the Drawing Board?' *Academy of Management Annals*, 7(1), 1-60.

Woodman, R. W., Sawyer, J. E. & Griffin, R. W. (1993). 'Toward a theory of organizational creativity'. *Academy of Management Review*, 18(2), 293-321.

Yuan, F. & Woodman, R. W. (2010). 'Innovative behavior in the workplace: The role of performance and image outcome expectations'. *Academy of Management Journal*, 53(2), 323-342.

Zhang, X. & Bartol, K. M. (2010). 'The influence of creative process engagement on employee creative performance and overall job performance: a curvilinear assessment'. *Journal of Applied Psychology*, 95(5), 862-873.

Zhou, J. & Hoever, I. J. (2014). 'Research on Workplace Creativity: A Review and Redirection'. *Annu. Rev. Organ. Psychol. Organ. Behav.*, 1(1), 333-359.

Zhou, J. & Shalley, C. E. (2008). 'Expanding the scope and impact of organizational creativity research'. *Handbook of organizational creativity*, 28, 125-147.

Chapter 7

Building Higher-Order Capabilities: Insights from Resource-Scarce Environments

Dr. Pavan Soni

E-mail: innovation.evangelist@gmail.com

Abstract: Innovation management is one of the most important capabilities for an organization. It is especially true with growing levels of environmental dynamism and complexity. However, there remains a scant understanding on how firms build such higher-order capabilities, and the role of the manager in doing so. This question becomes even more relevant in emerging economies which are mired by widespread resource scarcity and weak institutional setups. The research attempts to delve into the process of capability creation by adopting a case study-based approach to analyze how select firms in India have developed capabilities of managing a systematic innovation programme. By studying six large organizations across three industries over a period of 20 years, insights are offered on the role a manager plays in building a robust innovation management regime in the organization.

Keywords: Innovation Management, New Capability Creation, Resource-scarce environments, Emerging Economies, Case study research.

1. Introduction

Over the past few years, the discourse in strategic management research has gravitated towards understanding the 'genesis' of firm's competitive advantage. One of the capabilities of interest is that of managing innovation in an organizational context. The pursuit assumes even greater importance when one seeks to understand the means through which firms create de novo capabilities by overcoming path dependence, and, more so, while being in resource-scarce settings.

With significant research being performed on and in emerging economies, which are typically characterized as resource-scarce and institutionally-deficient, there remains an imperative to understand how firms operating in such environments build higher-order capabilities. This has remained a relatively unexplored and increasingly pertinent topic. Another concern that the scholarly community shares is that the resource-based view, or its distributaries, such as dynamic capabilities literature, does not adequately explain the 'role of the manager' on how exactly the manager's influence capability creation and, hence, a firm's competitive performance. In the light of these avenues of investigation, the thesis attempts to offer a model of capability creation that explicates the managerial role while contextualizing the process to the firm's external environment which is resource deficient. The approach adopted is as follows.

Firstly, a conceptual model of capability creation is proposed that builds on the extant research on a resource-based view, the capabilities literature, the firm's task environment, and managerial roles. To sharpen the focus, the aim is to study the creation of firm-specific and higher-order capabilities, such as new product development. Secondly, a logico-deductive approach is adopted to arrive at a capability creation model which comprises of four key managerial activities and a set of firm-level sub-processes within each one of the activities. The four managerial activities are- orientation, acquisition, orchestration, and deployment.

The orientation refers to 'building the foundation and the enablers for subsequent capability creation,' and the four sub-processes are creating a stretch, sensing and shaping opportunities, introducing variation and selection, and implementing learning systems. The acquisition refers to 'seeking constituent resources and competencies from outside the firm,' and the three sub-process are picking from strategic factor markets, forging network ties with the proximal environment, and accessing distant environments. The orchestration indicates 'configuring the existing bundle in isolation, or in association with the incoming resources and capabilities, to form newer capabilities,' and the five sub-process involved in orchestration are concentrating and protecting, recombining the existing, bundling the old with the new, improvisation, and retirement of assets. Finally, deployment refers to 'leveraging the extant or new competencies to address specific opportunities', and the three sub-processes under this stage are exploiting the existing, replicating across adjacencies, and learning by doing.

It is then argued how the 'sequence' of managerial activities and 'salience' of sub-processes vary with firms operating in different environmental conditions, characterized on the basis of environmental munificence (resource-availability), dynamism, and complexity. This leads to five different models, corresponding to the various environmental configurations. Further, propositions are offered on the capability creation process and how it gets influenced by the firm's external environment.

Next, an empirical model of capability creation is generated by adopting an inductive logic, where six Indian firms across three industries are studied while depicting three different environmental configurations. The evolution of unique firm-specific and higher-order capabilities around new product development are mapped over a twenty-year period in each firm. The three industries are auto-ancillary, IT services and pharmaceuticals, and the respective firms in each are ANAND Group and Tata AutoComp, Infosys and Wipro, and Biocon and Dr. Reddy's Lab. By adopting perceptual measures, the auto ancillary industry is characterized as an environment which is low on both dynamism and complexity, IT services as one being high on dynamism but low on complexity, and the pharmaceutical industry as a highly complex and dynamic setting. A case study-based method with replication logic is adopted to study the capability creation process in each of the six firms, and then abstractions are drawn on the sequence of managerial activities and salience of sub-processes for each of the environmental configurations. Over 114 interviews are conducted, and close to 500 artifacts from secondary sources are studied to arrive at the detailed cases and models. Each case is about 40 pages long and is coded in-line with the empirical codes generate beforehand.

Finally, the two models, the conceptual and the empirical, are contrasted to offer a refined set of propositions on capability creation. The various points of departure between the theoretic predictions and the empirical findings are explained in terms of managerial roles and firm-level sub-processes on how they shape the capability creation process and their contingency with the firm's external environment. The key insights derived from the exercise are as follows. Firstly, capability creation process can be decomposed into specific steps that a manager can influence. Secondly, the process of capability creation changes with the environment, as characterized by its munificence, dynamism, and complexity. Thirdly, there are certain sub-processes of capability creation that are agnostic of the firm's external environment. These include-creating a stretch, accessing distant environments, bundling the old with the new, and learning by doing. These elements are present in all the empirical models, across environmental configurations.

The thesis proposes to make contributions to both the theory of strategic management research and strategy as a practice. As for the conceptual contributions, the first one is to further the microfoundations project by elucidating the process of capability creation, and bringing to fore the role of the manager, an aspect that the field deems as the current research gaps. Secondly, the research brings back the importance of firm's external environment in the discourse on capability creation, which has largely been around dynamism, and not so much on munificence or complexity. On account of the contribution to practice, the cases share several best practices for managing new product development and influencing innovation capabilities drawn from the first-hand insights from industry-leading firms. Further, the study offers actionable insights for practicing managers in emerging economies.

2. Background

The research attempts to answer the question on how firms operating in re-source-scarce environments build higher-order capabilities, such as innovation management. The thrust is on the managerial activities and the firm-level subprocesses that lead to capability creation.

Nature of capabilities

Capability could be thought of as 'firm's capacity to deploy resources, usually in combination, using organizational processes, to affect the desired end' (Amit and Schoemaker, 1993: 35). Some of the key attributes of a capability could be identified as – *Purposeful, Embedded, Inimitable, Repeatable,* and *Reliable.* Further, based on the significance of a capability to the firm, one could think of two broad typologies of capabilities- *degree of specificity,* and the *level of complexity.* Regarding the extent of specificity to the business, capabilities could be thought of as either *firm-specific* or generic. A firm-specific capability would have a high level of specificity as compared to a generic capability (Leonard - Barton, 1992). Based on these proposed capability types, on the basis of their complexity, one could broadly classify capabilities as *lower-order* versus *higher-order* capabilities (Zollo and Winter, 2002).

The interest in this research is on firm-specific, higher-order capabilities, such as innovation management or new product development.

Talking of the origins of capabilities, in one of the earliest commentaries on the origins of capabilities, Dierickx and Cool (1989) proposed the model of 'internal asset accumulation' as a means of capability creation. From a knowledge management perspective, Grant offered that new capabilities are created by 'integrating the specialist knowledge bases of a number of individuals' (1996: 377). From a learning perspective, Winter (2000) explained how aspirations trigger learning and lead to capability creation. In a later work, Eisenhardt and Martin decomposed the process of capability creation into the steps of 'integrating, reconfiguring, gaining and releasing resources to match or create market change' (2000: 1107).

Clearly, internal accumulation and sourcing, through networks and alliances, seems to be the dominant ways of new capability creation.

Managerial role in capability creation

In terms of the managerial role in capability creation, in an early discourse on capabilities, Hamel and Prahalad (1994) identified two primary activities of the manager: creating strategic intent, and resource leverage. Later, Teece et al. (1997) highlighted the managerial activities of integrating internal and external competencies, learning to build new skills, and reconfiguring and transforming firm's assets to build new capabilities. To this Eisenhardt and Martin (2000) ascribed managers with the responsibilities of altering, or manipulating, the resource base through integrating, reconfiguring, gaining, and releasing resources to generate value-creating strategies. Moreover, Helfat and Peteraf (2003) identified six key ways in which managers could alter a firm's capabilities-retirement, retrenchment, renewal, replication, redeployment, and recombination.

It is only recently that the importance of manager as a resource and capability mobilizer has come into the discourse of strategic management. In one of the seminal works in this direction, Sirmon et al. defined resource management as 'the comprehensive process of structuring the firm's resource portfolio, bundling the resources to build capabilities, and leveraging those capabilities with the purpose of creating and maintaining value for customers and owners' (2007: 273). They identified the three sub-elements as structuring, bundling and leveraging.

In a more detailed follow-up, Sirmon et al. (2011) defined structuring as comprising of acquiring, accumulating, and divesting resources to form the firm's resource portfolio; bundling as integrating resources to form capabilities through stabilizing, enriching, and pioneering; and leveraging through mobilizing, coordinating, and deploying.

However, there are two shortcomings in the depiction by Sirmon et al. (2007, 2011). Firstly, the explanation does not illustrate why, in the first place, a manager should go about capability creation, or the 'trigger' for new capability creation is not clear. The authors assume that conditions exist for a new capability to be created. Secondly, the depiction of managerial roles doesn't pay attention to the firm's external environment (munificence, dynamism, and complexity) in terms of the contingency effect on the managerial roles in capability creation. Of the three key environmental dimensions, only that of munificence and dynamism are dealt with, and that too, only narrowly.

Limitations in literature

To sum up the literature review, the following insights emerge. Firstly, capabilities could be characterized as being purposeful, embedded, inimitable, repeatable, and reliable. This qualification is important in the light of identifying what truly qualifies as a capability versus an ad hoc approach to problem solving, or just a routine. Secondly, capabilities could be classified, in several other ways, into the dimensions of specificity to the firm, and the level of complexity. One could deem capabilities as firm-specific or generic on one vector, and higher-order or lower-order on the other vector.

Thirdly, the literature offers several attempts of arriving at the sources of capabilities, including dynamic capabilities, lifecycle view, knowledge-based view, or network view, amongst others. However, there still is a missing process model of the origin of capabilities. Fourthly, in terms of how managers influence capability creation, there is abundant research on the aspects of cognition and behavior, but not so much is researched about the volition, or the managerial actions meant to influence capabilities. Finally, the research on firm's task or external environment suggests the parsimonious dimensions as munificence, dynamism, and complexity.

Based on the literature review, the following research model is suggested (Figure 7.1).

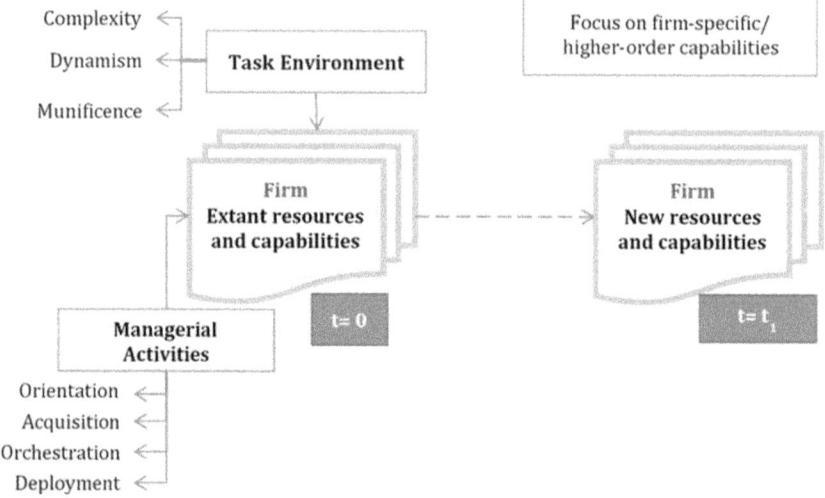

Figure 7.1 Research model depicting the task environment, managerial activities, and the creation of capabilities

The capability creation process is studied across the scenarios of 1) low-munificence, low-dynamism, and low-complexity; 2) low-munificence, high-dynamism, and low-complexity; 3) low-munificence, low-dynamism, and high-complexity; and finally, 4) low-munificence, high-dynamism, and high-complexity.

3. Research design

The objective of the research is two-fold. Firstly, identify the managerial activities and firm-level sub-processes that shape the formation of firm-specific, higher-order capabilities, such as innovation management. Secondly, elaborate how the sequence of activities and salience of sub-processes vary with the firm's task environment in terms of munificence, dynamism, and sali-ence. The focus is on environments with low levels of munificence, or in other words, have low resource availability.

Methodology

The study adopts *multiple case studies* and *holistic design* (single unit of analysis per case) for identification and studying the capability creation process (Yin, 1994). It is based on the approach of *theoretical replication* (predicting contrasting results but for predictable reasons), instead of literal replication (predicting the same result). Further, the choice of different industry contexts enables a more informed understanding of the sequence of managerial activities and salience of sub-processes, as contingent on the firm's external environment. Further, the level of analysis of the investiga-tion is the firm and the unit of analysis is the higher-order capability, pri-marily that of innovation management.

Data source and nature of data

The identification of firms and the capabilities of the case study research is a three-step process.

Firstly, the industries are identified where firms have managed to build higher-order capabilities, and secondly, in those industries, the most im-pactful firms are identified that have demonstrated enduring and largely inimitable capabilities. Moreover, it is ensured that the industries offer sufficient contrast in terms of variation of the environment to tease out the impact of environmental characteristics on the firm's capability creation process. Finally, in the third stage, the candidate capabilities are identified to be studied in detail.

For the mapping of industries to the environmental characteristics to be studied, perceptual measures are adopted which emerge mostly from pri-mary and secondary interviews with the industry leaders (Boyd et al., 1993).

Based on the assessment of the industries which have demonstrated world-class capabilities, in an Indian context, three industries are identi-fied- Auto ancillaries, IT services, and Pharmaceuticals. A few firms in each of these industries have demonstrated superior performance, at a global level, for a sustained period. In each of the three industries, specific re-sources that are low on munificence are identified and discussed, and how the firms have managed to create enduring higher-order capabilities.

A total of six firms were identified for empirical investigation. In the au-to ancillary sector, the two firms are New Delhi-based ANAND Group, and Pune-based Tata AutoComp Systems; in the IT services industry, the two firms are Bangalore-based Infosys and Wipro; and the pharmaceutical industry, the two firms are Bangalore-based Biocon and Hyderabad-based Dr. Reddy's.

The capabilities of interest are as follows.

ANAND Group: Managing a systemic and systematic innovation programme

Tata AutoComp: Technology indigenization through joint ventures

Infosys: Ability to co-create emerging technology solutions with clients

Wipro: Managing a systemic and systematic technology incubation programme

Biocon: 'Design for manufacturability' of biotechnology products

Managerial activities:

1) Orientation,

2) Acquisition,

3) Orchestration, and

4) Deployment

Firm-level sub-processes:

1) Creating a stretch,

2) Sensing and shaping opportunities,

3) Introducing variation and selection,

4) Implementing learning systems,

5) Picking from strategic factor markets,

6) Forging network ties with proximal environment,

7) Accessing distant environments,

8) Concentrating and protecting,

9) Recombining the existing,

10) Bundling the old with the new,

11) Improvisation,

12) Retirement of assets,

13) Exploiting the existing,

14) Replicating across adjacencies, and

15) Learning by doing

Data analysis

The primary source of information gathering included interviews, either face to face, or telephonic. In total, 114 interviews were conducted, totaling to 94 hours and 14 minutes of duration. All the interviews were recorded and later transcribed. These transcriptions were then sent back to the respective interviewees to get a concurrence on the implied meaning. Before incorporating the quotes into the cases, once again, a concurrence was secured on the appropriateness of the quote in the context of the case.

As for the secondary information, the key sources were annual reports, company bulletins, presentations/ minutes of the meetings, company press releases, and media articles. It covered a total of 471 published and unpublished sources across the six firms. The data is analyzed using Atlas.ti 7.0

4. Conclusion

The research is an effort to answer the question on how firms build capabilities when operating in resource scarce environments? The focus was on managing innovation in a systematic and systemic manner.

Based on the field observations, a few insights are offered on the capability creation process. The research is contextualized to a resource-scarce setting, and the attempted was to, firstly, elucidate the managerial activities and firm-level sub-processes that lead to new capability creation, and, secondly, tease out how the capability creation process varies with the firm's external environment. There are three insights offered by the research.

Capability creation process can be decomposed into well-defined steps

The starting point of the research was to propose a model of capability creation, and while doing so, a parsimonious framework was offered to depict a set of managerial activities and firm-level sub-processes that influence firm-level capability creation.

The empirical research, based on the case study led inductive process, validated the notion that indeed the capability creation process could be structured around a finite set of activities. The empirical exercise demonstrated that most of the firm-level activities could be attributed to one of the initially identified codes under the various managerial activities. This offered conviction that indeed the capability creation process could be decomposed into a finite set of sub-processes. Table 7.1 depicts the model of capability creation.

Table 7.1 General model of capability creation

Orientation	Acquisition	Orchestration	Deployment
• Creating a stretch • Sensing and shaping opportunities • Introducing variation and selection • Implementing learning systems	• Picking from strategic factor markets • Forging network ties with proximal environment • Accessing distant environments	• Concentrating and protecting the existing • Recombining the existing • Bundling the old with the new • Improvisation • Retirement of assets	• Exploiting the existing • Replicating across adjacencies • Learning by doing

Capability creation process changes with firm's external environment

The second key objective of the research was to assess whether the process of capability creation changes from one firm to another if the two operate in significantly different environmental conditions. Three critical environmental dimensions were identified, munificence, dynamism, and complexity, and propositions were offered on how the sequence of managerial activities and salience of firm-level sub-processes would change with different environmental configuration. Table 7.2 shows how the salience of various firm level sub-processes change with the environmental context.

Table 7.2 Summary of how sequence/salience varies with external environment

Scenario			Industry	Stage I	Stage II	Stage III	Stage IV
Munif- icence	**Dyna- mism**	**Com- plexity**		Sub- processes	Sub- processes	Sub- processes	Sub- processes
Low	Low	Low	Auto ancillary	**Orienta- tion** Creating a stretch Sensing shaping	**Acquisition** Distant environ- ments	**Orchestra- tion** Bundling	**Deploy- ment** Learning by doing
Low	High	Low	IT services	**Orienta- tion** Creating a stretch Sensing and shap- ing	**Acquisition** Distant environ- ments	**Orchestra- tion** Concen- trating Improvis- ing Bundling	**Deploy- ment** Learning by doing Replicat- ing
Low	High	High	Pharma	**Orienta- tion** Creating a stretch Introduc- tion varia- tion Learning systems	**Orchestra- tion** Concen- trating Bundling Recombin- ing	**Acquisi- tion** Distant environ- ments	**Deploy- ment** Learning by doing

Capability creation process has certain environment-agnostic steps

While these seem to be a distinct sequence of activities leading to capability crea- tion in each environmental condition, there, however, remains a certain set of sub- processes consistent across the various configurations. These could be thought of as steps to capability creation agnostic of the state of firm's external environment.

Based on the empirical findings, the four consistent elements are- creating a stretch, accessing distant environments, bundling the old with the new, and learning by doing. These seem to be the most elemental components of capability creation.

'Creating a stretch,' that often takes the shape of leaders' vision, and ambition remains the starting point of any efforts in creating a substantive capability. Simi- larly, faced with a resource-scarce environment, 'accessing distant environments' becomes a natural choice for the firm, as this takes the form of alliances, joint- research, or close associations with advanced customers. Also, 'bundling the old with the new' is the dominant means through which the firm fuses the extant with the incoming, and finally, 'learning by doing' befits the low-munificence setting where the firm doesn't necessarily have the resource to learn before doing.

Table 7.3 depicts the elements in each of the contexts.

Table 7.3 Elucidation of four environment-agnostic steps to capability creation across the six cases

Firm	Creating a stretch	Accessing distant environments	Bundling the old with the new	Learning by doing
ANAND Group	Founder's commitment to people and partnerships	Joint-ventures for advanced technologies	Embedding innovation practices (learned from network ties)	Innovation at Gabriel India (process innovation followed by product)
Tata AutoComp Systems	Forging a JV on equal footing (50/50 and Joint-R&D setup in India)	Engaging with advanced firms (through the JV model)	Setting up joint engineering centers with JV partners	Product indigenization at Tata Toyo (JV expansion and R&D setup in India)
Infosys	Creating a compelling brand for SETLabs, though publication and patenting	Co-creating technology assets along with Microsoft. Joint research with universities abroad.	oring co-creation opportunities.	Planting client innovation centers while building on co-creation opportunities
Wipro	Premji's vision and management style	Learning from clients on technology and management. Forging select alliances. Adopting an eco-system approach to innovation	Technology incubation at the CTO Office	Launch of Wipro Holmes to address the firm's objective of achieving non-linear growth
Biocon	Founder's vision and competence (Kiran Mazumdar-Shaw)	Forging alliances to fill competence gaps	Building on externally sourced expertise to enter into biotherapeutics	Insulin programme. Launch of ALZUMAb based on joint research with CIMAB
Dr. Reddy's	A scientist-entrepreneur as the founder (late Dr. Anji K Reddy)	Collaboration for R&D (starting with co-licensing).	Exploring US generics to fund R&D (complementing acquisition with in-house R&D)	Biosimilars programme build from scratch without resorting to alliances or inorganic means.

5. Implications and future research

Contribution to both the research on strategic management and the practice of strategy are presented here.

Contribution to research on strategic management

The study envisages two contributions to the research on strategic management. The first is in furthering the microfoundations project, and the second is to bring back the importance of task environment in strategic management research.

This study contributes towards furthering the pursuit of deciphering the foundations of new capabilities. It proposes specific managerial actions and sub-processes that influence capability creation. While most of these managerial activities are well known (Sirmon et al., 2007; Hamel and Prahalad, 1994), however, putting those in the context of capability creation is a novel contribution. Similarly, it was identified how the managerial actions trigger certain firm-level processes that enable capability creation, which offers further insight into the process itself.

Another salient contribution of the study is to bring to fore the impact of the firm's external environment on the approach the manager adopts for capability creation. More specifically, it is argued for the role low-munificence environments plays in capability creation. The task environments increasingly become less munificent or low on their resource carrying capacities, and with the competition increasingly shifting to the emerging markets, this dimension becomes critical for competition. The study lays out well argued and observed manners in which firms operating in different environmental conditions adopt distinct approaches to capability creation. The explication of how environment shapes the capability creation trajectories brings back the importance of the environment to the dominant discourse in strategic management.

Contribution to the practice of strategic management

The two questions raised in the research were- firstly, how does a manager shape capability creation? and secondly, how does the environment influence capability creation? Since the investigation was on the aspects that a manager could influence, the study has a direct relevance to practice.

The empirical findings are a result of interviews with over 150 senior managers across three industries and six firms. In the process of capturing the process of capability creation, there were several best practices documented on the ways firms shape culture, engage in alliances, set up incentive systems, and processes to bring about new capabilities. Coming from the real-world cases and especially from firms that have done well over long periods of time, there are clear takeaways for the practicing managers.

Further, creating new capabilities does not come easy, especially when a firm operates in an environment which is starved of critical-to-compete resources. Since, emerging markets in Asia, Latin America, and Eastern Europe, all share similar resource constraints, such practices have direct relevance to managers competing in such scenarios.

Hence, both on account of the managerial role, and the environmental influence, the study offers some tractable insights.

References

Amit, R., and Schoemaker, P. J. (1993). 'Strategic assets and organizational rent'. *Strategic management journal*, 14(1), 33-46.

Boyd, B. K., Dess, G. G., and Rasheed, A. M. (1993). 'Divergence between archival and perceptual measures of the environment: Causes and consequences'. *Academy of Management Review*, 18(2), 204-226.

Dierickx, I., and Cool, K. (1989). 'Asset stock accumulation and sustainability of competitive advantage'. *Management Science*, 35(12), 1504-1511.

Eisenhardt, K. M., and Martin, J. A. (2000). 'Dynamic capabilities: What are they'. *Strategic Management Journal*, 21(1), 1105-1121.

Grant, R. M. (1996). 'Toward a knowledge - based theory of the firm'. *Strategic management journal*, 17(S2), 109-122.

Hamel, G., and Prahalad, C. K. (1994). *Competing for the Future*. Harvard Business Press.

Helfat, C. E., and Peteraf, M. A. (2003). 'The dynamic resource - based view: Capability lifecycles'. *Strategic Management Journal*, 24(10), 997-1010.

Leonard - Barton, D. (1992). 'Core capabilities and core rigidities: a paradox in managing new product development'. *Strategic Management Journal*, 13(S1), 111-125.

Sirmon, D. G., Hitt, M. A., and Ireland, R. D. (2007). 'Managing firm resources in dynamic environments to create value: Looking inside the black box'. *Academy of management review*, 32(1), 273-292.

Sirmon, D. G., Hitt, M. A., Ireland, R. D., and Gilbert, B. A. (2011). 'Resource orchestration to create competitive advantage breadth, depth, and life cycle effects'. *Journal of Management*, 37(5), 1390-1412.

Teece, D. J., Pisano, G. and Shuen, A. (1997). 'Dynamic capabilities and strategic management'. *Strategic Management Journal*, 18(7): 509–533.

Winter, S. G. (2000). 'The satisfying principle in capability learning', *Strategic Management Journal* 21(10/11), 981-996.

Yin, R. (1994). *Case study research: Design and methods*, Beverly Hills.

Zollo, M., and Winter, S. G. (2002). 'Deliberate learning and the evolution of dynamic capabilities'. *Organization science*, 13(3), 339-351.

Chapter 8

Investigating Innovation Champions in the Nonprofit Sector

Courtney Molloy*

E-mail: courtney.molloy@newcastle.edu.au

Abstract: Innovation champions are critical actors driving and facilitating organizational innovation. This study extends champion investigations by exploring this phenomenon more broadly to include top-down and bottom-up champions operating in the unique but under-explored nonprofit sector. Furthermore, this study investigates the role of organizational level context (culture and leadership) in shaping championing. Specifically, champion behaviors, motivation and impact are investigated in small and medium sized human services nonprofit organizations. A qualitative, case study methodology was employed, with six cases selected to deeply explore championing within different organizational contexts. Empirical findings indicate similarities, and important differences, with extant champion literature. In particular, the greater external focus of championing, which related to idea generation, persistence, connectivity and influence is a novel finding and extends the literature beyond an intra-organizational focus. Further, champion motivation was found to be more nuanced than previous studies reflect, adding a significant contribution to champion and nonprofit literature. In terms of impact, champions drove important innovative projects, but also engendered critical organizational, and in some cases sectoral change, findings which challenge a relatively narrow focus on what champions achieve.

Keywords: innovation champion, champion of innovation, nonprofit innovation, context and innovation.

1. Introduction

Innovation champions are important actors driving and facilitating innovation within organizations (Anderson and Bateman 2000; Bankins et al. 2017; Howell and Higgins 1990a; Schon 1963), but empirical substantiation of champion impact remains limited (Howell, Shea and Higgins 2005; Walter et al. 2011). Furthermore, most champion research has been conducted in large, for-profit organizations with an emphasis on new-product or technological innovations. Although the extant literature provides important insights regarding championing, investigations offering finer-grained, contextual detail are required (Markham and Griffin 1998). In particular, exploration in organizations of different sizes and in different sectors is essential to understand how these contextual elements influence championing. Equally important is the exploration of championing of innovations that might be less well-defined than the more tangible innovative projects that have been the focus of previous research (Frost and Egri 1991; Howell and Boies 2004; Howell and Shea 2006). This chapter provides a summary of a research project (Molloy 2017) which empirically explored championing in the Australian, nonprofit context, with a specific focus on human services organizations.

Understanding innovation in nonprofits is important. Nonprofit organizations make significant contributions to Australia's economy, both in terms of input to GDP and to employment (Productivity Commission 2010). Beyond the economic contribution, and arguably of greater importance, is the social value that nonprofits deliver. Nonprofits play a highly active role in our community both directly through service provision and more broadly through their influence and advocacy (Dalton and Butcher 2014). Furthermore, nonprofits play a critical role in creating and shaping social capital (Passey and Lyons 2006) and afford individuals the opportunity to contribute to a chosen cause or mission (Wollebaek and Selle 2002).

This research focuses specifically on human services organizations within the nonprofit sector (Berzin, Pitt-Catsouphes and Gaitan-Rossi 2016). Human services organizations are defined by the Productivity Commission (2010, p. XVII) as "those services that seek to improve individual and community well-being through the provision of care, education and training and community services." In addition to the far-reaching contributions to civil society identified above, numerous authors have highlighted the increasingly important role of human services nonprofits in social service delivery due to the withdrawal of government from welfare service provision (Baulderstone and Earles 2009; Shea and Wang 2016).

Human services nonprofits are, as described above critical players in the delivery of essential social services and in shaping civil society. In Australia, there have been significant changes to government funding models which are threatening the capacity of human services organizations to make such important contributions (Baulderstone and Earles 2009; Evans, Richmond and Shields 2005). These funding changes are reflective of the broader neoliberal shift evident internationally (Baines et al. 2014; Goodwin and Phillips 2015) which is driving increased competitiveness, a desire for growth, the implementation of business-like practices and attempts to boost market-derived income amongst human service organizations (Hwang and Powell 2009; Smith 2008). Of substantial importance is how these shifts affect the delivery of social services (Butcher and Freyens 2011). Although no conclusive evidence has been provided, there is concern that these organizations, who are a crucial contributor to the social welfare of communities, may lose sight of their mission as they adjust in order to financially survive (Ebrahim and Rangan 2014; Jones 2007).

Understanding how innovation might facilitate a nonprofit contribution to social value through these turbulent times is therefore critical. Innovation may enable nonprofits to maintain a social focus and remain sustainable during this period of significant dynamism (Dart 2004; Jaskyte and Dressler 2004; McDonald 2007). Championing research outside of the for-profit sector is, however, scant and what does exist is directed towards the public sector (Bankins et al. 2017; Bartlett and Dibben 2002). How champions operate and cope within the unstable nonprofit environment fills an important gap, adding insight to for-profit championing literature.

2. Background

It is important before further discussion to identify how the focal unit of study, the innovation champion, is defined. Howell and Higgins (1990a) argue that championing should be viewed on a continuum and adopting a definition that allows scope for this is important. This study adopts the definition constructed by Howell and Higgins (1990b) which combines key elements from a synthesis of definitions presented in the literature and offers sufficient detail for identification purposes: "An individual who informally emerges in an organization (Schon 1963) and makes "a decisive contribution to the innovation by actively and enthusiastically promoting its progress through the critical [organizational] stages" (Achilladelis, Jervis and Robertson 1971, p. 14)". It is important to note that although the majority of champion research focuses on individuals who drive innovation and innovative projects upwards, from lower levels of an organization (e.g., Howell and Higgins 1990a; Markham and Griffin 1998; Schon 1963), because of the dearth of research exploring innovative behavior and specifically championing in the nonprofit sector, this research did not delimit championing to only that of bottom-up activity, but allowed for the inclusion of top-down champions.

For the most part, extant literature has identified what champions do, but has yet to understand how they do it (Howell, Shea and Higgins 2005). Relatedly, champion motivation has been identified as important, but there is a lack of investigation which explores exactly what drives champions. Moreover, champions are described as courageous individuals driving important innovations through organizations (Chakrabarti 1974; Frost and Egri 1991; Schon 1963) and there has been some empirical substantiation of champion impact, but none which verifies the extensiveness of their effect (Markham 1998). These three components form the core focus of this research, specifically, conducting a deep exploration of champion behaviors, motivation and impact. Furthermore, this study sought to add to the understanding of championing more deeply by exploring the influence of context on these individuals. To do so, an exploration of championing in the nonprofit sector was conducted, with a focus on organizational-specific contextual elements, namely culture and leadership. Figure 8.1 provides a visual representation of the key components of this study.

Figure 8.1 Conceptual framework – championing and context

Behaviors

Studying behaviors is identified as an ideal and appropriate way to identify champions and understand what they actually do (Markham, Green and Basu 1991). Champion behavior has undergone initial investigation, generating important insights from which this study builds. However, given the lack of previous champion research in the nonprofit context, it is important to develop a structure for exploring champion behaviors that are guided by the literature, but not prescriptive. The work of Howell, Shea and Higgins (2005) and the broader champion literature found this study's investigation of championing in the nonprofit context. A review of existing literature identified four broad categories to describe not just what champions do, but further inform our understanding of how they behave. These categories are labeled 'idea generation,' 'persistence,' 'connecting' and 'influencing.' Each of these categories represents an important component of championing described in the literature but are under-investigated. This study, therefore, begins to build a response to calls in the literature to develop a more comprehensive understanding of how champions operate (Howell and Shea 2006; Walter et al. 2011).

Motivation

Of significant importance when developing an understanding of an innovation champion is insights into why they choose to undertake championing behavior.

In the innovation process, champions may compete with, or even threaten, organizational power bases and structures, which potentially creates personal risk and stress (Howell 2005; Howell and Higgins 1990b). Understanding why champions emerge and remain motivated is useful in helping organizations know how to attract, reward, retain and support champions. Despite the potential significance of better understanding what drives champions, much of the discussion in extant studies is non-specific, with the intrinsic nature of champion motivation often expressed without adequate explanation (Howell and Boies 2004; Taylor et al. 2011). To begin to remedy this lack of understanding, self-determination theory (SDT) (Deci and Ryan 1985; Ryan and Deci 2000) is applied in this study, being a relevant lens that aligns with extant research exploring the motivation of nonprofit employees and also innovation champions.

Impact

Champions are acknowledged as heroes performing brave acts in the face of opposition and adversity (Frost and Egri 1991), with numerous authors stressing their positive influence in organizations (e.g., Coakes, Smith and Alwis 2011; Howell and Shea 2006; Schon 1963). Nevertheless, there has been an overreliance on anecdotal evidence and conceptual propositions to support these assertions, with more empirical substantiation of champion impact required (Howell, Shea and Higgins 2005; Markham 1998; Walter et al. 2011). As Walter et al. (2011, p. 587) conclude, there is insufficient evidence still "that champions contribute positively to the success of innovation." Notwithstanding the disagreement in the literature regarding the exact nature of champion impact, there appears to be agreement that champions do have at least some impact. For this reason alone, further research is needed to explore how and when the presence of champions is positive, and, potentially negative.

Context

Linking the study of individual innovative behavior with organizational level variables is important to further our understanding of how context influences innovation (Felin and Foss 2006). Identifying the context within which an innovation champion operates is acknowledged as particularly valuable, but is distinctly lacking in extant research (Anderson and Bateman 2000). The nonprofit context presents a theoretically interesting and practically relevant context to explore championing. There are features of nonprofit organizations that differentiate them from for-profit and public sector organizations (Hull and Lio 2006), and importantly, there are critical shifts occurring in the nonprofit sector which are intensifying the complexity for achieving organizational success (and even survival) in this sector (Goodwin and Phillips 2015).

These sectoral shifts are intensifying the impetus for innovation (McDonald 2007) and, along with the differentiating qualities of nonprofit organizations, suggest that championing may be both different and important for this sector.

Nonprofit organizations are however themselves diverse (Alcock and Kendall 2011; King 2017). As such, the internal contextual component of this study focused on the environment within the organizational boundaries that might influence championing. Culture and leadership were identified as significant in better understanding this relationship. Both are understood to be highly influential over organizational innovation, but the nature of these influences remains unclear (Crossan and Apaydin 2010; Frohman 1998; Khazanchi, Lewis and Boyer 2007).

3. Research design

This research relies upon qualitative data collected through multiple case studies. Case study research is defined by Easton (2010, p. 119) as "a research method that involves investigating one or a small number of social entities or situations about which data are collected using multiple sources with the intention of developing a holistic description through an iterative research process." Put another way, case study research seeks to investigate the situation in its entirety in order to develop a holistic understanding (Dooley 2002). Innovation champions are inextricably linked with their organizational environment and attempting to understand innovation champions without an appreciation of this context may provide narrow insight (Anderson and Bateman 2000). Furthermore, given the multi-layered nature of this investigation, the multiple case approach was expected to be most appropriate in allowing both the influence of nonprofit context to be explored across cases and for the potential variation of organizational context to be elucidated by cross-case comparison.

Selection of cases needed to balance the complexity of identifying the unique and potentially rare presence of an innovation champion (Howell and Higgins 1990b; Shane 1994), with the needs of generating sufficient data to conduct a deep exploration. Qualitative sampling is aimed at selecting cases that will provide an opportunity for learning (Marshall 1996). It is the selection of "information-rich cases" that Patton (2015, p. 53) argues affords qualitative research its "logic and power." In total, the research comprised six cases and included 46 interviewees, with six to nine interviewees sought per case. A range, rather than set number of interviewees, was identified as the number of relevant interviewees would potentially vary across organizational sizes and structures and the number of champions identified within each organization.

In each case, qualitative data was gathered via in-depth interviews. Innovation as a socio-political process is ambiguous and fluid in nature, the intricacies of which Frost and Egri (1991) contend, cannot be fully appreciated using quantitative methods. Qualitative data affords insights into dynamic and "complex social processes" (Eisenhardt and Graebner 2007, p. 26), which was essential for understanding innovation champion behaviors, impact and motivations as they occurred within a particular sector and organizational contexts, which are arguably both complex and dynamic in nature. Qualitative interviews provide the means to gather data on phenomena that are infrequent and difficult to observe (May 2010), which is relevant given the potential difficulty in predicting and observing the depth and breadth of championing behavior (Howell 2005). For the purposes of this study, a semi-structured interview guide was developed which allowed for variation and new questions and topics to emerge throughout the interviews (Merriam and Tisdell 2016). This was important as it allowed respondents scope to steer the discussion, but the discussions were guided by extant champion literature to ensure conversations explored the research questions and key topics.

Data analysis

Since there was existing literature on the major themes which the research addressed, high-level codes were developed based on these pre-existing understandings. Within these broader themes, the data, however, was coded more descriptively according to the perceptions and issues raised by interviewees. This meant that the researcher could observe divergence and convergence with the literature, which was important in identifying new ideas and confirming extant theory (Eisenhardt 1989). Overall, this approach was directed by the thematic analysis approach outlined by Braun and Clarke (2006).

Following the coding process, data was further analyzed through the preparation of detailed workbooks through which cross-case themes began to emerge. Multiple case study research requires both within and cross-case analysis (Merriam and Tisdell 2016). As such, each case was first treated as a stand-alone research investigation and data analyzed according to the contextual elements of that particular case. The researcher's deep immersion in the data through the extensive data analysis process was essential in identifying key themes. These were then explored across the cases to illuminate similarities and patterns as well as particularities that were evident in single or a few of the cases. Cross-case matrices (Miles and Huberman 1994) were developed to illuminate contextual and championing elements, which aided the researcher in 'eye-balling' the differences and similarities.

4. Conclusion

This research offers unique contributions to champion literature and the under-explored nature of innovation in the nonprofit sector, providing theoretical insights into how champions behave, are motivated and impact upon nonprofit organizations. Furthermore, this study importantly sought to understand how context influences championing. To briefly summarise, the findings suggest that the external shifts in the nonprofit sector are a significant driver of both top-down and bottom-up championing activity and were driving an urgency within the sector that champions were responding to. Within this context, the organizational financial positioning, leadership and culture then shaped how championing was undertaken. That is, the types of innovation champions pursued and the manner in which they attempted to push through an idea was significantly influenced by key internal stakeholders, including the board and CEO and also the broader organizational culture. The findings relevant to each of the three key areas, behaviors, motivation and impact, are briefly summarised below.

Behaviors

As identified earlier, champion behavior in this research was explored via four key areas: idea generation, persistence, connectivity and influence. Overall, the study's outcomes demonstrate that champion behaviors in the nonprofit context were highly varied, and, are contextually influenced. The key findings for each of the four behaviors are outlined below (see Molloy 2017 for further detail).

Firstly, for 'idea generation,' champions tapped into the organizational knowledge of others to help them improve and test ideas. More extensively, champions used external sources to identify ideas implemented elsewhere, including in other countries, which was recognized as providing information that was 'best practice' and ahead of the local market. Overall, the process of idea generation was generally unstructured and less systematic than is often defined in the literature (Gottfridsson 2014). Rather, champions articulated a process involving conversations with others, the combination of several ideas, along with the identification of specific knowledge or a specific opportunity, which coalesced to form the idea they championed.

Secondly, for many champions, 'persistence' meant working through challenging government policy, persevering through lack of understanding and awareness within the for-profit community and dealing with nonprofit stakeholders with a mission focus conflicting with their own. This is a noteworthy outcome as such external barriers have not been recognized in extant champion literature. Of note also is that one champion's persistence was described as at times, going too far. This commentary aligns with the findings of Walter et al. (2011), who identified that champion persistence was positive up to a point, but taken too far, negatively impacted on innovation outcomes.

To explore 'connecting,' the concepts of boundary spanning and networking were identified as relevant lenses through which to explore this category. Champions acted as inter-organizational boundary spanners and importantly played the role of 'cultural broker' (Trevillion 1991, p. 50), as they were critical in interpreting the perspectives of other parties effectively and translating this interpretation into an idea that was appropriate in their organizations. The external networking of champions was decisive for many reasons, including building long-term relationships and driving shorter term, transactional and project based outcomes. To do this, champions utilized existing networks, relied upon formal networking groups and leveraged chance encounters. This is an important contribution as extant literature has primarily focused on internal champion connectivity and there has more broadly been little explanation of how social processes in networking contribute to innovation (Pittaway et al. 2004).

Finally, there were few clear patterns regarding champion 'influencing', which is reflective of the lack of clarity within the literature (Ferris et al. 1994; Markham 1998). Some specific insights from the influence behaviors of champions in this study are important. Firstly, the way in which champions of innovation "canvassed" a board member before formally presenting a new concept to the entire board enhanced their capacity to gain formal board approval for ideas. This may be particularly important in better understanding how nonprofit CEO's can influence boards to accept innovative ideas. Relatedly, whereas champion literature primarily focuses on internal and upward influencing activity, champions in this study actively influenced external stakeholders. Finally, although discernible patterns did not emerge regarding the way in which champions attempted to influence, it was found that champions intentionally developed their influence approach in a way that was relevant for their target. The findings support that of Anderson and Bateman (2000), who highlighted the complexity of champion influence and reinforced the need for deep, contextual investigations which could specify the nuances involved.

Motivation

The motivation of champions in this study varied, highlighting the complex nature of motivation for innovative activity and also for the motivation of those working in the nonprofit sector. Regarding their motivation, the champions in this study could be divided into three categories: motivated to champion primarily by the social outcomes of their activity (identified regulation), primarily by the process of championing (intrinsic motivation) and by both social outcomes and intrinsic simultaneously and at different times (identified regulation and intrinsic) (Ryan and Deci 2000). That champions in the non-profit sector were driven not only by social outcomes, but were at times motivated purely by the activity of championing (intrinsic), is an important contributor to the nonprofit motivation literature (Chen 2014) and also provides valuable insight into innovation champion motivation, where a somewhat simplistic explanation assumed intrinsic motivation.

Impact

Three theoretical categories of champion impact were identified, as well as more direct project outcomes that help explain champion impact in the nonprofit sector. Each is discussed briefly below.

In two cases particularly, an important champion impact was to drive 'unlearning' of the 'welfare mentality' of their organizations in order for innovation to be accepted and more readily implemented. It is argued in the literature that for organizations to enact effective responses to significant external dynamism, organizational members must not only learn new knowledge, but must forget previous knowledge and ways of thinking as they become irrelevant (Hedberg 1981). Investigating behaviors driving organizational unlearning offers critical contributions to the nonprofit literature, as previous research has directed little attention toward how organizations enact these 'logic' changes (Maier, Meyer and Steinbereithner 2016).

Bricolage is defined by Baker and Nelson (2005, p. 33) as "making do by applying combinations of resources already at hand to new problems and opportunities." Champions used the physical resources, knowledge and skills of other individuals and organizations to fill their individual or organizational resource gaps. Moreover, they used their networks to aid the identification of potential opportunities and assist in selling ideas. These practices expanded the resources available to a champion, extending their championing impact considerably. That is, champions, in acting as bricoleurs (Levi-Strauss 1966), were exposed, and had access, to a much broader set of opportunities because of their bricolage activity.

Finally, champions in this study created impact through the external focus they stimulated, which occurred in two main ways: through idea generation activities which brought external information into their organizations; and in the direct linkages they created with external stakeholders. The ability of champions to develop more permeable boundaries (Frishammar and Åke Hörte 2005) through the external focus they drove offered positive contributions to their organizations' innovative capacities directly and indirectly. This finding is important for organizations in all sectors, as operating outside of organizational boundaries is widely noted in innovation literature as critical to innovation and even organizational survival (Chesbrough 2003; Holmes and Smart 2009).

Champions were, however, also driving specific projects, that were directly driving social change and positive outcomes within the community. These activities contributed to new methods of delivering social services in their region and new approaches within their specific area of service delivery nationally. Champions were thus important in the sector for driving socially transformative innovation (Netting, O'connor and Fauri 2007). This finding is an important contribution to the broader champion literature, indicating that champions may be influential outside of organizational boundaries in driving changes at an industry level.

5. Implications and future research

Practical implications

The findings of this study suggest that champions are critical actors within nonprofit organizations. The implications of champion impact could be significant for nonprofits for building sustainability and enhancing capacity to contribute positively to the social outcomes of the community. Specifically, champion persistence through conservative board decision-making may be especially valuable in driving innovation as boards are highly influential in shaping how a nonprofit embraces a "social-innovation-oriented" culture (Shier and Handy 2016, p. 123). By forcing boards to respond to their innovative ideas, champions may be influential in driving, at a strategic level, greater openness to innovation with their boards, which could have longer term implications for the innovativeness of their organizations.

There is a predominant expectation that market derived income will be important for the future survival of nonprofits (Hume and Hume 2015; King 2017). Reflecting this expectation, a core driver of championing within the cases was to diversify revenue streams. The emphasis on market derived income as a facilitator of innovation is, however, according to Berzin et al. (2015), unnecessarily narrow. Similarly, the implications of nonprofits embracing business-like practices has received mixed assessments (Hodge and Piccolo 2005), yet the movement appears to be occurring across much of the sector (Lurtz and Kreutzer 2016; Maier, Meyer and Steinbereithner 2016) and was similarly evident within the case organizations. Given the uncertainty regarding the implications for these sectoral changes, championing that is directed towards driving market-derived income and more business-like practices need to be carefully considered alongside an organization's strategic direction and mission orientation. This reinforces previous recommendations for monitoring champion activity given the influence that champions have over resourcing and strategic attention (Howell and Shea 2006; Markham and Aiman-Smith 2001).

Nevertheless, the positive potential of championing was evident and the findings suggest that leadership and organizational cultures that are conducive to championing are important. Leaders are highly influential both directly, and in their impact on culture, over organizational innovation (Boal and Hooijberg 2001; Jaskyte and Dressler 2004; Martin and Simons 2002). The complexity of how leaders facilitate champion activity was notable. One common thread, however, was the importance of providing champions with autonomy so their activity could be responsive to internal and external dynamics. Such autonomy was particularly important in facilitating the unstructured idea generation and external engagement of champions. This outcome supports the earlier findings of Holmes and Smart (2009) who identified that increased inter-organizational collaboration was related to instances where boundary spanning was informal, rather than organizationally directed. In addition, the ability of champions to act as bricoleurs (Levi-Strauss 1966) was related to the autonomy afforded by organizational leaders, both at the board and CEO level. Providing champions with the freedom to openly explore ideas and the means to bring such ideas to fruition may be particularly essential in the resource-constrained contexts of small and medium sized nonprofit organizations (Zappala and Lyons 2008).

This research has also provided important contributions that are useful in understanding how, at an individual level, championing can be facilitated. The analysis sheds new light on champion motivation and our understanding of employee motivation in nonprofits. Findings indicate that prosocial motivation was not always evident, nor even necessary, to drive championing in nonprofits that could bring about positive social outcomes. This potentially broadens the scope for recruitment activity aimed at driving innovation within nonprofits. Providing leaders and boards continue to guide activity towards the organizational mission, individuals who might lack strong social motivation but hold relevant industry or innovation expertise could be influential drivers of innovation in nonprofits. On the other hand, champions who base their motivation on mission-related outcomes may be negatively impacted by the shift towards business-like practices and mission-drift. As a whole, applying SDT (Ryan and Deci 2000) and having a more nuanced understanding of individual motivation, may assist leaders in more effectively identifying and supporting champions.

Limitations and future research

Although this inquiry was an in-depth exploration of championing in the nonprofit sector, the number of cases included may limit generalization to the broader nonprofit population, particularly in different sub-sectors and in larger nonprofit organizations. However, generalisability to theory remains a relevant outcome of such qualitative inquiry and the inclusion of contextual elements may further enable relevant application of the findings to other contexts (Welch et al. 2011). Future research could explore championing in other nonprofit sub-sectors and within larger nonprofits to further understand how these contextual variations might influence championing.

A further limitation is the cross-sectional research design. Championing is best understood as a process and therefore longitudinal research may be more conducive to understanding champion impact and to more fully encapsulate the nuances and impact of context. Since this research captured data at one point in time for each case, there are limitations in the interpretation of the findings to indicate causality of contextual components on championing and of the impact of champions. Future research could explore championing across the lifecycle of an innovation project to better understand how champion behaviors may change throughout the process and to more directly investigate the nature of champion impact.

Relatedly, the assessment of impact is another limitation and highlights the need for further research. Although the investigation of impact was purposefully conducted to capture the broader implications of championing, and did so, this also resulted in limitations in the specificity of findings. One area in which the assessment of champion impact was underdeveloped was the lack of an external perspective incorporated, given the importance of champion external activity. Future research should incorporate the perspectives of both internal and external stakeholders to better understand the role and impact of external champion activity. Despite these limitations, the broad approach employed remains relevant for future research and reinforces the need for reconceptualizing social innovation in a way that encompasses both internal and external organizational activity that directly and indirectly engenders positive social outcomes (Berzin, Pitt-Catsouphes and Gaitan-Rossi 2016).

Finally, findings from this study suggest that external connectivity was an important contributor to organizational innovation. In contrast, Jaskyte and Lee (2006) found that innovativeness of nonprofits was not increased by inter-organizational relationships built upon the sharing of knowledge and resources. Given these conflicting findings and the potentially important role of inter-organizational activity, further research to better understand the processes and impact of external connectivity is needed. Moreover, as the sector becomes increasingly competitive, understanding how "coopetition" can be employed to facilitate open innovation is critical (Wemmer, Emrich and Koenigstorfer 2016, p. 344).

Concluding remarks

Nonprofit organizations play a critical role in the delivery of important social services and are central players in shaping community understanding of social issues. There is a risk, however, that the changes occurring in the non-profit sector will leave little room for innovative behavior and advocacy efforts. Nonprofits must, therefore, remain cognisant of the impact that shifting policy is having on their decision-making. The ability of nonprofits to uphold their mission and address social inequality is made more difficult within an increasingly connected, competitive and resource constrained context. Addressing social issues today requires a fundamental shift not just in operational activity but in the very way these issues are conceived. As Neumeier (2009, p. 27) stated: "The narrow gauge mindset of the past is insufficient for today's wicked problems. We can no longer play the music as written. Instead, we have to invent a whole new scale." It may be that champions, as drivers of innovation, provide the vehicle through which nonprofits construct such a scale, so as to navigate the neo-liberal push for efficiency whilst upholding the values that are fundamental to their very existence.

References

Achilladelis, B, Jervis, P & Robertson, A., (1971*). A study of success and failure in industrial innovation*, University of Sussex Press, Sussex, UK.

Alcock, P & Kendall, J., (2011). 'Constituting the third sector: Processes of decontestation and contention under the UK Labour governments in England', *VOLUNTAS: International Journal of Voluntary and Nonprofit Organizations*, vol. 22, no. 3, pp. 450-69.

Anderson, LM & Bateman, TS., (2000). 'Individual environmental initiative: Championing natural environmental issues in U.S. business organizations', *Academy of Management Journal*, vol. 43, no. 4, pp. 548-70.

Baines, D, Cunningham, I, Campey, J & Shields, J., (2014). 'Not profiting from precarity: The work of nonprofit service delivery and the creation of precasiousness', *Just Labour*, vol. 22.

Baker, T & Nelson, RE., (2005). 'Creating something from nothing: Resource construction through entrepreneurial bricolage', *Administrative Science Quarterly*, vol. 50, no. 3, pp. 329-66.

Bankins, S, Denness, B, Kriz, A & Molloy, C., (2017). 'Innovation Agents in the Public Sector: Applying Champion and Promotor Theory to Explore Innovation in the Australian Public Service', *Australian Journal of Public Administration*, vol. 76, no. 1, pp. 122-37.

Bartlett, D & Dibben, P., (2002). 'Public sector innovation and entrepreneurship: Case studies from local government', *Local Government Studies*, vol. 28, no. 4, pp. 107-21.

Baulderstone, J & Earles, W., (2009). 'Changing relationships: How government funding models impact relationships between organisations', *Third Sector Review*, vol. 15, no. 2, p. 17.

Berzin, S, Pitt-Catsouphes, M & Gaitan-Rossi, P., (2015). 'Defining our own future: Human service leaders on social innovation', *Human Service Organizations: Management, Leadership & Governance*, vol. 39, no. 5, pp. 412-25.

—— (2016). 'Innovation and sustainability: An exploratory study of intrapreneurship among Human Service organizations', *Human Service Organizations: Management, Leadership & Governance*, vol. 40, no. 5, pp. 540-52.

Boal, KB & Hooijberg, R., (2001). 'Strategic leadership research: Moving on', *The leadership quarterly*, vol. 11, no. 4, pp. 515-49.

Braun, V & Clarke, V., (2006). 'Using thematic analysis in psychology', *Qualitative research in psychology*, vol. 3, no. 2, pp. 77-101.

Butcher, J & Freyens, BP., (2011). 'Competition and collaboration in the contracting of family relationship centres', *Australian Journal of Public Administration*, vol. 70, no. 1, pp. 15-33.

Chakrabarti, AK., (1974). 'The role of champion in product innovation', *California Management Review*, vol. 17, no. 2, pp. 58-62.

Chen, CA., (2014). 'Nonprofit managers' motivational styles: A view beyond the intrinsic-extrinsic dichotomy', *Nonprofit and Voluntary Sector Quarterly*, vol. 43, no. 4, pp. 737-58.

Chesbrough, H., (2003). 'The logic of open innovation: managing intellectual property', *California Management Review*, vol. 45, no. 3, pp. 33-58.

Coakes, EW, Smith, PAC & Alwis, D., (2011). 'Sustainable innovation and right to market', *Information Systems Management*, vol. 28, no. 1, pp. 30-42.

Crossan, MM & Apaydin, M., (2010). 'A multi-dimensional framework of organizational innovation: A systematic review of the literature', *Journal of Management Studies*, vol. 47, no. 6, pp. 1154-91.

Dalton, BM & Butcher, J., (2014). 'The rise of big charity in Australia', paper presented to Association for Research on Nonprofit Organizations and Voluntary Action, Denver, CO, 19-22 Nov.

Dart, R., (2004). 'Being "business-like" in a nonprofit organization: A grounded and inductive typology', *Nonprofit and Voluntary Sector Quarterly*, vol. 33, no. 2, pp. 290-310.

Deci, EL & Ryan, RM., (1985). 'The general causality orientations scale: Self-determination in personality', *Journal of research in personality*, vol. 19, no. 2, pp. 109-34.

Dooley, LM., (2002). 'Case study research and theory building', *Advances in Developing Human Resources*, vol. 4, no. 3, pp. 335-54.

Easton, G., (2010). 'Critical realism in case study research', *Industrial marketing management*, vol. 39, no. 1, pp. 118-28.

Ebrahim, A & Rangan, VK., (2014). 'What impact?', *California Management Review*, vol. 56, no. 3, pp. 118-41.

Eisenhardt, KM., (1989). 'Building theories from case study research', *Academy of Management Review*, vol. 14, no. 4, pp. 532-50.

Eisenhardt, KM & Graebner, ME., (2007). 'Theory building from cases: Opportunities and challenges', *Academy of Management Journal*, vol. 50, no. 1, pp. 25-32.

Evans, B, Richmond, T & Shields, J., (2005). 'Structuring neoliberal governance: The nonprofit sector, emerging new modes of control and the marketisation of service delivery', *Policy and Society*, vol. 24, no. 1, pp. 73-97.

Felin, T & Foss, N., (2006). 'Individuals and organizations: Thoughts on a micro-foundations project', *Research Methodology in Strategy and Management*, vol. 3, pp. 253-88.

Ferris, GR, Judge, TA, Rowland, KM & Fitzgibbons, DE., (1994). 'Subordinate influence and the performance evaluation process: Test of a model', *Organizational behavior and human decision processes*, vol. 58, no. 1, pp. 101-35.

Frishammar, J & Åke Hörte, S., (2005). 'Managing external information in manufacturing firms: The impact on innovation performance', *Journal of Product Innovation Management*, vol. 22, no. 3, pp. 251-66.

Frohman, AL., (1998). 'Managers at work: Building a culture for innovation', *Research-Technology Management*, vol. 41, no. 2, pp. 9-12.

Frost, PJ & Egri, CP., (1991). 'The political process of innovation', *Research in organizational behavior*, vol. 13, pp. 229-95.

Goodwin, S & Phillips, R., (2015). 'The marketisation of human services and the expansion of the not-for-profit sector', in G Meagher & S Goodwin (eds), *Markets, rights and power in Australian social policy*, Sydney University Press, Sydney, NSW.

Gottfridsson, P., (2014). 'Different actors' roles in small companies service innovation', *Journal of Services Marketing*, vol. 28, no. 7, pp. 547-57.

Hedberg, B., (1981). 'How organizations learn and unlearn', in PC Nystrom & WH Starbuck (eds), *Handbook of organizational design*, Oxford University Press, Oxford, vol. 1, pp. 3–27.

Hodge, MM & Piccolo, RF., (2005). 'Funding source, board involvement techniques, and financial vulnerability in nonprofit organizations: A test of resource dependence', *Nonprofit Management and Leadership*, vol. 16, no. 2, pp. 171-90.

Holmes, S & Smart, P., (2009). 'Exploring open innovation practice in firm-nonprofit engagements: a corporate social responsibility perspective', *R&D Management*, vol. 39, no. 4, pp. 394-409.

Howell, JM., (2005). 'The right stuff: Identifying and developing effective champions of innovation', *Academy of Management Executive*, vol. 19, no. 2, pp. 108-19.

Howell, JM & Boies, K., (2004). 'Champions of technological innovation: The influence of contextual knowledge, role orientation, idea generation, and idea promotion on champion emergence', *Leadership Quarterly*, vol. 15, no. 1, pp. 123-43.

Howell, JM & Higgins, CA., (1990a). 'Champions of change: Identifying, understanding, and supporting champions of technological innovations', *Organizational Dynamics*, vol. 19, no. 1, pp. 40-55.

—— (1990b). 'Champions of technological innovation', *Administrative Science Quarterly*, vol. 35, no. 2, p. 317.

Howell, JM & Shea, CM., (2006). 'Effects of champion behavior, team potency, and external communication activities on predicting team performance', *Group and Organization Management*, vol. 31, no. 2, pp. 180-211.

Howell, JM, Shea, CM & Higgins, CA., (2005). 'Champions of product innovations: Defining, developing, and validating a measure of champion behavior', *Journal of Business Venturing*, vol. 20, no. 5, pp. 641-61.

Hull, CE & Lio, BH., (2006). 'Innovation in non-profit and for-profit organizations: Visionary, strategic, and financial considerations', *Journal of Change Management*, vol. 6, no. 1, pp. 53-65.

Hume, C & Hume, M., (2015). 'The critical role of internal marketing in knowledge management in not-for-profit organizations', *Journal of Nonprofit & Public Sector Marketing*, vol. 27, no. 1, pp. 23-47.

Hwang, H & Powell, WW., (2009). 'The rationalization of charity: The influences of professionalism in the nonprofit sector', *Administrative Science Quarterly*, vol. 54, no. 2, pp. 268-98.

Jaskyte, K & Dressler, WW., (2004). 'Studying culture as an integral aggregate variable: Organizational culture and innovation in a group of nonprofit organizations', *Field methods*, vol. 16, no. 3, pp. 265-84.

Jaskyte, K & Lee, M., (2006). 'Interorganizational relationships', *Administration in Social Work*, vol. 30, no. 3, pp. 43-54.

Jones, MB., (2007). 'The multiple sources of mission drift', *Nonprofit and Voluntary Sector Quarterly*, vol. 36, no. 2, pp. 299-307.

Khazanchi, S, Lewis, MW & Boyer, KK., (2007). 'Innovation-supportive culture: The impact of organizational values on process innovation', *Journal of Operations Management*, vol. 25, no. 4, pp. 871-84.

King, D., (2017). 'Becoming business-like: Governing the nonprofit professional', *Nonprofit and Voluntary Sector Quarterly*, vol. 46, no. 2, pp. 241-60

Levi-Strauss, C., (1966). *The savage mind*, University of Chicago Press, Chicago, IL.

Lurtz, K & Kreutzer, K., (2016). 'Entrepreneurial orientation and social venture creation in nonprofit organizations: The pivotal role of social risk taking and collaboration', *Nonprofit and Voluntary Sector Quarterly*, vol. 46, no. 1, pp. 92-115.

Maier, F, Meyer, M & Steinbereithner, M., (2016). 'Nonprofit organizations becoming business-like: A systematic review', *Nonprofit and Voluntary Sector Quarterly*, vol. 45, no. 1, pp. 64-86.

Markham, SK., (1998). 'A longitudinal examination of how champions influence others to support their projects', *Journal of Product Innovation Management*, vol. 15, no. 6, pp. 490-504.

Markham, SK & Aiman-Smith, L., (2001). 'Product champions: Truths, myths and management', *Research Technology Management*, vol. 44, no. 3, pp. 44-50.

Markham, SK, Green, SG & Basu, R., (1991). 'Champions and antagonists: Relationships with r&d project characteristics and management', *Journal of Engineering and Technology Management*, vol. 8, no. 3-4, pp. 217-42.

Markham, SK & Griffin, A., (1998). 'The breakfast of champions: Associations between champions and product development environments, practices and performance', *Journal of Product Innovation Management*, vol. 15, no. 5, pp. 436-54.

Marshall, MN., (1996). 'Sampling for qualitative research', *Family Practice*, vol. 13, no. 6, pp. 522-6.

Martin, J & Simons, R., (2002). 'Managing competing values: Leadership styles of mayors and CEOs', *Australian Journal of Public Administration*, vol. 61, no. 3, pp. 65-75.

May, T., (2010). *Social Research*, 4th edn, McGraw-Hill International, Maidenhead, UK.

McDonald, RE., (2007). 'An investigation of innovation in nonprofit organizations: The role of organizational mission', *Nonprofit and Voluntary Sector Quarterly*, vol. 36, no. 2, pp. 256–28.

Merriam, SB & Tisdell, EJ., (2016). *Qualitative research: A guide to design and implementation*, Jossey-Bass, San Francisco, CA.

Miles, MB & Huberman, AM., (1994). *Qualitative data analysis: A sourcebook*, Beverly Hills: Sage Publications.

Molloy, C., (2017). 'Investigating innovation champions in the nonprofit sector', Doctor of Philosophy thesis, University of Newcastle, <https://ogma.newcastle.edu.au/vital/access/manager/Repository/uon:31085>.

Netting, FE, O'connor, MK & Fauri, DP., (2007). 'Planning transformative programs: Challenges for advocates in translating change processes into effectiveness measures', *Administration in Social Work*, vol. 31, no. 4, pp. 59-81.

Neumeier, M., (2009). *The designful company: How to build a culture of nonstop innovation*, New Riders, Berkeley, CA.

Passey, A & Lyons, M., (2006). 'Nonprofits and social capital: Measurement through organizational surveys', *Nonprofit Management and Leadership*, vol. 16, no. 4, pp. 481-95.

Patton, MQ., (2015). *Qualitative research and evaluation methods: Integrating theory and practice*, 4th edn, Sage, Thousand Oaks, CA.

Pittaway, L, Robertson, M, Munir, K, Denyer, D & Neely, A., (2004). 'Networking and innovation: a systematic review of the evidence', *International Journal of Management Reviews*, vol. 5, no. 3-4, pp. 137-68.

Productivity Commission., (2010). Contribution of the not-for-profit sector, Canberra.

Ryan, RM & Deci, EL., (2000). 'Intrinsic and extrinsic motivations: Classic definitions and new directions', *Contemporary Educational Psychology*, vol. 25, pp. 54–67.

Schon, DA., (1963). 'Champions for Radical New Inventions', *Harvard Business Review*, vol. 41, no. 2, pp. 77-86.

Shane, SA., (1994). 'Are champions different from non-champions?', *Journal of Business Venturing*, vol. 9, no. 5, pp. 397-421.

Shea, J & Wang, JQ., (2016). 'Revenue Diversification in Housing Nonprofits:Impact of State Funding Environments', *Nonprofit and Voluntary Sector Quarterly*, vol. 45, no. 3, pp. 548-67.

Shier, ML & Handy, F., (2016). 'Cross-sector partnerships: Factors supporting social innovation by nonprofits', *Human Service Organizations: Management, Leadership & Governance*, vol. 40, no. 3, pp. 253-66.

Smith, SR., (2008). 'The challenge of strengthening nonprofits and civil society', *Public Administration Review*, vol. 68, no. s1, pp. 132-45.

Taylor, A, Cocklin, C, Brown, R & Wilson-Evered, E., (2011). 'An investigation of champion-driven leadership processes', *The leadership quarterly*, vol. 22, no. 2, pp. 412-33.

Trevillion, S., (1991). *Caring in the community*, Longman, London, UK.

Walter, A, Parboteeah, KP, Riesenhuber, F & Hoegl, M., (2011). 'Championship behaviors and innovations success: An empirical investigation of university spin-offs', *Journal of Product Innovation* Management, vol. 28, no. 4, pp. 586-98.

Welch, C, Piekkari, R, Plakoyiannaki, E & Paavilainen-Mantymaki, E., (2011). 'Theorising from case studies: Towards a pluralist future for international business research', *Journal of International Business Studies*, vol. 42, no. 5, pp. 740-62.

Wemmer, F, Emrich, E & Koenigstorfer, J., (2016). 'The impact of coopetition-based open innovation on performance in nonprofit sports clubs', *European Sport Management Quarterly*, vol. 16, no. 3, pp. 341-63.

Wollebaek, D & Selle, P., (2002). 'Does participation in voluntary associations contribute to social capital? The impact of intensity, scope, and type', *Nonprofit and Voluntary Sector Quarterly*, vol. 31, no. 1, pp. 32-61.

Zappala, G & Lyons, M., (2008). 'Not-for-profit organisations and business: Mapping the extent and scope of community-business partnerships in Australia', in J Barraket (ed.), *Strategic issues for the not-for-profit sector*, UNSW Press, Sydney, NSW, p. 16.

Chapter 9

Design and Evaluation of a Process Model for the Early Stages of Product Innovation

Patrick Brandtner*

E-mail: patrick.brandtner@fh-steyr.at

Abstract: Today's business world is highly dynamic, competitive and hardly predictable, leading to shorter product lifecycles, higher degrees of uncertainty and ultimately to high failure rates in New Product Development. Most often, this is due to deficiencies in managing the Front End of Innovation (FEI). As substantial work has been done in relation to the later stages of the FEI, the stages of opportunity identification and analysis have been neglected, especially in terms of identifying and depicting process-related factors and activities in practitioner relevant, formal process models. This research identifies and analyzes FEI principles, differentiates between process and non-process principles and combines process-related ones in a comprehensive, theoretically grounded and practically applicable process model. The pivotal contribution of the research is identification and structuring of process related strategic FEI key activities. Ex-post evaluation results confirm the practical relevance of the developed process model and its syntactic, semantic and pragmatic quality.

Keywords: Front End of Innovation, Process Model Development, Design Science Research, Innovation Management, Corporate Foresight, Strategic Issue Management, Corporate Foresight, Innovation Process Model, Strategic Innovation Management.

1. Introduction

A global and volatile environment accompanied by constantly changing customer requirements and fierce competition poses major challenges to organizations. Increased costs of raw materials, the recent economic crisis, high failure rates in New Product Development (NPD) processes and shorter innovation cycles further increase the difficulties and burdens organizations have to face. It is becoming increasingly difficult for companies to succeed at such a high velocity, uncertain and often highly unpredictable environment without being able to quickly and flexibly react to potential or impending changes. These developments and the resulting consequences clearly stress the necessity for strategically oriented and efficiently conducted innovation management (Filieri 2013).

High failure rates in New Product Development (NPD) are most often due to deficiencies in effectively and efficiently managing the early stages of the innovation process. To systematically improve the effectiveness and efficiency of an organization's innovation activities, these early stages of the innovation process – which are known as the "Front End of Innovation" (referred to as FEI) or "Fuzzy Front End of Innovation" - offer the greatest potential (Stevens 2014; Aagaard, Gertsen 2011). The FEI is the initial stage of the innovation process, takes place before the actual NPD process and usually ends when a go or no-go decision regarding the launch of a new product (pre-) development process is taken (Stevens 2014, p. 431). Existing findings indicate that improving the FEI process offers the largest potential for improving an organization's innovation capability as a whole with the least effort (Aagaard, Gertsen 2011). Several authors refer to the FEI as "the root of success" for organizations involved with discontinuous product innovation (Reid, Brentani 2004) and clearly state that high failure rates in the NPD process are often related to too little effort put in the FEI activities (Cooper 2011; Verworn 2009; Khurana, Rosenthal 1998). This indicates that the FEI is critical for innovatory success and long-term competitiveness (Oliveira, Rozenfeld 2010).

In the course of the current thesis, the FEI is defined based on the definitions proposed by Koen et al. (Koen et al. 2014a; Koen et al. 2001;) and Poskela (Poskela 2007) as follows: The FEI includes the activities that come before the formal and well-structured NPD process and consists of strategically oriented activities (opportunity identification, opportunity analysis) and the more operative ideation and concept development process (idea genesis, idea selection and concept and technology development).

The problem addressed in this thesis is how to systematically structure the strategic parts of the FEI in the form of a process model, coupled with the motivation to evaluate research results in practice and to validate their applicability in an organizational environment. The underlying design hypothesis is that structuring the early, strategically oriented parts of the FEI by focusing on process key activities increases FEI performance from an expert's point of view. The current thesis postulates a positive impact of formalization at the FEI. Nevertheless, the need for both integrating process but also addressing non-process factors is recognized and addressed. Hence, the thesis focusses on deriving and defining exactly such key activities that can be structured and formalised (process factors) but also identifies the non-process factors relevant at the FEI.

Considering the above, it becomes clear that the FEI is, on the one hand, an important research area that already received quite some attention. On the other hand, there is no clear consensus on how exactly the FEI and its boundaries can be defined. Discrepancies concerning an advisable approach to the Front End can be found in literature. Existing literature mainly focussed on the idea generation stage, other stages at the Front End have received little attention (Wowak et al. 2016; Košmrlj et al. 2015a; Riel et al. 2013). The amount of holistic and practical approaches on how to manage the FEI is low (Markham 2013) and there are still few empirical studies clarifying Front End practices (Gregor, Hevner 2015; Aagaard, Gertsen 2011). According to Koen et al. there have only been eight empirical studies so far that specifically focussed on the FEI and even these are limited to a certain degree. Most focussed on one specific FEI project or were conducted in relatively small organizations (Koen et al. 2014a). In conclusion, there is a need for further research on the FEI and the significance of developing new theories and proposals that support effective implementation of the FEI is immense - from a scientific perspective as well as from a practical one. In this context, structuring the FEI by specifically addressing key tasks and activities at this early stage is emphasized as an approach offering high potential (Markham, 2013).

2. Background

Most authors describe the process at the FEI as a sequential process that consists of single sub-phases including iterations among and within them (e.g., Griffiths-Hemans 2006; Khurana, Rosenthal 1998). Other scholars do not particularly focus on the sequential order of the different activities and phases at the FEI, but rather concentrate on recurring key activities (Koen et al. 2001). Within the conducted literature review, several process models describing the phases and activities at the FEI were collected. Various models started with an idea generation phase (e.g., Cooper 2008; Griffiths-Hemans 2006), but most began with an initial more or less strategically oriented scanning process respectively with opportunity identification and analysis (Riel et al. 2013; Oliveira, Rozenfeld 2010; Khurana, Rosenthal 1998).

Most of the FEI process models provided in literature are activity based and sequential in nature. They divide the FEI process into separate stages with defined starting and ending points (Vahs, Brem 2015). Such models follow a linear course, suggest conducting task by task, allow for easy access of recommended activities and seem to provide transparency and predictability (Sandmeier et al. 2004; Khurana, Rosenthal 1998). Nevertheless, they run the risk of not corresponding to reality, of not considering creative exchange, of not allowing for or of not fostering feedback loops and of lacking flexibility (Gaubinger et al. 2015). Such models do not distinguish between project related and process oriented tasks and activities and the according framework creating tasks and activities. In this thesis, sequential, activity based FEI process models are considered useful for describing the FEI process and its single activities and tasks. However, they do not allow for distinguishing between project specific and cross project activities and are not capable of deriving appropriate and concrete organizational measurements (cf. Koen et al. 2001; Khurana, Rosenthal 1998). Strictly sequential FEI process models are not suited in the context of the current thesis. The shortcomings of such models have also been emphasized by various other authors, who propose iterative and integrative process approaches to the FEI (Sandmeier et al. 2004; Koen et al. 2001; Khurana, Rosenthal 1998).

"Integrative" FEI process models seek to allow for clearly distinguishing between supporting, continuous and cross-project activities (so-called "foundational elements", "framework conditions" or non-process factors) and project-specific activities (process factors) (Khurana, Rosenthal 1998). Such models strongly emphasize an iterative approach to the FEI and explicitly allow feedback loops between the stages. In line with the research objective of the current thesis integrative approaches to the FEI are more suitable than merely activity-based ones.

In conclusion, substantial work has been done in relation to the later stages of the FEI (from idea generation onwards), while the preceding stages of opportunity identification and analysis have been neglected (Wowak et al. 2016). Especially in terms of identifying and depicting process-related factors and activities in practitioner relevant, formal process models, little to no research has been done so far. The amount of holistic and practical approaches on how to manage the FEI is low (Markham, 2013) and there are still few empirical studies clarifying FEI practices (Gregor, Hevner 2015). The few existing process models covering the stages preceding idea generation fail to deliver practicable and concrete sets of guidelines and measures for practitioners (Gaubinger, Rabl 2014). The following table 9.1 summarizes the research gaps identified in the course of the literature review and contrasts these with the thesis' goals:

Table 9.1 Summary of identified literature gaps and goals of the thesis

Literature aps	Goals of the thesis
The significance of developing new theories supporting effective implementation of the FEI is immense (Wowak et al. 2016; Brandtner et al. 2015b; Koen et al. 2014a; Riel et al. 2013). There are still few empirical studies clarifying FEI practices and even those are often limited (Gregor, Hevner 2015; Brandtner et al. 2014; Koen et al. 2014a; Markham 2013; Aagaard, Gertsen 2011).	This research thesis contributes to the FEI within the field of Innovation Management by developing a theoretically grounded and practically oriented process model. This model is based on scientific literature, on the results of an exhaustive focus group study and on continuous practitioner involvement. Process model evaluation is done from an ex-ante as wells as from an ex-post perspective.
Previous work on the FEI mainly focussed on idea generation only and neglected the preceding phases of opportunity identification and analysis (Košmrlj et al. 2015a; Wowak et al. 2016; Brandtner et al. 2015a).	The current thesis specifically focusses on the stages of opportunity identification and analysis. Idea generation, evaluation and concept development have already received quite some attention in scientific literature.

The few existing FEI process models which cover the stages preceding idea generation fail to deliver practicable and concrete sets of guidelines and measures for practitioners (Gaubinger, Rabl 2014; Košmrlj et al. 2015b).	This research aims at developing a practicable process model for the strategically oriented parts of the FEI by providing a structured approach to process FEI factors and by identifying non-process factors. Practicability and value for practitioners is analyzed in the course of ex-post evaluation.

3. Research design

The highly unstructured and often ill-defined FEI is characterized by unstable requirements, complex relationships and interactions among subcomponents of the problem (Stevens 2014). This is a good example for what is called a wicked application domain. Such domains are characterized by the existence of vicious circles, risks that new solutions may introduce new problems or by a lack of self-evident solution options (Goldkuhl, Röstlinger 2009). This is typically addressed by design science research (Hevner et al. 2004). In line with the discussion presented above, with the identified problem statement, the defined research objective and the developed research questions, design science research (DSR) can be considered as an appropriate and applicable research methodology in this specific research setting. Several DSR process and procedures can be found in literature. In the course of the current thesis, the six-step design science research methodology (DSRM) by Peffers et al. (Peffers et al. 2007) is taken as a reference framework. The components of the DSRM were synthesized by Peffers et al. based on seven research papers and provide a set of phases for implementing design science research methodology following a sequential process. The six steps of the DSRM include (1) problem identification and motivation, (2) definition of the objectives for a solution, (3) design and development, (4) demonstration, (5) evaluation and (6) communication. A particularity of the DSRM method is that both the starting and the end point of the research can be modified and adapted to the type of problem and the respective research objectives (Peffers et al. 2007). Figure 9.1 provides an overview of the DSRM applied to the current research, demonstrates the outputs of each research question along the design science research process and includes the research techniques used to address the research questions:

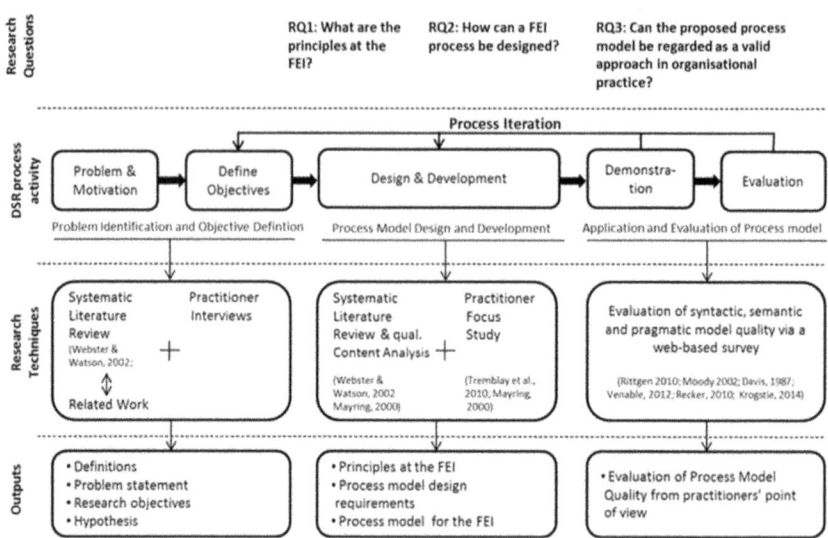

Figure 9.1 Summary of the research approach

Based on the identified problem statement, the main objectives of the current research are to (1) identify principles at the FEI, to (2) derive process model design requirements based on these and to (3) develop and (4) evaluate a formal process model specifically supporting process FEI key activities. Regarding the methodological approach, the thesis follows an adoption of the six-step design science research methodology (DSRM) by Peffers et al. (2007). First, the research problem is identified and the importance and motivation of the research is justified. Based on this, expected outcomes and research objectives are defined. Second, the design requirements related to process model activities and structure are derived based on theoretical and practical FEI principles and the process model is developed. Third, the process model is evaluated ex-ante (design inherent) and ex-post (quality of final artefact, i.e. the process model). Throughout the research process, research validity and reliability are ensured by applying appropriate, scientifically grounded methods and approaches. To this end, the knowledge has to be documented in a way that allows for making inferences on the artefact's suitability and its correctness of design. In the present case, this is achieved in two ways: firstly, it is assured that the research problem is both rigorous and relevant. Secondly, FEI principles derived from literature are aligned with principles derived from practice. Thus, the evaluation approach is capable of validating incremental design decisions right from the beginning of the research process. Reliability of the research is ensured by following structured, acknowledged, repeatable and transparent approaches: The collection of theoretical FEI principles followed the systematic literature review (SLR) process by Webster and Watson (2002). Practical FEI principles were collected applying the focus group procedure by Tremblay et al. (2010). The aggregation and alignment of principles was done based on the qualitative content analysis (QCA) approach proposed by Mayring (2000) and the ex-post evaluation built on an adoption of the TAM (Venkatesh and Davis, 2000).

4. Conclusion

The main result of the thesis is the develop process model for the strategic Front End of Innovation. Besides that, a main finding is that the design hypothesis (i.e. that the strategic FEI can be structured by the provision of a comprehensive process model) could not only be confirmed by literature but also by the survey results. The process model is developed based on the results of focus group study, building on existing FEI processes in organizational practice and following the structural requirements of Corporate Foresight and Strategic Issue Management. More precisely, the basic structure of the process model derives from the FEI processes existing in organizational practice and the ideal typical process structure in practice, the six-process model design requirement blocks ("key activities") and the general structure of CF frameworks (Input-Analysis-Output-Strategy. The combination of the results of these building block leads to a four-step structure: inputs have to be collected, information gathered has to be analyzed and findings or output has to be forwarded to the subsequent stages at the FEI respectively to innovation strategy definition. The structure of the process model also addresses the general innovation process and the FEI specific process requirements elaborated in the thesis. These requirements, which call for e.g. parallel tasks, interconnections, loops and iterative rather than strictly sequential activity chains, influence process model structure at sub-activity level. The following figure 9.2 provides the structural overview of the six key activity groups (represented by the EPC symbol for process-paths), their interconnections and the linkage to the subsequent processes of corporate strategy planning, idea generation and the operative NPD process:

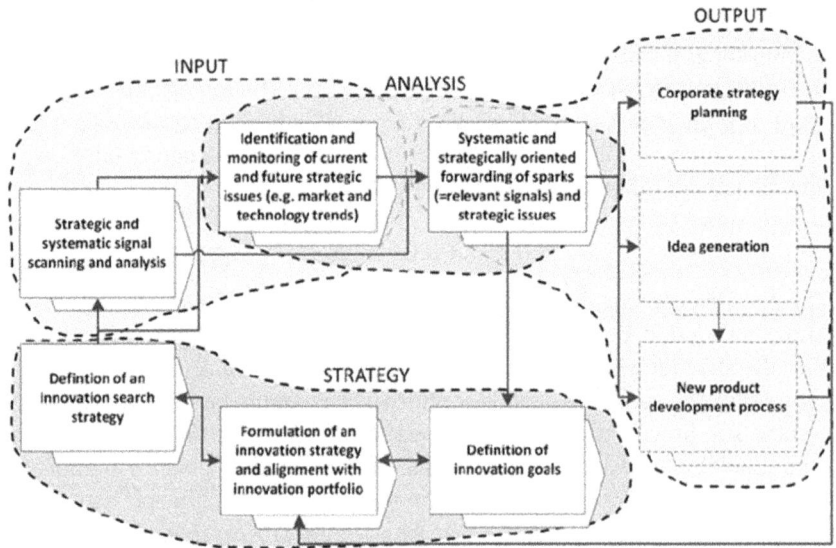

Figure 9.2 Structural overview of the develop process model

The full process model consists of six key activity groups and 19 sub-activities. For each key activity group, an overview of sub-activities is depicted in the form of the respective EPC-based process model part. Each sub-activity is then described in detail in table-form. Due to the page limitation of this paper, the detailed description of sub-activities and the full EPC-based process model is not presented here, but can be found in the full thesis. Regarding process model quality, the ex-post evaluation provides us with valuable insight. Practitioners participating in the survey state that the process model provides 1) a clear structure for projects and decisions at the FEI, 2) has high potential for organizational practice, 3) can establish not yet existing interfaces between innovation management and corporate strategy planning and 4) would definitely be applied and implemented in practice, provided the required resources are available. However, it is also stated in textual comments that the process model may be difficult to communicate to non-domain experts. Several comments indicate that it may be challenging to justify the amount of resources necessary to implement the process model.

5. Implications and future research

In terms of impact on theory and the provision of new or improved evidence, the thesis contributes in several ways. As discussed, the amount of empirical studies clarifying Front End practices and specifically dealing with the strategic FEI is low. To identify principles at the strategic FEI and to gain an understanding of FEI processes and activities in practice, a comprehensive focus group study was conducted. The results of this study are summarised in the thesis and deliver new insights on empirically constructed knowledge about the FEI. The results of artefact evaluation constitute new empirical knowledge about the strategic FEI and provide additional contributions to knowledge base in the form of new evidence regarding FEI process model quality. The conducted survey is the first to provide detailed and scientifically collected quality results for a strategic FEI process model. The textual comments collected during the web-based survey allow for deriving specific practitioner and expert feedback regarding selected items of process model quality. This allows, for example, identifying potential future research starting points.

New or improved concepts or theories are provided in the form of (1) principles at the strategic FEI derived from theory and practice, (2) design requirements for process and non-process based support of the strategic FEI, (3) process key activities at the strategic FEI and (4) the process model specifically addressing these key activities by applying the concept of Corporate Foresight (CF) and Strategic Issue Management (SIM). The research thesis contributes to the domain of Innovation Management by identifying FEI principles based on scientific literature, on the results of an extensive focus group study and on continuous practitioner involvement. By identifying both process and non-process principles for the strategic FEI, future research on this issue is provided with extensive information and knowledge about this early stage of the innovation process. Furthermore, the division of FEI principles into process and non-process principle groups provides potential starting points for future research on, e.g., the non-process design requirements and FEI principles at the FEI. The process model provides researchers and practitioners with insights into the formally depictable activities at the strategic FEI. The research contributes to the IS domain in the form of describing and depicting the area respectively the specific process in which potential future information systems for the strategic FEI will operate. In this context, the developed process model is a prerequisite for planning and designing complex systems of this sort.

In terms of employing a new or improved methodology to do analysis or interpretation, the thesis contributes in several ways. Firstly, the research methodology of the thesis is adapted based on the acknowledged DSR framework by Peffers (2007). It proves to be suitable for the research and enables a transparent, comprehensible and replicable way of developing a process model for the strategic FEI. The transparent research methodology provides insights on artefact construction and contributes, e.g., to the DSR domain. This and the research framework applied support other researchers concerned with similar research problems in conceptual modeling in developing and applying appropriate research approaches and methodologies. Secondly, the combination of findings from theory and practice in the form of the derived FEI principles, of process model design requirements and of process model structure and elements represents a transparent, coherent and applicable methodology to do analysis, interpretation and collation of theoretical and empirical knowledge.

Practical Implications

Ex-post evaluation results confirm the practical relevance of the developed process model and its syntactic, semantic and pragmatic quality. At the operational level of organizational innovation management practice, the ultimate result of the thesis, i.e., the process model, guides organizations in structuring and specifically addressing the key activities at the strategic FEI. Existing FEI process models either do not cover the stages preceding idea generation or fail to deliver practicable and concrete sets of guidelines and measures for practitioners. The process model provides in-depth details, formally described activities and a clear structured process for the strategic parts of the FEI. Each of the process related challenges and the critical success factors observable in current practice is incorporated in process model design. The results of ex-post evaluation confirm the correctness, completeness and usefulness of the process model. Practitioners state that they would apply and implement it in practice, provided the required resources are available. The actual implementation of the process model would enable organizations to 1) add structure and continuity to the complex strategic FEI, to 2) establish strategically oriented and on-going scanning and monitoring functions, 3) to clearly allocate responsibilities and define communication and decision making paths, to 4) link strategic and operative level FEI activities and ultimately to 5) establish a formal connection between innovation management and corporate strategy planning.

Summary and Future Work

Examining the results, contributions and limitations of the thesis, several future research opportunities and the need for further empirical studies arise. As the thesis is focussed on product innovation, such research could for example focus on the elaboration of process-based support for public and service sector. The need for investigating the strategic FEI in other sectors is still high and findings could contribute to the knowledge base. Furthermore, future research projects could extend or alter the scope of the process model, by for example extending it to include or cover corporate strategy planning or the actual NPD process as well. Future work could also lay a specific focus on evaluating the process model with experts from medium and small sized enterprises. This would not only be interesting but would also contribute to the understanding of differences and similarities between large sized and small respectively medium sized enterprises.

The strategically oriented parts of the FEI are highly complex and dynamic; process models for this part of the innovation process should rather visualise and address specific key activities than just provide an all-inclusive and only-true formal process for all aspects of the FEI. The author does not want to postulate such an only true solution for this part of the innovation process. Further research could focus on evaluating the actual performance and quality of the process model after its implementation in organizational practice. In addition to the ex-post evaluation results gained in the thesis, this could provide valuable contributions to continually develop and adapt the process model.

Future work could also support strengthening understanding of FEI principles by conducting a quantitative study specifically focussing on this subject. Depending on the respective subject of the study and depending on its sample size, several contributions to knowledge base could be gained. For example, it would be interesting to analyze the level of coherence of FEI principles in organizations of different sizes, of different industries, from different countries and of different stages of the organizational lifecycle. Against the background of the thesis' focus on process FEI factors, the need for in-depth analysis and empirically grounded studies regarding principles of and approaches to the non-process FEI factors is high. Considering the nature of the non-process FEI factors identified in the thesis, several research domains could contribute to this issue. For example, research in the organizational culture domain could investigate exactly which attributes and patterns of organizational culture are required at the strategic FEI. Likewise, research in the organizational learning domain or in the area of knowledge management could also contribute significantly to the body of knowledge on the strategic FEI. By for example focussing on intra and interpersonal, on intra and intergroup or on intra and inter-organizational aspects at the strategic FEI, valuable insights could be gained. Based on the results and findings of this thesis, other areas (like for example research on entrepreneurship, human behavior, network management or corporate development and corporate venturing) could produce relevant knowledge too.

Additional future research challenges at the strategic FEI could also be found at a more micro level: future studies could analyze the influence of factors like project size, technology type and degree of innovation, level of uncertainty or interrelations between different projects on strategic level FEI activities. Other efforts could be made to develop and implement ICT based support for the activities of the process model. In this context, the process model developed in the thesis can serve as theoretical and conceptual background. Furthermore, it represents the framework for integrating and combining single tools into one coherent software platform covering the key process activities at the strategic FEI.

The findings gained in this thesis address an interesting domain and focus on a still under-researched part of the innovation process. The design hypotheses defined at the beginning of the thesis could be confirmed: Key activities and tasks at the strategic FEI can be structured and systematically addressed and supported by a formal process model. The findings of ex-post evaluation confirm the semantic and pragmatic quality of the developed artefact and practitioners deem the process model to be useful and relevant in organizational practice.

References

Aagaard, A. and Gertsen, F. (2011). 'Supporting Radical Front End Innovation: Perceived Key Factors of Pharmaceutical Innovation'. *Creativity and Innovation Management* 20 (4), pp. 330-346.

Brandtner, P., Gaubinger, K., Auinger, A., Helfert, M. and Rabl, M. (2014). *Dealing with Uncertainty in Innovation Management - An empirical analysis of activities and method use in innovative organizations.* Proceedings of ISPIM 2014, Dublin, Ireland, p. 13.

Brandtner, P., Helfert, M., Auinger, A. and Gaubinger, K. (2015a). '*Conducting focus group research in a design science project: Application in developing a process model for the front end of innovation.* In Systems, Signs & Actions 9 (1), pp. 26-55.

Brandtner, P., Helfert, M., Auinger, A. and Gaubinger, K. (2015b*). Multi-criteria Selection in Design Science Projects - A Procedure for Selecting Foresight Methods at the Front End of Innovation,* Proceedings of DESRIST 2015, Dublin, Ireland, pp. 295-310.

Cooper, R. G. (2008). 'Perspective: The Stage-Gate® Idea-to-Launch Process - Update, What's New, and NexGen Systems*'. *Journal of Product Innovation Management,* 25 (3), pp. 213-232.

Cooper, R. G. (2011). *Winning at new products. Creating value through innovation.* 4th ed. New York: Basic Books.

Filieri, R. (2013). 'Consumer co-creation and new product development: a case study in the food industry'. *Marketing Intelligence & Planning,* 31 (1), pp. 40–53.

Gaubinger, K. and Rabl, M. (2014). 'Structuring the Front End of Innovation'. In Oliver Gassmann, Fiona Schweitzer (Eds.), *Management of the Fuzzy Front End of Innovation.* Cham: Springer, pp. 15-30.

Gaubinger, K., Rabl, M., Swan, S. and Werani, T. (2015). *Innovation and product management. A holistic and practical approach to uncertainty reduction.* Cham: Springer Texts in Business and Economics

Goldkuhl, G. and Röstlinger, A. (2009). *Argumentative Design - towards further grounding in Design Rationale.* VITS working paper, IEI, Linköping University.

Gregor, S. and Hevner, A. R. (2015). 'The Front End of Innovation: Perspectives on Creativity, Knowledge and Design'. In Proceedings of DESRIST 2015, Dublin, Ireland, May 20-22, 2015, vol. 9073. pp. 249-263.

Griffiths-Hemans, J. (2006). 'Setting the Stage for Creative New Products: Investigating the Idea Fruition Process'. *Journal of the Academy of Marketing Science*, 34 (1), pp. 27-39.

Hevner, A. R., March, S. T., Park, J. and Ram, S. (2004). 'Design Science in Information Systems Research'. *MIS Quarterly* 28 (1), pp. 75-106.

Khurana, A. and Rosenthal, R. (1998). 'Towards holistic "front ends" in new product development'. *Journal of Product Innovation Management*, 15 (1), pp. 57.74.

Koen, P. A., Ajamian, G.; Burkart, R., Clamen, A., Davidson, J. and D'Amore, R. et al. (2001). 'Providing Clarity and a Common Language to the "Fuzzy Front End"'. *Research technology management*. 44 (2), pp. 46-55.

Koen, P. A., Bertels, H. M. J. and Kleinschmidt, E. J. (2014), 'Managing the Front End of Innovation - Part I'. *Research Technology Management*, 57 (2), pp. 34-43.

Košmrlj, K., Širok, K. and Likar, B. (2015a). 'Addressing the Fuzzy Front End of Innovation in an Innovative Manner'. Proceedings of Management International Conference. Portoroz ̌, Slovenia, pp. 175-176.

Košmrlj, K., Širok, K. and Likar, B. (2015b). *The art of managing innovation problems and opportunities*, Koper: Faculty of Management.

Markham, S. K. (2013). 'The Impact of Front-End Innovation Activities on Product Performance'. *Journal of Product Innovation Management*, 30 (S1), pp. 77-92.

Mayring, P. (2000). 'Qualitative Content Analysis'. *Qualitative Social Research*, 1 (2), p. 10.

Oliveira, M. G. and Rozenfeld, H. (2010).' Integrating technology roadmapping and portfolio management at the front-end of new product development'. *Technological Forecasting and Social Change*, 77 (8), pp. 1339-1354.

Peffers, K., Tuunanen, T., Rothenberger, M. and Chatterjee, S. (2007). 'A Design Science Research Methodology for Information Systems Research'. *Journal of Management Information Systems*, 24 (3), pp. 45-77.

Poskela, J. (2007), 'Strategic and Operative Level Front-End Innovation Activities - Integration Perspective'. *International Journal of Innovation & Technology Management*, 4 (4), pp. 433-456.

Reid, S. E., Brentani, U. (2004). 'The Fuzzy Front End of New Product Development for Discontinuous Innovations: A Theoretical Model'. *Journal of Product Innovation Management*, 21 (3), pp. 170-184.

Riel, A., Neumann, M., and Tichkiewitch, S. (2013). 'Structuring the early fuzzy front-end to manage ideation for new product development'. *CIRP Annals - Manufacturing Technology*, 62 (1), pp. 107-110.

Sandmeier, P.; Jamali, N.; Kobe, C.; Enkel, E.; Gassmann, O.; Meier, M. (2004). *Towards a structured and integrative front-end of product innovation*. Zürich: ETH-Zürich.

Stevens, E. (2014). 'Fuzzy front-end learning strategies: Exploration of a high-tech company'. *Technovation* 34 (8), pp. 431-440.

Tremblay, M. C., Hevner, A. R. and Berndt, D. J. (2010). 'Focus Groups for Artifact Refinement and Evaluation in Design Research'. Communications of the Association for Information Systems 26, pp. 599-618.

Vahs, D. and Brem, A. (2015). *Innovationsmanagement*. 5th ed. Stuttgart: Schäffer-Poeschel.

Venkatesh, V. and Davis, F. D. (2000). 'A Theoretical Extension of the Technology Acceptance Model: Four Longitudinal Field Studies'. Management Science (46), pp. 186-204.

Verworn, B. (2009). 'A structural equation model of the impact of the "fuzzy front end" on the success of new product development'. *Research Policy* 38 (10), pp. 1571-1581.

Webster, J. and Watson, R. T. (2002). 'Analyzing the past to prepare for the future: writing a literature review'. *MIS Quarterly* 26 (2), pp. xiii-xxiii.

Wowak, K. D., Craighead, C. W., Ketchen, D. J., Hult, G. and Tomas M. (2016). 'Toward a "Theoretical Toolbox" for the Supplier-Enabled Fuzzy Front End of the New Product Development Process'. *Journal of Supply Chain Management*, 52 (1), pp. 66-81.

Chapter 10

Firm Responses to Disruptive Innovations

Amber Geurts*

E-mail: amber.geurts@aalto.fi

Abstract: In a time of fast technological change, firms are increasingly confronted with (digital) innovations that challenge and disrupt their business as usual. Rather than assuming incumbents to be displaced by start-ups that introduce such disruptive innovations, it is important to understand how firms can address the challenges of such disruptions. The different theoretical and empirical explorations of this dissertation provide new insights into firms and their responses to disruptions. The findings of this dissertation emphasize that even though disruptive innovation has far-reaching consequences for firms and industries, firms are able to purposefully pursue a certain, recognized opportunity by taking up agency in how they manage the challenges created by the disruption. This explains how and why similar firms develop different organizational responses to the same disruptive innovation, while different firms develop similar responses to such disruptions. The results of this dissertation offer interesting avenues for future research into the dynamics of firms' responses to disruptive innovations.

Keywords: awareness-motivation-capability framework; coopetition; disruptive innovation; digital innovation; mixed method; music industry; opportunity recognition; organizational identity; organizational responses; technology & innovation management.

1. Introduction

For music publishers, the rise of digital downloading, piracy and the falling of CD sales resulted in a crisis in the music industry, wherein firms had to deviate from their historical legacy in physical music recording and publishing (Moreau, 2013). For EMI Music the digitization of music meant a dramatic reversal of fortune; despite attempts to restructure, almost a century's experience in music recording and publishing turned out to inhibit a shift to new technologies resulting in the bankruptcy of EMI Music in 2012 (Business Week, 2008; 2012). Universal Music, on the other hand, set forward a clear focus on digital, enabling the firm to even increase its market share during the disruption (Billboard, 2015; Music & Copyright, 2014). Even though both firms faced the *same* situation of a rapidly changing business environment created by the introduction of digital disruptive innovations (Christensen, 1997; Tushman and Anderson, 1986; 1990), their responses are *different*.

In a time of fast-technological change, firms are increasingly confronted with technological developments that have disruptive effects on firms' business models and performance. As a result, the strategic positions of incumbents are disturbed while windows of opportunities are simultaneously opened for newcomers that aim to exploit the disruptive technologies (i.e., *disruptive innovations*, Christensen, 1997; Christensen and Roosenbloom, 1995). By now, more industries – i.e., the music, newspaper, book, retail, travel and financial industry (Grossman, 2016)- face the challenge to respond to such technological disruptions to ensure their long-term viability (i.e., *firm responses*, Charitou and Markides, 2003).

While the challenges of coping with disruptive innovations have inspired researchers to examine entrant-incumbent dynamics during disruption (i.e., Christensen, 1997; King and Baartagtokh, 2015; Markides, 2006; Nagy, Schuessler and Dubinsky, 2016), numerous exemptions in research and in managerial practice prevail (i.e. Bergek et al., 2013; Golder and Tellis, 1993; Hill and Rothaermel, 2003; King and Tucci, 2002; Rothaermel, 2001; Tripsas, 1997). If responding to disruptive innovations is so important, how and why do firms (come to) respond so differently, even when confronted with the same disruption? This gap in extant research indicates the need to explore firms' responses to disruptive innovations in greater depth and breadth.

In my dissertation, I, therefore, focus on what firms actually do when it recognizes or is confronted with, the inimical consequences of (the same) disruption, assuming that even when firms face the *same* situation of a rapidly changing business environment created by the introduction of a disruptive innovation, their responses widely *differ*. To address the question how and why firms (come to) respond differently to the same disruptive innovations, I therefore open up the "black box" of firms' responses to disruptive innovations using a mixed method approach of both qualitative and quantitative research methods (Eisenhardt, 1989; Fowler, 2013; Miles and Huberman, 1994). The digital disruption of the music industry (Moreau, 2013) provides a particularly useful and timely research setting for investigating firm responses to the same disruption(s), which eliminates potential contingencies based on industry or disruptive innovation characteristics at the same time (Charitou and Markides, 2003). By doing so, my dissertation provides an in-depth exploration of the different contingencies that stand at the origin and the evolution of these different responses that help firms to cope with disruptive innovations.

2. Background

The purpose of my dissertation is to address the overarching research question to obtain new insights and managerial implications with regard to firms and their responses to disruptions. At its core, it draws upon the work on *Disruptive*

Innovations as developed by Christensen (1997; 2003). The central argument of his work is that disruptive technologies enable the introduction of *disruptive innovations* that are able to destroy a firm's existing (technical) competences, skills and knowledge base (Tushman and Anderson, 1986, 1990) and to disrupt its value network and business models (Christensen, 1997; Christensen and Raynor, 2003). Disruptive innovations fundamentally challenge, and even render obsolete, the required skills, capabilities and knowledge applied by firms in the "old" technological paradigm (Christensen et al., 2015). Disruptive innovations are thus not only different but also in conflict with existing ways of doing business (Charitou and Markides, 2003; Kamien and Schwartz, 1982) and require the development and establishment of very different and new capabilities, competences, knowledge and value networks (Christensen, 1997).

We, therefore, took stock of the extant literature on entrant-incumbent dynamics in both radical technological change (i.e., Ansari and Krop, 2012; Eggers and Kaul, 2018) and disruptive innovation research (i.e., Assink, 2006; Christensen et al., 2015). In this literature, inertial (cognitive) constraints and the liabilities of devalued and obsolete competences often handicap established firms in their adaptability to disruption (Christensen and Roosenbloom, 1995; Leonard-Barton, 1992). Main predictions, therefore, find that incumbents' market leadership will be replaced by new entrants that introduce disruptive innovations based on new technologies (Christensen, 2006; Christensen et al., 2015; Markides, 2006; Schumpeter, 1994).

Nevertheless, within organizational practice and the extant literature on disruptive innovation numerous anomalies to this "standard model" of entrant-incumbent dynamics during disruption prevail. They indicate that *some* incumbents are able to survive (i.e., Bergek et al., 2013; Hill and Rothaermel, 2003; King and Tucci, 2002; Rothaermel, 2001; Roy and Sarkar, 2016; Tripsas, 1997), and that *some* new entrants struggle to rise to market dominance (i.e., Golder and Tellis, 1993; Ozcan and Eisenhardt, 2009; Suarez and Lanzolla, 2005). As a result, discussions regarding the relevance, applicability and generalizability of disruptive innovation theory continue, leaving firms bewildered with regard to the firm responses that enable them to respond to the challenges of disruptiveness (Christensen et al., 2015; Danneels, 2004; King and Baartagtokh, 2015; Nagy et al., 2016).

In the three empirical studies that make up my dissertation, I contribute to the ongoing discussions within disruptive innovation research by asking: how and why do firms (come to) response so *differently*, even when confronted with the *same* disruption? In my dissertation design I therefore purposefully choose to explore multiple firms' responses to the same disruptive innovation: the digital disruption of the music industry. Using a mixed method approach of both qualitative and quantitative research methods (Eisenhardt,

1989; Fowler, 2013; Miles and Huberman, 1994), this dissertation design enables me to open up the "black box" of firms' responses to the same disruptive innovation and explore the contingencies that stand at the origin and evolution of their different responses in more depth and breadth.

In the first empirical study of this dissertation I, therefore, explore the origin of different organizational responses to disruptive innovations by addressing how the type of response to disruptive innovations (Charitou and Markides, 2003) might be contingent upon organizational drivers as specified in the extant literature (see e.g. Ansari and Krop, 2012; Assink, 2006; Christensen et al., 2015; Eggers and Kaul, 2018). Drawing upon the *awareness-capabilities-motivations* framework, we explore the unique, different and interactive effects of these drivers (Chen, 1996; Chen, Su and Tsai, 2007) using a survey study among independent record companies in the Netherlands (N=118).

In the second empirical study of this dissertation, which consists of various in-depth case studies, I add to the extant disruptive innovation literature theorizing about the role of organizational identity when firms are faced with identity-challenging disruptions (Albert and Whetten, 1985; Ashforth and Mael, 1989; Tripsas, 2009). Furthermore, the multiple case study design enables me to provide one of the first comparative views on the role of organizational identity when responding to identity-challenging disruptions. Drawing upon organizational identity theory (Albert and Whetten, 1985; Ashforth and Mael, 1989), I explore the concept of "organizational identity shift," or the extent to which a firm adapts its enduring, central and distinctive aspects of its organizational identity after an identity-challenging shock like a disruption.

Finally, in the third empirical study of this dissertation, I go beyond addressing individual firm responses and organizational transformation processes by showing how firm responses are situated within a larger ecology of interdependent firms. I draw upon the coopetition literature, which explores the simultaneous engagement in both cooperation and competition among firms (Bengtsson and Kock, 2014; Brandenburger and Nalebuff, 1996; Gnyawali and Park, 2009), to focus on how firms can develop their own disruptive capacity, despite their status as incumbent or new entrant rather than disruptor (Ansari, Garud and Kumaraswamy, 2015). Using an in-depth case study of coopetition in the Dutch music market, I provide one of the first accounts of how coopetitive forces (Bengtsson and Kock, 2014; Gnyawali et al., 2016) play a role in firms' responses to disruptive innovations.

3. Research design

The empirical setting of this dissertation is one specific disruptive research context: the digital disruption of the (Dutch) music industry. The music industry provides an excellent opportunity to investigate firm responses to the same disruption(s) in a recent time frame (Alexander, 2002; Mol, Wijnberg and Carroll, 2005). After all, the rise of disruptive new technologies in sound compression and file sharing at the end of the 1990s enabled the introduction of innovative new platforms such as Napster, KaZaA and Limewire in the music industry. The virtually free music offered on many of these initial services mainly attracted young, online consumers. The introduction of new technological developments around 2006, such as mobile phones, portable MP3 devices and the rise of social networks, enhanced the new performance metrics of digitized music especially its portability and share-ability. These technological developments, alongside the increasing quantity and quality of music being offered online, accelerated the development of legal downloading music services such as iTunes (US launch in 2003, NL launch in 2006), and streaming platforms such as Spotify (Swedish launch in 2008, NL launch in 2010) or Deezer (French launch in 2007, NL launch in 2012) that resonated among increasingly more mainstream consumers (Aguiar and Waldfogel, 2015; Moreau, 2013). For firms operating in the music industry, the digitization of music resulted in a dramatic reversal of fortune (Leyshon et al., 2005; Moreau, 2013): established competitiveness patterns and traditional competences like the production of physical albums or access to important traditional retailers and intermediaries were challenged, and world-wide revenues were cut in half (NVPI, 2000-2015; IFPI 2016).

The Dutch music industry is particularly suitable as a research setting as the structure of this industry and the effects of digitization largely resembles patterns found in larger, foreign music industries (Mol, Chiu and Wijnberg, 2012). At the same time, the Netherlands is one of the front runners when it comes to digital music exploitation, especially in comparison to current market leaders such as the UK, France, Germany and Italy (IFPI, 2016), see Table 10.1. Studying firm responses in the Dutch music industry, therefore, presents a unique and timely research setting, which eliminates potential contingencies based on industry, country or disruptive innovation characteristics at the same time (Charitou and Markides, 2003; Govindarajan and Kopalle, 2006).

The three empirical studies of this dissertation use three vastly different empirical approaches: a quantitative survey study, qualitative comparative case studies and finally a qualitative, in-depth (group) case study ((Eisenhardt, 1989; Fowler, 2013; Miles and Huberman, 1994). Each study uses primary and secondary data from a variety of sources including those that have been collected in close collaboration with businesses in the Dutch music industry. Together, the collected data enables an unprecedented opportunity to address the overarching research questions of this dissertation to obtain new insights and managerial implications with regard to firms and their responses to disruptions.

Table 10.1 Market size and the market share (turnover) of digital music

	Global Market share (turnover)	% Market share digital
1	United States	United States
2	Japan	Canada
3	Germany	Australia
4	United Kingdom	South Korea
5	France	*Netherlands*
6	Australia	UK
7	Canada	Brazil
8	South Korea	France
9	Brazil	Italy
10	Italy	Germany
11	Netherlands	Japan

Source: IFPI 2014 & 2015

4. Conclusion

Coping with the challenges of disruptive innovations is essential to ensure the viability of firms in the long-term. To open up the "black box" of firm responses to disruptive innovations, I addressed the questions how and why firms (come to) respond differently to the same disruptive innovations by conducting three empirical studies within the same disruptive research context: the digital disruption of the Dutch music industry. The results of each of the empirical studies of my dissertation provide their own, unique findings that advance our understanding of firms' responses to disruptive innovations.

Together, the main finding from the three empirical studies of my dissertation is: prior research has largely neglected how disruption generates distributed opportunities, and these opportunities are not limited to disruptors (Ansari, Garud and Kumuraswamy, 2015) or new entrants (Hang, Garnsey and Ruan, 2015) alone. Ironically, when firms are confronted with disruptive innovation even the firms most affected by disruption are able to respond to the challenges of disruption: *opportunity recognition* (Shepherd, McMullen and Ocasio, 2016) during disruptive innovation plays a decisive factor in firms' adaptability during disruption, that is separate from factors discussed in extant disruption literature such as prior knowledge and routines, information access, cognition and abilities (Ansari and Krop, 2012; Assink, 2006; Bergek et al., 2013; Eggers and Kaul, 2018).

For example, the first empirical study of my dissertation, a quantitative survey study (N=118), indicated that defensive and offensive responses to disruptive innovations are driven by completely different drivers. These drivers therefore largely influence the identification and pursuit of 'new' business opportunities, which are created by the disruptive innovation. The second empirical study of this dissertation, which builds on comparative case studies, further highlighted that firms only perceive as an opportunity those opportunities that are consistent with their shifted self-identity as firms strive for identity-relevant action in response to the identity-challenging disruptive innovation. Finally, the third empirical study of my dissertation, the in-depth case study, indicated that as a disruption shakes up existing markets and affects established competitive dynamics (i.e., "old" industry players are challenged by disruptors and by new businesses with growth aspirations), firms might look to one another, including (former) competitors, to pursue opportunities that lie beyond the possibilities of the firm before the disruption.

Taken together, the studies of this dissertation thus indicate that prior research has largely neglected how disruption generates distributed opportunities, which are not limited to disruptors (i.e., Ansari et al., 2015) or new entrants (i.e., Hang, Garnsey and Ruan, 2015) alone. Recognizing this key role of opportunity recognition during disruption foregrounds that there is not a single "best" response to disruption. Rather, opportunities can be identified and pursued when firms, be it incumbent, new entrant or disruptor, see (disruptive) advantages. This active search for, and selection of, opportunities by all explains why some firms, but not others, identify and act upon specific opportunities. As a result, the various different firm responses to disruptive innovations should not be treated as "anomalous cases." Instead, such exemptions indicate that firms act upon the different opportunities presented when disrupted. These findings, therefore, show that even though disruption has far-reaching consequences for firms and industries, firms are able to purposefully pursue a certain, recognized opportunity by taking up agency in how they manage the challenges, conflicts *and* opportunities created by disruption.

5. Implications and future research

In a time of fast technological change, firms across industries are increasingly confronted with (digital) disruptions that challenge and disrupt their business as usual. Choosing and implementing meaningful responses to such (digital) disruptions has, therefore, become an increasingly important task for managers. The application of different theoretical approaches to disruption innovation theory within the same empirical context provides the opportunity to obtain new insights and managerial implications regarding firms and their responses to disruptive innovations. The results of this dissertation yield several practical implications and avenues for future research into the dynamics of firms' responses to disruptive innovations.

Practical implications

For managers choosing and implementing meaningful responses to disruptive innovations that disturb the traditional ways of doing business, my results indicate that firms, including incumbents, are not passive agents overthrown by disruption. Rather, firms are active agents that purposefully pursue distributed opportunities created by the disruptive innovation. As a result, opportunity recognition during disruptive innovation plays a key role in managerial decision making. This finding also foregrounds that there is not a single "best" response to disruption for either incumbent, new entrant or disruptor. Rather, opportunities can be identified and pursued when firms and their managers, be it incumbent, new entrant or disruptor, see (disruptive) advantages. These opportunities that can be actively searched for, selected and seized can lie within the vast opportunity space that includes both the disruptive and the traditional business model. By taking up agency in how a firm manages the challenges or conflicts of disruption, a firm can purposefully act upon the different opportunities presented when disrupted. These results specifically apply to firms in the music industry that are confronted with digital, disruptive innovations, and for other industries confronted with digital, disruptive innovations.

Future research

My dissertation has used different empirical methods to address firm responses to disruptive innovations. Although my findings clearly have important theoretical and practical implications for firms dealing with disruptive innovations, I hope that the insights yielded by this work will inspire additional research into the relationship between disruption and firm responses. We identify three future research areas.

First, empirical findings are drawn from firms in one industry and country, which were confronted with the same disruptions in a relatively recent time frame. Although the industry (music industry) and the disruption (digitization of music) are considered exemplary in a number of different ways and the setting was used to address industry, country and disruption contingencies that could influence my results (cf. Danneels, 2004; Charitou and Markides, 2003), future research should explore whether the findings of the studies can be more broadly generalized across countries, industries and (type of) disruptions in order to account for differences that are unique to the situation, industry or disruption faced. By including a closer investigation of the mid to long-term financial performance of different types of responses, one could also address whether, when and under what circumstances certain types of responses are better than others. The collection of longitudinal data can also guide future research into exploring if, when and how firms' responses may evolve over time, perhaps as a result of disruption or industry changes or because the chosen response does not pay off in the long run. Such an approach could enable a closer investigation of firm differences in organizational learning under disruption and identify the signals firms use to change their strategy (Argote and Spektor, 2011).

Second, our investigation of firm responses to disruptive innovations should be considered within the limitations of a cross-sectional, exploratory research design (Lindell and Whitney, 2001; Miles and Huberman, 1994). It is important to acknowledge that firm responses to disruptiveness are a longitudinal process, influenced by social contexts and events that existed and/or happened before and/or during the confrontation with a disruption. In support of this notion, the data collected for this dissertation are limited in acknowledging preferences for certain types of responses that emerged earlier, or that emerged from the social network of the firm. Longitudinal research projects in real time would be useful in clarifying causal relationships and feedback loops. Social network analysis could determine the influence of the social network.

Third, our investigation of firm responses to disruptive innovations indicated that 'becoming or being a disruptor' is not limited to disruptors alone. Future research could, therefore, address the role of established incumbents as a source of disruptive technological change (Eggers and Kaul, 2017) and provide a closer examination of how incumbents can develop their disruptive capacity. In addition, the failure of early disruptors like Napster and KaZaA indicate that the road to becoming a full-fledged disruptor has not been explored extensively yet. Future research could address the disruptors path (Ansari et al., 2015), by studying the transitions of "simple" innovators to full-fledged business disruptors over time.

References

Aguiar, L. and Waldfogel, J. (2015). *Streaming reaches flood stage: does Spotify stimulate or depress music sales?* Working paper 21653, National Bureau of Economic Research.

Albert, S. and Whetten, D. A. (1985). Organizational identity. In: Cummings, L. L. & Staw, B.M.(eds.), *Research in organizational behavior*, 7, pp. 263-295. Greenwich, CT: JAI Press.

Alexander, P. J. (2002). 'Peer-to-Peer File Sharing: The Case of the Music Recording Industry'. *Review of Industrial Organization*, 20(2), pp. 151-161.

Anderson, P. and Tushman, M. L. (1990). 'Technological Discontinuities and Dominant Designs: A Cyclical Model of Technological Change'. *Administrative Science Quarterly*, 35(1), pp. 604-633.

Ansari, S. Garud, R. and Kumaraswamy, A. (2015).' The disruptor's dilemma: TiVo and the U.S. television ecosystem'. *Strategic Management Journal*, 37(9), pp. 1829-1853.

Ansari, S. and Krop, P. (2012). 'Incumbent Performance in the Face of a Radical Innovation: Towards a Framework for Incumbent Challenger Dynamics'. *Research Policy*, 41(8), pp. 1357-1374.

Argote, L. and Spektor, E. M. (2011). 'Organizational Learning: From Experience to Knowledge'. *Organization Science*, 22(5), pp. 1123-1137.

Ashforth, B. E. and Mael, F. (1989). 'Social identity theory and the organization'. *Academy of Management Review*, 14(1), pp. 20-39.

Assink, M. (2006). 'Inhibitors of disruptive innovationcapability: a conceptual mode'l. *European Journal of Innovation Management*, 9(2), pp. 215-233.

Bengtsson, M. and Kock, S. (2014). 'Coopetition — Quo vadis? Past accomplishments and future Challenges'. *Industrial Marketing Management*, 43(2), pp. 180–188.

Bergek, A., Berggren, C., Magnusson, T. and Hobday, M. (2013). 'Technological discontinuities and the challenge for incumbent firms: destruction, disruption or creative accumulation?'. *Research Policy*, 42(6), pp. 1210-1224.

Brandenburger, A. and Nalebuff, B. (1996). *Co-opetition*. New York: Doubleday.

Business Week (2008). *EMI to cut one third of staff*. Available at: http://www.businessweek.com/stories/2008-01-15/emi-to-cut-one-third-of-staffbusinessweek-business-news-stock-market-and-financial-advice (accessed 1 September 2014).

Business Week (2012). *Key developments in proposed sale of EMI-group*. Available at: http://www.businessweek.com/ap/2012-04-17/key-developments-in-proposed-sale-of-emi-group (accessed 1 September 2014).

Charitou, C. D. and Markides, C. C. (2003). 'Responses to Disruptive Strategic Innovation'. *MIT Sloan Management Review*, 44, pp. 55-63.

Chen. M-J. (1996). 'Competitor Analysis and Interfirm Rivalry: Toward a Theoretical Integration'. *Academy of Management Review*, 21(1), pp. 100-134.

Chen, M-J., Su, K-H. and Tsai, W. (2007).' Competitive Tension: The Awareness Motivation-Capability Perspective'. *Academy of Management Journal*, 50(1), pp. 101-118.

Christensen, C. M. (1997). *The Innovator's Dilemma: When New Technologies Cause Great Firms to Fail*. Boston, MA: Harvard Business School Press.

Christensen, C. M. (2006). 'The ongoing process of building a theory of disruption'. *Journal of Product Innovation Management*, 23(1), pp. 39-55.

Christensen, C. M., Raynor, M. E. and McDonald, R. (2015). 'What is Disruptive Innovation?'. *Harvard Business Review*, 93, pp. 44-54.

Christensen, C. M. and Rosenbloom, R. (1995). 'Explaining the attacker's advantage: technological paradigms, organizational dynamics and the value network'. *Research Policy*, 24(2), pp. 233-257.

Danneels, E. (2004). 'Disruptive Technology Reconsidered': A Critique and Research Agenda. *Journal of Product Innovation Management*, 21(4), pp. 246-258.

Eggers, J.P. and Kaplan, S. (2009). 'Cognition and renewal: Comparing CEO and organizational effects on incumbent adaptation to technical change'. *Organization Science*, 20(2), pp. 461-477.

Eggers, J.P. and Kaul, A. (2017, forthcoming). 'Motivation and Ability? A behavioral perspective on the pursuit of radical invention in multi-technology incumbents'. *Academy of Management Journal*, forthcoming.

Eisenhardt, K. M. (1989). 'Building theories from case study research'. *Academy of Management Review*, 14(4), pp. 532-550.

Fowler, F. J. (2013). *Survey Research Methods*. Fifth Edition, Sage Publications.

Gnyawali, D. R., Madhavan, R., He, J., and Bengtsson, M. (2016). 'The competition-cooperation paradox in inter-firm relationships: A conceptual framework'. *Industrial Marketing Management*, 53, pp. 7-18.

Gnyawali, D. R. and Park, B. R. (2009). 'Co-opetition and Technological Innovation in Small And Medium-Sized Enterprises: A Multilevel Conceptual Model'. *Journal of Small Business Management*, 47(3), pp. 308-330.

Golder, P. N. and Tellis, G. J. (1993). 'Pioneer advantage: Marketing logic or marketing legends?'. *Journal of Marketing Research*, 30(2), pp. 158-170

Govindarajan, V. and Kopalle, P. K. (2006). 'Disruptiveness of innovations: measurement and an assessment of reliability and validity'. *Strategic Management Journal*, 27(2), pp. 189-199.

Grossman, R. (2016). 'The Industries That Are Being Disrupted the Most by Digital'. *Harvard Business Review*, March 21. Available at: https://hbr.org/2016/03/the-industries-that-are-being-disrupted-the-most-by-digital# (accessed 1 September 2016).

Hang, C. C., Garnsey, E and Ruan, Y. (2015). 'Opportunities for disruption'. *Technovation*, 29, pp. 83-93.

Hill, C. W. L. and Rothaermel, F. T. (2003). 'The Performance of Incumbent Firms in the Face of Radical Technological Innovation'. *Academy of Management Review*, 28(2), pp. 257-274.

IFPI (2014). Digital Music Report 2014. Available at: http://www.ifpi.org/downloads/Digital Music-Report-2014.pdf (accessed 1 May 2016).

IFPI (2015). *Digital Music Report 2015*. Available at: http://www.ifpi.org/downloads/Digital-Music-Report-2015.pdf (accessed 1 May 2016). IFPI (2016). Digital Music Report 2016. Available at: http://www.ifpi.org/downloads/GMR2016.pdf (accessed 1 May 2016).

King, A. A. and Baatartogtokh, B. (2015). How Useful Is The Theory of Disruptive Innovation?. *MITSloan Management Review*, 57, pp. 77-90.

King, A. A. and Tucci, C. L. (2002). 'Incumbent Entry into New Market Niches: The Role of Experience and Managerial Choice in the Creation of Dynamic Capabilities'. *Management Science*, 48(2), pp. 171-186.

Leyshon, A., Webb, P., French, S., Thrift, N. and Crewe, L. (2005). 'On the reproduction of the music economy after the interne. *Media, Culture & Society*, 27(2), pp. 177-209.

Markides, C. (2006). 'Disruptive Innovation: In Need of Better Theory'. *Journal of Product Innovation Management*, 23(1), pp. 19-25.

Miles M. B. and Huberman A. M. (1994). *Qualitative Data Analysis: An Expanded Sourcebook*. 2nd edn. Thousand Oaks, CA: Sage.

Mol, J., Chiu, M. M. and Wijnberg, N. (2012). 'Love Me Tender: new entry in poplar music'. *Journal of Organizational Change Management*, 25(1), pp. 88-120.

Mol, J., Wijnberg, N. M. and Carroll, C. (2005). 'Value Chain Envy: Explaining New Entry and Vertical Integration in Popular Music'. *Journal of Management Studies*, 42(2), pp. 251-276.

Nagy, D., Schuessler, J. and Dubinsky, A. (2016). 'Defining and identifying disruptive innovations'. *Industrial Marketing Management*, 57, pp. 119-126.

NVPI (2000-2016). *NVPI audiomarkt algemeen*. Available at: http://www.nvpi.nl/sites/default/files/ (accessed 25 April 2014).

Rothaermel, F. T. (2001). 'Incumbent's advantage through exploiting complementary assets via interfirm cooperation'. *Strategic Management Journal*, 22(6-7), pp. 687-699.

Shepherd, D. A., McMullen, J. S. and Ocasio, W. (2016). 'Is that an opportunity? An attention model of top managers' opportunity beliefs for strategic action'. *Strategic Management Journal*, 38(3), pp.626-644.

Tripsas, M. (1997). 'Unraveling the process of creative destruction: Complementary assets and incumbent survival in the typesetter industry'. *Strategic Management Journal*, 18(1), pp. 119-142.

Tripsas, M. (2009).' Technology, Identity and Inertia through the Lens of the "Digital Photography Company"'. *Organization Science*, 20(2), pp. 441-460.

Tushman, M. L. and Anderson, P. (1986). 'Technological Discontinuities and Organizational Environments'. *Administrative Science Quarterly*, 31(3), pp. 439-465.

Notes

We follow previous work to broadly define disruptive innovations as new products, processes or business models that utilize (disruptive) new technologies (Christensen, 1997; 2006). Such innovations are initially inferior to existing mainstream technologies on dominant product attributes that mainstream customers value and are therefore considered financially unattractive to incumbents (Ansari and Krop, 2012; Christensen, 2006; Markides, 2006). As they also introduce novel features, initially liked by a niche segment, mainstream customers are ultimately attracted after considerable (technological) advancements and improvements of the disruptive innovation over time (Christensen, Raynor and McDonald, 2015; Govindarajan and Kopalle, 2006).

Chapter 11

A Framework for Accelerated Product Innovation in a Big Data Environment

Yuanzhu Zhan*

E-mail: Yuanzhu@liverpool.ac.uk

Abstract: Today, the case for accelerated innovation has become increasingly compelling at both theoretical and practical level. Among the enabling factors behind this acceleration are the proliferation of information and communication technologies, the increasing amounts of data available to businesses that can now be brought to bear on innovation-related activities, and the new business models that have emerged in response to these technological changes. Accordingly, this research aims to extend the literature by developing a conceptual framework about how, specifically, big data initiatives can contribute to accelerated innovation in high-technology industries. Then it will offer evidence from different case companies and explain how innovation can most appropriately be accelerated in different kinds of big data environments. Particularly, the proposed study will focus on the leading high-tech Chinese companies as these companies have been observed to be aggressively experimenting with data-intensive, novel innovation models in their product innovation activities.

Keywords: Accelerated Product Innovation; Big Data; New Product Development; Data Analytics; Framework Development; Innovation Phases; Case Study; Chinese Companies.

1. Introduction

According to Cooper (1986) product innovation - the development of new and improved products - is crucial to the survival and prosperity of the modern business. A new product is usually defined as one that has been on the market three years or less and that is visibly different to the customer from previous offerings with new features, functionality or performance characteristics (Cooper and Kleinschmidt, 2011). Today, to keep up with the increasingly rapid pace of change in the marketplace, a growing number of companies around the world have begun to re-engineer their innovation and R&D processes to make new product development (NPD) dramatically faster and less costly (Hagel and Brown, 2011; Williamson and Yin, 2014; McKinsey, 2015). The literature has accordingly called for "accelerated product innovation" – which we define here as novel tactics and processes which can lead to higher speed to market and lower new product costs in NPD – as a key strategic capability (Millson et al.,

1992; Langerak et al., 1999; Williamson and Yin, 2014), and a growing body of evidence (e.g., Day and Wensley, 1988; Stanko et al., 2012; McKinsey, 2015) suggests that significant competitive advantage will be increasingly conferred on "first mover" firms that play a leading role in their market segment. In this kind of highly competitive environment, an abbreviated NPD cycle time plays a vital role in a firm's ability to be first to the market with a new product or offering (Stanko et al., 2012). The case for accelerating the rate of innovation is bolstered further still by evidence showing that faster NPD capabilities are also required for firms just to be successful as "fast followers" and later entrants (Ernst, 2002; Ahmad et al., 2015). Also, important benefits can be achieved by firms that learn to manage accelerated NPD (Barczak, 2012) as resources are utilized more creatively and efficiently, costs are reduced, and work-in-process bottlenecks are minimized (Millson et al., 1992; Cooper, 2014; Adner and Kapoor, 2010).

Traditionally, NPD has been viewed as a firm-driven activity in which individual companies are responsible for coming up with ideas for new products and, onward from that, deciding which ones should be commercialized and developed (Van Kleef, 2005; Cooper, 2011; Barczak, 2012). But advances in information and communication technologies (ICTs) are enabling new initiatives to be explored, and are materially transforming the NPD domain (Noble et al., 2013). Specifically, data from different sources can be captured and used to improve several aspects of NPD processes and workflows. IBM (2013) reports that 90% of the data that exists in the world today was created in the last two years, and some projections estimate that the total amount of data in the world will reach 35 zettabytes by 2020 (Wong, 2012). This is, therefore, the era of "Big Data" (Chan et al., 2015).

And just as important as the amount of data available is the diversity of the conduits from which it can be collected. Firms can now access potentially valuable digital information from a diverse range of sources that includes click streams, videos, tweets, and other unstructured sources to extract new ideas, or to improve their understanding about their products, customers, and markets (Tan et al., 2015; Noble et al., 2013). A recent survey revealed that 59% of respondents who described their organization as "data-driven" said that their company is more profitable than competitors (Economist, 2015). Among the characteristics that these organizations had was that their NPD and strategic decisions are guided by data rather than by intuition or personal experience (Chen et al., 2012). In such an environment, data analytics – that is, capturing useful information from data to inform decision making – has given rise to a novel approach to product innovation that is enhancing NPD processes in several important ways (Sanders, 2014). Data analytics can involve qualitative and quantitative techniques that leverage a suite of technologies to enhance productivity and business gains (Chen et al., 2012). These problems and considerations lead to the following research questions concerning in NPD:

1.   What are the best approaches for accelerated innovation in a big data environment?

2.   How can data analytics be applied to support accelerated innovation?

It is worth pointing out that there has also been a surprising amount of convergence in the literature with regards to how this area is being developed. The overwhelming majority of these earlier contributions in the area of accelerated product innovation have sought to identify potential success factors by analyzing relatively large samples and quantitative methodological approaches (Callahan and Moretoon, 2001; Stanko et al., 2012; Eling et al., 2013). By stark contrast, there has been a relative paucity of investigations in this area that have used case research, and that have explicitly explored approaches for accelerated product innovation in a big data environment. Therefore, a systematic study of the implications of data-supported accelerated product innovation approaches on NPD could greatly extend knowledge in this respect (Bharadwaj and Noble, 2015).

2. Background

Exactly how the data is extracted and categorised to identify and analyze patterns can vary significantly according to a firm's specific organizational requirements (Lavalle et al., 2011) or market environment factors (Millson et al., 1992; Liu and Jiang, 2016), but companies applying data analytics in this area agree that it is yielding benefits in spite of these differences. For example, predictive data analytical techniques have reduced the time healthcare companies typically need to bring a new drug to market, from 13 years to between 8 and 10 years (McKinsey, 2011). Capgemini (2012) estimates that the process improvements enabled by data analytics may lead to an average 26% performance improvement over a three-year period. These new tools have also been found to deliver substantial operational and strategic impacts on business process innovation both at the firm level and at the supply-chain level (Trkman et al., 2012), thereby helping the adopting firms to achieve an additional competitive advantage over industry rivals.

In today's "big data" era, tonnes of data constitutes an infrastructural resource that could be used in several ways to produce different products and services (Wong, 2012; McKinsey, 2011, Sanders, 2014). However, we are unaware of other research that attempts to bring together big data initiatives on these increasingly important accelerated product innovation approaches. The literature remains divided with regards to the specific ways in which companies should apply big data to support accelerated product innovation in new product development processes (Dahan and Hauser, 2002; Wong, 2012; Aloysius et al., 2016). Emerging evidence indicates that accelerated product innovation has already delivered a broad range of benefits in the marketplace, including greater opportunities to incorporate the latest technology, increased market share, the ability to generate higher returns, and more accurate forecasts of customer needs (Hagel and Brown, 2011; Williamson and Yin, 2014; McKinsey, 2015; Calder et al., 2016). While providing high-level evidence of these benefits, however, these contributions have failed to systematically investigate the specific mechanics of how firms can apply big data to realize these benefits. Therefore, a systematic study of the implications of data-supported accelerated product innovation approaches on NPD could greatly extend knowledge in this respect (Bharadwaj and Noble, 2015).

The literature in this area points to several important ingredients that seem to be helpful in bringing about various aspects of accelerated product innovation (Millson et al., 1992; Henard and Szymanski, 2001; Griffin, 1993; 2002; Zirger and Hartley, 1994; Ali et al., 1995; Eisenhardt and Tabrizi, 1995; Kessler and Chakrabarti, 1999; Langerak et al., 2008; Cankurtaran et al., 2013). There is still disagreement on their relative importance, and an integrated perspective and prescriptive framework have remained elusive as a result. For instance, while several studies have found that process formalization and process concurrency are important determinants for accelerating NPD (Tatikonda and Montoya-Weiss, 2001), others have found no significant effects (Zirger and Hartley, 1996; Barczak et al., 2008). Similarly, while some findings emphasize the importance of a probe and learning approach in accelerating product development (Eisenhardt and Tabrizi, 1995), others have reported that iteration does not significantly affect NPD acceleration (Callahan and Moretton, 2001).

Other important contributions in this area focus on specific aspects of speed. Prior studies on accelerated product innovation were mainly focused on NPD speed (Zirger and Hartley, 1994; Eisenhardt and Tabrizi, 1995; Kessler and Chakrabarti, 1996; Callahan and Moretton, 2001; Griffin, 2002; Langerak et al., 2008), generally focusing on how quickly an idea moves from conception to a product in the marketplace and measuring the ability of firms to move quickly through the NPD process (Chen et al., 2005). As noted by Kessler and Bierly (2002), and Chen et al. (2005), most studies on accelerated product innovation focus on its antecedents. Although different terms such as time-to-market (Chen et al., 2005), cycle time (Ittner and Larcker, 1997), innovation speed (Kessler and Chakrabarti, 1999), and speed to market (Meyer and Utterback, 1995) have been used to portray accelerated product innovation, the larger number of prior studies focused on the impact of speed on performance outcomes (i.e., profit and quality). These studies have not been consistent in their findings, with studies finding positive (Ali et al., 1995; Chen et al., 2005; Cooper and Kleinschmidt, 1994; Kessler and Bierly, 2002; Langerak and Hultink, 2005), negative (Crawford, 1992; Karau and Kelly, 1992; Sethi, 2000), nonsignificant (Meyer and Utterback, 1995; Ittner and Larcker, 1997; Griffin, 2002), and U-shaped relationships (Lukas and Menon, 2004; Langerak and Hultink, 2006). What is more, the overwhelming majority of these earlier contributions in the area of accelerated product innovation have sought to identify potential success factors by analysing relatively large samples and quantitative methodological approaches (Kessler and Chakrabarti, 1999; Callahan and Moretoon, 2001; Swink et al., 2006; Stanko et al., 2012; Eling et al., 2013). In contrast, there has been a relative paucity of investigations in this area that have used case research, and that have explicitly explored approaches for accelerated product innovation in a big data environment.

3. Research Methodology

There are two main stages to this study's research design. The first is a rudimentary conceptual framework, derived from a comprehensive literature study and empirical survey with academics and industrialists. The second is a qualitative study centering on observations and interviews with managers of five world-leading high-tech companies in the manufacturing, telecommunication, electronics, and software sectors. Following a naturalistic approach, this study focuses more on "what" goes on in the research context, and less on "how" events are socially brought into being (Silverman, 2014). The interviews are topical as they look for facts, descriptions, and examples that help answer a set of specific research questions (Rubin and Rubin, 2011). Comparative case study research (Yin, 2009) was selected as the most appropriate methodology for this investigation because of the expected context-specific nature of the phenomena and research questions being investigated.

This study investigates the questions through case-based research. Chinese companies were chosen as the research population for this investigation for three reasons. Firstly, several Chinese companies—like, for example, Xiaomi, the second largest smartphone manufacturer in the country, or Tencent, a leading internet company—have been observed to be aggressively experimenting with data-intensive, novel innovation models that have demonstrably accelerated and achieved cost benefits in their product innovation activities (Williamson and Yin, 2014). In fact, the country's activities on this front have been so impressive that McKinsey (2015), the global consulting firm, has specifically called for other countries to take note of and learn from the Chinese accelerated innovation model. Secondly, the Chinese economy has grown rapidly over the past several decades. The confluences of the world's largest population and the dramatic growth in per capita consumption have propelled China to become the second-largest economy by Gross Domestic Product in a relatively short period of time (BCG, 2015; McKinsey, 2015). As a result, Chinese organizations are operating in an increasingly demanding consumer market environment that is catalyzing these types of innovation (McKinsey, 2015) as the country tries to meet its "innovation imperative." Thirdly, most research into new product development has focused on Western economies and companies (Stanko et al., 2012; Eling et al., 2013; Roberts and Candi, 2014). Because of the size and rapid growth rate of its economy, however, China has emerged as an important new context for new product development. The specific nuances of how accelerated innovation occurs within the Chinese context are therefore extremely relevant on both a practical and theoretical level but have been largely overlooked in the literature. In this way, this paper sheds light on a knowledge gap that needs to be addressed (Wei and Morgan, 2004; Yang et al., 2012).

During the data collection, this study applied empirical field research in different world-leading high-tech companies. Our sampling is deliberately restricted to high-tech companies, which were focusing on accelerated innovation and applying a variety of data sources in support. These two characteristics offer the most suitable context given that our interest centers on the organizational issues associated with the link between accelerated innovation and big data environment in high-tech companies. Interviews were conducted with both managers (e.g., R&D managers, heads of innovation, senior managers and project managers) as well as with a selection of R&D team members. In addition to the interviews, the author observed these R&D teams, participated in internal presentations and workshops, and collected internal secondary material. According to McDonald (2005), observations can provide unique insights into day-to-day working practices because they shift the emphasis to the direct study of contextualized actions. The author had full access as an observer to most of the teams during a period of product development or while the teams applied data analytics. Therefore, the author was able to observe the teams in their natural setting (Schultze, 2000) to understand how they work. Besides, available documentation such as the external facilitators' reports were consulted where appropriate.

In terms of the data analysis, all the qualitative data were collected and systematically processed through the steps proposed by Lincoln and Guba (1985) and Locke (2001): data reduction, focused coding, and data display. In the first step, the author identified areas pertaining to the dominant themes for accelerated innovation in a big data environment. In the second step, the author focused on coding extracted passages relating to the main themes as well as the sub-themes. In the final step, data display, the author made tables and lists of passages and monitored the internal cohesion of the codes. The coding was an iterative process among the three authors which went through several rounds of coding, and after each coding round the data were compared and discussed.

4. Conclusion

The main outcome of this research has been the development and verification of a framework which helps managers in attaining accelerated product innovation in a big data environment. Results from the case studies demonstrated that the approaches included in the framework were highly rated by industrialists. Also, the implications of big data for product innovation were explored and the main efforts, success factors as well as managerial challenges were clearly summarised and identified. In the rest of this section, the findings from the case studies pertaining to the accelerated product innovation framework and big data are described.

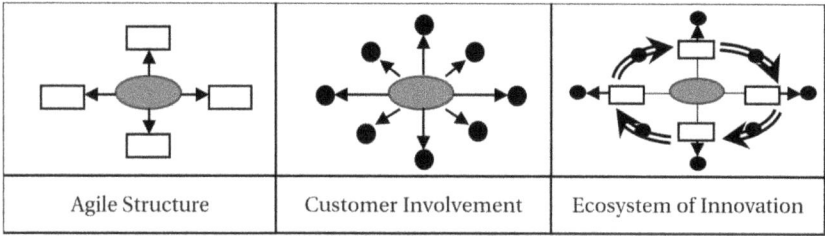

| Agile Structure | Customer Involvement | Ecosystem of Innovation |

Figure 11.1 Framework for accelerated product innovation in a big data environment

On the one hand, a three-phase framework based on prior studies and empirical research was developed and verified (see Figure 11.1). The approaches identified in the framework can be applied throughout all the phases of NPD and can be summarised by three innovation phases: (1) Agile Structure; (2) Customer Involvement; and (3) Ecosystem of Innovation. It is termed the ACE framework which we believe represents a paradigm shift to help firms to achieve accelerated product innovation in a big data environment. The framework allows firms to unlock the power of big data and make product innovation faster and less costly. The cases demonstrated that the framework provided practical approaches for managers to attain accelerated product innovation in a big data environment. For example, Case A was able to launch a range of new products in less than five months, at a total cost of $2 million. The company estimated that competitors using traditional design approaches have to invest around $20 million over twelve months to complete a similar set of new designs. In each case, the framework can provide companies with the guidance to handle data from various sources and formats, as well as to push intelligence from these data to various channels so as to support product innovation. Although prior research has examined different antecedents or success factors associated with various aspects of the NPD speed, no studies have investigated the approaches for accelerating innovation in today's big data environment. Therefore, the fact that many companies today have not identified these approaches systematically indicates that this is not 'common knowledge' and that practitioners and academics could benefit from applying this framework to similar accelerated innovation.

On the other hand, this study explores and provides an understanding of how to apply big data successfully in facilitating product innovation. It examines perceived benefits, the success factors for implementation and managerial challenges linked with big data in accelerated product innovation. Among the cases, the benefits of using big data to support product innovation are identified as follows. First, risk and market uncertainties can be reduced by using big data analytics. Market feedback in a variety formats and from different sources can be acquired in the early development stages. Second, harvesting big customer data allows previously unrecognized customer needs or combinations of needs to be identified. Market share will go to 'first mover' firms which can respond to customers quickly and meet their needs. Thirdly, big data can be used to generate great ideas from a variety sources. Lead customers (or innovative users) often act as co-creators and support product innovation managers in developing and bringing 'winning products' to the market. Fourthly, big data enables a company to contact potential customers in different ways. Fifthly, it also lends itself to customer loyalty and retention; for example, through online participation in product innovation, customers gain a better understanding of a new product but also become attached to the product to which they have made a contribution. It is a compelling experience which creates commitment and trust. Customer involvement in product innovation not only improves a company's product performance, but also serves as a means of building and enhancing relationships with both potential and existing customers. Finally, big data can provide product innovation teams with a broader basis for their decisions. By applying big data analytics, it is possible to increase the number of test options and to institute parallel testing of product alternatives among a variety of customers; moreover, this can be done repeatedly throughout the different phases of product innovation.

5. Implications and future research

Rather than attempting to build a theory about the whole product innovation process, this research stood in the position of the high-tech industries and specifically concentrated on incremental innovation in Chinese companies, in order to develop a better understanding of the research topic. This study contributes to the innovation literature by clearly defining the concept of accelerated product innovation. It further develops a framework with different approaches for accelerated product innovation in a big data environment. The framework can be applied throughout all the phases of product innovation, based on the framework developed this research contributes to existing research in several ways.

5.1. Implications for research

This research develops and demonstrates a distinct theoretical lens – a framework for accelerated product innovation in a big data environment – allowing for the new perspective on accelerated product innovation to be applied in empirical studies. There is no magic formula for accelerated product innovation. However, firms could expand their existing competence in many ways by tapping into the knowledge afforded by big data. The developed framework is based on information elicited from the literature and the unique product innovation approaches adopted by five successful Chinese firms. It provides a blueprint for using big data to make product innovation faster and less costly. Compared with existing product innovation approaches, the framework developed places particular emphasis on efficiency and cost saving (particularly in time-to-market and new product costs). It demonstrated that it can facilitate better planning and organization of parallel work teams and groups that may be involved in accelerated product innovation.

This study extends the accelerated product innovation boundaries pointed out by Williamson and Yin (2014) and provides further evidence to ascertain the vital role of the fast improve-and-relaunch process within an innovation ecosystem in product innovation. More specifically, this framework contributes to an increasingly vital body of literature discussing the importance of accelerated product innovation (Day and Wensley, 1988; Stanko et al., 2012; Williamson and Yin, 2014; McKinsey, 2015) and big data (McKinsey, 2011; Tan et al., 2015). Firms are leveraging big data to embed customer sentiment in product innovation. To stay competitive, Cooper (2014) points out that the next generation of product innovation process should be leaner, faster, adaptive and flexible. This research extends the traditional product innovation boundaries by providing a clear definition of accelerated product innovation and provides evidence of the vital role of accelerated product innovation in a big data environment. This enables firms to move away from product-focused innovation and to turn their attention to innovation around the customer experience. For example, the paradigm-shifting customer involvement innovation phase enables firms to find ways to innovate – unlocking the power of big data to improve customer understanding and make product innovation faster and less costly.

To our knowledge, this is the first attempt that incorporates the big data initiatives and applies it in a synergistic fashion with accelerated product innovation. Although the term big data is not new (Cecere, 2013; Zhou et al., 2014), the application of big data in facilitating accelerated product innovation is a relatively new area. The evidence provided in the research reveals the promise of this combinatorial approach, which we believe is worth further developmental efforts from product innovation and big data scholars. However, the implementation of the framework may put considerable strain on an organization. We posit that any stress presented by the introduction of these approaches will be more than compensated for by the time and cost reductions achieved in the modification of the product innovation process.

5.2. Implications for practice

In addition to the theoretical contributions as discussed above, the findings of this research could also guide company managers and strategists on how to achieve accelerated product innovation in a big data environment, and how to apply big data to facilitate accelerated product innovation using the prior experience of the case studies. The study is intended as a framework for R&D innovation managers to apply their resources to feature and product innovation in a fast and effective way through reducing the time-to-market and new product costs. Based on the examples in the case study, company managers can maximize positive outcomes from the approaches identified in the framework. Our study shows that managers agreed with the developed framework that enables them to capture the logic behind the variety of decisions made over the course of the accelerated product innovation process. Although the specific problem might be unique, they felt reassured that an approach to addressing it was well known. Also, the incorporation of big data into the fast improve-and-relaunch ecosystem can be significant. We identified a number of implications of implementing a customer-supported fast improve-and-relaunch process in the cases, including a decrease in new product costs, an increase in speed to market, better understanding of customers' needs (and connection with customers), and a change in leadership and team organization. The managers commented that the framework developed captures the main features for accelerated product innovation in a big data environment.

Moreover, the empirical findings show that the approaches of the developed framework are undoubtedly the most useful approaches for accelerated product innovation in high-tech industries, especially those that require big investments and a high degree of formalization. The role of big data in the developed framework was found to strengthen important activity approaches and segments. The effect of influential innovation phases streaming into the framework, from external and internal sources, increases with big data due to informationalization. However, the empirical study as well as the theory (Keon et al., 2001) highlight that the embedded corporate culture, governance and strategies directly influence the role of big data within the process. Nonetheless, the circular accelerated product innovation framework is more flexible than more sequential processes, thus better suited to adopt big data into its process of generating concepts in NPD.

Furthermore, this research points to the vital role of big data in helping firms to enhance product innovation (Davenport, 2014). First of all, it allows organizations to launch new products to market as quickly as possible. Secondly, it helps organizations to determine the weaknesses of the product earlier in the development cycle. Thirdly, it allows functionalities to be added to a product that customers are willing to pay a premium for, while eliminating features they don't want. Last but not least, it identifies and then prioritizes customer needs for specific markets. To stay competitive, Cooper (2014) points out that the next generation of product innovation process should be leaner, faster, adaptive and flexible. This study shows how firms could utilize big data to achieve that. However, the ACE framework developed is impossible in the absence of a strong leader, who can establish autonomous organizational structures that recognize and support product innovation. Thus, managers need to adopt a strong business orientation toward product innovation and embed this orientation in their organization's operating systems and cultural values (Verganti, 1997; Sarpong and Maclean, 2012).

5.3. Limitations and future research

In this research, we have only examined the framework by studying specific innovation projects within the five case companies. Therefore, future empirical studies can be conducted at the organizational level to identify the implications of the framework. According to Frambach and Schillewaert (2002), studies of organizational adoption of the framework in different disciplines can provide a better identification of factors to influence the acceptance of new products by organizations. Also, the cases were conducted on Chinese companies; it is not known to what extent the approaches for accelerated innovation can be generalized beyond the Chinese context. Thus, data from other country contexts are required to enhance confidence in the generalisability of these findings. In addition, relevant business models, as well as strategies, need to be developed to support accelerated innovation and the fast improve-and-relaunch process within an innovation ecosystem. Although the findings of this research focus on high-tech industries (high-tech manufacturing, telecommunications, electronics and software), we believe they can be generalized to any industry that applies data analytics and employs R&D in its product development and enables their businesses to be connected to the

Internet. Additionally, we pay attention to the approaches needed to achieve accelerated innovation in this research and we found that the fast improve-and-relaunch process can be generalized and applied to other properties of the service or product. So far, the development of a high-level framework for such a complicated phenomenon as accelerated innovation may highlight some obvious connections while failing to capture others. The developed framework is mainly focused on investigating approaches to accelerated innovation, where different data analytics were applied to support each of them. Therefore, the framework may not work where there is no data or data analytics to support it. We are hopeful, though, that this broad framework will provide a means to help integrate the wealth of research on innovation in order to advance both research and practice.

References

Adner, R. Kapoor, R. (2010). 'Value creation in innovation ecosystems: How the structure of technological interdependence affects firm performance in new technology generations'. *Strategic management journal 31*(3): 306-333.

Ahmad, S., D. N. Mallick, and R. G. Schroeder. (2013). 'New product development: impact of project characteristics and development practices on performance'. *Journal of Product Innovation Management 30*(2): 331-348.

Ali, A. A., R. Krapfel. and D. Labahn. (1995). 'Product innovativeness and entry strategy: impact on cycle time and break-even time'. *Journal of Product Innovation Management* 12: 54-69.

Aloysius, J.A., Hoehle, H., Goodarzi, S. and Venkatesh, V., (2016). 'Big data initiatives in retail environments: Linking service process perceptions to shopping outcomes'. *Annals of Operations Research* 1-27.

Barczak, G. (2012), 'The Future of NPD/Innovation Research', *Journal of Production Innovation Management*, Vol. 29 No. 3, pp. 355-357.

Barczak, G., E. J. Hultink., and F. Sultan. (2008). 'Antecedents and consequences of information technology usage in NPD: A comparison of Dutch and US companies'. *Journal of Product Innovation Management* 25(6): 620-631.

BCG, (2015). *The most innovative companies 2015*, The Boston Consulting Group.

Bharadwaj, N., and C. H. Noble. (2015). 'Call for Papers Innovation in Data-Rich Environment's. *International Journal of Product Innovation Management* 32 (3): 476-78.

Calder, B.J., Malthouse, E.C. and Maslowska, E., (2016). 'Brand marketing, big data and social innovation as future research directions for engagemen't. *Journal of Marketing Management*, 32(5-6): 579-585.

Callahan, J. and B. Moretton. (2001). 'Reducing software product development time'. *International Journal of Project Management* 19(1): 59-70.

Cankurtaran, P., F. Langerak, and A. Griffin. (2013). 'Consequences of New Product Development Speed: A Meta-Analysi's. *Journal of Product Innovation Management* 30 (3): 465-486.

Capgemini. (2012). *Unlocking the Power of Data and Analytics: Transforming Insight into Income, Capgemini,* available at: http://www.uk.capgemini.com/resources/business-process-analytics-unlocking-the-power-of-data-and-analytics-transforming-insight (assessed Oct 08, 2015).

Cecere, L. (2013), '*Big Data Handbook: How to unleash the big data opportunity',* Supply Chain Insight LLC.

Chan, H. K, X. Wang, E. Lacka, M. Zhang. (2015). 'A mixed-method approach to extracting the value of social media data'. *Production and Operations Management.* doi/10.1111/poms.12390

Chen, H., Chiang, R. and Storey, V. (2012), 'Business Intelligence and Analytics: From Big Data to Big Impact', *MIS Quarterly,* Vol. 36 No, 4, pp. 1165-1188.

Chen, J., R. Reilly, and G. Lynn. (2005). 'The impacts of speed-to-market on new product success: The moderating effects of uncertainty'. *IEEE Transactions on Engineering Management* 52 (2): 199-212.

Cooper, R. G. and Kleinschmidt, E. J. (2011). *New products: the key factors in success,* Marketing Classics Press, USA.

Cooper, R.G. (2014). '"What's Next? After Stage-Gate"', *Research Technology Management,* Vol. 57 No. 1, pp. 20-31.

Cooper, R.G. (1986). 'New product performance and product innovation strategies'. *Research Management,* May/June, 17–25.

Crawford, C.M., (1992). 'The hidden costs of accelerated product development'. *Journal of Product Innovation Management* 9(3): 188-199.

Dahan, E., and J. R. Hauser. (2002). 'The virtual customer'. *Journal of Product Innovation Management* 19 (5): 332-53.

Davenport, T.H. (2014). *Big Data at Work.* Boston, MA: Harvard Business School Publishing.

Day, G. S., and R, Wensley. (1988). 'Assessing advantage: a framework for disposing competitive superiority'. *Journal of Marketing.* 52-53.

Eisenhardt, K., and B. Tabrizi. (1995). 'Accelerating adaptive processes: Product innovation in the global computer industry'. *Administrative Science Quarterly* 40 (1): 84-110.

Eling, K., F. Langerak. and A. Griffin. (2013). 'A Stage-Wise Approach to Exploring Performance Effects of Cycle Time Reduction'. *Journal of Product Innovation Management* 30(4): 626-641.

Ernst, H. (2002). 'Success Factors of New Product Development: A Review of the Empirical Literatur'e. *International Journal of Management Reviews* 4 (1): 1-40.

Frambach, R. T. and N. Schillewaert. (2002). 'Organizational innovation adoption: A multi-level framework of determinants and opportunities for future research'. *Journal of Business Research* 55(2): 163-176.

Griffin, A. (1993). 'A metrics for measuring product development cycle time'. *Journal of Product Innovation Management,* 10 (2): 112-125.

Griffin, A. (2002). 'Product development cycle time for business-to-business products'. *Industrial Marketing management* 31 (4): 291-304.

Hagel, J., and J. S. Brown. (2011). 'Creation nets: harnessing the potential of open innovation'. *Journal of Service Science (JSS)* 1(2): 27-40.

Henard, D. H. and D. M. Szymanski. (2001) 'Why some new products are more successful than others'. *Journal of Marketing Research* 38(3): 362-375.

IBM, (2013). "What is big data? – Bringing big data to the enterprise", *IBM*, available at: www.IBM.com (accessed February 03, 2015).

Ittner, C. D., and D. F. Larcker. (1997). 'Product development cycle time and organisational performance'. *Journal of Marketing Research* 34 (1): 13-23.

Kessler, E. H., and A. K. Chakrabarti. (1999). 'Speeding up the pace of new product development'. *Journal of Product Innovation Management* 16 (3): 231-47.

Langerak, F., A. Griffin, and E. J. Hultink. (2010). 'Balancing development costs and sales to optimise the development time of product line additions'. *Journal of Product Innovation Management* 27 (3): 336-48.

Langerak, F., and E. J. Hultink. (2006). 'The impact of product innovativeness on the link between development speed and new product profitability'. *Journal of Product Innovation Management* 23 (3): 203-14.

Langerak, F., E. J. Hultink, and A. Griffin. (2008). 'Exploring mediating and moderating influences on the links among cycle time, proficiency in entry timing, and new product profitability'. *Journal of Product Innovation Management* 25 (4): 370-85.

Langerak, F., E. Peelen, and E. Nijssen. (1999). 'A laddering approach to the use of methods and techniques to reduce the cycle time of new-to-the-firm products'. *Journal of Product Innovation Management*, 16(2), pp.173-182.

LaValle, S., Hopkins, M.S., Lesser, E., Shockley, R. and Kruschwitz, N. (2011), "Big Data Analytics: the new path to value", *MIT Sloan Management Review*, Vol. 52 No. 1, pp. 1-22.

Lijun Liu, Zuhua Jiang, (2016) 'Influence of technological innovation capabilities on product competitiveness', *Industrial Management & Data Systems*, Vol. 116 Issue: 5, pp.883-902.

Lincoln, Y. S., and E. G. Guba. (1985). *Naturalistic inquiry.* Beverly Hills. CA: Sage.

Locke, J. (2001). *Grounded theory in management research.* London: Sage.

McDonald, S. 2005. 'Studying actions in context: A qualitative shadowing method for organisational research'. *Qualitative Research* 5: 455-73.

McKinsey. (2011). *Big Data: The Next Frontier for Innovation, Competition, and Productivity,* McKinsey Global Institute: 1-137, San Francisco, USA.

McKinsey. (2015). *The china Effect on Global Innovation.* McKinsey Global Institute, October 2015.

Menon, A., J. Chowdhury. and B. Lukas. (2002). Antecedents and outcomes of new product development speed: An interdisciplinary conceptual framework. *Industrial Marketing Management* 31 (4): 317-28.

Meyer, M. H., and J. M. Utterback. (1995). 'Product development cycle time and commercial success'. *IEEE Transactions on Engineering Management* 42 (4): 297-304.

Millson, M. R., Raj, S. P. and Wilemon, D. (1992). 'A survey of major approaches for accelerating new product development'. *Journal of Product Innovation Management* 9: 53-69.

Noble, C.H., M. N. Bing, and E. Bogoviyeva. (2013). 'The Effects of Brand Metaphors as Design Innovation: A Test of Congruency Hypotheses'. *Journal of Product Innovation Management 30*(S1):126-141.

Sanders, N.R., (2014). *Big data driven supply chain management: A framework for implementing analytics and turning information into intelligence.* Pearson Education, New Jersey.

Sarpong, D. and Maclean, M. (2012). 'Mobilising differential visions for new product innovation', *Technovation*, Vol. 32, pp. 694-702.

Schultze, U. (2000). 'A confessional account of an ethnography about knowledge work'. *MIS Quarterly* 24: 3-41.

Sethi, R., Smith, D. C., & Park, C. W. (2001). 'Cross-functional product development teams, creativity, and the innovativeness of new consumer product's. *Journal of Marketing Research*, *38*(1), 73-85.

Silverman, D. (2008). *Interpreting Qualitative Data: Methods for analysing talk, text and interaction*, 3rd Ed. Los Angeles, CA: Sage.

Stanko, M. A., F. J. Molina-Castillo, J. L. Munuera-Aleman. (2012) 'Speed to Market for Innovative Products: Blessing or Curse?', *Journal of Product Innovation Management 29* (5): 751-765.

Swink, M., S. Talluri. and T. Pandejpong. (2006). 'Faster, better, cheaper: A study of NPD project efficiency and performance tradeoffs'. *Journal of Operations Management* 24(5): 542-562.

Tan, K. H., Zhan, Y., Ji, G., Ye, F. and Chang, C. (2015). 'Harvesting big data to enhance supply chain innovation capabilities: an analytic infrastructure based on deduction graph', *International Journal of Production Economics*, Vol. 165, pp. 223-233.

Tatikonda, M. V., and M. M. Monotoya-Weiss. (2001). 'Integrating operations and marketing perspectives of product innovation: the influence of organisational process factors and capabilities on development performance'. *Management Science* 47 (1): 151-72.

The Economist. (2015). The Business of Data. *The Economist Intelligence Unit Limited*, available at: https://www.eiuperspectives.economist.com/sites/default/files/images/Business%20of%20Data%20briefing%20paper%20WEB.pdf (accessed Dec 21, 2015).

Trkman, P., Ladeira, M. B., Oliveira, M. and McCormack, K. (2012). 'Business Analytics, Process Maturity and Supply Chain Performance', *Lecture Notes in Business Information Processing*, Vol. 99, pp. 111-122.

Van Kleef, E., H. C. M. Can Trijp, and P. Luning. (2005). 'Consumer research in the early stages of new product development: A critical review of methods and techniques'. *Food Quality and Preference* 16: 181-201.

Verganti, R. (1997). 'Leveraging on systemic learning to manage the early phases of product innovation projects', *R&D Management*, Vol. 27 (4), pp. 377-392.

Wei, Y. and N. A. Morgan. 2004.' Supportiveness of organisational climate, market orientation, and new product performance in Chinese firms'. *Journal of Product Innovation Management* 21 (6): 375-88.

Williamson, P. J. and Yin, E. (2014). 'Accelerated Innovation: The New Challenge From China', *MITSloan Management Review*, Vol. 55 No. 4, pp. 27-34.

Chapter 12

A Framework to Evaluate the Impact of ICT Usage on Collaborative Product Development Performance in Manufacturing Firms

C. W. Chathurani Silva*

E-mail: chathurani@sjp.ac.lk

Abstract: Manufacturers are increasingly adopting collaborative product development (CPD) to achieve competitive advantage through joint synergies. Information and Communication Technology (ICT) is the major enabler of CPD activities in product conceptualization, development, and commercialization stages. Since most ICT implementations are costly, a deeper understanding of the impact of ICT usage on CPD performance is immensely useful for managing ICT resources in product innovations. Drawing on the relational resource-based view and the organizational information processing theory, this study developed a model including multidimensional ICT usage, CPD performance measurements, and possible moderating project characteristics, for comprehensively evaluating the ICT impact on CPD performance. The results confirmed that ICT usage in terms of frequency, proficiency, and intensity has a positive direct impact on new products' quality, commercial success, and time performance, and an indirect impact on these outcomes through collaboration performance. In addition, the study explored moderating effects of project complexity and uncertainty on these associations.

Keywords: Collaborative product development (CPD); ICT impact; CPD performance; collaboration performance; organizational information processing theory; relational resource-based view; manufacturing; frequency; proficiency; intensity.

1. Introduction

Innovation has become a necessity for existence in today's industrial business environment. The success of manufacturing companies mainly depends upon their ability to introduce new or improved products to the market speedily and at a relatively low cost. Organizations are keen to identify appropriate structural mechanisms and strategies to facilitate the generation of successful new products. Promising ideas and the expertise required to develop new products may be present with a company's stakeholders such as suppliers, customers, competitors, or staff. Developing new or improved products by joining complementary resources and experience of one or more external (e.g., suppliers and customers) and/or internal partners (cross-functional teams) with mutual goals is known as collaborative product development (CPD) (Büyüközkan and Arsenyan, 2012).

Information and communication technologies (ICTs) provide the key media for processing required information and facilitating communication between CPD partners (Curşeu et al., 2008, Montoya et al., 2009). Real-time communication, concurrent operations, and increased information access facilitated by intensive use of ICT help firms to overcome social, technical and organizational barriers against CPD (Boutellier et al., 1998, Swink, 2006). However, the increased use of ICT tools incurs significant costs to companies. The effectiveness of using ICT tools in CPD projects may vary depending on the requirement for processing information, determined by the characteristics of the projects. However, access to product-related information sometimes leads to issues such as leakage of proprietary knowledge and loss of control over the product development process (Hoecht and Trott, 2006, Littler et al., 1995). Therefore, adjusting the extent of communication and exchanging information via ICTs based on the requirements of CPD are vital for project success while these are quite challenging (Boutellier et al., 1998, Hoegl, 2005).

ICT impact on project performance can be direct as well as indirect through collaboration or collaboration outcomes such as knowledge-sharing (Banker, Bardhan, and Asdemir, 2006; Thomas, 2013). However, several limitations have been identified in previous studies in relation to: evaluating the impact of ICT usage or degree of using ICT tools on a new product's quality, time performance, and commercial success, and understanding the factors mediating and moderating these effects. Uncovering a detailed picture of the impact of ICT usage on collaborative product development performance could fill in existing gaps in the literature. Therefore, this study adopts more informative ICT usage evaluation criteria, broad CPD performance aspects, and project characteristics that could moderate the association between ICT usage and CPD performance. The study uses qualitative (interviews) and quantitative (secondary and primary) data to explore the current context of using ICT in CPD projects and to examine the direct, indirect, and moderated impact of ICT usage on CPD performance. The main research questions addressed in this study are:

1) How do manufacturing firms manage ICT usage in terms of frequency, proficiency, and intensity, for improving their collaborative product development activities?

2)   Does ICT usage have a significant impact on CPD performance?

3)   Do the project characteristics representing the information processing requirement in CPD projects significantly moderate the relationship between ICT usage and CPD performance?

1.3. Aim and purpose of the study

The primary objective of this study is to explore a comprehensive view of the impact of ICT usage on collaborative product development performance. Little empirical evidence is available in respect to the direct effect of ICT usage on project outcomes (Barczak et al., 2007; Kawakami et al., 2015) and collaboration (Peng et al., 2014), and the indirect effect through collaboration (Banker et al., 2006) on project outcomes are the main reasons for this investigation. Several scholars have suggested the importance of adopting a multi-dimensional ICT usage measurement for better revealing ICT impact (Chen et al., 2009; Durmusoglu and Barczak, 2011; Fichman, 2001). Therefore, this study incorporates three dimensions of ICT usage (frequency, proficiency, and intensity of use) and collaborative product development performance to attain the above objective. In addition to the performance criteria used in previous studies (quality, time, and/or commercial success) (e.g. Barczak et al., 2007; Durmusoglu and Barczak, 2011; Kawakami et al., 2015), this study incorporates collaboration performance that reflects the degree of achieving inter-firm relational-based outcomes of CPD (Büyüközkan and Arsenyan, 2012; Cousins and Lawson, 2007) rather than NPD collaboration (Banker et al., 2006; Peng et al., 2014). Hence, the CPD performance defined in this study represents the degree to which a product development project achieved its new product performance in terms of quality, commercial success, and time as well as collaboration performance.

Furthermore, the study aims to uncover the moderating effect of project characteristics on the relationship between ICT usage and collaborative product development performance. Previously, researchers have highlighted the need for understanding how the impact of ICT usage on the performance of product development projects varies based on factors that affect the information processing requirement of the projects (e.g., Thomas, 2013). Understanding these effects in relation to different dimensions of CPD performance will enable manufacturing firms to better utilize their ICT resources for the success of collaborative product development projects.

2. Background

Rapid developments in ICT make the collaborative product development process more complex to manage. However, heavy dependence on ICT itself may also cause some issues such as difficulty to change patterns of use (Montoya et al., 2009) and unnecessary leakage of commercially sensitive information (Hoecht and Trott, 2006). Past research has evaluated the usage of different ICT tools in CPD projects (e.g., de Grosbois et al., 2012, Markham and Lee, 2013). Some of these studies explored ICT usage based on the characteristics of the projects (e.g., de Grosbois et al., 2012, Corso and Paolucci, 2001). Very little research has focused on evaluating the frequency (Montoya et al., 2009) and proficiency (Chen, Tsou, and Huang, 2009) of ICT use and utilization of the functionalities of the tools (Kern and Kersten, 2007) in CPD programmes. However, the criteria of manufacturers for selecting ICT tools for CPD programmes, the importance of different ICT usage aspects (e.g., frequency, proficiency, and intensity), the positive outcomes of using ICT in CPD, and the barriers to achieving these outcomes have not been sufficiently explored in the literature.

The impact of ICT usage on CPD project performance has been discussed previously in product innovation research. Most of the studies focused on the impact of one (Banker et al., 2006) or several individual ICT tools (Durmusoglu and Barczak, 2011; Peng, Heim, and Mallick, 2014) while very few discussed overall ICT usage (Barczak et al., 2007). Research on the ICT-CPD performance relationship has mainly evaluated the direct effect of ICT usage on final project success associated with quality, financial, or time performance (e.g., Barczak et al., 2007; Durmusoglu and Barczak, 2011). These studies found little or no significant impact of ICT on some performance aspects (e.g., speed-to-market). Operationalizing ICT usage as the number of tools used in a project (or a project phase) is a major limitation found in most empirical investigations (e.g., Barczak et al., 2007; Durmusoglu and Barczak, 2011). The reason seems to be the difficulty of estimating the actual usage of different ICT tools in a selected CPD project or a phase. Fichman (2001) emphasized that multidimensional measurement of ICT usage leads to a clearer exploration of the role of these tools in innovation. Researchers have suggested the use of additional dimensions of ICT usage such as communication frequency and proficiency of use to reveal a more detailed picture of the effect of ICT on project performance (Durmusoglu and Barczak, 2011; Thomas, 2013). Recently, Kawakami et al. (2015) uncovered a positive effect of frequency of ICT use on NPD task proficiency which in turn improves NPD performance.

Research suggesting both a direct and an indirect impact of ICT usage on new product performance is rare to find in the literature. For example, Banker et al. (2006) found that PLM systems have an indirect impact on project performance through collaboration. In a study, Peng et al. (2014) found that communication and collaboration tools such as e-mail and groupware and product data and knowledge management tools do not significantly support collaboration between partners, while project management tools support this in low complex projects. However, these researchers have not examined the ICT usage-CPD performance association or the mediating effect of collaboration. Thomas (2013) found that e-mail supports knowledge exchange in CPD, which in turn increases project performance than rich communication media such as video conferencing and Web meetings. Although knowledge exchange is a basic element of collaboration, no study focusing on the direct ICT impact on the collaboration process performance comprising all its key elements (e.g., knowledge/information sharing, benefits sharing, risks sharing, and trust creation) (Büyüközkan and Arsenyan, 2012; Camarinha-Matos et al., 2009) or indirect impact through all these elements on new product performance was found in the literature.

Since ICT tools incur substantial costs to companies and intensive use of these tools leads to unnecessary information outflows, careful management of ICT usage to simply meet the information processing requirements of CPD projects would be worthwhile. Recent research has highlighted the need to investigate factors moderating the effectiveness of ICT usage, which may help in the proper management of ICT in CPD programmes (Durmusoglu and Barczak, 2011; Thomas, 2013). Project characteristics such as complexity and uncertainty represent the degree of the information processing requirement in CPD projects (Peng et al., 2014, Heim et al., 2012). However, very few studies addressing the relationship between ICT usage and CPD performance have examined the moderating effect of such project characteristics on this association. For example, Peng et al. (2014) studied the moderating effect of project complexity on the association between several ICT tools and NPD collaboration. Their study revealed that the associations are relatively strong when products are large, and weak when the project is novel and the interdependence of tasks is high. However, no empirical evidence for the moderating effects on the direct association between ICT usage and new product performance dimensions (e.g., quality, time, and financial success) or indirect association through collaboration-based performance was found.

In conclusion, four major gaps were identified in the existing literature. Prior studies addressing the impact of ICT usage on CPD performance have (1) not sufficiently explored the importance of multidimensional aspects of overall ICT usage in improving CPD programmes of manufacturing firms; (2) not incorporated CPD performance reflecting both final project performance and collaboration performance; (3) observed several inconclusive evidence for the association between ICT usage and CPD performance aspects; (4) paid little attention to the moderating effect of project characteristics on the direct and indirect associations between ICT usage and new product outcomes resulting from collaboration outcomes.

3. Research design

CPD is a business activity that involves several networked firms aiming for the success of a collective product innovation effort. The relational resource-based view (RRBV) argues that collaborative firms can achieve competitive advantage through relation-specific assets, effective governance, knowledge-sharing routines, and complementary resources and capabilities. It stimulates understanding that the intangible resources such as knowledge and trust shared by collaborative firms support achieving a sustainable competitive advantage (Lavie, 2006, Dyer and Singh, 1998). Drawing on this theory, the current study suggests that the effective use of ICT positively impacts on both product development and the collaboration processes of CPD and helps manufacturing firms to improve both tangible (e.g., profits) and intangible (e.g., knowledge-sharing) CPD outcomes. The RRBV supports theorizing both the direct and indirect effects of ICT usage on new product performance, through collaboration performance.

According to the organizational information processing theory (OIPT), the information processing capability of a firm needs the right balance with the information processing requirement of the tasks performed by the firm, in order to achieve higher organizational performance (Galbraith, 1984, Daft and Lengel, 1986). Since ICT is the key means for communication, collaboration, and product development in CPD, its usage in terms of frequency, proficiency, and intensity reflects the information processing capability of firms undertaking CPD projects. A CPD project's information requirement may depend on the degree of complexity, uncertainty, and urgency of the project. Therefore, drawing on OIPT, this study argues that ICT usage has varied effects on CPD performance for different levels of project characteristics that represent the information processing requirement of the projects.

First, the study developed and utilized a model for evaluating the impact of ICT usage on CPD performance based on RRBV, OIPT, and reviews of the literature. Second, it collected qualitative data from manufacturing and ICT vendors through interviews and analyzed the data using directed qualitative content analysis. The findings offered industrial evidence for the effectiveness of managing ICT usage in improving CPD programmes and identified barriers to the effective use of ICT in CPD. This answered the first research question and helped the examining and fine-tuning of the initial conceptual model which contained several new constructs (e.g., collaboration performance and intensity of ICT use) with practitioners' perspectives.

Next, secondary data obtained from the 2012 NPD best practices survey (i.e., Comparative Performance Assessment Study or CPAS) conducted by the Product Development and Management Association (PDMA) were analyzed using the hierarchical multiple regression approach. This preliminary study answered the second research question and evaluated the impact of ICT usage, with a different source of data. This analysis was important for studying the capability of previously used ICT measurement criteria in revealing the impact of ICT usage and to justify the importance of a multi-dimensional measurement (frequency, proficiency, and intensity of ICT use) proposed in the present study. In the final stage, an online survey on globally operated CPD projects was conducted to investigate the conceptualized direct, indirect, and moderated effects of ICT usage on CPD performance. The empirical data were analyzed using partial least square structural equation modeling (PLS-SEM), and the results were discussed providing deeper insights into the impact of ICT usage on CPD performance. This answered the second and third research questions concerning all direct, indirect and moderated effects of ICT usage on collaborative product development performance. Figure 12.1 presents the research model finalized based on the findings of the preliminary studies and tested in the final quantitative research phase.

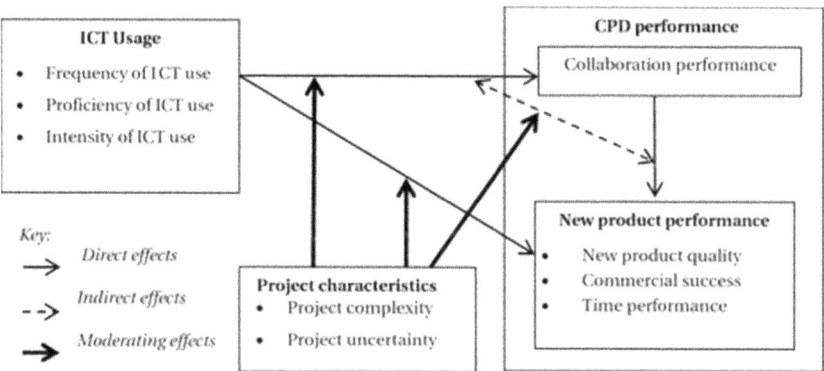

Figure 12.1 Finalized framework for evaluating the impact of ICT usage on CPD performance

4. Conclusion

Findings of the qualitative preliminary study adequately answered the first research question focusing on managing manufacturing firms' ICT usage for improving their CPD activities. Differences in the use of ICT are observed mainly due to: the technological levels of companies and managements' understanding and confidence in the positive impact of using these tools in CPD programmes. When selecting ICT tools for CPD, manufacturers primarily consider the size and distribution of their product development network, the degree of partner involvement, the nature of information transferred (knowledge intensity), and the frequency of new product introductions. Manufacturers of all types highly value the convenience, transparency, and traceability offered by simple ICT tools such as e-mail and Skype. Furthermore, the ability of an ICT tool to offer the benefits of face-to-face communication is an important criterion for selecting and using the tool in manufacturers' CPD projects. The study supported hypothesizing a positive impact of ICT usage on all the CPD performance aspects (collaboration performance, quality, commercial success, and time performance). Furthermore, the study identified several technical (e.g., version update problems), human (e.g., little knowledge in using advanced tools) and other barriers which can reduce the effective use of ICT in CPD. These other barriers were further divided into four categories, namely, context-specific (e.g. less effectiveness of ICT tools when customers are unable to provide correct specifications), outcome-related (e.g. difficulty of recovering high costs of ICT tools), organizational (frequent changing of ICT tools), and collaboration-based (e.g. failure to share information as required due to not using ICT tools appropriately) barriers.

The preliminary quantitative study that used PDMA's CPAS (2012) data examined a research model which includes several concepts related closely to the constructs in the main research model (collaboration instead of collaboration performance), and no moderating effects were tested due to lack of required data. The study examined the direct and indirect impact of individual ICT tools on overall NPD performance, through collaboration. It revealed a significant positive direct impact of PDM systems and project management tools on overall NPD performance. In addition, online communities/net ethnography/virtual shopping/semiotics, PDM systems, collaborative design systems, groupware, customer requirement analysis software, and online focus groups/online surveys, indicated significant positive effects on NPD collaboration which in turn improves NPD performance. However, the descriptive statistical analysis performed after the main hypotheses tests suggested that in high-tech industries, all types of ICT tools are likely to have a positive impact on NPD performance. Not adopting an informative multidimensional ICT usage measurement has been suggested as the key reason for the little ICT impact observed in this research phase.

In the final quantitative phase of the study, all the hypotheses asserting the direct and indirect positive impact of ICT usage on new product performance (quality, commercial success, and time performance), through collaboration performance were supported. This concludes that ICT usage comprising of frequency, proficiency, and intensity has a significant positive direct and indirect impact through collaboration performance on new product quality, commercial success, and time performance of CPD projects. This confirms the findings of the preliminary qualitative study, related to outcomes of ICT usage with more sound statistical evidence. According to the results, the contribution of ICT towards improving collaboration performance and new product quality is larger than improving financial and time-related outcomes. Collaboration performance enabled by ICT usage mostly helps in improving quality and time performance of CPD projects while having a moderate level positive influence on commercial success.

The study revealed that project complexity significantly moderates the direct and indirect relationships between ICT usage and new product quality. The direct impact of ICT usage on new product quality is weaker for more complex projects. However, the indirect impact of ICT usage on new product quality, through collaboration performance, is stronger for the complex projects. According to the results, no other moderating effects were significant. However, a detailed review of the statistical results suggests similar (to the above effect on new product quality) moderating effect of project complexity on the association between ICT usage and commercial success and positive moderating effects of project uncertainty on the associations between ICT usage and collaboration performance, and time performance. Under greater project uncertainties, ICT usage has a relatively larger impact on CPD projects' time performance and lower impact on collaboration performance.

5. Implications and future research

This study which explored a broad view of the impact of ICT usage on CPD performance with both qualitative and quantitative evidence has several significant contributions to the current body of knowledge. These are:

- broadening current understanding on managing ICT usage in terms of frequency, proficiency, and intensity, for improving CPD activities in manufacturing sector,

- developing a framework including improved ICT usage and CPD performance constructs and project characteristics to evaluate the direct and indirect impact of ICT usage on new product performance, through collaboration performance

- exploring the moderating effect of project characteristics on the relationship between ICT usage and collaborative product development performance, and

- contribution to the underlying theories of the study: RRBV and OIPT

The findings provide useful implications for CPD practitioners particularly in high-tech and medium-high-tech manufacturing industries that typically collaborate internally and externally in product innovations.

5.1. Using ICT for increasing performance of CPD projects

Understanding the direct impact of overall ICT usage on new product performance in terms of quality, commercial success, and time performance would be important for practitioners in ICT investment decisions and in managing ICT resources for the success of product development programmes. As the study implies, ICT tools improve manufacturers' ability to innovate products with increased design specification compliance, more customer-desired features, and enhanced technical performance. This occurs because ICTs significantly exceed human abilities in effective information recall, exchange, and processing which are important to make effective decisions. Cost reduction mechanisms such as computer-enabled simulation, performance evaluations, communication, and market research, supported by ICTs ensure higher profits, market share, and overall commercial success in CPD. Managements that utilize ICT resources to ensure high technical proficiency of their R&D staff will have better ability to achieve time targets in the new product conceptualization, development, and commercialization.

The direct impact of ICT usage and indirect impact through the collaboration outcomes on new product performance make CPD practitioners better informed about the value of ICT in their product innovation projects. ICT tools are the key means that facilitates all the design, development, market research, project management, communication, and collaboration activities within contemporary CPD teams. Managers should ensure increased frequency and proficiency of using these tools and effective utilization of their functionalities for maintaining relationships that are more trustworthy and help the sharing of project risks, benefits, information, and knowledge. Improved collaboration performance with ICT primarily assists in enhancing quality and increasing product development speed rather than ensuring higher commercial success. As suggested by the qualitative preliminary study, using ICT tools for increasing face-to-face contact with virtually involved members, obtaining frequent feedback from suppliers, and timely exchange of quality information, largely help CPD practitioners to achieve better performance. In addition, sharing of project risks and benefits such as new market opportunities and discounts on key material procurements enable manufacturers to claim good prices for their new products.

The results related to individual ICT usage aspects offer some key insights to product development managers. Frequent use of communication and collaboration ICT in early product development stages importantly assists managers in reaching greater collaboration performance and financial returns. Manufacturing firms should pay special attention to improving the proficiency of their R&D staff in using advanced ICT tools and to ensuring easy adoption of those tools. In addition, encouraging CPD participants to use various functionalities in knowledge, information, and the project management ICT tools, and the frequent use of ICT for market research activities, are important since these have a higher impact on all CPD performance aspects. However, it is noted that increased frequency of using project management tools does not largely help in improving product development times while it significantly improves other performance aspects (collaboration, quality, and commercial success). Managers can significantly increase the quality of new products rather than commercial success and time performance by effectively utilizing the features and functionalities in product design and development ICT tools.

5.2. Use of ICT in CPD projects with different information processing requirements

The moderating effects revealed in this study provide valuable implications for effectively managing CPD projects with different information processing requirements. As the study suggests, usage of ICT tools directly contributes to improving quality in simple projects more than in complex projects. In complex CPD projects where many distributed partners are intensively involved, many parts are to be designed, and various design constraints and task interdependencies exist, managers face lots of challenges in achieving performance, due to cultural differences, communication and language barriers, and varied technological proficiencies. Therefore, increasing project performance in terms of quality and commercial success through increased use of ICT tools can be relatively difficult in such complex projects. However, the study also suggests that the collaboration performance enhanced through the use of ICT assists managers in dealing with obstacles related to the complexity of projects in achieving quality. Extensive involvement of customers, more responsibility assigned to component suppliers, and including external team members with unique technical skills are typical in complex CPD projects (Clift and Vandenbosch, 1999). In such projects with higher information processing requirements, using ICT tools effectively to increase collaboration with the partners is critical to ensure a high level of customer satisfaction, technical performance, and overall quality of the new product as well as greater success in the market. Since there is no evidence of a moderating impact of project complexity on the association between ICT usage and time performance, it is important to note that increased ICT use is similarly important for achieving time targets of CPD projects with any level of complexity.

Although a strong empirical evidence for the moderating impact of project uncertainty was not found, the study offers some important implications concerning the ICT usage effectiveness in projects with varied uncertainties. When projects involve novel technologies, R&D teams usually have greater information ambiguities and a need for tacit knowledge to be transferred. However, there is a little opportunity for transferring this knowledge since ICT tools mainly support the exchange of knowledge available in codified format. Therefore, achieving higher collaboration performance with the use of ICT can be relatively difficult when running projects with high uncertainty. Nevertheless, CPD teams tend to be more committed and rush to process more information via ICT tools when the product/process technology or market is new to them. Consequently, such uncertain projects will have a greater chance for being completed within the expected timeframes. However, managers cannot expect substantial variations in the contribution of ICT use towards improving new product quality or commercial success of projects based on their uncertainties. Therefore, to achieve quality and financial objectives, increased ICT usage in terms of frequency, proficiency, and intensity is equally important for CPD projects with any level of uncertainty in the product technology, process technology, or market.

5.3. Suggestions for future research

The industries excluded in the main study (low-tech and service industries) may have differences in the direct, indirect and moderating effects investigated, thus require further examination in future. Although this study does not suggest significant differences in ICT impact across specific industries considered (electronic, automotive, etc.), future studies could investigate these differences in detail using larger samples from each industry. Comparisons of the results of such studies with the present findings would be worthwhile to explore differences in the effectiveness of ICT usage across technology levels and product types. The findings related to individual ICT types could be further reviewed by way of more focused studies on individual ICT tools, by appropriately adjusting the suggested measurement criteria (frequency, proficiency, and intensity) for evaluating the usage of these tools. Further examination of the moderating effects of project characteristics on the associations between ICT usage and CPD performance dimensions is recommended for future studies as this is the only research that has attempted to evaluate many of these effects. Including projects with more variations in terms of complexity and considering additional dimensions of uncertainty such as technological and market turbulence would be useful in those studies to uncover the moderating effects with improved accuracy. To overcome limitations in the present cross-sectional research design, evaluating similar hypotheses using project-based longitudinal data and comparing the results with the current findings are recommended.

References

Banker, R. D., Bardhan, I. & Asdemir, O. (2006). 'Understanding the impact of collaboration software on product design and development'. Information Systems Research, 17, 352-373.

Barczak, G., Sultan, F. & Hultink, E. J. (2007). 'Determinants of IT usage and new product performance'. The Journal of Product Innovation Management, 24, 600-613.

Boutellier, R., Gassmann, O., Macho, H. & Roux, M. (1998). 'Management of dispersed product development teams: The role of information technologies'. R&D Management, 28, 13-25.

Büyüközkan, G. & Arsenyan, J. (2012).' Collaborative product development: a literature overview'. Production Planning & Control, 23, 47-66.

Chen, J.-S., Tsou, H. T. & Huang, A. Y.-H. (2009). 'Service delivery innovation antecedents and impact on firm performance'. Journal of Service Research, 12, 36-55.

Corso, M. & Paolucci, E. (2001). 'Fostering innovation and knowledge transfer in product development through information technology'. International Journal of Technology Management, 22, 126-148.

Curşeu, P. L., Schalk, R. & Wessel, I. (2008). 'How do virtual teams process information? A literature review - and implications for management'. Journal of Managerial Psychology, 23, 628-652.

Daft, R. L. & Lengel, R. H. (1986). 'Organizational information requirements, media richness and structural design'. Management Science, 32, 554-571.

De Grosbois, D., Kumar, U. & Kumar, V. (2012). 'Extent of Internet-based Technology Use in New Product Development Projects in Canada and the United States'. Jindal Journal of Business Research, 1, 1-19.

Durmusoglu, S. S. & Barczak, G. (2011). 'The use of information technology tools in new product development phases: Analysis of effects on new product innovativeness, quality, and market performance'. Industrial Marketing Management, 40, 321-330.

Dyer, J. H. & Singh, H. (1998). 'The relational view: Cooperative strategy and sources of interorganizational competitive advantage'. Academy of management review, 23, 660-679.

Fichman, R. G. (2001). 'The role of aggregation in the measurement of IT-related organizational innovation'. MIS quarterly, 427-455.

Galbraith, J. R. (1984). 'Organization design: An information processing view'. Army Organizational Effectiveness Journal, 8, 21-26.

Heim, G. R., Mallick, D. N. & Peng, X. D. (2012). 'Antecedents and Consequences of New Product Development Practices and Software Tools: An Exploratory Study'. IEEE Transactions on Engineering Management, 59, 428-442.

Hoecht, A. & Trott, P. (2006). 'Innovation risks of strategic outsourcing'. Technovation, 26, 672-681.

Hoegl, M. (2005). 'Buyer-supplier collaboration in product development projects'. Journal of Management, 31, 530-548.

Kawakami, T., Barczak, G. & Durmusoglu, S. S. (2015).' Information Technology Tools in New Product Development: The Impact of Complementary Resources'. Journal of Product Innovation Management, 32, 622-635.

Kern, E.-M. & Kersten, W. (2007). 'Framework for internet-supported interorganizational product development collaboration'. Journal of Enterprise Information Management, 20, 562-577.

Lavie, D. (2006). 'The competitive advantage of interconnected firms: An extension of the resource-based view'. Academy of management review, 31, 638-658.

Littler, D., Leverick, F. & Bruce, M. (1995). 'Factors affecting the process of collaborative product development: A study of UK manufacturers of information and communications technology products'. Journal of Product Innovation Management, 12, 16-32.

Markham, S. K. & Lee, H. (2013). 'Product Development and Management Association's 2012 Comparative Performance Assessment Study'. Journal of Product Innovation Management, 30, 408-429.

Montoya, M. M., Massey, A. P., Hung, Y.-T. C. & Crisp, C. B. (2009). 'Can you hear me now? Communication in virtual product development team's. Journal of Product Innovation Management, 26, 139-155.

Peng, D. X., Heim, G. R. & Mallick, D. N. (2014). 'Collaborative Product Development: The Effect of Project Complexity on the Use of Information Technology Tools and New Product Development Practices'. Production and Operations Management, 23, 1421–1438.

Swink, M. (2006). 'Building collaborative innovation capability'. Research Technology Management, 49, 37-47.

Chapter 13

The Effects of Procedural Knowledge Transparency on Adoption in Corporate Social Networks

Bjørn J. M. Jensen*

E-mail: bjensen@poweredbyaction.org

Abstract: This dissertation investigated how a type of organizational knowledge sharing, procedural knowledge transparency (PKT), affected innovation adoption rates of members of a corporate social network (CSN) within a large Scandinavian organization. It also explored the mediation of these effects by different types of sensemaking and moderation by performance transparency in the form of badges. Content analysis was used to identify and classify instances of PKT, different modes of communication, sensemaking, intention to adopt, and adoption. A logistic regression model tested the main effect of PKT and was found to be significant at the discourse-level and at the user-level on both intent to adopt and adoption. The data proved insufficient in answering whether performance transparency affected adoption rates. A linear regression mediation model tested the mediating sensemaking variables and found that sensemaking mediates the effects of PKT on intent to adopt and adoption. Overall, the study found support that posts that contained PKT indeed did affect intent to adopt and adoption and was mediated to a great effect by sensemaking efforts of individuals. These findings have several implications for identifying and studying the value of CSNs.

Keywords: Transparency, Procedural Knowledge Transparency, Innovation, Sensemaking, Adoption, Corporate Social Networks, Enterprise Social Networks, Collaboration, Knowledge Sharing, Organizational Communication, Innovation Management.

1. Introduction

A central concern for any organization to innovate is to use internal capabilities to maximum advantage, e.g. by spurring innovation (West and Gallagher, 2006, p. 321). One of the ways of doing that is fostering online collaboration (Yoo, Boland, Lyytinen and Majchrzak, 2012) by making employees' knowledge or "know-how" visible (Leonardi, 2014); referred to as *Procedural Knowledge Transparency (PKT)*. Organizations that foster transparency in multiple ways are more likely to generate innovative ideas internally by bringing tacit knowledge to light (Leonard and Sensiper, 1998). Looking at PKT in the context of Corporate

Social Networks (CSNs)[1] is highly relevant. In the face of increasing difficulty in internalizing innovation (Calantone, Cavusgil and Zhao, 2003), these have become essential platforms for companies for spurring and retaining know-how, informal training and acculturation of novices, aiding in generating new products through communities of practice (Marion, Barczak and Hultink, 2014), and generally increasing organizational efficiency and resilience (Turban, Bolloju and Liang, 2011). This explains the massive uptake in the use of CSNs in recent years (Deloitte, 2013). As organizations are increasingly becoming digitally connected and work becoming more distributed, making communication visible online in the form of posts, conversations, and messages, has become crucial to enable collaboration and innovation online (Leonardi, 2014). Furthermore, to aid the motivation to participate, gamification elements have been used to make the contributor's performance transparent using, e.g. badges (Deterding, Dixon, Khaled and Nacke, 2011). However, the effects of having CSNs have been mixed, specifically because of continuously low participation rates among employees (Li, 2015). This indicates that the benefits of having a CSN are perceived to be mixed at best by management, perhaps even by employees. Existing literature paints the same picture of CSNs as having the potential to facilitate but also hinder knowledge sharing (Gibbs, Rozaidi and Eisenberg, 2013; Kane, Alavi, Labianca and Borgatti, 2014; Leonardi, Huysman and Steinfield, 2013; Majchrzak, Faraj, Kane and Azad, 2013; Oostervink, Agterberg and Huysman, 2016). Yet, whether CSNs make good platforms for employee innovation remains unclear (Kankanhalli, Ye and Teo, 2008; Recker, Malsbender and Kohlborn, 2016). Transparency, or lack thereof, is at the heart of this conundrum. Prior studies from Leonardi (2014) found that "documentation of the knowledge required to complete one's own work is not a natural or routine part of most tasks" (p. 18). Furthermore, this is "the largest impediment for organization-wide knowledge sharing" (p. 18) – a key factor for organizational innovation and performance (Recker, et al., 2016; Teece, 2009). This problem is being addressed within very few CSNs by using gamification and continuous encouragement from management and administrators, with seemingly great success in terms of collaboration and adopted ideas amongst its employees and management. One of these is the CSN platform, *Resonance,* which was deployed in 2012 within a large Scandinavian corporation and ran until 2014. A novel aspect of this platform was the procedural knowledge-sharing nature. Since most of the work in the company was "front-line," practical and hands-on, the communication

---

1. Corporate Social Networks refers to social media networks that resemble e.g. Facebook but are used internally in a corporation. They often go under the name Corporate Social Networks (CSNs) (Li, 2015), Enterprise Social Networks (ESNS) (See Leonardi, 2014; Treem and Leonardi, 2012) or Enterprise Social Media (Kane, 2015).

within the CSN was very procedure and process-oriented ("how I did this" or "how I handled this situation").

This type of communicative PKT we assume helps participants in CSNs in three ways: 1: it improves organizational communication and coordination, 2: it fosters new ideas by revealing what has and what has not been done, and 3: it increases production efficiency. Even though this type of PKT in communication can be seen on CSNs such as *Yammer*, *Jive*, and *Chatter*, little is known about how it affects individual innovation and adoption. Considering the users and purveyors of CSNs are using these platforms primarily to derive organizational value from the information they find (Raghavan, 2002, p. 91), research on these and their value-adding activities is still surprisingly scarce (Leonardi et al., 2013, p. 2). This leaves a theoretical gap in explaining how PKT fosters innovation in the form of novel ideas that can be adopted and bring value to a company. We aim to elucidate how this specific type of communicative transparency fostered innovation in a CSN through the following 6 research questions:

RQ1: Does Procedural knowledge transparency affect intention to adopt new practices in online corporate social networks?

RQ2: Does Procedural knowledge transparency affect adoption of new practices in online corporate social networks?

RQ3: Does performance transparency moderate the effects of procedural knowledge transparency and sensemaking on intention to adopt of innovation in online corporate social networks?

RQ4: Does performance transparency moderate the effects of procedural knowledge transparency and sensemaking on adoption of innovation in online corporate social networks?

RQ5: Does sensemaking mediate the effect of procedural knowledge transparency or intent to adopt practices in online corporate social networks?

RQ6: Does sensemaking mediate the effect of procedural knowledge transparency on adoption of practices in online corporate social networks?

2. Background

To answer the research questions, the dissertation uses three central concepts: PKT, Sensemaking, and Innovation (as Intent to Adopt and Adoption). The following section presents a brief background to our problem, what is known about it through existing literature, and how it informs the conceptual model, presented at the end of this section.

Adoption and Intent to Adopt as Organizational Innovation (DV)

Individual innovation has long remained one of the ultimate factors for the long-term survival of any organization (Ancona and Caldwell, 1987). At the user and discourse level, there has been considerable interest in tracking down and identifying factors contributing to "innovative behavior" through, e.g., path analysis (Scott and Bruce, 1994). We refer to innovation as "intent to adopt" and "adoption" as organizational innovation classically refers to "…adoption of certain novel or not yet tried ideas and practices" (Amabile, 1988; Daft, 1978; Zaltman, Duncan and Holbek, 1973). It is demonstrated through expressing compatibility of an innovative practice, or "…the degree to which an innovation is perceived as being consistent with the existing values, past experiences, and needs of the receivers." (Rogers and Shoemaker, 1971, p. 15). After receiving such expressions do not necessarily mean that the individual will automatically adopt a certain practice, knowledge, or idea. Yet, it demonstrates an intention to adopt when compatibility and fit between the proposed practice, knowledge, or idea, are perceived to be present (see Yen, Wu, Cheng and Huang, 2010). An important distinction is made between adoption and intention to adopt. First, adoption is a behavior indicating that an individual has and/or is already using a proposed idea, type of knowledge, or process. Intention to adopt is when an individual indicates that s/he will adopt/use an idea, type of knowledge, or process later. This is done through communication. The dissertation focuses on the individual and internal sources of company innovation, specifically from the employees. The next section focuses on PKT, the primary independent variable that affects and may predict subsequent individual innovation adoption.

Procedural Knowledge Transparency (IV)

PKT is a concept derived from existing literature (Anderson and Lebiere, 1998; Leonardi, 2014) that refers to transparency as the visibility of what individuals do or did in a certain situation which can help members adopt new behaviors. It is a relatively new concept whose predecessors are in the literature on enterprise social networks. Yet, it also draws on organizational knowledge literature, and specifically how knowledge is articulated and transferred from one individual to another. It explicates how visibility of online communication binds together the increasingly distributed nature of today's workforce (Leonardi, 2014). Finally, it also highlights the invisible nature of work to everyone but its own practitioners (Nardi and Engeström, 1999), and how visibility of communication as a work activity can improve, e.g. product and process innovation (Majchrzak,

Cooper and Neece, 2004) through the encouragement of documenting work processes as mentioned earlier. In short, the degree of visibility and granularity of an idea, process, or behavior that was done in the past is assumed to have an effect on subsequent innovation adoption or intent to adopt.

Sensemaking (M)

This variable might mediate the effect of PKT on adoption and intent to adopt. Sensemaking is the process of patterning and articulating disparate information into a new structure (Weick, Sutcliffe and Obstfeld, 2005, p. 413). In CSNs (and life in general) individuals are confronted with too many cues to notice and will only extract cues with relevance for them (Weick, 1995). In this study, the CSN in question encouraged employees to share procedures or "how they did something in a certain case." Tacit knowledge, in some cases even explicit knowledge, can be hard to articulate when asked to do so. A critical factor for triggering this articulation through sensemaking is when we are told to consciously deliberate about something, in this case, our own work processes (Griffith, 1999). Sensemaking is triggered through novelty (novel processes), discrepancies between the expected and observed, and conscious deliberation, or, when we are aware we are thinking about it, such as after we are told to (Fiske and Taylor, 1991). Communication is central to sensemaking and talks it into existence for further action (Taylor and Van Every, 2000, p. 58), making sensemaking a social process – what a person does depends on others (Resnick, Levine, and Teasly, 1991), meaning that to understand sensemaking is to pay more attention to coordination cues (Weick, 1995). Following recommendations from Weick and colleagues (2005, p. 413), we do that through describing the process of sensemaking to occur in interaction through articulation. This dissertation builds upon the concept of articulation as a representation of sensemaking, i.e. an utterance such as "this is a good idea, but…" indicates that the individual is still trying to make sense of the situation and whether the idea fits his or her work processes, while "this makes sense" or "this is a great idea that I can use" is a primer for later adoption, indicating that indeed, sensemaking is taking place and the individual is now taking into account how it could be adopted in his or her practice and is making an actual value judgment. It reflects the aggregated cues that s/he extracted from the environment prior to the response to PKT and before the decision to adopt or not, and then iterate. Because the exposure to PKT represents just one of the cues chosen by the individual in the sensemaking process and this process is ongoing in the decision to whether the individual adopts a procedure or not, we suspect that this very process will mediate the effects of PKT as it represents an ongoing decision making process, where a decision to adopt or not is a function of the cues the individual chose to utilize at that point in time. Taken together, the full model (Figure 13.1) assumes that

PKT has a direct effect on the dependent variables, Adoption and Intent to Adopt, and that this effect is mediated by Sensemaking, and moderated by Performance Transparency[2].

The effects of PKT on adoption are going to be investigated at two levels: the user-level and the discourse-level. These differ significantly at the conceptual level and warrant investigation of differences in communication patterns. At the discourse level, focus is on the global discourse practice level, i.e., the overall content individuals in the CSN engage in through turn-taking (Van Dijk, 1997). Finding high-quality content that constitutes instances of the concepts previously outlined requires looking at process and content at the user-level. This level consists of individual communication behaviors. This methodological choice is necessary to address the fact that looking at global discursive practices may attribute too much power to Discourse (big D, because it is a macro-level view) (Alvesson and Karreman, 2000). By looking at individual-level (or micro-view) of interactions, it serves to disprove or confirm if the overall discursive practices happen within the micro-level interactions (Alvesson and Karreman, 2000). With such an analysis at both levels, it enables a more thorough look at how the concepts permeate throughout the organization.

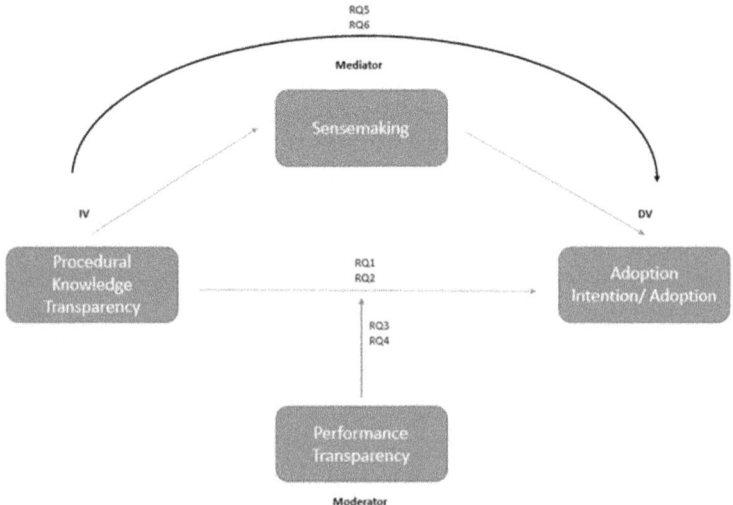

Figure 13.1 Theoretical Model

---

2.   As mentioned in the abstract, the data proved insufficient in answering if performance transparency moderated the effect of PKT on adoption. However, for those interested in performance transparency as a starting point, the definition originates from literature on gamification (see Deterding et al., 2011) and literature on reputation in online communities (see e.g. Majchrzak et al., 2013).

3. Research design

To test the abovementioned theory that PKT affects individual adoption of ideas/behavior/processes after potential mediation of sensemaking, archival data were obtained from a CSN called *Resonance* in a large public service corporation headquartered in Scandinavia. It was used between 2012-2014 to foster innovation among front-line workers by encouraging individuals to share actions/processes/ideas and/or deeds that represented the company's values and at the same time encouraged other people to pick up these processes (adoption or intention to adopt). The dissertation's approach was primarily quantitative, but with qualitative parts.

We obtained and cleaned a large dataset which ended up including 349 unique users who contributed with 1558 "deeds" (posts), and 295 unique users who contributed with 1589 comments to these deeds. The total number of individuals registered and having logged in on this CSN was 1139. The data were organized, collected, thematically analyzed (Boyatzis, 1998) and re-analyzed to ensure that themes representing the variables were prevalent and supported the theoretical foundation for these: PKT, advice, sensemaking, adoption, and intention to adopt. We furthermore dissected transparency into one-to-many communication, one-to-one communication, step by step communication, and predictive and/or educated guess. This parsing, informed by literature on tacit and explicit knowledge, was done to look into R-square changes and which aspects of PKT were most influential on adoption and intent to adopt.

The level of analysis was the post and its language. Due to the nature of the dataset, comments were already linked to deeds, allowing for coding of sensemaking and adoption of an idea, behavior, or process in these. PKT was determined linguistically by an active verb phrase indicating a process. Every instance of a theme, even if in the same sentence or post, was counted to quantify the findings. To ensure intercoder reliability (Krippendorff, 2013), two Scandinavian coders were hired to pre-test until reaching reliability, then code the entire data set, not only to ensure high reliability (which was $\alpha>.700$ for all codes), but to ensure that they picked up on the cultural nuances of Scandinavians in conversation. As an example, emojis are use more frequently and bear multiple meanings in the context of a given conversation.

Finally, after all instances of themes were counted (these were binary and reflected as 0 and 1), logistic regression was used and data were analyzed at the individual user-post-level and transformed to the discourse level. Reliability, validity, and power were all extremely satisfactory and necessary control variables (gender, front-line vs. office workers) were implemented. Likewise, we tried to include performance badges as moderators of adoption (i.e., if a post is from an individual with an "ideator of the month" badge then it might have more weight on subsequent adoption), but the data proved unsuitable. Overall, results were highly interesting.

4. Conclusion

We found that PKT is consistently a significant predictor for intent to adopt and adoption. Sensemaking mediates this relationship, both at the individual and discourse level. This answered the first two major research questions. Sensemaking played a large role in the increase of this rate as a mediator at the user-level; especially when discussions revealed agreement or posed a counter suggestion to an original idea posted, this positively affected the rate of adoption whereas disagreement did not, and actually had a negative effect. It should be mentioned that before the transformation of the discourse-level data to user-level data, there were unusually high log-odds for agreement stemming from few counts of agreement. After the transformation, however, it appears as these results normalized themselves, but skew was still higher than the other transformed variables, meaning that the results of this variable should be viewed with that in mind. Advice, different from PKT, had a modest effect on intent to adopt and pure adoption and suggests that, in *Resonance*, influence on adoption came indirectly rather than via pure advice. In fact, it was negatively correlated and decreased the likelihood of that outcome. Individuals were less likely to think about adopting an idea when they were given advice. Gender, interestingly, did not influence the outcome, while front-line workers versus desk workers had an effect on intent to adopt. In short, in answering research question five and six, it was found that there were several variants of the sensemaking mediator that were more influential than others in leading to intent to adopt and pure adoption. In conjunction with Griffith's (1999) propositions, more concrete features of communication (i.e., PKT and its associated variables of step-by-step communication and predictive and educated guesses) were more likely to influence intent to adopt and adoption rather than advice. Research questions three and four remained unanswered as the types of badges were not individually classified in the data set and multiple new badge rollouts were implemented over the course of the CSNs 2-year lifetime. The significant effects of each independent variable on the dependent variables overall are documented in Table 13.1 with betas for the user-level results and log-odds at the discourse level.

Table 13.1 Parameter Estimates Found Significant for Key Predictor Variables

Independent Variable	DV and Level of Analysis			
	Intent to Adopt		Adoption	
	User	Discourse	User	Discourse
Procedural Knowledge Transparency	0.146	2.569	0.1537	2.393
Frontline versus Desk		1.635		
Communication, Mode One to Many		0.357		
Communication, Mode One to One				1.930
Communication, Mode Step by step				2.129
Predictive and or Educated Guess				1.769
Advice		0.394		
Agreement Sensemaking	0.811		0.758	
Disagreement Sensemaking				
Countersuggestion Sensemaking		4.577	0.106	

* Discourse-level analysis parameters are log-odds, user-level analysis are betas.

On a broad scale, the findings suggest that in a large public organization that primarily relies on "front-line" workers to maintain large machinery and be customer-facing, a CSN may well be a very appropriate medium for sharing process-specific information to optimize and increase best practice adoption. Furthermore, the dissertation highlighted that there are in fact, active externalizations of tacit knowledge that lead to successful adoption, or at least consideration from others. This corresponds with the earlier mentioned method of articulating knowledge as well as we possibly can (Haldin-Herrgard, 2000) and demonstrates theoretically the value of feedforward as a link to adoption. Especially when looking at the significance of the related variables, predictive and educated guesses, outlining the steps of a process and addressing one individual rather than many, these are influential in predicting adoption too, both in tandem with procedural knowledge transparency and without, explaining the high R-squared in all models run. Thus, they contribute to a broader understanding of what drives influence in CSNs. This is a preliminary step towards understanding how certain types of information conditions shape adoption in CSNs and suggests that certain speech acts are more likely to predict adoption of a proposed idea.

Finally, the findings suggest that these fundamentally different types of utterances on a CSN can be efficiently classified through rigorous content analysis and evaluated subsequently via logistic regression to determine their
value added in the form of adoption by another employee. The methodology
itself in checking for presence of certain types of utterances and distinguishing these apart may serve to further distill how many value-adding utterances
appear within a CSN. The findings are documented in Table 13.2.

Table 13.2 Confirmatory Answers (x) to RQs

Research Question	DV and Level of Analysis			
	Intent to Adopt		Adoption	
	User	Discourse	User	Discourse
RQ1: Does Procedural knowledge transparency affect intention to adopt new practices in online corporate social networks?	×	×	×	×
RQ2: Does Procedural knowledge transparency affect adoption of new practices in online corporate social networks?	×	×		×
RQ3: Does performance transparency moderate the effects of procedural knowledge transparency and sensemaking on intention to adopt of innovation in online corporate social networks?	.			
RQ4: Does performance transparency moderate the effects of procedural knowledge transparency and sensemaking on adoption of innovation in online corporate social networks?				
RQ5: Does sensemaking mediate the effect of procedural knowledge transparency or intent to adopt practices in online corporate social networks?	×	×	×	×
RQ6: Does sensemaking mediate the effect of procedural knowledge transparency on adoption of practices in online corporate social networks?	×	×	×	×

5. Implications and future research

This study successfully proved that there are indeed significant effects of PKT shared in CSNs on employee adoption and that this relationship is mediated by individual sensemaking. The combination of existing transparency components such as visibility, theories of sensemaking as a process, feedback and feedforward (Arnold et al., 2006), linguistic markers, and theories of innovation diffusion proved to be highly fit for analyzing different utterances at the post level and for CSN data in general. Using Rogers' (2003) and Rogers and Shoemaker's (1971) diffusion of innovation theory in the sense that communication is a significant driver of adoption of others' ideas, innovations, and/or behavior proved sufficient as an outcome variable for exploring how value may be created and spread within a CSN. Perhaps the most crucial addition to theory is that the dissertation demonstrates the idea of the individual as a creator of transparency in their communication and refocuses this as a basis for social action and influence, witnessed in our mediator and outcome variables. With current literature focusing on affordances of visibility as the basis for transparency, this dissertation adds to the literature that it is not only "making information visible" on the technological side of a CSN, but also encouraging individuals to make certain types of information, here procedural knowledge, visible. In the end, the volition to share such knowledge emerges at the individual level. From there it is distributed through text, digested by others and then adopted. Here, the results confirmed that there is merit to the gap highlighted by Griffith (1999) that new insights and redesign are motivated (by PKT in this study) and indeed affected in the sensemaking process, with significant mediation in agreement, and smaller, yet also significant mediation when counter suggestions arise. Furthermore, the results confirmed that employees are drivers of idea generation and very focal for determining which ideas are strategically important enough to adopt, or at least think about adopting.

From a methodological standpoint, the dissertation offered a "prototype" of how one would go about analyzing from whom good ideas emerge within a CSN and by whom they are adopted, by identifying the textual components through content analysis and using simple binary indicators. Furthermore, this study provides a good roadmap for future studies into transparency effects and further conceptualizing it. It also serves as a roadmap for exploring new and empirically untested concepts unfold within CSNs. Despite having a sufficiently large sample, theoretically, there was reason to believe that there might not be a high number of instances of any outcome variable, combined with the exploratory nature of the theories and perhaps lack of sufficient numbers of empirically established concepts in the literature. In this case, normality of the data could be hard to reach. If these indicators emerge from initial suspicions, then based on this dissertation, the use of binary or continuous variables for logistic regression would be recommended to avoid too skewed data as it evaluates the odds ratio of an outcome variable occurring when predictor variables are taken into account.

Finally, despite a few methodological limitations, this study is important as it demonstrates a simple working metric for how good ideas are created. Furthermore, it explains how they can be characterized in terms of content, where they come from in the organization, how they are strategically negotiated and directed, and when they lead to adoption or influence people to think about adopting an idea, process, or behavior, both at the discourse-level and at the user-level. While this study exemplified that good work, processes can be richly documented and shared within a CSN and value is derived at the individual level, thus addressing the gap of how to achieve value derivation from CSNs (Raghavan, 2002), participation remains a key problematic for management. This study confirmed that too. Nonetheless, it represents a crucial step in identifying organizational innovation at the broader discourse level and individual behavior and communication level in a CSN and measuring its value based on employee adoption. Indeed, it illuminates that the key innovation driver for the organization lies within its employees' communication patterns and social influence and may provide a valuable metric for innovation success, allowing management to gauge the innovative pulse of its employees.

References

Alvesson, M. and Karreman, D. (2000). 'Varieties of Discourse: On the Study of Organizations through Discourse Analysis', *Human Relations*, 53(9), pp. 1125-1149.

Amabile, T. M. (1988). 'A Model of Creativity and Innovation in Organization', in Cummings, L.L. & Staw, B.M. (eds.) *Research in Organizational Behavior*. Greenwich, CT: JAI Press, pp. 123-167.

Ancona, D. G. and Caldwell, G. F. (1987). 'Management issues facing new-product teams in high technology companies', *Advances in Industrial and Labor Relations, 4*, pp. Greenwich, CT: JAI Press.

Anderson, J. R. and Lebiere, C. (1998). *The Atomic Components of Thought*. Hillsdale, NJ: Erlbaum.

Arnold, V., Clark, N., Collier, P. A., Leech, S. A. and Sutton, S. G. (2006) 'The differential use and effect of knowledge-based system explanations in novice and expert judgment decisions', *Mis Quarterly*, pp. 79-97.

Boyatzis, R. E. (1998). *Transforming qualitative information: Thematic analysis and code development*. Thousand Oaks, CA: Sage.

Calantone, R. J., Cavusgil, S. T. and Zhao, Y. (2002). 'Learning orientation, firm innovation capability, and firm performance', *Industrial Marketing Management*, 31(6), pp. 515-524.

Daft, R. L. (1978). 'A Dual-Core Model of Organizational Innovation', *Academy of Management Journal*, 21, pp. 193-210.

Deloitte (2013). *Technology, Media & Telecommunications Predictions 2013.* Available at: http://www2.deloitte.com/global/en/pages/technology-media-and-telecommunications/articles/tmt-predictions-collection.html.

Deterding, S., Dixon, D., Khaled, R. and Nacke, L. 'From game design elements to gamefulness: defining gamification'., *the 15th International Academic MindTrek Conference: Envisioning Future Media Environments*

Fiske, S. and Taylor, S. (1991). *Social cognition (2nd ed.).* New York: Mcgraw-Hill Book Company.

Gibbs, J. L., Rozaidi, N. A. and Eisenberg, J. (2013). 'Overcoming the "Ideology of Openness": Probing the Affordances of Social Media for Organizational Knowledge Sharing', *Journal of Computer-Mediated Communication*, 19(1), pp. 102-120.

Griffith, T. L. (1999). 'Technology Features as Triggers for Sensemaking', *The Academy of Management Review*, 24(3), pp. 472-488.

Kane, G. C., Alavi, M., Labianca, G. and Borgatti, S. P. (2014). 'What's Different About Social Media Networks? A Framework And Research Agenda', *MIS Quarterly*, 38(1), pp. 275-304.

Kankanhalli, A., Ye, H. J. and Teo, H.-H. (2015). 'Comparing Potential and Actual Innovators: An Empirical Study of Mobile Data Services Innovation', *MIS Quarterly*, 39(3), pp. 667-682.

Leonard, D. and Sensiper, S. (1998). 'The role of tacit knowledge in group innovation', *California management review*, 40(3), pp. 112-132.

Leonardi, P. M. (2014). 'Social Media, Knowledge Sharing, and Innovation: Toward a Theory of Communication Visibility', *Information Systems Research*, 25(4), pp. 796-816.

Leonardi, P. M., Huysman, M. and Steinfield, C. (2013). 'Enterprise Social Media: Definition, History, and Prospects for the Study of Social Technologies in Organizations', *Journal of Computer-Mediated Communication*, 19(1), pp. 1-19.

Li, C. (2015). 'Why No One Uses the Corporate Social Network', *Harvard Business Review*.

Majchrzak, A., Cooper, L. P. and Neece, O. E. (2004). 'Knowledge Reuse for Innovation', *Management Science*, 50(2), pp. 174-188.

Majchrzak, A., Faraj, S., Kane, G. C. and Azad, B. (2013). 'The Contradictory Influence of Social Media Affordances on Online Communal Knowledge Sharing', *Journal of Computer-Mediated Communication*, 19(1), pp. 38-55.

Marion, T. J., Barczak, G. and Hultink, E. J. (2014). 'Do Social Media Tools Impact the Development Phase? An Exploratory Study', *Journal of Product Innovation Management*, 31, pp. 18-29.

Nardi, B. and Engeström, Y. (1999). 'A Web on the Wind: The Structure of Invisible Work', *Computer Supported Cooperative Work*, 8(1-2), pp. 1-8.

Oostervink, N., Agterberg, M. and Huysman, M. (2016). 'Knowledge Sharing on Enterprise Social Media: Practices to Cope With Institutional Complexity', *Journal of Computer-Mediated Communication*, 21(2), pp. 156-176.

Raghavan, P. (2002). 'Social Networks - From the Web to the Enterprise', *IEEE Internet Computing*, January - February 2002.

Recker, J., Malsbender, A. and Kohlborn, T. (2016). 'Using Enterprise Social Networks as Innovation Platform's, *IT Professional*, 18(2), pp. 42-49.

Resnick, L. B., Levine, J. M. and Teasley, S. D. (1991). *Perspectives on socially shared cognition*. NE, Washington DC: American Psychological Association

Rogers, E. M. (2003). *Diffusion of Innovations*. 5th edn. New York: Free Press.

Rogers, E. M. and Shoemaker, F. F. (1971). *Communication of innovations*. New York: Free Press.

Scott, S. G. and Bruce, R. A. (1994). 'Determinants of Innovative Behavior: A Path Model of Individual Innovation in the Workplace', *Academy of Management Journal*, 37(3), pp. 580-607.

Taylor, J. R. and Van Every, E. J. (2000). *The Emergent Organization: Communication as Its Site and Surface*. Mahwah, N. J.: Erlbaum.

Teece, D. J. (2009). *Dynamic capabilities and strategic management: organizing for innovation and growth*. OUP Oxford.

Turban, E., Bolloju, N. and Liang, T.-P. (2011). 'Enterprise Social Networking: Opportunities, Adoption, and Risk Mitigation', *Journal of Organizational Computing and Electronic Commerce*, 21(3), pp. 202-220.

Van Dijk, T. A. (1997). *Discourse as social interaction*. Sage.

Weick, K. E. (1995). *Sensemaking in Organizations*. London: Sage.

Weick, K. E., Sutcliffe, K. M. and Obstfeld, D. (2005). 'Organizing and the Process of Sensemaking', *Organization Science*, 16(4), pp. 409-421.

West, J. and Gallagher, S. (2006). 'Challenges of open innovation: the paradox of firm investment in open-source software', *R&D Management*, 36(3), pp. 319-331.

Yen, D. C., Wu, C.-S., Cheng, F.-F. and Huang, Y.-W. (2010). 'Determinants of users' intention to adopt wireless technology: An empirical study by integrating TTF with TAM', *Computers in Human Behavior*, 26(5), pp. 906-915.

Yoo, Y., Boland, R. J., Lyytinen, K. and Majchrzak, A. (2012). 'Organizing for Innovation in the Digitized World', *Organization Science*, 23(5), pp. 1398-1408.

Zaltman, G., Duncan, R. and Holbek, J. (1973). *Innovations and Organizations*. New York, NY: Wiley.

Chapter 14

Technology Planning for Aligning Emerging Business Models and Regulatory Structures - the Case of Electric Vehicle Charging and the Smart Grid

Kelly R. Cowan

E-mail: kcowan@pdx.edu

Abstract: Smart grid has been described as the Energy Internet: Where Energy Technology meets Information Technology. The incorporation of such technology into vast existing utility infrastructures offers many advantages, including new smart appliances, energy management systems, better integration of renewable energy, value-added services, and new business models, both for supply- and demand-side management. However, while smart grid offers the promise of revolutionizing utility delivery systems, many questions remain about how such systems can be rolled out at the state, regional, and national levels. Technology Roadmapping may be a valuable approach for understanding factors that could affect smart grid technology and product development, as well as key business, policy and regulatory drivers. This research builds upon existing roadmapping processes by considering an integrated set of factors, including policy issues, which are specifically tuned to the needs of smart grids and have not generally been considered in other types of roadmapping efforts.

Keywords: Smart Grid; Grid Modernization; Technology Roadmapping; Technology Planning; Utility Planning; Business Model; Electric Vehicle; Electric Vehicle Charging; Transportation Electrification; Transactive Energy.

1. Introduction

Electrical utility grids are important parts of the energy delivery systems that keep the modern world as we know it running. They are vital parts of our economies, powering the production of goods and services, and they are strategic assets, important for protecting the health, well-being, and security of populations which have come to rely upon modern technological infrastructure. In the U.S. alone, electrical utilities accounted for nearly $400 billion in revenues in 2016 (EEI, 2017). But, nearly all of our electrical utility systems are also in need of modernization. Smart grid is a class of technologies that offers many promising benefits for the modernization of electrical power delivery systems. The following are just a few of the benefits offered by smart grid: (1) Improvement in operating efficiencies of electricity grids at all levels of the system; (2) Improvement of communications and controls within the power system for all actors, including generators, transmitters, system operators, distributors, and end-users; (3) Opportunities for new value-added services related to control and management of energy; (4) and increased system reliability by replacing obsolete hardware that is nearing the end of its useful service life (Hammerstrom et al., 2006). With the average age of electrical transformers in the US power grid now at 42 years, out of a maximum design life of 40 years, critical elements of the power system are now at risk, and there is a strong need to modernize aging infrastructure for the power grid (Rouse and Kelly, 2011; Hussler et al., 2010).

Current power grids, especially in the United States, are being used well past their designed lifetime. Updates to these systems are important to address energy inefficiency, reliability, and security vulnerabilities of the 21st century. It is possible to use the emerging technology smart grid technology product platform on many types of utility systems, including gas, water, and electricity delivery systems, but this research will focus only on smart electricity grids.

Power grid modernization offers the opportunity to implement technologies with new capabilities that may have been difficult or impossible in the past. From remotely operated energy management system, self-monitoring and self-healing systems, to smart electric vehicles, smart grid can open a myriad of new opportunities for businesses, consumers, and decision makers (Fox-Penner, 2009, Stimmel, 2015). Therefore, it is critical to examine how smart grid is likely to develop in the future, what its effects may be, and to create a detailed roadmap showing how this vision might occur.

The next section will describe the smart grid industry and related technologies in greater detail. The need for development of roadmaps to guide the deployment of smart grid technologies will then be discussed, including current efforts in Oregon and the US Pacific Northwest. This field is very broad, so only a limited number of technologies and the capabilities they provide will be described, with an emphasis on technologies that are currently being introduced and seen as important in the region. In particular, this research will focus on how smart grid technologies can be used to meet key regional goals, such as enabling the integration of renewable energy, which according to recently enacted legislation, must now provide 25% of the energy mix in Oregon by 2025 (Jenkins et al., 2007). Thus, the following questions will be specifically explored.

What factors are most significant in motivating the adoption of smart grid technologies? How can important emerging smart technologies, like electric vehicles, be used to integrate renewable energy into the power system? What policies can encourage businesses and individuals to participate in such systems?

The topic described above raises a number of interesting questions that are important to explore both in the industry practitioner literature and the academic research literature. First, how can a tool such as technology roadmapping be extended to include a policy layer, business services model layer, and an expanded product market needs layer, which includes the ability to consider appropriate technology performance metrics. The research further raises the question of the interaction between technology push versus market pull. It then extends these concepts by considering how they might be affected by policy and business model push-pull dynamics.

1. How can technology roadmapping be used to improve regional smart grid planning?

2. How can technology roadmapping be extended to better integrate technology planning, business model development, and regulatory and policy considerations for smart grid?

3. What are the best ways to encourage the adoption of emerging smart grid technologies that meet critical regional needs, such as the use of electric vehicles to help with the integration of renewable energy?

This research can provide insights to help planners understand which factors are most likely to promote diffusion and adoption of smart grid technologies and their use for the integration of renewable energy. It offers valuable extensions to the concept of technology roadmapping by integrating consideration of regulatory and policy issues, business model development, and technology research and development. It explores the interactions between traditional technology push and market pull dynamics by adding consideration of the policy and business model push-pull relationships. It then helps to build an understanding about how these factors inform one another to improve chances of successful deployment of technology.

2. Background

While the term "smart grid" has been in widespread use since at least 2005, it has not always been consistently used (Amin and Wollenberg, 2006). Smart grid is not a single thing, or an exact end state. It is a process of gaining more advanced capabilities to improve upon the features that the electric utility grid that has evolved over the last century.

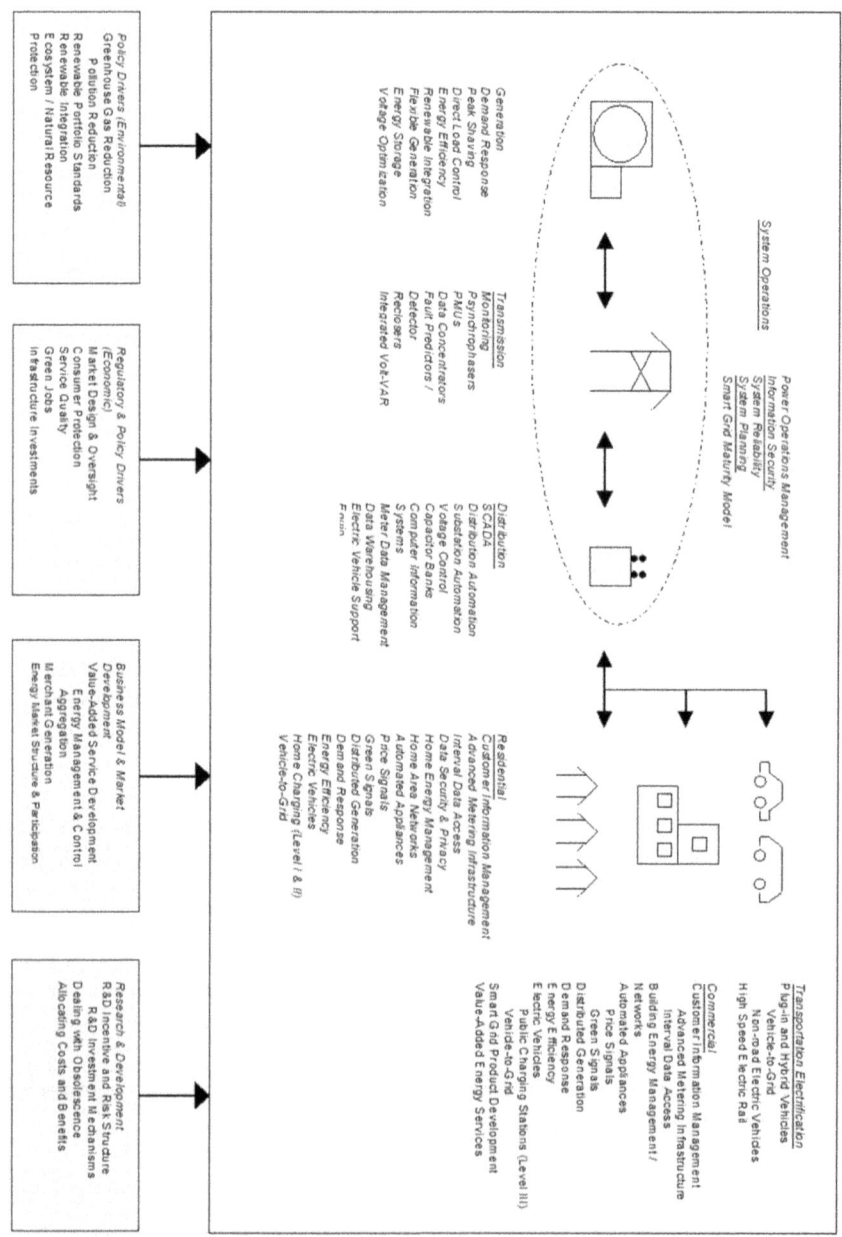

Figure 14.1 Key Elements and Drivers Contributing to Smart Grid

Smart grid technologies cover a wide range of functions, so it would be difficult to describe all the technologies that comprise it in detail. However, its main categories and functional areas consist of the generation, transmission, distribution, and systems operation functions which are shown in the figure 14.1. The figure 14.1 also shows key policy, market, business model and technology drivers that are influencing the evolution of the industry.

Unlike many other technology-intensive industries, the electric power industry has been highly regulated, almost since the time that Thomas Edison opened the first commercial power station in lower Manhattan in 1882 (Cramer, 2001). With high barriers to entry, high capital requirements, and generally positive economies of scale in production, the industry has many key characteristics of natural monopolies (Filippini, 1998). It benefits from network effects, making it cheaper to serve customers when they are all part of the largest possible network of interconnections (Fox-Penner, 2010). Once the health, safety, environmental, and economic benefits of electrification became widely known, states began establishing regulatory compacts to extend the benefits of electric power to all citizens (Fox-Penner, 2010). This was generally done by creating monopoly services territories with utilities agreeing to an "obligation to serve" under regulated rates. Early industry pioneers, like Samuel Ansull, felt the industry could benefit from the stability and protection of a regulated monopoly structure, thus setting a tone that has remained to the present day (Insull and Keily, 1915).

Roadmapping is a term used in many industries, but it is not always interpreted in the same way. For the purposes of this research, the technology roadmapping process pioneered by Motorola in the 1980's is the main concept that will be extended (Willyard and McClees, 1987b). The concept was further refined in the 1990's (Bray and Garcia, 1997) and a standard approach, known as the T-Plan was developed in early 2000 (Phaal et al., 2001, Phaal et al., 2004). Second generation roadmaps for disruptive technologies were developed by Walsh (Walsh, 2004). In addition, a process known as an S-Plan was developed to provide an overview of the strategic landscape for a potential technology product. Such roadmaps are useful for identifying key technologies and gaps that exist in a strategic and technology planning processes (Holmes and Ferrill, 2005b).

Roadmaps show key possibilities for relationships between technologies and products over time. Most successful roadmaps attempt to integrate the perspectives of "technology push" and the "market pull (Nauda and Hall, 1991b)." In the case of the development of smart grid roadmaps, integration of these perspectives is critical. While the Schumpeterian view that essential change within an industry depends strongly on the type and quality of technology developed in that new industry (Schumpeter and Opie, 1934), it also must meet important and well-defined market needs, as described by Schmookler (Coombs et al.,

1987). Regulatory and policy factors can exert both a push and a pull on the traditional technology-push and market-pull perspectives. At times, policy may combine with technology push to create a sort of "policy-push," which nudges technology to do more to meet an important policy goal, such as increased fuel efficiency vehicles or zero emission vehicles, for example.

It is possible that this may cause technologies to fall out of alignment with market pull demands of consumers, such as with those who prefer larger but less fuel-efficient vehicle for other reasons, such as horsepower and cargo capacity. At other times, policy may take the form of a pull, attempting to get technology more aligned with market preferences than it otherwise might be given new technological capabilities that have been developed. For the purposes of this research, as we consider the possible role of policy in balancing the technology push and market pull perspectives, it is useful to consider a "policy push-pull" dynamic that would be able to act back and forth on these other two perspectives. This can be visualized as the Regulatory and Policy Push / Pull arrow in the following 14.2 on balancing perspectives for planning in the utility industry.

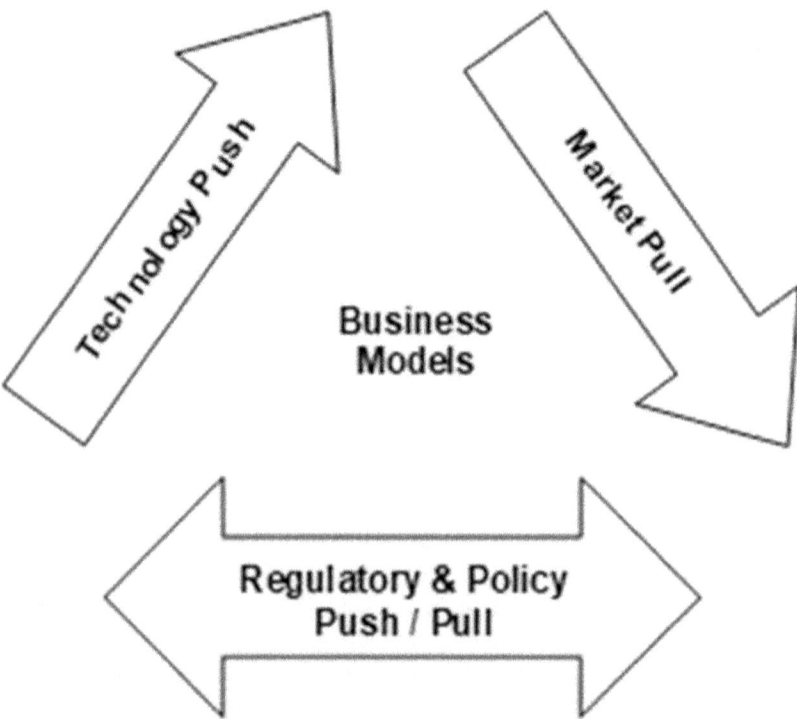

Figure 14.2 Balancing Planning Perspectives in Regulated Industries

Business models are shown occupying the central space in the above diagram, as they are reliant on technology, market, and policy factors. They can be seen as a means for implementing successful combinations of these factors. The exact combination of factors can be visualized as a shape, if you will, that represents the space made available by the dynamic action of the other three factors. For the purposes of this research, this visual metaphor is essential for understanding the central importance of business models and the essential nature of an integrated approach to understanding successful technological innovation. Furthermore, while these points are likely applicable to a wide range of industries, the central role of regulation and policy on the utility industry, and the impact it exerts on shaping business models are seen as a reason why it may be particularly important for this research.

3. Research design

The Research Gaps, Research Goals and Research Questions determined after performing all the analysis up to this point in this study are summarized below.

The Research Objective is to develop an integrated planning process to address technology, business models, regulatory, and policy issues for electric vehicle smart charging systems to meet utility needs in regions like the Pacific Northwest. Based on these objectives, three main research questions are created to guide this study. The first research question is: What are the highest priority technologies, gaps and barriers for creating EVSC systems that meet business, regulatory, and regional energy policy objectives? The second research question is: Is TRM an appropriate tool for understanding technology, business, regulatory, and regional energy policy objectives? The third research question is: RQ3: Can TRM be combined with business modeling and prioritization to better understand key requirements for creating a plan for EVSC in the PNW that meets business, regulatory, and regional energy policy objectives? The next section then explains the industry focus for this study.

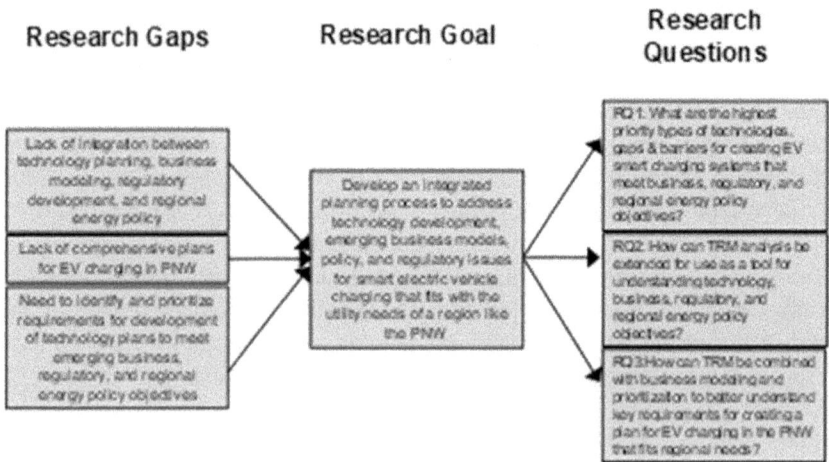

Research Gaps   **Research Goal**   **Research Questions**

Figure 14.3 Summary of Research Gaps, Goals, and Questions

The following diagram outlines the key steps needed to conduct the research described in the paper up to this point. Additional detail about each of the steps is then provided in the next sections.

		Phase 1	Phase 2	Phase 3	Phase 4
Documents		Technology Planning for Business, Regulatory & Policy Integration	Start-up Business Model Development	Industry Analysis	Prioritization & Verification	Analysis & Synthesis
Methods		Research Design Diagram	Business Concept Development	Modified 5 Forces (Reg Indus), Profit Modeling	TRM Constrcution & Prioritization	Integrated TRM & Analysis
Processes		Literature, Experts (6-8)	Literature, Email Virtual Panel (6-8)	Literature, Email Virtual Panel (6-8)	Workshop (12-16)	Research Synthesis, Expert Feedback (12-18)
Description		Utility Experts, Pol Anlyts, EV/V2G Bus & Tech Experts	Utility Execs, Pol Anlyts, EV/V2G Bus Experts	Utility Execs, Pol Anlyts, EV/V2G Bus Experts	Utility Experts, Pol Anlyts, EV/V2G Bus & Tech Experts	Data Analysis, Validation & Conclusions
Validation		Content & Face Validity Tools	Content Validity Tools	Content Validity Tools	Criteria Validity Tools	Criteria Validity Tools
Examples		Complete B&R Model and Complete Prioritized TRM	Stakeholder-Objective Matrix, Business Sub-Models, Business Summary, Stakeholder Perspectives, and Business Model Overview	Modified 5 Forces Model, Business-Stakeholder Alternatives Matrix, Industry Factor Alternatives Matrix, Statics & Dynamic Business Models	Grouped Drivers, Impact Matrices, Initial TRM and Prioritization	Final Integrated TRM, Analysis or Alternatives and Priorities

Figure 14.4 Research Outline

The overall goal of this research is to conduct technology planning for business, regulatory and policy integration. This is shown in the second column of the research outline above. Conducting this research requires a comprehensive review of the literature streams, an expert panel of utility and policy experts, as well as a panel of technology and business experts. Expert judgment is used to assess factors required to create business models and consider other relevant business and regulatory factors. Data gathered for the research will have to be verified and validated or consistency and reliability. It is then used to construct a technology roadmap and prioritize the items on that roadmap. All this information is then analyzed to create an integrated and prioritized roadmap that considers business, regulatory, and technology factors.

The research process used for this study will consist of four phases:

1. Start-up Business Model Development;

2. Industry Analysis;

3. Prioritization and Verification; and

4. Analysis and Synthesis.

Methods, Processes, Descriptions, Validation Techniques, and Examples of specific deliverables are also summarized in the Research Outline table.

Strategic alignment of the business model and policy frameworks is particularly important for regulated industries like electric utilities (Rouse and Kelly, 2011, Shively and Ferrare, 2010). Utilities generally have large capital costs, high barriers to entry, and increasing efficiencies of scale. This gives them many characteristics of natural monopolies. With rapid technology advances in the utility sector, one key issue is the need to overcome chronically low levels of R&D investment in the industry, estimated at around 0.25% of revenues (NSF, 2010). Thus, it is necessary to incorporate an understanding of utility regulation and planning processes (Rawson and Sugar, 2007, Chuang, 2011) to create alignment (Duann et al., 1994, Rose et al., 1997) between business models and policy frameworks (Nauda and Hall, 1991a), and technology development (Galvin et al., 2009).

Unique energy policy planning issues exist in Pacific Northwest due to multiple regulatory frameworks at the state (Brown and Satler, 2010), federal (NPCC, 1994), and regional (Hussler et al., 2010, Thukral et al., 2008) levels. Implementing improved smart grid roadmaps will take considerable amounts of discipline spanning knowledge (Daim and Oliver, 2008, Cowan and Daim, 2009, Daim et al., 2012). A multiple perspectives view (Linstone and Turoff,

1975, Saaty, 2000, Salmeron and Herrero, 2005) is critical for creating robust planning models in the utility industry (Dragoon, 2011, Nickell, 2009), (Willyard and McClees, 1987a) and incorporate these inputs into a roadmapping process that an understanding of utility regulation and planning processes to create strategic alignment between business models and policy frameworks. TRM methods need to be adapted to unique regulatory frameworks for regional utility industries (Bray and Garcia, 1997, Phaal et al., 2004). Overall, there is a strong need for robust, multiple perspective planning models in the utility industry that create strategic alignment between business models, policy, and regulatory requirements.

4. Conclusion

The main outcome of this research is the development of a process to help integrate technology roadmapping with business modeling, as well as regulatory and policy planning, and to thus enable a better understanding of opportunities for emerging technologies in emerging environments. This process is expected to be especially important for dealing with highly regulated industries, such as the utility sector, which has historically had one of the lowest rates of research and development investment of any major technology-based industry, only 0.25% of revenue (NSF, 2010). There are many reasons for this, including common regulatory structures, and various justifications for such regulatory structures, as discussed in previous sections. However, the result of this investment pattern has clearly been a slow, careful deployment of technology, which has focused on durable, well-understood devices and systems that have often been deployed and operated for decades at a time. While this may have had some favorable effect of protecting utility ratepayers from investing in risky or uncertain new technologies, it has also caused the industry to remain one that is still largely analog and manual in an age where many if not most other technologies are becoming digital and automated. To develop and successfully deploy critical new energy-related technology in the 21st century, at a time of increasing concern and urgency over rising energy costs and environmental damage caused by current technology, careful planning will be required. New methods which gracefully integrate technology, business, regulatory, and policy considerations into a holistic planning approach may prove extremely useful. Creating a framework to assist with such efforts is a primary aim of this research.

This research also focuses on the emerging smart grid industry, since smart grid technologies appear to have great potential to drive future innovation in the electric utility sector. This framework could be applied to many other emerging technology and industry environments as well, but new tools are needed to tailor the development process to a variety of unique requirements. This research offers one such set of tools and processes to achieve this goal.

Several types of roadmaps were created to examine different aspects of this research. First, an overall roadmap was created that shows the combined effect of business, consumer, regulatory, and market factors over the entire 10-year time span of the roadmap. The roadmap shows many key elements that relate to ownership structure and primary profit mechanism for stakeholders involved in implementing aspects of the roadmap. These mechanisms included: Direct fees for vehicle charging and/or parking fees; membership fees and fees for other bundled and premium services, such as internet access or auxiliary vehicle power hook-up fees; advertiser fees or fees for consumers to opt-out of advertisements; ancillary service fees, which provide essential services to utilities, such as voltage and frequency regulation; or energy efficiency optimization contracts and energy aggregation contracts, which allow a network operator to manage and optimize energy use over a grid or micro-grid. The roadmap was then broken into two parts. Section A shows a Business and Regulatory focused version of the roadmap. Section B shows Consumer and Market focused version of the roadmap. Options for financing and distribution methods related to each business model were then considered under the discussion of business models and in Appendix F, where each of the business model specifications is described. Analysis was then done on what business models may be used to implement various aspects of the roadmaps that have been developed. To summarize the main business model challenges, expert input was gathered to create a taxonomy of business models appropriate for the issues discussed in the roadmap construction process. The models were divided into Investor-Owned structures, Utility-Owned structures and Aggregator-Owned structures. This research provides tools to help stakeholders interested in exploring details about each of the 31 business model variations to quickly sort through large amounts of information related to each of the industry options most relevant to them. This allows them to determine appropriate paths to achieve their goals.

5. Implications and future research

This research is intended to help improve the processes for envisioning and planning the introduction of emerging technologies into industries like the electrical utility sector. Historically, this industry has been slow to embrace modern information and communication technologies, due to a variety of factors, including relatively durable regulatory structures that have long been common in many parts of the world, as well as a difficulty creating products that have appropriate business models to meet regulatory and policy needs. A key goal of this research is to better integrate technology development with regulatory, policy, and business model development, to increase the likelihood of successful innovation. Within the utility industry, introduction of technologies related to grid modernization, or smart grid, have a particularly strong relevance to this research. However, development of a method that is useful in that area is also expected to have implications for improvements in many other industries, which have a variety of regulatory structures. This research performed a case study on the development of an integrated technology roadmapping process for electric vehicle charging. Specific analysis of details of that case are provided in Chapter 7 and summarized in the previous section. In addition to specific practical recommendations regarding the case study, this research provides a number of other important contributions to several fields of knowledge.

This research reviewed and analyzed many literature streams. It examined the current state of knowledge regarding smart grid technology and the emerging smart grid industry. In the process, it also examined the history of the U.S. electrical utility industry, as well as some of the relevant literature on utility economics. Integrated Resource Planning is another literature stream that was examined in the process of understanding how technology has been developed and deployed in this sector. Literature on energy policy and regulation was examined, as well as specific analysis regarding the policy landscape that has developed for the Pacific Northwest region of the U.S. Closely tied to policy and regulatory issues, new frameworks, such as transactive energy structures were explored, and this, in turn, was specifically related to electric vehicle charging and vehicle-to-grid technology specifically. The technology roadmapping literature was also examined as a unifying concept for envisioning the technology development and deployment over time. Efforts specifically related to "smart grid roadmaps" were examined, and it was determined that few if any of the previous efforts in that literature stream would resemble those used in the technology roadmapping literature. Therefore, this research fills a gap by providing a technology roadmap on electric vehicle charging.

Furthermore, this research ties together important technology adoption concepts regarding "technology push" and "market pull" and offers several new concepts relevant to regulated industries, like electrical utilities. In addition to technology roadmaps balancing the technology push and market pull perspectives, it is proposed that regulated industries also have a significant "regulatory and policy push / pull" force that mediates between the technology push and market pull perspectives. Regulation can, for instance, distort market conditions, as well as place constraints on technology. Business models--which attempt to find a practical combination to solve the problem of competing technology, market, regulatory and policy forces--are affected by these simultaneous dynamics.

This research also examined relevant literature related to business models and tied it in to technology development business concept development, and analysis of industry forces. A set of general categories and characteristics were developed regarding the forces affecting the industry. A taxonomy of 31 business models were then develop and coded so that they could be easily distinguished and compared. These ideas were then connected to the technology roadmapping and prioritization process. Analytical tools were provided to show how specific roadmap elements over short-, medium-, and long-term planning horizons related to each business model. This provides an important resource for comparing elements of existing business models on the roadmap and helping stakeholders who wish to better understand this complex area. By providing a systematic framework for categorizing and comparing models as they relate to the roadmaps, it provides an excellent platform for adding further detail about models or as well as providing possible insights on the development of new models. More about this is addressed in the final section on limitations and further work.

There are a number of important assumptions for the selection of expert panels for judgment quantification. These include the following:

1. All experts are assumed to be knowledgeable and be able to give independent judgments in their areas of expertise.

2. Biases of experts are expected to balance within panels of experts.

This study is designed to develop a process for improving technology planning by integrating technology roadmapping and prioritization, business modeling, and regulatory and policy analysis. The following limitations should be considered:

1. The research case study is limited to specific smart grid technologies, such as emerging vehicle-to-grid technologies that are current being experimented with in demonstration projects in Oregon and the Pacific Northwest. While future studies may indicate that the findings of this research are applicable to other technologies and other regions, the current case study has not considered other technologies or regional contexts.

2. The outputs of this research rely on the subjective judgments of the experts. Limited knowledge and biases might affect the validity of the model.

This research offers a number of potential areas for future work. First, additional details could be added regarding any specific technologies, business models, or other roadmap elements analyzed in this study. Many of the topics studied are complex and additional research could be done on one of these areas alone. Business models, for example, could be developed in further detail, or additional models could be developed. This study provides an organized framework for categorizing and comparing roadmap elements. The more that people continue to build upon that framework, the more valuable it becomes. The method could also be applied to other smart grid or utility-related technologies. This could provide important insights both about specific emerging technologies and help understand how they might impact other similar technologies that may soon be developed or deployed. It could also be applied to other regulated industries outside the smart grid and the utility sector. It is expected to be generally applicable to other regulated industries, but case studies are needed to demonstrate this. It could also be compared to other roadmapping techniques and analytical methods. It would be valuable to see if industry practitioners are able to use the method to achieve improved results over other methods.

References

Amin, S. M. & Wollenberg, B. F. (2006). 'Toward a Smart Grid'. *IEEE Power & Energy*, 4, 66.

Bray, O. H. & Garcia, M. L. (1997). 'Technology Roadmapping: The Integration of Strategic and Technology Planning for Competitiveness', Portland, OR, PICMET (Portland International Conference on Management of Engineering and Technology).

Brown, A. & Satler, R. (2010). Smart Grid Issues in State Law and Regulation. Galvin Electricity Initiative.

Chuang, A. (2011). 'California Utility Vision and Roadmap for the Smart Grid of 2020: Final Project Report' [Online]. Sacramento, CA: California Energy Commission (CEC).

Coombs, R., Saviotti, P. & Walsh, V. (1987). *Economics and Technological Change*, Totowa, N.J., Rowman & Littlefield.

Costello, K. W. & Burns, R. E. (2000). 'Regional Transmission Organizations and the Coordination of Regional Electricity Markets: A Review of FERC Order 2000', Columbus, Ohio, National Regulatory Research Institute.

Cowan, K. R. & Daim, T. U. (2009). 'Comparative Technological Roadmapping for Renewable Energy'. *Technology in Society*, 31, 333-341.

Cramer, C. (2001). *Thomas Edison*, San Diego, CA, Greenhaven Press.

Daim, T. & Oliver, T. (2008). 'Implementing Technology Roadmapping Process: A Case Study of a Government Agency'. *Technology Forecasting & Social Change*, 75, 687-720.

Daim, T. U., Amer, M. & Brenden, R. (2012). 'Technology Roadmapping for Wind Energy: Case of the Pacific Northwest'. *Journal of Cleaner Production*, 20, 27-37.

Dragoon, K. (2011). *RE: Lowest Cost Balancing Resources.*

Duann, D. J., Chen, B., (c.1994). National regulatory research, i. & national association of regulatory utility, A Survey of Recent State Initiatives on EPACT and FERC Order 636, Columbus, Ohio, National Regulatory Research Institute.

EEI (2017). *Industry Data: Statistical Highlights.* Edison Electric Institute.

Filippini, M. (1998). 'Are Municipal Electricity Distribution Utilities Natural Monopolies?'. *Annals of Public and Cooperative Economics*, 69, 157.

Fox-Penner, P. (2010). Smart Power: Climate Change, Smart Grid, & the Future of Electric Utilities.

Galvin, R. W., Yeager, K. E. & Stuller, J. (2009). *Perfect Power: How the Microgrid Revolution Will Unleash Cleaner, Greener, and More Abundant Energy*, New York, McGraw-Hill.

Hammerstrom, D. J., Gephart, J. M. & Pacific Northwest National Laboratory, R. W. A. (2006). 'Smart Technology Brings Power to the People'. *Power Engineering International*, 14(10):45-46.

Holmes, C. & Ferrill, M. (2005a). 'The Application of Operation and Technology Roadmapping to Aid Singaporean SMEs Identify and Select Emerging Technologies'. *Technological Forecasting and Social Change*, 72, 349.

Hussler, C., Tang, M. & Picard, F. (2010). 'Taking the Ivory from the Tower to Coat the Economic World: Regional Strategies to make Science Useful'. *Technovation*, 30, 508-518.

Insull, S. & Keily, W. E. (1915). Central Station Electric Service: Its Commercial Development and Economic Significance, Chicago.

Jenkins, J., Bauman, J. & Bissonette, J. (2007). Renewable Energy Standard Powering Oregon's Future.

Linstone, H. A. & Turoff, M. (1975). *The Delphi Method: Techniques and Applications*, Reading, MA, Addison-Wesley Publishing Company.

Nauda, A. & Hall, D. (1991a). *Strategic Technology Planning - Developing Roadmaps for Competitive Advantage.* PICMET 1991. Portland, OR: PICMET.

Nickell, B. M. (2009). Wind Dispatchability and Storage - Interconnected Grid Perspective. EERE (Energy Efficiency & Renewable Energy Department).

NPCC., (2007). 'Northwest Wind Integration Action Plan', NPCC (Northwest Power & Conservation Council)

NSF., (2010). 'Funds for Industrial R&D as a Percent of Net Sales of Companies Performing Industrial R&D in the United States'. Washington, DC: National Science Foundation (NSF).

Phaal, R., Farrukh, C. & Probert, D. (2001). T-Plan: The Fast-Start to Technology Roadmapping - Planning your Route to Success, Cambridge, University of Cambridge, Institute for Manufacturing.

Phaal, R., Farrukh, C. J. P. & Probert, D. R. (2004). 'Technology Roadmapping - A Planning Framework for Evolution and Revolution'. *Technological Forecasting and Social Change.*, 71, 5.

Rawson, M. & Sugar, J. (2007). 'Distributed Generation and Cogeneration Policy Roadmap for California. Sacramento', CA: California Energy Commission.

Rose, K., Burns, R. E. & Graniere, R. J. (1997). Research Report: Summary of Key state Issues of FERC orders 888 and 889, Columbus, OH, National Regulatory Research Institute.

Rouse, G. & Kelly, J. (2011). Electricity Reliability: Problems Progress and Policy Solutions. Galvin Electricity Initiative.

Saaty, T. L. (2000). *Fundamentals of Decision Making and Priority Theory with the Analytic Hierarchy Process*, Pittsburgh, PA, RWS Publications.

Salmeron, J. L. & Herrero, I. (2005). 'An AHP-Based Methodology to Rank Critical Success Factors of Executive Information Systems'. *Computer Standards and Interfaces*, 28, 1-12.

Schumpeter, J. A. & Opie, R. (1934). *The Theory of Economic Development: An Inquiry into Profits, Capital, Credit, Interest, and the Business Cycle*, Cambridge, MA, Harvard University Press.

Shively, B. & Ferrare, J. (2010). *Understanding today's electricity business*, Laporte, CO, Enerdynamics.

Stimmel, C. L. (2015). Big data analytics strategies for the smart grid.

Thukral, I. S., Von Ehr, I. J. R., Walsh, S., Groen, A. J., Van der Sijde, P. & Akmaliah Adham, K. (2008). 'Entrepreneurship, Emerging Technologies, Emerging Markets'. *International Small Business Journal*, 26, 101-116.

Walsh, S. T. (2004). 'Roadmapping a Disruptive Technology: A Case Study'. *Technological Forecasting and Social Change*, 71, 161-185.

Willyard, C. & Mcclees, C. (1987a). 'Motorola's Technology Roadmap'. *Research Management*, 13-19.

Chapter 15

From Gamestorming to Mobile Learning: a Conceptual Framework and a Gaming Proposition to Explore the Design of Flourishing Business Models

Albert Lejeune*

E-mail: lejeune.albert@uqam.ca

Abstract: The thesis starts with a literature review, conceptual framework building and research problem definition. This research contrasts Business Models (BMs) developed under a more traditional computational-interpretative cognitive view with BMs for a flourishing future (BMFs) calling for new preconditions, namely situated cognition and macrocognition. In this way, actors design a BMF through their sensorimotor interface to socio- and physical materiality where meaning emerges from multiple interactions. Also, a BMF becomes a shared public object open to social competence development in a situation where macrocognition principles apply. Thus, the Flourishing – Artificiality – Cognition (FAC) framework is produced to better understand differences between BM and BMF. Results from action research both with MBA students and managers are presented. Then, an open platform architecture, namely SustAbd©, is proposed through a reflection on the game design process.

Keywords: Business Model; Sustainability; Cognition; Macrocognition; Materiality; Game storming; Mobile Learning; Action Research; Design.

1. Introduction

Managers and MBA students are taking stock that, year after year, the natural environment finds its way into managerial practices, strategy and business models. Compared to the strategy concept, a business model (BM) seems to be an abstract artefact detached from any organizational context. In contrast to the inherent subjectivity of the strategy concept, a BM reaches a kind of objective status because it is computable: in the end, a BM, as a mix of corporate finance and corporate strategy formalized within a spreadsheet, generates costs and revenues. With this in mind, this thesis explores the interactions between a BM, the physical environment and cognition, where BMs tend to become BMFs or BMs for a flourishing future like as defined by Ehren-feld (2008) and Ehrenfeld and Hoffman (2013).

However, instead of 'pure' BMFs' emergence, we can observe these days the birth and evolution of a kind of 'green' management that's constrained and limited inside organizational hierarchies determined to prove the reality of their 'green façade.' The stakes are high; sustainability discourses are every-where. The VW Group demonstrated its commitment to sustainability on its corporate website, was ranked first—in 2013—on the Dow Jones Sustainabil-ity Index for automakers sector. Then, in fall 2015, came the VW dieselgate in the U.S. regarding the TDI motor. Reading about the VW case (Monti et al., 2016) shows us that: First, VW had a well-developed CSR (Corporate Social Responsibility) function; second, a leader who declared that VW was becom-ing a world leader in sustainability; and, third, VW received the 'Green Car of the Year' (2009) label for the Jetta TDI and was ranked among the best com-panies in terms of sustainability.

So, what went wrong? First, 'sustainability' is so vague a concept and word that we—like Ehrenfeld (2008)—must back off from using the word. Second, a BM cannot be really 'green' or flourish inside a hierarchy where it must gen-erate the economic and strategic drive for strategists and shareholders look-ing for returns. Instead, the 'green' or flourishing dimension as defined by Ehrenfeld (2008) should be shared by different categories of actors inside and outside the hierarchy.

'Green' mental states should be shared by people with suppliers, custom-ers and stakeholders across enterprises inside a business ecosystem. The appeal that ecological transparency has for customers illustrates such a 'green' mental state. And a growing awareness of the physical limits of the planet, computed by ecological footprint measurement, is also a sharable mental state. In defining the concept of macrocognition as a shared mental state, Huebner (2013, 2014) offers a way to disentangle the tensions—and fallacies—between the BM and the hierarchy that leads to the development of 'green façade.' Quoting Huebner (2014): "Macrocognition cannot happen inside a hierarchy."

The design of a flourishing BM is like unchartered territory. If a few au-thors give some indications regarding the design of a new business model, only a few papers are considered as explicitly bringing sustainability to a BM. From a cognitive science angle, the objective of this thesis is to under-line the role of (inter)subjective invariants (i.e., values, beliefs, attitudes…) vs. external invariants (i.e., fixed categories) in a BMF design where compu-tation offers a too limited view but situated cognition is key. The goal is the specification of an architectural target using an original framework enabling the design of a game that facilitates collaboration and macrocognition between actors often experiencing incompatible visions and diverging interests but belonging to the same ecological space. What are the options for designing such an intelligent environment?

At least four types of intelligent environments are already deployed for sustainability training. First, sustainability science ontology could be the heart of an intelligent tutorial system. Second, the serious games approach could be chosen as games are developed to train managers to Global Reporting Initiative (GRI) reporting practices. Third, gamestorming with the business model canvas (BMC) (Osterwalder, 2004) is the approach behind sustainable BMs developed with the SSBMG group in Toronto. Finally, situated cognition can be applied to mobile learning. In this thesis, we first try to become acquainted with gamestorming to generate specifications for a mobile learning system enabling situated cognition and macrocognition. However, the projected system should relate to a sustainability science ontology.

2. Background

We see BMs' evolution over time in three steps: value BM (VBM), architectural BM (ABM) and sustainable BM or BM for a flourishing future (BMF).

(Digital) Value BM or VBM

The reasons why BMs came to designate a tool to compute and find selling arguments for e-business ventures are both theoretical and practical. Theoretically, following Copeland et al. (1990: p. ix):

> "In the last decade, two separate streams of thinking and activity—corporate finance and corporate strategy—have come together with a resounding crash. Corporate finance is no longer the exclusive preserve of financiers. Corporate strategy is no longer a separate realm ruled by CEOs". The link between strategy and finance has become very close and clear. Practically, Copeland et al. (1990) underline the role of "computing technology and analytical techniques that make it easier than ever before to identify potential targets" for mergers and acquisitions (pp. 18-19). Computing technology meant first and foremost the use of the VisiCalc software, a software developed by Dan Bricklin and inspired by a BM design problem.

The BM concept began to be heavily used in the business world around 1995 when entrepreneurs began designing electronic companies whose economic profits seemed so evident before the Internet bubble of 2000. At the time, BM designers adopted 'thin' design principles and practices. In the business world, BM reaches a kind of objective status because it is computable: in the end, a BM generates costs and revenues. In fact, BM is mostly a practical—not academic—concept (Eyquem-Renault, 2011); it's more of an explicit recipe than an identity-developing strategy. A BM canvas (BMC) considers the customer interface, offerings, costs and revenues computation and the activity system. BMC developers came from the MIS discipline that developed formal BM ontologies (Osterwalder, 2004). Cognitively speaking, a BM is a 'thing' (a mental representation) computed thanks to external invariants—BM canvases are made of key business categories—while subjective invariants promoting the subject role are outside the main BM paradigm. The absence of subjective invariants in BM design hampers the emergence of BM designed for strong sustainability.

Architectural BM or ABM

Following Teece (2010: p. 173), a BM, "if it is not a spreadsheet or computer model, might well become embedded in a business plan and in income statements and cash flow projections. But, clearly, the notion refers in the first instance to a conceptual, rather than a financial, model of a business." For Teece (2010), a BM is nothing less than the organizational and financial 'architecture' of a business. Zott and Amit (2010) essentially view a BM as an activity system; they describe it using two sets of parameters, design elements and design themes. Zott and Amit (2008) also posit that a business model, while often regarded as a paradox in business literature (Klang et al., 2014), is the modern complement of strategy formulation in business ecosystems and, in some way, a substitute for organizational structure. A BM's unit of analysis is bound only by the vast business ecosystem out of which it is emerging.

BM for a flourishing future or BMF

The quest for strong sustainability equates with the quest for a 'flourishing' business future (Laszlo and Sorum Brown, 2014), as stated by Ehrenfeld (2008) in his 'flourishing' manifesto. Ehrenfeld wrote on his blog: "Those who follow me know I am backing off from using the word 'sustainability' because it has become merely a jargon word with little or no meaning or a euphemism for continuing to do the same thing as before with perhaps some slight improvement." Conversely, a BMF requires the presence of conditions for situated cognition and macrocognition that are missing from traditional BMs. Corporate BM design and transformation relate to the power of a few influential and/or intelligent people, like senior executives, international consultants, and brilliant academics. The strategic drive created by an efficient BM fits a business hierarchy.

This thesis' stance is that traditional BMs belong to the computation/interpretation paradigm but the design and implementation of a BMF should require more than computation as cognitive processes and should include situated cognition and macrocognition. Our research angle is the following: a BMF—like a BM—is a cognitive artefact. But as a BM is developed under a more traditional computational-interpretative cognitive view, a BMF asks for new preconditions, namely situated cognition and macrocognition. In this way, actors design a BMF through their sensorimotor interface to socio- and physical materiality where meaning emerges from multiple interactions. Also, a BMF becomes a shared public object open to social competence development in a situation where macrocognition principles apply.

A BM can be described as the blueprint of a firm's business logic (Lüdeke-Freund, 2009a) and explains the rationale of how companies create, deliver and capture value. The key focus is on the firm and its exchange partners, in terms of illustrating the link between the firm and "the larger production and consumption system in which it operates" (Boons et al., 2013: p. 1; Lüdeke-Freund, 2009). Clearly, the BMF concept is still debated as a functional concept (Engeström and Sannino, 2012) because BMs in themselves are multifaceted and because sustainability opposes weak sustainability tenants to strong sustainability defenders and, finally, to 'flourishing' BM explorers. BMFs are still under debate, particularly when researchers oppose classical market techno-materiality (carbon market), socio-materiality (activity system) and physical materiality (physical environment, such as carbon cycles). Does 'end of pipe' regulation really equate to sustainability promotion? And do carbon markets equate to a sustainable initiative? It depends on one's definition of sustainability and on one's position as a stakeholder in the sustainability debate: polluter vs. environmentalist, citizen vs. regulator, etc.

3. Research design

Checkland (1985) introduced framework F definition as a key first step in action research (AR) while composing his 'Soft Systems Methodology' (SSM). In this research, a framework F - called FAC - enables VBM, then ABM and BMF design challenges to be discussed. We position BMF design in a 3D framework using Flourishing, Artificiality and Cognition axes (Figure 15.1). Per Checkland (1985), M declares the methodology to apply F to A, areas or fields of interest. In this thesis, there are two As: a teaching experiment with EMBA students and a table game specifically developed for managers working in the sustainable development unit (SDU) of a large Canadian city. M, in this thesis, as a methodological approach, is a mix of action research (participant observation, video and interviews coded in NVivo) and design science. Action research is the guide to apply F in A under M; design science (DS) is the guide to bring the lessons learned a step forward into the definition of a future artefact's specifications.

FAC Framework

This thesis' framework contribution is to integrate the cognitive dimension while positioning BMs vs BMFs. As a mix of finance, strategy and information technology, BMs are first designed for computing value creation and capture. On the contrary, BMFs are still functional concepts (Engeström and Sannino, 2012) having a subjective meaning for different people and an intersubjective meaning for different groups (possibility of macrocognition). This thesis thus posits three challenging design choices (Figure 15.2):

- The types of materiality (flourishing axis),

- The artificiality of designed objects (artificiality trajectory axis),

- The designer's or designers' cognitive modes (cognition axis).

Research Problem

Sustainability is still a debated 'functional' concept (Engeström and Sannino, 2012) interacting with computational BMs induced by GRI reporting practices. There isn't an easy way to create a BMF design because sustainability is about science and physical materiality while BM is a (non-scientific) practical value creation/capture pattern (made to stay as it is conceived) based on a combination of market immateriality and activity system socio-materiality.

We take a cognitive science point of view because literature in the field agrees on two observations: 1. lack of understanding of sustainability, and 2. lack of capabilities to design strongly sustainable business models. The sustainability-flourishing challenge is first a matter of cognition, both individual and organizational. 'Understanding,' with 'Remembering,' are referred to by Anderson and al. (2001) as the fundamental cognitive process while, at the other end of its taxonomy progression, 'Creating' sits at the top of the cognitive processes. It can be hypothesized that the whole range of cognitive processes and knowledge types are questioned by the introduction of sustainability in BMs. The research problem is thus formulated using learning theories established by Anderson et al. (2001) and Kolb and Kolb (2005).

Research Objectives

1. Evaluate traditional BM gamestorming usefulness in the context of BMF design. Even if this thesis' objective is not to discuss traditional BM design, research design will let students and managers use a traditional BM canvas in the context of BMF design. This thesis' results may shed some light on traditional BM canvas transposition in a BMF design context.

2. Experiment FAC research framework robustness by organizing practical experiments. This experimentation is done in two different contexts. First, there is an ontologizing approach within an EMBA classroom to develop methods and practices of collaboration, even inverted teaching, around an energy company case. This experiment is designed to push the envelope on the cognition axis. Second, a table game is invented and played by city sustainability managers who will need to use a BM canvas to develop a BMF. Here, fluid navigation is the essence, especially between discourses and BMF's products and services. This thesis' results may contribute to defining the learning processes implicit in various activities intended to stimulate BMF design like gaming, gamification, serious gaming and gamestorming.

3. Transfer lessons learned into high-level virtual tutor requirements. Experiments, observations and analysis will generate results regarding any BM and BMF differences interpretable in the FAC framework on cognition, artificiality and flourishing themes. In other words, third objective is to define and transfer key use cases that could be instructive into a UML language to specify a virtual robot dedicated either to gamestorming or mobile learning.

4. Conclusion

In the FAC framework, the F axis is named 'Flourishing' following Ehrenfeld and Hoffman's (2013) view of sustainability. 'Artificiality' axis (the X-axis) comes from the philosophy of design. Interpreting Krippendorff's (1997, 2007) understanding of design progression from concrete to abstract, it is possible to position a BM's elements along an 'artificiality trajectory' where designers start with a concrete product and end with a project and an abstract discourse, or the reverse. Finally, the cognition axis C considers four designers' cognitive modes from computation to interpretation, situated cognition and macrocognition (Figure 15.1).

Figure 15.1 displays BM categories for different materiality types. For example, for 'Products,' the 'Products' cube 49 brings data to three dimensions: 1. An artificiality level (the products are concrete elements), 2. a materiality level (at techno-materiality level, products are products' data and metadata) and 3. a cognition level (in this case, a computation level where products' costs and revenues are calculated or life cycle computed). At the artificiality level, the challenge is to produce a coherent discourse and/or a vision and/or a backcasting approach. At the materiality level, the challenge is to produce 'green' products through 'green' processes and 'green' activity systems inside a circular economy. At the cognition level, the challenge is to move forward, beyond computation and interpretation, toward situated cognition and macrocognition as cognitive modes.

'Services' are next to products while 'Interfaces' regroup customer channels and supply chains. The 'organizational change' dimension clearly belongs to the socio-materiality level and leads to new interactions between members of organizations inside more lateral structures enabling new organizational behaviors. If some aspects of 'organizational change' can be computed (training costs etc.), its execution calls for interpretation as cognitive mode to evacuate all related ambiguities.

The Cognition axis (the Z Axis: Designers' Cognitive Modes) makes clearer the differences about what is happening cognitively to BM vs. BMF designers: BM designers are measuring and interpreting business logic while BMF designers are adding to that sensing and discussing—individually and/or as a community—what is happening to their 'place' in terms of sustainability and value generation/capture. In fact, BM being mostly a practical concept without any spatial dimension, managers and/or shareholders/stakeholders discuss, design and compute their BMs as they have the legitimacy to act that way. So, one extremity of the cognition axis is assimilated into individual computation inside an organizational hierarchy set up to achieve the goals or realize the intentions of a few powerful and/or intelligent people (Huebner, 2014). By contrast, the other extremity is illustrated by a community of people, living in and inhabiting a 'place,' who meet the conditions of macrocognition (Huebner, 2014). Both powerful people and situated communities are benefitting from technologies enabling cognitive extension (Clark, 2008). Both groups are practicing computation and interpretation as cognitive modes. However, logical modes may differ. The literature shows (Moore, 2007) that, if sustainability management is often a matter of induction/deduction between theory and facts using predefined categories, it is rather formulated and executed in an abductive logical mode in leading 'green' cities.

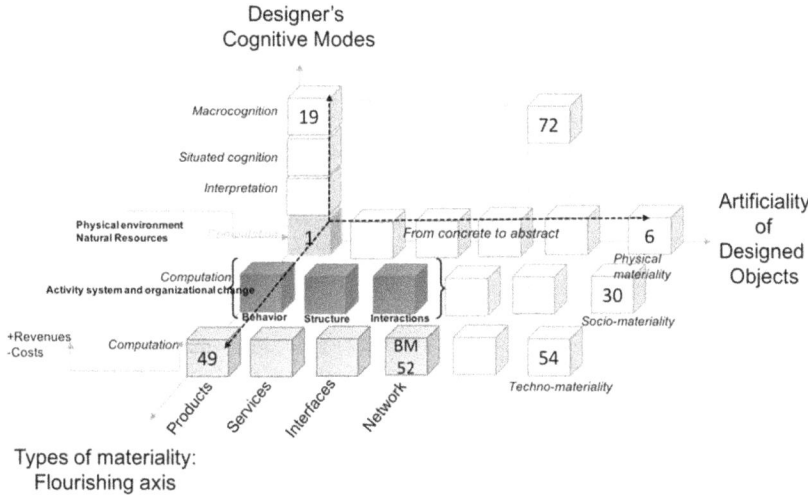

Figure 15.1 From Cube 1: Three Challenges from the Physical Environment

5. Implications and future research

Per Moore (2007), managers who reason with logical deduction construct idealized models, that is pre-political and "thin" models rather than "dense" models. These models are static, do not reflect the Bruntdland report (1987) and offer only one possible form of democracy: liberal capitalism. In a way, models and lists referring to sustainability can be useful as heuristic and analytical tools. However, they tend to suppress public speaking required to motivate action in a 'place'. In fact, following Moore (2007), sustainability models and lists are produced by social scientists who studied the past through rational methods of deduction (models) and induction (lists). However, planners and urban planners—in the study by Moore (2007)—seem to be much more productive than social scientists, generating a sustainable future using abduction as a logic design.

BM, as an artefact, lies in the middle of Krippendorff's 'Trajectory of Artificiality' between customer interface and innovation project levels: "There is no need to force users to know what designers know about an artefact, but there are good reasons for designers to know the conceptions that users have available to approach the artefact they are asked to design. (Krippendorf, 2007: p. 18).

Abduction as Logical Mode

At one extremity (computation), the Cognition axis in the FAC grid represents the analytical aspect of the scientific method: hypothesis, experiment and theory constitute the way science examines the real to create knowledge. At the other extremity (situated cognition, macrocognition), knowledge must be used to create a new reality through new artefacts. In this case, science is a science of synthesis using abduction as a logical mode to solve complex problems. With sustainability science, the work of Kumazawa et al. (2009) has designed the structure of knowledge and helps thinking in this direction. They focus on the challenges of structuring knowledge in the science of sustainability; they identify requirements for structuring knowledge while providing a reference model and developing a mapping tool based on ontologies.

BMC and BMF as Conceptual Artefacts

As previously stated, BMs and BMFs are cognitive artefacts. Their nature is that of a designed object (and some designs are better than others), as an object playing a cognitive role (and therefore an object whose design must support this feature), as an external object with which we interact (and therefore part of the perspective of situated cognition) and as a public object that several people can use at the same time (and therefore part of the macrocognitive perspective). The concept of BMs and BMFs as cognitive artefacts could anchor everything we can say about BMFs from a cognitive point of view.

Future Research: Implementing the FAC Framework

A general criticism from evaluation committee members was that the FAC framework was underexplored, specifically on the cognition dimension. So, the first step would be to better describe mental states defining players' cognition modes from computation to macrocognition. Finally, future research should:

- Experiment Logim@s© game with a new population, on multiple sites, in real time

- Enhance game functionalities

- Design original games from different table game models or from video games

- Develop gamestorming platform elements

- Connect platforms with sustainability science ontology

- Connect platforms with computer assisted abduction tools

- Experiment the approach on business ecosystem scale

- Develop the virtual tutor through player-tutor dialogues

- Monitor macrocognition conditions and ease social reasoning during the debriefing period.

Contribution of this Research, Limits and Conclusion

This research was mostly exploratory. The starting point was BMC gamestorming's popular success vs. field research surveys confirming that a BMF was a managerial challenge illustrating both a lack of design capabilities and a lack of understanding of sustainability. By opposing BMC 'thin' design and BMF 'thick' design, we introduced socio- and physical materiality to form the FAC grid which uses Krippendorff's 'Artificiality Trajectory.' Contrasting the way discourse tries to sell a new BM, vision proposes a new organizational architecture while backcasting identifies piecemeal changes leading actors to a desirable and flourishing future. These research propositions were developed and tested through course material and the development of an original game. From the observations that were made, a BMF gamestorming platform design was proposed with a virtual tutor definition designed to be a substitute for a human tutor.

This research neither creates nor proves any theory. The researcher used action research and kept a design science stance. However, gamestorming ideas emerged from numerous interactions in the field as well as a sound literature review at the intersection of BMs, sustainability and cognition. Both the literature review and field research are the foundations of the FAC framework. SustAbd© development could use extant technologies like intelligent tutors, the Universal Abduction Studio, the Sustainability Science ontology created in Japan, much of the recently developed knowledge in new business models and sustainability and big data tools. However, free exchanges with professionals in real settings using simple table games seems to be a low-cost but high-return way to better define and build SustAbd©.

References

Anderson, L. W., Krathwohl, D. R., Airasian, P. W., Cruikshank, K. A., Mayer, R. E., Pintrich, P. R., … Wittrock, M. C. (2001). *A taxonomy for learning, teaching, and assessing: A revision of Bloom's taxonomy of educational objectives*, abridged edition. White Plains, NY: Longman.

Baskerville, R. L., and Wood-Harper, A. T. (2016). A Critical Perspective on Action Research as a Method for Information Systems Research. In L. P. Willcocks, C. Sauer, and M. C. Lacity (Eds.), *Enacting Research Methods in Information Systems: Volume 2* (pp. 169–190). Springer International Publishing.

Boons, F., and Lüdeke-Freund, F. (2013). 'Business models for sustainable innovation: state- of-the-art and steps towards a research agenda'. *Journal of Cleaner Production, 45,* 9– 19.

Boons, F., Montalvo, C., Quist, J., and Wagner, M. (2013). 'Sustainable innovation, business models and economic performance: an overview'. *Journal of Cleaner Production, 45,* 1–8.

Checkland, P. (1985). 'From optimizing to learning: A development of systems thinking for the 1990s'. *Journal of the Operational Research Society,* 36(9), 757–767.

Chesbrough, H. (2010). 'Business model innovation: opportunities and barrier's. *Long Range Planning,* 43(2), 354–363.

Clark, A. (2008). *Supersizing the Mind: Embodiment, Action, and Cognitive Extension: Embodiment, Action, and Cognitive Extension.* Oxford University Press, New York, NY.

Clark, W. C., and Dickson, N. M. (2003). 'Sustainability science: The emerging research program'. Proceedings of the National Academy of Sciences, 100(14), 8059–8061.

Copeland, T., Koller, T., and Murrin, J. (1990). *Valuation. Measuring and managing the value of companies.* McKinsey and Company, Inc.

Ehrenfeld, J. (2008). *Sustainability by Design: A Subversive Strategy for Transforming Our Consumer Culture.* Yale University Press, New Haven, CT.

Ehrenfeld, J., and Hoffman, A. (2013). *Flourishing: A Frank Conversation about Sustainability.* Stanford University Press, Redwood, CA.

Engeström, Y., and Sannino, A. (2012). 'Concept formation in the wild'. *Mind, Culture, and Activity, 19*(3), 201–206.

Eyquem-Renault, M. (2011, December 6). *Analyse pragmatique du business model et performances de marché dans l'entrepreneuriat technologique,* Ph.D. Thesis. École Nationale Supérieure des Mines de Paris, Paris.

Huebner, B. (2013). 'Socially embedded cognition'. *Cognitive Systems Research, 25,* 13–18.

Huebner, B. (2014). *Macrocognition: A Theory of Distributed Minds and Collective Intentionality.* Oxford University Press, New York, NY.

Klang, D., Wallnöfer, M., and Hacklin, F. (2014).'The Business Model Paradox: A Systematic Review and Exploration of Antecedents'. *International Journal of Management Reviews,* 16: 454–478.

Kolb, A. Y., and Kolb, D. A. (2005). 'Learning styles and learning spaces: Enhancing experiential learning in higher education'. *Academy of Management Learning and Education,* 4(2), 193–212.

Krippendorff, K. (1997). 'A Trajectory of Artificiality and New Principles of Design for the Information Age'. *Design in the Age of Information, A Report to the National Science Foundation (NSF),* 91–96.

Krippendorff, K. (2007). 'An Exploration of Artificiality'. *Artifact, 1*(1), 17–22.

Kumazawa, T., Saito, O., Kozaki, K., Matsui, T., and Mizoguchi, R. (2009). 'Toward knowledge structuring of sustainability science based on ontology engineering'. *Sustainability Science, 4*(1), 99–116.

Laszlo, C., Brown, J., Robson, L., Saillant, R., and Sherman, D. (2014). *Flourishing Enterprise: The New Spirit of Business.* Stanford University Press, Sebastopol, CA.

Lüdeke-Freund, F. (2009). Business Model Concepts in Corporate Sustainability Contexts: From Rhetoric to a Generic Template for 'Business Models for Sustainability', *Centre for Sustainability Management (CSM), Leuphana Universität Lüneburg, ISBN*, 978–3.

Monti, C. et al. (2016). *Volkswagen's Clean Diesel Dilemma.* WDI Publishing, University of Michigan, Case 1-430-484.

Moore, S. A. (2007). *Alternative routes to the sustainable city: Austin, Curitiba, and Frankfurt.* Lexington Books, Toronto, ON.

Osterwalder, A. (2004). The Business Model Ontology-a proposition in a design science approach. *Academic Dissertation, Université de Lausanne, École Des Hautes Études Commerciales.*

Osterwalder, A. and Pigneur, Y. (2002). "An eBusiness Model Ontology for Modeling eBusiness" BLED 2002 Proceedings. Paper 2. http://aisel.aisnet.org/bled2002/2

Osterwalder, A., and Pigneur, Y. (2010). *Business Model Generation: A Handbook For Visionaries, Game Changers, And Challengers.* Wiley.

Osterwalder, A., Pigneur, Y., and Tucci, C. L. (2005). 'Clarifying business models: Origins, present, and future of the concept'. *Communications of the Association for Information Systems, 16*(1), 1.

Teece, D. J. (2007). 'Explicating dynamic capabilities: the nature and microfoundations of (sustainable) enterprise performance'. *Strategic Management Journal, 28*(13), 1319– 1350.

Teece, D. J. (2010). 'Business Models, Business Strategy and Innovation'. *Long Range Planning, 43*(2–3), 172–194.

Zott, C., and Amit, R. (2008). 'The fit between product market strategy and business model: implications for firm performance'. *Strategic Management Journal, 29*(1), 1–26.

Zott, C., and Amit, R. (2010). 'Business model design: an activity system perspective'. *Long Range Planning, 43*(2), 216–226.

Chapter 16

Chinese Multinational Enterprises' R&D "Going out": a Prelude to Inclusive Globalization

Sheng Wu*

E-mail: wusheng12b@mails.ucas.edu.cn

Abstract: This dissertation breaks the conventional thinking that "Globalization is for selected groups of countries or industrial sectors," and proposes a new philosophy of globalization, evidenced by Chinese Multinational Enterprises' (MNE) Research and Development (R&D) "going out" movement. It demonstrates trends and incentives of Chinese MNEs' overseas R&D activities, depicts the evolution of Chinese MNEs' global R&D networks, and theorizes the organizational configurations system which applies to MNEs in global range. It proposes a proposition that Chinese MNEs' overseas R&D activities have changed the old economic order, unveiling a new phase of "Inclusive Globalization," a globalization bringing opportunities to all.

Keywords: R&D globalization; incentives; locations; networks; R&D organizational configurations; Chinese MNEs; R&D "going out" strategy; inclusive globalization.

1. Introduction

Globalization has extended the geographical reach of firms and taken international competition into new trajectories. The globalization of Research and Development (R&D), the most knowledge-intensive corporate function, has been harnessed by companies to capture knowledge and market opportunities internationally (UNCTAD, 2005). While Chinese firms are late-comers in establishing overseas R&D subsidiaries (Sun, von Zedtwitz and Simon, 2007), against the backdrop of the *"Going Out" Strategy* and the *"Innovation-Driven Development" Strategy*, Chinese MNEs' overseas R&D investment has surged in recent years. The study on R&D globalization in Chinese MNEs' scenarios will contribute to academic discussion and management practices, due to China's increasingly important role in the global economy.

Development trend of Chinese MNEs' overseas R&D

Based on statistics from 1500 Chinese firms that established foreign R&D subsidiaries over the past five years (2012-2016) in 88 countries across the world,[1] trends of the overseas R&D of Chinese MNEs are identified as follows:

- First, the quantity of Chinese MNEs' overseas' R&D subsidiaries increased rapidly. (see Figure 16.1) Their parent firms are widely but unevenly distributed in China (See Figure 16.2).

- Secondly, Chinese MNEs' overseas' R&D subsidiaries have been widely distributed in both developed and developing countries, including the 10 least-developed countries (LDCs) (See Figure 16.3).

- Thirdly, the majority of MNEs are from the manufacturing (756), electronics (390), and Internet (66) industries, which is in line with China's traditional industry pattern as well as China's new industrial development trajectory shaped by government policy (See Figure 16.4).

---

1.   Source of statistics: Ministry of Commerce of P.R. China. Data collection method is elaborated in Part 3.

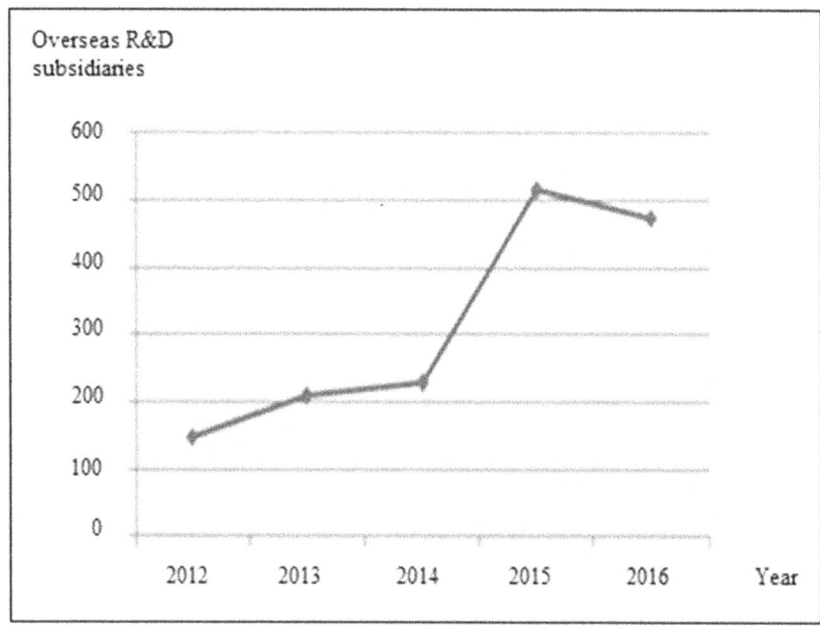

Figure 16.1 Number of overseas R&D subsidiaries

Figure 16.2 Regional distribution of parent firms

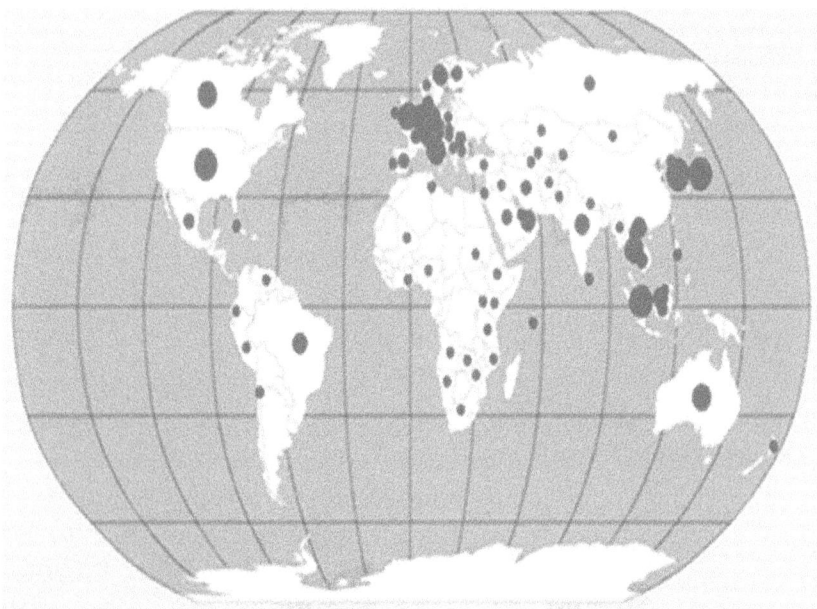

Figure 16.3 Global distribution of overseas R&D subsidiaries

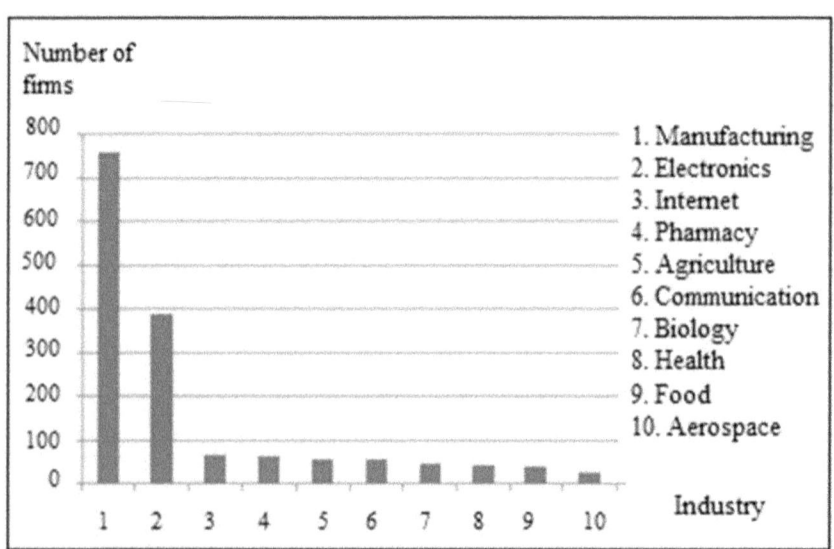

Figure 16.4 Industrial distribution of overseas R&D subsidiaries

(Statistics source of the four figures: Ministry of Commerce of China)

Motives of Chinese MNEs' R&D "going out" and its relation to globalization

Existing studies on the motives of overseas R&D investment by MNEs from Western countries focus on firm level. The motives observed and evidenced were market-supporting (Cordell, 1973; Niosi, 1999) and production-supporting (Casson and Singh, 1993). Study during the period starting in the 1990s until the early 2000s reflected that motives for obtaining new technology and developing new products had become increasingly significant (Von Zedtwitz &Gassmann, 2002). MNEs became active in both "asset-exploiting" and "asset-expanding" types of overseas R&D subsidiaries (Fagerberg, 2005).

The new tide of Chinese MNEs' overseas R&D investment rose in a different historical context. Chinese MNEs have been encouraged to establish overseas R&D subsidiaries by the national development policies, the *"Going out" strategy* and the *"Innovation-driven development"* strategy.[2] The Chinese central and provincial governments have issued a series of concrete measures to compel and subsidize "going out" for R&D. At the country level, the hand of the government has imposed powerful driving and shaping forces upon the tide. As a result, Chinese MNEs' overseas R&D investment has demonstrated different characteristics: firstly, while internationalization of R&D requires enterprises to have a certain level of resources and capacities, and large MNEs are considered to be main driver of R&D globalization in Western countries' scenario (OECD, 2008), a large number of small Chinese enterprises with limited capacities were able to quickly join the tide with government support. (Rui &Yip, 2008); secondly, Chinese MNEs have become pioneers in exploring overseas R&D in developing countries; thirdly, while Western MNEs tended to establish overseas R&D subsidiaries within their advantageous industries, China's top ten industries in R&D "going out" included both advantageous industries and some fledgling industries nurtured by the Chinese government.

Globalization is conventionally viewed as "globalization of selected groups of countries or industrial sectors" (Narula, 2003). The literature on economic "catch-up" categorizes countries into three groups. The first group is developed countries, which have converged in income, consumption and technology levels in the past decades. The second group contains more advanced industrialized

---

2. "Going out" strategy (1999-present) aims at promoting Chinese investments abroad. The Government has introduced several schemes to assist companies in exploiting international markets. "Innovation-driven development" strategy (2012-present) aims at making innovation the primary driving force for development. The Government has issued guidelines, turning China into an innovative nation by 2020, into the forefront of innovative countries by 2030, and into a world powerhouse of innovation by 2050 (Source: The State Council Information Office of P.R. China).

developing countries, which are catching up with the first group. The third group contains countries that have "fallen behind." in both a relative and absolute sense (Hikino and Amsden, 1994). That is to say, the convergence brought by globalization is "selective" (Narula, 2003). Chinese MNEs' overseas R&D has involved many developing countries, including LDCs, into the landscape of globalization, while Western MNEs only "selected" the first group (for technology and market) and the second group (for market).

Furthermore, China's top ten industries in R&D "going out" enlisted some low-tech and traditional industries, including manufacturing, agriculture and clothing. China is a "World Factory" and a largely agricultural country; labor-intensive industries, such as clothing industry, play an important role in the Chinese economy. During R&D "going out," Chinese MNEs have globalized these traditional and basic industries. This trend echoes the relationship between industrial capacities for obtaining new technology, and economic development in Lundvall (1997)'s "Learning Economy" theory. Learning Economy theory was established in the late 1990s, while R&D internationalization was transitioning into R&D globalization. The theory holds that the learning capability is crucial to the success of individuals, enterprises and countries. One crucial understanding of learning economy is that "it is not necessarily a high-tech economy." "Leaning is an activity which takes place in all parts of the economy, including so-called low-tech and traditional sectors" (Maskell, 1996). This feature of "Learning Economy" was absent from Western MNEs' R&D internationalization but distinctively presented by Chinese MNEs.

While globalization brings challenges and opportunities to Chinese MNEs, Chinese MNEs' overseas R&D also challenges the conventions of globalization. Therefore, an insight into R&D globalization in the context of China, a typical "Learning Economy," can advance theory development and reveal new policy and managerial implications.

2. Background

Theoretical basis of overseas R&D investment

Internationalization of Enterprises is carried out through International Business (IB) and Foreign Direct Investment (FDI). Overseas R&D investment is a special type of FDI and Innovation activities. As a form of internationalization of enterprises, it falls in the internationalization theory system. Therefore, the overseas R&D investment theory system is multi-disciplinary in nature (see Figure 16.5), and can be observed from perspectives as follows:

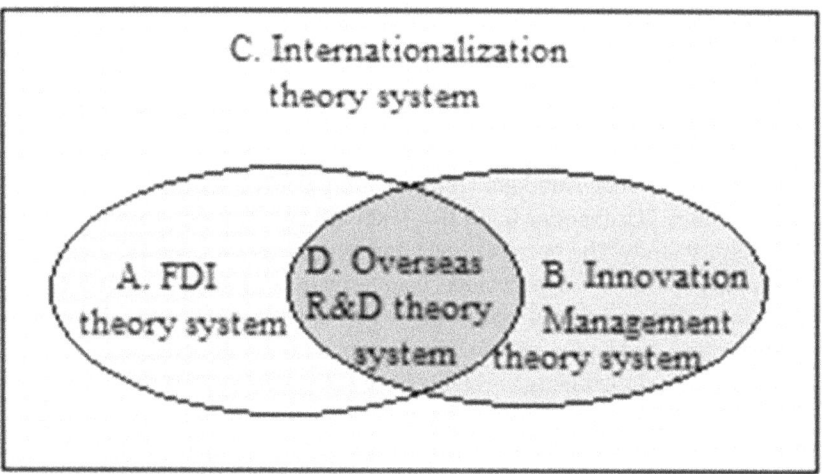

Figure 16.5 Nature of Overseas R&D theory system

A. FDI theory system: The major theories in the system include Monopolistic Advantage (Hymer, 1960), Product Life Cycle (Vernon, 1966), Internalization Theory (Buckley and Casson, 1976), Eclectic and Comparative Advantage (Kojima, 1973) and Paradigm of International Production (Dunning, 1977). Theories concerning developing countries include: Localized Technological Change (Lall, 1983), Technological Innovation and Industrial Upgrading (Cantwell &Tolentino, 1990), Cycle of Investment Development (Dunning, 1977), linkage-leverage-learning (LLL) (Mathews, 2006). In this system, Dunning's Eclectic Paradigm has been most widely revisited.

B. Innovation Management theory system: The theory lent by this study is "Learning Economy" by Lundvall (1977), a theory forward-looking into the relationship between innovation and globalization. "Learning Economy" is defined as an economy which the ability to learn is crucial for the economic success of individuals, firms, regions and national economies.

C. Internationalization theory system: The theory employed by this study is Uppsala Model. It proposed that enterprises internationalization is a gradual process; "All factors that hinder the flow of market information" is defined as "psychological distance," and the cultural and language difference affect the mode of FDI (Johanson and Vahlne, 1977; 2009).

D. Overseas R&D theory system: Since 1980s to 1990s, many Western scholars applied FDI theories in their study of overseas R&D activities. Dunning's Eclectic Paradigm (1977) laid foundations for this theory system. Other FDI theories have also been applied in a small number of empirical study. The overseas R&D theory system has taken shape with several gaps: first, this system has been established mainly based on FDI theories that were generated from Western countries' context. Theories addressing developing countries' scenario are not sufficient. Second, all of the existing theories are evolving from FDI theory system. As R&D and Innovation is an issue that concerning economics, sociology, psychology, and engineering (Fagerberg, 2005), the current theory system is in lack of multi-disciplinary approaches. Thirdly, the theories in the system still remain in observing the phenomenon in a static way, without enough attention paid to the increasingly dynamic, complex environment.

Literature review

The earliest literature on MNEs' overseas R&D activities can be traced to Ronstadt's (1978) study on American MNEs' overseas R&D subsidiaries. With the advent of Western MNEs' R&D internationalization peak in the 1990s to the early 2000s, and Emerging Markets Enterprises' (EMEs) rising outward FDI of R&D later, extensive study has been conducted around several thematic areas, including: 1. the incentives of R&D internationalization (Rugman, 1981; Miravitlles et al., 2013; Piperopoulos et al., 2017); 2. the choice of location for overseas R&D activities (Hewitt, 1980; Kummar, 1995; Ivarsson and Alvstam, 2017); 3. the organization of R&D units and the functions of overseas R&D subsidiaries (Gerybadze and Reger, 1999; Andersson and Pedersen, 2010; Fuller, Akinwande and Sodini, 2017); 4. overseas R&D networks (Perrino and Tipping, 1989; De Prato and Nepelski, 2012); 5. country-specific features of overseas R&D investment (Von Zedtwitz and Gassmann, 2002); and 6. the knowledge spill-over effect of overseas R&D (Audretsch and Feldman, 1996; Zhang, Di Minin and Quan, 2010). Although a large amount of literature has been devoted to this issue, effective organization and management of international R&D still remains difficult to MNEs. (Moitra and Krishnamoorthy, 2004) The former literature has demonstrated features and research gaps as below:

- The thematic areas are closely related to each other. For example, attention on the incentives of the overseas R&D activities is a common theme for study. While being a research topic itself, it is also core to other research questions.

- There has been an abundance of empirical study applying Dunning's Eclectic Paradigm, but most of them used the theory in the context of Western MNEs. While Dunning (2011) had pointed out, many of the explanations of the 1970s and early 1980s need to be modified as the world's scenario has changed, the attempt to reflect a more dynamic environment is not sufficient. Theoretical discussions and empirical research on Chinese MNEs are few and remain in a marginalized status. (Von Zedtwitz, 2005)

- Most recently, Cano-kollmann, Cantwell and Hannigan (2016) brought the knowledge linkage concept into R&D internationalization; holding that, due to the convergence of technology, the knowledge linkage between innovation systems need more attention. In the future, adopting the knowledge flow route of "parent company–subsidiaries" or community-based linkage, will greatly affect the actors (Thomas, 2016). This forward-looking perspective has been reflected in existing literature.

In view of the theory and empirical research gap, and a necessity to reflect new conditions and clues for future development, this study adopts multidisciplinary approach to add a dynamic dimension to observe the overseas R&D investment process, so as to push forward understanding of the growing phenomenon from a theoretical and empirical perspective.

3. Research design

The overall research is designed around the fundamental debate in the Economic Geography, i.e., whether "the competitiveness of the companies is more related to the locations or to the networks." Drawing on Syllogism, this research starts from an analysis of Chinese MNE's overseas R&D location choices, then exam of their overseas' R&D networks, and eventually sublimates from the previous two components, reaching a new theoretical system on the organizational configuration of R&D globalization. (see Figure 16.6)

Syllogism	Proposition 1	Proposition 2	Propostion 3
Structure	location	network	organizational configurations
Approach	macro-perspective quantitative	micro-perspective qualitative	synthetical

Figure 16.6 Research roadmap

Component 1: Determinants of locational choice of Chinese MNEs' overseas R&D investment

Based on a dataset from 1500 Chinese MNEs, which established overseas R&D subsidiaries in the recent 5 years (2012-2016), this component analyzes the locational determinants for Chinese MNEs' overseas R&D investment, and whether and how it differs from the overseas R&D investment peak led by the MNEs in Western countries in the past century. A theoretical framework integrating Dunning's (1977; 1998) eclectic paradigm and the Uppsala Model (Johanson &Vahlne, 1977; 2009) was constructed. The eclectic model is employed to examine whether the host countries' advantages and disadvantages, in terms of market size, Science and Technology (S&T) resources, communication infrastructure and policy regime, correlates with Chinese MNCs' location choice. The Uppsala Model is used to spot where national culture fits in the dynamism (Earley and Gibson, 2002; Oyserman, Kemmelmeier and Coon, 2002) and how it is intertwined with the internationalization process as a mediator (see Figure 16.7).

The data on Chinese MNEs' overseas R&D subsidiaries is collected from the "Going-out Strategy" platform, Ministry of Commerce of China, which consists of registration information of Chinese MNEs which established overseas subsidiaries. After filtering the registration records by business scope, a dataset of 1500 MNEs that established overseas R&D subsidiaries (2012-2016) was obtained. Due to the availability of host countries' data, this estimation chooses 49 representative host countries for analysis. The variables and indicators' data source are listed in table 16.1.

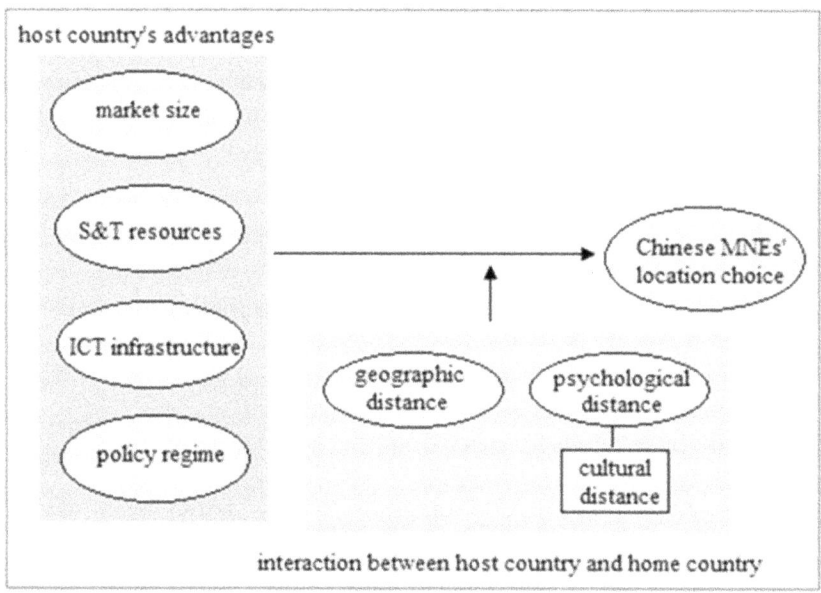

Figure 16.7 Theoretical framework on location determinants of Chinese firms' overseas R&D subsidiaries

Table 16.1 Variables, indicators and data source

	Variables	**Indicators**	**Data source**
Host countries' factors	market sizes	Gross Domestic Product (GDP)	World Bank (WB)
	S&T resources	residents and patent number ratio	World Bank (WB)
	ICT infrastructure	broadband penetration rate	International Telecommunication Union (ITU)
	policy environment	intellectual property protection index	Global Competitiveness Report of World Economic Forum (WEF)
	ecological resources	Countries' ecological remainder/deficit	Global Footprint Network
Interaction process	bilateral geographic distance		CEP II database
	cultural distance		Hofstede Centre

A multiple linear regression model is established. The number of Chinese MNEs' overseas R&D subsidiaries in a certain host country is the dependent variable, the host country advantages are independent variables. How the bilateral geographical distance and cultural distance moderates the R&D international process are examined. The ecological resources of the host counties are a controlled variable.

$$Y_{i=}\alpha_0+\alpha_1 Z_i+\mu_i \tag{1}$$

(1) is a linear regression formula with the control variable Z;

$$Y_i=\alpha_0+\alpha_1 Z_i+\beta_1 X_{1i}+\beta_2 X_{2i}+\beta_3 X_{3i}+\beta_4 X_{41}+\mu_i \tag{2}$$

(2) is a linear regression formula with independent variables X_{ki} (k=1,2,3,4)

$$Y_i=\alpha_0+\alpha_1 Z_i+\beta_1 X_{1i}+\beta_2 X_{2i}+\beta_3 X_{3i}+\beta_4 X_{4i}+\gamma j_0 M_j+\gamma j_1 M_j \times X_{1i}+\gamma j_2 M_j \times X_{2i}+\gamma j_3 M_j \times X_{3i}$$
$$+\gamma j_4 M_j \times X_{41}+\mu_i \tag{3}$$

(3) adds in moderating variables M_j. Y_i denotes the number of Chinese firms' overseas R&D subsidiaries in country i. Z_i denotes the value of the control variable in country i. X_{ki} is No. k affecting factors in country i. μ donates random error. Analysis is conducted by eviews 8.0.

Component 2: Case study on Huawei's global R&D network

The second component adopts a Network Analysis method to examine how Huawei, a leading Chinese company in R&D globalization, developed its global R&D network. Using UCINET 6.0, this study visualizes Huawei's over-seas R&D network, where the nodes are the overseas R&D units' locations, and the lines between locations reflect the cooperation between R&D units. (see Figure 16.8) 17 host countries of Huawei's overseas R&D subsidiaries are divided into 5 categories according to their advantages, so that their position and activities can be observed within the network.[3] Based on annual data

---

3.   Host countries with advantage in market are coded as M, including Brazil, Po-land, Hungary and Indonesia; those with advantage in S&T are coded as T, in-cluding Germany, France, American, Sweden, and Britain; those with ad-vantage in human resource are coded as H, including Russia, Finland, Cana-da, Spain and India; those with advantage in geography, are coded as G, in-cluding Turkey and Italy; those with advantage in industrial chain as C. R&D units in home country is coded as P. The analysis results are shown in Figure 16.8 and Figure 16.9.

(2009-2016) of patent cooperation among the R&D unites, evolution diagrams of Huawei's global R&D network are drawn (see Figure 16.9). The data source is the United States Patent and Trademark Office (USPTO). By searching for multi-location invented patents with Huawei as the assignee, and the location of investors as being from the 17 host countries of Huawei's overseas R&D units, a dataset of Huawei's global patent collaboration within its R&D network was obtained. The result contains 242 patent cooperation, which took place in 70 cities, among Huawei's 10 R&D units at home and abroad.

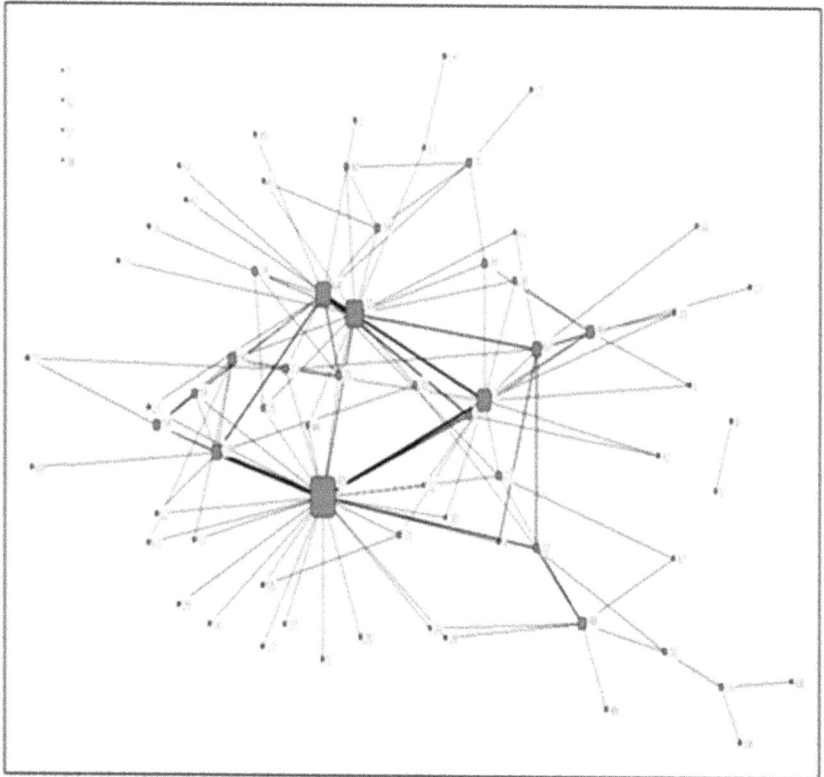

Figure 16.8 Huawei's global R&D network

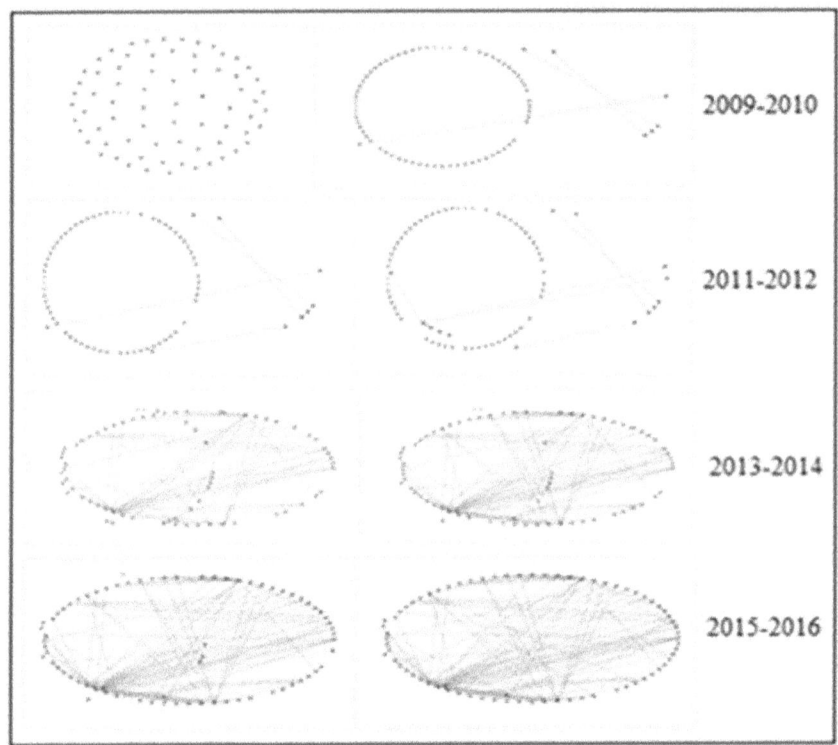

Figure 16.9 Evolution of Huawei's global R&D network

Component 3: Global R&D organizational configurations system

The third component synthesizes the findings from the previous two components and establishes a framework of organizational configuration modes for R&D globalization, which applies for MNEs in a global range. The data source is synthesized from datasets in the previous two components and relevant enterprises' annual report, documents and archives. Analysis is conducted by extracting relevant results from previous steps and conducting a comparative study with reference to the framework of R&D organizational configuration system initiated by Gassmann and Von Zedtwitz (1999), in order to explore whether in the Chinese MNEs' R&D globalization process uses the five organizational configuration modes defined by Gassmann and Von Zedtwitz (1999); and to excavate the mechanism of organizational configuration modes adaptation.

4. Conclusion

Finding 1

The major incentive of Chinese MNEs' overseas R&D investment is for overseas markets. The S&T resources of the host countries are attractive to Chinese MNEs. However, the orientation of technology-seeking in establishing overseas R&D subsidiaries is much weaker than market orientation, and it is further weakened by the barriers created by geographic and cultural distance. In host countries with comparatively bigger geographic and cultural distance, Chinese MNEs have a high tendency to establish overseas R&D subsidiaries, in order to support the local market in host countries and resolve the "not-invented here syndrome" (Von Zedtwitz and Gassmann 2002). Chinese MNEs pay high attention to the host countries intellectual property protection policy environments, regardless of the geographic and cultural distance of the host countries.

Table 16.2 Regression results: Determinants of location choice of Chinese MNEs' overseas R&D

Models	Model 1(OLS)	Model 2(OLS)	Model 3(OLS)	Model 4(OLS)	Model 5 (OLS)	Model 6 (OLS)	Model 7 (OLS)	Model 8 (OLS)
(Constant)	1.04 E-16	3.73 E-07	2.33 E-07	7.56 E-07	-1.37 E-07	0.3173 ***	-0.0181 ***	0.0195 ***
ECOLOGICAL RESOURCES	-0.169	-0.1730	-0.1639	0.0077	-0.0440	-0.1397 ***	-0.1214 ***	-0.1458 ***
INTELLECTURAL PROPERTY PROTECTION		0.2152	0.1151	0.0992	0.0313	0.2018 ***	0.1674 ***	0.1946 ***
INTERNET PENETRATION			0.1386	-0.0342	-0.0326	0.1560 ***	-0.1335 ***	-0.1803 ***
PATENT/ RESIDENT RATIO				0.7622 ***	0.0140	0.0831	-0.8605 ***	-0.7350 ***
MARKET SIZE					0.9390 ***	0.9334 ***	0.9742 ***	0.9475 ***
GEOGRAPHIC DISTANCE							0.0645	
CULTURAL DISTANCE								0.1180
DIS*IP PROTECTION							0.0848	

DIS*INTERNET							-0.2267 ***	
DIS*PATANT							-0.4654 ***	
DIS*MARKET							1.0357 ***	
CUL DIS*IP PROTECTION								0.0621
CUL DIS*INTERNET								-0.1784
CUL DIS*PATENT								-0.9016 ***
CUL DIS*MARKET								0.4340 ***
R2	0.028	0.0747	0.0839	0.5984	0.9136	0.9990	0.9996	0.9995
Adjusted R2	0.008	0.0345	0.0228	0.5619	0.9036	0.9988	0.9994	0.9992
F value/Wald	1.377	1.8590	1.3742	16.391	91.051	5303.690	5269.149	4182.990
P value	0.246	0.1673	0.2627	0.0000	0.0000	0.0000	0.0000	0.0000

(* $P<0.1$, ** $P<0.05$, *** $P<0.01$)

Finding 2

Huawei has established an advanced global R&D network over the past two decades. In this network, each R&D unit node is well connected; HQ and the units in technologically-advantageous countries have the highest betweenness centrality and highest Taylor index rank, and thus stronger control power and bigger influence over the network. Based on the network indicators[4], the evolution of Huawei's global R&D network can be divided into four phases: first, *the initial phase (2009-2010)*: the network was initiated in France, and the interaction between units in France and Sweden was first reflected by patent collaboration; second, *the primary phase (2011-2012)*: R&D units in home country cities entered the network. Units in technologically-advantageous countries, including France, UK, and the US are active actors; thirdly, *the rapid-developing phase*

---

4. Network indicators referred to include: number of actors, density, network centralization, clustering coefficient, number of components, number of components with more than 2 nodes, and scale of largest component.

(2013-2014): the number of actors and the interactions among actors increased rapidly. Fourthly, *the sophisticated phase (2015-2016)*: The number of isolates in the network is small. Extensive interactions had been established among actors. The number of active actors increases at a steady pace, and the positions of actors in the network have been formulated.

Through observing actors' status in the network by category, it is found that technologically-advantageous actors are the initiators and drivers in early phases. In the maturing phases of the network, technologically-advantageous actors remain as the main force, and market–advantageous actors appeared as non-major forces of the network. The category of actors diversifies at a steady pace; on the occasion of several telecom giants' downsizing, the network took in human resources-advantageous actors. Huawei has had a successful strategy in production internationalization, starting from developing countries under hard conditions and extending production territories over the world. While an "innovation management system is different from traditional management system" (O'Connor et al., 2008), Huawei avoided the inertia of a production internationalization route and established a new pattern strategy for R&D globalization.

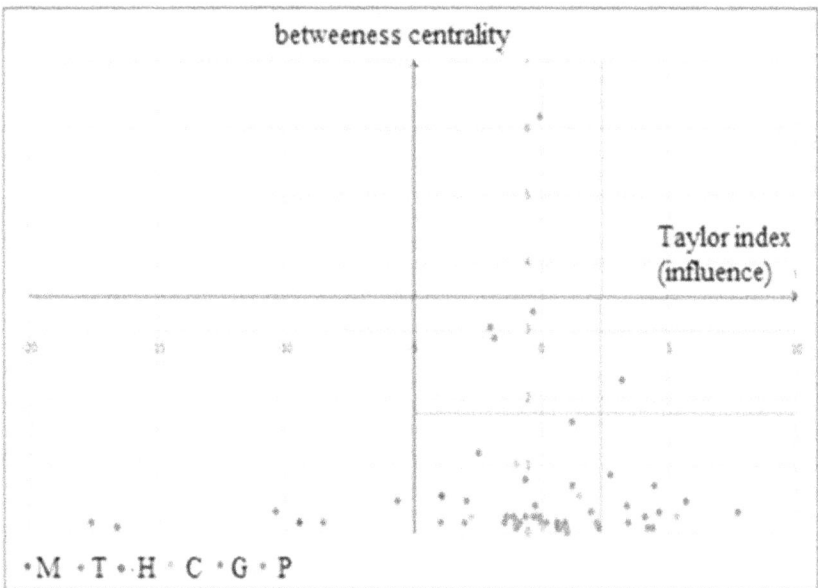

Figure 16.10 betweenness centrality and influencer

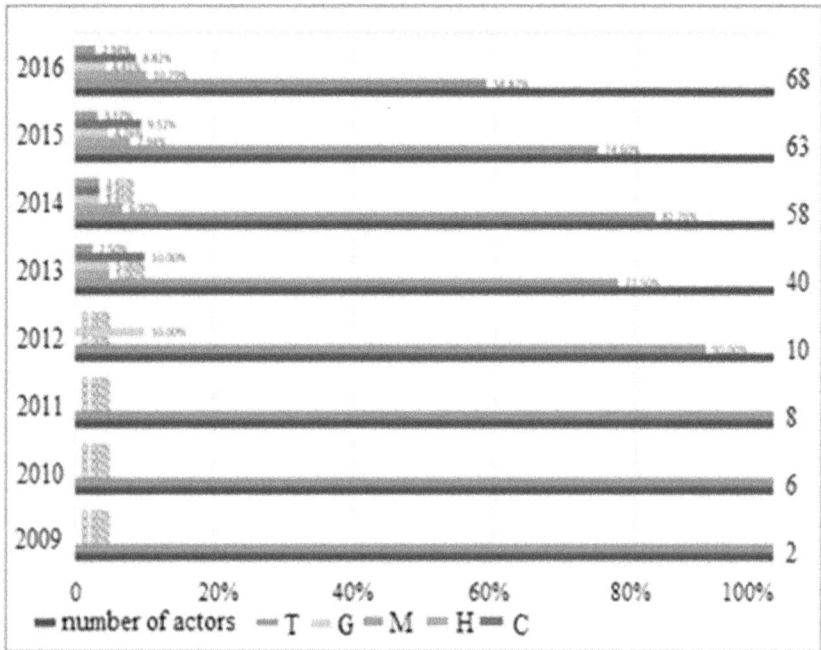

Figure 16.11 entry of actors into the network

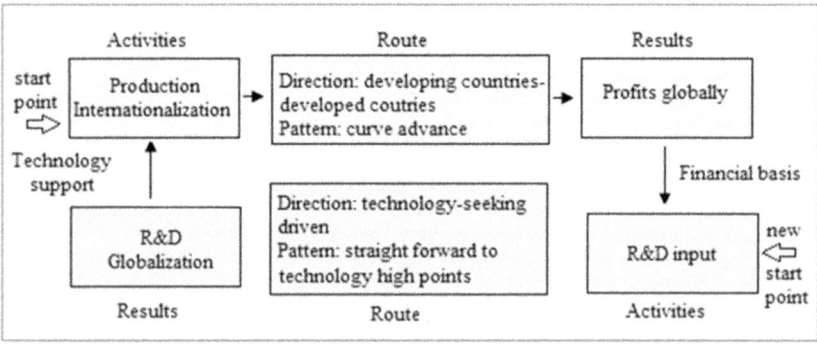

Figure 16.12 Huawei's strategic route for production internationalization and R&D globalization

Finding 3

Based on previous concepts (Gassmann &Von Zedtwitz, 1999), this study develops a more comprehensive global R&D organizational configuration system, in which the mechanism of adoption of the modes are built-in. This system points out that adaptation of global R&D organizational configuration modes is confined to enterprises' internal resources and capacity level. Small enterprises with limited resources adopt Polycentric Decentralized R&D mode or R&D Hub mode. Under these modes, global R&D is organized in a comparatively scattered manner, and the enterprises' R&D strategy is more tactical in nature and more market-oriented. Enterprises with more resources enter a higher level of modes, including Ethnocentric Centralized R&D, Geocentric Centralized R&D, and Integrated R&D Network. Under the high-level modes, enterprises carry out R&D organization and operation in a more strategic and systematic way, and with increasing strong technology-seeking orientation (see Figure 16.12).

An equation based on this mechanism is established. Q denotes global R&D efficiency, V1 denotes global R&D input, V2 denotes R&D output, C denotes an enterprise's research capacity, and W denotes the resources and time cost associated with certain organizational configuration modes. Global R&D efficiency maximizes when the cost associated with certain organizational configurations mode minimizes, and the enterprise's R&D capacity and R&D input reach the highest level (see Figure 16.13). Therefore, there are two channels to enhance MNEs' global R&D efficiency: first, to improve enterprises R&D capacity. R&D capacity determines knowledge conversion rate and the internal cost of knowledge creation. It is the ultimate distinction between enterprises (Cantwell, 1995). Second, to increase R&D input and choose the most cost-saving R&D organizational configurations with the enterprises' resources scope.

$$Q = \frac{V_2}{V_1} = \frac{V_1 \times C - W}{V_1} = C - \frac{W}{V_1}$$

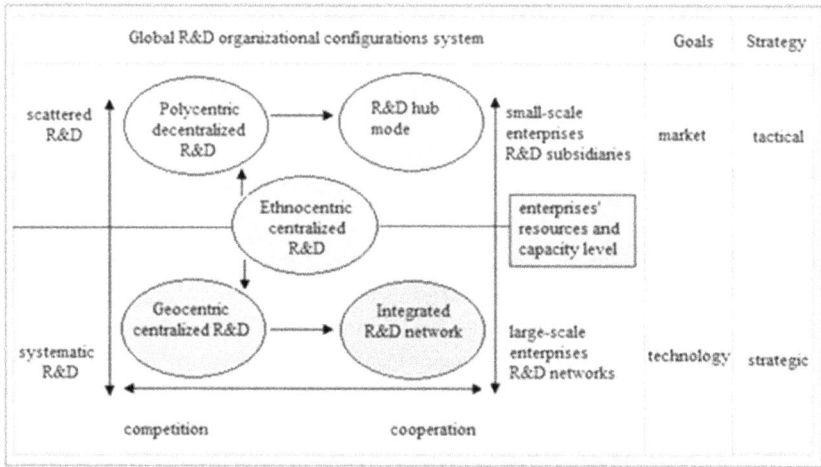

Figure 16.13 Global R&D organizational configurations system and adoption mechanism

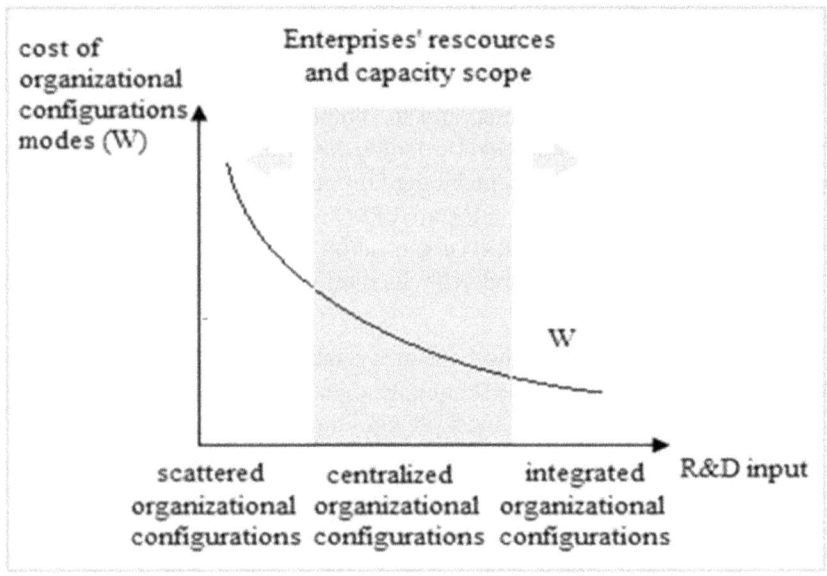

Figure 16.14 Adoption of global R&D organizational configurations modes

This deductive reasoning arrives at the conclusion that, while both the locations and networks of R&D globalization are important in building the competitiveness of MNEs, the two routes of knowledge flow — "parent company-subsidiaries" and network linage — co-exist, making today's globalization more complex and diverse than ever. It is crucial to note that MNEs at different development levels and with different R&D investment capacities need to choose a suitable R&D organizational configuration mode, in order to optimize its R&D efficiency.

5. Implications and future research

Managerial implications

The identified determinants of locational choices for Chinese MNEs' overseas R&D investment demonstrate a difference from the stereotype that Chinese firms set up overseas R&D subsidiaries as a "short-cut" for obtaining technology: rather, the primary incentive for Chinese firms R&D "going out" is for supporting a global market. Chinese MNEs' R&D "going out" is rational behavior decided by the market need. At the same time, it is worth noting that while the R&D "going out" is viewed as a "window of opportunity" for China to catch up with advanced technology and realize economic transformation at a national level, currently, MNEs have a comparatively less-strong orientation for technology-seeking in establishing overseas R&D subsidiaries, and this orientation is further weakened as geographic and cultural distance increases. Guidance and measures are needed to encourage the Chinese enterprises to balance a market-supporting orientation with a knowledge seeking orientation, in order to achieve both the aims of enhancing enterprises' competitiveness and fulfill the national development agenda.

The evolution route and dominion of Huawei's global R&D network demonstrates how Chinese MNEs can carve out strategic paths for R&D globalization which fit their scenarios. Breaking the scope of conventional hotspots for FDI, Huawei pioneered overseas R&D activities in vast development countries to create new opportunities for R&D globalization. Huawei's success story on global R&D strategic management reflects the Chinese MNEs' enterprising spirit, open vision and innovative approach to clear target.

The most suitable organizational configuration modes for global R&D is determined by an individual enterprise's internal resources and capacity. In order to maximize R&D performance, enterprises need to adopt the most-compatible organizational configuration mode. A large number of Chinese MNEs have limited internal capacities and belong to the manufacturing industry, so they adopted primary level organizational configuration modes. Chinese MNEs must fully realize that, while these primary level organizational configuration modes give a quick entry into R&D globalization, they also bring downsides, including low R&D efficiency and repetition of work. It is important to enhance the R&D organizational configuration level, in order to develop an optimal R&D strategy. Measures optimizing global R&D performance include: enhancing an enterprise's internal R&D capacity, increasing input in R&D, and choosing the most cost-saving organizational configuration mode allowed by a certain amount of R&D input. Optimizing global R&D organizational configurations is a gradual process.

Chinese MNEs have pioneered a convention-breaking path in R&D globalization, and prelude a new economic order, "inclusive globalization."

Future research

This study examines Chinese MNEs' overseas R&D location choice from macro-perspective. It has not further analyzed each determinants' specific effect. Further exploration can be conducted in this regard. Like all network analysis based on patent data, the study on Huawei's global R&D network has limitations (Ter Wal and Boschman, 2008), as the Network Analysis method presumes that the data on the network is complete. The network drawn in this study has not reflected Non-patent inventors' participation. Therefore, future research may explore a method that captures reality in this respect. Furthermore, this study proposes that China has become a typical "learning economy" and has preluded a new "Inclusive Globalization." New theories and empirical study are to be established under this new philosophy of globalization.

References

Andersson, U. & Pedersen, T. (2010). 'Organizational design mechanisms for the R&D function in a world of offshoring'. *Scandinavian Journal of Management*. 26(4), 431-438.

Buckley, P. J. & Casson, M. C. (1976). *The future of multinational enterprise*. London, Macmillan.

Cano-Kollmann, M., Cantwell, J., Hannigan, T. J., Mudambi, R. & Song, J. (2016). 'Knowledge connectivity: An agenda for innovation research in international business'. *Journal of International Business Studies*. 47 (3), 255-262.

Cantwell, J. (1995) 'The globalization of technology: what remains of the product cycle model?' *Cambridge journal of economics*. 19: 155-155.

Cantwell, J. & Tolentino, P. E. E. (1990). *Technological accumulation and third world multinationals*. Department of Economics, University of Reading. Number: 139.

Casson, M. & Singh, S. (1993) 'Corporate research and development strategies: the influence of firm, industry and country factors on the decentralization of R&D'. *R&D management*. 23(2), 91-108.

Cordell, A.J. (1973) 'Innovation, the multinational corporation: some implications for national science policy'. *Long Range Planning*. 6(3), 22-29.

De Prato, G. & Nepelski, D. (2012). *Global R&D network. A network analysis of international R&D centres*. Joint Research Centre (Seville site). Report number: JRC79478.

Dunning, J. H. (1977). Trade, location of economic activity and the MNE: A search for an eclectic approach. *The international allocation of economic activity*. London, Palgrave Macmillan. 395-418.

Dunning, J. H. (1998). 'Location and the multinational enterprise: a neglected factor?' *Journal of international business studies*. 29(1), 45-66.

Dunning, J. H. (2011). 'The eclectic paradigm as an envelope for economic and business theories of MNE activity'. *International Business Review*. 9(2), 163-190.

Earley, P. C. & Gibson, C. B. (2002) *Multinational work teams: A new perspective*. Milton Park, Routledge.

Fagerberg, J. (2005) *The Oxford handbook of innovation*. Oxford, Oxford university press.

Fuller, D. B., Akinwande, A. I. & Sodini, C. G. (2017). 'The globalization of R&D's implications for technological capabilities in MNC home countries: semiconductor design offshoring to China and India'. *Technological Forecasting & Social Change*, 120, 14-23.

Gassmann, O., & Von Zedtwitz, M. (1999). 'New concepts and trends in international R&D organization'. *Research policy*. 28(2-3), 231-250.

Gerybadze, A. & Reger, G. (1999). 'Globalization of R&D: recent trends in the management of innovation in transnational corporations'. *Research Policy*. 28(2-3), 251-274.

Hewitt, G. (1980). 'Research and development performed abroad by US manufacturing multinationals'. *Kyklos*. 33(2): 308-327.

Hikino, T. & Amsden, A. H. (1994). 'Staying behind, stumbling back, sneaking up, soaring ahead: late industrialization in historical perspective'. In: Baumol, W. J., Nelson, R. R. & Wolff, E. N. (eds.) *Convergence of productivity: Cross-national studies and historical evidence*. Oxford, Oxford University Press. pp. 285-315.

Hymer, S. (1960). 'On multinational corporations and foreign direct investment'. *The Theory of Transnational Corporations*. London, Routledge for the United Nations.

Ivarsson, I. & Alvstam, C. G. (2017). 'New technology development by Swedish MNEs in emerging markets: the role of co-location of R&D and production'. *Asian Business & Management*.16 (1), 1-25.

Johanson, J. & Vahlne, J. E. (1977). 'The internationalization process of the firm: a model of knowledge development and process of the firm: A model of knowledge development and increasing foreign market commitments'. *Journal of International Business Studies*. 8(1), 23-32.

Johanson, J. & Vahlne, J. E. (2009). 'The Uppsala internationalization process model revisited: From liability of foreignness to liability of outsidership'. *Journal of international business studies*. 40(9), 1411-1431.

Kojima, K. (1973). 'A macroeconomic approach to foreign direct investment'. *Hitotsubashi Journal of Economics*. 14(1), 1-21.

Kumar, N. (1995) *Intellectual Property Protection, Market Orientation and Location of Overseas R&D Activities by Multinational Enterprises*. United Nations University, Institute for New Technologies, 673–688.

Lall, S. (1983). *The new multinationals*. New York: Wiley.

Lundvall, B. Å. & Borrás, S. (1997). *The globalizing learning economy: Implications for innovation policy*. Luxembourg: Office for Official Publications of the European Communities.

Maskell, P. (1996). *Localized low-tech learning in the furniture industry*. DRUID Working Paper, no. 96-17, Department of Industrial Economics and Strategy, Copenhagen Business School, Copenhagen.

Mathews, J. A. (2006). 'Dragon multinationals: New players in 21st century globalization'. *Asia Pacific journal of management*. 23(1), 5-27.

Miravitlles, P., Guitarttarrés, L., Achcaoucaou, F. & Núñezcarballosa, A. (2013). 'The role of the environment in the location of R&D and innovation activities in subsidiaries of foreign multinationals'. *Innovation*. 15(2), 170-182.

Moitra, D. & Krishnamoorthy, M. B. (2004). 'Global innovation exchange'. *Research-Technology Management*. 47(4), 32-38.

Narula, R. (2003). *Globalization and technology: Interdependence, innovation systems and industrial policy*. Hoboken, John Wiley & Sons.

Niosi, J. (1999) 'The internationalization of industrial R&D: from technology transfer to the learning organization'. *Research Policy*.28 (2), 107-117.

O'Connor, G. C., Ravichandran, T. & Robeson, D. (2008). 'Risk management through learning: management practices for radical innovation success'. *Journal of High Technology Management Research.* 19(1), 70-82.

OECD. (2008) *The Internationalisation of Business R&D: Evidence, Impacts and Implications.* Available from: www.oecd.org/sti/scitech.htm [Accessed 15 January 2017].

Oyserman, D., Kemmelmeier, M., & Coon, H. M. (2002). Cultural psychology, a new look: Reply to Bond (2002), Fiske (2002), Kitayama (2002), and Miller (2002). *Psychological Bulletin.* 128(1), 110-117.

Perrino, A. C. & Tipping, J. W. (1989). 'Global management of technology'. *Research-Technology Management.* 32(3), 12-19.

Piperopoulos, P., Wu, J. & Wang, C. (2017). 'Outward FDI, location choices and innovation performance of emerging market enterprises'. *Research Policy.* 47(1), 232-240.

Rugman, A. M. (1981). *Inside the multinationals: The economics of international markets.* London, Croom Helm.

Ronstadt, R. C. (1978). 'International R&D: the establishment and evolution of research and development abroad by seven US multinationals'. *Journal of International Business Studies.* 9(1), 7-24.

Rui, H. & Yip, G. S. (2008). 'Foreign acquisitions by Chinese firms: A strategic intent perspective'. *Journal of World Business.* 43(2), 213-226.

Sun, Y.F., Von Zedtwitz & Simon, D. F. (2007) 'Globalization of R&D and China: an introduction'. *Asia Pacific Business Review.* 13(3), 311-319.

Ter Wal, A. L. & Boschma, R. A. (2009). 'Applying social network analysis in economic geography: framing some key analytic issues'. *The Annals of Regional Science.* 43(3), 739-756.

Vernon, R. (1966). 'International Investment and International Trade in the Product Cycle'. *Quarterly Journal of Economics.* 80. 190-207.

UNCTAD. (2005) 'Corporations and the internationalization of R&D'. *World Investment Report.* Available from:http://unctad.org/en/Pages/PublicationArchive.aspx=693[Accessed 15 January 2017]

Von Zedtwitz, M. & Gassmann, O. (2002) 'Market versus technology drive in R&D internationalization: four different patterns of managing research and development'. *Research Policy.* 31(4), 569-588.

Zhang, J., Minin, A. D. & Quan, X. (2011). A comparison of international R&D strategies of Chinese companies in Europe and the U.S. *Proceedings of First IEEE International Technology Management Conference,* ITMC 2011, 27-30 June 2011, San Jose, U.S.A. Piscataway, IEEE. pp. 149-157.

Chapter 17

The Impact of Strategic Alliances and Internal Knowledge Sources on the Manufacturing Firms' Innovation and on Their Financial Performance: a Comparison between Brazil and Europe

Fábio O. Paula*

E-mail: fabioop@iag.puc-rio.br

Abstract: This study aimed to explain the relationships among internal and external R&D, innovation performance and financial performance in Brazilian and in some European countries' firms and compare both realities to bring lessons about how Brazilian firms may improve their performances. We proposed a theoretical model and tested it with a sample of 2,810 Brazilian manufacturing firms and with a sample of 2,745 manufacturing firms of 14 European countries (Bulgaria, Cyprus, Czech Republic, Spain, Croatia, Portugal, Hungary, Slovenia, Norway, Lithuania, Romania, Italy, Slovakia and Estonia) and compared the results. The analysis allowed to identify similarities and differences in the relationships among the constructs and brought interesting lessons for academics and managers.

Keywords: Innovation Performance; Internal R&D; External R&D; Absorptive Capacity; Strategic Alliances; Financial Performance; Manufacturing Firms; Structural Equation Modelling (SEM); Bayesian Estimation; Brazil; Europe.

1. Introduction

The capacity to innovate is considered by academics and managers as an essential capability to improve firms' performance and increase firms' chances of survival in an environment increasingly competitive and full of uncertainties. With the increasing complexity and diversity of technologies, it is becoming hard for organizations to work in isolation. Thus, besides developing innovations internally, firms increasingly seek to develop partnerships to innovate more effectively, which has shown positive results in several cases (e.g., Belussi, Sammarra and Sedita, 2010). Additionally, some firms achieve more success than others in their efforts to innovate, both internally and through alliances, which is corroborated by several authors who found a positive relationship between innovation and financial performance (e.g., Cheng and Huizingh, 2014).

Another relevant factor for the success of innovation is the environment, starting by the country. Brazil is at the 69th position in the 2016 ranking of the most innovative countries of the Global Innovation Index (Dutta, Lavin and Wunsh-Vincent, 2016). In contrast, European countries dominate the top positions of the list, with 15 countries among the 25 most innovative. However, country issues are not the only reasons why Brazilian firms do not have the same innovative potential as European firms. Cases of Brazilian firms that reach a world-leading innovative level, such as Embraer in the aviation industry (Figueiredo, Silveira and Sbragia, 2008) illustrate it. Firms' strategies, resources and capabilities may be among the other causes.

Considering these facts, it is relevant to explore the similarities and differences in the innovation processes of firms from Brazil and from more innovative countries, including the relationships among the innovation antecedents (e.g. firms' knowledge and innovation capabilities), the firms' innovation strategy (the mix of internal R&D and strategic alliances that provide R&D inputs), innovation performance (IP) and financial performance (FP). This may help the Brazilian firms to improve IP and learn more about the conditions under which innovation positively affects FP. Additionally, it may help the Brazilian government to implement more effective policies to support innovation. To achieve this goal, this study proposes to compare firms from Brazil and from some selected European countries to answer the following research questions:

Q1 - How do internal knowledge sources and strategic alliances influence product and process innovation performance in manufacturing firms?

Q2 - Does innovation performance have a positive impact on these firms' financial performance?

Q3 - What is the influence of the environment on these relationships in the context of Brazil and of some selected European countries?

To answer these research questions, this study proposed a model based on a literature review of innovation management, strategic alliances and performance and tested it with a sample of 2,810 Brazilian manufacturing firms and compared it with the results of the model tested with a sample of 2,745 manufacturing firms from 14 European countries (Bulgaria, Czech Republic, Cyprus, Spain, Croatia, Portugal, Hungary, Slovenia, Norway, Lithuania, Romania, Italy, Slovakia and Estonia).

The main academic contributions of this manuscript consist in integrating the concepts of internal and external R&D, IP and FP in a theoretical model; understanding if the presence of manufacturing firms in a more innovative environment, such as the selected European countries, favors the IP of these firms, even if these countries are not advanced but moderate innovators, compared to Brazil, which is a low innovator; and exploring the effect of these different contexts on the alliances, on the internal knowledge sources and on the way the IP affects these firms' FP. This study takes innovation theory a step further in analyzing the different impacts of alliances and internal knowledge sources in product and process innovation to ensure better performance. The comparison between Brazil and some European countries helps researchers to understand the similarities and differences of these relationships in different contexts, which increases the validity and applicability of the theory. It also serves as a reference for future studies about innovation, alliances and performance due to the extensive bibliographic research.

For practitioners, the work has relevance because it proposes a model that helps to choose the strategies that manufacturing firm may adopt (e.g., investments in internal R&D, more efficient alliance types) to develop product and process innovations effectively and make innovation positively influence FP. The study may also, by comparing the results in the selected European countries and in the Brazilian context, help the Brazilian firms' managers to overcome the challenges posed by the environment through the lessons learned from these European countries' companies. It may also help the Brazilian government agencies to formulate better innovation policies.

2. Background

Internal and External R&D and Financial Performance

Strategic alliances represent important external sources of R&D. Alliances can be used to develop open innovation that, according to Chesbrough (2003), is "the use of internal and external flows of knowledge to accelerate internal innovation and expand markets for external use of the innovation, respectively." The reasons to invest in innovative collaboration are diverse, such as access to complementary assets, transference of tacit and codified knowledge and spread of R&D costs (Faems, Van Looy and Debackere, 2005). A positive relationship between external sources of R&D and IP have been found in various empirical studies (e.g., Belussi et al., 2010). Some researchers have also found an inverted U-shape relationship (Duysters and Lokshin, 2011) between external R&D and IP. The positive relationship inverts with high levels of external R&D because of the increasing coordination and monitoring costs to avoid misappropriation (Hallen, Katila and Rosenberger, 2014). A firm can execute open innovation with seven types of partners: i) suppliers, ii) customers, iii) competitors, iv) consultants, v) private R&D institutes, vi) universities and other forms of higher education, and vii) government and public research institutes (OECD, 2008). Several authors studied the influence of different types of partnerships on IP and found positive results (e.g., von Hippel, 1988; Un, Cuervo-Cazurra and Asakawa 2010; Soh and Subramanian, 2014). Internal R&D, on its turn, is mentioned in the literature mostly as impacting positively innovation (e.g., Hagedoorn and Wang, 2012). In a longitudinal research with start-ups, Stam and Wennberg (2009) found a positive relationship between internal R&D and new product development. The authors also found a relationship between R&D activities and firm growth in high-tech industries.

Innovation Performance and Financial Performance

A positive relationship between IP and FP has been consistently found in the academy. Innovation is essential for a firm's survival in uncertain environments (Teece, 2007). When a radical innovation in the industry occurs, performance of the incumbents tends to decrease, whereas new ventures usually pioneer the introduction of innovation (Hill and Rothaermel, 2003). Tomlinson (2010) found a positive relationship between product and process innovation and factors that may indicate performance, such as firm size and sales growth. Some authors detected that open innovation activities performed by firms have a positive relationship with customer performance and FP (Cheng and Huizingh, 2014).

The influence of the country

The environment has an important influence in all aspects that evolves a firm. The environmental uncertainty may influence the adoption of innovation by firms (Goerzen, 2007) and the motivation to form strategic alliances (Dickson and Weaver, 1997). The innovation process is strongly affected by country differences. For the innovation strategy of a firm to succeed, leading to a satisfactory IP, it must fit the characteristics of the environment in which the firm is inserted and must be able to leverage firm's resources and capabilities (Bell and Figueiredo, 2012). Some authors, studying the innovation process of latecomer firms in developing economies, found that the path for these companies is totally different from the process followed by firms of developed countries (Kim, 1997). Therefore, the choices about strategic alliances and the balance between internal and external R&D are strongly dependent on the reality of the country where the firm competes. But the country is not only influential because of its economic development stage. The NSI is also of great importance in a firms' decisions about internal and external R&D, IP and consequentially, its FP. The interaction among the institutes that compose the NSI determines the innovative performance of the national firms. This network of institutions includes the government, with its policies and programs, universities, research institutes and local firms - competitors, clients, suppliers and complementors (Nelson, 1993).

3 Research design

To answer the research questions, a theoretical model (see Figure 17.1) and hypotheses based on an extensive literature review of the innovation management and strategy fields were proposed. The hypotheses are in Table 17.1:

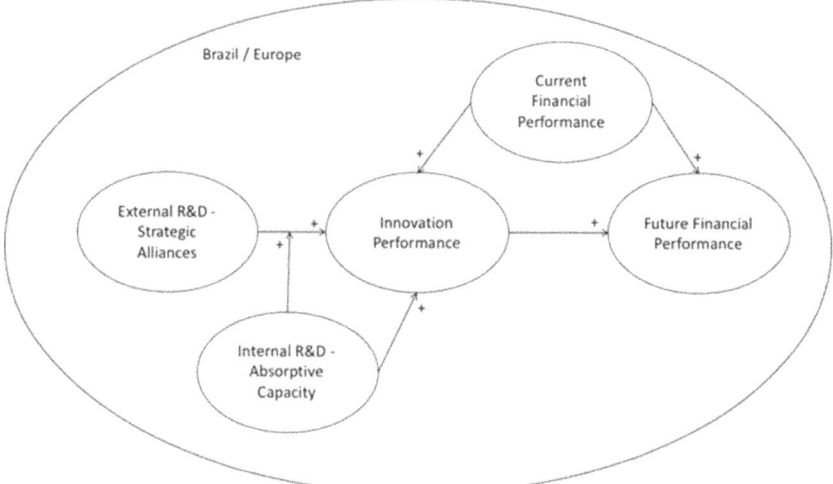

Figure 17.1 Theoretical model

Table 17.1 Model's hypotheses

Hypothesis 1	The more a firm invests in external R&D, the higher the firm's innovation performance.
Hypothesis 2	The more a firm invests in internal R&D, the higher the firm's innovation performance.
Hypothesis 3	The higher a firm's level of internal R&D, which improves its absorptive capacity, the higher is the positive effect of the investments in external R&D on the firm's innovation performance.

Hypothesis 4	The higher a firm's innovation performance, the higher the firm's future financial performance.
Hypothesis 5a	The fact that a firm is located in Brazil or in Europe affects differently the innovation strategy, represented by its choices of internal and external R&D.
Hypothesis 5b	The fact that a firm is located in Brazil or in Europe affects differently its innovation performance.
Hypothesis 5c	The fact that a firm is located in Brazil or in Europe affects differently its current and future financial performance.
Hypothesis 6a	The higher a firm's current financial performance, the higher the firm's innovation performance.
Hypothesis 6b	The higher a firm's current financial performance, the higher the firm's future financial performance.

The Brazilian sample consisted of 2,810 firms that conducted innovation activities from 2009 to 2011 of the Brazilian innovation survey PINTEC 2011 (IBGE, 2016). The European sample had 2,745 manufacturing firms of 14 countries (Bulgaria, Czech Republic, Cyprus, Spain, Croatia, Portugal, Hungary, Slovenia, Norway, Lithuania, Romania, Italy, Slovakia and Estonia) of the Community Innovation Survey (CIS) 2010 (European Commission, 2016), which considered the years from 2008 to 2010. The constructs were operationalized by variables from PINTEC 2011 in the case of Brazilian firms and CIS 2010 in the case of European firms. The variables for each construct are shown in table 17.2. The hypotheses were tested using structural equation modeling (SEM) and Bayesian estimation separately for the Brazilian and the European firms. Some adaptations in the models were necessary because of variables' restrictions.

Table 17.2 Model's variables – Brazil and Europe

Proxy name	Brazil / EU	Proxy format
Construct Innovation Performance		
% Turnover from new products/services	Brazil / EU	0 to 100%
Introduction of product innovation	Brazil / EU	Yes / No
Introduction of process innovation	Brazil / EU	Yes / No
Innovative degree of product innovation	Brazil / EU	0) No product/process innovation; 1) New to the firm; 2) New to the country; 3) New to the European market (EU); 4) New to the world
Innovative degree of process innovation	Brazil / EU	

Radicality degree of product innovation	Brazil / EU	0) No product/process innovation; 1) Innovation is incremental; 2) Innovation is radical
Radicality degree of process innovation	Brazil / EU	
Innovation impact: 15 indicators (BR) and 10 indicators (EU)	Brazil / EU	0) Irrelevant; 1) Low; 2) Medium; 3) High
Construct External R&D - Strategic Alliances		
Importance of partnership by partner type: 1) Suppliers; 2) Clients (in EU, clients of private and public sector are separated); 3) Competitors; 4) Firms of the group; 5) Consulting firms; 6) Universities or research institutes; 7) Professional capacitation and technical assistance centers; 8) Test, trial and certification centers; 9) Government (EU)	Brazil / EU	0) Irrelevant; 1) Low; 2) Medium; 3) High
Governmental support	Brazil	Yes / No
Constructs Previous Financial Performance and Future Financial Performance		
Turnover growth	Brazil / EU	Turnover (year)/Turnover (year-1)
Value added growth	Brazil	Value added (year)/Value added (year-1)
Firm growth	Brazil / EU	N. employees (year)/N. employees (year-1)
Construct Internal R&D – Absorptive Capacity		
Internal R&D spending/total turnover (R&D intensity)	Brazil / EU	0 to 100%
R&D training expenses/total turnover	Brazil	0 to 100%
R&D training activities	EU	Yes / No
R&D personnel level of education	Brazil	0 to 1. Formula: (Num. Doctors * 3 + Num. Masters * 2 + Num. Graduates)/total number of R&D staff
Importance of internal R&D	EU	0) Irrelevant; 1) Low; 2) Medium; 3) High

4. Conclusion

We examined the standard regression weights of the relationships between the constructs in Table 17.3 and Table 17.4 to analyze the hypotheses respectively for the Brazilian firms and European firms. Hypothesis 1 was confirmed in both models. This indicates that External R&D from strategic alliances is positively related to the innovation performance of manufacturing firms in different environments, with different NSIs and diverse levels of innovation development.

In contrast, the test of the relationship between internal R&D and innovation performance in hypothesis 2 presented different results on the two samples. It was confirmed in the selected European countries and was rejected in Brazil. This result may be indicating that the firms of the selected European countries' sample may be in a more evolved stage in the accumulation of innovative capabilities, which allows them to generate more significant incremental and radical innovations by their internal efforts and knowledge. As supposed, a lower level of innovative capabilities from the firms in the Brazilian sample forces them to focus on copying and making simple modifications on existing products and processes or rely on the knowledge of more technological developed partners.

Hypothesis 3, on the other hand, was supported for Brazilian manufacturing firms and rejected for the selected European countries' firms. There are several possible reasons why this difference emerged. Going deeper into the model's results of the Brazilian case indicates that the only factor of absorptive capacity that had a significant moderation effect in the relationship between strategic alliances and innovation performance was the level of education of the employees. Data about the level of education of employees was not available in the selected European countries' sample, the reason why such proxy was not used in the European model. This fact led to the conclusion that, for environments with firms of modest or low levels of innovation capability (such as the countries studied), the accumulated knowledge, represented by the level of education, is more important than the level of effort of the firm, represented by R&D intensity and training expenses. However, it is mandatory that firms continue to invest more in internal R&D as higher levels of this variable have a direct positive effect on innovation performance and increase the accumulated knowledge through time, which improves their absorptive capacity.

The comparative analysis of hypothesis 4 brought less valuable conclusions. This hypothesis was rejected in Brazil and in the selected European countries. In the selected European countries, the relationship between innovation and financial performance was not significant. In Brazil, however, it was negative. This negative relationship may have happened because a lag of two years for future financial performance that did not allow to identify the positive effects of the new products and services in the firm's growth but allowed to capture the negative impact of the redirection of resources from marketing and sales to innovation activities and of the costs of collaboration management.

Table 17.3 Results of SEM – Brazilian firms

Brazilian Manufacturing Firms (n = 2,810)			
Relationship	*Std. Regression Weight*	*Sig. *** p < 0.05*	*Hypothesis test*
Ext. R&D → IP	0.105	***	H1: Supported
Int. R&D → IP	0.004	-	H2: Rejected
Ext. R&D x Int R&D(AC) → IP	0.993	***	H3: Supported
IP → FFP	-0.897	***	H4: Rejected
CFP → IP	0.001	-	H5a: Rejected
CFP → FFP	0.259	-	H5b: Rejected

*** p < 0.05

Table 17.4 Results of SEM – European firms

All 14 Countries (n = 2,745)						
	FP - turn_growth			FP - emp_growth		
Relationship	*S.R.W.*	*Sig.*	*Hyp. test*	*S.R.W.*	*Sig.*	*Hyp. test*
Ext. R&D → IP	0.398	***	H1: Supported	0.400	***	H1: Supported
Int. R&D → IP	0.056	***	H2: Supported	0.051	***	H2: Supported
Ext R&D x Int R&D → IP	-0.027	-	H3: Rejected	-0.029	-	H3: Rejected
IP → FP	-0.009	-	H4: Rejected	-0.010	-	H4: Rejected

*** p < 0.05

5. Implications and future research

Theoretical implications

In the case of Brazil, a positive direct relationship between strategic alliances and innovation performance was detected. Internal R&D, on the other hand, did not influence innovation performance directly. However, it positively moderated the relationship between strategic alliances and innovation, which is consistent with the absorptive capacity theory (Cohen and Levinthal, 1990). Contrary to the theory, innovation performance had a negative influence on the future financial performance. This negative relationship may have been caused by the two-year lag between the proxies of the two constructs of the model, that did not identify an increase in revenues achieved by the new products and services but captured the negative effect of the redirection of resources from marketing and sales to innovation activities, such as internal R&D, and of the managerial costs of the strategic alliances.

For the selected European countries, the empirical analysis detected a positive relationship between internal and external R&D (from strategic alliances) and innovation performance separately. Contrary to the expectations, it did not find a moderation of internal R&D on the relationship between strategic alliances and innovation performance. This was probably caused by the low absorptive capacity of the firms in the European countries studied compared to the most innovative countries in Europe and in the world. Innovation performance did not influence financial performance. This may have been caused by the absence of a time-lag between the measurement of the proxies of these two constructs, which did not to allow to identify an increase in revenues from new products and services, that takes some time to be perceived.

A deeper analysis of absorptive capacity showed that, when the level of education is considered (only in the Brazilian model), which represents in some sort the dimension accumulated knowledge of this capability, it effectively moderates the relationship between strategic alliances and innovation performance. This implies that, for low or moderate innovators, the dimension of accumulated knowledge is more effective than the dimension firm's efforts for the development absorptive capacity. However, an improvement in both dimensions is necessary to allow these firms to reach the level of absorptive capacity of the world-leading firms, which would improve their innovation process and increase their innovation performance.

Practical implications

The Brazilian environment is inhospitable for innovation, imposing a big challenge for firms that want to innovate. This contributed to low investments in internal R&D and high levels of licensing and copying. As licensing and copying does not impact the process to a high degree as the development of more radical innovations, process innovation has been neglected. The main lesson is that, in catching-up countries like Brazil, the government and the industry players should work together with a consistent strategy to overcome the local issues and make the industry and its firms become world-leader innovators. Brazilian companies should invest more in internal R&D, which may promote a faster catch-up, allowing to generate more innovation directly from its own efforts while accumulating innovation capabilities and absorptive capacity. Also, firms should choose their partners carefully, giving preference to market partners, like clients and competitors, although not neglecting the partnerships with universities and research institutes in basic and applied research. However, they should not amplify too much the number of partners' types, which promotes a decrease in the innovation performance because of the increasing complexity of the management of the alliances' portfolio. Another important lesson is that process innovation must not be neglected. Governmental programs that are more focused on product innovation should also incentive process innovation, so as firms should put more efforts on it to achieve more short-term financial return, as process innovation usually brings faster financial results than product innovation.

For both manufacturing firms from Brazil and from the 14 European countries of our sample, which presented moderate or low levels of innovative capabilities and absorptive capacity, this study demonstrated that, if the main goal is an immediate improvement in the innovation performance level, they should focus on either internal or external R&D. However, if the main goal is improving in the long-term, beginning to strengthen their internal R&D is effective in improving the firms' absorptive capacity while achieving a satisfactory innovation outcome. This strategy will allow them to adopt more complex strategies, balancing internal and external R&D, effectively in the future, when the absorptive capacity level becomes high.

Recommendations for future studies

Although this study contributed to exploring the influence of internal and external R&D on innovation and financial performance in Brazil and in several European countries, it was only a starting point and several research opportunities are presented for the future. A first opportunity that arises is to study other European countries that participated of the CIS survey and could not be included in this research, such as the biggest economies of the continent (e.g., Germany, France, UK) and some of the most innovative countries (e.g., Sweden, Denmark, Finland, Holland), among others. Adding these European countries may enable comparison with developed countries in which the mainstream theories of innovation fit better with Brazil and less developed European economies, in which the innovation theories must be adapted to the reality of catching-up countries and try to identify the reasons why these differences happen.

One additional possibility to extend the research is to run the model for other countries that applied surveys similar to CIS and PINTEC. Several countries in all continents and at different innovative stages are in this situation, such as Argentine, Belarus, China, Colombia, Dominican Republic, Ecuador, Lesotho, Malaysia, Palestine, Paraguay, Philippines, Serbia, Tunisia, Uganda,

Ukraine, Russia, South Africa, New Zeeland, Canada, South Korea, Turkey, Switzerland, Mexico, Chile, Uruguay, etc.

Another opportunity regards running the model for firms of different industrial sectors. As only manufacturing firms were used, the service sectors, the extractive sectors and so forth were not considered and possibly would present different results that could generate interesting conclusions. Another possibility is merging several CIS and PINTEC surveys to create a panel dataset to improve the capacity to analyze the causal relationships with longer time-lags among the constructs. Antecedents such as internal and external R&D could be from one time-frame, innovation performance from another and financial performance from another one. CIS started to be applied in 1992 and has eight versions nowadays. PINTEC has been applied since 2000, and the last one (PINTEC 2014) is the sixth version of the survey. The surveys had changes through time and a longer time-frame includes more complexity as some historical events may have influenced the events and should be considered. However, with this type of panel database, possibly the positive influence of innovation performance on financial performance could be captured, for example in a five-years' or in a ten-years' time-lag. It also would allow us to differentiate current and future financial performance in the European model.

The last suggestion is to use data from different surveys that investigated innovation activities, such as the Business Environment and Enterprise Performance Survey – BEEPS, conducted by the World Bank conjointly with the European Bank for Reconstruction and Development (European Bank for Reconstruction and Development, 2016). This survey investigated several phenomena related to innovation activities and to financial performance at the firm-level, besides having information about the characteristics of firms of transition countries from Eastern Europe, Asia and Africa based on the year 2011.

References

Bell, M. and Figueiredo, P., (2012). 'Building Innovative Capabilities in Latecomer Emerging Market Firms: Some Key Issues'. *Innovative Firms in Emerging Market Countries*, pp.24–109.

Bellamy, M. A., Ghosh, S. and Hora, M., (2014). 'The influence of supply network structure on firm innovation'. *Journal of Operations Management, 32*(6), pp.357–373.

Belussi, F., Sammarra, A., and Sedita, S. R., (2010). 'Learning at the boundaries in an "Open Regional Innovation System": A focus on firms' innovation strategies in the Emilia Romagna life science industry'. *Research Policy, 39*(6), pp.710-721.

Cheng, C. C., and Huizingh, E. K., (2014). 'When is open innovation beneficial? The role of strategic orientation'. *Journal of Product Innovation Management, 31*(6), pp. 1235-1253.

Chesbrough, H.(2003). *Open innovation: The new imperative for creating and profiting from technology.* Harvard Business Press.

Cohen, W. M., and Levinthal, D. A., (1990). 'Absorptive capacity: A new perspective on learning and innovation'. *Administrative Science Quarterly,* pp.128-152.

Dickson, P. and Weaver, K., (1997). 'Individual-Level Moderators of Alliance Use'. *Academy of Management Journal, 40*(2), pp.404–425.

Dutta, S., Lanvin, B., and Wunsch-Vincent, S. (2016). *The global innovation index 2016: Winning with global innovation.* Johnson Cornell University.

Duysters, G., and Lokshin, B., (2011). 'Determinants of alliance portfolio complexity and its effect on innovative performance of companies'. *Journal of Product Innovation Management, 28*(4), pp.570–585.

European Bank For Reconstruction And Development., (2016). *Business Environment and Enterprise Performance Survey (BEEPS),* 2016 Retrieved from: http://ebrd-beeps.com.

European Commission, (2016). *Community Innovation Survey (CIS)* Retrieved from: http://ec.europa.eu/eurostat/web/microdata/community-innovation-survey.

Faems, D., Van Looy, B., and Debackere, K., (2005). 'Interorganizational collaboration and innovation: Toward a portfolio approach'. *Journal of Product Innovation Management, 22*(3), pp.238–250

Figueiredo, P., Silveira, G., and Sbragia, R., (2008). 'Risk sharing partnerships with suppliers: the case of Embraer'. *Journal of Technology Management and Innovation,* 3(1), pp.27-37.

Goerzen, A., (2007). 'Alliance Networks and Firm Performance: the Impact of Repeated Partnerships'. *Strategic Management Journal, 28*(5), pp.487–509.

Hagedoorn, J. and Wang., N., (2012). 'Is there complementarity or substitutability between internal and external R&D strategies?' *Research Policy, 41*(6), pp.1072–1083.

Hallen, B., Katila, R. and Rosenberger, J., (2014). 'How do social defences work? A resource-dependence lens on thechnology ventures, venture capital investors, and corporate relationships'. *Academy of Management Journal, 57*(4), pp.1078–1101.

Hill, C. and Rothaermel, F., (2003). 'The performance of incumbent firms in the face of radical technological innovation'. *Academy of Management Review, 28*(2), pp.257–274.

von Hippel, E., (1988). *The sources of innovation.* New York: Oxford University Press.

Instituto Brasileiro de Geografia e Estatística (IBGE), (2016). *PINTEC – Pesquisa de Inovação,* Retrieved from: http://www.pintec.ibge.gov.br.

Kim, L., (1997). *Imitation to innovation: The dynamics of Korea's technological learning.* Harvard Business Press.

Lin, C., Wu, Y.J., Chang, C., Wang, W. and Lee, C.Y., 2012. 'The alliance innovation performance of R&D alliances—the absorptive capacity perspective'. *Technovation, 32*(5), pp.282-292.

Mowery, D.C., Oxley, J.E. and Silverman, B.S., (1996). 'Strategic alliances and interfirm knowledge transfer'. *Strategic Management Journal, 17*(S2), pp.77-91.

Nelson, R., (1993). *National innovation systems: a comparative analysis.* Oxford University Press.

Organization of Economic Co-operation and Development (OECD), (2008). *Open innovation in global networks.* OECD.

Soh, P. and Subramanian, M., (2014). 'When do firms benefit from university-industry R&D collaborations? The implications of firm R&D focus on scientific research and technological recombination'. *Journal of Business Venturing, 29*(6), pp.807–821.

Stam, E. and Wennberg, K., (2009). 'The roles of R&D in new firm growth'. *Small Business Economics, 33*(1), pp.77–89.

Teece, D., (2007). 'Explicating dynamic capabilities: The nature and micro-foundations of (sustainable) enterprise performance'. *Strategic Management Journal, 28*(3), pp.1319–1350.

Tomlinson, P., (2010). 'Co-operative ties and innovation: Some new evidence for UK manufacturing'. *Research Policy, 39*(6), pp.762–775.

Un, C., Cuervo-Cazurra, A., and Asakawa, K., (2010). 'R&D collaborations and product innovation'. *Journal of Product Management Innovation Management, 27*(5), pp.673–689.

Chapter 18

Reverse Innovation: Towards a New Global Innovation Model for Multinationals

Marine Hadengue*

E-mail: marine.hadengue@polytechnique.edu

Abstract: Western multinationals can no longer limit themselves to their historic markets (the United States, Canada or Western Europe). Indeed, these markets, affected by the recent economic crises and lack of growth, are today saturated and therefore no longer have sufficient development potential. Conversely, other markets are booming. The middle class of several emerging economies such as Brazil, China, and India is growing considerably, creating very attractive new markets.

In that context, multinationals started to do reverse innovation. An innovation is called reverse if it is first adopted in an emerging economy before being trickled up in an advanced economy. Since reverse innovation is a recent phenomenon, the doctoral dissertation contributes to the theoretical understanding and positioning of this new innovation model. In practical terms, the doctorate aims at identifying the key factors for the success of such a strategy. The focus is on Western multinationals and more specifically on the health sector.

Keywords: Innovation Management; Reverse Innovation; Multinationals.

1. Introduction

The fact that emerging countries are considered today by many Western companies as the new incubators of innovation represents an important paradigm shift. In 2010, a special issue of The Economist on innovation in emerging countries, entitled "The world turned upside down", already predicted that this paradigm shift would have major consequences for local markets, but also and above all for the rest of the world (The Economist, 2010). Reverse innovation is one of those consequences.

Taking advantage of their presence and R&D strength in the field, Western companies had the opportunity to innovate in an original context, in a frame of reference different from the one they were used to. In tune with the local realities of these new markets, namely the constraints of price, infrastructure, sustainability, regulation or again the cultural preferences of consumers, they have been pushed out of their comfort zone in terms of innovation paradigms and have succeeded in proposing disruptive innovations, products of great value, which they could hardly have developed in a Western context (Markides, 2012).

Then, companies began to do what is now called reverse innovation. An innovation is said to be reverse if it is first adopted in an emerging economy before being subsequently brought back and marketed in an advanced economy (Govindarajan and Trimble, 2012a). This concept, originally introduced in (2009) by Immelt, Govindarajan and Trimble in an article from the Harvard Business Review, has gained considerable popularity since then.

Reverse innovation is both an old and a new idea (Burger-Helmchen, Cohendet, and Nebojsa, 2013). Some compared the practice of reverse innovation to what Japan and South Korea had experienced after World War II, as they were at the time emerging markets quickly becoming leaders in the field of innovation. To this argument, the fathers of the concept reply that the income gap between the United States and these countries was much smaller than the gap that exists today between China or India and the United States (Govindarajan and Ramamurti, 2011). Others have claimed that certain innovation concepts, prior to the reverse innovation, overlap the latter in a more or less important way (Zeschky, Winterhalter, and Gassmann, 2014). Yet, despite these overlaps, reverse innovation brings along new dimensions, the most notable of them are (1) the inclusion of the *emerging markets* dimension in the transfer of innovations and more particularly the fact that this transfer is from the *South to the North* (2) the disruptive dimension, i.e. the fact that these innovations are not necessarily frugal innovations or less efficient innovations, but rather original innovations having emerged in a new context, borrowing also from new constraints.

Among all industry sectors, it appears that the health industry is particularly conducive to the practice of reverse innovation (Crisp, 2014). The most famous example is the electrocardiograph developed by General Electric for rural areas in India. With the constraints of price, autonomy, transportability and ease of use, local R&D teams have developed a portable electrocardiograph that is easy to use and runs on batteries but is 20 times cheaper than the one proposed in the West. This innovation now equips the majority of ambulances and emergency rooms in the United States. Another less well-known example of reverse innovation is that of new medical equipment designed by a Canadian team in Botswana to facilitate rapid diagnosis of diarrheal diseases, where these are particularly deadly especially in children. This medical equipment is also widely used in Canada today.

Although the literature on reverse innovation is growing, the majority of studies are still limited to identifying successful examples of this new strategy. As the phenomenon is new, very little work has been done to investigate reverse innovation in greater depth. Directly addressing the new international innovation strategies put in place by companies to ensure their future competitiveness, the study of reverse innovation is indeed difficult. Still in a phase of imitation and trial-and-error, many companies are reluctant to share their experiences of reverse innovation, and therefore, the access to data and the publication of results, remain arduous.

In this context, the dissertation contributes to the advancement of knowledge in this field by focusing mainly on the practice of this new model of international innovation by Western multinationals.

2 Background

Recent economic crises have somewhat changed the established order. Affected by a significant lack of growth, advanced markets are now largely saturated (Charue-Duboc and Midler, 2016) and therefore no longer have sufficient development potential for their multinationals. Conversely, other markets are booming. Emerging countries such as Brazil, China and India are seeing their middle classes grow considerably, creating new and very attractive markets.

But conquering these new markets and the consumers that compose them is not trivial for Western companies. Indeed, consumers in emerging countries are in demand for more accessible products (less expensive, easier to use, etc.), but meeting different specific criteria, and without compromising quality (Prahalad and Mashelkar, 2010). There are currently five major constraints which characterize - and differentiate - these emerging markets and their consumers (Govindarajan and Trimble, 2012b): (1) the demand for cheaper products that are at least as good, (2) a significant lack of infrastructure, (3) severe requirements in terms of sustainability of innovations in a context of a strong awareness of the importance of environmental preservation, (4) different regulations and finally (5) the uses or cultural preferences which are sometimes very distinct.

The strategy adopted by some Western multinationals to transfer end-of-life or degraded products to these markets (to respond to a strong price constraint, for example) has therefore proved to be inadequate. In other words:

"Developing world customers can not be differentiated from rich world customers because they have less money. They also have unique needs. To win in emerging markets, you have to understand those needs, and innovate to meet them. (Trimble, 2012)

The gaps exposed above, although fostering innovation, thus represent new constraints for Western R&D teams, forcing them to think out of the box and to come out with breakthrough innovations instead of incremental ones. It exists a significant number of concepts that have been used to describe this phenomenon. A popular one is *frugal innovation*. It characterizes the process by which products "that respond to severe resource constraints (...) and have extreme cost advantages compared to existing solutions" (Zeschky, Widenmayer, and Gassmann, 2011b: 39) emerge. Another one is *disruptive innovation* defined as "innovation that results in worse product performance in mainstream markets" or "typically cheaper, simpler, smaller and frequently more convenient to use" version of an existing product (Christensen, 1997; Christensen and Bower, 1995).

Because the frugal innovation concept emphasizes the importance of considering environmental constraints in the innovation process, it is usually associated with emerging market innovation and could represent the first step of reverse innovation. The case of disruptive innovation is trickier. As pointed out in Govindarajan and Trimble (2009) and then more extensively in Corsi and Di Minin (2014), reverse innovation and disruptive innovation only overlap in specific circumstances. More precisely, as not all emerging market innovations are disruptive ones, the disruptive innovation framework only allows us to better understand and interpret some innovations rising from emerging markets.

Thus, assuming that reverse innovation relates to a paradigm shift and given the pioneering nature of its practice for Western multinationals, abundant literature has emerged. In order to enhance creativity and facilitate the first step of reverse innovation, i.e., innovate for the needs of a developing country or region and market the innovation over there, some authors have highlighted the importance of implementing new management strategies. These new strategies include offshoring of R&D units in emerging markets (Agarwal and Brem, 2012), building local growth teams (LGTs) in order to bring diversity and foster the adaptation to the local environment (Corsi and Di Minin, 2014; Corsi et al., 2014; Govindarajan and Euchner, 2012; Immelt et al., 2009) and using a clean-slate/zero-based strategy to enable the emergence of new relevant and appropriate ideas and concepts (Govindarajan and Ramamurti, 2011; Govindarajan and Trimble, 2012b).

Partnerships between companies from high-income countries and emerging countries have also been mentioned by the literature as a key approach to accurately target customer needs, effectively market new solutions in these new markets and overcome the liability of foreignness (Dubiel and Ernst, 2012; Govindarajan and Euchner, 2012; Laperche and Lefebvre, 2012). Considering local customers as lead-users has also been mentioned as a facilitator during the design phase of a reverse innovation (Judge, Hölttä-Otto, and Winter, 2015). Finally, a positive impact of some subsidiaries' organizational attributes has been found. It includes among others a strategic R&D orientation, a local integration and an important autonomy of local subsidiaries (Borini, Oliveira, Silveira, and Concer, 2012; M. Zeschky, Widenmayer, and Gassmann, 2014).

Another facet of the literature has focused on the consequences of practicing reverse innovation. From an economic point of view, reverse innovation could drive *reverse spillovers* -reverse knowledge transfer, i.e. from the south to the north- (Adriaens, De Lange, and Zielinski, 2013; Esko, Zeromskis, and Hsuan, 2013; Govindarajan and Ramamurti, 2011; Lee and McNamee, 2014; Radojevic and Peerally, 2013). Reverse innovation can also result in leapfrogging in emerging markets, which occurs when innovators skip over legacy technologies to adopt frontier technologies (Burger-Helmchen et al., 2013; Govindarajan and Ramamurti, 2011).

Taking these elements into account, it is clear that reverse innovation is not just a new way of doing innovation; it is also a new way of thinking about the innovation process as a whole. Most importantly, because the mature innovation will be marketed in both emerging markets and (subsequently) advanced ones, the practice of reverse innovation by Western multinationals implies a more complex and holistic innovation process. This fact changes somewhat our frontiers of knowledge about innovation and its management in general. The doctoral dissertation proposes to deepen our understanding of this phenomenon.

Specifically, the following research questions are asked:

1) To what extent do multinationals practice reverse innovation today and what are the implications for technology transfer between developed and emerging markets?

2) What are the challenges associated with the practice of reverse innovation and what are the risk mitigators?

3) What impact does the multinational network configuration (internal and external) have on the practice of reverse innovation?

The doctoral dissertation is composed of four articles. The first one is a systematic literature review of the concept of reverse innovation. The next three articles answer the research questions mentioned above. The following table 18.1 presents the organization of the dissertation.

Table 18.1 Summary of the research organization

	Article 1	**Article 2**	**Article 3**	**Article 4**
Original Title	Reverse Innovation: A Systematic Review of the Literature	Reverse Innovation and Reverse Technology Transfer: From Made in China to Discovered in China in the Pharmaceutical Sector	Avoiding the Pitfalls in Reverse Innovation: Lessons learned from Essilor	Reverse Innovation: An MNC's Network Perspective
Research Question (s)	How is reverse innovation positioned in existing literature?	Has China become a new center of innovation? To what extent do multinationals practice reverse innovation and what are the implications for knowledge transfer?	What are the challenges associated with the practice of reverse innovation and what are the risk mitigators used to promote the success of this strategy?	What influence does the configuration of the network (internal and external) of the multinational have on the practice of reverse innovation?
Key Concepts	Reverse Innovation, Systematic Review, Trickle-up innovation, Emerging Markets, Multinational Corporations, Globalization	Innovation, Reverse Innovation, Technology Transfer, Spillovers, Pharmaceutical Companies, China	Reverse Innovation, Global Innovation, Emerging Markets, Product Cannibalization, Not-invented-here Syndrome, Reverse Product Localization	Reverse Innovation, Multinational Corporations, Network, Knowledge Flows, Power bargaining, Resources Configuration
Research Objectives	Establish the state of the art of reverse innovation	Determine the extent to which multinationals practice reverse innovation and the effects of this practice on technology transfer between developed and emerging markets	Analyze in greater depth the practice of reverse innovation to identify the challenges associated with it and the keys to overcome these challenges	Propose a theoretical framework for reverse innovation by identifying the multinational company's internal and external dynamics which favor the practice of this strategy
Publication Status	Published in the *International Journal of Emerging Market (2017)*	Published in *Management International (2015)*	Published in *Research-Technology Management (2017)*	Under review

3. Research design

Since reverse innovation is a recent phenomenon, the doctoral dissertation aims to contribute to the understanding and theoretical positioning of this new model of innovation, but it also aims to identify the key factors for the success of such a strategy. To do this, a mainly qualitative methodology is used. This research design, particularly appropriate for studying emerging phenomena, seemed the most appropriate.

Two main factors explain this choice. First, since the theorization of the phenomenon is largely incomplete, the observation and description of the practice of reverse innovation are still necessary to better understand this strategy and its implications for organizations. In addition, the practice of reverse innovation still relatively uncommon, companies are, for the most part, reluctant to share their management experiences of this new innovation strategy internationally, making it difficult to build important databases.

The weak theoretical positioning of the concept coupled with this scarcity of data clearly calls for more qualitative work. Only in the following stage, and when a larger number of companies have gained experience in the practice of reverse innovation, quantitative research will make it possible to test the different hypotheses that have emerged from exploratory research.

The following table 18.2 shows the different methodologies used in each article composing the doctoral dissertation. In each case (and if applicable), the key literature of the methodology in question, the unit of analysis considered, but also the data used are specified.

It should be noted that the research design of Article 2 represents an exception to the general methodology of the thesis. Indeed, a mixed research methodology (quantitative then qualitative) was used. A quantitative statistical analysis is performed on three levels of patents, and then an analysis of official speech content is conducted. More details are given in the table 18.2 below.

Table 18.2 Summary of methodologies used in the dissertation (by article)

	Article 1	Article 2		Article 3	Article 4
Main objective of the article	Establish the state of the art on reverse innovation	Determine the extent to which multinationals practice reverse innovation and the effects of this practice on technology transfer		Analyze deeper the practice of reverse innovation	Propose a theoretical framework for reverse innovation
Methodology	Systematic Review of the Literature	Mixed Methodology		Case Study	Conceptual Study
		Descriptive statistics	Content analysis		

Key Methodological Literature	Briner and Denyer, 2012; Tranfield, Denyer, and Smart, 2003	-	Gioia, Corley, and Hamilton, 2012; Krippendorff, 2012	Yin, 2014	-
Analysis unit (s)	The concept of reverse innovation	Patents	The practice of reverse innovation and reverse technology transfer	The cases of reverse innovation at Essilor: Myopilux, Azio / India, Ready-to-Clip and Gemcoat lenses	The influence of the multinational's network configuration on the practice of reverse innovation
Data	377 documents (scientific articles, books, book chapters, theses)	Patents in general, patents in the pharmaceutical sector and patents published by the ten largest pharmaceutical companies	The official discourse of the 10 largest pharmaceutical companies in terms of revenues in 2014	Interviews with Essilor employees + additional data	Existing literature
Data sources	A set of scientific databases	WIPO and SIPO	Specialized Internet media, corporate websites, annual reports, interviews with sector stakeholders	More than 20 interviews conducted at different hierarchical levels for more than one year + brochures, internal reports, internal emails and annual reports	n/a

4. Conclusion

As a whole, this doctorate contributes to the theorization of reverse innovation, but also to the improvement of its practice.

First, it is clear from the thesis that reverse innovation is an emerging phenomenon: a new model of global innovation for companies that is attracting increasing interest in the scientific community. As the literature on the subject is abundant and unstructured, the thesis participates, through the construction of a theoretical framework, to the organization of the field and knowledge surrounding this phenomenon and it allows for a better structuring of current and future research. More than 350 documents (in English and French) were collected via several databases and then were analyzed. This work made it possible to understand how reverse innovation was both an old and a new phenomenon and to better position it the literature. In order to portray a global vision of the concept, a conceptual framework was also built. This has led to several suggestions for future research. Three of them have been addressed in the doctoral dissertation - they constitute the three research questions of the doctorate mentioned above.

The dissertation then contributes in demonstrating a significant shift in balance: Western markets are no longer the only ones targeted by multinationals. Indeed, the latter are now also interested in consumers in the middle classes of emerging economies. To verify this statement, patent data were collected and analyzed at three levels:

1) patents in general

2) patents in the pharmaceutical sector and finally

3) patents published by the ten largest companies which have recently invested in China. Patents filed in China must be filed in Chinese, the third level of analysis required to trace the patents in that language.

Pushing the reflection beyond this observation, the dissertation shows that Western multinationals practice reverse innovation, but also make reverse technology transfers. This represents an important paradigm shift in terms of knowledge transfer: they are no longer exclusively North-South, but also South-North. A content analysis of the top ten, in terms of revenues, pharmaceutical company's official discourse was conducted. This official discourse was retrieved via specialized Internet media reporting interviews with senior officials, corporate websites, annual reports, and face-to-face interviews with industry stakeholders. The coding, via a text analysis software, of several hundred pages of speech made it possible to verify that these multinationals practiced or intended to practice reverse innovation and reverse technology transfer.

In practical terms, the dissertation also proposes management tools to promote the success of reverse innovation in organizations. The multinational Essilor was then chosen to carry out a case study. Interviews were conducted with company employees and many internal documents, such as e-mails or reports, as well as marketing brochures or the company's annual reports, were collected to triangulate the data. Four cases of reverse innovation and their associated challenges were then identified.

Through the reverse innovation cases analyzed, ten challenges encountered during these projects were identified. They have been categorized into four broad groups:

1) internal corporate challenges such as the fact that head office employees perceive innovations in emerging market subsidiaries as poor quality products,

2) market-related challenges such as the risk that some innovations brought from emerging countries may cannibalize the traditional products of the company,

3) the challenges related to the sensitivity of customers such as the fact that the image they have of the company can be negatively affected if the products it offers come from emerging markets and finally

4) the challenges related to regulatory gaps between developed and emerging countries and ethical issues that may arise. The solutions put in place by Essilor to prevent or overcome these various obstacles have also been identified.

This study is the first to offer an in-depth analysis of four reverse innovation projects. In addition, it highlights an innovative company that practices reverse innovation and is willing to share its experience. It is conceivable to imagine that such an example could possibly encourage the commitment of other companies to participate in future similar studies.

The thesis finally proposes the very first theoretical framework of reverse innovation. This framework, articulated around the redefinition of reverse innovation as a process composed of two distinct but indivisible stages, allows a better understanding of the concept. By studying the potential impact of the multinational's network configuration (Ghoshal and Bartlett, 1990) on the practice of reverse innovation, the dissertation highlights the paradoxical and therefore complex nature of reverse innovation management in terms of knowledge transfers, power bargaining and also resource allocation.

Building on seminal works, for example, Andersson, Forsgren and Holm (2007)'s paper on subsidiaries' autonomy, and putting them into the context of reverse innovation, the dissertation challenges certain established practices. Indeed, if some configurations (for example, a subsidiary's embeddedness in the emerging market) could foster the first step of reverse innovation, i.e., to innovate for the emerging market, they could, at the same time, impede the second step of the reverse innovation process, i.e. the return of this innovation into the advanced market.

This angle brings a different dimension to the concept of reverse innovation but more importantly forces us to question many of our previous assumptions in terms of innovation management.

5. Implications and future research

"The electric light did not come from the continuous improvement of candles". (Oren Harari)

In conclusion, the overall goal of the doctorate was to improve the understanding of reverse innovation. Attempting to make a contribution both theoretically and practically, the articles making up the body of the doctoral dissertation have each responded to different issues. It has contributed to the research community by improving the theoretical positioning of reverse innovation, but it has also benefited practitioners by providing management tools.

But all these findings raise several new questions not yet investigated in the dissertation. Indeed, it is clear that a significant proportion of reverse innovations that have been identified as major successes are, first and foremost, social innovations [1]. General Electric's compact electrocardiograph and portable ultrasound scanner, Essilor's Ready-to-Clip glasses, Parmalat's bagged milk for malnourished children, and Renault's economical Dacia Logan car are some excellent examples. Less expensive than conventional products in the same category, these innovations, often easier to use, sometimes portable and energy-autonomous, have improved the quality of life or even saved lives in emerging countries, for which they were designed, but also in advanced economies. In total, out of more than 60 reverse innovations listed in the dissertation's appendix, about a third of them can be considered as social innovations.

Some of these innovations have been put in place by non-profit organizations whose primary mission is exclusively social. This is the case with the MIT Mobility Lab's Leveraged Freedom Chair all-terrain wheelchair or Partners In Health's health care program for the underprivileged. But in other cases, large multinationals are at the origin of these social innovations (General Electric, Essilor, Parmalat, Renault, etc.). This observation raises major questions: why so many reverse innovations are also social innovations, whereas the multinationals from which they emerge are not, in principle, social enterprises? Do these social innovations respond to the same (social) needs in emerging or developing markets as in developed markets? If social innovation is traditionally associated with incremental innovation since the organizations at its origin have few resources (Gundry, Kickul, Griffiths, and Bacq, 2011), what about reverse innovations of a social character developed by multinationals? Finally, is it possible to consider that reverse innovation is a promising strategy for the creation of radical global social innovations? Although these questions call for further research, the following paragraphs attempt to give some clues or at least some development possibilities.

The key here probably lies in the nature of the constraints facing Western companies wishing to conquer these new markets and more specifically in the reorientation of their mission of innovation. The imperative of developing cheaper, sustainable and at least equally performing products, the significant lack of on-site infrastructures, the regulations, but also the sometimes very different uses or cultural preferences of these new markets are the main constraints mentioned by the theory of reverse innovation (Govindarajan and Trimble, 2012b). Among these constraints, at least two (little or no infrastructure and very limited financial means) represent alone the basic elements responsible for the majority of social needs in the world (World Bank, 2006). Thus, to overcome these obstacles, and regardless of the industry, the practice of reverse innovation by Western multinationals will potentially generate new solutions that are, in essence, social innovations.

It is interesting to note that, in many cases, new areas of value are developed during the creative process of reverse innovation. Thus, reverse innovations do not necessarily meet the same need in emerging or developing economies as in advanced economies. The compact electrocardiograph or the portable ultrasound scanner, each originally intended for rural, remote Indian populations, is now used in ambulances and emergencies in the United States because of its transportability and low cost. Parmalat sachet milk for malnourished children is now a sustainable environmental solution in developed countries. Finally, Renault's Dacia Logan, originally designed for consumers in Eastern Europe, was a relief option for French families whose incomes had been reduced by the economic crisis. For others, the affordable prices at which these vehicles were sold in France represented the possibility of acquiring a second car.

In other words, not only do these social reverse innovations lead to significant improvements in performance and costs, transforming the markets of emerging countries, but they also create new market opportunities in advanced markets. They are, by definition, radical innovations (Leifer, O'Connor, Rice, and O'Connoer, 2001).

Although literature traditionally describes social innovations as incremental innovations, mainly due to the lack of resources available to social enterprises (Gundry et al., 2011), the case of reverse innovations seems to call for different reasoning. Multinationals are indeed among the richest organizations in terms of human and material resources, and these resources, coupled with the dynamics of reverse innovation management, push back the traditional limits of social innovation. Thus, the empowerment of local subsidiaries, the establishment of a new innovation ecosystem involving head office employees, but also new employees directly from local markets and the reformulation of a new mission of innovation (Govindarajan and Trimble, 2012a, 2012b; Hadengue, De Marcellis-Warin, von Zedtwitz, and Warin, 2017) are all new strategies for these companies. They make it possible to challenge traditional paradigms and to break cognitive schemas, thus favoring the emergence of new ideas and potentially radical innovations (Agogué, 2013; Dewar and Dutton, 1986).

Of course, it is possible that some reverse innovations are social innovations without being radical or radical without being social. It is also possible that some are neither. The tea-flavored toothpaste originally developed by Colgate-Palmolive for China, which later became a worldwide success, is an example. However, it seems reasonable to admit that reverse innovation is a process whose intrinsic properties can potentially stimulate the emergence of global social innovations.

To conclude, these different observations refer back to the question of the impact of constraints on the degree of creativity of an organization. There seems to be no consensus in the innovation management literature on this issue (Caniëls and Rietzschel, 2015). If organizational constraints seem to diminish creativity (Amabile, 1998; Amabile, Schatzel, Moneta, and Kramer, 2006), design constraints or environmental constraints could tend to stimulate the creative process (Arrighi, Le Masson, and Weil, 2015).

In the case of reverse innovation, it seems that the new constraints faced by Western multinationals are the main determinants of the innovative nature of new products that emerge from the creative process. In other words, the context in which these innovations are developed and then commercialized stimulates creativity and allows the emergence of original solutions, sometimes social or even radical.

Taking up the work done in the fourth article of the thesis and breaking down the reverse innovation into two distinct stages, it could be accepted that creativity is stimulated by different constraints at each of these stages. The demand for inexpensive, efficient, autonomous, sustainable products, etc. stimulates the creative process during the first stage. R&D teams are forced to redefine the mission of innovation and get out of their traditional cognitive schemas.

In a following second stage, other constraints both external and internal to the organization can stimulate the creativity needed to repatriate these new products in developed markets (Hadengue et al., 2017). At the external level, it is possible to think for example of the risk of cannibalization of traditional products of the company. Internally, the perception by head office employees of poor product quality from subsidiaries located in emerging or developing markets can be a significant challenge. In the latter case, creative solutions within the company must be put in place to overcome these prior judgments or attitudes. Thus, it is clear that the study of the reverse innovation practice taking the angle of creativity could possibly come to enrich this literature.

Overall, all these issues regarding the social or even radical character of reverse innovations as well as the impacts of this new global innovation process in terms of creativity, open the way for an important agenda of research. Indeed, reverse innovation appears to be a must-have for Western multinationals that want to survive in a world where emerging economies are taking up considerably more market space than before. But this new innovation model is hard to achieve and more work is needed to successfully guide companies in the process.

References

Adriaens, P., De Lange, D., and Zielinski, S. (2013). *Reverse Innovation for the New Mobility*. SSRN Scholarly Paper no. ID 2297912, Rochester, NY: Social Science Research Network. http://papers.ssrn.com/abstract=2297912.

Agarwal, N., and Brem, A. (2012). Frugal and reverse innovation - Literature overview and case study insights from a German MNC in India and China. *2012 18th International ICE Conference on Engineering, Technology and Innovation (ICE 2012), 18-20 June 2012*, 11 pp. IEEE.

Agogué, M. (2013). *L'innovation orpheline: lutter contre les biais cognitifs dans les dynamiques industrielles*. Paris: Presses des Mines.

Amabile, T. M. (1998). 'How to Kill Creativity'. *Harvard Business Review*, 76(5): 76–87.

Amabile, T. M., Schatzel, E. A., Moneta, G. B., and Kramer, S. J. (2006). 'Corrigendum to "Leader behaviors and the work environment for creativity: Perceived leader support"'. *The Leadership Quarterly*, 17(6): 679–680.

Andersson, U., Forsgren, M., and Holm, U. (2007). 'Balancing Subsidiary Influence in the Federative MNC: A Business Network View'. *Journal of International Business Studies*, 38(5): 802–818.

Arrighi, P.-A., Le Masson, P., and Weil, B. (2015). 'Addressing Constraints Creatively: How New Design Software Helps Solve the Dilemma of Originality and Feasibility'. *Creativity and Innovation Management*, 24(2): 247–260.

Borini, F. M., Oliveira, M. de M., Jr, Silveira, F. F., and Concer, R. de O. (2012). 'The reverse transfer of innovation of foreign subsidiaries of Brazilian multinationals'. *European Management Journal*, 30(3): 219.

Burger-Helmchen, T., Cohendet, P., and Nebojsa, R. (2013). 'L'innovation inverse : un retournement du principe de diffusion internationale des innovations ?' *Le Management International à l'écoute du local*: 131–149. Gualino Editeur.

Caniëls, M. C. J., and Rietzschel, E. F. (2015). 'Organizing Creativity: Creativity and Innovation under Constraints'. *Creativity and Innovation Management*, 24(2): 184–196.

Charue-Duboc, F., and Midler, C. (2016). 'Management de l'innovation et globalisation'. *Le journal de l'école de Paris du management*, (118): 38–45.

Christensen, C. M. (1997). *The Innovator's Dilemma: When New Technologies Cause Great Firms to Fail*. Boston, MA: Harvard Business School Press.

Christensen, C. M., and Bower, J. L. (1995). 'Disruptive Technologies: Catching the Wave'. *Harvard Business Review*, 73(1): 43–53.

Corsi, S., and Di Minin, A. (2014). 'Disruptive innovation ... in reverse: adding a geographical dimension to disruptive innovation theory'. *Creativity and Innovation Management*, 23(1): 76–90.

Corsi, S., Di Minin, A., and Piccaluga, A. (2014). 'Reverse innovation at speres a case study in China'. *Research Technology Management*, 57(4): 28–34.

Crisp, N. (2014). 'Mutual learning and reverse innovation–where next?' *Globalization and Health*, 10(1): 14.

Dewar, R. D., and Dutton, J. E. (1986). 'The Adoption of Radical and Incremental Innovations: An Empirical Analysis'. *Management Science*, 32(11): 1422–1433.

Dubiel, A., and Ernst, H. (2012). 'Success Factors of New Product Development for Emerging Markets'. *The PDMA Handbook of New Product Development*: 100–114. John Wiley and Sons, Inc.

Esko, S., Zeromskis, M., and Hsuan, J. (2013). 'Value chain and innovation at the base of the pyramid'. *South Asian Journal of Global Business Research*, 2(2): 230–250.

Ghoshal, S., and Bartlett, C. A. (1990). 'The Multinational Corporation as an Interorganizational Network'. *The Academy of Management Review*, 15(4): 603–625.

Govindarajan, V., and Euchner, J. (2012). 'Reverse Innovation: An Interview with Vijay Govindarajan'. *Research Technology Management*, 55(6): 13–17.

Govindarajan, V., and Ramamurti, R. (2011). 'Reverse innovation, emerging markets, and global strategy'. *Global Strategy Journal*, 1(3–4): 191–205.

Govindarajan, V., and Trimble, C. (2009). 'Is Reverse Innovation Like Disruptive Innovation?' *Harvard Business Review*. https://hbr.org/2009/09/is-reverse-innovation-like-dis.

Govindarajan, V., and Trimble, C. (2012a). *Reverse Innovation: Create Far from Home, Win Everywhere*. Boston, MA: Harvard Business Press.

Govindarajan, V., and Trimble, C. (2012b). 'Reverse innovation: a global growth strategy that could pre-empt disruption at home'. *Strategy and Leadership*, 40(5): 5–11.

Gundry, L. K., Kickul, J. R., Griffiths, M. D., and Bacq, S. C. (2011). 'Creating Social Change Out of Nothing: The Role of Entrepreneurial Bricolage in Social Entrepreneurs' Catalytic Innovations'. *Social and Sustainable Entrepreneurship*, vol. 13: 1–24. Emerald Group Publishing Limited.

Hadengue, M., De Marcellis-Warin, N., von Zedtwitz, M., and Warin, T. (2017). 'Avoiding the Pitfalls in Reverse Innovation - Lessons from Essilor'. *Research-Technology Management*, 60(3): 40–47.

Immelt, J., Govindarajan, V., and Trimble, C. (2009). 'How GE is disrupting itself'. *Harvard Business Review*, 87: 56–65.

Judge, B. M., Höltta-Otto, K., and Winter, V., Amos G. (2015). 'Developing World Users as Lead Users: A Case Study in Engineering Reverse Innovation'. *Journal of Mechanical Design*, 137(7): 071406–071406.

Laperche, B., and Lefebvre, G. (2012). 'The globalization of Research and Development in industrial corporations: Towards "reverse innovation"?. The cases of General Electric and Renault'. *Journal of Innovation Economics and Management*, n°10(2): 53–79.

Lee, A., and McNamee, R. C. (2014). 'In Search Of A Theoritical Framework For Reverse Innovations'. *Academy of International Business. Annual Meeting. Proceedings*, 0_1,3-5,7,9-294,296-326. Academy of International Business (AIB).

Leifer, R., O'Connor, G. C., Rice, M., and O'Connoer, G. C. (2001). 'Implementing Radical Innovation in Mature Firms: The Role of Hubs'. *The Academy of Management Executive (1993-2005)*, 15(3): 102–113.

Markides, C. C. (2012). 'How Disruptive Will Innovations from Emerging Markets Be?' *MIT Sloan Management Review*, 54(1): 23–25.

Phills, J. A., Deiglmeier, K., and Miller, D. T. (2008). 'Rediscovering Social Innovation'. *Social Innovation Review*, Fall.
https://ssir.org/articles/entry/rediscovering_social_innovation.

Prahalad, C. K., and Mashelkar, R. A. (2010). Innovation's holy grail. *Harvard Business Review*, 88(7–8): 132–141.

Radojevic, N., and Peerally, J. A. (2013). 'Reverse Innovation and the Bottom of the Pyramid Proposition: New Clothes for Old Garbs?' *Quality Innovation: Knowledge, Theory, and Practices* (1 edition). Hershey, PA: IGI Global.

The Economist. (2010), April 15. The world turned upside down. *The Economist*. http://www.economist.com/node/15879369.

Trimble, C. (2012). 'Reverse innovation and the emerging-market growth imperative'. *Ivey Business Journal*, 76: 19.

World Bank. (2006). *Social development and infrastructure: working in partnership for sustainable development*: 1–41. no. 49410, Washington, DC: World Bank.

Zeschky, M. B., Winterhalter, S., and Gassmann, O. (2014). 'From cost to frugal and reverse innovation: Mapping the field and implications for global competitiveness'. *Research Technology Management*, 57(4): 20–27.

Zeschky, M., Widenmayer, B., and Gassmann, O. (2011). 'Frugal innovation in emerging markets'. *Research-Technology Management*, 54: 38–45.

Zeschky, M., Widenmayer, B., and Gassmann, O. (2014). 'Organising for reverse innovation in Western MNCs: the role of frugal product innovation capabilities'. *International Journal of Technology Management*, 64(2): 255–75.

Chapter 19

Never Venture, Never Win!
The Chinese Rush to Innovation
and Regional Development

Antonio Crupi*

E-mail: antonio.crupi@santannapisa.it

Abstract: The purpose of the thesis is to study the influence that innovation, and especially the public policies for boosting innovation, generated on the economic regional development. The main idea behind the research is to concentrate the analysis of innovation and regional development on the Chinese framework, in order to identify the functioning of the innovation drivers in such a peculiar context. The study aims to stress how the interactions between the different actors in the innovation system are re-shaping the firms' behavior and how the great participation of the public sector in the production of innovation is acting like a booster for the regional development, through the intervention on the innovative level of the country.

Keywords: Innovation; Regional Innovation System; Regional Development; China, Public and Private Investments, Patents, Nanotechnologies; Regional Policies; Intellectual Property; Employment; R&D investment; FDI.

1. Introduction

The attention to the scientific production as a booster for the technology development is a phenomenon in continuous growth among the most developed countries and the fast-growing economies. Literature in innovation is often centered on cross-country evaluations of innovative implementation based on the structures and dynamics of national innovation systems through comparative studies (Freeman, 2002; Lundvall, 1992; Nelson, 1993).

Countries in the World present a heterogeneous innovative framework. Innovation implementations differ not only between countries but also within the countries (Acs et al., 2002; Evangelista et al., 2001; Fritsch, 2002). Analysing large countries, according to Edquist (2010), the national innovation system approach risks to be less relevant because of the stressed differences at regional level.

The aim of the thesis is to investigate the impact of the innovation on the economic regional development. In doing so, the analysis is mainly focused on the national and regional policies issued by the Chinese Central Government and the Regional Governments in order to boost the innovative level of the country.

Thus, the idea behind the research is to concentrate the analysis of innovation and regional development on the Chinese framework, in order to identify the functioning of the innovation drivers in such a peculiar context. The study's goal, on the one hand, is to stress how interactions between the different actors in the innovation system are re-shaping the firms' behavior. On the other hand, is to highlight how the great participation of the public sector in the innovation production is acting like a booster for the regional development, thanks to the improvement of the innovative level of the country.

China, being one of the largest fast-growing economies in the world is one of the most innovative economic landscape. The country is in rapid transformation also thanks to a rapid increment of the economic and technological development; this implies that the national innovation system is under transition from a central planned to a market-driven system (Li, 2009).

As a matter of fact, starting from the new millennium, China has made a huge effort to drive the internal economy from the industry-based model to the innovation-driven one, experimenting an impressive growth in technological capability. Those efforts have led the country up to the top in the global scenario making China one of the most productive countries in the world in terms of innovation (Baglieri et al., 2012). Thus, such an increment is the result of unique interactions between national and regional governments, universities, and domestic and foreign firms (Liu and White, 2001). Moreover, the Chinese system can also be considered unique in terms of connections between the private and the public sectors.

Chinese innovation system is characterized by several peculiarities that make it different from other advanced economies (Baglieri et al., 2014). Mainly, from the technology development point of view, in the last decades, China has experimented an exceptional increase in the technological capacity. Indeed, one of the most peculiar aspects of the thesis is the attention given on one of the most common tools used to measure the innovative level of the country: the number of patent applications. Indeed, as well demonstrated by the previous literature on the subject that China has increased dramatically the number of applications during the last decades even overtaking the United States in 2011 and becoming a global leader. The entire theoretical framework of this study is based on these considerations. In developing my research framework and, in turn, grounding the research hypotheses in it, I considered the effort made by the government in boosting the innovation and the effort made in protecting this innovation generated as focal to this study.

The starting point is given by the consideration, thanks to a clear political strategy, China is reshaping its economy from being industry-based to innovation- driven. The Government is making all the possible effort in the first phase to fill the technological gap with the most advanced economies in the World. In the second phase to take the innovation leadership and to maintain it re-determining the geography on innovation. In doing so, it is one of the most relevant aspects of the Intellectual Property Protection (IPP). Well-known, in the past years, as a counterfeiter China is pivoting drastically this trivial idea.

Investing in innovation and using massively the IPP China is defining the ground rules. On the one hand, the Government is incentivizing the patent activity in order to demonstrate the technological superiority of the country. On the other hand, thanks to the international IPP (China is an active member of the WTO since the 2001) is holding up the most influent economic competitors around the World forcing them in recognizing China as a major interlocutor.

Formally the thesis is divided into four parts. Firstly, it offers a general overview of the theoretical framework. By going through the literature on "innovation" and "regional development," I investigated the publications issued in accordance with these two keywords. By performing a co-citation network analysis, I then investigated the new trends in terms of related literature.

Secondly, I analyze the contribution to innovation given by universities. This part investigates how the effort made in R&D private expenditure and in S&T public expenditure affects the universities' patent production in terms of quantity and quality.

Then I focus my attention on the analysis of the public policies in terms of subsidies offered by the regional governments in order to stimulate patent applications. I investigate the impact generated by innovation production (patents) on the regional economic growth, highlighting the influence generated by the subsidy program for the development of indigenous inventions.

Finally, I study the relationships between innovation and regional employment measuring the impact generated by innovation, at regional level, on the employment and on the salaries gained by employees.

2. Background

The modern era is totally shaped on global competition and the concept of innovation is linked with the idea of cutting the geographic distance. It seems a paradox studying the phenomenon of innovation at regional level because it is well known as the improvement in technology and competition made the traditional role of location less influent (Porter, 2000).

By contrast, the idea of innovation itself has deep roots in territorial experiences of industrial clusters and localized knowledge spillovers (Doloreux and Parto, 2004). The geographic location assumes new significance given the fact that resources, funds and technology are well accessible in the local market and firms do not need to be located anymore close to the large market that they are serving and also governments are losing their prevalence in influencing the global market.

Following this, the concept of regional dimension is assuming greater importance and is representing a new way of considering national and local economies, according to the role played by the different level of governments and institutions involved in the development. As a matter of fact, innovation is the result of the collaboration between institutional, political and social actors and the regional dimension is the place in which economy and innovation interact (Storper, 1997). The rising interest for the regional dimension, as proxy to analyze the innovation-driven economies, started from considering the central role played by the local resources in boosting innovative capabilities of the local environment and the competitiveness of firms. The present paper highlights the importance of the geographic proximity as a strategic factor that helps the improvement of the general innovative level of the system. As a matter of fact, proximity is the way thanks to which the knowledge has spread among the private and public actors and is also the key for firms and universities to adapt and reshape their behavior in order to get the highest profit.

As stated by Porter (1998) in a global economy the competitive advantage is the result of local extremely specialized abilities and knowledge linked to institutions, partners and customers inside the regions. This is also stated in other studies that show how firms innovative outputs are related to regional endemic characteristics such as the level of specialization of the labour force, the accessibility to the labour market, the presence of spillover effects and the institutional and policy makers support (Cooke, 2001; Tödtling and Trippl, 2005). But innovation does not involve only firms and local capabilities. It is also a matter of social and institutional relationships. On the one hand, the social panorama determines the economic, socio-cultural and political dynamics strengthening the innovation and learning capabilities and increasing the value of the capital composed also by social interactions and connections within the community (Storper, 1997).

On the other hand, at an institutional level, innovation will arise with higher proficiency thanks to the proximity to the knowledge source. In this view the geographic location plays a key role, indeed, in terms of a local unit of analysis, the literature identifies the concept of cluster as an element of observation (Porter, 2000). Regional clusters are composed by firms operating in same or similar technological field, public institutions such government, education institutions and logistic services (Porter, 1998). The cluster works like a unique synergic entity in which innovation is boosted by the knowledge spillover given by the geographic proximity that helps the flows of information at every level.

On the grounds of the just cited theories, the aim of the thesis is to give a general overview of the most important studies that link the concept of regional development to the concept of innovation. This will provide a general framework of the pillars on which this literature is based and analyze the impact of innovation on regional development in a specific environment (Cesaroni et al., 2017). Thus, the research setting of the present work is China. Chinese economic and innovative landscape is in rapid transformation thanks to a rapid increment of the economic and technological development, this implies that the national innovation system is under transition from a central planned to a market-driven system (Li, 2009). Following the approach suggested by Li (2009) the thesis considers Chinese regions as independent, innovative systems and analyzes the role-played by Universities, as knowledge generator, in regional development in fast growing emerging economies.

One of the most utilized tools to measure the level of innovation is the number of registered patents; China has been experimenting with a massive increment of patenting activity interesting scholars from all around the World; the phenomenon has been studied from different points of view. The most targeted issue in the studies is still how the quantity increase affected the general qualitative level of the outputs. The present research work suggests different interpretations.

Firstly, it studied how the public and private expenditure in R&D affect the principal characteristics of the patents and how university-industry collaboration impact on the Regional Innovation System. Secondly, it studied the impact of the innovation outputs on the general economic growth. Isolating the contribution given to the innovation, in terms of the number of patents registered, the analysis shows the impact on the regional economic growth also according to the regional patent subsidy programs issued by the different regions across the years. Lastly, the analysis shows the impact generated by innovation in terms of public and private R&D expenditure and the number of patents registered on the regional development taking into account a specific target: the level of employment and the total wage bill at regional level.

In doing so, the research points out the attention on two different levels. The first is the institutional level analyzing the differences, on the economic growth, made by universities or private patents. The second level is the

regional one, investigating the efforts given by the patent promotion policies. Since the end of 90s Chinese central government pushes regional authorities in issuing policies devoted to the promotion of "domestic invention" so regions, within the first decade of the new millennium, adopted
incentives to the patent activity.

3. Research design

The thesis in the different chapters adopts different methodological strategies
in order to respond to different research hypotheses.

Firstly, the thesis investigating the role played by R&D public and private
investments on the patents' characteristics. In order to do so, the first quantitative chapter responds to the following research hypotheses:

- Hypothesis 1: Public expenditures in S&T impact positively on
  the number of Chinese university granted patents;

- Hypothesis 1.2: Private investments in R&D impact positively
  on the number of Chinese university granted patents

- Hypothesis 2: Public expenditures in S&T and private investments in R&D positively influence patent claims

- Hypothesis 3: Public expenditures in S&T and private investments in R&D positively influence patent citations.

Hypotheses have been tested on a particular case. The chapter uses for the
investigation a sample composed by all the Chinese universities that have
been issued, from 2000 to 2016, more than 10 patents in Carbon Nanotubes,
counting overall 10,633 patents.

The model used is a structured dynamic panel model with fixed effect and
robust standard errors for clustering the regional differences. The equation to
be estimated and analyzed is:

$$Y_{it} = \alpha + \beta_1 Pub_{i,t} + \beta_2 Hindex_{i,t} + \beta_3 Dcoassi_{i,t} + \beta_4 GRP_{i,t} + \beta_5 S\&Texp_{i,t}$$
$$+ \beta_6 S\&Texp2_{i,t} + \beta_7 S\&Tperspubl_{i,t} + \beta_8 RDprivexp_{i,t}$$
$$+ \beta_9 FFE_{i,t} + \varepsilon_i$$

Where the dependent variable is alternatively: NPAT, Claims and Citations.
Variables are explained in the following table 19.1.

Table 19.1 list of variables model 1

Variable	Type	Explanation	Source
NPAT	Dep.	N. of patents in CNT granted	Qpat-Orbit database
Claims	Dep.	N. of Claims University/Region	Qpat-Orbit database
Citations	Dep.	N. of Claims University/Region	Qpat-Orbit database
Pub	Control	N. of Universities' publications	Web of knowledge database
Hindex	Control	H-index of universities' publications	Web of knowledge database
GRP	Control	Gross Regional Product	Chinese Statistical Bureau Database
Coassi	Indep.	Dummy for patent co-ownership	Qpat-Orbit database
S&Texp	Indep.	Public expenditures in S&T per Region	Chinese Statistical Bureau Database
S&Texp2	Indep.	S&Texp squared	Self-elaboration
S&Tperspubl	Indep.	Employees in S&T public institutions and universities per Region	Chinese Statistical Bureau Database
RDprivexp	Indep.	Private expenditures in R&D per Region	Chinese Statistical Bureau Database

Secondly, the thesis investigating: on the one hand, the role played by innovation and especially public and private patents on economic regional development. On the other hand, the role played by the patents subsidy regional program on economic regional growth. In order to do so the second quantitative chapter responds to the following research hypotheses:

- **Hypothesis 1:** The greater the innovative effort of local universities, the higher the regional economic growth.

- *Hypothesis 1.1:* The impact of local universities' innovative effort of regional economic growth presents diminishing returns.

- **Hypothesis 2:** The greater the innovative effort of local firms, the higher the regional economic growth.

- *Hypothesis 2.1:* The impact of local firms' innovative effort of regional economic growth presents diminishing returns.

- **Hypothesis 3:** The more regional governments promote local innovative activity, the higher the regional economic growth.

The study combines three different databases: the first one at regional level structured with the National Statistical Office database, the second made by the universities patent data from Q-pat database and the third one a dummy variables database, made by self-elaborations, in which are reported the year of introduction of the different policies at regional level. The final dataset has a balanced panel structure and comprehends a temporal range of twenty years, from 1996 to 2016.

The model utilized is a structured dynamic panel model using fixed effect with robust standard errors in order to cluster the differences between regions. The estimated equation is:

$$
\begin{aligned}
growthGRP_{i,t} = \ & \alpha + \beta_1 Patentuniv_{i,t} + \beta_2 Patentuniv2_{i,t} \\
& + \beta_3 Patentindust_{i,t} + \beta_4 Patentindust2_{i,t} \\
& + \beta_5 lnGRP_{i,t-1} + \beta_6 Fixedassets_{i,t} + \beta_7 FFE_{i,t} \\
& + \beta_8 Population_{i,t} + \beta_9 Nhigheredu_{i,t} + \beta_{10} PolicyA_{i,t} \\
& + \beta_{11} PolicyB_{i,t} + \beta_{12} PolicyC_{i,t} + \varepsilon_i
\end{aligned}
$$

Variables are explained in the following table 19.2.

Table 19.2 list of variables model 2

Variable	Type	Explanation	Source
growthGRP	Dep.	Annual GRP growth rate per capita	Chinese Statistical Bureau Database
Patentuniv	Indep.	N. of patents granted by universities per region	Qpat-Orbit database
Patentuniv2	Indep.	Patentuniv squared	Self-elaboration
Patentindust	Indep.	N. of patents granted by industries per region	Chinese Statistical Bureau Database
Patentindust	Indep.	Patentindust squared	Self-elaboration
L.lnGRP	Control	Natural log of GRP per capita (t-1)	Chinese Statistical Bureau Database
Fixedassets	Control	Total Fixed Assets per Region	Chinese Statistical Bureau Database
FFE	Control	N. of Foreign Funded Enterprises per Region	Chinese Statistical Bureau Database

Population	Control	Tot. resident population per Region	Chinese Statistical Bureau Database
Nhigheredu	Control	N. of Institutions of Higher Education	Chinese Statistical Bureau Database
PolicyA	Indep.	Dummy for filling patent request policy	Self-elaboration
PolicyB	Indep.	Dummy for examination request policy	Self-elaboration
PolicyC	Indep.	Dummy for grant-contingent policy	Self-elaboration

Finally, the thesis ends with the investigation of the impact of innovation on regional employment and on the wages bill. In order to do so the third quantitative chapter responds to the following research hypotheses:

- ***Hypothesis 1.1:*** Innovation impacts positively on the employment level.

- ***Hypothesis 1.2:*** Innovation impacts positively on the local growth through a positive influence on the wages' bill.

- ***Hypothesis 2.1:*** Public investment on Science and Technology influences the innovative level of the region.

- ***Hypothesis 2.2:*** Private investment on R&D influences the innovative level of the region.

Data have been extracted from the Chinese National Statistical Bureau and organized in a balanced panel database. Data cover a time range from 1996 to 2015. To empirically test the hypotheses, the chapter performs a two stage least square model with fixed effects.

The estimated equation is:

$$\lceil y_{i,t} = \beta_0 + \beta_{1,i} lnGRP_{i,t} + \beta_{2,i} FDI_{i,t} + \beta_{3,i} Patents_{i,t} + u_i$$

$$\{ Patents_{i,t} = \gamma_0 + \gamma_{1,i} lnGRP_{i,t} + \gamma_{2,i} FDI_{i,t} + \gamma_{3,i} R\&D_{i,t} + \gamma_{4,i} Hedu_{i,t} + \gamma_{5,i} S\&T_{i,t} + \varepsilon_i$$

Where: Y represents alternatively the number of employed persons *(Empl)* and the total wage bill of employed persons *(Wage)*. Variables are explained in the following table 19.3.

Table 19.3 list of variables model 3

Variable	Explanation	Source
Empl	Number of Employed Persons per Region	Chinese Statistical Bureau Database
Wage	Total Wage Bill of Employed Persons per Region	Chinese Statistical Bureau Database
Patents	N. of domestic patents applications accepted	Self-elaboration
lnGRP	Natural log of GRP per capita	Chinese Statistical Bureau Database
FDI	Tot. investments of Foreign Funded Enterprises per Region	Chinese Statistical Bureau Database
R&Dpriv	Expenditures in R&D of Industrial Enterprises	Chinese Statistical Bureau Database
Hedu	N. of Institutions of Higher Education	Chinese Statistical Bureau Database
S&Texp	Public expenditures in S&T per Region	Self-elaboration

4. Conclusion

As shown in table 19.4 public effort in S&T generates a positive impact on the number of patents filed by universities. However, the role of private firms seems controversial, since foreign direct investments at the regional level show a negative impact on the dependent variable and R&D expenditure of private firms is not statistically associated to the number of university patents. Thus, the more private firms invest in R&D at the regional level, the fewer universities develop patented research outcomes. The negative effect of FDIs is confirmed and results show that R&D investments of private firms negatively affect university patenting. The second regression considers the average of the number of claims of university patents at the regional level as dependent variable. The larger the number of claims included in a patent, the broader its applicability, that is, the higher the possibility to apply that patent in diverse application fields. According to such an interpretation, results show that public investments in S&T induce universities to develop more general-purpose technologies (patents with higher number of claims). By contrast, private investments in R&D do affect negatively the number of claims of university patents. It seems that foreign firms had in the past to locate their manufacturing facilities in China mainly to take advantage of the reduced labour cost. During the last years, by contrast, foreign firms locate their facilities in China (also) to profit from local research capabilities and to collaborate with local Chinese universities. In doing so they influence universities' patenting policy, by pushing for more specialized patents. The same pattern seems to apply to local private firms, whose investments in R&D induce universities to develop patents characterized by a lower number of claims (i.e., more specialized patents). In turn, in those regions where local private firms invest more in R&D and the presence of foreign direct investments is higher, universities generate patents that respond to the direct needs of the market. Finally, the third regression considers the number of forward citations received from patent as dependent variable. The more citations a patent receives, the greater is the influence that the patent has on the technological arena. Here, public S&T expenditures do have a positive impact on the number of citations of university patents. So, when local governments invest more in S&T, local universities develop more impactful research outcomes. By contrast, the impact of private R&D expenditure and of foreign direct investments on patent citations is negative. Again, similarly to the case of claims, these results seem to confirm that in those regions where the presence of private (local or multinational) firms is more intensive, universities tend to pro-mote research that responds to the needs of the local technology market, albeit being less general and less impactful.

Table 19.4 results model 1

Variable	NPAT		Claims		Citations	
Pub	3.64***	4.10***	2.86***	2.49**	2.13**	1.60
	(0.001)	(0.000)	(0.005)	(0.014)	(0.036)	(0.112)
Hindex	0.32	-0.31	0.32	0.03	0.11	-0.28
	(0.752)	(0.757)	(0.752)	(0.980)	(0.910)	(0.783)
Coassi	-1.72 *	-1.80*	-1.53	-1.55	-1.24	-1.33
	(0.090)	(0.073)	(0.128)	(0.122)	(0.217)	(0.187)
GRP	-1.97*	-1.43	-1.19	-0.86	-0.69	-0.27
	(0.052)	(0.156)	(0.235)	(0.393)	(0.493)	(0.788)
S&Texp	2.46	4.24***	4.28***	2.86***	4.87***	3.69***
	(0.016)	(0.000)	(0.000)	(0.005)	(0.000)	(0.000)
S&Texp2	-	-2.41**	-	-1.06	-	-1.78*
		(0.017)		(0.290)		(0.077)
S&Tperspubl	1.59	1.09	0.81	0.98	-2.78***	0.38
	(0.116)	(0.278)	(0.420)	(0.330)	(0.006)	(0.702)

RDprivexp	-1.67 (0.101)	-2.99*** (0.003)	-2.88*** (0.005)	-2.86*** (0.005)	-2.48** (0.015)	-2.96*** (0.004)
FFE	-2.29** (0.025)	-3.65*** (0.000)	-2.75*** (0.007)	-2.92*** (0.004)	-2.48*** (0.015)	-2.97*** (0.004)
Obs.	215		207		192	
F	(8,67) 8.94	(9,138) 13.66	(8,133) 6.92	(9,132) 6.28	(8,117) 0.025	(9,116) 6.48

Table 19.5 shows the results for the second set of hypotheses. In the first regression, the number of patent granted by universities generates a negative impact on the regional development. Moreover, the findings on the policies imply that the first two incentives: the filling step and the examination request do not give any return in terms of direct economic impact. The third step of the program, instead, being granted-contingent, implies a positive return on the economic growth. It is interesting to notice how the universities patent outcome affects also the initial level of the GRP that indicates that the effort made in innovation by universities does not help the regions less developed in growing faster. The second regression isolates the industrial innovation productivity considering the impact of the number of patents generated by the industries on the economic growth. According to the regression results, the efforts of the industries do not give any benefit, per se, to the regional development but they confirm the neoclassical growth theory reported by Rodriguez-Pose and Peralta (2015) according to which due to the constant or lessening returns to investment, less developed regions tend to grow faster. The policies result confirms the tendency seen in the precedent model that only the granted-contingent subsidy generates a positive impact. The third regression considers at the same time the patents production of universities and industries. In order to further investigate the effects caused by the policies the regression has been performed two times. The first time the policies are analyzed at the time t, in the second time the policies are considered at the time t-1 in order to catch up the influence after one year of policies implementation. The regression confirms substantially the findings of the precedents with the negative effect of the universities patents and the limited positive influence of the industries patent. The findings on the policies are interesting. Introducing the one-year lag the first incentive policy becomes significant.

Table 19.5 results model 2

Variable	GrowthGRP	GrowthGRP	GrowthGRP	
Patentuniv	-2.94*** (0.007)	-	-3.53*** (0.001)	-3.14*** (0.004)
Patentuniv2	2.61** (0.014)	-	3.74*** (0.001)	3.35*** (0.002)
Patentindust	-	-0-33 (0.746)	1.83* (0.078)	1.47 (0.151)
Patentindust2	-	1.09 (0.283)	-0.70 (0.491)	-0.48 (0.635)
L.lnGRP	3.01*** (0.005)	-3.28*** (0.003)	-2.66** (0.013)	-3.45*** (0.002)
Fixedassets	-5.87*** (0.000)	-6.23*** (0.000)	-5.93*** (0.000)	-5.92*** (0.000)
FFE	2.60** (0.015)	1.46 (0.156)	2.52** (0.018)	2.46** (0.020)
Population	-3.77*** (0.001)	-3.61*** (0.001)	-4.55*** (0.000)	-3.84*** (0.001)
Nhigheredu	8.59*** (0.000)	9.28*** (0.000)	8.98*** (0.000)	8.98*** (0.000)
PolicyA	1.40 (0.172)	1.41 (0.168)	1.49 (0.147)	-
PolicyB	1.03 (0.310)	1.10 (0.283)	1.20 (0.239)	-
PolicyC	2.93*** (0.007)	3.07*** (0.005)	3.06*** (0.005)	-
L.PolicyA	-	-	-	1.99* (0.056)
L.PolicyB	-	-	-	1.06 (0.298)
L.PolicyC	-	-	-	3.16*** (0.004)
Obs.	446	446	446	420
F	(10,28) 44.30	(10,28) 26.42	(12,28) 33.31	(12,28) 39.95

The third model has been run in two stages. The first stage considers the dependent variable as the number of employees in the second model and the wage bill of the region. Since the independent variable used to measure the technology level of the region is the number of patents accepted at the regional patent the second stage isolates the variables that influence the technology production embedded into the patents. Thus, tables 6 and 7 show the results of the first and second stage. The table 19.6 shows the positive impact generated by the S&T and the R&D expenditure on the patent production. Results confirm that the increased effort made by public and private in boosting the research and development activities led to a positive increment of the patents production. Here it is possible to observe how patents impact on the employment and on the total wage. Of course, indirectly is showed the stimulus given by the expenditure in science and technology and research and development carried out by public and private actors to the local development. The model entirely confirms the thesis according to which innovation impact positively on the local development and, how is specifically showed in the paper, on employment. The original intuition behind these results is that the model showed the contribution of both lines of investment: public and private. Eventually is worthy to notice the behavior of the FDI that positively influence the wage but not the employment. The finding confirms the transformation of the Chinese economic landscape from industry to technology-driven economy in which specialization instead of the basic manpower is promoted and foreign enterprises are not outsourcing specialized knowledge and not just simple manufacturing industry.

Table 19.6 results model 3 – first least square

Variable	(1) Patents	(2) Patents
lnGRP	1.31 (0.193)	1.31 (0.193)
FDI	1.64 (0.104)	1.64 (0.104)
R&Dpriv	7.48*** (0.000)	7.48*** (0.000)
Hedu	-1.05 (0.297)	-1.05 (0.297)
S&Texp	3.93*** (0.000)	3.93*** (0.000)
Obs.	217	217
F	(5,181)	(5,181)
	136.30	136.30

Table 19.7 results model 3 – second least square

Variable	(1) Empl	(2) Wage
Patents	7.95*** (0.000)	8.11*** (0.000)
lnGRP	0.82 (0.414)	3.30*** (0.000)
FDI	-0.53 (0.596)	3.25*** (0.001)
Obs.	217	217
F	(30,183) 3.41	(30,183) 16.02

5. Implications and future research

Clearly, Chinese innovation landscape growth has not been fostered by any single event. China has gradually redesigned the policies, institutions and incentives required to stimulate innovation in academia and business. Economic reform and a relatively stronger legal system have together created a more patent-friendly environment and have fostered the surge of patenting. The thesis contributes to the literature and brings implications for both scholars and policy makers.

In the first paper, the results offer an interesting and somehow unexpected interpretation. While the effect of public investments in S&T on university research activity largely meets expectations, the effect of private R&D investments seems counterintuitive (and largely contrasting our hypotheses). What emerges from the analyzes is that private firms do strongly impact on universities' patenting activity. Firstly, universities file a lower number of patents with respect to regions with a lower level of private investment in R&D. Secondly, patents have different characteristics, being less generic (more specialized) and less impactful (lower number of citations). At the end of the day, private firms push the universities' and public research centers' research agenda according to their own industrial and technological orientation (Crupi et al., 2017).

The results bring some suggestions also to policy makers. Firstly, the R&D investment is amongst the fundamental driving force of the patent applications growth. However, a simple increase in R&D investments does not necessarily imply a transformation from "technological follower" to "technological leader" and a change in efficiency of innovation capabilities. It is evident that other factors play important roles such as those related to the interactions and communications amongst actors. Secondly, in many cases, the policies' objective should not be to simply increase investments in R&D but rather to foster appropriate long-term partnerships between universities and industry. In more details, institutional practices and national resources should focus on ensuring the conditions that allow new knowledge and technologies to be easily and rapidly absorbed and adapted by industries.

Those results also bring some theoretical contributions. They confirm the study by Xie and Zhang (2015) in that private firms have been the engine of innovation and contributed to delineating the role of firms in the growth of Chinese University patents growth. As emphasized by those authors, this role had been neglected due to lack of firm-specific patent data. Findings are also consistent with Hong's study (2008) that highlighted the relevance of universities in the Chinese innovation system, described a strong connection between industry and university, and emphasized regional peculiarities in the knowledge transfer from university to industry.

Since they distinguish the contribution to the patent generation of public expenditure from private investments, the results contribute to solving the concern of Hu and Mathews (2008) and Huang and Wu (2012). The former authors documented that despite educating a well- trained labor force and generating a significant number of spin-offs, R&D investments have played less of a role in building innovative activity than would be expected. The latter authors identified R&D expenditures and universities' personnel as important drivers of patenting in the nanotechnology sector. At the same time, they retained uncertain whether and when local industry has benefitted from investments in R&D.

More importantly, results shed new light on the private firms' capacity to absorb tacit knowledge from academia. It is generally accepted that for successful relationships between firms and industry should be facilitated by an adequate level of absorptive capacity (Zahra and George, 2002). The concept of "absorptive capacity" is a familiar one in innovation debates and was first introduced by Cohen and Levinthal (1990) to describe an individual firm's "ability to recognize the value of new information, assimilate it and apply it to commercial ends." Its dimensions span from the acquisition of external knowledge to more specific abilities in order to assimilate, transform and apply knowledge (Camison and Fores, 2010). Our findings suggest that according to their absorptive capacity, private investments in R&D influence university research activities. In other words, as additionally demonstrated by claims and citations, firms press university to produce knowledge codified in patents that they are able to acquire, assimilate, transform and apply.

The results in the second chapter shed new light on the university patent production. Speculating it is possible to assume that the negative influence on the local development is because the most important universities tend to maintain strong one-to-one connections with big firms located outside Chinese territory (Hong Kong, Taiwan, Singapore and similar), which generates a drainage of public resources. Thus, the effort made by universities in terms of public research and innovation does not directly nor immediately influence the regional economic development. Moreover, the variables utilized to catch up the phenomenon do not intercept the secondary or posteriori ingenerated aspects of the development. As a matter of fact it is imaginable that the high level reached in innovation production offers to the universities a massive public exposure and a focused worldwide attention. China, becoming the leader in patent production, attracted the scientific and the economic community.

Similar assumptions can be made about the policies. The results show the scarce significance of the policies in terms of direct impact on the economic growth, even if for the lagged model there is an increment with respect to the filling subsidy program. In light of these results, it can be said that regional economic development in China, with respect to the observed period, did not respond entirely to the solicitations of the patent subsidy program. The outcome of the program on the regional growth is limited or ineffective.

The program aimed to increment the number of the granted patent, and it achieved this goal according to the literature and the statistics, leading China as the most prolific country in patents applications, but the program does not affect, immediately the economic growth.

Obviously, policies implemented by China in the last decades have totally reshaped the economic landscape, influencing the behavior of the different actors: public, private and foreigners. The push given by the change in the political and institutional panorama led China to international accreditation. The clear economic vision in the long-run makes the country faithful for private (domestic and foreign) investments thanks also to the government's massive investment in science and technology promotion. What emerged in the third chapter, from the policy implications side, is firstly that the private and public substantial investments create the basis for a technology development which led China to accredit itself in the international scientific panorama reaching in a decade the role of leader in patent applications. Secondly that the technological progress impacts positively on the local development measured in terms of employment and total wage bill and finally the role of FDI is more incisive in raising the level of the wage.

These findings bring up some insights for the policy maker. First of all, the impact given by the change in the formal panorama with the modernization of the institutional structures and tools to catch up the technological challenge. Secondly, that the push given by the augmented public investment in S&T generated a diffuse trust among private and international investors that participate in national economic and technological growth. Lastly, the transformation of China from follower to leader in technology has been well interpreted outside the country because the foreigner investors seem to be more interested in pursuing a higher degree of specialization in the labor market instead of basic manpower.

From the theoretical implications point of view, the findings of the analysis corroborate and implement previous researches on technology and employment. Previous studies focused their attention on the relationship between innovation and employment at firms' level or as a private initiative driven phenomenon. The findings shed new light on the contribution given by the public choice of investing in science and technology and on the spillover effects given as consequence of this choice. In other words, they demonstrate the strong linkage between public effort in technology and employment passing through the augmented private investment share and the enhanced technology capacity of the national innovation system.

Innovation is one of the most important goals pursued by the Chinese government in the last decades. The enormous effort made by China to reduce the technology gap first, and to become a global leader after, reshaped the entire economic panorama at national and regional level. Technology has been demonstrated to be a strategic driver for the local development and this research work contributes to enriching the research field on regional development by analyzing the singular relationship between public and private sectors and the impact of the innovation activity of Chinese organizations on local economic development. It offers clear policy suggestions by emphasizing the relevant role that technology development has on regional wealth. Furthermore, it suggests that private investments are key in this direction, especially if complemented with public investments in Science and Technology.

The study presents limitations and it would be essential to understand the complexity of the relationship between innovation and employment in the light of a strategic, economic and legal national framework. Nevertheless, further investigation is needed to explore the complementary effect between private and public intervention.

References

Acs, Z.J., Anselin, L., Varga, A., (2002). 'Patents and innovation counts as measures of regional production of new knowledge'. *Res. Policy* 31, 1069–1085. https://doi.org/10.1016/S0048-7333(01)00184-6

Baglieri, D., Cesaroni, F., Orsi, L., (2014). 'Does the nano-patent "Gold rush" lead to entrepreneurial-driven growth? Some policy lessons from China and Japan'. *Technovation* 34, 746–761. https://doi.org/10.1016/j.technovation.2014.07.009

Baglieri, D., Cinici, M.C., Mangematin, V., (2012). 'Rejuvenating clusters with "sleeping anchors": The case of nanoclusters'. *Technovation* 32, 245–256. https://doi.org/https://doi.org/10.1016/j.technovation.2011.09.003

Cesaroni, F., Baglieri, D., Crupi, A., (2017). 1.19 – Closing Distances Between Academia and Market, in: Comprehensive Medicinal Chemistry III. pp. 520–528. https://doi.org/10.1016/B978-0-12-409547-2.12304-2

Cohen, W.M., Levinthal, D.A., (1990). 'Absorptive Capacity: A New Perspective on Learning and Innovatio'n. *Adm. Sci. Q.* 35, 128–152. https://doi.org/10.2307/2393553

Cooke, P., (2001). 'Regional Innovation Systems, Clusters, and the Knowledge Economy'. *Ind. Corp. Chang.* 10, 945–974. https://doi.org/10.1093/icc/10.4.945

Crupi, A., Cesaroni, F., Baglieri, D., (2017). Firms ab. capacity and universities patenting activity. Findings from Chinese CNT sector. Acad. Manag. Proc. 2017. https://doi.org/10.5465/AMBPP.2017.16290abstract

Doloreux, D., Parto, S., (2004). Regional Innovation Systems: a Critical Synthesis 38. https://doi.org/ISSN 1564-8370

Edquist, C., (2010). 'African journal of science, technology, innovation and development.', *African Journal of Science, Technology, Innovation and Development.* Taylor and Francis.

Evangelista, R., Iammarino, S., Mastrostefano, V., Silvani, A., (2001). 'Measuring the regional dimension of innovation. Lessons from the Italian Innovation Survey'. *Technovation* 21, 733–745. https://doi.org/10.1016/S0166-4972(00)00084-5

Freeman, C., (2002). 'Continental, national and sub-national innovation systems—complementarity and economic growth'. *Res. Policy* 31, 191–211. https://doi.org/10.1016/S0048-7333(01)00136-6

Fritsch, M., (2002). 'Measuring the Quality of Regional Innovation Systems: A Knowledge Production Function Approach'. *Int. Reg. Sci. Rev.* 25, 86–101. https://doi.org/10.1177/016001702762039394

Hong, W., (2008). 'Decline of the center: The decentralizing process of knowledge transfer of Chinese universities from 1985 to 2004'. *Res. Policy* 37, 580–595. https://doi.org/https://doi.org/10.1016/j.respol.2007.12.008

Hu, M.-C., Mathews, J.A., (2008). 'China's national innovative capacity'. *Res. Policy* 37, 1465–1479. https://doi.org/10.1016/j.respol.2008.07.003

Huang, C., Wu, Y., (2012). 'State-led Technological Development: A Case of China's Nanotechnology Development'. *World Dev.* 40, 970–982. https://doi.org/10.1016/j.worlddev.2011.11.013

Li, X., (2009). 'China's regional innovation capacity in transition: An empirical approach'. *Res. Policy* 38, 338–357. https://doi.org/10.1016/j.respol.2008.12.002

Liu, X., White, S., (2001). 'Comparing innovation systems: a framework and application to China's transitional context'. *Res. Policy*.

Lundvall, B., (1992). *National Systems of Innovation* (London: Pinter). Links.

Nelson, R., (1993). *National innovation systems: a comparative analysis.*

Porter, M., (1998). *Clusters and the new economics of competition.*

Porter, M.E., (2000). 'Location, Competition, and Economic Development: Local Clusters in a Global Economy'. *Econ. Dev. Q.* 14, 15–34. https://doi.org/10.1177/089124240001400105

Storper, M., (1997). *The regional world: territorial development in a global economy*. Guilford Press, New York.

Tödtling, F., Trippl, M., (2005). 'One size fits all: Towards a differentiated regional innovation policy approach'. *Res. Policy* 34, 1203–1219. https://doi.org/10.1016/j.respol.2005.01.018

Xie, Z., Zhang, X., (2015). 'The patterns of patents in China'. *China Econ. J.* 8, 122–142. https://doi.org/10.1080/17538963.2015.1046219

Zahra, S.A., George, G., (2002). 'Absorptive Capacity: a Review, Reconceptualization, and Extension'. *Acad. Manag. Rev.* 27, 185–203.

Chapter 20

Innovation Management Systems: Systematic Structuration, Semantic Interoperability and Multi-Dimensional Measurement for Continuous Performance Improvement

Lamyaa EL BASSITI*

E-mail: lamyaa.elbassiti@gmail.com

Abstract: Believing that the most pressing problems organizations face today are characterized by unprecedented levels of complexity and interdependence, leads to the breakdown of the conventional problem-solving paradigm focusing on incremental improvements, and go about leveraging from the currently experienced change by innovating systematically and successfully. However, despite the countless efforts and spending, many organizations do not generate satisfactory results. This problem does not lie in a lack of ideas, but more in a holistic, integrated and unified framework allowing innovation actors to ensure a sustainable impact through a steady flow of innovation, which calls organizations to manage all the aspects fostering the innovation capabilities as well as the necessary tools and techniques supporting the innovation activities. This thesis focuses on these problems areas and contributes five expansive theoretical constructs and three practical tools to assist modern organizations to systematically structure their innovation processes and activities, semantically represent the nascent knowledge domain of innovation, and continuously measure and then improve their innovation performance with a multi-dimensional perspective.

Keywords: Idea Management; Innovation Structuration; Innovation Interoperability; Innovation Performance; Modern Organization; Complexity Theory; Emergence; Creativity-based Experience; Knowledge Dynamics; Knowledge Management; Semantic Web; Ontology.

1. Introduction

Over the last decades, innovation has grown in importance as a competitive advantage for contemporary organizations. Ideas and Innovation Management Systems (IMS) are poised to become the catalyst that can help them to compete at levels never before possible. Various analyzes of the vendor landscape have shown rapid adoption growth of these systems in many organizations in recent years (Gliedman et al., 2013; Drakos et al., 2013). Although in some cases, they have been coupled with developing some competencies and organizational capabilities, the current state of the art shows that conducting innovation within modern organizations, seen as complex systems, still remains problematic. Narrowing the focus of the research, firstly the concept of *modern organization* has been investigated in order to better identify the trends to look for and understand the broadness of the topic to be addressed. Afterward, we have focused on the *phenomenon of innovation* as it is the contemporary response to the increasing complexity and change that face modern organizations. Then, the requirements to structure, formalize, manage and measure innovation rose, which has led to the exploration of the *knowledge organization* and *performance measurement* areas. Based on these investigations, the various shortcomings we found in the management of innovation were aggregated under the following key points:

1) **Structuration of Innovation Process:** An increasing number of organizations spend more and more on innovation, but many of these initiatives don't generate satisfactory profit. This problem does not lie in a lack of ideas, but more in a successful innovation management process spanning from idea generation to product use (du Preez and Louw, 2008). Many researchers (Chiesa et al., 2009) have for many years shown the importance of structuration of the innovation process; in particular, its early stages often referred as "fuzzy"; in the ultimate success of innovation. Thus, there is crucial need to reduce uncertainty and bring order to the chaotic character of innovation.

2) **Identification of Innovation Activities:** Previous researchers have mostly focused on innovation management from the strategic level (i.e. managerial problems and success factors) and they have completely neglected the operative level (i.e. key activities) (Khurana and Rosenthal, 1997; Cooper and Kleinschmidt, 1987). However, it has been found that the conceptualization and identification of key activities help to make the innovation process more explicit, which supports improving the performance of innovation management and enhances the innovation ability within organizations. Thus, there is a need to specify the main activities required to deal with the challenge of achieving breakthrough innovations and tap into new sources of sustainable growth.

3) **Conceptualization of Innovation Domain:** Understanding the process of innovation is to understand factors that facilitate or inhibit the success of innovations. The best understanding of how these factors are related will lead to an efficient management framework supporting the innovation lifecycle (Van de Ven, 1986). So, there is a need for a meaningful clustering of the innovation knowledge which can be taken as a unifying structure for giving knowledge a common representation and semantics. In other words, there is a need to an integrated model intended to be a domain vocabulary for representing the key concepts of innovation and their relationships, facilitating knowledge acquisition from subject matter experts, and sharing domain knowledge.

4) **Organization of Innovation Knowledge:** Schumpeter, commonly known as the father of innovation studies, has made a key contribution to our understanding about how knowledge produces innovations. He has argued that an innovation rarely involves a single idea, but rather bundles of knowledge that are brought together into a whole. That is to say, most innovations are not novel in themselves but they are novel combinations of elements that already exist (Salter and Alexy, 2013). Likewise, current perspectives of innovation management view it as an interactive and networked system that spans organizational boundaries to draw on knowledge, experiences and capabilities from diverse sources (Tidd et al., 2005). However, relevant knowledge is not easily obtained as it is distributed, of tacit nature and highly context-specific and then requires particular capabilities to be absorbed. Thus, there is a need to deliver a single point of reference for innovation knowledge management and provide a formalization that can be applied for achieving interoperability within and across different organizations and knowledge systems.

5) **Measurement of Innovation:** Commonly, the success of an innovation depends on the quality of the best opportunity selected (Girotra et al., 2010), because organizational resources are, usually, limited and cannot be wasted in the development of unpromising ideas (Cooper, 1985; Justel et al., 2007). Yet, while best idea identification is undoubtedly important, it is only one aspect of an organization's innovativeness and it is the measurement of the overall innovation aspects that is crit-

ical to ensure a sustainable impact. Thus, there is a need to identify the key dimensions that can form a systematic basis to support the engagement of relevant actors in dialogue within an eco-socio-cultural and environmental context; in order to find out new connections, explore new symbolic values and new patterns of interaction, and contribute to the definition of new beliefs and standards supporting and promoting a more holistic and integrated approach to measurement and then continuous performance improvement.

Rather than investigating each area individually and apart from identifying the main problems, we have espoused a holistic view and formulated three complementary research questions to guide the direction of our research work.

Research Question 1: "how innovation can be structured to allow a systematic management of innovation within a modern organization?"

Research Question 2: "how innovation can be semantically represented to stimulate experience sharing, new knowledge emergence and innovation interoperability?"

Research Question 3: "how innovation can be measured to assist modern organizations in their efforts to continuously improve their innovation performance and impact?"

The remainder of this chapter unfolds as follows: The background of this research work and the foundations in the contribution areas are summarized in Section 2. Next, the research design and the methodological choices that guided the conduct of this research work are presented (Section 3). Then section 4 expands the different contributions delivered by this thesis and the results of their empirical investigations. We conclude this chapter by summing up the contributions and suggesting future directions of research (Section 5).

2. Background

Narrowing the focus of the research, firstly the concept of *innovation structuration* has been investigated in order to better identify the trends to look for and understand the broadness of the topic to be addressed. Afterward, we have focused on the *innovation interoperability* as it provides a promising response to the increasing complexity related to knowledge dynamics management that faces the modern organization. Then, the requirements to measure innovation performance rose, which has led to the exploration of the *performance management* areas.

2.1 Innovation Structuration

The academic literature and management practice reveal a shift in the way analysts understand the concept of "*innovation.*" This shift is not revealed as a cohesive trend; rather it comprises contributions from a wide range of academic disciplines and empirical evidence. Yet despite the value of innovation, it is only over the past two decades that considerable progress has been made in understanding the key features of successful innovation. Such progress has hinged on taking a *complexity perspective.* This new perspective is concerned with the study of emergent order in what otherwise may be considered as very disorderly systems (Sherif, 2006). Although until recently the power and ubiquity of complex systems were not understood, these key aspects are especially important for contemporary organizations as they allow and encourage creative responses to emerge from changing environments (Morel and Ramanujam, 1999; Steele, 2003).

People are familiar with the use of models to clarify their intentions. So, using models to structure innovation will provide a good conceptual basis for developing an effective management framework. In order to be able to keep the flexibility and the adaptability required to deliver innovations with a sustainable impact, a set of 9 characteristics has been considered. Based on these 9 characteristics we compared a selection of the most known innovation process models with the goal of understanding their strengths and weaknesses. Table 20.1 below presents a summary of this comparison.

Table 20.1 Innovation Management Process Models Comparison (El Bassiti et al., 2017)

Innovation Management Process Model \ Criterion	Creativity	Knowledge Management	Collaboration	Learning and Wise Judgment	Context	Innovation Memory	Feedback	Formal Gates	Dynamic Balancing
Holistic Approach	√	×	×	×	√	×	√	×	×
Funnel Model	×	×	×	×	×	√	×	×	×

NCD Model	×	×	×	×	√	×	√	×	×
Process Model	×	×	×	×	√	×	×	√	×
Idea Fruition Process	√	×	×	×	√	×	√	×	×
Innovation Value Chain	√	×	×	×	×	×	×	×	×
Stage-Gate Model	×	×	×	×	√	×	×	√	×
GI2MO Life Cycle	√	√	×	×	√	√	√	×	×

As it can be observed, although relevant, the studied models have shown several shortcomings. Mainly, they don't adapt gracefully to the "emergence" characteristic of innovation, which is shaped by eco-socio environmental factors. Although supporting knowledge sharing in some cases, they don't support contextualization and flexibility required for creative problem-solving.

2.2 Innovation Interoperability

Based on the fact that useful knowledge today is widely distributed, weakly structured, heterogeneous and grows very quickly, open innovation challenges traditional notions of KM. So, within an open context, there is a clear need to be some sense of what of the available knowledge resources should be mapped. Further, more and more innovation systems appear, so it becomes imperative to establish a common vocabulary that facilitates access and reuse of knowledge and to coordinate efficiently the actors involved in the innovation process. Pagano et al. (2013) regard interoperability as "a problem affecting the interaction of entities at various levels." Accordingly, we define "*innovation interoperability*" as the ability of people, systems and organizations to smartly investigate experiences as well as inter- and intra-organizational interactions and critically exploit the deduced knowledge to meet current needs and develop new opportunities for unforeseen circumstances. To deal with such challenge ontologies; being the foundational component of semantic technologies, providing a "formal and explicit specification of a shared conceptualization" (Studer et al., 1998); have been proposed to provide efficient solution to support the integration of the innovation process with heterogeneous knowledge sources.

Lawson and Samson (2001) argue that a successful innovation is based on a set of core elements and processes that are similar across industries and organizations. Accordingly, we consider every innovation deliverable as an interoperable experience distinguished by an aggregation of "*unique knowledge units*" involving a "*similar set of activities.*" This challenging duality of uniqueness and similarity can be addressed through the development of a granular ontology, based on the concept of *flexibility* to cater for uniqueness and the notion of *uniformity* to cater for similarity. Accordingly, we identified a set of five criteria that must underlie a generic representation of innovation. Based on these factors we evaluated a selection of the most known innovation ontologies. Table 20.2 below provides a summary of this evaluation:

Table 20.2 Innovation Ontologies Evaluation (El Bassiti, 2017)

Ontology \ Criterion	Management Flexibility	Validation Uniformity	Functional Completeness	Perspicuity	Precision/ Granularity
Iteams Ontology	×	×	×	√	√
OntoGate Ontology	√	√	×	×	×
Idea Ontology	×	×	×	√	√
GI2MO Ontology	√	√	×	×	√

As a result of the investigation, we conclude that the presented ontologies, although they have a similar objective to represent innovation semantically, they differ in conceptual depth, practical focus, terminology, and target audience. Each model is either specific to a domain or focuses mainly on a specific aspect of the innovation process. Although there are few -extensive- efforts trying to provide a specific view, there is no comprehensive model that can be applied to the innovation knowledge modeling, its lifecycle phases or its deliverables in a holistic manner.

2.3 Innovation Performance

Simons (1990) emphasized that measurement can be used as a strategic tool to motivate and inspire new behaviors, to have the potential to support team autonomy, as well as stimulating communities for the generation and implementation of creative ideas. Despite its potential to facilitate management, measurement is considered as a challenging area in practice and measuring innovation is particularly challenging as innovation is multidimensional, complex and unpredictable (McCarthy et al., 2006). In addition, empirical studies have found that many organizations tend to focus only on the measurement of innovation inputs and outputs in terms of spending, speed to market and numbers of new products, and ignore the quality of the process in-between (Adams et al., 2006).

As well, the measurement of its underlying knowledge dynamics is still emerging and misses workable method and metrics. Neely (2004) has pointed out that the "measurement crisis" is the result of "drowning in data." Consequently, there is too great attempt being made to quantify features which do not really lend themselves usefully to quantification. A key challenge is then the lack of a sound, holistic and systematic model of innovation performance against which measures can be set and action decided.

In order to increase the reliability, adoptability and usability for different actors involved in the innovation effort, we purposefully chose a set of twenty-five dimensions that have largely been used in the different performance measurement models. Using these dimensions, we investigated a selection of the most known performance measures to identify the most suitable model to meet the specific requirements of innovation. Table 20.3 below provides a summary of this investigation.

In analyzing the suitability of the presented dimensions for the development of a systematic and performance-focused innovation representation most were narrow in approach. However, collectively they formed a strong basis for a promising performance driven framework. As such, we bring up the critical need to identify the key dimensions that can underlie a systematic, synthetic and integrative framework supporting an accurate performance measurement and fostering a continuous performance improvement, with a focus on innovation with a sustainable impact.

Table 20.3 Innovation Performance Models Review (El Bassiti a Ajhoun, 2016)

Innovation Performance Models	Diamond Model	Open Funnel Model	Innovation Value Chain	Oslo Manual	Quality Function Deployment	Arthur D. Little's Innovation Excellence	Value Creation Model	EIRMA Framework	Performance Measurement Matrix	Results and Determinants Model	Balanced Scorecard Indicator	Performance Prism Model	European Quality Foundation Perfection
Financial	√	√	√	√	√	√	√	√	√	√	√	√	√
People	×	×	×	×	√	×	×	×	×	×	√	√	√
Market	×	√	×	×	√	×	√	×	×	×	×	×	×

Process	√	√	×	×	×	×	×	√	×	×	√	√	√
Policies	×	×	×	√	×	×	×	×	×	×	×	×	√
Efficiency & Productivity	×	×	×	×	×	×	√	×	×	√	×	√	√
Flexibility	×	×	×	×	×	×	×	×	×	×	×	√	×
Learning	√	×	×	×	×	×	×	×	×	×	√	√	√
Linkage	√	×	×	√	×	×	×	×	×	×	×	×	×
Vision/ & Strategy	√	√	×	×	×	√	√	×	√	×	√	√	√
External Environment	×	√	×	×	×	×	×	√	√	×	×	×	√
Leadership	×	×	×	×	×	×	√	×	×	×	×	×	√
Internal Business	×	×	×	×	×	×	√	×	√	×	√	×	×
Institutional Factors	√	√	×	√	×	×	√	×	√	×	×	√	×
Requirements	×	×	×	×	√	×	×	×	×	×	×	×	×
Resources	×	×	×	×	×	√	×	×	×	√	×	×	√
Competencies	×	×	×	×	×	√	×	×	×	×	×	√	×
Technology	×	√	×	×	×	√	√	×	×	×	×	×	×
Inputs	×	√	√	×	√	×	×	√	×	×	×	×	×
Outputs	×	√	√	×	×	×	×	√	×	×	×	×	×
Competitiveness	×	×	×	×	×	×	×	×	√	√	×	√	√
Quality	×	√	×	×	×	×	×	×	×	√	×	√	√
Growth	×	√	×	×	×	×	×	×	×	×	√	×	×
Idea Management	×	√	√	×	×	√	×	×	×	×	×	×	×

3. Research design

The subject of this thesis is interdisciplinary, spanning from organizational change to innovation management and studying the knowledge organizations systems in use, towards achieving continuous performance improvement based on accurate and systematic measurement. Although such interdisciplinarity is useful and required in order to provide a well-rounded view of the problem at hand, it suggests a challenge since a wide variety of research paradigms, strategies and methodologies from different disciplines have to be applied.

3.1. Research Objectives

This research work aims to contribute to knowledge within three different and correlated research areas, following two major and interrelated research fields, which are *Information Systems* and *Organizational Studies*. The main research objectives of this study can, be enumerated as follows:

1) **Innovation Structuration:** The innovation process entails a variety of activities, from idea generation to the exploitation of a new or improved product, and these activities need to be clearly identified and managed somehow (Trott, 2011). Thus, our first objective is to identify which *activities* are most essential for conducting systematic innovation with sustainable impact. On the other hand, maximizing existing resources to achieve cost reductions, lower risks and shortened development cycles by increasing speed and quality in the innovation process are all desirable conditions of an efficient innovation process (Nixon, 1998). Thus, our second objective is to design a structured *lifecycle model* giving a holistic understanding of innovation interactions, milestones and deliverables. A special focus will be given to the learning activity behind the innovation lifecycle. Thus, our third objective is to simulate the *learning engine* underpinning the organizational capacity for innovation, in a way that provides a trade-off between granting conditions for creativity and exercising control.

2) **Innovation Interoperability:** To counter the limitations experienced with existing approaches to innovation knowledge management, one such enabling capability is opening innovation process to external stakeholders (Borgatti and Cross, 2003; Fritsch, 2001). But, the numerous contributions produced by networked users have to be structured and linked. This issue can be overcome by using *Semantic Technologies* providing a whole stack of tools to structure, link and exchange social content (Bojars et al., 2008). Thus, our fourth objective is to develop a *modular ontology* that supports experience-based creativity[1] by enhancing the management of tacit and highly distributed knowledge using semantics combined with knowledge modeling mechanisms.

---

1.   *Experience-based creativity* means the creativity triggered by past experiences designed as formal knowledge sources.

3) **Innovation Measurement:** While many argue that too much measurement will stifle the spirit of innovation, accurate measurement is still considered as pivotal for every business success because assessing the progress and evaluating the impact allow the organization to change its direction before mistakes become expensive or great opportunities are missed. However, the existing approaches don't satisfy the specific requirements of innovation within a complex system and don't support the measurement of the overall innovation capability (Muller et al., 2005). Thus, our fifth objective is to define an integrated basis for a *multi-dimensional approach to innovation measurement,* which allows managers to monitor and gauge their innovation performance, detect faults and identify repairs.

3.2. Research Paradigm

Along this research journey we adopted a ***mixed scientific perspective*** combining behavioral and design logics, and a research paradigm closer to ***interpretive*** and ***critical*** assumptions than to positivist one. The reason is that this study does not strive to confirm an existing phenomenon or to measure it against another one; However, it seeks to bring meaning and structure to a chaotic and complex phenomenon (innovation and the related concepts and relationships) through an IS and OS lenses. The study also includes epistemological elements pertaining to critical thought – not only to study innovation as a set of interrelated activities within an organizational context but also to inform how innovation is conducted within and across organizations.

3.3. Research Strategy

This study organizes the domain knowledge by inferring innovation concepts and their relationships, generating theoretical constructs to represent these concepts/relations, and then using these constructs to develop tools for practical application. Such an approach is considered as a hypothesis-building exercise which mostly lends itself to the ***retroductive*** research strategy. However, retroduction is just the first stage of an inquiry (Atkinson, 2011). The hypothesis must then be tested using both induction and deduction, as ***inductive*** strategy can only make a prediction or suggest a solution (by amalgamating previous solutions or by proposing a new one), while a ***deductive*** strategy is used to test the solution and confirm its validity. As a result, this research journey adopted a ***mixture of research strategies*** to formulate the conceptual constructs -hypothetically- underlying the innovation domain and translate them into practical tools.

3.4. Research Methodology

While qualitative approaches have been criticized for being overly subjective and lacking in replicability and generalizability, quantitative approaches have also been criticized for lacking representative validity within social environments (Hewson, 2006). Since this research work does not seek to prove, disprove or compare phenomena but rather to discover the underlying structures of a nascent domain of knowledge, and in order to satisfy the hypothetical and demonstrative nature of our research questions, this study has adopted a ***mixed research methodology*** mixing both quantitative and qualitative data in a single study.

3.5. Data Collection

Based on the methodological choices, the different constructs resulting from this research work have been first submitted for scrutiny through a set of 11 *peer-reviewed publications*. Then, they have been presented to subject matter experts (16 innovation professionals from industry and academia across four countries: UK, Malaysia, Australia and US) through three *online surveys* (questionnaires and interviews). Next, a set of *prototype solutions*, translating the conceptual constructs into useful products, has been developed. Finally, a *business case study* has been carried, within a rapidly growing firm in the building sector in Morocco, to examine practically the delivered constructs and tools through four complementary scenarios.

4. Research Findings and Implications

Based on the analysis of the shifts global mindset manifest, and following today's transition towards a new era of flexible forms of managing and organizing, we propose a conceptual framework for designing the innovation activities and processes and managing the underlying knowledge dynamics. Maybe it is difficult to get a precise design of the innovation phenomenon because the contemporary notion of "innovation" is still "a very slippery concept." However, a holistic picture was drawn from the exploration of the distinguishing characteristics of the new economy and the new millenary. This PhD thesis has contributed with *five expansive theoretical constructs* and *three practical tools* to *structure* and semantically *represent* the nascent knowledge domain of innovation, which will assist modern organizations to manage *measure* and improve their innovation performance in a sustainable manner. These contributions have been conceived to be integrated into a coherent framework, we called "***Generic Innovation Designing -GenID-Framework***," providing a ground to build a new, holistic, generic and more comprehensive approach to systematically manage and continuously improve the organizational capability to innovating for a sustainable impact.

4.1. Innovation Structuration: Complexity-Driven Designing

Through this PhD thesis, we proposed usage of innovation theories and models to provide a generic and holistic understanding of the innovation concept within a modern organization, considered as a complex context. Based on this understanding, the main contributions are: (1) a set of *Main Activities* supporting the majority of processes involved in the innovation journey; (2) a generic *Lifecycle Model* that provides a conceptual engine to integrate the innovation phases, stages, interactions and deliverables; and (3) a *Learning Engine Model* that enables learning to occur and flow, and alignment to be kept with the internal as well as the external context of the organization along the innovation lifecycle. These knowledge models allowed us to develop (4) an *Idea Management System* that served as a prototype to prove their feasibility and usefulness. It has also been used in the 1st scenario of the accomplished business case study to showcase our approach to innovation Structuration and allow more flexibility and best understanding of the conduct of innovation.

4.1.1. Innovation Main Activities Models

Unlike previous modes of scientific thought, the complexity perspective entails a change in mindset away from understanding the whole by understanding its individual parts, towards considering the whole as different and less than the sum of its parts. While this feature of complexity has been considered an argument for systems thinking, the necessity for variety and multi-reasoning pathways and methodologies to explore possibilities of what could be, and to create desired outcomes that benefit the whole seems to call for a design mindset that is solution focused and action-oriented. This involves "***creative imagination***" not just from one person or even a few people, but instead from everyone. In this way, the thoughts of each one will gain enough space to take on their own significance, yet they remain connected to the larger group field. Such "***collaborative working***" will allow the capacity of human collectives to make wise choices and to orient them around a living sense of the future that truly matters to them, which requires enhanced capacity of "***intentional learning***" to understand the complexity of a situation as well as the ability to make sense and simplify so that action can be taken. As such, there is an urgent need to be endowed with an ability to exercise "***wise judgment***" in order to achieve a balanced perception of innovation based on the assumption that economic, social, and environmental matters are interrelated. These are the sine qua non activities (Figure 20.1) required to success a systematic structuration and management of innovation for a sustainable impact.

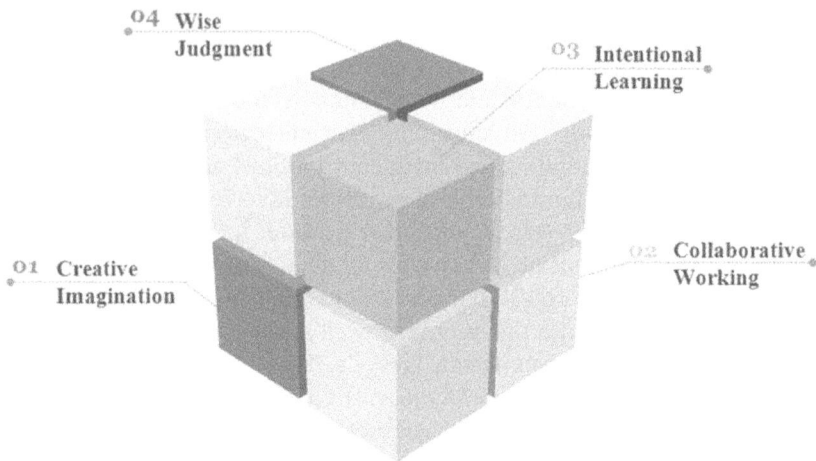

Figure 20.1 GenID Main Activities Model

4.1.2. Innovation Lifecycle Model

Our complexity-driven perspective to innovation designing aims to shift the concept of innovation from a narrow vision focusing on economic boundaries and thresholds, to a wider perspective where a new balance is continually being sought between social, economic and environmental challenges and goals. Accordingly, innovation can be conceptualized as the co-production of knowledge arising from the collaboration of multiple knowledge providers. In this view, we structure innovation as a "*lifecycle model*" (Figure 20.2) identifying *six principal stages* grouped into *two main phases* (***design*** and ***adoption***) and distinguishing *two major deliverables* (***idea*** and ***innovation***). Each stage delineates three *iterations* underpinning the main activities of innovation. Each stage is followed by a "***Gate***", a decision point that allows for pause and then to synthesize the current state of progress to the whole. At the heart of the lifecycle, we define the "***learning engine***" that will be detailed in the next sub-section.

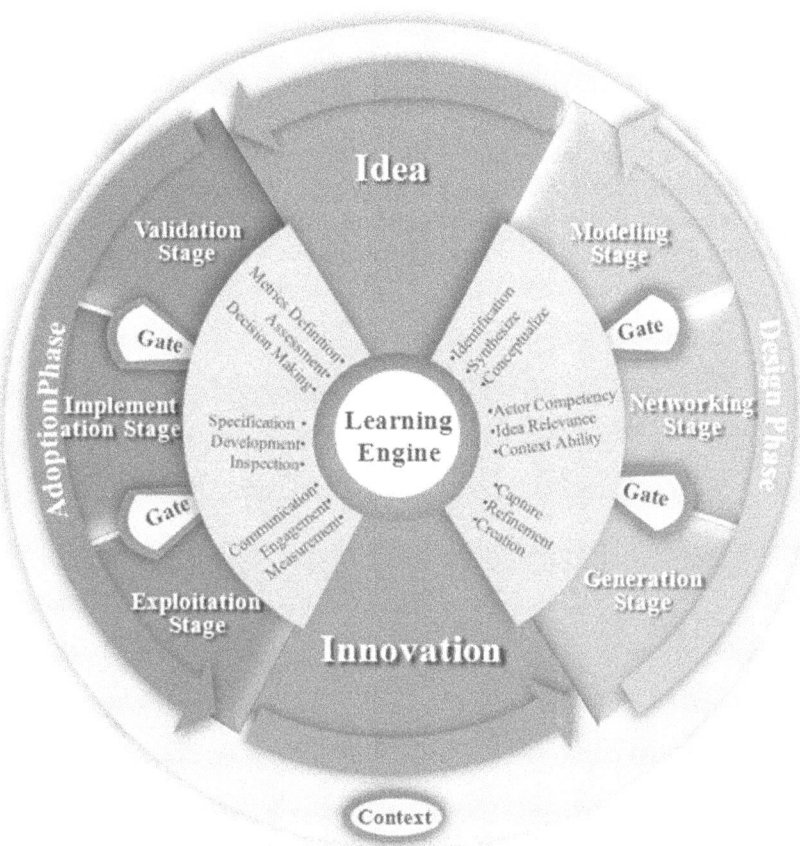

Figure 20.2 GenID Lifecycle Model

4.1.3. Innovation Learning Engine

The **"learning engine"** (Figure 20.3) aims to use structured feedbacks to perform three complementary processes: "*Feedback coordination*" that provides the mechanism driving and guiding the output performance of a deliverable to conform to desired effects. The feedback process is conceived as continuous or iterative loops, gathering information from a state, applying control signals to obtain the desired performance, measuring the difference and coordinating this control to achieve a better state. "*Learning*" that aims to acquire knowledge or skills from experiences. The learning process aims to purposefully collate feedbacks into learning items and topics to be used to illuminate the improvement process. These learning items and topics can also be used for the improvement of individual knowledge and skills and therefore the innovation status. In addition, they can be used to enrich the organizational learning memory used to reduce risks, build organizational capability and continuously improve the organizational innovation performance. "*Improvement*" that aims to allow innovation actors to bring a chain of small improvements, modifications and additions as the feedbacks and learning are gathered, rather than a single jump. These three processes are followed by a key iteration, we called a "*Gate*", where one of the potential decisions (Go, Go Back or No Go) is taken.

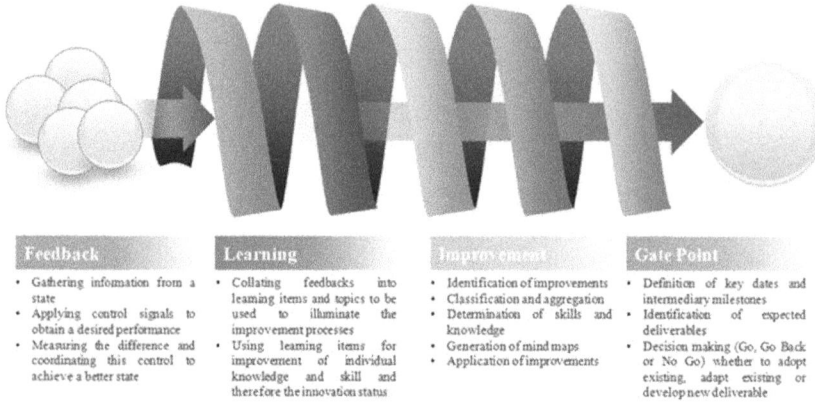

Feedback	Learning	Improvement	Gate Point
• Gathering information from a state	• Collating feedbacks into learning items and topics to be used to illuminate the improvement processes	• Identification of improvements	• Definition of key dates and intermediary milestones
• Applying control signals to obtain a desired performance	• Using learning items for improvement of individual knowledge and skill and therefore the innovation status	• Classification and aggregation	• Identification of expected deliverables
• Measuring the difference and coordinating this control to achieve a better state		• Determination of skills and knowledge	• Decision making (Go, Go Back or No Go) whether to adopt existing, adapt existing or develop new deliverable
		• Generation of mind maps	
		• Application of improvements	

Figure 20.3 GenID Learning Engine

4.2. Innovation Interoperability: Modular Semantic Representation

Understanding the process of innovation and the underpinned activities has led us to identify the key concepts underlying a generic representation of innovation and how these concepts could be related. The result was (1) a *Generic Modular Innovation Ontology* that has been designed to serve as a unifying structure for giving knowledge a common representation and semantics. This ontology has been used to develop (2) an *Idea Dependency Visualizer* that served as a prototype to prove the feasibility and usefulness of the developed ontology. It has also been used in the 2nd scenario of the accomplished business case study to showcase our approach to innovation interoperability, by allowing interactive visualizations and hierarchical clustering to explore emerging patterns in the networks of the generated ideas.

4.2.1. Generic Innovation Designing -GenID-Ontology

Based on our complexity-driven perspective to innovation designing we consider innovation as an *emergent process* characterized by characterized by an emergent "*context*" with no predefined identity, properties or behavior; an emergent "*actors*" with unpredictable roles or prior knowledge; an emergent "*knowledge objects*" with no best structure or sequence. Based on these distinctive features we elicit the three key dimensions required to build a domain vocabulary to represent the innovation concept: (1) "***innovation actor***" which refers to the involved individuals, organizations or communities in the innovation effort; (2) "***innovation core-idea***" which refers to the aggregation of knowledge objects delivered and used by an innovation actor to generate an idea; (3) "***innovation context***" which refers to the contextual variables -either internal or external- impacting the innovation process. Each of these three dimensions has been developed as an ontology module that can fit together with other modules into an overall ontology -as depicted in Figure 20.4 to guide an effective and efficient management of innovation. Further details about these sub-ontologies will be provided in the following sub-sections.

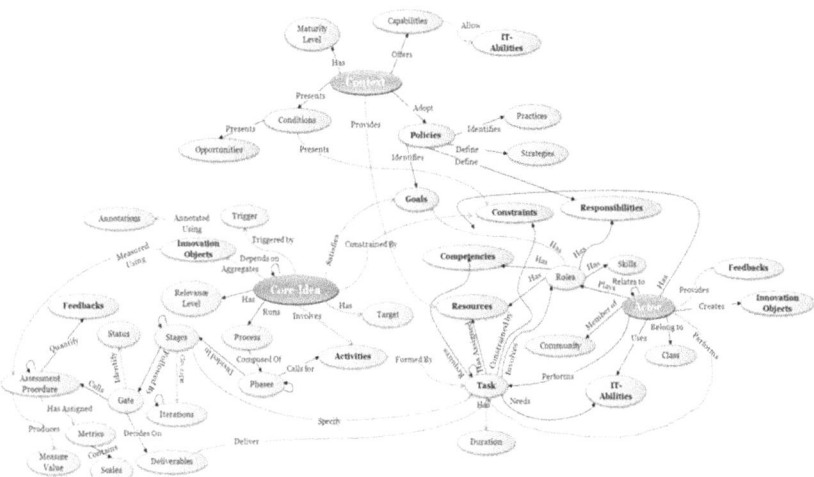

Figure 20.4 GenID Ontology Main Concepts

4.2.2. Innovation Actor Sub-Ontology

GenID Actor sub-ontology (Figure 20.5) aims to represent the different kinds of innovation actors (individual, organization or community) and their interactions within the innovation process, in order to support effective management of their involvement. *GenID Actor* concept can be represented as an "***individual***" which refers to a person who participates in the *emergence*, *design* and *adoption* of an idea; an "***organization***" which refers to a complex assemblage of individuals and their interactions (e.g. responsibilities, social structures, objectives, resources); a "***community***" which refers to a purposeful cluster of individuals or organizations, temporarily bound together through a unifying long-term mission, a common goal or a shared activity. This sub-ontology seeks to allow analyzing the innovation actor competencies; selecting and hiring qualified actors; assigning suitable roles to the proper actors which aid in obtaining appropriately focused communities as needed in each phase, stage or iteration throughout the innovation process; exchanging frequent feedback related to goal attainment; and linking the actors' abilities, recognition, rewards with the organization's profitability.

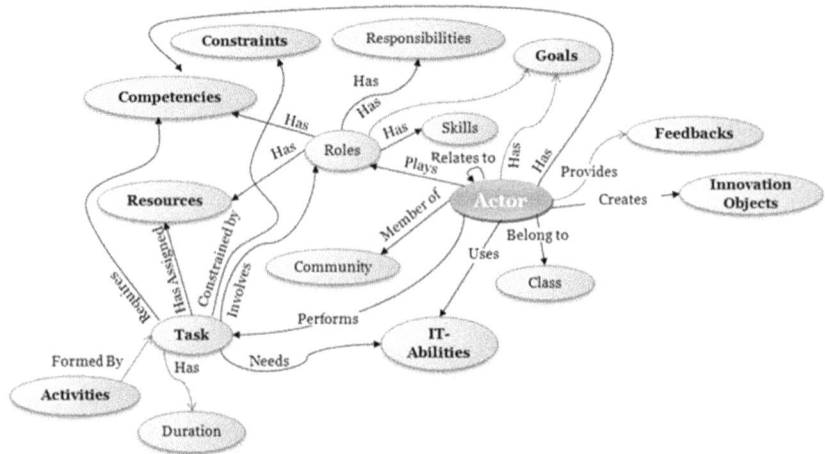

Figure 20.5 GenID Actor Sub-Ontology Knowledge View

4.2.3. Innovation Core-Idea Sub-Ontology

GenID Core-Idea sub-ontology (Figure 20.6) aims to represent the conceptual and practical knowledge usable by an innovation actor to perform a set of tasks in order to deliver a noteworthy outcome. *GenID core-idea* concept can be represented as one or an aggregation of the four following elements: an "***knowledge entity***": a *set of knowledge units* that can be used, re-used or referenced during the innovation lifecycle; a "***behavior***": a set of *actions* performed by an actor on a particular entity; a "***process***": a set of *activities* occurring within a given context as a result of transforming inputs into outputs in a defined order; a "***class***": a set of qualitative or quantitative *descriptions* of a knowledge entity, behavior, or process. This sub-ontology seeks to allow easy handling and quick locating of relevant innovation items; breaking individual as well as organizational innovation content down into small chunks, so each innovation object can be used independently and (re)used efficiently in various innovation contexts; and providing *self-contained* components *aggregating all the required information*, so they can be easily understood, computationally searched and then quickly modified according to the innovation actor's requirements. This *micro-based approach* is legitimate as we suggest that any innovation can be built from reusable components of cognition, which are created just once but can be used several times separately in different contexts.

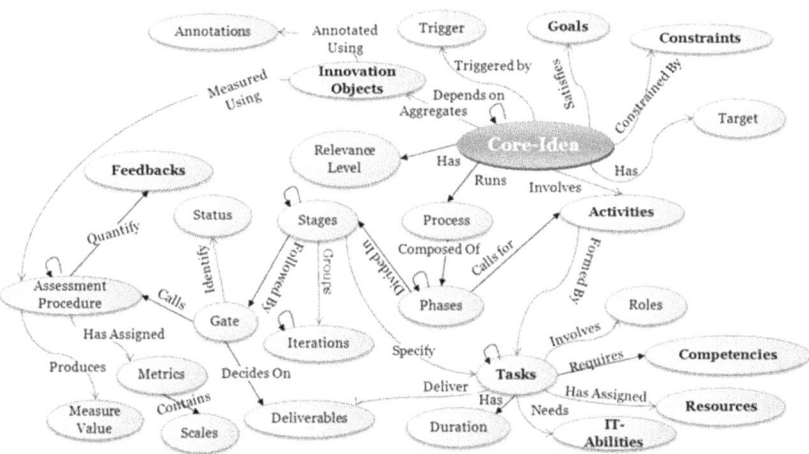

Figure 20.6 GenID Core-Idea Sub-Ontology Knowledge View

4.2.4. Innovation Context Sub-Ontology

GenID Context sub-ontology (Figure 20.7) aims to represent the organizational abilities allowed to innovation actors to perform innovation activities and deliver noteworthy outcomes. As a basis for a wider conceptualization of an innovation context, *GenID Context* concept can be represented as the aggregation of three fundamental elements: "***resources***" that refer to a set of tangible and intangible assets, in particular intellectual assets, supporting the accomplishment of innovation activities; "***policies***" that refer to the principles, rules and moralities guiding the decision-making along the innovation lifecycle; "***capabilities***" that refer to the systematic knowledge practices and tools, in particular technologies, turning organizational vision into action and enhancing the organizational innovation performance. This sub-ontology seeks to allow representing *organizational ability* with a wider perspective that is not only restricted to the use of technologies but that pertains to the development of a contextual ability endowed with the adequate resources, appropriate policies and advanced capabilities.

Figure 20.7 Innovation Context Sub-Ontology Knowledge View

4.3. Innovation Performance: Multi-Dimensional Approach to Measurement

Managing is not enough to ensure innovation success, accurate measurement and continuous improvement as well mater. In accordance with the above contributions reflecting our perception to innovation management, our contributions in this area are: (1) a set of three integrated and interrelated *Dimensions* underlying a *Multi-dimensional Approach to Innovation Measurement.* These dimensions supported by the above constructed models to innovation structuration and interoperability allowed us to develop (2) an *Idea Scoring System* identifying set of *Idea Measurement Indicators* that served as a prototype to prove the feasibility and usefulness of the designed approach to innovation measurement. It has also been used in the 3rd scenario of the accomplished business case study to inform the idea management system and continuously improve the decision-making.

4.3.1. Multi-Dimensional Model of Innovation Performance

Since innovation is a complex and multidimensional phenomenon, modern organizations can overcome the innovation performance management gap by defining a synthesized framework that represents this diversity using a *multi-dimensional approach.* Accordingly and based on the investigation, aggregation and clustering of the performance dimensions gathered from the literature and the performance models presented above (Table 20.9) we defined a tri-axial model comprised of a set of three interrelated and integrated dimensions to be used as a basis of a multi-dimensional approach to innovation performance management: (1) "***innovation actor competency***" that aims to organize the innovation actors and their related roles and activities into meaningful, exhaustive, and mutually-exclusive clusters based on their competencies; (2) "*innovation core-idea relevance*" that aims to organize the relevant knowledge sources and deliverables of the innovation effort along the innovation continuum; (3) "*innovation context ability*" that aims to organize the contextual factors that impact the innovation performance and enhance the organizational continuous renewal ability. The exploration of each dimension is detailed below in the following sub-sections.

4.3.2 Innovation Actor Competency Dimension

The notion of "*competency*" is defined as the ability to perform a specific task or come out with a noteworthy deliverable. Accordingly, we defined an "*innovation actor competency*" as an aggregation that can be objectively measured or subjectively recognized of *knowledge* (i.e. conceptual or theoretical cognitions), *skills* (i.e. procedural or applied knowledge), *wills* (i.e. intentions or motivations), *experiences* (i.e. verifiable knowledge about past activities that would inform potential abilities in similar situation) and *personal traits* (i.e. specific characteristics like attitude, physical ability) required to perform an innovation activity, fulfill a life-cycle stage, or bring a significant deliverable.

4.3.3. Innovation Core-Idea Relevance Dimension

The notion of "*relevance*" is defined as the goodness and efficacy to provide new insights, influence the development and generate sustainable impact. As such, we suggest that the "*innovation core-idea relevance*" should be decided according to its *consistency* (i.e., contribution level to the integrity of the mother idea), *dependency* (i.e., relatedness to other core-ideas), *completeness* (i.e. contribution level to the elaboration of the mother idea), *appropriateness* (i.e. contribution level to the usability and feasibility of the mother idea), *compatibility* (i.e. contribution level to the alignment with organizational goals), *innovativeness* (i.e. contribution level to the novelty and originality of the mother idea), *riskiness* (i.e. severity of expected risk from the adoption of the mother idea), *hardness* (i.e. contribution level to the required workload) and *effectiveness* (i.e. contribution level to the potential benefit of the mother idea).

4.3.4. Innovation Context Ability Dimension

The notion of "*ability to renew*" is defined as the capability to adapt to external changes by creating internal change that impacts innovation performance within modern organizations. In other words, it is the capability to learn and innovate sustainably by continuously transforming knowledge and ideas into new outputs for the global benefit. In order to provide the innovation actors with a predefined roadmap for ongoing performance measurement and then improvement from "*not able to do it*" towards "*able to continuously improve it*", we defined five distinct levels of the "***innovation context ability***": (a) *awareness* - to understand what innovation means; (b) *acceptance* - by tongue and heart of whatever the adopted innovation policy implies; (c) *believe* - in innovation sincerely, with honesty, to actually mean it and to have no doubt about its promises (d) *enactment* – to engage by deeds and to do it solely for the sake of worthy wealth creation and sustainable impact (e) *enjoyment* - to enjoy innovation, its implications, requirements and what it stands for.

4.4. Practical Implications

Practically, this research work is intended to be useful for all types of organizations (large or small, private or public), whatever their work area and in any sector of activity. It is a way to create awareness on the importance of the required effort and promote the growth of an innovation culture that could make this effort easier. It will boost fast and intuitive management of innovation activities and deliverables within a complex environment while keeping an eye on the quality perspective. In sum, implementing a GenID approach to innovation management will benefit modern organizations of all kind by enhancing their capability to have a sustainable impact and participate in the global-wealth creation. Indeed, at an even deeper level, this research work will enable modern organizations:

- At the *individual level*, to gain a clear picture of actor's competencies across the innovation context and along the innovation continuum, to generate target competency profiles and identify competency gaps, to perform the suitable matching of actor's competencies to innovation roles and actions, and to carry out required training and professional development.

- At the *knowledge level*, to increase productivity by locating noteworthy deliverables, to reduce the time and rework waste, to enable fast-tracking, to build the sole of an educational framework and learning modules, and to conduct awareness sessions across the innovation actors, encouraging the development of e-learning materials covering all disciplines and roles.

- At the *organizational level*, to establish the organization's innovation adoption readiness, to identify organizational bottleneck and innovation hampering causes, to discover untapped potential that can be used to foster the innovation effort, and to identify compliance gaps due to missing standards and protocols that need to be developed.

5. Conclusion and Future Research

The research project presented in this chapter set out with a goal to identify a generic, holistic and integrated approach to innovation management. It has been managed to provide relevant contributions to state of the art on three main areas: *"Innovation Structuration,"* *"Innovation Interoperability"* and *"Innovation Performance."* These contributions have been conceived to be integrated into a coherent framework we called *"Generic Innovation Designing -GenID- Framework."* This approach allows *systematic structuration* with a complexity perspective, *semantic representation* with a modular approach and *multi-dimensional measurement* with a continuous performance improvement intention. Benefiting from previous research and applicable theories - and reflecting our experiential knowledge and thought experiments - this research work adopted a pragmatic research design and a mixed research strategy. The results from the conducted experiments and empirical investigation have delivered proof for usefulness and relevance of all contributions, though, further experiments with specific and large use cases in both industry and academia are planned.

In terms of directions for future work the conceptual and practical contributions of this research project can be extended following three main sections:

1) **Innovation Structuration** – Further research could be done on how to leverage from *enterprise linked data* in order to link the GenID Learning engine with various data silos of the organization as well as other open information sources like blogs and forums. Another line of future work could be to leverage from *business intelligence* and *natural language processing techniques* to import information from the *Social Web* (SW) and analyze them together with the well formatted ideas submitted by different innovator actors. Furthermore, *social networking* could be used to highlight new interactions between individuals and communities and new approaches to the spread of knowledge and ideas, while SW data could be used to rank already submitted ideas. In addition, GenID approach to innovation structuration could be used to build a unified approach to innovation teaching and training as well as to establish a solid base for a formal innovation learning process.

2) ***Innovation Interoperability*** – Further work will be made to use
    GenID Ontology for *similarity* detection, *clustering, networking*
    and *recommendation* of relevant innovation entities (i.e. core-
    ideas, actors and contextual conditions). Another extension would
    be to develop a custom *annotation* model to capture and visually
    represent complex innovation processes. These annotations
    could also be used to develop metrics for innovation performance
    measurement. Yet, the introduction of new elements to GenID
    Ontology will make the annotation process difficult. So, potential
    future lines of research could be to *extend* the ontology and add
    new concepts in a fully *automatic way.* As well, it could be inter-
    esting to leverage from *semantic search* and *data mining* technol-
    ogies to make automatic annotations (e.g. by searching for se-
    mantic similar innovations, then mining annotations from the
    profiles of the retrieved innovations, before using the learned an-
    notations for auto-annotation). In addition, an *online innovation
    dictionary* could be defined and expanded to include a large
    number of terms and descriptions, in order to reduce terms' am-
    biguity and enable development of interconnected competency
    assessments, learning modules and performance workflows.

3) ***Innovation Performance*** – While the commonly used metrics
    to idea measurement are not fully accurate about the com-
    ments related to an idea, there is a need to consider the *eval-
    uation of opinions* expressed in comments as it can deliver
    relevant knowledge that could influence the adoption deci-
    sion. In other words, there is a need to investigate the *opinion
    mining* area in order to be able to provide an *opinion rating* of
    every comment attached to an idea. In doing so, supplemen-
    tary tool for judging ideas' performance can be used besides
    the existing idea assessment metrics. However, most review-
    ers and decision makers are faced with an overwhelming
    amount of comments, which exceeds their ability to analyze
    and make conclusions in reasonable time. Thus, using an *au-
    tomated opinion mining algorithm* will provide more valuable
    help. Another extension could be to develop an *accreditation
    program* clarifying innovation performance milestones and
    providing individuals and organizations with *metrics* to assess
    and continuously improve their innovation performance. In
    addition, GenID approach to innovation measurement can be
    used to structure and standardize the innovation assessment,
    as well as establish a solid basis for an *innovation policy model*

that could facilitate collaboration between different organizations and knowledge systems.

References

Adams, R., Bessant, J. and Phelps, R. (2006). 'Innovation management measurement: A review'. *International Journal of Management Reviews*, 8(1), 21-47.

Atkinson, D. (2011). *Approaches and Strategies of Social Research, Essay for Reasearch Methods Class*. RMIT.

Bojars, U., Breslin, J.G., Peristeras, V., Tummarello, G. and Decker, S. (2008). 'Interlinking the social web with semantics'. *Intelligent Systems*, IEEE, 23(3), 29-40.

Borgatti, S.P. and Cross, R. (2003). 'A relational view of information seeking and learning in social networks'. *Management Science*, 49, 432-445.

Chiesa, V., Frattini, F., Lamberti, L. and Noci, G. (2009). 'Exploring management control in radical innovation projects'. *European Journal of Innovation Management*, 2(4), 416-443.

Cooper, R.G. and Kleinschmidt, E.J. (1987). 'New products: What separates winners from losers?' *Journal of Product Innovation Management*, 4(3), 169-184.

Cooper, R.G. (1985). 'Selecting winning new product projects: Using the New Prod system'. *Journal of Product Innovation Management*, 2(1), 34-44.

Drakos, N., Fenn, J. and Rozwell, C. (2013). 'Who's Who in Innovation Management Technology'. *Gartner*, January.

du Preez, N.D. and Louw, L. (2008). 'A framework for managing the innovation process'. Conference Proceeding, Portland International Conference on Management of Engineering & Technology (PICMET), 546-558.

El Bassiti (2017). 'Generic Ontology for Innovation Domain towards "Innovation Interoperability". *Journal of Entrepreneurship Management and Innovation* (JEMI), 13(2), 105-126.

El Bassiti, L. and Ajhoun, R. (2016). 'Continuous Performance Improvement of Innovation: Bridging the Gap between Creativity and Measurement'. 28th International Business Information Management Conference (IBIMA), 4248- 4262.

El Bassiti, L., El Haiba, M. and Ajhoun, R. (2017). 'Generic Innovation Designing -GenID- Framework: Towards a more Systematic Approach to Innovation Management'. 18th European Conference on Knowledge Management (ECKM), 2, 1097-1106.

Etzkowitz, H., and Leydesdorff, L. (2000). 'The Dynamics of Innovation: From National Systems and "Mode 2" to a Triple Helix of University-Industry-Government Relations'. *Research Policy*, 29(2), 109-123.

Fritsch, M. (2001). 'Innovation by networking: An economic perspective', in Koschatzky, K., Kulicke, M. and Zenker, A. (Eds.): *Innovation networks-Concepts and challenges in the European perspective*, Heidelberg, Germany: Physica, 25-34.

Girotra, K., Terwiesch, C. and Ulrich, K.T. (2010). 'Idea generation and the quality of the best idea'. *Management science*. 56(4), 591-605.

Gliedman, C., Burris, P. and Wang, N. (2013). *The Forrester Wave: Innovation Management Tools*. Forrester, Q3.

Hewson, C. (2006). *Mixed Methods Research*. London: SAGE.

Justel, D., Vidal, R., Arriaga, E., Franco, V., Val-Jauregi, E. (2007). 'Evaluation method for selecting innovative product concepts with greater potential marketing success'. International Conference on Engineering Design (ICED).

Khurana, A., Rosenthal, S.R. (1997). 'Integrating the fuzzy front end of new product development'. *Sloan Management Review*, 38, 103-120.

Lawson, B. and Samson, D. (2001). 'Developing innovation capability in organizations: A dynamic capabili-ties approach'. *International Journal of Innovation Management*,5(3), 377-400.

Lee, A.S. (2001). 'Editorial'. *MIS Quarterly*, 25(1), iii-vii.

McCarthy, I.P., Tsinopoulos, C., Allen, P. and Rose Anderssen, C. (2006). 'New product development as a complex adaptive system of decisions'. *Journal of Product Innovation Management*, 23(5), 437-456.

Morel, B. and Ramanujam, R. (1999). 'Through the looking glass of complexity: the dynamics of organizations as adaptive and evolving systems'. *Organization Science*, 10(3), 278-293.

Muller, A., Valikangas, L. and Merlyn, P. (2005). 'Metrics for innovation: guidelines for developing a customized suite of innovation metrics'. *Strategy & Leadership*, 33(1), 37-45.

Neely, A. (2004). 'Performance measurement: the new crisis', in Crainer, S. and Dearlove, D. (Eds.*): Financial Times Handbook of Management*, Pearson Education Ltd, Harlow.

Nixon, B. (1998). 'Research and development performance measurement: a case study'. *Management Accounting Research*, 9(3), 329-355.

Pagano, P., Candela, L. and Castelli, D. (2013). 'Data interoperability'. *Data Science Journal*, 12, GRDI19-GRDI25.

Salter, A. and Alexy, O. (2013). 'The nature of Innovation', in Dodgson, M., Gann, D. and Phillips, N. (Eds.): *The Oxford Handbook of Innovation Management*, Oxford: OUP.

Sherif, K. (2006). 'An adaptive strategy for managing knowledge in organizations'. *Journal of Knowledge Management*, 10(4), 72-80.

Simons, R. (1990). 'The role of management control systems in creating competitive advantage: New perspectives'. *Accounting, Organizations and Society*, 15(1/2), 127-143.

Steele, M.D. (2003). *Margins count: systems thinking and cost*. AACE International Transactions, PM.03: 03.1-03.5.

Studer, R., Benjamins, V. and Fensel, D. (1998). 'Knowledge Engineering: Principles and Methods'. *IEEE Transactions on Data and Knowledge Engineering*, 25(1-2), 161–197.

Tidd, J., Bessant, J. and Pavitt, K. (2005). *Managing Innovation: Integrating Technological, Market and Organisational Change*. John Wiley & Sons, Chichester.

Trott, P. (2011). *Innovation management and new product development*. New Jersey: Prentice Hall.

Van de Ven, A.H. (1986). 'Central problems in the management of innovation, management science'. *Organization Design*, 32(5), 590-607.

Chapter 21

First Things First -
Think before You Decide the How,
What and Who of Idea Screening

Johan Netz*

E-mail: johan.netz@kau.se

Abstract: This thesis investigates the decision-making process when screening new ideas in the Front-End Innovation phase. In the thesis two alternative decision-making approaches are explored, the intuitive and rational approach. The empirical findings demystify the concept of intuition by connecting it to the use of five underlying (rational) criteria. The results increase our understanding of the use of rational and intuitive decision-making when screening ideas during the FEI phase, as well as questioning the traditional view of intuition, as a decision-making tool that is only reliable if applied by those with a vast amount of experience and expertise. The reported findings indicate for example, that users with an understanding of the idea context are able to intuitively identify the ideas that decision-making experts identify as the top (best) ones. Hence, managers faced with a situation where they are being inundated with new ideas can turn to non-experts for help.

Keywords: Idea Management; Innovation; Intuition; Rationality; Criteria; Idea Assessment; Idea Screening; Idea Evaluation; Decision-making; Front-End Innovation.

1. Introduction

The focus of this thesis is studying how firms initially decide which new ideas should be selected for further development or rejected, during the Front End Innovation (FEI) phase of the innovation process (Koen et al., 2001). The decision-making activities (i.e., idea screening) leading to an initial selection of ideas in the FEI phase are highlighted and described as among the most important (Calantone et al., 1999, Cooper, 2007, Markham, 2013), but challenging tasks to master (Barczak et al., 2009), since they have such a huge impact on the subsequent development phases (Cooper, 2014). There are two main reasons for this; firstly, not all ideas are good, and no firm has the resources to develop every single idea proposed to it (Kock et al., 2015, Ozer, 1999, Sharma, 1999). Secondly, the development of ideas into finalized innovations is crucial when it comes to gaining and sustaining competitive advantage (Drucker, 2014, Griffin, 1997, Schumpeter, 1934). A firm that is not able to compete against the new innovations introduced by its competitors will likely fail in the long run. Thus, it is important to be careful when initially deciding which ideas to select and develop into future possible innovations, in order to eliminate weak ideas and retain those that have a substantial chance of becoming successful (Alam and Perry, 2002, Florén and Frishammar, 2012, Girotra et al., 2010, Hammedi et al., 2011).

However, with the introduction of IT-based Open Innovation or OI concepts (Chesbrough, 2006), for generating new ideas such as IBM's *Innovation Jam* (Bjelland and Wood, 2008), Starbuck's *My Starbucks Idea* (Sigala, 2012) or Dell's *Idea storm* (Bayus, 2012), the challenges associated with the initial idea screening increase. By paving the way for anyone to contribute new ideas, a firm can potentially end up being flooded with ideas (Bjelland and Wood, 2008, Pisano and Verganti, 2008, Ringo, 2007). Hence, collecting new ideas is not the problem for most firms; rather, how to select is the most interesting ideas to develop (Magnusson et al., 2014, van den Ende et al., 2015). OI can thus be seen as both a possibility (i.e., getting new perspectives on ideas) and a threat (i.e., the increased number of ideas make the initial idea selection difficult). When the number of new ideas collected from an OI concept increases, the group of decision-makers responsible for FEI idea screening (and assumed being fairly constant), will face three key challenges. The first challenge is linked to the rational decision-making approach and the use of criteria, which is described as the established way of working when screening ideas during the FEI phase (Crawford and Di Benedetto, 2008, Hammedi et al., 2011, Koen et al., 2002). Two issues relating to the use of criteria are, (a) knowing which criteria to use and (b), how to weigh and evaluate the different criteria assessments.

Secondly, should an intuitive decision-making approach be used in favor of a rational (criteria) approach? In a scenario, of being overwhelmed with new ideas, it could, at first glance, seem legitimate to recommend that an intuition based approach would be more useful compared to an rational approach, since intuitive decisions are faster than rational decisions (Akinci and Sadler-Smith, 2012). However, comparative studies of the differences and/or similarities between intuitive and rational criteria decision-making during FEI idea screening are scant (Eling et al., 2015, Magnusson et al., 2014, Pétervári et al., 2016), although it has been argued that a connection does exist between intuitive and rationally-based decisions (Epstein, 1994, Epstein, 2003, Sowden et al., 2015). Thus, further studies relating to this topic are needed in order to produce sound recommendations as to which decision-making approach to use (Björk et al., 2016).

Thirdly, is the challenge of the decision-makers responsible for FEI idea screening becoming a bottleneck. Since the increased ratio between ideas per decision-maker, when using OI concepts, will increase the time needed to complete the screening. A prolonged FEI phase can obviously delay later stages of the innovation process, and in a highly competitive marketplace, this could lead to missed marketing opportunities, e.g., being first to market (Magnusson et al., 2014). One way of addressing this issue is to involve additional individuals to help in screening all new ideas. These additional assessors (labeled non-decision-makers) could assist by reducing the number of ideas that decision-makers should focus on more thoroughly. The non-decision-makers could, for example, make an initial rough selection in order to sift out the worst ideas; they could be potential users or employees. However, even though research into this topic is growing, the question of whether or not it would be appropriate to involve non-decision-makers during FEI idea screening, and also if they can act as a proxy for decision-makers is in need of additional research (Magnusson et al., 2016).

Based on the above discussion, this thesis aims to expand current knowledge of the use of rational and holistic intuitive decision-making during the FEI phase. The focus of the thesis also relates to the general call to expand current knowledge regarding FEI activities (Boeddrich, 2004, Koen et al., 2001, van den Ende et al., 2015, Eling et al., 2014, Björk et al., 2016). The purpose of the thesis is as follows:

To contribute towards better understanding the use of rational and holistic intuitive decision-making approaches when screening ideas during the front-end innovation phase, and to explore the involvement of non-decision-makers in the screening process.

2. Background

When screening ideas during the FEI phase, two alternative decision-making approaches are mentioned in the literature, the rational and intuitive approaches (Eling et al., 2015). These two approaches are often described on the basis of the dual-processes theory (Evans and Stanovich, 2013, Sowden et al., 2015). Evans (2003) summarizes this as "... *two minds in one brain*" (p 458). Dual-process theorists have argued that humans rely on two underlying cognitive systems when reasoning, in turn leading to a final decision (Evans, 2008). These systems are called System-1 and System-2, where System-1 is described as the intuitive system and System-2 as the rational system (Kahneman, 2003, Epstein, 1994, Evans, 2003, Sloman, 1996, Stanovich and West, 2000).

The rational (System-2) approach, portrayed as the common decision-making approach when screening ideas (Crawford and Di Benedetto, 2008, Hammedi et al., 2011, Koen et al., 2002), can be described as an analytical process (Sadler-Smith and Shefy, 2004), during which the idea is assessed against various predefined criteria (Hart et al., 2003, Magnusson et al., 2014, Wheelwright and Clark, 1992). Advocates of the rational approach argue that rational criteria analysis is superior to intuitively-based decisions, since rational decisions are seen as more elaborated (Behling and Eckel, 1991, Meehl, 1954), and also enhance the overall innovation success rate (Eling et al., 2016). However, and even though it is argued that having well-defined decision-making criteria when assessing ideas, is very important (Cooper, 1999, Griffin, 1997), knowledge of which criteria to use when assessing ideas during FEI is under debate. Summarizing years of research, it becomes clear that no guidelines exist for what specific criteria to use when screening ideas in FEI phase (Balachandra and Friar, 1997, Carbonell-Foulquié et al., 2004, Hart et al., 2003, Magnusson et al., 2014). Additionally, is the challenge of how to aggregate the different assessments; i.e., how to weight the various criteria (Magnusson et al., 2016, Soukhoroukova et al., 2012). This challenge is crucial since a change in weights can alter the final selection of ideas for further development.

An intuitive (System-1) approach, on the other hand, can be described as a holistic hunch about the idea (Akinci and Sadler-Smith, 2012, Miller and Ireland, 2005). Intuitive decision-making is a more rapid decision-making technique than using the rational approach (Akinci and Sadler-Smith, 2012). It is based on the decision-makers prior knowledge, acquired over time in a certain domain or context (Sadler-Smith and Shefy, 2004, Salas et al., 2010). It is argued that when confronting huge or insufficient amounts of information during a limited timeframe, intuitive decisions seem preferable (as discussed by Hodgkinson et al., 2009). However, comparative studies of the possible differences, similarities or connections between the two approaches as regards the idea selection outcome is scant (Eling et al., 2015, Magnusson et al., 2014, Pétervári et al., 2016). Hence, clear and evolved recommendations regarding which decision-making approach to use when selecting ideas during the FEI phase are lacking. According to Pétervári et al. (2016), future research efforts regarding the use of intuition when selecting ideas should be given special attention. In the end, use of the different decision-making approaches might have an effect on the actual decision-making outcome, i.e. idea selection.

Regardless of the discussions for what decision-making approach to use, the issue of having large numbers of ideas to screen is still one of the greatest challenges facing firms that collect ideas using an OI approach. From a practical point of view, a simple solution to this challenge would be to increase the number of assessors taking part in the screening process. These additional assessors (labeled non-decision-makers), could assist by reducing the number of ideas that decision-makers should focus on more thoroughly. However, which individuals should be asked to participate as assessors when screening ideas has not been fully investigated as yet (Magnusson et al., 2016, Riedl et al., 2010). Two groups that are frequently highlighted as key resources in assisting with idea screening during FEI are *users* (Toubia and Florès, 2007, Magnusson et al., 2016), and *employees* (Feldmann et al., 2013). From the literature, it is clear that both users and employees should be considered as a useful knowledge source to utilize. But does, for example, the weighting of different criteria differ between different types of assessors? Having this type of data would make it possible to give better recommendations to practitioners regarding how to organize a screening activity that involves non-decision-makers.

From the discussion above, several questions can be raised. However, based on the findings in the five papers this thesis is built on, three general research questions are addressed, these are formulated as follows:

RQ1: What criteria do decision-makers take into account when intuitively (holistically) screening ideas during the FEI phase?

RQ2: Does the weighting of criteria differ between decision-makers and non-decision-makers, and if so how?

RQ3: How is idea screening affected on the basis of which decision-making approach is applied (rational or intuitive) and on the basis of who conducts it (decision-maker or non-decision-maker)?

The three different research questions thus correspond to the thesis purpose, as well as to the three different key challenges discussed in the introduction.

3. Research design

To answer the research questions and fulfill the overall purpose of the thesis both qualitative and quantitative methods have been used. The first research question is addressed using a qualitative approach, while the second and third research questions are studied using a quantitative approach. The empirical data is based on three different studies, using either a qualitative or quantitative approach, or a combination of them. Three global Swedish firms; Telia (telecom provider), Ericsson (telecom equipment manufacturer) and Volvo (commercial vehicle manufacturer), were involved in the three different studies (including 192 ideas and 127 participants, see figure 21.1 below for a visualization).

Research projects   **Appended papers**   **Research questions**

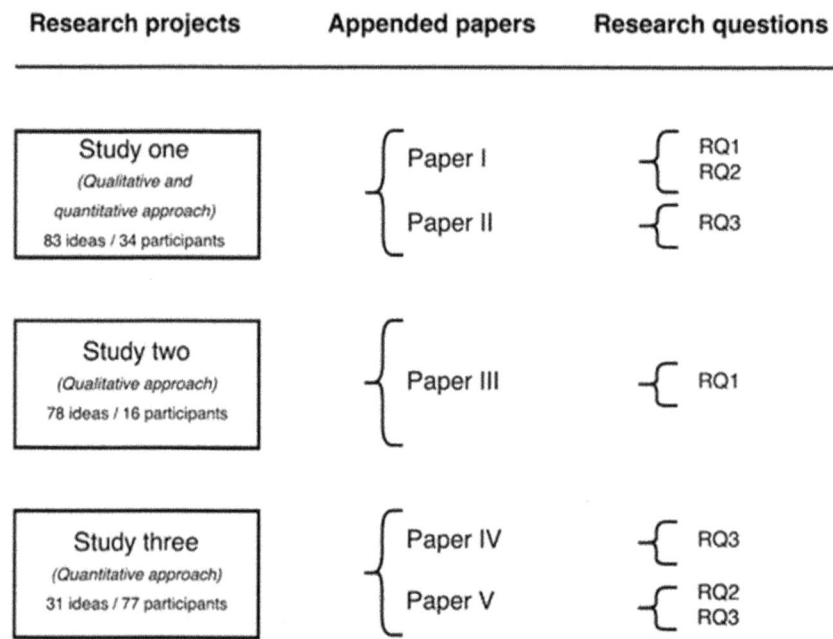

Figure 21.1 Connections between projects, papers and research questions.

To answer the first research question which can be described as exploratory, an inductive qualitative approach was applied, using the talk-aloud method (Fonteyn et al., 1993, Ericsson and Simon, 1993), to Papers I and III. The aim of the Talk-aloud method is not judging the outcomes of a participant's cognitive process, but exploring the decision-making process itself (Ericsson and Simon, 1993). Summarizing the research on idea screening, using a rational (criteria) approach, show that the results are mostly based on retrospective data collection methods, meaning that the decision-makers studied try to recall which criteria they have been using when screening ideas. However, individuals who are asked, for example, to verbalize their cognitive processes which lead to a decision, in retrospect, can be biased (Nisbett and Wilson, 1977), thus leading a researcher towards incorrect assumptions. Data collected using the Talk-aloud method is however seen as reliable since it is labeled as concurrent data (Ericsson and Simon, 1980). Information that is verbalized, for example during an actual idea screening activity, is labeled concurrent data, while information provided by participants, who are asked to recall and verbalize their cognitive processes from situations that have occurred in the past, is labeled retrospective data (Ericsson and Simon, 1980). It has been shown that the concurrent Talk-aloud method outperforms the retrospective method by providing clearer descriptions of the decision-making steps between the "stimulus introduction" (in this case the introduction of the ideas) and the final decision being made (Kuusela and Pallab, 2000). Additionally, all the ideas were presented in a randomized order to the individual assessors. The reason for presenting the ideas in this way was to manage the "order-effect bias" that can occur (Perreault, 1975). The collected Talk-aloud data was analyzed using Thematic Analysis (Boyatzis, 1998), following the recommendations of Braun and Clarke (2006).

To answer the second and third research questions, which explores whether or not differences exist among the different groups of peoples (i.e., decision-makers and non-decision-makers), when screening ideas, a quasi-experimental design was applied (Mertens, 2014, Shadish et al., 2002). In relation to the quantitative approach applied to questions two and three, Paper II is based on deductive hypotheses testing. Papers I, IV and V on the other hand had an inductive focus, implying an iterative process, moving between data and theory (Bryman and Bell, 2011), since the existing literature, regarding each paper's aim, did not permit the use of a deductive approach (due to a lack of extensive theoretical foundations). The experiments conducted in Papers I, II, IV, and V strongly resemble each other and the same idea-randomization procedure was used during the experiments, as mentioned in the Talk-aloud method above. All participants were asked to individually assess the ideas, using an online IT platform, by initially making an intuitive assessment followed by a rational criteria assessment. The setup of having the participants depart from an intuitive decision-making approach before conducting a rational assessment is in line with Shapiro and Spence (1997), and Eling et al. (2015) arguments that this setup increases the decision quality. Initially, three different criteria were used in Study 1, Originality, User-value and Producibility, based on the works of Magnusson (2009). After the qualitative Study 2, two additional criteria were identified and added to Study 3 (i.e., Strategic-fit and Profitability).

4. Conclusion

In relation to the first research question, an initial contribution is the demystification of the concept of intuition, in the context of screening product or service ideas. Based on the Think-aloud sessions, it was found that decision-makers' holistic decisions were predominantly based on five criteria; *Originality, User-value, Producibility, Strategic-fit* and *Profitability*. These five criteria explained between 50 and 80 percent of the variations of the holistic assessments made by non-decision-makers. Hence, showing that a holistic assessment might not always be intuitive but still includes some sort of underlying reasoning processes. The finding thus adds to the debate about the connection between intuitive and rational decision-making (see, e.g.

Fredrickson, 1985, Sadler-Smith and Shefy, 2004, Sadler-Smith and Sparrow, 2008, Salas et al., 2010). However, further studies of the application of intuitive decision-making are needed, especially since it was also shown that the holistic assessments made by decision-makers and non-decision-makers were similar in terms of the relative ranking of the top ideas. The latter thus questioning intuition as something that should only be used by highly-experienced experts (Hayashi, 2001, Kahneman and Klein, 2009).

Furthermore, the finding that many decision-makers involve financial and market aspects (i.e., profitability) when holistically screening ideas are also interesting. In the innovation literature, several authors argue that there are difficulties using financially- and market-related criteria in the FEI idea screening (Cooper, 2014, Lynn et al., 1996, O'Connor, 1998). Despite this, decision-makers were found to involve these aspects. This could lead decision-makers into taking a short-term perspective when holistically screening ideas, i.e., favor ideas that could have a positive impact on the next set of financial statements. Hence, an idea might be rejected too early, if it does not include enough information to assess its potential profitability. According to Cooper (2014), firms should thus use more flexible criteria, i.e., not making a final decision when not enough information is at hand at the time of the decision. However, more research is required before solid recommendations can be made regarding how, for example, profitability criteria should be used when screening ideas during the FEI phase.

In relation to the second research question, regarding the weighting of different criteria, the current literature is scant (Magnusson et al., 2016, Soukhoroukova et al., 2012). The findings add to the discussion about criteria weighting, by establishing a statistical relationship between holistic (intuitive) assessments and rational criteria assessments. Thus, when screening ideas, assessors highlight user-value as the most important criterion. This finding is interesting from an idea-generation perspective since it emphasizes the importance of idea creators focusing on what user-value their ideas can bring (Dean et al., 2006). Another interesting finding that relates to criteria weighting is that some non-decision-makers (frontline employees) only focused (significantly) on three of the five criteria when screening ideas; i.e., user-value, strategic-fit and originality. Thus, depending who makes the assessment, it is advisable to use different criteria; for instance, strategic-fit is possibly more difficult for users to evaluate, because of their unawareness of internal company strategy (Magnusson et al., 2016).

In relation to the third research question, it was found that assessor's orientation towards a technical or user perspective affects the assessments. Thus, if a rational criteria decision approach is applied, then different groups would most certainly reach different conclusions (i.e. in terms of absolute scores). This finding is highly interesting since no research has been found that compares different assessor groups who assess ideas using the same assessment method. However, when focusing on the relative holistic rankings of ideas, the results show that companies can employ non-decision-makers, as proxies for in-house decision-makers, to select the top (best) ideas for further elaboration when intuitively assessing ideas (Magnusson et al., 2016). Thus, in line with previous findings from Toubia and Florès (2007). Furthermore, the results contribute to the open and user innovation literature, which traditionally discuss users as a source of new ideas, by showing that both users and non-decision-making employees are also able to contribute to the assessment of ideas. Hence, a firm that has been flooded with new ideas, could by involving non-decision-making users and/or employees, significantly reduce the amount of ideas that the in-house decision-makers will ultimately have to focus on.

5. Implications and future research

For managers, in control of the FEI idea-screening process, it is important to put time and effort into how the idea screening should be commenced once the ideas have been collected. An initial step should be making sure that the ideas being subjected to screening are, in fact, ready or complete enough to be assessed. If an idea is incomprehensible to an assessor, it would not be wise to try to assess it regardless of the decision-making approach used. It could thus be argued that, before screening even starts, ideas that are not "complete enough" should undergo a refinement stage to improve and/or even reshape the original idea. However, this would increase the time needed during the FEI phase and thus calls for a more systematic way of categorizing ideas based on their readiness for critical assessment. This is, however, outside the scope of this thesis. If, on the other hand, ideas were to be screened immediately, the systems used to screen them, should include a function permitting assessors to develop the original idea. One way to do this could be to make it possible to include mini-scenarios which some decision-makers created in the Talk-aloud sessions. Their scenarios could, for example, be formalized (e.g. recorded or written down) so that other assessors could increase their comprehension of the idea in question. These mini-scenarios could also be used when further developing ideas into more robust concepts during later development stages. Besides the obvious importance of making sure that ideas are ready to be critically assessed, proper decision-making should also be based on the type of idea to be screened (i.e. incremental or radical), as well as on who will be taking part in screening (i.e. what knowledge they have).

Additional research is needed to understand how different ideas are perceived and comprehended by assessors. Comprehension can be defined as a person's capability of discerning appropriate meaning (Smith and Taffler, 1992). Ideas lacking adequate information at the time of screening will increase the difficulties of assessing them properly (Kornish and Ulrich, 2014). Thus, idea descriptions which are posted, for example, on an online OI forum should carry enough information to make them understandable to the assessors screening them. Previous research argues in favor of the importance of an idea's specificity and clarity, suggesting that a complete idea should include answers to the *who*, *what*, *where*, *why* and *how* questions, as well as clearly linking the problem and the solution description to each other (Dean et al., 2006). Thus, ideas that are not complete will force assessors to either request additional information or make assessments based on their presumptions, associations and interpretations of these ideas. The latter case may mislead both comprehension and subsequent assessment according to Moreau et al. (2001). However, it might not always be possible to ask the idea creator for additional information about the idea description, for example, if the idea creator is an outsider (e.g., a user) who is not easily accessible. Thus, assessors could be forced to make decisions based on the limited information they have.

Furthermore, it would be interesting to investigate how the elaboration of idea descriptions would affect assessments. This could, for example, be done using an experimental design whereby the same original idea is presented in two different ways (unelaborated vs. elaborated). The results could, for instance, be used to instruct how ideas should be written in order to maximize the likelihood of them being interpreted in the way the idea creator intended them to be. In addition to the ideas, the findings in Paper III, regarding how individual traits seems to affect the willingness to generate mini-scenarios, are also something that I would address in future research. Do, for instance, these individuals differ in their actual assessments? If they differ, should the screening team then be organized on the basis of how individual assessors can maximize their individual performance? Knowing more about how individual traits might affect how ideas are interpreted could enhance the way firms organize their FEI activities. For example, a firm that has identified individuals who are more creative could, for instance, involve these in the initial development of the raw ideas, as suggested by Stevens et al. (1999). Individuals who are more conservative might, on the other hand, be involved when the initial raw idea has matured (i.e., being developed) into a more robust concept.

Regarding who should be taking part in screening, I think, it will be good if more people are involved since this would broaden the perspectives. As an analogy, the creation of a football team can be used. When forming a football team, it is necessary to find the right mixture of players since not everyone can be a goal scorer. You need a goalkeeper, as well as defenders, midfielders, and attackers, and some of these will have different tasks in their respective positions (e.g., acting as the playmaker). The same thought is applicable when working with the FEI phase. Ideas that are generated might not be complete, i.e., they are unable to "score a goal" by themselves, they need the help of the team. Furthermore, it is not always the case that the idea's originator is able to develop the idea by him-/herself into an assessable concept; he/she might need help from a creative midfielder. However, if the idea is assessed by a person with a negative attitude to new things (e.g., a brutal defender), the chances are that the idea will be rejected and the idea creator might not want to participate in future idea generation activities due to, for example, the lack of constructive feedback. During the Talk-aloud studies in Paper III, these challenges were noted. To clarify, it is important to have players (i.e., decision-makers) who are willing and who dare to question the need for new ideas, since no firm has the resources to develop every single new idea into a final-ized innovation. However, being too harsh during the first screening of an idea might also lead to missed opportunities. Thus, like a football coach or a manager of the idea screening, it is important to set up the team in a way that maximizes the chances of scoring, in other words identifying ideas that have a substantial chance of becoming successfully-developed innovations (i.e. having the right person do the right thing at the right time).

When taking an even wider perspective on the FEI phase and screening, it would be recommendable for firms to become more precise about what it is they want. If knowing, from the beginning, which types of ideas are desired, it would be easier to steer (prime) the idea generators towards a specific direction. This would likely increase the quality of the ideas (Ward 2004). However, contemporary research indicates that it is not preferable if it is based upon financial criteria, i.e., using cost reductions when priming idea generators (Olsson et al., 2017). Thus, the difficulty of incorporating financial criteria into the screening process is similar to having it during the actual idea generation phase. Financial aspects are not unimportant and have a role to play; however, it might not be the best criterion to use during the initial FEI phase of the innovation process. Finally, it is important to note that an idea for an innovation might not turn out to be the same as the finalized innovation itself. Therefore, it is important to think about what the idea is really all about before deciding its ultimate future (in terms of either being rejected or accepted for further development). Thus, the problem of obtaining vast numbers of new ideas might be due to a lack of thought about what is being sought in the first place. Research has shown that the quality of the ideas has a high impact on the success rate of the innovation process (Kornish and Ulrich, 2014). Thus, this substantiates why idea quality should be emphasized over the advancing of high numbers of generated ideas in the first place (Markham, 2013). Furthermore, having a well thought out strategy for what is desired when ideas are being generated will improve the chances of identifying good ones (Kock et al., 2015) Consequently, *think before you decide.*

Acknowledgment

This summary is based on the thesis, Netz, J., 2017. *First things first-think before you decide: The how, what and who of idea screening* (Doctoral dissertation, Karlstads universitet).

Permanent link: http://urn.kb.se/resolve?urn=urn:nbn:se:kau:diva-63719

References

Akinci, C. and Sadler-Smith, E. (2012). 'Intuition in management research: A historical review'. *International Journal of Management Reviews*, 14, 104-122.

Alam, I. and Perry, C. (2002). 'A customer-oriented new service development process'. *Journal of Services Marketing*, 16, 515-534.

Balachandra, R. and Friar, J. H. (1997). 'Factors for success in R&D projects and new product innovation: A contextual framework'. *IEEE Transactions on Engineering Management*, 44, 276-287.

Barczak, G., Griffin, A. & Kahn, K. B. (2009). 'Perspective: Trends and drivers of success in NPD practices: Results of the 2003 PDMA best practices study*'. *Journal of Product Innovation Management*, 26, 3-23.

Bayus, B. (2012). 'Crowdsourcing New Product Ideas Over Time: An Analysis of Dell's Ideastorm Community'. *Management science*, 59, 226-244.

Behling, O. & Eckel, N. L. (1991). 'Making sense out of intuition'. *The Executive*, 5, 46-54.

Bjelland, O. M. & Wood, R. C. (2008). 'An Inside View of IBM's "Innovation Jam"'. *MIT Sloan management review*, 50, 32-40.

Björk, J., Magnusson, M., Magnusson, P., Olsson, L. E. & Sukhov, A.' The What, Who, When, Where and How of Idea Assessment'. The Proceedings of The 2016 ISPIM Forum, 2016 Boston, USA. ISPIM.

Boeddrich, H. J. (2004). 'Ideas in the workplace: a new approach towards organizing the fuzzy front end of the innovation process'. *Creativity and innovation management*, 13, 274-285.

Boyatzis, R. E. (1998). *Transforming qualitative information : Thematic analysis and code development*, Thousand Oaks, CA, Sage Publications.

Braun, V. & Clarke, V. (2006).' Using thematic analysis in psychology'. *Qualitative Research in Psychology*, 3, 77-101.

Bryman, A. & Bell, E. (2011). *Business research methods*, Oxford, Oxford Univ. Press.

Calantone, R. J., Benedetto, C. A. & Schmidt, J. B. (1999). 'Using the analytic hierarchy process in new product screening'. *Journal of Product Innovation Management*, 16, 65-76.

Carbonell-Foulquié, P., Munuera-Alemán, J. L. & Rodriguez-Escudero, A. I. (2004). 'Criteria employed for go/no-go decisions when developing successful highly innovative products'. *Industrial Marketing Management*, 33, 307-316.

Chesbrough, H. W. (2006). *Open innovation: The new imperative for creating and profiting from technology*, Boston, MA, Harvard Business Press.

Cooper, R. G. (1999). 'The invisible success factors in product innovation'. *Journal of product innovation management*, 16, 115-133.

Cooper, R. G. (2007). 'New Products—What Separates the Winners from the Losers and What Drives Success'. In: Kahn, K. B. (ed.) *The PDMA Handbook of New Product Development*. Hoboken, NJ: Wiley.

Cooper, R. G. (2014). 'What's Next?: After Stage-Gate'. *Research-Technology Management*, 57, 20-31.

Crawford, C. M. & Di Benedetto, C. A. (2008). *New products management*, Boston, MA, McGraw-Hill Education.

Dean, D. L., Hender, J. M., Rodgers, T. L. & Santanen, E. L. (2006). 'Identifying Quality, Novel, and Creative Ideas: Constructs and Scales for Idea Evaluation'. *Journal of the Association for Information Systems*, 7, 646-699.

Drucker, P. (2014). *Innovation and entrepreneurship: Practice and principles*, London, Routledge.

Eling, K., Griffin, A. & Langerak, F. (2014). 'Using Intuition in Fuzzy Front-End Decision-Making: A Conceptual Framework'. *Journal of Product Innovation Management*, 31, 956-972.

Eling, K., Griffin, A. & Langerak, F. (2016). 'Consistency Matters in Formally Selecting Incremental and Radical New Product Ideas for Advancement'. *Journal of Product Innovation Management*, 33, 20-33.

Eling, K., Langerak, F. & Griffin, A. (2015). 'The Performance Effects of Combining Rationality and Intuition in Making Early New Product Idea Evaluation Decisions'. *Creativity and Innovation Management*, 24, 464-477.

Epstein, S. (1994). 'Integration of the cognitive and the psychodynamic unconscious'. *American Psychologist*, 49, 709-724.

Epstein, S. (2003). 'Cognitive-experiential self-theory of personality'. In: Millon, T. & Lerner, M. J. (eds.) *Handbook of psychology*. New York: Wiley.

Ericsson, K. & Simon, H. (1980). 'Verbal reports as data'. *Psychological Review* 87, 215-251.

Ericsson, K. A. & Simon, H. A. (1993). *Protocol analysis*, Cambridge, MIT press.

Evans, J. (2003). 'In two minds: dual-process accounts of reasoning'. *Trends in Cognitive Sciences*, 7, 454-459.

Evans, J. (2008). 'Dual-processing accounts of reasoning, judgment, and social cognition'. *Annual Review of Psychology*, 59, 255-278.

Evans, J. & Stanovich, K. E. (2013). 'Dual-process theories of higher cognition: Advancing the debate'. *Perspectives on psychological science*, 8, 223-241.

Feldmann, N., Gimpel, H., Kohler, M. & Weinhardt, C. 'Using crowd funding for idea assessment inside organizations: Lessons learned from a market engineering perspective'. In: Agarwal, R., Selen, W., Roos, G. & Green, R., ed. *Cloud and Green Computing* (CGC), 2013 Third International Conference, 2013. IEEE, 525-530.

Florén, H. & Frishammar, J. (2012). 'From preliminary ideas to corroborated product definitions: Managing the front end of new product development'. *California Management Review*, 54, 20-43.

Fonteyn, M. E., Kuipers, B. & Grobe, S. J. (1993). 'A Description of Think Aloud Method and Protocol Analysis'. *Qualitative Health Research*, 3, 430-441.

Fredrickson, J. W. (1985). 'Effects of decision motive and organizational performance level on strategic decision processes'. *Academy of Management journal*, 28, 821-843.

Girotra, K., Terwiesch, C. & Ulrich, K. T. (2010). 'Idea generation and the quality of the best idea'. *Management Science*, 56, 591-605.

Griffin, A. (1997). 'PDMA research on new product development practices: Updating trends and benchmarking best practices'. *Journal of Product Innovation Management*, 14, 429-458.

Hammedi, W., Van Riel, A. C. & Sasovova, Z. (2011). 'Antecedents and Consequences of Reflexivity in New Product Idea Screening*'. *Journal of Product Innovation Management*, 28, 662-679.

Hart, S., Hultink, E. J., Tzokas, N. & Commandeur, H. R. (2003). 'Industrial Companies' Evaluation Criteria in New Product Development Gates'. *Journal of Product Innovation Management*, 20, 22-36.

Hayashi, A. M. (2001). 'When to TRUST Your GUT'. *Harvard Business Review*, 79, 59-65.

Hodgkinson, G. P., Sadler-Smith, E., Burke, L. A., Claxton, G. & Sparrow, P. R. (2009). 'Intuition in Organizations: Implications for Strategic Management'. *Long Range Planning*, 42, 277-297.

Kahneman, D. (2003). 'A Perspective on Judgment and Choice: Mapping Bounded Rationality'. *American Psychologist*, 58, 697-720.

Kahneman, D. & Klein, G. (2009). 'Conditions for Intuitive Expertise: A Failure to Disagree'. *American Psychologist*, 64, 515-526.

Kock, A., Heising, W. & Gemünden, H. G. (2015). 'How Ideation Portfolio Management Influences Front-End Success'. *Journal of Product Innovation Management*, 32, 539-555.

Koen, P., Ajamian, G., Boyce, S., Clamen, A., Fisher, E., Fountoulakis, S., Johnson, A., Puri, P. & Seibert, R. (2002). 'Fuzzy front end: Effective methods, tools and techniques'. In: Belliveau, P., Griffin, A. & Somermeyer, S. (eds.) *The PDMA Toolbook for New Product Development*. 2nd ed. New York: John Wiley & Sons.

Koen, P., Ajamian, G., Burkart, R., Clamen, C., Davidson, J., d'Amore, R., Elkins, C., Kathy, H., Incorvia, M., Johnson, A., Karol, R., Seibert, R., Slavejkov, A. & Wagner, K. (2001). 'Providing clarity and a common language to the "fuzzy front end"'. *Research Technology Management*, 44, 46-55.

Kornish, L. J. & Ulrich, K. T. (2014). 'The importance of the raw idea in innovation: Testing the sow's ear hypothesis'. *Journal of Marketing Research*, 51, 14-26.

Kuusela, H. & Pallab, P. (2000). 'A comparison of concurrent and retrospective verbal protocol analysis'. *The American journal of psychology*, 113, 387.

Lynn, G. S., Morone, J. G. & Paulson, A. S. (1996). 'Marketing and discontinuous innovation: The probe and learn process'. *California Management Review*, 38, 8-37.

Magnusson, P. R. (2009). 'Exploring the Contributions of Involving Ordinary Users in Ideation of Technology-Based Services*'. *Journal of Product Innovation Management*, 26, 578-593.

Magnusson, P. R., Netz, J. & Wästlund, E. (2014). 'Exploring holistic intuitive idea screening in the light of formal criteria'. *Technovation*, 34, 315-326.

Magnusson, P. R., Wästlund, E. & Netz, J. (2016). 'Exploring users' appropriateness as a proxy for experts when screening new product/service ideas'. *Journal of Product Innovation Management*, 33, 4-18.

Markham, S. K. (2013). 'The Impact of Front-End Innovation Activities on Product Performance'. *Journal of Product Innovation Management*, 30, 77-92.

Meehl, P. E. (1954). *Clinical versus statistical prediction: A theoretical analysis and a review of the evidence*, Minneapolis, MN, University of Minnesota Press.

Mertens, D. M. (2014*). Research and evaluation in education and psychology: Integrating diversity with quantitative, qualitative, and mixed methods*, Thousand Oaks, CA, Sage.

Miller, C. C. & Ireland, R. D. (2005). 'Intuition in strategic decision making: Friend or foe in the fast-paced 21st century?' *Academy of Management Executive*, 19, 19-30.

Moreau, C. P., Lehmann, D. R. & Markman, A. B. (2001). 'Entrenched knowledge structures and consumer response to new products'. *Journal of Marketing Research*, 38, 14-29.

Nisbett, R. E. & Wilson, T. D. (1977). 'Telling more than we can know: Verbal reports on mental processes'. *Psychological review*, 84, 231-259.

O'Connor, G. C. (1998). 'Market Learning and Radical Innovation: A Cross Case Comparison of Eight Radical Innovation Project's. *Journal of Product Innovation Management*, 15, 151-166.

Olsson, L. E., Magnusson, P. R. & Sukhov, A. (2017). Don't prime for creativity under cost-saving constraints! The 24th Innovation and Product Development Management Conference (IPDMC). Reykjavik, Iceland.

Ozer, M. (1999).' A survey of new product evaluation models'. *Journal of Product Innovation Management*, 16, 77-94.

Perreault, W. D. (1975). 'Controlling order-effect bias'. *The Public Opinion Quarterly*, 39, 544-551.

Pétervári, J., Osman, M. & Bhattacharya, J. (2016). 'The Role of Intuition in the Generation and Evaluation Stages of Creativity'. *Frontiers in Psychology*, 7.

Pisano, G. P. & Verganti, R. (2008). 'Which kind of collaboration is right for you'. *Harvard Business Review*, 86, 78-86.

Riedl, C., Blohm, I., Leimeister, J. M. & Krcmar, H. (2010). 'Rating scales for collective intelligence in innovation communities: Why quick and easy decision making does not get it right'. In Proceedings of Thirty First International Conference on Information Systems, December 12-15 2010 St. Louis, MO.

Ringo, T. (2007). 'IBM explores new frontiers in collaborative innovation'. *Research Technology Management*, 50, 6-7.

Sadler-Smith, E. & Shefy, E. (2004). 'The intuitive executive: Understanding and applying 'gut feel' in decision-making'. *Academy of Management Executive*, 18, 76-91.

Sadler-Smith, E. & Sparrow, P. R. (2008). 'Intuition in organizational decision making'. In: Hodgkinson, G. P. & Starbuck, W. H. (eds.) *The Oxford Handbook of Organizational Decision Making*. Oxford: Oxford University Press.

Salas, E., Rosen, M. A. & Diazgranados, D. (2010). 'Expertise-Based Intuition and Decision Making in Organizations'. *Journal of Management*, 36, 941-973.

SchumpeteR, J. A. (1934). *The Theory of Economic Development.*

Shadish, W. R., Cook, T. D. & Campbell, D. T. (2002). *Experimental and quasi-experimental designs for generalized causal inference*, Boston, MA, Houghton Mifflin.

Shapiro, S. & Spence, M. T. (1997). 'Managerial intuition: A conceptual and operational framework'. *Business Horizons*, 40, 63-68.

Sharma, A. (1999). 'Central Dilemmas of Managing Innovation in Large Firms'. *California Management Review*, 41, 146-164.

Sigala, M. (2012). 'Social networks and customer involvement in new service development (NSD) The case of www. mystarbucksidea. Com'. *International Journal of Contemporary Hospitality Management*, 24, 966-990.

Sloman, S. A. (1996). The empirical case for two systems of reasoning. Psychological bulletin, 119, 3-22.

Smith, M. & Taffler, R. (1992). 'Readability and understandability: Different measures of the textual complexity of accounting narrative'. *Accounting Auditing & Accountability Journal*, 5, 84-98.

Soukhoroukova, A., Spann, M. & Skiera, B. (2012). 'Sourcing, Filtering, and Evaluating New Product Ideas: An Empirical Exploration of the Performance of Idea Markets'. *Journal of Product Innovation Management*, 29, 100-112.

Sowden, P. T., Pringle, A. & Gabora, L. (2015). 'The shifting sands of creative thinking: Connections to dual-process theory'. *Thinking & Reasoning*, 21, 40-60.

Stanovich, K. E. & West, R. F. (2000). 'Individual differences in reasoning: Implications for the rationality debate?' *Behavioral and Brain Sciences*, 23, 645-665.

Stevens, G., Burley, J. & Divine, R. (1999). 'Creativity + Business Discipline = Higher Profits Faster from New Product Development'. *Journal of Product Innovation Management*, 16, 455-468.

Toubia, O. & Florès, L. (2007). 'Adaptive idea screening using consumers'. *Marketing Science*, 26, 342-360.

Van den Ende, J., Frederiksen, L. & Prencipe, A. (2015). 'The Front End of Innovation: Organizing Search for Ideas'. *Journal of Product Innovation Management*, 32, 482-487.

WheelWright, S. C. & Clark, K. B. (1992). *Revolutionizing product development: quantum leaps in speed, efficiency and quality*, New York, NY, Free Press.

Chapter 22

Consumer Resistance to Innovations - Essays on Antecedents, Manifestations and Ways of Overcoming It

Nadine Hietschold*

E-mail: nadine.hietschold@business.uzh.ch

Abstract: Although conventional wisdom associates innovations with societal progress and company success, consumer responses to innovations often include resistance. While previous research in innovation management has extensively studied success factors of adoption and diffusion, consumer resistance literature is less advanced. Specifically, a conceptualization of different resistance forms according to cognitive, emotional and behavioral elements is missing and a differentiated approach to address different forms of resistance is lacking. In this thesis, I specifically focus on a behavioral extreme form of active resistance (i.e., innovation resistance leaders) and on emotional resistance (i.e., fear and anger). I use different methods to understand antecedents, manifestations and ways of addressing active resistance and emotional resistance. I contribute to extant literature with a holistic but fine-grained approach to consumer resistance.

Keywords: consumer resistance; innovation resistance; innovation adoption; innovation diffusion; resistance leader; active resistance; negative emotion; consumer emotion; fear; anger.

1. Introduction

To buy or not to buy –that is the question consumers face when innovations are launched to the market. Although conventional wisdom associates innovations with societal progress and company success, consumer responses to innovations are often hesitant and reluctant. A review of peer-reviewed research studies published between 1945 and 2004 found that failure rates of new products ranged between 30 % and 49 %, depending on the innovation context (Castellion and Markham, 2013). Other sources even report failure rates as high as 90 % (e.g., Gourville, 2006). Consumer resistance is one main reason for innovation failure (Labrecque, Wood, Neal, and Harrington, 2017), because "the success of innovations depends ultimately on consumers accepting them" (Hauser, Tellis, and Griffin, 2006, p. 688). If consumers do not accept innovations, purchase and use them, companies cannot generate revenues to compensate their R&D expenditures. Consequently, new product failures lead to substantial financial losses amounting to billions of Euros and US-Dollars per year in countries such as Germany and the U.S. (Heidenreich, Kraemer, and Handrich, 2016). Further negative consequences of innovation failure for firms are a loss of reputation and competitiveness (Heidenreich and Spieth, 2013).

The list of promising innovations that encountered consumer resistance and failed on the market is long. For example, the Segway was promoted to revolutionize the way people move around in cities. Although famous technocrats such as Steve Jobs endorsed the self-balancing scooter, the Segway could not regain the 100 million US-Dollars spent on its research and development. Especially end-consumers were resistant to adopt this new mode of mobility. Segway expected to sell 500,000 units per year but was only able to sell 30,000 in six years (Gourville, 2006; WIRED, 2015). Moreover, Google Glasses –Google's approach to augmented reality– was hyped by the Time Magazine as one of the best inventions of the year 2012. Diane von Furstenberg even wore a pair at the New York Fashion Week 2012. However, Google Glasses could not take off, it received sharp criticism and a low demand from consumers, and Google announced the selling stop of Google Glasses in early 2015 after barely two years on the market (The New York Times, 2015). In addition to these new products, entire technologies encounter consumer resistance as well. For example, after decades of protests of consumers and anti-nuclear movements, the German government decided to opt out of nuclear energy in 2011 (SPIEGEL ONLINE, 2011). Consumer resistance to innovations and technology has not only implications for industries but also for politics and society in general. For example, to fight the Zika virus, genetically engineered mosquitos were going to be released on a trial side in Key Haven, Florida. Although the responsible company Oxitec received approval from the Food and Drug Administration (FDA), resistance and a referendum by local residents made Oxitec change the site of the trial to Monroe County (The Guardian, 2016). Hence, even innovations targeted to fight diseases that pose a threat to society might still encounter consumer resistance. Respective innovation failures do not only affect producers and individuals but restrain the population from potential benefits (e.g., limited contagion).

Despite the huge implications of consumer resistance for companies and society, the research field of consumer resistance is still in its infancy (Gurtner, 2014). Previous research mainly focused on innovation adoption including its motivating factors and positive outcomes (Heidenreich et al., 2016). "However, understanding why people do not adopt is arguably at least as important as knowing about those who do adopt" (Szmigin and Foxall, 1998, p. 460). The neglecting of consumer resistance has two roots. First, previous literature suffers from a historically developed pro-innovation bias. Scholars assume that innovations are beneficial, that they should be adopted by all consumers and should not be rejected. This bias leads to the ignorance of resistance and to limited knowledge about important aspects of resistance regarding the diffusion of innovations (Rogers, 2003). Second, the pro-change bias refers to the scholars' assumption that consumers are open to change and interested in evaluating new products (Talke and Heidenreich, 2014), although initial resistance is a normal and common consumer response. A search in scientific database Google Scholar illustrates the imbalance of the current research focus. Entering "innovation adoption" as coherent keyword combination results in 46,600 hits ("innovation diffusion" generates 58,300 hits) but searching for the keywords "innovation resistance" results in 2,410 hits only ("consumer resistance" generates 12,000 hits). Similarly, "technology acceptance" generates 110,000 hits and "technology resistance" 1,990 hits only.

The research in this thesis seeks to contribute to the field of consumer resistance by applying different research methods that investigate different perspectives of the concept of consumer resistance. This research approach helps to draw a more holistic picture of consumer resistance; it develops new theories and closes existing research gaps. The thesis includes four essays, and two of them are described in more detail here. Essay 1 focuses on **active resistance** (by Hietschold, N.; Reinhardt, R.; Gurtner, S.) and essay 2 on **emotional resistance** (by Hietschold, N.; Gurtner, S.; Spanjol, J.).

2. Background

Active innovation resistance (essay 1)

Whereas passive resistance is more profoundly researched in the context of consumer resistance to innovations (e.g., Heidenreich and Handrich, 2014), fewer research activities focus on active resistance, conceptualized as a deliberately formed attitude and an active oppositional behavior. Although several authors address the barriers and risks that lead to a negative attitude (e.g., Wiedmann, Hennigs, Pankalla, Kassubek, and Seegebarth, 2011), behavioral extreme forms are not researched in the context of innovation resistance. It remains nebulous how active innovation resistance emerges, how it is spread and who active resisters are. Research in the context of innovations has already demonstrated that specific individuals can impact innovation development and diffusion substantially. For example, opinion leaders exert a considerable amount of influence on the opinion of others and can accelerate innovation diffusion (Lu, Jerath, and Singh, 2013). Previous research extensively studies characteristics and behaviors of such individuals (e.g., Cho, Hwang, and Lee, 2012). However, previous research has not yet studied innovation resistance leaders, who are particularly relevant to the fate of innovations (Moldovan and Goldenberg, 2004). Hence, the first essay investigates active resistance and especially innovation resistance leaders. The essay answers the research questions (RQ):

RQ 1.1: Who are innovation resistance leaders?

RQ 1.2: Why do innovation resistance leaders resist?

RQ 1.3: How do innovation resistance leaders spread resistance?

Emotional innovation resistance (essay 2)

Although research acknowledges the importance of emotions in decision-making (e.g., Lerner et al., 2015) and innovation adoption (e.g., Wood and Moreau, 2006), previous definitions of consumer resistance only included behavioral and cognitive components (Talke and Heidenreich, 2014). Hence, the second essay adds to this literature and focuses on emotional resistance including not only emotional manifestations but also their causes and consequences. In this way, the second essay establishes the relationship between the emotional, cognitive and behavioral dimensions of consumer resistance. Moreover, scholars call for the need to differentiate between discrete emotions (e.g., fear and anger) instead of focusing on general effect (i.e., generic negative valence) in marketing research (Garg, Wansink, and Inman, 2007). Consumers differ in their negative emotions experienced and react to communication strategies differently (Jin, 2009). Therefore, firms require different ways to overcome resistance to different negative emotions. Focusing on fear and anger as representative emotions, the second essay answers the research questions (RQ):

RQ 2.1: How do specific negative emotions emerge?

RQ 2.2: What consumer cognitions and behaviors result from specific negative emotions?

RQ 2.3: How do consumers (emotionally) react to various strategies?

According to appraisal theory, emotions are a result of different perceptions of the current situation (e.g., the innovation event) (Smith and Ellsworth, 1985). Cognitive appraisals are interpretations of the situation with reference to the impact on the individuals' well-being (Bagozzi, Gopinath, and Nyer, 1999). Anger and fear are two key emotions in the context of consumption. Appraisal theory indicates that fear results from perceptions of (a) uncertainty, (b) threat and (c) situational control (*hypothesis 1*). In contrast, anger is elicited by appraisals of (a) certainty, (b) norm violation and (c) other blame (*hypothesis 2*) (Lerner and Keltner, 2000). Different emotions also lead to different behavioral action tendencies, self-regulation, and coping mechanisms. For example, anger is more likely to result in hostile and confrontational actions such as attacks or negative word of mouth (*hypothesis 3*), whereas fear more likely leads to avoidance behavior (*hypothesis 4*) (Yi and Baumgartner, 2004).

Emotion can either be regulated through reappraisal or response modulation (i.e., suppression of negative emotions, avoidance or rumination) (Gross, 2002). However, previous research agrees that reappraisal is the most effective strategy. Reappraisal as the change of the cognitive meaning and situational re-interpretation can decrease the emotional experience and consequently, also the emotional expression. We test two reappraisal strategies, one designed to attenuate the dominant appraisal dimensions of fear (i.e., information provision) and the other to reduce anger (i.e., perspective taking). We also test suppression of negative emotions through the induction of positive emotions (i.e., happiness). We expect information provision to be most effective to reduce fear as it reduces the appraisal of uncertainty (*hypothesis 5*). We expect perspective taking to be most effective to reduce anger, as it might reduce blame attribution (*hypothesis 6*). We expect the induction of happiness to be effective in the short-term to reduce anger and fear (*hypothesis 7*).

3. Research design and findings

Multiple case study research to understand resistance leaders (essay 1)

When little is known about a phenomenon and the context is complex, inductive approaches such as case study research are adequate to build new theory (Eisenhardt, 1989). We selected eight cases of consumer resistance according to the rationale of theoretical sampling (Glaser and Strauss, 2009). The three sample criteria were (1) different application levels (i.e., technologies, product categories and branded products), (2) different consumer concerns towards the innovations (e.g., functional risks, health risks or norm violations) and (3) two different local settings (i.e., North America and Germany). Our cases cover three technologies (i.e., nanotechnology, agricultural genetic engineering and cloud computing), three product categories (i.e., e-cigarettes, electric cars and E10 bioethanol fuel) and two branded products (i.e., Windows 8 and Google Street View). After selecting the innovation cases, we identified resistance leaders. For each case, we searched in online news articles for individuals who (1) are presented in the media as most famous or as the personalized face of the resistance or (2) are quoted in the media repeatedly as critics. In line with the triangulation rationale, case study research uses multiple sources for data collection (Yin, 2009). Our study included three rounds of data collection: (1) interviews with resistance leaders, (2) follow-up interviews with resistance leaders as well as interviews with close key informants of the resistance leaders, and (3) a systematic secondary data analysis. The data material comprises 20 primary interviews, 46 secondary audio or video interviews and speeches, 478 news articles, 48 books or book chapters, 148 blog articles or twitter accounts, 18 brochures or white papers and 35 webpages. Using a Grounded Theory approach, we coded the data material with the help of the software MAXQDA, resulting in more than 5,000 coded text passages. Within-case analysis resulted in a description of each case. Subsequently, using cross-case analysis, we compared the results between the cases and searched for patterns of certain typologies of resistance leaders and the resistance process. All three authors studied the data material in detail, discussed the patterns of the cross-case analysis and built the theoretical model in a joint discussion.

We identified two types of resistance leader, who we conceptualize as initiators and aggregators and who differ in their purposes and the resistance process. **Initiators** are driven by a missionary purpose (i.e., advance a societal vision), they are among the first to notice a problem after an innovation launch and scale up the resistance movement through media (i.e., initiation process). **Aggregators** are driven by a consumerist purpose (i.e., help and support consumers), they join an initial movement after a critical mass of negative voices has been reached and amplify consumers' opinions through media (i.e., aggregation process). Our theory on resistance leaders further demonstrates why resistance leaders resist (i.e., their criticism of innovations, the type of innovations criticized, goals, societal roles), how they resist (i.e., their life tasks, measures of resistance, communication in media, engagement drivers) and who resistance leaders are (i.e., perception of traits, self-perceived engagement origins).

Why do innovation resistance leaders resist? Initiators criticize innovations because of their potential negative long-term effects on society (e.g., increasing gap between the rich and the poor) and aggregators criticize innovations due to their immediate and direct negative effects on consumers (e.g., performance deficiencies). Initiators appear in innovation cases of technologies and product categories. In contrast, aggregators emerge in innovation cases of branded products with which consumers have direct contact. Initiators seek social change and governmental regulations. Aggregators seek to eliminate consumer grievances in a shorter run. To this end, aggregators aim for modifications of the innovation. Hence, initiators are societal change agents and fighters against harmful societal structures and aggregators represent the voice of the consumers and act as advocates and problem-solvers for consumers.

How do innovation resistance leaders resist? The processes of resistance diffusion (i.e., initiation and aggregation) are embedded in superordinate life tasks of the resistance leaders. Each innovation case constitutes only one point in time within this life task. Initiators pursue a specific mission and create a corresponding broader movement around this mission. For example, one initiator aims for a world with only free software that does not control the user. Along the path of this mission, innovations interfere with this mission (e.g., cloud computing, because the users do not have control over their data). Aggregators do not have a specific mission that includes a final objective. However, they are guided by general, unspecific ethical principles (e.g., resolve consumers' confusion). Aggregators specifically focus on innovation cases and jump from one case to the next trying to solve the consumer problems (e.g., Windows 8, because it caused confusion within users). Hence, whereas aggregators specifically focus on the evaluation of innovations as their main task, initiators only criticize innovations as a byproduct of their overall mission.

Initiators and aggregators largely use the same measures to organize resistance. Resistance leaders are embedded in organizational structures of NGOs or technology assessment groups. Resistance leaders profit from the organizational structures in terms of resources and networks but have enough freedom in the organizational structures to act independently. Resistance leaders engage in profound analyzes of the situation (e.g., scientific research) and are well connected to various other institutions. However, initiators use more distribution measures than aggregators. Initiators have a mission to spread and therefore, continuously travel the world to give lectures and speeches. Interestingly, initiators sometimes go beyond pure criticism of the innovation and suggestions of alternative concepts –they become innovators and develop alternative solutions themselves. Moreover, resistance leaders use several tactics to communicate (e.g., exaggerated risk demonstrations, metaphors, and neologisms). Resistance leaders stay dedicated because the subject they fight for fascinates them, because of events that can be characterized as successes and because they perceive their work as eventful, entertaining as well as an interesting endeavor.

Who are innovation resistance leaders? Resistance leaders are knowledge seekers and have expert knowledge in the area of their resistance. They are tech-savvy, persistent, stubborn, eloquent, persuasive, and courageous and possess a strong sense of justice. In addition, initiators are maverick, idealistic and sometimes even ideologically biased. The strong dedication of resistance leaders comes from childhood experiences, engagement in young years, events where they have been affected themselves, the professional background and from the experience that an alternative solution was superior.

Experiments to understand negative consumer emotions (essay 2)

We used a set of experiments in the context of a fictional functional food in-novation to test our hypotheses. We used surveys including scenarios and constructs measured with established scales. We tested differences between scenarios with ANOVA. In the **pre-test**, we developed two scenarios that have been manipulated according to the appraisal dimension either to elicit anger or fear. The scenarios tell John's experiences with a new functional food inno-vation. We relied on a sample (n=187) from Amazon Mechanical Turk (mTurk), a crowdsourcing platform. We measured self-reported emotions (i.e., emo-tion-picking and emotion-rating) after participants viewed one of the two randomly assigned scenarios. The emotion-picking task asked participants to pick the dominant emotion John would experience (fearful, angry, both fear-ful and angry, neither fearful nor angry). The emotion-rating tasks asked par-ticipants to rate the intensity of the negative emotions anger and fear John would experience on a nine-point Likert scale. Participants picked the emo-tion fearful clearly more often in the fear scenario than the anger scenario and the emotion angry clearly more often in the anger scenario than the fear sce-nario. However, in contrast to the results of the emotion-picking task, the emotion-rating task could only achieve the desired manipulation with the sub-sample of participants who picked one dominant emotion (i.e., fearful or angry) and not with the full sample. The reason for the vague differentiation between anger and fear in the emotion-rating task is that many participants experience multiple emotions simultaneously. In line with previous research, fear and anger often co-occur. To understand the mechanisms of the negative emotions better, it was important to separate participants who experience single emotions ("deliberate feelers") and participants who experienced mixed emotions ("overwhelmed feelers") in subsequent experiments. We assumed that deliberate feelers and overwhelmed feelers process the infor-mation inherent in a situation differently. Deliberate feelers have been ex-pected to be more analytic, to process information in more depth, and to prefer affective thinking less and overwhelmed feelers have been expected to be more holistic, to process information more heuristically, and to prefer affective thinking stronger (*hypothesis 8, 9 and 10*).

In **experiment 1**, we used responses from n=285 mTurk participants to test our hypotheses. Participants answered questions on appraisal dimensions, behaviors and individual differences after seeing one of the three randomly assigned scenarios (i.e., fear scenario, anger scenario, and control scenario). We could replicate the findings from the pre-test regarding the emotion-picking and emotion-rating tasks. In addition, we found certainty, norm viola-tion and other blame to be significantly higher in the anger scenario than the fear scenario (confirming hypotheses 1a, 2a, 2b and 2c, but rejecting hypotheses 1b and 1c). Moreover, we could confirm hypotheses 3 and 4, because the constructs 'negative word of mouth', 'complaining to the firm,' 'complaining to third parties' and 'attack' as a course of action were rated significantly higher in the anger scenario. Purchase intention (i.e., non-adoption) was equally low in both scenarios and 'no action' was higher in the fear scenario. Finally, we found that deliberate feelers process information in more depth and overwhelmed feelers have a stronger preference for affective thinking (confirming hypotheses 9 and 10 but rejecting hypothesis 8).

In **experiment 2**, we used the same procedures as in experiment 1, but randomly included one of the three ads 'information provision', 'company perspective' or 'happiness' directly after the scenarios to evaluate their effectiveness in reducing negative emotions. The ad 'information provision' communicates the results of an independent study that could clearly reject health risks. The ad 'company perspective' shows that the company takes (financial) risks to guarantee consumers' well-being. The ad 'happiness' solely shows pictures of happy people eating croissants. We compared the results of experiment 1 to experiment 2 in order to measure the effectiveness of the communication strategies in this 2 x 4 between-subject design (scenario x ad). In a separate pre-test (n=45), we ran a manipulation check for the ads, confirming that each ad represents the intended content. Responses from n=168 mTurk participants showed that the ad information provision was more effective to reduce fear than the other ads. In addition, the ad perspective taking was more effective to reduce anger than the other ads (confirming hypothesis 5 and 6). However, both ads are effective to reduce fear and anger. In addition, we found that happiness could reduce fear but not anger (partly confirming hypothesis 7). As cell sizes of the scenario conditions were small, we wanted to confirm the results in a third experiment.

In **experiment 3**, we changed the John-perspective to the I-perspective (i.e., participants answered questions from their own perspective). In addition, as the aim of this experiment was to test the effectiveness of the strategies, we waived to test how emotions arise from different perceptions of appraisal. Therefore, we revised the scenarios in a form that explicitly stated the emotions anger or fear. We applied a 2 x 4 within-subject design. Participants randomly saw the fear scenario or the anger scenario. We then measured emotions and subsequently, participants saw one of the three ads or no ad (i.e., control scenario). We measured emotions again after seeing the ad. Measurement inventories remained the same as previously. We recruited participants from mTurk (n=133) and from the Qualtrics Research Panel (n=821). For the analysis of the effectiveness of the ads, we only included participants who received an ad (excluding the control group) and clearly indicated that they dominantly felt fearful (n=162) or angry (n=95) before seeing an ad. With these participants, we could directly trace how the emotions fear and anger change after seeing an ad. For fearful participants, we found that the ad information provision reduces fear stronger than the ad company perspective or the ad happiness, confirming the results of experiment 2. Interestingly, the ad information provision also reduced anger most effectively, although the effect was not statistically significant. The results indicate that the ad information provision is most effective to reduce fear, but also to reduce anger. While the effectiveness of information provision on fear reduction is in line with appraisal theory, the effect on anger is surprising. We can explain these results in the following way. First, in contrast to the previous experiments, fear and anger have been strongly mixed in the anger scenario resulting in an overlap of these two emotions. Second, anger is generally harder to reduce than fear.

4. Conclusion

Extending innovation diffusion theory (essay 1)

The essay develops new and important theoretical foundations on individuals in the formation of consumer resistance –resistance leaders. Previously, literature did not account for behavioral extreme forms of resistance, although active opponents can significantly influence an innovation's fate. The research identified two different types of innovation resistance leaders (i.e., initiators and aggregators) who differ in their purposes and processes of resistance diffusion. This finding extends innovation diffusion literature by better explaining innovation diffusion processes. The two archetypes of resistance leaders and their thorough characterization is an essential building block to understand diffusion rates and saturation points. This research shows that it is not the mere individual who independently decides do adopt or reject an innovation, but rather a complex system of leaders and followers. Therefore, we also add to theory that proposes social components to influence adoption and rejection decisions of individuals (Gatignon and Robertson, 1985). We theorize that it is the two types of resistance leaders that shape two different resistance diffusion processes that counteract positive opinion leaders and innovation contagion processes. The findings also add to innovation adoption and consumer resistance research, as we identified a type of resister that is different from Rogers' laggards and we were able to conceptualize their nature. Our theoretical model of resistance leaders demonstrates where the resistance leaders' engagement comes from (i.e., antecedents) and which cognitive and behavioral manifestations it entails.

Anchoring emotions conceptually in consumer resistance (essay 2)

The second essay investigates emotional resistance, a previously neglected dimension of consumer resistance. Our research approach advances knowledge in the domain of emotional resistance as it is the first to empirically show how emotions emerge in the context innovation, how different emotions (i.e., fear and anger) evolve to create different forms of resistance (i.e., active vs. passive) and how communication strategies can be used to counteract resistance. Furthermore, we advance emotion theory by identifying personality traits that differentiate individuals who experience multiple emotions at the same time from those who predominantly experience a single emotion. This distinction has the potential to explain mixed results in previous studies of emotion discrimination and the effects of emotions in a variety of contexts. In addition, we were able to provide evidence that emotion regulation theory is transferable from an intrapersonal context to a setting of interpersonal interactions and we confirm that the mechanisms of reappraisal are most effective to reduce negative emotions.

General contributions

Each of the essays provides a piece to validate and further expand a holistic picture of consumer resistance. The most important contribution of this thesis is to demonstrate that different manifestations of consumer resistance can be distinguished on a cognitive, emotional and behavioral level. In addition, the thesis is the first to demonstrate that various manifestations of consumer resistance (e.g., active and passive resistance) are caused by systematically different antecedents and likely require different ways to be overcome. Essay 2 indicates for both passive and active resistance how cognition, emotion and behavior are related and how levels of these dimensions differ between passive and active resistance. Essay 1 specifies the relation between cognition and behavior in-depth for the case of resistance leaders.

5. Implications and future research

Future research agenda

This research presents a major step to a complete understanding of consumer resistance to innovations. However, each essay is constrained by specific limitations from a methodological perspective and also from the findings' theoretical boundaries. Hence, future research should build on the results and dig deeper on several issues. To understand **active resistance**, future research has to quantitatively validate the aggregator-initiator theory and investigate whether this theory is also valid in non-mass media local contexts. In addition, further research should investigate how large the resistance leaders' influence is indeed on innovation failure. Finally, future research would benefit from a resistance leader scale that can be used to identify and measure such active opponents. To understand **emotional resistance**, future research should conceptually model how and when emotions influence innovation decision as well as how appraisal patterns of discrete emotions change in different contexts. Moreover, we could not reveal the mechanisms of reappraisal in emotion regulation. Future research should further our understanding how firm strategies are able to reduce negative emotions. To find the best ways to overcome resistance, a meta-analysis should validate the effectiveness of different strategies.

Table 22.1 Future research agenda

Active resistance	Emotional resistance
• Validation of initiator-aggregator theory with data from social networks • Investigation of resistance leaders in local contexts including personal interactions • Understanding the influence of resistance leaders on innovation failure (e.g., the effect of negative comments on the companies' stock performances) • Scale development for the resistance leader construct	• Model development at which stages and how emotions influence adoption and resistance decisions • Understanding how appraisal patterns of fear and anger change in different contexts • Investigation of the mechanisms of reappraisal as strategy to regulate discrete negative emotions • Meta-analysis of the effects of firm response strategies to negative events on consumer reactions

Implications for management and policy

Management and policy need to identify and address consumer resistance adequately in order to prevent beneficial innovations from failure and in order to identify potential consumer risks and concerns in an early development phase. Decision-makers have to monitor social media and mass media for the appearance of resistance leaders early on. Moreover, decision-makers can identify negative emotions when monitoring media outlets with specific keyword searches. Negative emotions can also be identified using survey-based market research. Active resisters, especially resistance leaders, could then be included in innovation development to improve innovations. Decision-maker should listen to the consumers' concerns and develop solutions jointly to address these concerns.

Table 22.2 Strategies for decision-makers

Identify consumer resistance	Address consumer resistance
• Monitor mass media and social networks for (1) resistance leaders and consumer activists (2) indicators of negative emotions • Use survey market research (including both adopters and non-adopters) to reveal presence of discrete negative emotions	• Include resisters in different phases of innovation development • Apply the right communication strategy (e.g., information provision, positive emotion induction)

References

Bagozzi, R. P., Gopinath, M., & Nyer, P. U. (1999). 'The Role of Emotions in Marketing'. *Journal of the Academy of Marketing Science*, 27(2): 184-206.

Castellion, G., & Markham, S. K. (2013). 'Perspective: New Product Failure Rates: Influence of Argumentum ad Populum and Self-Interest'. *Journal of Product Innovation Management*, 30(5): 976-979.

Cho, Y., Hwang, J., & Lee, D. (2012). 'Identification of effective opinion leaders in the diffusion of technological innovation: A social network approach'. *Technological Forecasting and Social Change*, 79(1): 97-106.

Eisenhardt, K. M. (1989). 'Building Theories from Case Study Research'. *Academy of Management Review*, 14(4): 532-550.

Garg, N., Wansink, B., & Inman, J. J. (2007). 'The influence of incidental affect on consumers' food intake'. *Journal of Marketing*, 71(1): 194-206.

Gatignon, H., & Robertson, T. S. (1985). 'A Propositional Inventory for New Diffusion Research'. *Journal of Consumer Research*, 11(4): 849-867.

Glaser, B. G., & Strauss, A. L. (2009). *The Discovery of Grounded Theory: Strategies for Qualitative Research*. New York: Aldine.

Gourville, J. T. (2006). 'Eager Sellers and Stony Buyers: Understanding the Psychology of New-Product Adoption'. *Harvard Business Review*, 84(6): 98-106.

Gurtner, S. (2014). 'Modelling consumer resistance to mobile health applications', *Twenty Second European Conference on Information Systems*. Tel Aviv, Israel.

Gross, J. J. (2002). 'Emotion regulation: Affective, cognitive, and social consequences'. *Psychophysiology*, 39(3): 281-291.

Hauser, J., Tellis, G. J., & Griffin, A. (2006). 'Research on Innovation: A Review and Agenda for Marketing Science'. *Marketing Science*, 25(6): 687-717.

Heidenreich, S., & Handrich, M. (2014). 'What about Passive Innovation Resistance? Investigating Adoption-Related Behavior from a Resistance Perspective'. *Journal of Product Innovation Management*, Online First.

Heidenreich, S., Kraemer, T., & Handrich, M. (2016). 'Satisfied and unwilling: Exploring cognitive and situational resistance to innovations'. *Journal of Business Research*, 69(7): 2440-2447.

Heidenreich, S., & Spieth, P. (2013). 'Why Innovations Fail - The Case Of Passive And Active Innovation Resistance'. *International Journal of Innovation Management*, 17(5): 1-42.

Jin, Y. (2009). 'The effects of public's cognitive appraisal of emotions in crises on crisis coping and strategy assessment'. *Public Relations Review*, 35(3): 310-313.

Labrecque, J. S., Wood, W., Neal, D. T., & Harrington, N. (2017). 'Habit slips: When consumers unintentionally resist new products'. *Journal of the Academy of Marketing Science*, 45(1): 119-133.

Lerner, J. S., & Keltner, D. (2000). 'Beyond valence: Toward a model of emotion-specific influences on judgement and choice'. *Cognition & Emotion*, 14(4): 473-493.

Lerner, J. S., Li, Y., Valdesolo, P., & Kassam, K. S. (2015). 'Emotion and Decision Making'. *Annual Review of Psychology*, 66: 799-823.

Lu, Y., Jerath, K., & Singh, P. V. (2013). 'The emergence of opinion leaders in a networked online community: A dyadic model with time dynamics and a heuristic for fast estimation'. *Management Science*, 59(8): 1783-1799.

Moldovan, S., & Goldenberg, J. (2004). 'Cellular Automata Modeling of Resistance to Innovations: Effects and Solutions'. *Technological Forecasting and Social Change*, 71(5): 425-442.

Rogers, E. M. (2003). *Diffusion of Innovations* (5th ed.). New York: Free Press.

Smith, C. A., & Ellsworth, P. C. (1985). 'Patterns of cognitive appraisal in emotion'. *Journal of Personality and Social Psychology*, 48(4): 813-838.

SPIEGEL ONLINE. (2011). *Atomkraft ade,* Retrieved from http://www.spiegel.de/politik/deutschland/ende-eines-jahrzehnte-kampfs-atomkraft-ade-a-771403.html, 5th of June 2017.

Szmigin, I., & Foxall, G. (1998). 'Three Forms of Innovation Resistance: the Case of Retail Payment Methods'. *Technovation*, 18(6): 459-468.

Talke, K., & Heidenreich, S. (2014). 'How to Overcome Pro-Change Bias: Incorporating Passive and Active Innovation Resistance in Innovation Decision Models'. *Journal of Product Innovation Management*, 31(5): 894-907.

The Guardian. (2016). *Genetically modified mosquitoes could be released in Florida Keys by spring,* Retrieved from https://www.theguardian.com/us-news/2016/nov/26/zika-virus-genetically-modified-mosquitoes-florida, 1st of Janurary 2017.

The New York Times. (2015). *Why Google Glass Broke,* Retrieved from https://www.nytimes.com/2015/02/05/style/why-google-glass-broke.html?_r=0, 5th of June 2017.

Wiedmann, K.-P., Hennigs, N., Pankalla, L., Kassubek, M., & Seegebarth, B. (2011). 'Adoption Barriers and Resistance to Sustainable Solutions in the Automotive Sector'. *Journal of Business Research*, 64(11): 1201-1206.

WIRED. (2015). *Well, that did't work: the Segway is a technological marvel. Too bad it doesn't make any sense,* Retrieved from https://www.wired.com/2015/01/well-didnt-work-segway-technological-marvel-bad-doesnt-make-sense/, 5th of June 2017.

Wood, S. L., & Moreau, C. P. (2006). 'From fear to loathing? How emotion influences the evaluation and early use of innovations'. *Journal of Marketing*, 70(3): 44-57.

Yi, S., & Baumgartner, H. (2004). 'Coping with negative emotions in purchase-related situations'. *Journal of Consumer Psychology*, 14(3): 303-317.

Chapter 23

Entrepreneurial Opportunity Perception: Analysing the Effect of the Learning Style

Alexandros Kakouris*

E-mail: akakour@phys.uoa.gr

Abstract: The present dissertation deals with entrepreneurial opportunity perception by individuals. Based on an online experiment, quantitative results indicate that the effect of prior domain-specific knowledge on opportunity perception is moderated by the learning style of the individual. This effect is known as 'learning asymmetry' and has been previously articulated and tested in the technological domain. The present findings cross-validate the previous empirical results and also extend the concept in non-technological opportunities. Especially the diverging learning style was found supportive to both early (abstract) and late (concrete) stages of new business formation. The results also reveal how certain belief structures regarding the success factors for a new business vary amongst different kind opportunities or co-evolve in different stages of a new venture. Implications for innovation managers pertain to effective innovation team building within organizations.

Keywords: Entrepreneurial opportunity; opportunity perception; learning asymmetry; learning style; entrepreneurial beliefs; creativity; innovation; innovation management; innovation teams; Austrian economics.

1. Introduction

To cope with the management of innovation in the organizational context, a model regarding the origin of innovation has to be presumed. For a long time, innovation was assumed to emerge linearly, and rather naturally, through a four-stage model, i.e., the linear model of innovation (e.g., Godin, 2006), where applied research follows basic research with a succeeding development stage leading to the final production and diffusion one. Nonetheless, contemporary research based on companies' practices reveal a more complex pattern referred as the 'fuzzy front end' of innovation (Koen et al., 2001). In this model, different teams (non-focus groups) from different departments cooperate iteratively towards opportunity identification, opportunity analysis, idea genesis, idea selection and concept development. Once opportunity is inserted as a factor in the innovation process, the teams are actually expected to act entrepreneurially from the beginning. Ergo, the innovation process can be hardly constrained in R&D departments and depend on the rest aspects of the firm management; it may be encountered, at least partly, through corporate entrepreneurship practices (Stevenson and Jarillo, 1990). Once innovation teams are considered entrepreneurial at the same time, the generic question that underlies the managerial perspective of large companies is how to build efficient innovation teams. In the case of start-ups, micro or small enterprises, the whole entrepreneurial team (i.e., the partners along with a few highly motivated employees) may operate as an innovation team. Hence, the question refers to what makes these teams efficient? From the entrepreneurial viewpoint, the innovation team performance has to do with its capability to identify and pursue promising opportunities in the market. Given the high failure rates of innovation and the associated capital loss, innovative products need not be just new products but new products that pursue certain entrepreneurial opportunities. Therefore, the problem confronted in the present dissertation pertains to how to increase the entrepreneurial opportunity identification capability of innovation teams within organizations.

How opportunities are discovered and exploited has been a central question within entrepreneurship research. The concept of entrepreneurial opportunity was introduced by Shane and Venkataraman (2000) in their 'new' manifestation of entrepreneurship as an autonomous field of research. Short et al. (2010, p. 40) state that "without an opportunity, there is no entrepreneurship" while Gaglio and Katz (2001, p. 95) remark that "… understanding the opportunity identification process represents one of the core intellectual questions for the domain of entrepreneurship". For the last fifteen years, the 'individual-opportunity nexus' (Shane and Eckhardt, 2003) offers a framework to analyze the entrepreneurial phenomena admitting a cognitive base behind them. Nonetheless, the concept of entrepreneurial opportunity has raised a series of ontological and epistemological debates in literature and has appeared difficult, even formidable, for empirical research (Dimov, 2011). Generally, entrepreneurial opportunity identification and exploitation capability refer to the domain-specific (i.e., technological) knowledge of individuals in combination with their personal characteristics and preferences. Otherwise stated, there must be a 'cognitive fit' between the individual and the situation at hand and thus, the present dissertation confronts the problem of how such 'cognitive fits' occur depend on personal traits of individuals engaged in the innovation process.

It becomes apparent that asking from employees to come up with identified opportunities and new ideas is a non-straightforward process that intrudes innovation management problems relevant to team building, performance and eligibility. Innovation managers aiming at the continuous improvement of an organization should become aware of which personal preferences affect opportunity identification and exploitation facilitating possible 'cognitive fits' in each stage of the innovation process. Else, much of the selection and task assignment procedure is strictly based on knowledge and experience of the team members that introduces an implicit emulation of the focus-groups operation. The latter may be more appropriate to a later phase, the 'back end' of innovation (e.g., Günzel and Holm. 2013), where new ideas have to be implemented and embedded into the firm's strategy. Another problem associated with the customary innovation team building based on knowledge and experience is that knowledge is tacitly considered a 'static' construct. The present dissertation examines learning preferences as personal traits that shape the dynamic change of the knowledge base of individuals and especially whether these preferences affect the opportunity identification process. In this way, it aims at elucidating how entrepreneurial opportunities are perceived and accordingly how innovation managers could enhance the innovation team building process in order to follow more efficiently the 'front end' of innovation that is inherently a creative process.

2. Background

The principal question, introduced in the previous section, reads "what leads to the identification of entrepreneurial opportunities?" The relevance of innovation management lies in the 'human side' of innovation (e.g., O'Connor and McDermott, 2004) and the need to build and manage successful innovation teams within organizations. Team members are expected not to merely develop new products but also recognize the entrepreneurial opportunities these new products encounter in order to contribute to the overall innovation performance of a firm (cf. Adams, Bessant and Phelps, 2006). To this end, domain-specific knowledge has appeared a dominant factor in literature. Nevertheless, research is needed for additional parameters and features in cases where the required type of knowledge is not abundant, or the company decides to venture into new markets.

To reveal the source of entrepreneurial opportunities, the Austrian economics doctrine draws upon 'information asymmetries' (e.g., Akerlof's (1970) 'lemons') that cognitively becomes 'knowledge asymmetries' but dynamically seen can become 'learning asymmetries.' The last concept was introduced by Dimov (2003, 2007) and Corbett (2007) demanding further empirical validation since it has been under-researched. This fact motivated the present dissertation.

Schematically, the Austrian perspective for the effect of prior knowledge on opportunity recognition and exploitation is depicted through Shane's (2000) model shown in Figure 23.1. The left intervention refers to the initial opportunity perception process and the right one to opportunity exploitation, i.e., the idea generation. Once dealing with opportunity perception, only the left intersection is considered in the present research. Accordingly, the knowledge base of the individual and its variety shapes what is perceived as 'opportunity' based on market clues and the developments of technology. The analogy with the organization refers to the concept of the absorptive capacity (Cohen and Levinthal, 1990).

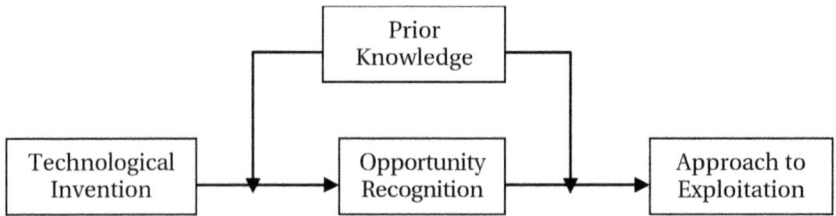

Figure 23.1 Shane's (2000) model for the effect of prior knowledge on opportunity recognition.

Furthermore, Hills, Shrader and Lumpkin (1999) have introduced a five-stage creativity model for opportunity recognition in the organizational context. Three stages (preparation, incubation, insight) refer to opportunity conception and another two (elaboration, evaluation) to opportunity formation. This model describes opportunity identification and exploitation as an iterative, back and forth process amongst these stages. The present survey examines opportunity conception, and thus, it refers to the first three stages.

The original work of Corbett and Dimov illustrated that the learning style (Kolb, 1984) moderates the effect of prior knowledge on opportunity recognition (i.e., the 'learning asymmetry' concept). Shane's (2000) findings and experiments of Corbett and Dimov were constrained in the technological domain. Learning asymmetry in this domain showed that the converging learning style facilitates opportunity identification. Surveying the same domain, Gemmell (2017) questioned the role of the diverging learning style, and especially the reflective observation mode, as it induces negative effects on the entrepreneurial performance. Nonetheless, Ardichvili, Cardozo and Ray (2003) included the 'type of opportunity' as a determinant of opportunity identification process in their creativity model. These scholars recognize three types of opportunity, namely 'Dreams,' 'Problem Solving,' 'Technology Transfer' and 'Business Formation,' depending on how overt the supply or the demand side of the opportunity is. Hence, the variable of Ardichvili et al. (2003) offers the possibility to examine the learning asymmetry concept in non-technological domains and conclude for the role of the learning style on opportunity identification throughout the entire spectrum of entrepreneurial opportunities. It also allows for comparisons between opportunity domains that demand different levels of creativity. Besides, the cognitive change of the knowledge base of an individual is known to be affected by her/his beliefs. Considering beliefs that refer to success factors of entrepreneurship (e.g., the ASKO structure of Kakouris, 2008; 2018a,b) the experiment on opportunity perception could also examine how certain belief structures participate in the process.

Extending the experiments of Corbett and Dimov, the present survey cross-validates their findings but also extends the idea of 'learning asymmetries' to non-technological sectors and integrates it into the entire spectrum of entrepreneurial opportunities. In parallel, it examines how belief structures regarding the success factors of a new venture vary between different kinds of opportunity or co-evolve in different stages of a new venture. The present survey advances the studies on entrepreneurial opportunity identification process and its findings suggest implications relevant to innovation management within organizations.

3. Research design

The present research adopts the positivist view aiming at providing empirical data on the entrepreneurial opportunity perception process. Due to the long-standing ontological debate about the objectivity / subjectivity of opportunity, assumptions on the existence of opportunities in the market have been made. This is consistent with the Austrian school of thought in economics. Dimov (2011) discussed the epistemological issue of empirical surveys on opportunity identification revealing two different and complementary approaches: the 'variance' versus 'process' explanations of opportunity. The former assumes that opportunities 'exist' and "focus on making inferences from the covariance patterns among particular variables without reference to the underlying generative mechanisms" (Dimov, 2011, p. 69) whilst the latter assume that opportunities are 'made' and "focus on the specific path – in terms of a sequence of events or concrete experiences – that observed cases follow from one state to another" (Dimov, 2011, p. 70). According to this classification, the present research is classified as a 'variance' explanation. Another assumption of the present research, coming from the Austrian perspective, is that opportunity perception is a serendipitous event. Thus, respondents exposed to pieces of technology or market information are able to perceive them as 'opportunities' without any particular or intensive search.

Along these lines, fourteen testable research hypotheses based on previous research were articulated. To test these hypotheses, respondents were invited to evaluate potential opportunities of different type and in return, they were receiving their learning style measurement. Opportunity items covered the four domains of Ardichvili et al. (2003) and they were finally aggregated per each domain. A particular vulnerability, confronted through three sequential pilot tests, pertained to the attractiveness of different opportunity items in order to control for financial reward or other peculiarities that might influence their selectivity and bias the results. In this way, opportunity items exposed to the final sample were found of comparable selectivity. The learning style of the respondents was measured through Kolb's LSI (v3.1) instrument (Learning Style Inventory, Kolb and Kolb, 2005) as well as their entrepreneurial beliefs regarding success factors of entrepreneurship (Kakouris, 2008; 2018a,b). Furthermore, a 'prior domain-specific knowledge' variable was developed through the field of study declared by the respondents. Beyond the rest demographics, adaptation and innovativeness indices based on Kirton's (1976) cognitive style were introduced along with creativity and entrepreneurial nascence indices (Kakouris, 2016). The final sample was randomly selected through snowballing techniques and consisted of 376 responses. The data were manipulated statistically through factor analyzes, correlations, hierarchical linear regression and structural equation modeling. Multiple checks through gender-stratified sub-samples were performed in order to eliminate any possible influences from the gender variable as it has been known to affect both the learning style and entrepreneurial opportunity selection.

Reliability of the results was certified through relevant measures (Cronbach's alpha, test-retest) whilst most of the known and expected correlations that concern the LSI instrument appeared. Typical hypothesis testing supported the majority of research hypotheses. The one for the learning asymmetry:

> Hypothesis 14 Kolb's learning style moderates the relationship between prior domain-specific knowledge and opportunity perception within Ardichvili et al. domains.

> was partially supported in 'Dreams' and 'Business Formation' opportunity domains of Ardichvili et al. (2003). This result, along with the support to the hypothesis that prior domain-specific knowledge is positively correlated with opportunity perception in the 'Technology Transfer' domain, cross-validates the concept of learning asymmetry in the technological sector and extends it into non-technological opportunity domains.

In sum, the methodology of the present research has been quantitative, based on an online questionnaire, followed typical hypothesis testing and can be classified as a 'variance' explanation in regard to Dimov's (2011) classification of empirical research relevant to entrepreneurial opportunity identification.

4. Conclusion

The main finding of the present thesis is the cross-validation of previous empirical results for the learning asymmetry concept in the technological domain (Corbett, 2007; Dimov, 2003, 2007) and its extension to the non-technological ones. Besides, co-evolution of success belief structures enriches the understanding of how different learning style and different belief individuals operate in different stages (or types) of innovative ventures.

Specifically, Ardichvili et al. (2003) distinguished 'Dreams' opportunities, where both the need in the market (demand side) and the product/service that fulfills that need (supply side) are unknown, from 'Problem Solving' opportunities. where the need in the market has been identified and the product/service that fulfills that need is sought. Similarly, they distinguish 'Technology Transfer' opportunities, where the product/service is defined, but the need in the market is sought, from 'Business Formation,' where both the need in the market and the product/service that fulfills that need are known. These four types of opportunity might also be seen as a gradual progression of any type of venture, i.e. business ideas start abstract and blurred ('Dreams'), proceed through either 'Problem Solving' or 'Technology Transfer' and finally become concrete and specific ('Business Formation'). The present findings indicate that, as expected, individuals with prior technological knowledge favor opportunities from the 'Technology Transfer' domain. In this opportunity domain, the converging learning style dominates. Nevertheless, those who lack such knowledge 'flee' to other domains of either 'Dreams' or 'Business Formation.' In the first option, they tend to develop ideas 'from the scratch' whilst in the second one they tend to 'replicate' known solutions. In the first option, they also like to pose the problems to be solved whilst in the second one they recognize the need for certain products or services that they cannot produce themselves and decide to cover the need either through importing or franchising. The unexpected result is that in both these non-technological domains, the learning style still moderates the effect of (lack of) domain-specific knowledge on opportunity perception (i.e., the learning asymmetry survives). Therefore, the learning asymmetry concept can be supported in the whole spectrum of entrepreneurial opportunities stating that not only knowledge but also learning preferences participate in the entrepreneurial opportunity identification process.

Remarkably, the belief structures regarding the success factors for new businesses vary amongst the opportunity domains of Ardichvili et al. (2003). In 'Dreams' and 'Problem Solving' domains, success beliefs are not crystallized whilst in the 'Technology Transfer' one these beliefs mostly concern effective business planning and marketing. In the 'Business Formation' domain, success beliefs mostly pertain to networking and fundraising. Following the evolutionary perspective, initially the enterprising or innovating team members can have any conception about business success factors, but those who are more eager in technology transfer and product development are more concerned about marketing and business planning whilst those who are keen to the final business formation stage promote the gathering of resources. The results for the belief structures, as cognitive elements that participate in learning, enrich the understanding of how different individuals perceive entrepreneurial opportunities.

Finally, through the previous results and analysis, a new role for the diverging learning style in the innovation process emerges. The reflective observation mode was found dominant in the 'Dreams' domain whilst the concrete experience one was found dominant in 'Business Formation'. The combination of these two modes defines the diverging learning style. Therefore, diverging style learners appear substantial for the initiation of an innovation project, where they utilize their reflective observation in brainstorming and problem posing, but also for the finalization of the project, where they utilize their concrete experience towards gathering the resources. In this way, diverging style learners may appear crucial for an innovation project independently whether they possess the domain-specific knowledge required in the new product development phase.

5. Implications and future research

The present findings support a concise and consistent view towards understanding the opportunity perception process in a cognitive framework with theoretical and practical implications to corporate entrepreneurship and innovation management. Intrapreneurs need to recognize and seize opportunities whilst innovation teams need to be aware of the opportunities they pursue in order to be more efficient in their new product or service development and beyond. The findings also support a new and essential role for diverging learning style in the pre- and post-product development phases of an innovative venture. Success belief structures appear active in the innovation process based on the pursuit of certain entrepreneurial opportunities. The present results need to be examined further through future research in different samples and in real organizational circumstances.

Theoretical implications

The theoretical contribution of the present dissertation is threefold. Firstly, it enriches the empirical evidence of Corbett's and Dimov's 'learning asymmetry' concept as a mechanism of entrepreneurial opportunity identification. It also extends the concept in the whole spectrum of opportunities. This contributes the Austrian economics perspective that builds upon 'information' and subsequently 'knowledge' asymmetry, and thus, it contributes towards theorizing in entrepreneurship. Relevant research has been scarce in literature due to the complexity of the notion of opportunity and the associated methodological difficulties (Dimov, 2011). Secondly, it offers a new methodological approach for experiments that aim at providing 'variance' explanations based on empirical data in the entrepreneurial opportunity identification process. The current methodology follows a pure Austrian perspective consistent with all underlying details as, for instance, the serendipitous discovery of opportunity. And thirdly, it associates, for the first time, beliefs (beyond knowledge and learning preferences) to the opportunity perception process utilizing the entire cognitive infrastructure. Beliefs are known to be of equal cognitive importance with knowledge as they actively participate in the transformation of mental schemes and the evolution of the knowledge base (i.e., learning) of the individual. Researchers in the field of entrepreneurial opportunity recognition are offered empirical evidence along with an extended cognitive infrastructure to design future experiments able to confront the innermost part of the entrepreneurial process which embraces the notion of the entrepreneurial opportunity and its identification. Similarly, scholars from the innovation management field are offered original results which pertain to the 'human side' of innovation and the effective pursuit of entrepreneurial opportunities compatible with the individual characteristics of innovation team members. These results can be further exploited in the theoretical context of the 'fuzzy front end' of innovation and its complexity.

Practical implications

Practical implications of the present results concern entrepreneurship education, policy making and innovation management within organizations. Focusing on the latter, the importance of the converging learning style in technology transfer opportunities has been validated. Its role in technological innovation remains unequivocally crucial. But also, the significance of the diverging learning style has been revealed in non-technological opportunities and in the pre- and post- product development stages of the innovation process. Consequently, diverging style learners should be present in innovation teams independently whether these individuals possess the required technological knowledge for prototyping and new product development. Noteworthy, the diverging learning style and thinking, that employs reflection, has been condemned in literature as idle or 'harmful,' especially for technological ventures (e.g., Gemmell, 2017) as learners of this style, may usually lack technological knowledge as well. The findings of the present thesis suggest its role has to be reconsidered in the innovation practice within organizations.

Furthermore, the 'flee' or 'wandering' effect amongst different types of opportunity may become beneficial in other aspects of innovation as, for example, problem discovery, brainstorming, creative ideation or resource management from diverging style learners who lack technological knowledge for new product development. These aspects are of equal importance since innovation is a complex process that exceeds the simple development of new products within the R&D department of an enterprise. Innovation that emerges as a holistic 'front end' process which penetrates different units of the organization and includes opportunity identification and idea generation can start from limited and ambiguous information unable to adequately describe the final product. Iterations during the ideation process can significantly alter the entrepreneurial opportunity perception of a team. And furthermore, just a prototype development is not sufficient for the successful completion of the innovation project without the production and promotion phases that require the organization of significant resources. Diverging style learners can also be efficient in double-loop organizational learning (Argyris and Schön, 1978) which is especially important for the knowledge management of the organization. Innovation processes may not be limited in simple problem-solving and single-loop learning – where converging style learners are known to be efficient – demanding reflective thinking on the problem itself. Adept innovation managers should be aware of the role of each learning style within these active learning processes.

Present findings on how different style learners can operate and collaborate in innovative business venturing ideas offer insights to organization's decision-makers on how to build efficient innovation teams. They also offer a theoretically sound tool based on the learning style, to venture capitals towards evaluating innovation teams. Similarly, the top-management of an ambidextrous organization may optimize its team-building capacity when it decides to produce, exploitatively or exploratively, innovative products or to significantly differentiate its product base. The present dissertation shows that entrepreneurial opportunity perception lies beneath these processes and is strongly related to the knowledge base, the learning preferences and the beliefs of the involved individuals. This is why I call entrepreneurial opportunity the 'Lydian stone' of entrepreneurship. Better opportunity perception enhances the viability of innovation wherever the latter is adopted as a vehicle to overcome rapid changes in the market and in the society.

Future research

Some of the limitations of the present survey could be relaxed in future research. For instance, a different set of opportunity items, corresponding to Ardichvili et al. domains, could be examined. Alternatively, the same set of opportunity items could be re-examined in a different country and culture to avoid any local influences in the results. Besides, the codification of opportunity items utilized in the present experiment may have constrained the influence of prior knowledge and experience on opportunity perception. This variable needs to be examined more thoroughly and more closely to specific technologies in order to identify its relevance in the future. The ASKO belief structures need also to be, enriched, refined and psychometrically adjusted in future research. Kirton's (1976) KAI instrument for the cognitive style could also be employed. Hence, future experiments will be designed accordingly.

It will also be a subject of future research to examine the present findings in real organizational environments. In situ experiments could be appropriate to validate whether operational innovation teams exhibit similar results. And finally, different experiments based on qualitative research and aiming at providing 'process' explanations of opportunity identification might be used for triangulation purposes. The latter will also reveal the role of the learning style in opportunity exploitation phase where the full process of experiential learning is expected to take place.

References

Adams, R., Bessant, J. and Phelps, R., (2006). 'Innovation management measurement: A review'. *International Journal of Management Reviews*, 8(1), pp. 21-47.

Akerlof, G.A. (1970). 'The Market for "Lemons": Quality Uncertainty and the Market Mechanism'. *Quarterly Journal of Economics*, 84(3), pp. 488–500.

Ardichvili, A., Cardozo, R., and Ray, S. (2003). 'A theory of entrepreneurial opportunity identification and development'. *Journal of Business Venturing*, 18(1), pp. 105–123.

Argyris, C., and Schön, D. A. (1978). *Organizational learning: A theory of action perspective* (Vol. 173). Reading, MA: Addison-Wesley.

Cohen, W. M., and Levinthal, D. (1990) 'Absorptive capacity: A new perspective on learning and innovation', *Administrative Science Quarterly*, 35 (1), pp. 128–152.

Corbett, A. C. (2007). 'Learning asymmetries and the discovery of entrepreneurial opportunities'. *Journal of Business Venturing*, 22(1), pp. 97-118.

Dimov, D. (2003). 'The Nexus of Individual and Opportunity: Opportunity Recognition as a Learning Process'. *Frontiers of Entrepreneurship Research*. Wellesley, MA: Babson College

Dimov, D. (2007). 'From opportunity insight to opportunity intention: The importance of person-situation learning match'. *Entrepreneurship Theory and Practice*, 31(4), pp. 561-583.

Dimov, D. (2011). 'Grappling with the unbearable elusiveness of entrepreneurial opportunities'. *Entrepreneurship Theory and Practice*, 35(1), pp. 57-81.

Gaglio, C. M., & Katz, J. A. (2001). 'The psychological basis of opportunity identification: Entrepreneurial alertness'. *Small Business Economics*, 16(2), pp. 95-111.

Gemmell, R. M. (2017). 'Learning styles of entrepreneurs in knowledge-intensive industries'. *International Journal of Entrepreneurial Behavior & Research*, 23(3), pp. 446-464.

Godin, B., (2006). 'The linear model of innovation: The historical construction of an analytical framework. Science', *Technology, & Human Values*, 31(6), pp.639-667.

Günzel, F. and Holm, A.B., (2013). 'One size does not fit all—understanding the front-end and back-end of business model innovation'. *International Journal of Innovation Management*, 17(01), pp.1-34.

Hills, G. E., Shrader, R. C., and Lumpkin, G. T. (1999). 'Opportunity recognition as a creative process'. *Frontiers of entrepreneurship research*, 19(19), pp. 216-227.

Kakouris, A. (2008). 'On initial implementations of innovation and entrepreneurship courses: a case study for undergraduates at the University of Athens'. In N. Marriot (Ed.), 3rd European Conference on Entrepreneurship and on Innovation, Winchester, UK (pp. 121-129). Reading UK: Academic Conferences Ltd.

Kakouris, A., (2016). 'Exploring entrepreneurial conceptions, beliefs and intentions of Greek graduates'. *International Journal of Entrepreneurial Behavior & Research*, 22(1), pp. 109-132.

Kakouris, A. (2018a). 'Inter-comparison between entrepreneurial courses: a two dimensional, dialectical representation of outcome'. *Entrepreneurship Education*, submitted

Kakouris, A. (2018b). 'Inter-comparison between entrepreneurial courses: applying the ASKO framework'. *Entrepreneurship Education*, submitted

Kirton, M. (1976). 'Adaptors and innovators: a description and measure', *Journal of Applied Psychology*, 61(5), pp. 622–629.

Koen, P., Ajamian, G., Burkart, R., Clamen, A., Davidson, J., D'Amore, R., Elkins, C., Herald, K., Incorvia, M., Johnson, A., Karol, R., Seibert, R., Slavejkov, A. and Wagner, K. (2001). 'Providing clarity and a common language to the "fuzzy front end"'. *Research-Technology Management*, 44, pp. 46–55.

Kolb, D. (1984). *Experiential learning: Experience as the source of learning and development*. Englewood Cliffs, NJ: Prentice-Hall.

Kolb, A.Y. and Kolb, D.A. (2005). The Kolb learning style inventory—version 3.1: 2005 Technical Specifications, Boston, MA: Hay Resources Direct. Available at: https://pdfs.semanticscholar.org/3cfe/53acc0eff44d736311d2402e9eadb2aa296f.pdf (Accessed: 25.03.2018)

O'Connor, G. C., and McDermott, C. M. (2004). 'The human side of radical innovation. *Journal of engineering and technology management*, 21(1-2), pp. 11-30.'

Shane, S. (2000). Prior knowledge and the discovery of entrepreneurial opportunities'. *Organization Science*, 11(4), pp. 448-469.

Shane, S., and Eckhardt, J. (2003). 'The individual-opportunity nexus'. In Z. Acs & D. Audretsch (Eds.), *Handbook of Entrepreneurship Research, An Interdisciplinary Survey and Introduction*, (pp. 161-191). Boston, Mass and London: Kluwer Academic Publishers.

Shane, S., and Venkataraman, S. (2000). 'The promise of entrepreneurship as a field of research'. *Academy of Management Review*, 25(1), pp. 217–226.

Short, J.C., Ketchen Jr, D.J., Shook, C.L., and Ireland, R.D. (2010). 'The concept of "opportunity" in entrepreneurship research: Past accomplishments and future challenges'. *Journal of Management*, 36(1), pp. 40–65.

Stevenson, H. H., and Jarillo, J. C. (1990) 'A paradigm of entrepreneurship: Entrepreneurial management', *Strategic Management Journal*, 11, pp. 17–27.

Chapter 24

Antecedents and Consequences of Exploration and Exploitation Decisions: Evidence from Corporate Venture Capital Investing

Eui Ju Jeon*

E-mail: euiju.jeon@aalto.fi

Abstract: This dissertation examines how performance feedback and corporate governance influence exploration and exploitation decisions and their performance consequences. In the first essay, I theorize on how poor firm performance influences exploration and exploitation decisions and how such decisions are affected by dedicated and transient ownership and by the boards' monitoring and advising intensities. This theory is empirically tested in the second essay based on CVC investments made by 286 U.S. companies during 1993-2013. In the third essay, based on the same sample, I examine how oscillating between explorative and exploitative CVC initiatives impacts firm performance. This dissertation contributes to the Behavioral Theory of the Firm and Corporate Governance research by introducing how shareholders and boards influence managerial decision-making in search, Ambidexterity research by studying how continuous change and inertia impact temporal spillover arising from oscillation, and CVC research by examining the antecedents and consequences of explorative and exploitative CVC initiatives.

Keywords: Exploration; Exploitation; Behavioral Theory of the Firm; Corporate Governance; Ambidexterity, Corporate Venture Capital.

1. Motivations

Corporate Venture Captial (CVC) is direct minority equity investment made by established firms (i.e., corporate investors) in privately held entrepreneurial startups. Scholars have largely viewed CVC as a vehicle for exploration (Keil et al., 2008; Schildt et al., 2005), which provides the corporate investors with the "windows on novel technology" (Dushnitsky and Lenox, 2006) and greater radical innovations (Van de Vrande et al., 2011). However, this view is incomplete as CVC investment can also take exploitative initiatives. While corporate investors can make *explorative* investments in startups from distant sectors with relatively novel and unfamiliar technology, they can also make *exploitative* investments in startups from nearby sectors with similar and familiar technology (Wadhwa and Basu, 2013). For instance, Walt Disney, a media and entertainment company, made explorative investments in electronics, photographic, data processing, and advertising startups, whereas Amgen, a pharmaceutical company, focused on exploitative investments in biotech startups. Although anecdotal evidence suggests that there is substantial variation in explorative and exploitative CVC initiatives, surprisingly the literature has not yet examined how such decisions are made and their performance consequences. I discuss these limitations in detail as follows.

First, CVC research provides little insight into how explorative and exploitative CVC investing decisions are made. Prior CVC research has discussed how CVC investing can be triggered by searching for solutions to resolve underperformance problems (Gaba and Bhattacharya, 2012; Ma, 2016). Accordingly, scholars have found that the discrepancy between the actual and expected performance prompts problemistic search and influences the decisions to establish or terminate CVC programs (Gaba and Bhattacharya, 2012; Ma, 2016). While this research provides insights on whether and when CVC investing is made, it lacks the insight on how and by whom the CVC resources are allocated between explorative and exploitative initiatives. To shed light on how resources are allocated, in addition to problemistic search mechanism, it may be useful to take into account the stakeholders of the CVC program. Insights from the corporate governance literature suggest that the interests of top managers in making strategic decisions may conflict with those of the shareholders and that the purpose of corporate governance is to influence a firm's strategic decision-making by aligning it with the shareholders' interests (Eisenhardt, 1989). Consistent with this perspective, research shows that shareholders and board of directors often seek to influence a variety of corporate strategy decisions (Hoskisson et al., 2002), particularly when firms perform below expectations (Tuggle et al., 2010). While these findings suggest that shareholders and board of directors may influence how firms make explorative and exploitative CVC investing decisions, prior research has not explored this proposition. By integrating insights from corporate governance research to the problemistic search mechanism, we can improve our understanding of how and by whom the CVC resources are allocated to exploration and exploitation.

Secondly, CVC research provides little insight on how explorative and exploitative CVC initiatives influence firm performance. By taking the ambidexterity perspective, prior research evidenced that when corporate venturing units conduct high levels of both exploration and exploitation, it results in longer survival (Hill and Birkinshaw, 2014). However, this research largely built upon the static assumption that the tension arising from executing both exploration and exploitation is persistent and time-invariant (Raisch and Birkinshaw, 2008). In contrast, evidence from the organizational change literature suggests that firms temporally separate, and oscillate between exploration and exploitation under changing resource constraints (e.g., Brown and Eisenhardt, 1997). It is important to consider the effect of oscillation because exploration and exploitation are complementary over time with regards to increasing firm performance as exploitation becomes an input to exploration and vice versa over time (Gilsing and Nooteboom, 2006). In particular, it is important to consider the impact of continuous change, which affects the positive temporal spillover arising from modification routines (e.g., Brown and Eisenhardt, 1997) and negative temporal spillover arising from organizational inertia (Hannan and Freeman, 1984). Without a sufficient understanding of the dynamic nature of exploration and exploitation in CVC investing, it is difficult to understand how organizations can oscillate between the two activities over time and increase their performance. By integrating insights from ambidexterity and continuous change research, we can improve our understanding of the outcomes of oscillating between explorative and exploitative CVC initiatives over time.

To sum up, this dissertation investigates how poor firm performance and corporate governance influence the direction of organizational change – in terms of explorative and exploitative CVC investing – and how such change over time influences firm performance.

2. Research Design

To answer the research question, I integrated insights from the literature on CVC, Behavioral Theory of the Firm (BTF), Corporate Governance, and Ambidexterity with those I gained from qualitative data analysis. Qualitative data were collected by performing twenty-five interviews with CVC Managers, Institutional Shareholders, and Investor Relations (IR) Managers. The interviews were carried out on the following two topics.

First, I interviewed eight IR managers from companies with active CVC programs and three institutional shareholders who have substantial equity positions in companies with active CVC programs. Through the interviews, I aimed to gain a better understanding of how institutional investors influence managerial decision-making processes. I conducted interviews with IR managers because they function as direct communication channels between institutional shareholders and senior managers (Bushee and Miller, 2012). During the interviews, I investigated the dedicated and transient shareholders' investment goals, their nature of the communication with senior managers, and their preferences with regards to making CVC investments. The interview respondents were selected from the companies with the largest annual CVC investments in 2014 and 2015 based on Global Corporate Venturing reports.

On average, each interview lasted about 35 minutes and all interview generated about 100 pages of printed transcripts.

Secondly, I conducted interviews with fourteen CVC program managers from companies with active CVC programs. I aimed to gain a better understanding of how explorative and exploitative CVC initiatives influence firm performance. More specifically, I inquired about the explorative and exploitative natures of CVC investing, decision makers who are involved in CVC investing, and how CVC performance is measured. I selected the interview respondents from the participants from the Global Corporate Venturing Symposium held in London, the United Kingdom in 2016. On average, each interview lasted about 30 minutes and all interview generated about 20 pages of summarized transcript.

Analysis of the interviews provided rich insights into the CVC decision-making process and its performance consequences. By combining the insights from the interviews and the literature, I developed a theoretical model where resource allocation decisions on exploration and exploitation are influenced by the interaction between poor firm performance and shareholders/boards and where the firm's market valuation is affected by the oscillation between exploration and exploitation initiatives. While the first essay was a theoretical piece, in the following second and third essays, I empirically tested the theoretical model based on the explorative and exploitative nature of 10,261 CVC deals made by 286 U.S. corporate investors during 1993-2013.

In the second essay, I tested the hypotheses that predict how negative performance feedback and institutional ownership impact the proportion of explorative CVC relative to total CVC. I ran the Generalized Estimating Equations (GEE) Fractional Probit model for panel data because the dependent variable, exploration share, was in the form of a fraction. Also, I ran the Random Effects Panel Linear Regression model as a robustness check. All of the independent variables were lagged by one period, which reduces concerns of reverse causality and removes the possibility of simultaneity bias.

In the third essay, I tested the hypotheses that predict how oscillation affect the corporate investor's market valuation. I ran the two-stage panel linear regression models to treat the endogeneity arising from the self-selection. Accordingly, in the first stage of the estimation, I regress of exploration share on institutional shareholders' ownership, earnings gap above and below aspirations, and the control variables used in essay 2. In the second stage, I regress of Tobin's Q, a continuous variable, on the predicted value of the ambidexterity variable based on the predicted values of the exploration share and exploitation share from the first stage. By taking a two-stage approach, I expect to remove the unobserved heterogeneity that drives the decisions of allocating resources to explorative and exploitative CVC initiatives. Also, all independent variables were lagged by one period to reduce the concerns of reverse causality and simultaneity bias.

3. Conclusion

The three essays of this dissertation are complementary with regards to developing and testing the new theory on the antecedents and consequences of explorative and exploitative CVC investing decisions. Following are the main theories and findings of the three essays.

Essay 1. Performance Feedback, Corporate Governance and the Direction of Change

In the first essay, I theorized how poor firm performance affects the direction of organizational change and how this relationship is moderated by the board of directors and shareholders. As a baseline proposition, following the predictions of the Behavioral Theory of the Firm (BTF) (Cyert and March, 1963), I argued that poor firm performance results in an increased likelihood of organizational change. By drawing from decision risk research (Kacperczyk, Beckman, and Moliterno, 2015), I theorized that under poor firm performance, risk-averse managers trigger more resources to be allocated to exploitation, whereas risk-seeking managers prompt more resources to be allocated to exploration.

Furthermore, by drawing on insights from corporate governance research, I developed theories that consider the moderating effects of shareholders and board of directors. Assuming that managers are largely risk-averse, I predicted that as the concentration of dedicated ownership increases in a poorly performing firm, the firm will alter its search trajectory by exploring more and exploiting less because dedicated shareholders prefer long-term growth in value creation and are more inclined to voice their interests when firm performance misses its expectation. In contrast, because transient shareholders prefer short-term returns and are more inclined to pose a credible threat of selling their stocks if performance misses its expectation, I argued that as the concentration of transient ownership increases in a poorly performing firm, the firm will alter its search trajectory by exploiting more and exploring less.

Moreover, I argued that as the level of the board's monitoring intensity increases in a poorly performing firm, the firm will shift its allocation of resources to more exploitation and lesser exploration because monitoring-intensive boards rely on financial controls, which motivates managers to become myopic and risk-averse. Lastly, I argued that as the level of the board's advising intensity increases in a poorly performing firm, the firm will allocate more resources to exploration and fewer resources to exploitation because advising-intensive boards rely on strategic controls, which motivates managers to become long-term oriented and risk-tolerant.

Essay 2. Performance Feedback, Shareholder Influence and the Direction of Change: Evidence from Corporate Venture Capital Investing

In the second essay, I tested the theories developed in the first essay. More specifically, I empirically examined how poor firm performance affects the direction of organizational change and how this relationship is moderated by the dedicated and transient shareholders in the context of CVC investing. I argued that poor firm performance leads to increased CVC investment intensity. Assuming that CVC program managers are typically risk-averse, I argued that poor firm performance leads to allocating resources to more exploitation and lesser exploration. I predicted that as the concentration of dedicated ownership increases in a poorly performing firm, the firm will allocate more CVC resources to exploration and lesser to exploitation. In contrast, I hypothesized that as the concentration of transient ownership increases in a poorly performing firm, the firm will allocate more CVC resources to exploitation and lesser to exploration. Empirical analysis of CVC investments made by U.S. corporate investors during 1993-2013 confirms that poor firm performance motivates firms to increase their CVC investment intensity and that this investment is directed at exploitation. Furthermore, the results show that as the concentration of dedicated ownership increases in a poorly performing firm, the firm alters its search trajectory by exploring more and exploiting less. On the contrary, the concentration of transient ownership had no effect.

Essay 3. Performance Implications of Oscillating between Exploration and Exploitation: Evidence from Corporate Venture Capital Investing

In the third essay, I examined how and under what conditions a firm's oscillation between explorative and exploitative CVC initiatives influences its performance. As a baseline hypothesis, drawing from the ambidexterity research (e.g., Raisch and Birkinshaw, 2008), I argued that the synchronous pursuit of both explorative and exploitative CVC initiatives (in the same period) leads to greater performance. Also, I argued that oscillating between explorative and exploitative CVC investing initiatives over time increases a firm's performance. By building on continuous change and organizational inertia research (e.g., Brown and Eisenhardt, 1997; Hannan and Freeman, 1984), I argued that the duration of continuous change has an inverted-U shaped relationship with firm performance. Furthermore, I argued that the amplitude of continuous change has a negative relationship with firm performance. Analysis of CVC investments made by U.S. corporate investors during 1993-2013 showed that both simultaneous ambidexterity and oscillation in CVC increases a firm's market valuation. Additionally, I found that the duration of continuous change has an inverted-U shaped relationship with a firm's market valuation. On the contrary, the effect of the amplitude of continuous change was not found.

4. Implications and Future Research

This dissertation contributes to the literature on Corporate Venture Capital, Behavioral Theory of the Firm, and Ambidexterity. I elaborate on the contributions as follows.

Contributions to Corporate Venture Capital Research

While scholars largely viewed CVC as a vehicle for exploration (Keil et al., 2008; Schildt et al., 2005), in this dissertation, I take into account that CVC investing initiatives may vary between exploration and exploitation not only across firms but also over time. I discuss the specific contributions to CVC research as follows.

First, CVC research has not yet examined how resource allocation decisions on exploration and exploitation are made. In the second essay, I showed that problemistic search and managerial risk preferences interact and influence the allocation of CVC resources to exploration and exploitation. Assuming that CVC managers are risk-averse, I found that performance shortfall relative to aspirations triggers firms to increase their CVC investment intensity, and such investment is directed at exploitation. This finding is an important addition to the literature on how decisions are made in CVC. While the literature found whether and when CVC programs are adopted or terminated (Gaba and Bhattacharya, 2012; Ma, 2016), I showed whether and when CVC intensity increases and where the resources are allocated. More importantly, I contribute to CVC research by investigating how dedicated shareholders participate in the CVC decision-making process. Prior CVC research illustrated how the established firm's senior executives, business units, the startups, and the venture capitals take part in the CVC decision-making process (Basu, Phelps, and Kotha, 2016; Keil et al., 2008). In this dissertation, I showed that dedicated shareholders influence managerial decisions to allocate more CVC resources to exploration and fewer resources to exploitation, in particular, when firm performance falls below aspiration levels.

Secondly, CVC research provides little insight on how explorative and exploitative CVC initiatives influence firm performance. In the third essay, I suggested that firms oscillate between explorative and exploitative CVC initiatives over time and such oscillation affects firm performance. I showed that not only striking a balance between explorative and exploitative CVC initiatives at the same period but also oscillating over periods enhance a firm's market valuation. Accordingly, while past CVC research has largely focused on the effect of simultaneous ambidexterity (Hill and Birkinshaw, 2014), I showed the positive performance effect of oscillation. Furthermore, by examining the period when continuous change takes place in the allocation of resources to exploration and exploitation, I found that the duration of continuous change has an inverted-U shaped relationship with a firm's market valuation. In brief, I showed that oscillating between explorative and exploitative CVC initiatives enhances firm performance, and in particular, moderate durations of continuous change enhances the performance the most.

Contributions to Behavioral Theory of the Firm Research

This dissertation contributes to the BTF research by theorizing and showing how the constituencies of corporate governance influence the managerial decision-making process and how the interaction between poor firm performance and managerial risk preferences affects the direction of organizational change. I elaborate on these contributions as follows.

First, the literature on BTF typically assumed that an organization is composed of a dominant coalition of managers that reigns over the strategic decision-making process, reflecting its own interests and preferences (Desai, 2016). By drawing on insights from corporate governance research, in the second essay, I showed that managerial decision-making process is an outcome of bargaining and negotiation between the managers and the shareholders. In particular, I found that dedicated shareholders gain legitimacy and voice their interests in the managerial decision-making process when performance falls below aspiration levels. Influence of dedicated ownership resulted in the firm's greater allocation of resources to exploration and lesser to exploitation in the face of negative performance feedback. Furthermore, in the first essay, I theorized on how the monitoring- and advising-intensive board of directors differentially influence the managerial decision-making process, particularly when performance falls below aspiration levels.

Secondly, BTF research has focused on explaining whether and when organizational change takes place, but it lacks the mechanism to predict how problemistic search affects decision-making with regards to the direction of change after the need for and type of change have been established (Greve and Zhang, 2016). In the first essay, by drawing on insights from decision risk research (Kacperczyk et al., 2015), I theorized on how the direction of change is affected by the interaction between the poor firm performance and the risk preferences of the managers implementing the change. Additionally, in the second essay, I found that risk-averse managers prefer to allocate more CVC resources to exploitation than exploration when faced with negative performance feedback.

Contributions to Ambidexterity Research

This dissertation contributes to the Ambidexterity research by theorizing and showing how the oscillation between exploration and exploitation, in particular, how 'continuous' oscillation enhances a firm's performance. I discuss the contributions in detail as follows.

First, prior ambidexterity literature provides little insight into how temporally separating exploration and exploitation impacts firm performance (Raisch and Birkinshaw, 2008). In the third essay, I studied how oscillating between exploration and exploitation over time influences a firm's performance. Although the ambidexterity literature discussed the oscillation based on case studies (e.g., Boumgarden et al., 2012), evidence-based on extensive longitudinal data has not been well established yet (e.g., Luger, 2014). By removing potential selection biases arising from resource allocation decisions, I found that striking the right balance between exploration and exploitation at the same period and over different periods enhances a firm's performance.

Secondly, past ambidexterity literature lacks the discussion of the costs of oscillating between exploration and exploitation and the potential limits to temporal spillovers resulting from such oscillation (e.g., Luger, 2014). In the third essay, by drawing on insights from the continuous change and organizational inertia literature (e.g., Brown and Eisenhardt, 1997; Hannan and Freeman, 1984), I examined how the continuous nature of oscillation impacts the benefits and costs of oscillation and eventually, firm performance. I found that the duration of continuous oscillation has an inverted-U shaped relationship with firm performance.

Managerial Implications

The findings of this dissertation provide insights to the managers who are involved in the CVC decision-making process. These managers primarily include but are not limited to senior executives who are participants of the CVC investment committee and the directors of the CVC program. One of the fundamental problems organizations face is the tendency to over-exploit (March, 2003). Organizations often fall into success traps by being stuck in an endless loop of exploitation. If organizations keep on exploiting when the environmental demands change, the products and technologies that were once successful become obsolete and organizations are likely to fail. The findings in the second essay suggest that dedicated shareholders can play a role in adjusting such over-exploitative tendencies and altering the direction of search towards exploration when firms are not performing well. This result implies that bringing in stakeholders that value exploration, such as dedicated shareholders, in the managerial decision-making process can be useful in reversing the managerial tendency to over-exploit.

Another fundamental problem that organizations face is how to strike the right balance between exploration and exploitation (Tushman and O'Reilly, 1996). The findings from the third essay suggest that indeed, oscillating between exploration and exploitation over time, particularly in a continuous fashion, enhance a firm's performance. It shows that the duration of continuous oscillation plays an important role in affecting both (1) the benefits that arise from enhanced coordination, focused attention, and agile response to environmental changes and (2) the costs that arise from changing the structures and routines of the CVC programs. The findings imply that engaging in continuous oscillation during six years enhances the firm market valuation the most.

Future Research Avenues

Here, I briefly discuss the several limitations of this dissertation that represent interesting avenues for future research. First, as the second and third essays are primarily based on empirical analysis of large-scale secondary data, they do not capture the intricate micro-level processes at play. For instance, in the second essay, while I assumed that managers and shareholders interact with each other during the periods of poor firm performance, I did not directly observe this micro-level process of interactions. Further investigation based on such micro-level data will be useful in explaining how managerial discretion is limited in times of poor firm performance and how managers and shareholders bargain or negotiate over the decisions to allocate resources to exploitation and exploration. Also, in the third essay, while I assumed that changes in the allocation of resources to exploitation and exploration involves changes in structures and routines, I did not directly observe this micro-level evolution of the structures and routines of the CVC program over time. I expect that qualitative inquiries of this micro-level data can shed insight on how oscillating firms can better design their structures and routines.

Secondly, in the first essay, I theorized on how negative performance feedback influences managerial decisions to allocate resources to exploitation and exploration and how such relationship is affected by the board of directors and shareholders. While I tested the moderating effects of shareholders in the second essay, it may be interesting for future research to test the propositions developed in the first essay on the influence of the board of directors. Furthermore, taking a broader perspective, it may be interesting to examine the influence of external governance mechanisms, such as the legal system, corporate control, external auditors, governance ratings, stakeholder activism, and media on managerial decision-making (Aguilera et al., 2015).

Thirdly, while the empirical examination of the second and third essays was made in the context of CVC, it can be extended to alternative contexts of external corporate venturing such as alliances and acquisitions. These contexts meet the conditions required to test the theories developed in this dissertation. For instance, a firm's performance shortfall relative to aspirations may trigger organizational change in the form of making alliances and acquisitions (Iyer and Miller, 2008). Also, substantial variation in exploitation and exploration is observed within and across firms for alliances and acquisitions (e.g., Luger, 2014; Hagedoom and Duysters, 2002). Moreover, ambidexterity is pursued in the context of alliances and acquisitions (Luger, 2014). Lastly, corporate governance entities have substantial influence over managerial decision-making with regards to making alliances and acquisitions (Connelly et al., 2010).

References

Aguilera, R. V., Desender, K., Bednar, M. K., & Lee, J. H. (2015). 'Connecting the dots: Bringing external corporate governance into the corporate governance puzzle'. *The Academy of Management Annals*, 9(1), pp. 483-573.

Basu, S., Phelps, C. C., & Kotha, S. (2016). 'Search and Integration in External Venturing: An Inductive Examination of Corporate Venture Capital Units'. *Strategic Entrepreneurship Journal*, 10(2), pp. 129-152.

Boumgarden, P., Nickerson, J., & Zenger, T. R. (2012). 'Sailing into the wind: Exploring the relationships among ambidexterity, vacillation, and organizational performance'. *Strategic Management Journal*, *33*(6), pp. 587-610.

Brown, S. L., & Eisenhardt, K. M. (1997). 'The art of continuous change: Linking complexity theory and time-paced evolution in relentlessly shifting organizations'. *Administrative Science Quarterly*, 42(1), pp. 1-34.

Bushee, B. J., & Miller, G. S. (2012). 'Investor relations, firm visibility, and investor following'. *The Accounting Review*, *87*(3), pp. 867-897.

Connelly, B. L., Tihanyi, L., Certo, S. T., & Hitt, M. A. (2010). 'Marching to the beat of different drummers: The influence of institutional owners on competitive actions'. *Academy of Management Journal*, *53*(4), pp. 723-742.

Cyert, R. M., & March, J. G. (1963). 'A behavioral theory of the firm'. *Englewood Cliffs, NJ*, pp. 169-187.

Desai, V. (2016). 'The Behavioral Theory of the (Governed) Firm: Corporate Board Influences on Organizations' Responses to Performance Shortfalls'. *Academy of Management Journal*, 59(3), pp. 860-879.

Dushnitsky, G., & Lenox, M. J. (2006). 'When does corporate venture capital investment create firm value?' *Journal of Business Venturing*, 21(6), pp. 753-772.

Eisenhardt, K. M. (1989). 'Agency theory: An assessment and review'. *Academy of Management Review*, 14(1), pp. 57-74.

Gaba, V., & Bhattacharya, S. (2012). 'Aspirations, innovation, and corporate venture capital: A behavioral perspective'. *Strategic Entrepreneurship Journal*, *6*(2), pp. 178-199.

Gilsing, V., & Nooteboom, B. (2006). 'Exploration and exploitation in innovation systems: The case of pharmaceutical biotechnology'. *Research Policy*, 35(1), pp. 1-23.

Greve, H. R. & Zhang, C.M. (2016). *Myopic reactions to performance feedback: Different decision makers, different decisions.* Working paper.

Hagedoorn, J., & Duysters, G. (2002). 'Learning in dynamic inter-firm networks: the efficacy of multiple contacts'. *Organization studies, 23*(4), pp. 525-548.

Hannan, M. T., & Freeman, J. (1984). 'Structural inertia and organizational change'. *American Sociological Review*, 49(2), pp. 149-164.

Hill, S. A., & Birkinshaw, J. (2014). 'Ambidexterity and survival in corporate venture units'. *Journal of Management*, 40(7), pp. 1899-1931.

Hoskisson, R. E., Hitt, M. A., Johnson, R. A., & Grossman, W. (2002). 'Conflicting voices: The effects of institutional ownership heterogeneity and internal governance on corporate innovation strategies'. *Academy of Management Journal*, 45(4), pp. 697-716.

Iyer, D. N., & Miller, K. D. (2008). 'Performance feedback, slack, and the timing of acquisitions'. *Academy of Management Journal, 51*(4), pp. 808-822.

Kacperczyk, A., Beckman, C. M., & Moliterno, T. P. (2015). 'Disentangling risk and change: Internal and external social comparison in the mutual fund industry'. *Administrative Science Quarterly, 60*(2), pp. 228-262.

Keil, T., Autio, E., & George, G. (2008). 'Corporate venture capital, disembodied experimentation and capability development'. *Journal of Management Studies, 45*(8), pp. 1475-1505.

Luger, J. (2014). *A longitudinal perspective on organizational ambidexterity.* Unpublished Doctoral dissertation. University of St. Gallen.

Ma, S. (2016). *The life cycle of corporate venture capital.* SSRN Working Paper.

March, J. G. (2003). 'Understanding organisational adaptation'. *Society and Economy, 25*(1), pp. 1-10.

Raisch, S., & Birkinshaw, J. (2008). 'Organizational ambidexterity: Antecedents, outcomes, and moderators'. *Journal of Management*, 34(3), pp. 375-409.

Schildt, H. A., Maula, M. V., & Keil, T. (2005). 'Explorative and exploitative learning from external corporate ventures'. *Entrepreneurship Theory and Practice*, 29(4), pp. 493-515.

Tuggle, C. S., Sirmon, D. G., Reutzel, C. R., & Bierman, L. (2010). 'Commanding board of director attention: investigating how organizational performance and CEO duality affect board members' attention to monitoring'. *Strategic Management Journal*, 31(9), pp. 946-968.

Tushman, M. L., & O'Reilly, C. A. (1996). ''The ambidextrous organizations: Managing evolutionary and revolutionary change. *California Management Review*, 38(4), pp. 8-30.

Wadhwa, A., & Basu, S. (2013). 'Exploration and resource commitments in unequal partnerships: An examination of corporate venture capital investment's. *Journal of Product Innovation Management*, 30(5), pp. 916-936.

Van de Vrande, V., Vanhaverbeke, W., & Duysters, G. (2011). 'Technology in-sourcing and the creation of pioneering technologies'. *Journal of Product Innovation Management, 28*(6), pp. 974-987.

Chapter 25

A Journey through University Technology Transfer, Organizational Learning and the Search for Innovation

Roberta Pellegrino

E-mail: pellegrinoro@gmail.com

Abstract: Innovation often starts with incisive scientific discoveries. What is the role of Academia in the creation of innovation? Who is paying for it and how does this work? The three papers in my dissertation represent different levels of analysis: Micro-level, Meso-level and Macro-level and each level concerns a different aspect of the broad topic of innovation within academia. Given the space constraints, in this chapter I will focus exclusively on the Macro-level of analysis and answer to these questions: how does the system of industrial and federal funding support the process of spreading innovation and how do they interact? To test my hypotheses, I use negative binomials models with unconditional fixed effect specification and longitudinal data (1991–2014) coming from more than 200 different North American institutions.

Keywords: R&D; University Technology Transfer; Discoveries; Patents; Licences; Federal Funding; Industrial Funding; Applied Research: Basic Research; Interaction Effect.

1. Introduction

In the summer of 2012, the University of Pennsylvania (Penn) and Novartis announced an exclusive global research and licensing agreement to further study and commercialize novel cellular immunotherapies. The agreement was worth 20 million dollars, and it followed a research team's 2011 publication of breakthrough results in a new personalized immunotherapy technique (Thomas, 2012). That partnership broke new ground in the growing trend of academic institutions collaborating with pharmaceutical companies where both parties could benefit: pharmaceutical companies have access to the expertise of top researchers at universities and can use basic research advances to develop new therapies and procedures in exchange for funding their research. It seems to be a mutually beneficial situation. However, the Perelman School at UPenn has not only managed to make deals and receive funding from the private sector, but it is also consistently among the nation's top recipients of federal funding from the National Institutes of Health, with $392 million awarded in the 2013 fiscal year.

Federal funding has been the main source for scientific research in the United States since after the second world war. This funding comes from government agencies and it has a crucial role in the process of creating innovation: it supplies faculty and research personnel with the necessary financial resources to begin discovery phases, innovation processes concerning all the disciplines, and facilitates the transfer of new technologies to all of the society (Monotti and Ricketson, 2003).

Despite its important role, and despite the critical role of public science, federal funding has been decreasing over the last years. More specifically, it declined 1,7% between 2014 and 2015, and since its highest peak, in 2011, it has fallen off nearly 13% (HERD Survey, 2015). The stasis in federal funding has led to increased worry that scientific research will suffer and that preliminary and risky activities will be no longer likely to be financed, turning the United States into a less innovative country and decelerating the pace of progress in science (Jahnke, 2015). In the meantime, in this last decade, the research environment has become more competitive, and universities and research centers have started looking and relying on other sources of funding, which has become increasingly important over the years. Among these sources, there is the private funding coming from the industry. Federal and industrial funding have both become crucial sources to carry on scientific research, but their relationship is still unclear. Do different sources of funding (federal and industrial) have a different impact on research outputs? Do these different sources of funding interact with each other and more specifically, do private and public funding get along or not in affecting research outputs?

The aim of this work is to answer to these research questions, to do this I will examine three different research outputs: the number of invention disclosures, the number of patents filed and the number of licenses options processed by 200 University Technology Transfer Offices (UTTO) in the United States.

Disentangling the relationship that exists between research funding inputs and its outputs is a formidable challenge. Research outputs are intended to produce knowledge, but the empirical measurement of science in the marketplace is laborious and complex (Heisey and Adelman, 2011). In fact, as a consequence of changes that have occurred over the past several decades, the character of universities' output has strongly changed, and they have become more commercially orientated (Monotti and Ricketson, 2003). The commercialization of science has been a source of concern within universities (Bok, 2003), but rules and research agendas have been changing and an increasing number of academic departments have been trying to boost their entrepreneurial mission (Baglieri and Lorenzoni, 2014).

In this study, I explore how federal funding and industry funding interact in the University Technology Transfer field and analyze how they differently affect research outputs. If this interaction exists, to know if and how it affects the research outputs might provide valuable evidence for university administrators, private corporations, and federal agencies involved in funding research.

To test my hypotheses, I use longitudinal data coming from the Association of University Technology Managers (AUTM) Licensing Survey (years 1991–2014) which represents more than 200 different North American institutions. I integrate the AUTM data with cross-sectional observations about the universities' ownership status (private or public) coming from the Carnegie Foundation for the Advancement of Teaching (CFAT). For the econometric analysis, I use negative binomials models with unconditional fixed effect specification. This kind of model, among other pros and cons, lets me take into account the high heterogeneity of the institutions of my sample. For each of the three dependent variables (disclosures, patents, licenses) I use, I include the interaction effect between the two main independent variables of this study's interest: federal and industrial funding.

The structure of this paper is as follows. The next session introduces the theoretical background with the hypotheses development. This is followed by the methods section introducing the data, the variables I used in this study and the empirical strategy. In the third section, I present the results. The final section provides the theoretical and practical implications and the limitations of this work.

2. Background

University funding: inputs and outputs

The United States government has provided the greater part of all funds devoted to basic research since the second world war and it has been widely studied how scientific research taking place in universities has been generating positive effects on both the social and industrial level (Bozeman 2000; Cohen et al. 2002). According to the 'Triple Helix' approach, university research is a crucial support for industrial competitiveness (Etzkowitz and Leydesdorff, 2000), and this is why a stronger university–industry–government collaboration has been established.

Despite the important and undisputed role of federal funding in American history, universities and research centers have started looking and also relying on industry funding, which has over the years become increasingly important. A good example of how certain universities started relying on private funding is Harvard, where university data demonstrates an evident conversion toward private funding: 75% of research is still funded by the government, but corporate research funding has tripled, to $41 million, from 2006 to 2013 (Jahnke, 2015). There has been a considerable accordance in the economic literature about the importance of university-industry collaboration (Cesaroni and Piccaluga, 2015) and about how governments should carry forward all the measures to ease the path of academic research to the market (Muscio et al., 2012). The new academic funding logic and its new dynamics have raised several issues: what are the advantages and what the disadvantages of this new collaboration happening between university and industry? What does this shift imply in regard to the way university technology transfer happens? There has been a considerable stream of literature focusing on these questions. Several authors indicated the potentially negative effects of academic research going toward industry funding (Perkmann et al., 2013) while others pointed that university–industry collaboration has little negative impact on academic research activities (Thursby and Thursby, 2001). Finally, some studies have shown that both universities and corporations might instead take advantage of this collaboration (Gulbrandsen and Smeby, 2005).

In this research, I call *research input* the funding, federal and industrial, used to conduct scientific inquiry and producing research outputs. Among many other research outputs, patenting and licensing of inventions have received a great deal of attention from the technology transfer literature and in the policy community (Phan and Siegel, 2006; Rothaermel et al., 2007). There are several other different and important research outputs which have been studied (Agrawal and Anderson, 2002; Agrawal, 2001;Pries and Guild, 2007; Lockett et al., 2005) but I will focus on patents, licenses, and invention disclosures.

The invention disclosure is usually the first action taken to start the technology transfer process, and it happens when the academic researcher discovers something new and officially register his scientific discovery/invention at the UTTO. After the disclosure, the scientist and the UTTO decide to hand over the protection of the intellectual property. In a certain way, therefore "a disclosure is the raw material needed to generate patents, products, and economic benefits" (Survey AUTM, 2014 p. 19). Not all the inventions which have been disclosed have a commercial value, and the TTO usually helps the scientist to find out how to exploit the discovery and if it is the case, to start the process to obtain the patent on that technology. TTOs might also contribute to promote the inventions to potential licensees and to negotiate the right accord of licensing. A License is a legal document that grants commercial rights to for-profit entities for the intellectual property owned by the academic institutions (Survey AUTM, 2014).

Even if it is hard to predict from which direction new discoveries will spring and to map the route which connects a specific kind of funding to scientific discoveries (Rosenberg, 1989), it is possible to say that private companies strongly count on federally funded research to enhance basic research (Narin et al., 1997; Salter Martin 2001) and that industry tends to finance commercially-oriented research more than federal funding does (Di Gregorio and Shane, 2003). The license, being one of the most remarkable outputs representing the commercialization of new technology, I expect industry funding to affect it more than industrial funding.

Hypothesis 1a - Federal funding has a stronger positive effect on invention disclosures than industrial funding does

Hypothesis 2a - Federal funding has a stronger effect on patents than industrial funding does

Hypothesis 3a - Industrial funding has a stronger effect on patents than federal funding does

While I described some of the research that explored the university-industry collaborations and some of its consequences, there has been a crucial factor that may have been left out as noticed by Muscio et al. (2012): what is the relationship between federal and industry funding and what is its effect on the research outputs? It has been shown by Jensen et al. (2010) that there is strategic complementarity between federal and industry funding and they also show how under certain sufficient conditions, they behave as strategic complements for university research. In addition, this complementarity would also imply that universities need federal funding to augment the impact of collaborations and fundraising opportunities with industry (Jensen et al., 2010; Dechenaux et al., 2011; Muscio, 2012).

Drawing on this theoretical background, I test the hypothesis on the interaction between federal and industry funding and explore how this affects the generation of these research outputs.

Hypothesis 1b - Federal funding moderates the relationship of industrial funding on disclosures

Hypothesis 2b - Federal funding moderates the relationship of industrial funding on patents

Hypothesis 3b - Federal funding moderates the relationship of industrial funding on licenses

3. Research design

Data and Sample

The data set I use in my analysis combines two sources: the licensing data from the Association of University Technology Managers (AUTM) Licensing Survey (years 1991–2014), and data on University characteristics collected by the Carnegie Foundation for the Advancement of Teaching (CFAT). The AUTM dataset contains information related to some of the main research outputs and come from 262 North American institutions. These 277 institutions are of two different types: universities (both public and private) and research centers. Due to its panel structure (22 years of observations) the AUTM dataset permits one to control for unobservable institution effects that may be correlated with the predictor variables allowing me to use the fixed effect models and to accomplish simultaneous estimation of models with lagged predictors. I describe the variables used for my analysis in the following table (Table 25.1).

Table 25.1 Variables and Definitions

Variable	Definitions
Federal Expenditures	Expenditures made in by the institution in support of its research activities that are funded by federal government. These grants are assigned through a competitive process and judged based on the quality and potential impact in a certain area.
Industrial Expenditures	Expenditures funded by for-profit corporations (not foundations or non profit organizations)
Other Funding	Expenditures coming from the University itself and from private foundations (No Profit)
Institutions Characteristics	
Type of Institution	Dummy variable equal to 1 if the institution is a University: 0 if it is US Hospital/ Res. Institutes
Public Institution	Dummy variable equal to 1 if the institution is public; 0 otherwise
Medical School	Dummy variable equal to 1 if there is a medical school in the organization; 0 otherwise
TTO Characteristics	
Full time employees	Count of number of full time employees working in the Technology transfer office
Research Outputs	

Disclosures	Include the number of disclosures, no matter how comprehensive, that are submitted during the survey year requested and are counted as received by the institution
Patents filed	Count of the number of patents filed in the year
License	Count the number of licenses or option agreements that were executed in the year indicated for all technologies
License Income received	License issue fees, payments under options, annual minimums, running royalties, termination payments, the amount of equity received when cashed-in
Startups formed	Startup companies formed during fiscal year that were dependent upon the licensing of institution's technology

Analysis

The dependent variables used in this paper are all counts of something: counts of disclosures, counts of papers, counts of licenses. Such variables are discrete, non-negative and typically highly skewed and it is for these reasons that conventional linear models are not appropriate (Allison, 2011). In order to analyze count data, it is more appropriate to use count models such as negative binomial models. The negative binomial models assume that the distribution of y_{it} is negative binomial rather than Poisson and it is a generalization of the Poisson, with an over-dispersion parameter.

I can turn the negative binomial model into a random or fixed effect model by specifying another term, *alpha.* Both random and fixed effect models follow the same equation:

$$y_{it} = \mu_t + \text{Fed\_Funding}_{it} + \text{Ind\_Funding}_{it} + \text{Control}_{it} + \varepsilon_{it} + \alpha_i$$

Using fixed effect models enables me to control for all the unchanging characteristics of the institutions in my sample, whether observed or unobserved. A negative consequence of this decision is that standard errors tend to be larger for fixed effect rather than for random effect models but as a reward for this issue, there is that each institution serves as its own control (Allison, 2011).

4. Conclusions

Table 25.2 Results

Results	
1a: Federal funding has a stronger effect on invention disclosures than industrial funding does	Accepted

1b: Federal funding moderates the relationship of industrial funding on disclosures	Accepted
2a: Federal funding has a stronger effect on patents than industrial funding does	Rejected
2b: Federal funding moderates the relationship of industrial funding on patents	Rejected
3a: Industrial funding has a stronger positive effect on licenses than federal funding does	Rejected
3b: Federal funding moderates the relationship of industrial funding on licenses	Accepted

Hypotheses 1a and 1b

These results provide considerable evidence that federal funding has a stronger effect on the number of invention disclosures than industrial funding has. Moreover, the result remains stable over eight different models and robustness checks. As I expected, the amount of federal funding received by each institution significantly predicts the number of disclosures. The main model shows, other things equal, that an increase in federal funding by one point means an increase of 23% (coefficient 0,23 highly significant with $p<0.01$) of invention disclosures. An increase in industrial funding by one point is instead associated with an increase of 2% (coefficient 0.02 significant with $p<0.05$).

According to the analysis, federal funding moderates the relationship of industrial funding on disclosures, and they have a positive effect on each other and the positive coefficient of the interaction term coefficient means that at larger values of federal funding, the value industrial funding of is also higher.

Hypotheses 2a and 2b

The second hypotheses are both rejected. Results provide evidence that federal funding does not have a stronger effect on the number of patents filed than industrial funding has. In fact, while the results in the first model show that federal funding has a more powerful positive effect on the number of patents filed, they do not remain significant over the three robustness checks. The same thing happens to the interaction effect which according to the results, does not have any effect on the number of patents filed each year.

Hypotheses 3a and 3b

In the hypothesis 3a, I state that industrial funding has a stronger effect on the number of yearly licenses than federal funding does. The results not just reject this hypothesis, but also state the opposite thesis. Industrial funding does not have a stronger effect on licenses than federal funding does, but the most surprising thing is that the coefficient of industrial funding is negative. What does it mean? It means that in the model, ceteris paribus, an increase in industrial funding by one point means a decrease of 5% (coefficient -0,053 highly significant with $p<0.01$) of license options. On the contrary, an increase in federal funding by one point means an increase of 20% (coefficient 0.198 highly significant with $p<0.01$). The results remain stable through four robustness checks, and industrial funding holds a negative coefficient and remains highly significant.

The last hypothesis, 3b, is accepted and confirms that industrial funding does moderate the relationship of federal funding on licenses. How do these two different sources of financing research interact with each other? The coefficient of the interaction effect is negative (- 0.06 highly significant with $p<0.01$), which means that they do not collaborate in helping the process of licensing. The negative passes five robustness checks. The negativity of the coefficient means that at larger values of federal funding, the value of industrial funding on licenses decreases, and vice versa, and even if the mechanism through which this happens is not entirely clear, I can infer that having more money is not generally good for any kind of research output and from where the money comes can be crucial.

5. Implications and future research

Scientific research generates an invaluable and crucial asset for national economies; it is "the energy that fuels the technology transfer engine" (AUTM Survey, 2014 p.16) and its primary source of funding is the U.S government. More frequent and stronger cuts will be happening in the next years, if we take as evidence the first budget plan released on March 16th by Trump's administration (Reardon et al., 2017). This disinvestment might lead to the slowing down of the progress in technology transfer that universities and industries have worked to accomplish so far. As a reaction, universities have started to increase their relationships with industry. In light of these facts, it is important to have a clear picture of how public and private funding interact. The aim of this paper was to explore two different paths. In the first path, I explored how the two main types of research funding, federal and industrial, affect three different research outputs: number invention disclosures, patents and licenses. In the second and more insidious path, I explored if and how federal and industrial funding interaction affects the three research outputs.

This study has both policy and managerial implications. It contributes to the ongoing debate on the private and public funding of universities and with these empirical results, it shows that a larger amount of funding does not always correspond to a larger amount of scientific output and in the production function of university research, federal and industrial funding do not always get along.

In fact, federal and industrial funding potentiate each other when it comes to generating disclosures, but not when it comes to generating licenses. In the first case, having more federal funding helps the industrial funding (and vice versa) to produce more disclosures, while in the second case, federal and industrial funding hinder each other. Their interaction is, in fact, negative and highly significant which means that the more federal funding there is, the less the industrial funding helps in producing licenses and vice versa. Surprisingly, when I examined the case of patents, both with industrial and federal funding, I did not find any measurable impact of federal or industry expenditures.

The mechanisms behind these effects are not entirely clear, but the technology transfer literature offers some explanations which it would be worth exploring further. Where do these conflicts between federal and industrial funding come from when it comes to generating licenses? Previous research has shown how many academics have established their own firms or have developed close relationships (often including relevant economic incentives) with private companies, bargaining their university research (Kenney and Patton, 2009). This mechanism contributes to the emergence of a 'gray market' for research outputs (Markman et al., 2008). More than 20% of the professors working in academia have started companies in their field of expertise without university licenses (Audretsch et al., 2006) and over 42% of the professors who applied for a patent bypassed the university technology transfer office (Markman et al., 2008).

Another possible mechanism to explain why funding coming from industry negatively affects the number of licenses, emerged from an informal conversation with a manager of the University of Pennsylvania's UTTO. I asked him what he thought of the results of my analysis and he answered that the biggest investments coming from industry are generally converted into one big license. This answer could explain why a larger amount of money coming from industry corresponds to a low number of licenses. Since this information came from an informal conversation, I would like to dig deeper into my future works and run further empirical analysis.

There is a long list of limitations of this study that need to be mentioned. First of all, my data represents just the University technology transfer situations in the United States, the empirical results are then limited to the U.S. context and can't be applied to the European situation. It might be interesting to discover whether or not this analysis produces the same results in Europe as well. Another issue concerns the estimation of the impact of research expenditures on research outputs. This can, in fact, take longer than expected and this is the reason why modeling the relationship between research inputs and outputs is so complex. A strong point of this study is the longitudinal structure of the data I used, and the sample size, which gave me enough statistical power and allowed me to analyze several lag structures, but still, the effect of federal and industry funding on licensing activities could be lagged in ways I am not able to predict. Integrating the quantitative analysis with qualitative data could have helped me to better understand the results and the mechanisms behind them and it will be a good reason to continue working on this topic.

References

Acs, Z. J., Audretsch, D. B., and Feldman, M. P. (1992). 'Real effects of academic research: comment'. *The American Economic Review, 82*(1), 363-367.

Adams, J. D., and Griliches, Z. (1996). *Research productivity in a system of universities* (No. w5833). National bureau of economic research.

Agrawal, A., and Henderson, R. (2002). 'Putting patents in context: Exploring knowledge transfer from MIT'. *Management science, 48*(1), 44-60.

Agrawal, A. K. (2001). 'University-to-industry knowledge transfer: Literature review and unanswered questions'. *International Journal of management reviews, 3*(4), 285-302.

Aghion, P., Dewatripont, M., and Stein, J. C. (2008). 'Academic freedom, private-sector focus, and the process of innovation'. *The RAND Journal of Economics, 39*(3), 617-635.

Allison, P. D., and Waterman, R. P. (2002). 'Fixed–effects negative binomial regression models'. *Sociological Methodology, 32*(1), 247-265.

Allison, P. D. (2011). Longitudinal data analysis using Stata. *Course lectures presented at: Longitudinal Data Analysis Using Stata PHL,* 25-26.

Arrow, K. (1962). 'Economic welfare and the allocation of resources for invention'. In *The rate and direction of inventive activity: Economic and social factors* (pp. 609-626). Princeton University Press.

Association of University Technology (2014). Licensing Survey, 1991-2014.

Audretsch, D. B., Keilbach, M. C., and Lehmann, E. E. (2006). *Entrepreneurship and economic growth.* Oxford University Press.

Auranen, O., and Nieminen, M. (2010). 'University research funding and publication performance—An international comparison'. *Research Policy, 39*(6), 822-834.

Baglieri, D., and Lorenzoni, G. (2014). 'Closing the distance between academia and market: experimentation and user entrepreneurial processes'. *The Journal of Technology Transfer, 39*(1), 52-74.

Blume-Kohout, M. E., Kumar, K. B., and Sood, N. (2009). *Federal life sciences funding and university R&D* (No. w15146). National Bureau of Economic Research.

Bok, D. (2009). *Universities in the marketplace: The commercialization of higher education.* Princeton University Press.

Bozeman, B. (2000). 'Technology transfer and public policy: a review of research and theory'. *Research policy, 29*(4), 627-655.

Brooks, H. (1986). 'National science policy and technological innovation'. *The Positive Sum Strategy: Harnessing Technology for Economic Growth. National Academy Press, Washington,* 119-167.

Bush, V. (1945). 'Science: The endless frontier'. *Transactions of the Kansas Academy of Science (1903), 48*(3), 231-264.

Carnegie Foundation for the Advancement of Teaching Carnegie Classifications Data File, February 2012

Cesaroni, F., and Piccaluga, A. (2015). 'The activities of university knowledge transfer offices: towards the third mission in Italy'. *The Journal of Technology Transfer, 41*(4), 753-777.

Coffman, W. R., Lesser, W. H., and McCouch, S. R. (2003). Commercialization and the scientific research process: The example of plant breeding. *Science and the University.*

Cohen, W. M., and Levinthal, D. A. (1989). 'Innovation and learning: the two faces of R&D'. *The Economic Journal,* 99(397), 569-596.

Cohen, W. M., and Levinthal, D. A. (1990). 'Absorptive capacity: A new perspective on learning and innovation'. *Administrative Science Quarterly,* 128-152.

Cohen, W. M., Nelson, R. R., and Walsh, J. P. (2002). 'Links and impacts: the influence of public research on industrial R&D'. *Management science, 48*(1), 1-23.

Colyvas, J., Crow, M., Gelijns, A., Mazzoleni, R., Nelson, R. R., Rosenberg, N., and Sampat, B. N. (2002). 'How do university inventions get into practice?'. *Management Science, 48*(1), 61-72.

Dechenaux, E., Thursby, J., Thursby, M. (2011). 'Inventor moral hazard in university licensing: the role of contracts'. *Research Policy* 40 (1), 94–104

Forero-Pineda, C. (2006). 'The impact of stronger intellectual property rights on science and technology in developing countries'. *Research policy, 35*(6), 808-824.

Goldin, C. (2001). 'The human-capital century and American Leadership: virtues of the past'. *The Journal of Economic History,* 61(2), 263–292.

Gulbrandsen, M., Mowery, D., and Feldman, M. (2011). Introduction to the special section: Heterogeneity and university–industry relations.

Gulbrandsen, M., Smeby, J.C. (2005). 'Industry funding and university professors' research performance'. *Research Policy* 34, 932–950.

Heisey, P. W., and Adelman, S. W. (2011). 'Research expenditures, technology transfer activity, and university licensing revenue'. *The Journal of Technology Transfer, 36*(1), 38-60.

Henderson, R., Jaffe, A. B., and Trajtenberg, M. (1998). 'Universities as a source of commercial technology: a detailed analysis of university patenting, 1965–1988'. *Review of Economics and Statistics, 80*(1), 119-127.

Huffman, W. E., and Just, R. E. (2000). 'Setting efficient incentives for agricultural research: Lessons from principal-agent theory'. *American Journal of Agricultural Economics, 82*(4), 828-841.

Jahnke, A. (2015). Who picks up the tab for science? Retrieved from *BU Today* http://www.bu.edu/today/2015/funding-for-scientific-research/

Jensen, R., Thursby, J., and Thursby, M. C. (2010). *University-industry spillovers, government funding, and industrial consulting* (No. w15732). National Bureau of Economic Research.

Just, R. E., and Huffman, W. E. (2006). The role of patents, royalties, and public-private partnering in university funding.

Lavie, D., Kang, J., and Rosenkopf, L. (2011). 'Balance within and across domains: The performance implications of exploration and exploitation in alliances'. *Organization Science, 22*(6), 1517-1538.

Lavie, D., and Rosenkopf, L. (2006). 'Balancing exploration and exploitation in alliance formation'. *Academy of Management Journal*, 49(4), 797-818.

Lee, Y. S. (2000). 'The sustainability of university-industry research collaboration: An empirical assessment'. *The Journal of Technology Transfer*, 25(2), 111-133.

Lockett, A., Siegel, D., Wright, M., and Ensley, M. D. (2005). 'The creation of spin-off firms at public research institutions: Managerial and policy implications'. *Research Policy*, *34*(7), 981-993.

Markman, G. D., Siegel, D. S., and Wright, M. (2008). 'Research and technology commercialization'. *Journal of Management Studies*, *45*(8), 1401-1423.

McMillan, G. S., Narin, F., and Deeds, D. L. (2000). 'An analysis of the critical role of public science in innovation: the case of biotechnology'. *Research Policy*, *29*(1), 1-8.

Monotti, A., and Ricketson, S. (2003). Universities and intellectual property: Ownership and exploitation.

Mowery, D. C., Thompson, N. C., and Ziedonis, A. A. (2014). 'Does University Licensing Facilitate or Restrict the Flow of Knowledge and Research Inputs Among Scientists?'. In *Arbeitspapier präsentiert am Workshop "Beyond spillovers.*

Muscio, A., Quaglione, D., and Vallanti, G. (2013). 'Does government funding complement or substitute private research funding to universities?'. *Research Policy*, *42*(1), 63-75.

Narin, F., Hamilton, K. S., and Olivastro, D. (1997). 'The increasing linkage between US technology and public science'. *Research Policy*, *26*(3), 317-330.

Payne, A. A., and Siow, A. (1998). 'Estimating the Effects of Federal Research Funding on Universities using Alumni Representation on Congressional Appropriations Committees'. *Advances in Economic Analysis and Policy*, 1-22.

Perkmann, M., Tartari, V., McKelvey, M., Autio, E., Broström, A., D'Este, P., and Krabel, S. (2013). 'Academic engagement and commercialisation: A review of the literature on university–industry relations'. *Research policy*, *42*(2), 423-442.

Perkmann, M., and Walsh, K. (2008). 'Engaging the scholar: Three types of academic consulting and their impact on universities and industry'. *Research Policy*, *37*(10), 1884-1891.

Phan, P. H., and Siegel, D. S. (2006). 'The effectiveness of university technology transfer'. *Foundations and Trends in Entrepreneurship*, *2*(2), 77-144.

Pries, F., and Guild, P. (2007). 'Commercial exploitation of new technologies arising from university research: start-ups and markets for technology'. *R&D Management*, *37*(4), 319-328.

Reardon, S., Tollefson, J., Witze, A., and Ross, E. (2017). 'US science agencies face deep cuts in Trump budget'. *Nature*, *543*(7646), 471-472.

Rosenberg, N. (1990). 'Why do firms do basic research (with their own money)?' *Research Policy*, *19*(2), 165-174.

Salter, A. J., and Martin, B. R. (2001). 'The economic benefits of publicly funded basic research: a critical review'. *Research policy*, *30*(3), 509-532.

Thomas, K. (2012), August 2. Novartis and Penn Unite on New Anticancer Path. *The New York Times*. Retrieved from http://www.nytimes.com

Thursby, J. G., Jensen, R., and Thursby, M. C. (2001). 'Objectives, characteristics and outcomes of university licensing: A survey of major US universities'. *The Journal of Technology Transfer*, *26*(1-2), 59-72.

Chapter 26

Processes and Ecosystems of Innovation with a Multi-KET Approach to Foster Technology Transfer and Commercialization of Nanotechnologies in the Field of Healthcare

Cristina Páez-Avilés*

E-mail: cristina@paez.ec

Abstract: This empirical study analyzed the technological diversity and innovation management strategies that might influence the process of cross-fertilization of Key Enabling Technologies (KETs), and in particular nanotechnology, that are currently being fostered by European initiatives such as Horizon 2020. To do so, texts and networks from nanotechnology-related projects were analyzed and project leaders interviewed. The outcomes of this research contribute to the analysis of successful transference and commercialization of multi-KETs in the field of nanotechnologies applied to healthcare by understanding the processes and ecosystems of innovation. Accordingly, it aims to contribute to the reduction of the gap between research and the marketplace and to expand the knowledge of current interest regarding innovation ecosystems for emergent technologies, regional systems of innovation and strategic innovation management.

Keywords: nanotechnology; KETs; technological diversity; innovation management; technology transfer; commercialization.

1. Introduction

Nanotechnology is an important and very promising field of research since it plays a significant role in economic, social and regional growth. This technology has been considered the greatest impulse of technological and industrial development of the 21st century and the resource for the next industrial revolution (Flynn and Wei, 2005; Rothaermel and Thursby, 2007; European Commission, 2011; RNCOS, 2013). Moreover, it is expected to be the fastest-growing industry in history (Morrow Jr, Bawa and Wei, 2007). Some predictions claim that nanotechnology is following a similar evolutionary pattern in industrial application as biotechnology (Rothaermel and Thursby, 2007; Niku-lainen and Palmberg, 2010), but with the potential to influence a broader range of industrial sectors (Roco, 2011).

Healthcare is one of the fields that have been greatly improved by nano-scale manipulation. In this context, the convergence of nanotechnology and biotechnology opens a challenging economic and scientific landscape leading to a huge market for nanomedicine-related products and services. Advances in nanomedicine have shown great potential to reduce rates of morbidity and mortality, revolutionizing global health (Pautler and Brenner, 2010; Gabellieri and Frima, 2011) and making available innovative, cheaper and faster bio-medical facilities, accurate diagnosis, less invasive procedures and more tar-geted drugs (Bjørn Larsen, 2011; Maine *et al.*, 2014).

Despite this continued growth, few scientific discoveries have impacted clinical practice, especially when compared to the significant, global progress made by genomics, proteomics and other disciplines (Whitesides, 2006; Fu *et al.*, 2011; Chin, Linder and Sia, 2012). The complete technological and innova-tive lifecycle of nano-products is not realizing its full potential due to a *gap* between academia, industry and the market known as the "**Valley of Death**" (Debackere, 2000; Flynn and Wei, 2005; J. D. Linton and Walsh, 2008; Europe-an Commission, 2012; Mahroum and Al-Saleh, 2013). This concept is aligned with the so-called **"European paradox"**, which suggests a contradiction be-tween higher levels of scientific performance on the one hand and the mini-mal contributions to industrial competitiveness and new venture entrepre-neurship in Europe on the other (Pavitt, 1998; Debackere, 2000; Flynn and Wei, 2005; J. D. Linton and Walsh, 2008; Mahroum and Al-Saleh, 2013).

Costs are often the principal barrier, especially in settings with lower levels of resources (Fu *et al.*, 2011). Moreover, some medical advances are yet to demonstrate the cost-effective benefits required to displace current technolo-gy or workflow (Neužil *et al.*, 2014). However, recent findings have shown that costs or technological barriers are not the only reasons for explaining why much of the science and technology developed in research laboratories is not commercialized (Jonathan D Linton and Walsh, 2008). Therefore, it is im-portant to consider that qualified R&D in academic and industry laboratories cannot determine the success of this technology by themselves (Roco, 2003).

Overcoming this gap to attain commercial success and the social return of re-search could be a difficult process if innovation challenges are not addressed. In fact, the future of industry will rely on its ability to innovate in high-tech activi-ties that can offer a differential added-value, rather than improving existing technologies and products (Juanola-Feliu *et al.*, 2012; Motyl and Filippi, 2014). The European Commission (EC) has considered these premises as a concern. As a result, the current European Framework Programme Horizon 2020 (H2020) is fostering innovation through the development and industrial uptake of Key Enabling Technologies[1] (KETs), which are considered strategic for a sustainable economy. Moreover, the cross-fertilization of KETs is being emphasized in this initiative in order to obtain new product properties or technological features that cannot be obtained with a single KET. Nanotechnology is part of this selected group of technologies, and since its industrial applicability is broad, its cross-fertilization with other KETs constitutes an important challenge.

Studies about the process of cross-fertilization of KETs are few (Kim *et al.*, 2014). Most of the approaches have focused on inter-disciplinarity (Schummer, 2004; Hacklin, Marxt and Fahrni, 2009; Porter and Youtie, 2009; Rafols and Meyer, 2010; Sedighi, 2013) or partial technological convergence (Dang *et al.*, 2010; No and Park, 2010). Previous works have also analyzed the cross-fertilization process by focusing on the inter-disciplinarity of research collaboration (Rafols and Meyer, 2010; Van Rijnsoever and Hessels, 2011; König *et al.*, 2013; Sedighi, 2013), especially in the emergent field of nanotechnologies (Rafols and Meyer, 2007, 2010; Juanola-Feliu *et al.*, 2012; You, Kim and Jeong, 2014; Páez-Avilés, González-Piñero and Juanola-Feliu, 2015). However, little attention has been paid to address innovation and technology transfer challenges for the successful commercialization of multi-KET outcomes.

In this regard, this work addresses these challenges by focusing on the field of healthcare. Nano-related European innovation projects have been analyzed in this work. Principal contributions have sought a better understanding of the processes and ecosystems of innovation and have therefore helped to reduce the Valley of Death gap between research and market.

2. Background

Combining diverse technological streams frequently underlies the development of new and significant inventions (Maine, Thomas and Utterback, 2014). Yet, not only the combination, but the convergence of technologies could generate and transform products that could be shared across diverse fields, resulting in radical innovations (Roco and Bainbridge, 2005; Björkdahl, 2009; Heide *et al.*, 2013). In this process, value is generated by sharing knowledge and equipment and from the alignment of different stakeholders and skilled specialists (Mangematin and Walsh, 2012; Organization for Economic Cooperation and Development OECD, 2014).

---

1.   Group of six technologies selected by the EC on the base of their economic, innovative and competitive potential in industry (European Commission, 2014).

As well as the concept of hybridization, the concept of *convergence of technologies* is often associated with the process of cross-fertilization. The rationale is that "convergence" specifically involves conflation between previously distinct knowledge, technology, product or industry domains (Jeong and Lee, 2015). According to Katz (1996), the concept of convergence has broad implications for economic welfare and could shape the structure of industry (Katz, 1996). Technological convergence has become a current phenomenon aimed at enhancing previous solutions for a specific product or service (Gauch and Blind, 2015). In line with this, it is expected that the convergence or cross-fertilization of KETs could drive radical change, supporting the development of other technologies (Australian Government, 2012). To this end, six KETs have been selected by the EC as most strategically relevant at H2020 as per their economic potential and their capital and technological intensity (European Commission, 2009; Aschhoff *et al.*, 2010; Butter *et al.*, 2014).

Individually, each KET has a huge potential for innovation. However, cross-fertilization of KETs could offer even greater possibilities for fostering innovation and creating new markets (Butter *et al.*, 2014). The relevance of this combining process lies in the creation of new unique product properties or technology features, which could not have been obtained with a single technology. This convergent scenario in areas such as microelectronics, microfluidics, micro-sensors and biocompatible materials enables the availability of cheaper and faster new medical devices of small dimensions (Juanola-Feliu *et al.*, 2012; Páez-Avilés, González-Piñero and Juanola-Feliu, 2015).

For an emerging technology like nanotechnology, creating sufficient *technological diversity* among its alternatives is important for its long-term success (Negro, Suurs and Hekkert, 2008; Van den Bergh, 2008; Van Rijnsoever *et al.*, 2015). Innovation is an evolutionary process of variation and selection (Edquist, 1997; Hekkert *et al.*, 2007). The diversity of a technology changes as new technological alternatives are created (Saviotti and Metcalfe, 1984; Murmann and Frenken, 2006; Van Rijnsoever *et al.*, 2015). If a new technological alternative represents a common technological design, diversity decreases. Technological alternatives that have a novel or less common design increase diversity (Abernathy, 1979; Frenken, Saviotti and Trommetter, 1999).

The creation of new technological alternatives often takes place in innovation projects in which different organizations such as firms, universities and research institutes collaborate (Cooke, Gomez Uranga and Etxebarria, 1997; Edquist and Hommen, 1999; Niosi, 2011). For emerging technologies, these innovation projects are often publicly supported, for example, through EU-funding. Hence, funding instruments can be used as a tool for policy makers to influence the level of technological diversity (Pandza, Wilkins and Alfoldi, 2011; Van Rijnsoever *et al.*, 2015), and thereby secure the long-term viability of the technology.

Simulations (Jonard and Yfldizoglu, 1998) and conceptual works (Edquist and Hommen, 1999) indicate that the creation and persistence of technological diversity depends on learning from their neighborhood and network externalities. Yet, there is little empirical evidence about the characteristics of innovation projects that influence diversity. Van Rijnsoever et al., (2015) demonstrated that diversity created by an innovation project is related to the network position and organizational composition of the project. Adding to insights from innovation systems (Hekkert *et al.*, 2007), Van Rijnsoever et al., (2015) argue that it is also important to consider the structure of the network to make a technology successful in the long-term. In European funded nanotechnology projects, Pandza et al., (2011) found a significant degree of collaborative diversity in terms of international and institutional affiliation in the research network. This should be beneficial to technological diversity creation, but they did not test this implication empirically.

Innovation management strategies are also essential activities in a convergent scenario such as the process of cross-fertilization of KETs. A previous study, focused on the convergence of Nano and Biotechnologies, by Maine et al., (2014), showed three central innovation management strategies in this convergence: 1) *to import ideas from broad networks*, 2) *to create environments for deep collaboration* and 3) *technology-market-matching*. The first strategy refers to the search and synthesis of concepts or ideas that could be taken from networks with different technology streams. The second strategy involves the dynamic collaborative flow of knowledge between R&D groups. Finally, these two strategies need to be complemented by considering market needs, which is the third strategy.

In addition to the analysis of technological diversity, this study is also grounded in the three aforementioned management strategies and takes into account other aspects related to network theories, absorptive capacity and the dynamic capabilities literature. The aim is to obtain an expanded vision of these three strategies and the possible influence they could have on the cross-fertilization of KETs.

3. Research design

As mentioned above, a new paradigm is needed for research, development and innovation activities in a convergent scenario of emerging technologies. For that purpose, the general aim of this study is to get insights about the innovation and technology transfer challenges that exist in the cross-fertilization of KETs, from fundamental research through to technological commercialization, in order to achieve a successful technology transfer process in nanotechnology. Moreover, since this research focuses on the application of nanotechnologies in the field of healthcare, the social return of public investment and the healthy living of end-users are highlighted.

On the one hand the study focussed on nanotechnologies applied to the field of healthcare, and on the other hand, it also looked at the process of cross-fertilization of KETs. For this purpose, nanotechnology-related projects for healthcare applications were selected from the Work Programme LEIT 2014-2015 of H2020 called "Nanotechnologies, Advanced Materials, Biotechnology and Advanced Manufacturing and Processing," which fosters the technological cross-fertilization of nanotechnologies, advanced materials, biotechnologies and advanced manufacturing systems (European Commission, 2015). The projects belong to the following four types of categories: Nanotechnology and advanced materials for more effective healthcare; Exploiting the cross-sector potential of nanotechnologies and advanced materials to drive competitiveness and sustainability; Bridging the gap between nanotechnology research and markets; Biotechnology-based industrial processes driving competitiveness and sustainability.

A total of 69 projects were obtained and 222 different organizations as coordinators and participants were identified. Some organizations participated in more than one project, so a total of 239 organizations were considered for the descriptive analysis.

The information retrieved from the selected projects was initially analyzed through descriptive statistics, network graphs and text mining approaches in order to have a complete overview of the study. For the first section, the change in technological diversity (dependent variable) caused by a project was related to the independent variables: degree of multi-disciplinarity, degree of clustering, knowledge base of organizations, diversity of organizations, number of organizations and geographical distance. In order to analyze the creation of technological diversity, a Topic Modelling approach was used. This is a novel text mining method for categorizing technological alternatives from text data. This method allows the calculation of diversity creation in a more efficient manner than in conventional qualitative approaches, and uses discrete probabilistic techniques for information retrieval, and text and data mining (Blei, Ng and Jordan, 2003). For the LDA analysis, the *lda* package of the R-program was used (Ponweiser, 2012). The hypotheses formulated in this section were tested with an Ordinal Logistic Regression Model.

For the second section of the study, project leaders were interviewed in order to reveal information about their innovation management strategies. The hypotheses about technological distances, technological efforts, access to information, previous collaboration, type of collaboration, market orientation, customer prioritization, and experience in Technological Readiness

Levels were tested only for those organizations within collaborative projects. To that end, Multiple Correspondence Analysis was used. This statistical descriptive mapping method is based on scaling dimensionality reduction for nominal qualitative and multivariate data (Abdi, 2007). It is based on analyzing the similarity of the data, which is graphically represented as points in two- or three-dimensional space. Observable differences can be viewed in a graph, which are percentage maps, composed of coordinate axes in a Euclidean space. This method is commonly used to analyze data from surveys (Husson, Lê and Pagès, 2010). For this analysis, the packages *FactoMineR* and *factoextra* from the R software were used (Lê, Josse and Mazet, 2008).

The analysis included the established variables and other qualitative supplementary variables such as the size of the organizations and the level of nanotechnology applicability in order to explore the relationships of these characteristics with cross-fertilization.

The methodology applied in both sections is summarized in Figure 26.1.

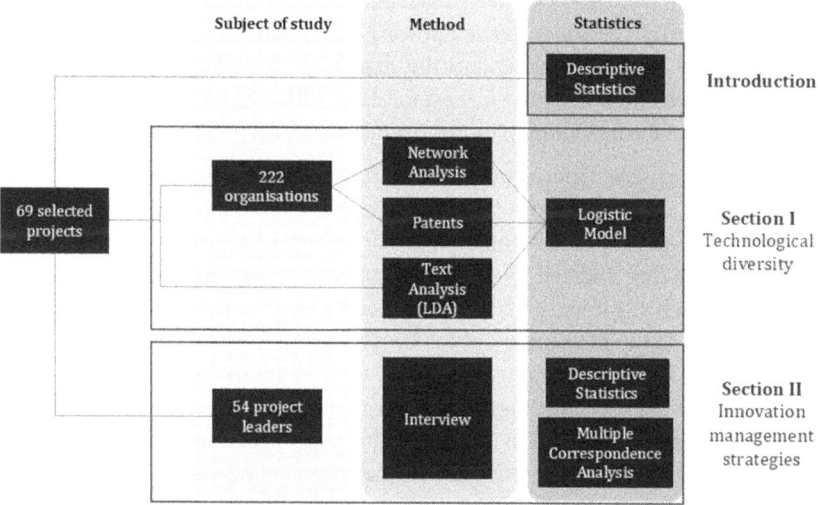

Figure 26.1 Summary of methodology used in the empirical study.

4. Conclusion

The nano-related innovation ecosystem has been analyzed in a European regional context through EU-funded nanotechnology innovation projects. Of the selected projects, it was found that most of the projects were granted to Spain, Germany, Italy, the UK and France. Specifically, Spain and Germany are the countries with major levels of shared cooperation. In addition, it was found that more than half of the participant organizations are private for-profit entities (principally SMEs), followed by higher or secondary education establishments and research organizations. Once again, we conclude that the current H2020 Programme puts the focus on innovation outputs and places the firms as innovating engines for sustainable and technology-driven economy growth.

The influence of characteristics of EU-funded nanotechnology projects on the creation of technological diversity was also analyzed. In addition to organizational diversity and the network of the project, novel variables that have a plausible influence on diversity creation were included. Results showed that the largest contribution to the creation of technological diversity comes from the multi-disciplinary nature of a project. These findings support the idea that the development of multi-disciplinary projects fosters the long-term success of nanotechnologies. In this regard, the multi-disciplinary collaboration found in previous findings is endorsed and suggested for use to boost the cross-fertilization of KETs.

The joint knowledge base of project partners and the geographical distance between them were also positively associated with technological diversity creation in the system of projects. The opposite has occurred regarding the number and diversity of organizations and the degree of clustering, which showed a negative association. These results establish that the structure of the network is also an essential consideration for the overall success of nanotechnologies.

On the other side, three innovation management strategies and their influence on the process of cross-fertilization of KETs were studied (**Figure 26.2**). From their analysis, it was concluded that higher levels of cross-fertilization of KETs are being boosted by customer-concerned and market-oriented projects, in which organizations prioritize access to external knowledge. It was also found that the network that best boosts the cross-fertilization of KETs has an informal structure, where knowledge is moderately heterogeneous. This endorses the previous findings from the case studies. Therefore, these results suggest that factors related to the absorptive capacities and dynamic capabilities of organizations are decisive in a technological convergent approach.

The suggested innovation ecosystem for developing health-related multi-KETs show that the suggested model includes a multi-disciplinary team and considers the *level of multi-disciplinarity* as relevant in order to avoid too much multi-disciplinarity. Additionally, the existence of a previous collaboration from the beginning of the value chain was not completely supported in the empirical study; therefore, more research is needed to endorse the concept of an *integrated mosaic-based* innovation community as the optimal model to transfer multi-KETs to the marketplace.

Finally, it was also identified that actors with higher levels of nanotechnology application are correlated with higher levels of cross-fertilization of KETs. Accordingly, this study confirms the transversal role of nanotechnologies, highlighting the imperative for implementation of this technology in the industrial sector.

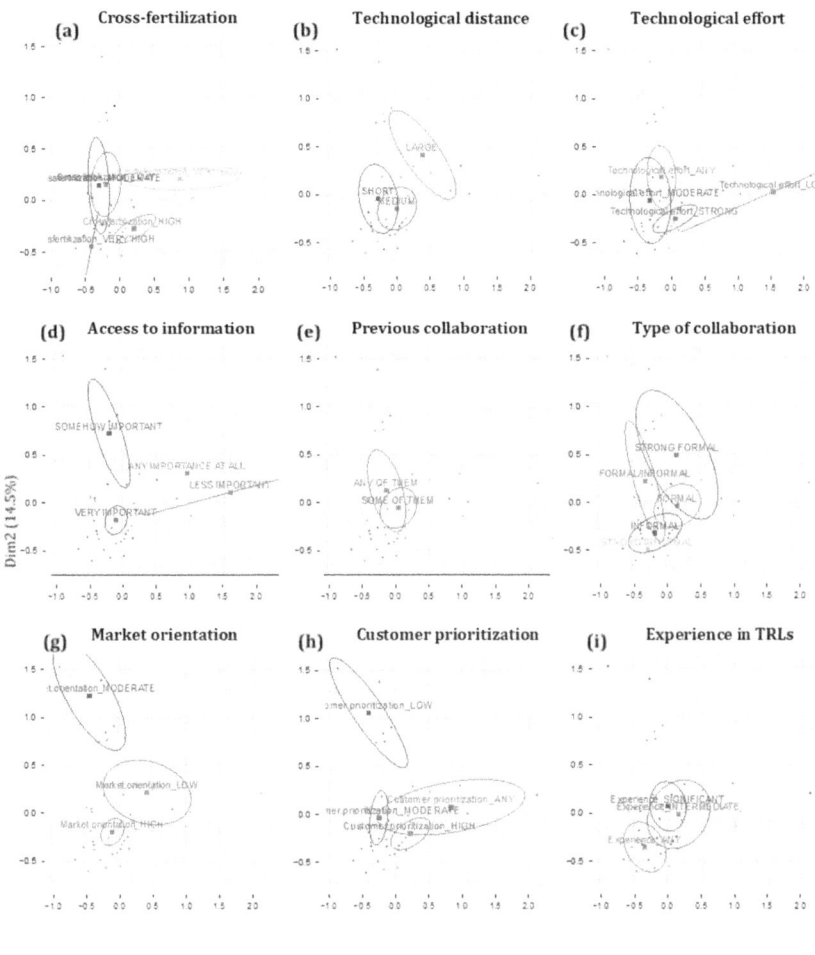

Figure 26.2 MCA for each categorical variable. Ellipses plot. Variables: (a) level of cross-fertilization, (b) technological distance, (c) technological effort, (d) access to information, (e) previous collaboration, (f) type of collaboration, (g) market orientation, (h) customer prioritization, and (i) experience in TRLs.

5. Implications and future research

This work analyzed the process and ecosystems of innovation in nanotechnologies by considering the cross-fertilization of KETs in the field of healthcare. In this regard, key issues and current concerns of innovation and technology transfer have addressed. By doing so, this work has sought to extend scientific, industrial and innovation knowledge attempting to answer the new challenges that are facing publicly-funded research.

The main addition to the literature is that the ***degree of multi-disciplinarity*** of a project and the size of the joint knowledge base of project partners are predictors of diversity creation. In this context, the hypothesis that different disciplines and broader knowledge bases increase the chances of recombinant innovation was supported. Second, the results mostly support earlier findings and the theoretical expectations with regards to the number of organizations in the project, the clustering coefficient and the effect of geographical distance. However, the claim that organizational diversity adds to technological diversity creation was not completely supported. Innovation system research argues that building networks is important for the success of emerging technology. These results verify the claim that it is also important to consider what the network should look like.

Accordingly, the results from the first section may serve as guidelines for policy makers, especially at the EU-level, for fostering the success of emerging technologies on the basis of their cross-fertilization and technology diversity creation. In order to encourage creation of technological diversity, emphasis should be placed on subsidizing: i) projects involving or developing multiple disciplines, ii) projects with organizations that show a strong background in nanotechnology knowledge, iii) projects with partners from different geographical regions, and iv) projects with a limited number of partners that are not too closely connected with each other. The first three are already explicit or implicit criteria in H2020. Yet these projects often involve large consortia. These results suggest that it is better for diversity if these consortia are smaller. Moreover, in some instances, partners are involved in multiple projects. Finally, in this first section, these results showed that these cases should be handled with care, as this can decrease technological diversity.

On the other hand, this study has empirically explored three ***innovation management strategies*** in the process of cross-fertilization of KETs. The first strategy is related to importing ideas from broad networks. This strategy was nuanced by considering a technological distance within the network, the technological effort organizations make to import ideas from the network and the value organizations give to having access to external information. Findings suggest that the level of cross-fertilization is higher when there are short or medium technological distances, when organizations make stronger technological efforts and when the access to external information is a very important reason for belonging to the network. These findings could support an open innovation strategy where organizations tend to be aware of and open to what their network could offer, rather than protecting their own knowledge.

The second strategy which was analyzed refers to the creation of a collaborative network: findings suggest that neither a previous collaboration nor a formal collaborative structure supports higher levels of cross-fertilization. Indeed, the authors believe that these considerations could be related to each other by taking into account that since no formal agreements are developed along the value chain, informal and spontaneous interactions are more likely to emerge in this situation. These findings are also consistent with the informal network literature, which gives more weight to the trust, commitment and mutual learning from informal dynamics in order to foster the convergence of creative ideas and technologies.

The third strategy which was analyzed took into account the level of orientation to market, customer prioritization and the experience in higher levels of Technological Readiness Levels (TRLs) where pilot production and product demonstration activities are prevalent. Evidence suggests that market-oriented and customer prioritized projects boost higher levels of cross-fertilization of KETs. In contrast, the claim that previous experience with higher levels of technological maturity favors cross-fertilization was not completely supported.

Another contribution of this work is regarding the significant role of nanotechnologies in the cross-fertilization of KETs. This study identified that organizations that apply nanotechnology knowledge in their own organization are the ones that produce higher levels of cross-fertilization. This result not only confirms the transversal and multidisciplinary nature of nanotechnologies, emphasizing its plasticity among different industries but more importantly, suggests an essential characteristic of highly cross-fertilized projects.

The results form this second section could be used as a guideline for policy makers and project leaders that aim to create innovation on the basis of the cross-fertilization of technologies. In this regard, consideration of this relationship could be strategic for management and policy making in a cross-fertilized context (Markard and Truffer, 2006; Stirling, 2007; Schoen *et al.*, 2012). Therefore, in order to encourage this process and consequently to leverage innovation projects, this study suggests considering projects where: i) organizations can share technological knowledge, which should not be too similar or too diverse from their partners', ii) organizations can make strong efforts to obtain broad knowledge, iii) having access to external sources of information is considered important, iv) where the network could have an informal collaborative structure, v) with projects with high market orientation and vi) where customers could be prioritized as part of their innovation strategy. Neither a previous collaborative experience, nor an experience in higher levels of TRLs seemed to correspond with higher levels of cross-fertilization. Considering these aspects, new scientific policies and strategies could be reshaped to address and support the growing industrialization of emergent cross-fertilized KETs.

These implications have sought to contribute to a better understanding of regional systems of innovation, which are aimed at solving major economic and societal needs. Accordingly, this research is aligned with the knowledge-based economy speech, grounded in the optimal change of the productive matrix of a region through the development of technological activities and the social return of investments in science. It should be stressed that the objectives of this research are also aligned with a traditional expression in Quichua (native language of Ecuador), which is an ancestral community goal: "**SUMAK KAWSAY**", which means equity and quality of life for all citizens.

Additionally, the relevance of collaborative interaction and environmental factors associated with the success of a medicine-related emerging technology were highlighted in this work by consolidating several actors in a Five-Helix innovation model. This concept emphasizes the pressing need to ensure closer cooperation between engineers, physicians, project and innovation managers, technicians and researchers. It also represents a different perspective regarding innovation communities and open innovation literature.

Findings from this research could also have implications for evolutionary economics regarding technological diversity creation in innovation systems. The data once again supports the idea that the innovation system literature is connected with social network approaches. In this regard, it has been shown that external collaboration plays an important role in emerging technologies.

Moreover, this work makes an original methodological contribution, which is the implementation of the probabilistic text modeling method LDA for analyzing the degree of a project's multi-disciplinarity. Even though this method is well-accepted by the research community, text analyzes are less frequent and have not been used before for studying technological diversity. This fact notwithstanding, this is the first work to use topic modeling for analyzing technological diversity at nano-related European projects in a convergent scenario of technologies. Additionally, since project information has been used as the data source, this study offers a differentiated methodology compared with publications and patents, which have been the common source of data used for analyzing innovation. Therefore, this work has considered complementary techniques by drawing from the increasing power of machine learning and computation.

This study could be considered the starting point of future research activities. Initial factors to be considered are the sample size and the sample setting. The reduced sample size in the empirical section was the result of the conditions of inclusion which were considered. Consequently the claims generated are restricted specifically for this sample, and this fact restrains the generalization of the results. It is therefore suggested that future research could include a larger element of analysis in order to obtain more reliable results and statistical power.

Furthermore, establishing a European regional setting could be a strength, but could also be a weakness. It is a strength from a European policy perspective that aims to take into account the impact of such policies in the region. However, national and regional initiatives could be hindered in this respect. Moreover, because of the different national priorities regarding technological policies, not all of the actors participate with the same number of projects according to each country. Therefore, conclusions in this domain must be handled with care and in a regional context. Assumptions cannot be applied to the entire innovation ecosystem, or even further, outsourced to other systems. In this regard, future research could include national projects and consider national and regional initiatives in order to expand the scope of the research.

it Is doubtless that to include other ***application areas of nanotechnologies*** would be an interesting approach. Since nanotechnology benefits a broad range of fields, future research could include a comparative analysis of the challenges of this technology in different industries such as energy, agro-food, advanced materials, etc. Additionally, this study is suitable to be applied to other ***innovation ecosystems or networks.*** For instance, it could be applied to studying technological platforms (e.g., the Spanish Technology Platform on Nanomedicine), knowledge and innovation communities (e.g., the KIC Health from the European Institute of Technology), or other regional innovation systems (e.g., the Research Innovation Strategies for Smart Specialization RIS3Cat). In this context, the methodologies applied in this research could be practical for these purposes since they have been demonstrated to be appropriate for a better understanding of the technological and management perspectives of innovation in nanotechnologies and other emergent technologies.

References

Abdi, H. (2007). 'Multiple correspondence analysis', *Encyclopedia of measurement and statistics*, 95(2), pp. 116–28.

Abernathy, W. (1979). 'The productivity dilemma', *Batiment International, Building Research and Practice*, pp. 2–2.

Aschhoff, B. *et al.* (2010). 'European Competitiveness in Key Enabling Technologies'.

Australian Government (2012). *Enabling technology futures : a survey of the Australian technology landscape.*

Van den Bergh, J. C. J. M. (2008). 'Optimal diversity: Increasing returns versus recombinant innovation', *Journal of Economic Behavior and Organization*, 68(3–4), pp. 565–580.

Björkdahl, J. (2009). 'Technology cross-fertilization and the business model: The case of integrating ICTs in mechanical engineering products', *Research Policy*, 38(9), pp. 1468–1477.

Bjørn Larsen, P. (2011). *Cross-sectoral analysis of the impact of international industrial policy on Key Enabling Technologies - European Commission.*

Blei, D. M., Ng, A. Y. and Jordan, M. I. (2003). 'Latent dirichlet allocation', *The Journal of Machine Learning Research.* JMLR.org, 3, pp. 993–1022.

Butter, M. *et al.* (2014). *Horizon 2020: Key Enabling Technologies (KETs), Booster for European Leadership in the Manufacturing Sector. Study for the ITRE Committee.* Brussels, Belgium. 21 August 2015).

Chin, C. D., Linder, V. and Sia, S. K. (2012). 'Commercialization of microfluidic point-of-care diagnostic devices.', *Lab on a chip*, 12(12), pp. 2118–34.

Cooke, P., Gomez Uranga, M. and Etxebarria, G. (1997). 'Regional innovation systems: Institutional and organisational dimensions', *Research Policy*, 26(4–5), pp. 475–491.

Dang, Y. *et al.* (2010). 'Trends in worldwide nanotechnology patent applications: 1991 to 2008.', *Journal of nanoparticle research : an interdisciplinary forum for nanoscale science and technology*, 12(3), pp. 687–706.

Debackere, K. (2000). 'Managing academic R&D as a business at K.U. Leuven: context, structure and process', *R and D Management*, 30(4), pp. 323–328.

Edquist, C. (1997). 'Systems of innovation approaches - their emergence and characteristics', *Systems of Innovation: Technologies, Institutions and Organizations*, (1989), pp. 1–35.

Edquist, C. and Hommen, L. (1999). 'Systems of innovation: Theory and policy for the demand side', *Technology in Society*, 21(1), pp. 63–79.

European Commission (2009). *Preparing for our future: Developing a common strategy for key enabling technologies in the EU.* Brussels.

European Commission (2011). *Successful European Nanotechnology Research: Outstanding science and technology to match the needs of future society.* Brussels, Belgium.

European Commission (2012). *Regional Innovation Scoreboard 2012 Report.* Belgium.

European Commission (2014). *Key Enabling Technologies, Web page.*

European Commission (2015). 'HORIZON 2020 Work programme 2014 - 2015. Leadership in enabling and industrial technologies: ii . Nanotechnologies , Advanced Materials , Biotechnology and Advanced Manufacturing and Processing'.

Flynn, T. and Wei, C. (2005). 'The pathway to commercialization for nanomedicine.', *Nanomedicine : nanotechnology, biology, and medicine*, 1(1), pp. 47–51.

Frenken, K., Saviotti, P. P. and Trommetter, M. (1999). 'Variety and niche creation in aircraft, helicopters, motorcycles and microcomputers', *Research Policy*, 28(5), pp. 469–488.

Fu, B. E. *et al.* (2011). 'Perspective on Diagnostics for Global Health', *IEEE Pulse*, 2(6), pp. 40–50.

Gabellieri, C. and Frima, H. (2011). 'Nanomedicine in the European Commission policy for nanotechnology.', *Nanomedicine : nanotechnology, biology, and medicine*. Elsevier Inc., 7(5), pp. 519–20.

Gauch, S. and Blind, K. (2015). 'Technological convergence and the absorptive capacity of standardisation', *Technological Forecasting and Social Change*. Elsevier Inc., 91, pp. 236–249.

Hacklin, F., Marxt, C. and Fahrni, F. (2009). 'Coevolutionary cycles of convergence: An extrapolation from the ICT industry', *Technological Forecasting and Social Change*, 76(6), pp. 723–736.

Heide, M. De *et al.* (2013). 'Vision and characteristics of multi KETs pilot lines', (September), pp. 1–58.

Hekkert, M. P. *et al.* (2007). 'Functions of innovation systems: A new approach for analysing technological change', *Technological Forecasting and Social Change*, 74(4), pp. 413–432.

Husson, F., Lê, S. and Pagès, J. (2010). 'Exploratory Multivariate Analysis by Example using R', *Chapman & Hall/CRC Computer Science & Data Analysis*, 40(April), p. 240.

Jeong, S. and Lee, S. (2015). 'What drives technology convergence? Exploring the influence of technological and resource allocation contexts', *Journal of Engineering and Technology Management*, 36, pp. 78–96.

Jonard, N. and Yfldizoglu, M. (1998). 'Technological diversity in an evolutionary industry model with localized learning and network externalities', *Structural Change and Economic Dynamics*, 9(1995), pp. 35–53.

Juanola-Feliu, E. *et al.* (2012). 'Market challenges facing academic research in commercializing nano-enabled implantable devices for in-vivo biomedical analysis', *Technovation*, 32(3–4), pp. 193–204.

Katz, M. L. (1996). 'Remarks on the Economic Implications of Convergence', *Industrial and Corporate Change*, 5(4), pp. 1079–1095.

Kim, K.-H. *et al.* (2014). 'The structure of bio-information-nano technology convergence from firms' perspective', *Foresight*. Edited by D. Tugrul U. Daim. Emerald Group Publishing Limited, 16(3), pp. 270–288.

König, B. *et al.* (2013). 'A framework for structuring interdisciplinary research management', *Research Policy*, 42(1), pp. 261–272.

Lê, S., Josse, J. and Mazet, F. (2008). 'Package " FactoMineR "', *Journal of Statistical Software*, 25(1), pp. 1–18.

Linton, J. D. and Walsh, S. T. (2008). 'A theory of innovation for process-based innovations such as nanotechnology', *Technological Forecasting and Social Change*, 75(5), pp. 583–594.

Linton, J. D. and Walsh, S. T. (2008). 'Acceleration and Extension of Opportunity Recognition for Nanotechnologies and Other Emerging Technologies', *International Small Business Journal*, 26(1), pp. 83–99.

Mahroum, S. and Al-Saleh, Y. (2013). 'Towards a functional framework for measuring national innovation efficacy', *Technovation*. Elsevier, 33(10–11), pp. 320–332.

Maine, E. *et al.* (2014). 'The emergence of the nanobiotechnology industry.', *Nature nanotechnology*. Nature Publishing Group, 9(1), pp. 2–5.

Maine, E., Thomas, V. J. and Utterback, J. (2014). 'Radical innovation from the confluence of technologies: Innovation management strategies for the emerging nanobiotechnology industry', *Journal of Engineering and Technology Management*. Elsevier B.V., 32, pp. 1–25.

Mangematin, V. and Walsh, S. (2012). 'The future of nanotechnologies', *Technovation*, 32(3), pp. 157–160.

Markard, J. and Truffer, B. (2006). 'Innovation processes in large technical systems: Market liberalization as a driver for radical change?', *Research Policy*, 35(5), pp. 609–625.

Morrow Jr, Bawa, R. and Wei, C. (2007). 'Recent advances in basic and clinical nanomedicine.', *Medical Clinics of North America*, 91(5), pp. 805–843.

Motyl, B. and Filippi, S. (2014). 'Integration of Creativity Enhancement Tools in Medical Device Design Process', *Procedia Engineering*. Elsevier B.V., 69, pp. 1316–1325.

Murmann, J. P. and Frenken, K. (2006). 'Toward a systematic framework for research on dominant designs, technological innovations, and industrial change', *Research Policy*, 35(7), pp. 925–952.

Negro, S. O., Suurs, R. A. A. A. and Hekkert, M. P. (2008). 'The bumpy road of biomass gasification in the Netherlands: Explaining the rise and fall of an emerging innovation system', *Technological Forecasting and Social Change*, 75(1), pp. 57–77.

Neužil, P. *et al.* (2014). 'From chip-in-a-lab to lab-on-a-chip: towards a single handheld electronic system for multiple application-specific lab-on-a-chip (ASLOC).', *Lab on a chip*. Royal Society of Chemistry, 14(13), pp. 2168–76.

Nikulainen, T. and Palmberg, C. (2010). 'Transferring science-based technologies to industry—Does nanotechnology make a difference?', *Technovation*. Elsevier, 30(1), pp. 3–11.

Niosi, J. (2011). 'Building innovation systems: an introduction to the special section', *Industrial and Corporate Change*, 20(6), pp. 1637–1643.

No, H. J. and Park, Y. (2010). 'Trajectory patterns of technology fusion: Trend analysis and taxonomical grouping in nanobiotechnology', *Technological Forecasting and Social Change*, 77(1), pp. 63–75.

Organisation for Economic Co-operation and Development OECD (2014). *Challenges and Opportunities for Innovation through Technology: The Convergence of Technologies*.

Páez-Avilés, C., González-Piñero, M. and Juanola-Feliu, E. (2015). *Innovation by Cross-Cutting KETs. Technology Transfer and Commercialization Challenges for Nanobiotechnology and Nanomedicine*. LAP Lambert Academic Publishing.

Pandza, K., Wilkins, T. A. and Alfoldi, E. A. (2011). 'Collaborative diversity in a nanotechnology innovation system: Evidence from the EU Framework Programme', *Technovation*, 31(9), pp. 476–489.

Pautler, M. and Brenner, S. (2010). 'Nanomedicine: promises and challenges for the future of public health.', *International journal of nanomedicine*, 5, pp. 803–9.

Pavitt, K. (1998). 'The inevitable limits of EU R&D funding', *Research Policy*, 27(6), pp. 559–568.

Ponweiser, M. (2012) 'Latent Dirichlet Allocation in R', (May), pp. 2–21.

Porter, A. L. and Youtie, J. (2009). 'How interdisciplinary is nanotechnology?', *Journal of Nanoparticle Research*, 11(5), pp. 1023–1041.

Rafols, I. and Meyer, M. (2007). 'How cross-disciplinary is bionanotechnology? Explorations in the specialty of molecular motors', *Scientometrics*, 70(3), pp. 633–650.

Rafols, I. and Meyer, M. (2010). 'Diversity and network coherence as indicators of interdisciplinarity: case studies in bionanoscience', *Scientometrics*, 82(2), pp. 263–287.

Van Rijnsoever, F. J. *et al.* (2015). 'Smart innovation policy: How network position and project composition affect the diversity of an emerging technology', *Research Policy*. Elsevier B.V., 44(5), pp. 1094–1107.

Van Rijnsoever, F. J. and Hessels, L. K. (2011). 'Factors associated with disciplinary and interdisciplinary research collaboration', *Research Policy*, 40(3), pp. 463–472.

RNCOS (2013). *Nanotechnology Market Outlook 2017*.

Roco, M. (2003). 'Converging science and technology at the nanoscale: opportunities for education and training', *Nature Biotechnology*, 21(10), pp. 1247–1249.

Roco, M. (2011). 'The long view of nanotechnology development: the National Nanotechnology Initiative at 10 years', in *Nanotechnology Research Directions for Societal Needs in 2020*. Springer Netherlands, pp. 1–690.

Roco, M. C. and Bainbridge, W. S. (2005). 'Societal implications of nanoscience and nanotechnology: Maximizing human benefit', *Journal of Nanoparticle Research*, 7(1), pp. 1–13.

Rothaermel, F. T. and Thursby, M. (2007). 'The Nanotech vs. the biotech revolution: sources of productivity in incumbent firm research', *Research Policy*, 36(6), pp. 832–849.

Saviotti, P. P. and Metcalfe, J. S. (1984). 'A theoretical approach to the construction of technological output indicators', *Research Policy*, 13(3), pp. 141–151.

Schoen, A. *et al.* (2012). 'The Network Structure of Technological Developments ; Technological Distance as a Walk on the Technology Map', in *STI Conference*, pp. 734–742.

Schummer, J. (2004). 'Multidisciplinarity, interdisciplinarity, and patterns of research collaboration in nanoscience and nanotechnology', *Scientometrics*, 59(3), pp. 425–465.

Sedighi, M. (2013). 'Interdisciplinary relations in some high-priority fields of science and technology: An analytical study', *Library Review*, 62(6), pp. 407–419.

Stirling, A. (2007). 'A general framework for analysing diversity in science, technology and society.', *Journal of the Royal Society, Interface / the Royal Society*, 4(15), pp. 707–19.

Whitesides, G. (2006). 'The origins and the future of microfluidics', *Nature*, 442(7101), pp. 368–373.

You, Y.-B., Kim, B.-K. and Jeong, E.-S. (2014). 'An exploratory study on the development path of converging technologies using patent analysis: the case of nano biosensors', *Asian Journal of Technology Innovation*. Routledge, 22(1), pp. 100–113.

Chapter 27

Innovation Hubs in Africa: Assemblers of Technology Entrepreneurs

Nicolas Friederici*

E-mail: nicolas.friederici@oii.ox.ac.uk

Abstract: Innovation hub organizations—or 'hubs'—have become prevalent in Africa: about 170 hubs were established between 2010 and 2016. This thesis asks how African hubs work, specifically how they shape relationships among technology entrepreneurs. Literature on innovation intermediation and incubation is reviewed to establish a theoretical framework. In-depth case study data (including 119 interviews) on six hubs were collected in Kigali, Harare, and Accra in 2014. The thesis finds that the six analyzed hubs were defined by nested, fluidly bounded entrepreneurial communities. Four hubs focused on technological products while two promoted entrepreneurships as a cause. The thesis theorizes hubs as *assemblers* of technology entrepreneurs: hubs assemble previously distant and different actors into communities. Assembly is unique to hubs: it is different from incubation and most forms of intermediation. Assembly fills meso-level theory gaps in research on the organization of entrepreneurship, explaining the intersection between entrepreneurship support organizations and local contexts.

Keywords: innovation hubs; assembly; incubation; innovation intermediaries; entrepreneurial communities; entrepreneurial networking; entrepreneurial ecosystems; technology entrepreneurship; Africa.

1. Introduction

Innovation hub organizations have become a prevalent way of supporting technology entrepreneurship and grassroots innovation (Giaccone and Longo, 2015; Toivonen and Friederici, 2015; Bachmann, 2014). Hubs aim to enable individual technologists, entrepreneurs, and freelancers to innovate, network, and start businesses. In practice, hubs are small operations with a simple functional setup: they usually consist of a Wi-Fi-connected space with hot desks, used for laptop-based work, training and mentorship sessions, events, and small innovation competitions like hackathons. Funders and sponsors of hubs are extremely varied: they include development organizations, local governments, and technology corporations, but also grassroots interest groups and philanthropic foundations (Friederici, 2014a).

The global rise of hubs has happened in conjunction with the diffusion of similar organizational forms, including coworking spaces, open innovation and creative labs, and makerspaces (Gryszkiewicz et al., 2017; Schmidt and Brinks, 2017; Seo-Zindy and Heeks, 2017; Gandini, 2015; Merkel, 2015). There are also functional overlaps with more 'networked' and community-oriented versions of traditional intermediaries, such as hub-like universities or networked and bottom-up incubators (Bøllingtoft, 2012; Youtie and Shapira, 2008; Bøllingtoft and Ulhøi, 2005; Hansen et al., 2000). Yet, in contrast to incubators (Aerts et al., 2007; Hackett and Dilts, 2004), hubs are typically 'open,' meaning that entrepreneurs and innovators do not have to pass selection and are given maximum discretion over their work. Hubs also tend to support the very beginning of the entrepreneurial process (i.e., individuals with an idea or loosely formed teams) rather than ventures that are already incorporated as firms. While it is difficult to precisely delineate hubs from coworking spaces (Friederici, 2018a), hubs more explicitly connect entrepreneurs with other groups in entrepreneurial ecosystems, such as mentors, government, investors, and funders (Littlewood and Kiyumbu, 2017; Gryszkiewicz and Friederici, 2014; Friederici, 2014b).

Notwithstanding a lack of conceptual clarity, hubs have become immensely popular in Africa (Friederici, 2018b; Jiménez and Zheng, 2017; De Beer et al., 2017; Kelly and Firestone, 2016; Gathege and Moraa, 2013). Desk research exercises by the World Bank and the GSMA (a global association of mobile network operators) resulted in counts of 173 and 314 African hubs in 2016, with most established since 2010 (du Boucher, 2016; Firestone and Kelly, 2016). In early 2018, the GSMA updated its figure to as many as 443 active hubs in Africa (Bayen and Giuliani, 2018).

Despite hubs' small physical size and limited budgets, African hub funders and other proponents soon developed rather elaborate narratives about hubs' transformational outcomes (Friederici, 2018b, 2014a). These actors have argued that hubs are far "more than just a space to work" (e.g., Ofori, 2016), in that they strengthen 'collaboration,' 'openness,' 'community,' 'creativity,' and 'diversity,' thereby improving conditions in 'tech communities.' The 'hub' metaphor thus appears to be rooted in the expectation that hubs can be central nodes in wider networks, letting people interact who would not otherwise do so.

These visions have coalesced in a sanguine narrative about African hubs, which can be summarized as the *network infrastructure expectation*. Hubs are imagined to effectively and cogently create the kinds of support structures for technology entrepreneurs that are missing in African contexts. Hubs are imagined to form the foundation of 'knowledge economies,' 'digital economies,' or 'ecosystems' (AfriLabs, 2015; Bright and Hruby, 2015). Yet, not everyone has accepted this optimistic view. In particular, hubs have increasingly been grouped together with business incubators and accelerators (Firestone and Kelly, 2016; Essien, 2015; Baird et al., 2013; Gathege and Moraa, 2013). The resulting *incubator expectation* sees 'hub' simply as a new label for organizations that support early-stage ventures. This perspective does not care so much about what happens inside of hubs and instead focuses entirely on outcomes. Following from the analogy with incubators, the expectation concludes that hubs should also be assessed like incubators: by tracking the marginal increase in performance (survival, revenues, capital raised, etc.) of client companies (Amezcua et al., 2013; Sherman and Chappell, 1998). However, African hubs have rarely created wildly successful ventures, and consequently, some have considered them an outright failure and hopeless endeavor (Essien, 2015).

The doctoral thesis summarized in this chapter (Friederici, 2017) takes a step back from debates about whether African hubs work. Concretely, the thesis argues that we can neither assess nor should we assert, whether hubs work, as long as we do not understand *what hubs do* and *how they work*. The thesis thus embarks on an open-ended, rigorous, and grounded inquiry into the workings of African hubs, in order to ultimately inspect the merit of different expectations that have been advanced and to do away with some of the conceptual confusion which has followed an earlier period of hype and excitement. In addition, by studying a new organizational form, the thesis wants to test if prior theory on related forms is equipped to explain hubs, proposing theory extensions wherever gaps become apparent.

Given the newness of and uncertainty around the phenomenon, the thesis uses deliberately broad research questions which are refined following a review of pertinent academic literature:

1.   How are technology entrepreneurs in African cities experiencing and engaging with hubs?

2.   How do African hubs work?

Answers to these questions about African hubs also speak to wider and significant concerns of contemporary technology and innovation management:

• How can organizations effectively manage independent innovative individuals (e.g., entrepreneurs and technologists) without formally selecting and controlling them?

• How are open innovation management organizations affected by challenging contexts?

2. Background

The present thesis studies hubs as a new type of organization that recently emerged in Africa, serving to manage grassroots innovation. To guide the empirical inquiry and theory development, the thesis first reviews expectations about innovation hubs as an organizational form. In the absence of an established academic literature, the thesis begins by examining practitioners' understandings of hubs. The thesis develops both a relational and ideational theory of the organizational form "hub" (Ruef, 1999): it identifies practitioners' expressed expectations about how hubs work and what makes them unique, as well as the emergence of The Impact Hub as a global and iHub Nairobi as an Africa-wide ideal type. Through a review of online media, the dissertation further shows that practitioners' ideal-typical understanding of iHub translated into a broader expectation that hubs across the continent could function as transformative "network infrastructures" for Africa's fledgling digital economy. Yet, the review also shows that some commentators started to take a different stance, framing hubs as nothing but ineffective business incubators—and thus not a new organizational form at all.

The thesis then reviews academic literatures on innovation intermediation to capture the network infrastructure expectation (e.g., Sapsed et al., 2007; Howells, 2006; Hargadon and Sutton, 1997) and incubation to reflect the incubator expectation (e.g., Bruneel et al., 2012; Bøllingtoft and Ulhøi, 2005; Hackett and Dilts, 2004). Overlaps and differences between the literatures are used to develop a theoretical framework with the potential to explain processes in hubs. Overlaps between the intermediation/incubation literature include:

1. The supported entrepreneurial actor is a firm, specifically a venture/startup or small enterprise.

2. The venture and intermediary/incubator have a service provider-client relationship.

3. The relationship between client venture and intermediary/incubator is typically formally specified (e.g., through a service provision contract).

4. The intermediary/incubator brokers between client venture and third parties.

5. Third parties are external to the intermediary/incubator organization.

6. Client venture capacities interdepend with intermediation/incubation effectiveness.

7. Client venture capacities interdepend with intermediation/incubation service offerings.

8. Client ventures' openness or attitudes towards intermediation/incubation affect the effectiveness of the process.

9. Goals and influences of intermediary/incubator funders can conflict with those of clients.

10. Client venture selection affects intermediation/incubation effectiveness.

Beyond expectations that are consistent across intermediation and incubation research, the incubation literature includes several more specific and micro-level predictions, but which are divided into a venture creation and a dyadic view (see Table 27.). The incubation literature further points towards the notion of "community" (Bøllingtoft and Ulhøi, 2005; Phan et al., 2005; Peters et al., 2004), which resonates with practitioners' expectations towards African hubs.

Based on the review, the research questions are refined to sharpen the analysis towards potentially unique and non-trivial elements in hub processes. The first research question regarding entrepreneurs' perceptions of hubs is reformulated to reflect that entrepreneurs are actors, but hub organizations as well, and to more clearly understand how entrepreneurs enter a relationship with hubs:

1a. How do African hub organizations interact with technology entrepreneurs?

1b. How do technology entrepreneurs participate in African hub organizations?

The second research question is refocused on the facilitation of relationships for entrepreneurs, which both the intermediation and the incubation literature emphasize. Yet, differences between the literatures suggest that relations among supported entrepreneurs should be analytically distinguished from relations with external non-entrepreneurial actors (i.e., third parties in brokerage processes). A separate research question is devoted to the question of 'communities' in hubs, which was important in practitioner expectations but which intermediation and incubation literatures left largely undiscussed:

2a. How do African hub organizations enable relationships among technology entrepreneurs?

2b. How do African hub organizations enable relationships between technology entrepreneurs and non-entrepreneurial partners?

2c. Do African hub organizations create or enable entrepreneurial communities, and if so, how?

Table 27.1 Theoretical framework based on incubator/incubation literature

Organization or process feature	Incubator / incubation	
Goal	Venture creation or development is immediate goal	
Supported entrepreneurial actor Distinction of internal/external actors	Ventures, small enterprises Binary (in / out), stable: incubatee ventures are internal, third parties are external	
Entry of entrepreneurs in process	Selection from among applicant ventures conducted by the incubator	
Means to determine entrepreneur status	Formal agreement (e.g., service provision contract)	
Facilitation of interactions with non-entrepreneurial actors	Directed brokerage (creation of a link between venture and external partners by incubator/staff)	
Services	Office/work space, business assistance, networking / brokerage of connections between startups and external partners by the incubator (or its manager)	
Organization or process feature	**Venture creation view**	**Dyadic / community view**
Process differentiation by entrepreneurs	Standardized staff-guided process	Staff-guided process adapted to incubatee (e.g., maturity)
Relationship between organization's staff and entrepreneur	Unidirectional relationship from incubator staff to venture	Interactive relationship between incubator staff and venture
Relationships among entrepreneurs	Incubatees independent from each other	Community of incubatees
Control over process	Incubator staff determine incubation	Incubatees shape incubation together with incubator staff
Boundary towards environment	Formally bounded towards external business community	Networks of incubatees reach across boundary of the incubator

3. Research design

The research goals for the thesis were to, first, establish descriptive evidence on African hubs as a new phenomenon, and second, theorize the innovation management process in hubs. To achieve both research goals (description and theory building), in-depth comparative case studies are chosen as methodology (Yin, 2009; Eisenhardt, 1989). Accra (Ghana), Kigali (Rwanda), and Harare (Zimbabwe) are selected as least-similar contexts (Bennett, 2004): contextual variation is increased as much as possible to maximize generalizability for those processes that are identified across all analyzed hub cases. The previously discussed hub ideal types (Impact Hub and iHub Nairobi) are then crystallized into a working definition of hubs, using only clearly observable organizational features. Based on the definition, six hub cases are sampled, incidentally two per city.

Data collection was conducted in line with key concepts in the research questions and theoretical framework. These suggested a focus on interpersonal relations of entrepreneurs and on small-scale social structures. Yet, the literatures underlying the framework cut across entrepreneurship, innovation management, innovation studies, and economic geography, leading to ambiguity regarding the appropriate level of analysis and implied understandings of structure and agency (cf., Phan et al., 2005). Accordingly, the dissertation takes care to develop a coherent analytical lens that can capture interpersonal relationship formation and the resulting structures across the city / contextual and organizational levels of analysis (Scott and Davis, 2016).

Drawing from a recent study with similar analytical issues (Marti et al., 2013), the thesis engages the sociological tradition of symbolic interactionism (Hallett, 2010; Hallett and Ventresca, 2006) to derive a micro-social interactionist lens (Blumer, 1986) that can guide data collection and analysis. Through this lens, all relevant units of analysis (actions, interpersonal ties, communities, organizations, contextual factors, etc.) are captured as per how they are interpreted and perceived as meaningful by individuals. Thereby, the thesis introduces a clear theory of individual and collective action, where individuals engage in "interpretative interaction" to "fit[] together their lines of action to one another," with "joint or collective action [as] an outcome of such a process of interpretative action" (Blumer, 1986, p. 16). Social structures are crystallizations of collectively enacted relationships, entrenched by repeated, compatible, "transindividual consistencies in action" (Martin, 2009, p. 5). Organizations are those social structures that have an explicit purpose as well as identity and actor qualities (Scott and Davis, 2016; King et al., 2010). "Organizationality" is a matter of degree; for instance, not every community is an organization, but communities can be equivalent or equifinal to organizations when they serve to pursue collective goals and/or develop actor qualities (Dobusch and Schoeneborn, 2015).

In sum, the thesis detects that innovation intermediary and incubator literatures lack a sufficiently rich theory of collective action and organization to answer the present research questions, and thus mobilizes foundational and recent organizational sociology to make up for these shortcomings.

Data collection thus focused on in-depth interviews, in which participants were asked about their ties to and interpretations of other social entities (hubs, incubators, associations, communities, etc.). Sampling focused on hub managers as well as hub-affiliated and unaffiliated individual technology entrepreneurs: they would be the main intended members (or clients) of African hubs, while supporting actors (mentors, investors, sponsors, etc.) were likely to play a more peripheral role. Interviews with 133 participants were conducted, roughly half being technology entrepreneurs and half hub staff and other support actors.

4. Conclusion

The dissertation derives rich empirical results, presented in one case study chapter and two results chapters. For each hub, case studies document the founding stage, participation dynamics, and managerial adaptations. They also outline differences between Kigali, Harare, and Accra as hub contexts.

The first results chapter presents the social structure of African hubs as an organizational form, generalized from the six cases. The chapter shows that entrepreneurs fall into three participation categories: *kernels of community*, *apprentices*, and *networkers*. As a result, hubs' overall social structure has nested levels: a *core community* of mostly novice entrepreneurs is enclosed by a *peripheral community* of various other technology entrepreneurship stakeholders. Internally and externally, the social structure of hubs is fluidly bounded (Schreyögg and Sydow, 2010), meaning that community members move towards or away from the core based on continual decisions as to what degree of engagement provides them with benefits. The boundary around core communities is stronger, while the boundary around peripheral communities is weaker and mostly symbolic (Scott, 2004; Lamont and Molnár, 2002). Fluid boundaries are permeable but have tangible social roles, namely to allow for routinized interaction and establish social norms (e.g., informal hierarchies and membership rules) within or across a given boundary (Brint, 2001).

The second results chapter presents variation in the social structures of the six hubs. Notably, communities varied by their level of *activation*: members of active communities had concern for each other and recognized communities as social entities, while members of inactive communities only shared a loose purpose. The chapter highlights distinct collective advantages of active communities (such as members' willingness to make sacrifices) and suggests community activation as an essential outcome of innovation management processes in hubs. In turn, the analyzed hubs facilitated different community levels and different kinds of interaction contents. The six hubs could be distinguished as *technology hubs* (depending on active core communities) and *entrepreneurship hubs* (relying on active peripheral communities). Communities in technology hubs reflected a focus on technical knowledge exchange; for instance, individual members co-specialized in coding languages, felt strong occupational identities (e.g., as software engineers), and had a clear sense of hierarchies based on seniority and expertise (Bailetti, 2012; Benner, 2003). In entrepreneurship hubs, hierarchical thinking was explicitly discouraged while inspiration and entrepreneurship promotion were emphasized. Entrepreneurship hubs thus depended on more general and lightweight entrepreneurial commitment, and thus stabilized more easily.

Building on the two results chapters, the thesis then proposes a generalized theory of the innovation management process in African hubs. Namely, it provides an explanatory account of how the identified social structures (core and peripheral communities with different interaction content and varying levels of activation) came into being, and how managerial action affected them. The thesis theorizes hubs as *assemblers of technology entrepreneurs*. 'Assembly' is used to connote a process of construction and gathering. As assemblers, hubs construct new social entities by gathering otherwise dispersed constituents: entrepreneurs and partners (mentors, support organizations, etc.) who are cognitively different or distant (i.e., they lack mutual awareness or have different knowledge and capacities). This implies that hubs are inherently limited by who and what is available in local contexts: a hub without access to capable and complementary entrepreneurs will be ineffective. Assembly consists of three mechanisms rooted in hubs' organizational action. First, hubs create an occasion for interactions between certain actor groups, thereby increasing the chance that relations get established (*convening*). Second, hubs explicitly encourage and facilitate particular relationships that would otherwise be more difficult or costly for members to establish (*interconnecting*). Third, hubs allow community formation based on members' mutual concern, sustained interactions, and shared meaning (*activating*). Assembly is triggered by a combination of typical organizational features of hubs, such as a freely usable coworking space, facilitative rather than interventionist hub manager engagement, and an open usage policy.

5. Implications and future research

Theory Implications

Assembly is conceptually positioned as a sub-form of innovation intermediation that is related to but different from brokerage and incubation (see

Table 27.2). Based on hub cases in Kenya, similar results were later produced by Littlewood and Kiyumbu (2017), providing further validation for
assembly theory. More broadly, the thesis shows that prior innovation intermediation literature lacks a sufficiently rich theory of organization, for
instance, regarding organizational boundaries and supra-individual entities
like communities. The use of a micro-social interactionist lens allowed the
thesis to identify heterogeneity in interaction contents and in the kinds of
social structures that hubs formed—elements which prior intermediation
literature had ignored. The thesis thus challenges innovation intermediation's implicit reductionist assumption that social structures should always
be understood as networks (Tran et al., 2011; Kirkels and Duysters, 2010;
Howells, 2006). It also extends sparse existing literature on how intra- and
extra-organizational dynamics overlap and influence each other in intermediation processes (Boari and Riboldazzi, 2014; Sapsed et al., 2007). Similarly, it sets a foundation for richer environmental contingency theory for
incubation literature (Mian et al., 2016; Phan et al., 2005). Relatedly, assembly represents an extension and integration of a scattered literature on the
role of organizations in shaping networks of individual entrepreneurs (Marti et al., 2013; Bøllingtoft and Ulhøi, 2005; Thornton and Flynn, 2003; Johannisson et al., 1994).

Table 27.2 Differences between broker-type intermediaries, incubators, and hubs

Differences between intermediaries/incubators and hubs		
Organizational feature	*Intermediary or incubator*	*Hub / assembly*
Relationship between organization and entrepreneur	Service provider—client	Community—member
Means to determine entrepreneur status	Formal agreement (e.g., service provision contract)	Informal agreement (e.g., regular attendance of events)
Distinction of inter-nal/external actors	Binary (in / out), stable	Continuous (degree), dynamic
Supported entrepre-neurial actor	Ventures, small enterprises	Individual novice entrepreneurs, newly formed teams
Facilitation of interactions	Directed (creation of a link between two specific others)	Directed and undirected (members initiate inter-actions but hub provides occasion)

Differences between broker-type intermediaries/brokerage and hubs/assembly		
Organizational feature	*Broker / brokerage*	*Hub / assembly*
Boundedness towards entrepreneurs	Intermediary and client organization are separate	Member becomes part of hub organization
Connecting different and distant actors	Client "plugs into" network of broker	Integrating actors into entrepreneurial community
Differences between incubators and hubs		
Organizational feature	*Incubator / incubation*		*Hub / assembly*
	Venture creation view	*Dyadic view*	
Goal	Venture creation or development is immediate goal		Venture creation or development is ultimate goal
Entry of entrepreneurs	Selection by the incubator		Self-selection by entrepreneurs
Process differentiation by entrepreneurs	Staff-guided, standardized	Staff-guided, adapted to incubatee	Idiosyncratic, largely entrepreneur-led process
Relationship between organization's staff and entrepreneur	Unidirectional from incubator staff to venture	Interactive	Interactive
Relationships among entrepreneurs	Independent incubatees	Community of incubatees	Core and peripheral community of members
Control over process	Incubator staff determine incubation	Incubatees shape incubation together with incubator staff	Entrepreneurs shape assembly process, hub staff loosely facilitate
Boundary towards environment	Formally bounded	Networks of incubatees reach outside of incubator	Fluidly bounded, peripheral community blends in with external environment

Assembly also contributes to a fragmented literature on entrepreneurial and professional communities (Marti et al., 2013; Fleming and Waguespack, 2007; Benner, 2003). Assembly builds on the communities-of-practice concept (Brown and Duguid, 1991, 2001), but also responds to critique (Grugulis and Stoyanova, 2011; Amin and Roberts, 2008; Roberts, 2006) by highlighting diversity in the nature, social functions, and strength of entrepreneurial communities. For instance, the thesis shows that core/localized communities can be more conducive to tacit and specialized knowledge exchange and to collaboration, while peripheral/city-wide communities may facilitate instrumental information exchanges and cognitive outcomes such as inspiration. Further, it illustrates that occupational identity is but one possible social bond: communities can also be assembled from diverse occupational groups as long as some shared purpose unites participants and enables their mutual concern. Most significantly, assembly offers a processual account of community formation, showing how communities are formed in the image of mental models, and then nurtured through combined and interdependent organizational and individual actions.

Practical Implications

The dissertation also informs practice. Namely, it points to a number of managerial issues arising from hubs' openness (that is, the fact that membership is self-selected). First, leaders of hubs and similar organizations have to be intimately familiar with entrepreneurial capacities and motivations in local contexts, and they need to mobilize participation where it is not forthcoming. Furthermore, contrary to hub funders' assertions that hubs are particularly "diverse," membership can be increasingly homogeneous over time, leading to cliques and exclusion of newcomers. In the same vein, the thesis flags self-selected membership in open organizations as a self-reinforcing mechanisms which can lead organizational change to become path-dependent (Schreyögg and Sydow, 2011; Sydow et al., 2009). This can result in lock-in effects in community formation, which hub funders and managers may be unable to control. Finally, the dissertation warns that measuring hubs' contribution to economic development is extremely difficult. The thesis instead provides practitioners with a list of guiding principles for the management of infrastructural organizations (like hubs) as opposed to interventionist ones (like incubators).

Future Research

This thesis shows important intersections between organizational research and key concepts from economic geography, such as geographically concentrated knowledge creation (Howells, 2012), anchor organizations (Agrawal and Cockburn, 2003), and buzz (Bathelt et al., 2004; Storper and Venables, 2004). The thesis highlights that organizational mechanisms (such as assembly) often underlie macro-level system concepts from economic geography. Much more work on such mechanisms is needed.

The thesis also demonstrated that organizational forms need to be more closely linked to processes in intermediation and incubation research. It suggested that intermediation and incubation were too widely defined and too ambiguous to discern between processes which differ in substantive ways.

For incubation research, the thesis highlighted a contradiction: despite increasing acknowledgment that entrepreneurs shape the incubation process together with incubator managers, incubator typologies continue to rely on service models which assume a one-sided and controlled incubation process. Future studies can thus learn from this thesis by focusing on differences between processes (at a granular analytical level), not between service models, to distinguish between intermediary and incubator organizations. The thesis suggests that comparing processes could yield more meaningful typologies, which will help manage expectations about what a particular organizational form can deliver and how it should be assessed.

A cross-disciplinary inquiry into organizational forms of innovation management could also address the question why certain forms begin to exist, and why they diffuse to some places more than to others. Incubators' existence is usually explained through some notion of market failure (Phan et al., 2005). In contrast to market failure arguments, the thesis included hints that an institutional reasoning might provide better answers to the question why hubs exist in Africa. It demonstrated, for instance, that hubs, at the time of implementation, were anything but a proven, functional tool to achieve a predetermined goal. Instead, African hubs appeared to be established based on aspirations to re-create role model hubs. Yet, ultimately, African hubs appeared to rarely work like the role models because locally specific implementation constraints came in the way. For future research, the thesis thus points to an interesting tension between an isomorphism of models versus a divergence in actualized processes across different contexts. An institutional theory lens could help capture how models get transferred and translated to different contexts (Dalpiaz and Tracey, 2013).

Thesis Originality and Conclusion

In sum, the dissertation summarized in this chapter is an original and compelling piece of organizational and innovation management research, breaking analytical ground in at least four ways. First, the dissertation proposes an empirically grounded and detailed original theory of how organizational and individual actions co-construct entrepreneurial communities. Second, by focusing on Africa, the thesis departs from most previous studies of technology innovation and entrepreneurship, which have focused almost exclusively on success stories in the Global North. Third, the thesis uses foundational organizational sociology to analytically connect and show parallels among a number of scattered phenomenon-driven studies from varied academic fields. Fourth, the thesis diligently executes a challenging theory development process, including a number of conceptual innovations, to explain a new phenomenon with fuzzy organizational and geographical boundaries.

Through these unique contributions, the thesis shows that hubs have been critically misunderstood. Hubs are indeed an exciting new type of innovation management organization, with the potential to assemble vibrant entrepreneurial communities. Yet, organizations like hubs depend on capable and motivated entrepreneurs in local contexts, leading to crucial limitations outside of hub managers' control. For research, this means that future theories must better explain the interplay of managerial visions, entrepreneurial actions, and contexts. For practice, organizational leaders must become aware of contextual limitations, and perfect curational strategies rather than insisting on control.

References

Adler, P. S. (2001). 'Market, Hierarchy, and Trust: The Knowledge Economy and the Future of Capitalism', *Organization Science*, vol. 12, no. 2, pp. 215–234 [Online]. DOI: 10.1287/orsc.12.2.215.10117.

Aerts, K., Matthyssens, P. and Vandenbempt, K. (2007). 'Critical role and screening practices of European business incubators', *Technovation*, vol. 27, no. 5, pp. 254–267 [Online]. DOI: 10.1016/j.technovation.2006.12.002.

AfriLabs (2015). *AfriLabs* [Online]. Available at http://afrilabs.com (Accessed 17 August 2015).

Agrawal, A. and Cockburn, I. (2003). 'The anchor tenant hypothesis: exploring the role of large, local, R&D-intensive firms in regional innovation systems', *International Journal of Industrial Organization*, The economics of intellectual property at universities, vol. 21, no. 9, pp. 1227–1253 [Online]. DOI: 10.1016/S0167-7187(03)00081-X.

Amezcua, A. S., Grimes, M. G., Bradley, S. W. and Wiklund, J. (2013). 'Organizational Sponsorship and Founding Environments: A Contingency View on the Survival of Business-Incubated Firms, 1994–2007', *Academy of Management Journal*, vol. 56, no. 6, pp. 1628–1654 [Online]. DOI: 10.5465/amj.2011.0652.

Amin, A. and Roberts, J. (2008). 'Knowing in action: Beyond communities of practice', *Research Policy*, vol. 37, no. 2, pp. 353–369 [Online]. DOI: 10.1016/j.respol.2007.11.003.

Bachmann, M. (2014). 'How the Hub Found Its Center', *Stanford Social Innovation Review* [Online]. Available at http://ssir.org/articles/entry/how_the_hub_found_its_center (Accessed 13 July 2016).

Bailetti, T. (2012). 'Technology Entrepreneurship: Overview, Definition, and Distinctive Aspects', *Technology Innovation Management Review*, vol. 2, no. 2, pp. 5–12.

Baird, R., Bowles, L. and Lall, S. (2013). *Bridging the "Pioneer Gap": The Role of Accelerators in Launching High-Impact Enterprises*, Aspen Network of Development Entrepreneurs & Village Capital.

Bathelt, H., Malmberg, A. and Maskell, P. (2004). 'Clusters and knowledge: local buzz, global pipelines and the process of knowledge creation', *Progress in Human Geography*, vol. 28, no. 1, pp. 31–56 [Online]. DOI: 10.1191/0309132504ph469oa.

Bayen, M. and Giuliani, D. (2018). '1000 Tech Hubs are Powering Ecosystems in Asia Pacific and Africa', *GSMA Mobile for Development* [Online]. Available at https://www.gsma.com/mobilefordevelopment/programme/ecosystem-accelerator/1000-tech-hubs-are-powering-ecosystems-in-asia-pacific-and-africa (Accessed 20 March 2018).

Benner, C. (2003). 'Learning communities in a learning region: the soft infrastructure of cross-firm learning networks in Silicon Valley', *Environment and Planning A*, vol. 35, no. 10, pp. 1809–1830 [Online]. DOI: 10.1068/a35238.

Bennett, A. (2004). 'Case Study Methods: Design, Use, and Comparative Advantages', in Sprinz, D. F. and Wolinsky-Nahmias, Y. (eds), *Models, Numbers, and Cases: Methods for Studying International Relations*, University of Michigan Press, pp. 19–48.

Blumer, H. (1986). *Symbolic Interactionism: Perspective and Method*, University of California Press [Online]. Available at http://www.amazon.ca/exec/obidos/redirect?tag=citeulike09-20&path=ASIN/0520056760 (Accessed 7 July 2016).

Boari, C. and Riboldazzi, F. (2014). 'How knowledge brokers emerge and evolve: The role of actors' behaviour', *Research Policy*, vol. 43, no. 4, pp. 683–695 [Online]. DOI: 10.1016/j.respol.2014.01.007.

Bøllingtoft, A. (2012). 'The bottom-up business incubator: Leverage to networking and cooperation practices in a self-generated, entrepreneurial-enabled environment', *Technovation*, vol. 32, no. 5, pp. 304–315 [Online]. DOI: 10.1016/j.technovation.2011.11.005.

Bøllingtoft, A. and Ulhøi, J. P. (2005). 'The networked business incubator—leveraging entrepreneurial agency?', *Journal of Business Venturing*, vol. 20, no. 2, pp. 265–290 [Online]. DOI: 10.1016/j.jbusvent.2003.12.005.

du Boucher, V. (2016). 'A few things we learned about tech hubs in Africa and Asia', *GSMA Mobile for Development* [Online]. Available at http://www.gsma.com/mobilefordevelopment/programme/ecosystem-accelerator/things-learned-tech-hubs-africa-asia (Accessed 3 September 2016).

Bright, J. and Hruby, A. (2015). 'The Rise Of Silicon Savannah And Africa's Tech Movement', *TechCrunch* [Online]. Available at http://social.techcrunch.com/2015/07/23/the-rise-of-silicon-savannah-and-africas-tech-movement/ (Accessed 28 October 2015).

Brint, S. (2001). 'Gemeinschaft Revisited: A Critique and Reconstruction of the Community Concept', *Sociological Theory*, vol. 19, no. 1, pp. 1–23 [Online]. DOI: 10.1111/0735-2751.00125.

Brown, J. S. and Duguid, P. (1991). 'Organizational Learning and Communities-of-Practice: Toward a Unified View of Working, Learning, and Innovation', *Organization Science*, vol. 2, no. 1, pp. 40–57 [Online]. DOI: 10.1287/orsc.2.1.40.

Brown, J. S. and Duguid, P. (2001). 'Knowledge and Organization: A Social-Practice Perspective', *Organization Science*, vol. 12, no. 2, pp. 198–213 [Online]. DOI: 10.1287/orsc.12.2.198.10116.

Bruneel, J., Ratinho, T., Clarysse, B. and Groen, A. (2012). 'The Evolution of Business Incubators: Comparing demand and supply of business incubation services across different incubator generations', *Technovation*, vol. 32, no. 2, pp. 110–121 [Online]. DOI: 10.1016/j.technovation.2011.11.003.

Dalpiaz, E. and Tracey, P. (2013). 'New venture creation and the use of cultural resources: The case of H-Farm', *Academy of Management Proceedings*, vol. 2013, no. 1, p. 10455 [Online]. DOI: 10.5465/AMBPP.2013.10455abstract.

De Beer, J., Millar, P., Mwangi, J., Nzomo, V. B. and Rutenberg, I. (2017). 'A Framework for Assessing Technology Hubs in Africa', *NYU Journal of Intellectual Property & Entertainment Law*, vol. 6, no. 2 [Online]. Available at http://jipel.law.nyu.edu/author/jeremydebeer/ (Accessed 16 May 2017).

Dobusch, L. and Schoeneborn, D. (2015). 'Fluidity, Identity, and Organizationality: The Communicative Constitution of Anonymous', *Journal of Management Studies*, vol. 52, no. 8, pp. 1005–1035 [Online]. DOI: 10.1111/joms.12139.

Eisenhardt, K. M. (1989). 'Building Theories from Case Study Research', *Academy of Management Review*, vol. 14, no. 4, pp. 532–550 [Online]. DOI: 10.5465/AMR.1989.4308385.

Essien, M. (2015). 'Startup Incubators in Africa and why they don't work', *Venture Capital for Africa* [Online]. Available at https://vc4africa.biz/blog/2015/04/21/startup-incubators-in-africa-and-why-they-dont-work/ (Accessed 13 January 2016).

Firestone, R. and Kelly, T. (2016). 'The Importance of Mapping Tech Hubs in Africa, and beyond', *Information and Communications for Development* [Online]. Available at http://blogs.worldbank.org/ic4d/importance-mapping-tech-hubs-africa-and-beyond (Accessed 1 September 2016).

Fleming, L. and Waguespack, D. M. (2007). 'Brokerage, Boundary Spanning, and Leadership in Open Innovation Communities', *Organization Science*, vol. 18, no. 2, pp. 165–180 [Online]. DOI: 10.1287/orsc.1060.0242.

Friederici, N. (2014a). *The Business Models of mLabs and mHubs: An Evaluation of infoDev's Mobile Innovation Support Pilots*, Washington, DC, infoDev, World Bank [Online]. Available at http://www.infodev.org/mobilebusinessmodels.

Friederici, N. (2014b). 'More Art than Science? Exploring the Roles of Technology Innovation Hubs for Urban Regions in Developing Countries', Valencia, Spain, Social Science Research Network [Online]. Available at https://papers.ssrn.com/abstract=3123868 (Accessed 10 April 2018).

Friederici, N. (2017). 'Innovation Hubs in Africa: Assemblers of Technology Entrepreneurs', Dissertation, Oxford, UK, Oxford Internet Institute, University of Oxford [Online]. Available at https://ora.ox.ac.uk/objects/uuid:2e5c9248-15b4-450a-958a-0ce87cf6e263.

Friederici, N. (2018a). 'Taking Stock of Innovation Hubs Literature, Plus Three Working Papers', *The Connectivity, Inclusion, and Inequality Group* [Online]. Available at http://cii.oii.ox.ac.uk/2018/02/14/taking-stock-of-innovation-hubs-literature-plus-three-working-papers/ (Accessed 10 April 2018).

Friederici, N. (2018b). 'Hope and Hype in Africa's Digital Economy: The Rise of Innovation Hubs', in Graham, M. (ed), *Digital Economies at Global Margins*, Boston, MA, USA, MIT Press.

Gandini, A. (2015). 'The rise of coworking spaces: A literature review', *Ephemera*, vol. 15, no. 1, pp. 193–205.

Gathege, D. and Moraa, H. (2013). *Draft Report On Comparative Study On Innovation Hubs Across Africa*, Nairobi, iHub Research [Online]. Available at http://research.ihub.co.ke/uploads/2013/may/1367840837__923.pdf.

Giaccone, S. C. and Longo, M. C. (2015). 'Insights on the innovation hub's design and management', *International Journal of Technology Marketing*, vol. 11, no. 1, pp. 97–119 [Online]. DOI: 10.1504/IJTMKT.2016.073318.

Grugulis, I. and Stoyanova, D. (2011). 'The missing middle: communities of practice in a freelance labour market', *Work, Employment & Society*, vol. 25, no. 2, pp. 342–351 [Online]. DOI: 10.1177/0950017011398891.

Gryszkiewicz, L. and Friederici, N. (2014). 'Learning from innovation hubs: fluidity, serendipity and community combined', *InnovationManagement.se* [Online]. Available at http://www.innovationmanagement.se/2014/12/15/learning-from-innovation-hubs-fluidity-serendipity-and-community-combined/.

Gryszkiewicz, L., Lykourentzou, I. and Toivonen, T. (2017). 'Innovation labs: leveraging openness for radical innovation?', *Journal of Innovation Management*, vol. 4, no. 4, pp. 68–97.

Hackett, S. M. and Dilts, D. M. (2004). 'A Systematic Review of Business Incubation Research', *The Journal of Technology Transfer*, vol. 29, no. 1, pp. 55–82 [Online]. DOI: 10.1023/B:JOTT.0000011181.11952.0f.

Hallett, T. (2010). 'The Myth Incarnate Recoupling Processes, Turmoil, and Inhabited Institutions in an Urban Elementary School', *American Sociological Review*, vol. 75, no. 1, pp. 52–74 [Online]. DOI: 10.1177/0003122409357044.

Hallett, T. and Ventresca, M. J. (2006). 'Inhabited Institutions: Social Interactions and Organizational Forms in Gouldner's Patterns of Industrial Bureaucracy', *Theory and Society*, vol. 35, no. 2, pp. 213–236 [Online]. DOI: 10.1007/s11186-006-9003-z.

Hansen, M. T., Chesbrough, H. W., Nohria, N. and Sull, D. N. (2000). 'Networked incubators. Hothouses of the new economy', *Harvard Business Review*, vol. 78, no. 5, pp. 74–84, 199.

Hargadon, A. and Sutton, R. I. (1997). 'Technology Brokering and Innovation in a Product Development Firm', *Administrative Science Quarterly*, vol. 42, no. 4, pp. 716–749 [Online]. DOI: 10.2307/2393655.

Howells, J. (2006). 'Intermediation and the role of intermediaries in innovation', *Research Policy*, vol. 35, no. 5, pp. 715–728 [Online]. DOI: 10.1016/j.respol.2006.03.005.

Howells, J. (2012). 'The geography of knowledge: never so close but never so far apart', *Journal of Economic Geography*, vol. 12, no. 5, pp. 1003–1020 [Online]. DOI: 10.1093/jeg/lbs027.

Jiménez, A. and Zheng, Y. (2017). 'Tech hubs, innovation and development', *Information Technology for Development*, vol. 0, no. 0, pp. 1–24 [Online]. DOI: 10.1080/02681102.2017.1335282.

Johannisson, B., Alexanderson, O., Nowicki, K. and Senneseth, K. (1994) 'Beyond anarchy and organization: entrepreneurs in contextual networks', *Entrepreneurship & Regional Development*, vol. 6, no. 4, pp. 329–356 [Online]. DOI: 10.1080/08985629400000020.

Kelly, T. and Firestone, R. (2016). *How Tech Hubs are helping to Drive Economic Growth in Africa*, Background Paper for the World Development Report 2016: Digital Dividends, Washington, DC, The World Bank [Online]. Available at https://openknowledge.worldbank.org/bitstream/handle/10986/23645/WDR 16-BP-How-Tech-Hubs-are-helping-to-Drive-Economic-Growth-in-Africa-Kelly-Firestone.pdf.

King, B. G., Felin, T. and Whetten, D. A. (2010). 'Perspective—Finding the Organization in Organizational Theory: A Meta-Theory of the Organization as a Social Actor', *Organization Science*, vol. 21, no. 1, pp. 290–305 [Online]. DOI: 10.1287/orsc.1090.0443.

Kirkels, Y. and Duysters, G. (2010). 'Brokerage in SME networks', *Research Policy*, vol. 39, no. 3, pp. 375–385 [Online]. DOI: 10.1016/j.respol.2010.01.005.

Lamont, M. and Molnár, V. (2002). 'The Study of Boundaries in the Social Sciences', *Annual Review of Sociology*, vol. 28, pp. 167–195.

Littlewood, D. C. and Kiyumbu, W. L. (2017) '"Hub" organisations in Kenya: What are they? What do they do? And what is their potential?', *Technological Forecasting and Social Change* [Online]. DOI: 10.1016/j.techfore.2017.09.031 (Accessed 6 February 2018).

Marti, I., Courpasson, D. and Dubard Barbosa, S. (2013). '"Living in the fishbowl". Generating an entrepreneurial culture in a local community in Argentina', *Journal of Business Venturing*, vol. 28, no. 1, pp. 10–29 [Online]. DOI: 10.1016/j.jbusvent.2011.09.001.

Martin, J. L. (2009). *Social structures*, Princeton, N.J., Princeton University Press [Online]. Available at http://public.eblib.com/choice/publicfullrecord.aspx?p=675884 (Accessed 11 February 2016).

Merkel, J. (2015). 'Coworking in the city', *ephemera: theory & politics in organization*, vol. 15, no. 1, pp. 121–139.

Mian, S. A., Lamine, W. and Fayolle, A. (2016). 'Technology Business Incubation: An overview of the state of knowledge', *Technovation*, Technology Business Incubation, vol. 50–51, pp. 1–12 [Online]. DOI: 10.1016/j.technovation.2016.02.005.

Ofori, O. (2016). 'hapaSpace is the newest co-working hub in Kumasi', *The African Dream* [Online]. Available at http://www.theafricandream.net/habaspace-is-the-newest-coworking-hub-in-kumasi/ (Accessed 3 September 2016).

O'Mahony, S. and Lakhani, K. R. (2011). 'Organizations in the Shadow of Communities', in Marquis, C., Lounsbury, M. D., and Greenwood, R. (eds), *Communities and Organizations*, Emerald Group Publishing Limited, vol. 33, pp. 3–36.

Peters, L., Rice, M. P. and Sundararajan, M. (2004). 'The Role of Incubators in the Entrepreneurial Process', *The Journal of Technology Transfer*, vol. 29, no. 1, pp. 83–91 [Online]. DOI: 10.1023/B:JOTT.0000011182.82350.df.

Phan, P. H., Siegel, D. S. and Wright, M. (2005). 'Science parks and incubators: observations, synthesis and future research', *Journal of Business Venturing*, Special Issue on Science Parks and Incubators, vol. 20, no. 2, pp. 165–182 [Online]. DOI: 10.1016/j.jbusvent.2003.12.001.

Roberts, J. (2006). 'Limits to Communities of Practice', *Journal of Management Studies*, vol. 43, no. 3, pp. 623–639 [Online]. DOI: 10.1111/j.1467-6486.2006.00618.x.

Ruef, M. (1999). 'Social Ontology and the Dynamics of Organizational Forms: Creating Market Actors in the Healthcare Field, 1966–1994', *Social Forces*, vol. 77, no. 4, pp. 1403–1432 [Online]. DOI: 10.1093/sf/77.4.1403.

Sapsed, J., Grantham, A. and DeFillippi, R. (2007). 'A bridge over troubled waters: Bridging organisations and entrepreneurial opportunities in emerging sectors', *Research Policy*, vol. 36, no. 9, pp. 1314–1334 [Online]. DOI: 10.1016/j.respol.2007.05.003.

Schmidt, S. and Brinks, V. (2017). 'Open creative labs: Spatial settings at the intersection of communities and organizations', *Creativity and Innovation Management*, vol. 26, no. 3, pp. 291–299 [Online]. DOI: 10.1111/caim.12220.

Schreyögg, G. and Sydow, J. (2010). 'CROSSROADS—Organizing for Fluidity? Dilemmas of New Organizational Forms', *Organization Science*, vol. 21, no. 6, pp. 1251–1262 [Online]. DOI: 10.1287/orsc.1100.0561.

Schreyögg, G. and Sydow, J. (2011). 'Organizational Path Dependence: A Process View', *Organization Studies*, vol. 32, no. 3, pp. 321–335 [Online]. DOI: 10.1177/0170840610397481.

Scott, W. R. (2004). 'Reflections on a Half-Century of Organizational Sociology', *Annual Review of Sociology*, vol. 30, no. 1, pp. 1–21 [Online]. DOI: 10.1146/annurev.soc.30.012703.110644.

Scott, W. R. and Davis, G. F. (2016). *Organizations and organizing: rational, natural and open systems perspectives*, Routledge [Online]. (Accessed 17 April 2016).

Seo-Zindy, R. and Heeks, R. (2017). 'Researching the Emergence of 3D Printing, Makerspaces, Hackerspaces and FabLabs in the Global South: A Scoping Review and Research Agenda on Digital Innovation and Fabrication Networks', *The Electronic Journal of Information Systems in Developing Countries*, vol. 80, no. 0 [Online]. Available at http://www.ejisdc.org/ojs2/index.php/ejisdc/article/view/1902 (Accessed 22 May 2017).

Sherman, H. and Chappell, D. S. (1998). 'Methodological Challenges in Evaluating Business Incubator Outcomes', *Economic Development Quarterly*, vol. 12, no. 4, pp. 313–321 [Online]. DOI: 10.1177/089124249801200403.

Storper, M. and Venables, A. J. (2004). 'Buzz: face-to-face contact and the urban economy', *Journal of Economic Geography*, vol. 4, no. 4, pp. 351–370 [Online]. DOI: 10.1093/jnlecg/lbh027.

Sydow, J., Schreyögg, G. and Koch, J. (2009). 'Organizational Path Dependence: Opening the Black Box', *Academy of Management Review*, vol. 34, no. 4, pp. 689–709.

Thornton, P. H. and Flynn, K. H. (2003). 'Entrepreneurship, Networks, and Geographies', in Acs, Z. J. and Audretsch, D. B. (eds), *Handbook of Entrepreneurship Research*, Kluwer Law International, pp. 401–433.

Toivonen, T. and Friederici, N. (2015). 'Time to define what a "hub" really is', *Stanford Social Innovation Review*, no. Online article [Online]. Available at http://www.ssireview.org/blog/entry/time_to_define_what_a_hub_really_is.

Tran, Y., Hsuan, J. and Mahnke, V. (2011). 'How do innovation intermediaries add value? Insight from new product development in fashion markets', *R&D Management*, vol. 41, no. 1, pp. 80–91 [Online]. DOI: 10.1111/j.1467-9310.2010.00628.x.

Yin, R. K. (2009). *Case study research: Design and methods*, 4th edition. Thousand Oaks, California Sage Publ.

Youtie, J. and Shapira, P. (2008). 'Building an innovation hub: A case study of the transformation of university roles in regional technological and economic development', *Research Policy*, Special Section on University-Industry Linkages: The Significance of Tacit Knowledge and the Role of Intermediaries, vol. 37, no. 8, pp. 1188–1204 [Online]. DOI: 10.1016/j.respol.2008.04.012.

Chapter 28

Exploring Knowledge Intensity in Entrepreneurship: A Quantitative Study of Knowledge, Innovation and Performance in Entrepreneurial Firms

Ethan A. Gifford*

E-mail: ethan.gifford@gu.se

Abstract: Using various quantitative methods, I conceptualize and then operationalize the entrepreneurial firm as consisting of both internal and external knowledge intensity, and that these are related to both to each other as well as to the firm's performance, both operational and economic. My work expands the boundaries of current theory on knowledge intensive entrepreneurship, as well as gives insight to policy makers and practitioners regarding how knowledge intensity in entrepreneurial contexts might be measured, as well as how it can be developed as a useful conceptualization based on firm level resources and capabilities and how they affect performance, and, potentially, economic and societal growth.

Keywords: Knowledge intensive entrepreneurship; innovation; entrepreneurship; firm performance; search; human capital; firm growth; resource-based view.

1. Introduction

For many years now, scholars and policy makers have argued that newly established business ventures should be seen as important engines for growth in modern economies. This is not a statement that provokes much argument in the present day, but this was not always the case. One need only compare our current understanding of economic growth with that which was prominent in the early to mid- 20th century. This was a time when policy makers in capitalist economies were largely content with putting their trust in neoclassical growth theory, something which largely failed to account for the entrepreneur and entrepreneurial activities such as the starting of a new business venture. Though much of the research community in modern economics still ascribes to largely non-dynamic models which exclude the entrepreneur, the view of entrepreneurship as a potential driver of economic growth has changed a great deal. This change in perception is in part thanks to the work done in the fields of evolutionary economics, entrepreneurship studies, and economic geography. Moreover, it is important to remember that how much an economy benefits from new ventures also depends on how these ventures contribute to, and what they provide to society. That is to say, entrepreneurship in and of itself may not be the answer to stimulating economic growth; however, some particular types of entrepreneurship may be better poised to do so. One such newly established typology is knowledge intensive entrepreneurial firms.

This type of firm is posited to actively use or apply novel forms of scientific and technological knowledge in its competitive and remunerative activities. The examples of this type of firm are numerous and quite varied: Corporate spin-off firms radically redeveloping or re-envisioning their parents' technology for new aims; Academic spin-off firms making their first step into a market with new technology based on new scientific developments; a firm providing business and technology services, such as an enterprise resource planning-based application and consultancy, honing and develop new systems and techniques to enhance their clients business and resource management; a new firm involved in food production harnessing new technological breakthroughs in feed and feeding procedures. In summary, the potential KIE firm knows no industrial bounds, which leads many to look at scrutinizing low- and medium-tech industries for knowledge intensive activities. What makes these firms such a driving force in societal development? It may be argued that it is how they harness this knowledge, and this is how this activity drives their growth, survival, and performance, which creates both implicit and explicit benefits for society. Highly knowledge intensive entrepreneurial firms that perform well are likewise assumed to contribute relatively more to society.

This thesis will attempt to clarify the interaction between the different properties possessed by such a firm, and how these properties interact with and influence one another. Simply put, it deals with *to what extent an entrepreneurial firm's knowledge intensity affects how the venture performs, and how different types of knowledge intensity and performance affect one another*, according to different metrics. What is meant by this is that there is not only more work needed in exploring relationships between knowledge intensity and how it affects, or associates with, performance, but that there is also a need to look deeper into the theory and the conceptualization of knowledge intensity, as well as performance itself (in which I include innovation performance) in order to explore the inner workings of the KIE phenomenon, and see what relationships exist both between and within.

This thesis explores the concept of knowledge intensive entrepreneurship (KIE) in Europe and how knowledge intensity and performance in entrepreneurial firms can be related. Knowledge intensive entrepreneurship is modeled as an application of resource-based theory, connecting pre-entry inputs like education and experience to external search activities to innovativeness and firm financial performance, growth, and survival.

2. Background

The link between knowledge and economic growth is one that is now well-established. Much of the literature in the fields of innovation and entrepreneurship has revolved around the impact of individual- and firm-level knowledge on economic growth and technical change in society (cf. Solow, 1957; Nelson and Winter, 1982; Romer, 1990; Metcalfe, 2002). Schumpeter (1934; 1939; 1942) and other growth theorists (cf. Young, 1928; Kuznets, 1954) established a connection between the knowledge resides in innovative firms, the actions of entrepreneurs, and the growth of the modern capitalist economy.

Schumpeterian innovation scholars see entrepreneurs and entrepreneurial ventures as crucial, dynamic, driving forces for economic activity. Despite extensive research over the past decades, how innovative, entrepreneurial firms contribute to economic growth remains a phenomenon that is not completely understood (Block et al., 2016), and a significant area of research and policy still thrives around these and other related issues. In light of this, it is not surprising that in recent years, young, dynamic, high-growth firms have been identified by inter- and non-governmental organizations (and many scholars) as particularly beneficial for economies, accounting for a significant amount of job creation and employment opportunities, not least in developed countries (OECD, 2015). While many have taken this observed phenomenon and tried to classify and understand the types of firms most responsible for growth generation, select research groups have attempted to pin down this typology of a new firm driving economic growth and technical change as being *knowledge intensive* as well as *entrepreneurial* (cf. Malerba et al., 2015).

This research has helped many to realize that knowledge intensity can be a multifaceted construct and that it is not something that only exists in the traditional high-technology industries (Smith, 2002; Hirsch-Kreinsen et al., 2008; Malerba et al., 2015). This notion has traditionally been a common conception within the literature surrounding innovation and entrepreneurship, and as represented in many studies of innovation and change in pharmaceutical, engineering, and other high-tech fields. Potentially manifesting in diverse sectors and activities, knowledge intensive entrepreneurial firms are said to be distinguished by their application of new knowledge or innovation (McKelvey and Lassen, 2013). The way in which one defines this type of firm is crucial for its identification and use in theory, practice and policy making. *The knowledge intensive entrepreneurial venture has been defined by some as a new firm that strategically uses new scientific, technological, or organizational knowledge to reap economic rewards and harness innovative opportunities* (Holmén et al., 2007; Malerba et al., 2015).

There has been a recent upswing in the importance of knowledge intensive entrepreneurship, 'high-potential entrepreneurship' (Delmar and Wennberg, 2010; Autio and Acs, 2007), or innovative or Schumpeterian entrepreneurship (Block et al., 2016). However, despite much theoretical and exploratory work being done to address these related concepts (Malerba, 2010; Malerba et al., 2015), there are still relatively few empirical, in-depth studies on the relationship between knowledge, innovation and performance of the firm.

The main theoretical point of departure is as follows: There is both an internal and an external component to a firm's knowledge intensity. Thus, two working definitions or conceptualizations may be introduced: Internal knowledge intensity: or, *the knowledge intensity that is largely inherent in a firm when it comes into being, rooted in different types of human capital investments and outcomes, as well as other knowledge-based factors have driven the firm to formation;* and external knowledge intensity: or, *the way and extent to which a firm searches out, relies on, and evaluates external knowledge post-formation.* I will go on to explore how these concepts are inter-related empirically, as well as how they affect different outcomes of performance in entrepreneurial firms, which are also inter-related. At the end of the thesis, these two knowledge intensity dimensions will be re-assessed according to the empirical results and discussions, and I will link them to both innovative and economic/business performance. The thesis has the following research objectives:

1. Explore the association between external knowledge intensity and innovative performance in the entrepreneurial firm

2. Explore the association between internal knowledge intensity and external knowledge intensity in the entrepreneurial firm

3. Explore the association between internal knowledge intensity and business performance of the entrepreneurial firm

4. Explore the association between innovative performance and business performance of entrepreneurial firms

One of the key propositions about knowledge intensive entrepreneurship is that the innovativeness of firms should be positively associated with economic growth and performance. In lieu of being able to compare the effects on whole economies, I carry out an investigation looking at whether the innovativeness of entrepreneurial firms is actually positively associated with firm-level growth, volume and performance.

Using these different objectives as a tool to structure the different intra- and inter-relationships between on both knowledge intensity and performance (including both innovation and business performance), I hope to find some confirmation that these relationships are both inter-linked and also influential. This should, in my view, aid in tackling such broad and complex realities as innovativeness, entrepreneurial firms, and the elusive relationship with economic growth and well-being by use of finely-honed research tools.

3. Research design

The data used is quantitative survey data collected during a wide-scale EU financed framework project (FP7 - AEGIS), with additional panel-based firm level data gathering by the author in order to investigate knowledge intensity, innovation, and performance in entrepreneurial firms. The survey response was 4004 firms. This sample was used in 2 of the overarching models. For the third and fourth research objectives, the survey data was combined with firm level registry data from 2010-2015. Both samples cover a broad range of high-tech, medium-tech, low-tech manufacturing firms, as well as business services, as knowledge intensive entrepreneurship may occur in any of these broad sectoral categories (Malerba et al., 2015). See Table 28.1 for a list of included NACE rev 1.1 sectors.

The relationships and associations analyzed are as follows:

- The relationship between external knowledge intensity (operationalized as search for and reliance on external knowledge sources), and innovative performance (operationalized as innovative goods and services proportional to sales and degree of radicalness of said innovations).

- The relationship between internal knowledge intensity (operationalized as pre-entry founder, employee, and organization resources and capabilities) and external knowledge intensity.

- The relationship between internal knowledge intensity and business performance (operationalized as annual number of employees and operating revenue over time, along with likelihood of survival)

- The relationship between innovative performance and business performance

The dissertation employs regression analysis in the form of fractional logit regression to analyze the different effects on innovation performance (a percentage-based variable); ordinary least squares regression models (using principal components as dependent variables) to measure the effects on external knowledge intensity; and generalized estimating equations (GEE) regression to analyze the different effects on business performance (based on size, growth and survival indicators).

Table 28.1 Sectors included in the samples

High-technology manufacturing sectors	NACE rev 1.1
Aerospace	35.3
Computers and office machinery	30
Radio-television and communication	32
Scientific instruments	33
Pharmaceuticals	24.4
Medium-to-high-technology manufacturing sectors	
Electrical machinery	31
Machinery and equipment	29
Chemicals	24 (except 24.4)
Low-to-medium-technology manufacturing sectors	
Wood and furniture	36
Basic metals	27
Fabricated metal products	28
Low-technology manufacturing sectors	
Paper and printing	21, 22
Textiles and clothing	17, 18, 19
Food, beverages, tobacco	15, 16
Knowledge intensive business service sectors	
Telecommunications	64.2
Computer and related activities	72
Research and development	73
Other business service sectors	
Legal/accounting; technical consulting; technical testing; labor recruitment and personnel; misc. business activities	74.1-74.4, 74.5, 74.8

4. Conclusion

Drawing inspiration from the literature on search and innovation (March, 1991; Katila and Ahuja, 2002; Laursen and Salter, 2006; Laursen, 2012), the first model looked at how the concepts of breadth of search and depth of search (in terms of number of different types of external knowledge sources) impact the innovative performance of knowledge intensive entrepreneurial firms, testing for curvilinear relationships. The dissertation then takes the next step by using principal components analysis to capture the specific categories of external knowledge that KIE firms value most, and how these are associated with innovation performance. Results yielded positive associations between the depth of external search with innovative performance and a partial inverse curvilinear association between breadth of external search and innovative performance. Interesting to note here is that for KIE firms, service innovations were not associated with reliance on value chain relationships like clients, customers or suppliers.

The second objective investigated how the internal knowledge intensity of the firm, through the pre-venture history of the founders, functional heterogeneity of founding teams, and human capital of employees, affects how firms search for external knowledge from different types of actors using the principal components derived in model 1 as the response variables. While some partial results were found in that founder experience and employee education seem to be the most important factors driving the importance of external knowledge sources (either specialized knowledge providers (Tether and Tajar, 2008), value chain partners, or publications and trade conferences) for knowledge intensive entrepreneurial firms.

For the third objective, positive yet inversely curvilinear associations between the beneficial aspects of functional heterogeneity of the founding team (in terms of the *knowledge scope* as introduced by Cantner, et al., 2010) with that of financial performance and survival, and negative linear associations between detrimental aspects of functional heterogeneity of the founding team (Cantner et al.'s *knowledge disparity (ibid.)*) with the same response variables.

Finally, concerning the fourth objective, positive associations were identified between the radicalness of innovations produced with that of financial performance over time and with the likelihood of entrepreneurial firm survival.

What can be derived from these results is as follows. The internal knowledge intensity of the entrepreneurial firm can be linked to business performance most clearly through the functional heterogeneity of the founding team, while other concepts like education and work experience of the employees and founders were less robustly linked. This tells us that the composition or the 'sum of all parts' of the interaction between the different founders has a pronounced relationship with how the firm performs over time and whether or not indeed it survives.

While no consistent relationships between internal knowledge intensity and external knowledge intensity were uncovered, many nuanced results were obtained, suggesting that the relationships are more complex and require further consideration and research. The two relationships that were confirmed were those between the education of the employees, as well as experience levels of founders (University, entrepreneurial, and same industry), with that of the business performance of the firm

On the other hand, external knowledge intensity, conceptualized as breadth and depth of search (Laursen and Salter, 2006) of entrepreneurial firms, is clearly associated, in a curvilinearly manner, with the innovative performance for firms in manufacturing industries. However, it is only associated in a linear fashion with the innovative performance of firms in service (KIBS and other) industries. This leads the researcher to conclude that the search dynamics of entrepreneurial firms are different depending on what type of activities are being performed by the firm, although it reinforces the conclusions of Laursen and Salter that search is curvilinearly related to performance in manufacturing activities even for very small firms.

Finally, the degree of radicalness of innovation was positively associated with business performance in entrepreneurial firms in this study. However, there is a high risk associated with this 'beneficial' relationship. Small, young firms that have high knowledge intensity, while having the potential to perform very well in the mid- to long-term, are at great risk, so while the higher the radicalness of innovations, the higher potential success rate, the risk of exit also increases.

So, while much has been uncovered about the relationships between knowledge intensity and performance in entrepreneurial firms by this dissertation, the work is just beginning.

5. Implications and future research

Recommendations for future research include more advanced modeling of complex latent factors constituting different forms of internal and external knowledge intensity, innovativeness, and performance on the part of entrepreneurial firms. Furthermore, drawing more extensively on existing tools such as resource-based theory might prove more enlightening than constructing new concepts and typologies to explain knowledge intensive entrepreneurship. Policy wishing to promote knowledge intensive entrepreneurship may find it beneficial to focus on the educational and experiential underpinnings of creating such firms in diverse industries. This can include low-

and medium-technology industries as well as different types of services, as results hold while controlling for sectoral and country differences.

Practitioners in these types of KIE firms need to expand their own understanding of how these knowledge harnessing and seeking processes take form; human action that may on many levels be unaccounted for or unconscious, in order to better harness their own resources and capabilities to the best effect, to improve their innovative potential, or to understand what drives their competitive advantage as a business. Policy makers need to refine and develop tools for advancing the research on and support of knowledge intensive entrepreneurial firms, as it has been established that blanket funding of sectors of economic activity where some baseline indicator of *knowledge intensity* has not proved very effective or efficient in stimulating growth. A more nuanced picture of which new firms require support and why, in which sectors they might be classified as acting in, and which technological and scientific resources they use and apply. States and NGOs need to become better at dealing with and designing policy measures for firms and industries that have 'high potential.' This can be aided by establishing methods for identifying and explaining activities of knowledge intensive entrepreneurial firms. For scholars, there are numerous critical goals for understanding the new face of entrepreneurship in the knowledge economy. Researchers need to improve how they classify firms and industries in terms of knowledge intensity, and, potentially address the issue that this might not be the most effective way to categorize, splice, and assign meaning and tangibility to progressive entrepreneurial economic activity. Lastly, my own work takes statistical techniques from psychology, political science and other highly quantified disciplines and applies them to innovation and entrepreneurship studies, many of which are in my view underutilized and given the high reliance on surveys and rating scales, deserve greater consideration as valid, reliable and effective research methods.

Knowledge intensive entrepreneurship as a research concept is a challenging one, but it is also a very important one. It is the essence of what many judge to be one of the main explanatory factors of economic change, growth, and well-being in the modern age. I have made some rather large assumptions about the nature of the connection between KIE success and economic development, prosperity, growth and well-being, and chosen to focus on the nature of knowledge intensity itself, and what it might mean if a resource based view is applied. It may be helpful to view it as a problem of resources and output when viewed from a policy standpoint as well, with firms as the population, and some type of natural selection mechanism choosing the winners instead of the nation-states and their policy makers. Providing fertile ground for knowledge intensive entrepreneurship in all types of sectors may be best achieved through broader policy measures than those that are popular at present. The AEGIS project represented an initial explorative venture into the phenomenon of knowledge intensive entrepreneurship, and many lessons have been learned about how this phenomenon might best be approached and grappled with. We have already begun to see an increased focus on prescribing more systemic approaches to fostering economic growth, urging policy makers to take a step back and consider the broad and complex situation involving promoting and retaining knowledge intensive activities. The EU projects AEGIS and KEINS have prescribed much the same medicine, and I can only add my voice to the tumult. Already, though, it seems as though policy is shifting gears towards new concepts: At the time of writing this section, the OECD is shifting to a focus on global productivity, and firms at the global productivity frontier. A paper by Andrews et al. (2015) advocates framework policies to aid productivity diffusion by sharpening incentives for firms to adopt new technologies and the reallocation of resources to more productive firms. These authors lay quite a heavy focus on both turnover as well as patenting stock as indicators of productivity, and the OECD (2015: 7) professes it expects productivity *"to be the main driver of economic growth and well-being over the next 50 years, via investment in innovation and knowledge-based capital."* I view this to be a bit of a misstep, in that productivity concerns were a large driving factor in investigating knowledge intensive activities, and it seems that policy makers may be falling back on a more, for them at least, easily understood characterization of economic growth agents.

It is my sincere hope that this direction does not disregard all that has been learned about knowledge-based, or knowledge-intensive entrepreneurship in the past few years, and that the context that knowledge intensity is made up of more than just education, although this does seem empirically to be one of the more robust components in terms of firm performance. Additional complications may arise due to the decreasing stability of liberal and globalizing economic policies that are occurring at the time of writing. The co-evolution of innovation policy and innovation research has brought about many changes in the way governments, researchers and entrepreneurs interact with science and technology in order to create knowledge in the past decades (Smith, 2005), and for the next step to occur there is a need for clarity of purpose and the ability to act among all involved. Learning to distinguish between different types of knowledge, and different types and degrees of knowledge intensity, is a crucial step in this development. In this respect, a more careful approach focused on the application and use of such knowledge, and how it diffuses in a different context, rather than just an overall motivation or incentive to adopt new technologies for new firms, might be of higher worth.

Hopefully, my work has shown that despite the fact that the EU is made up of diverse countries with differing institutional settings and heritage, and therein diverse sectoral systems, the constructs that I have used to represent knowledge intensive activity, by and large, are at least in some ways consistent across the region, regardless of sector and place. We see differences in magnitude of course, but often the effects are present anyway. Taking an evolutionary perspective, policy makers should be hesitant to 'pick winners' based on sectoral systems or to target entrepreneurial support based on 'knowledge intensity', for it can be seen here that the concept flows into all sectors, in all regions, and it is on average important for new woodworking ventures, logistic service providers, as well as biotech startups. Baseline support like improving educational infrastructure and employability of graduates ought to take priority over tailoring programs to drive up the amount of entrepreneurship. In the Schumpeterian sense, true entrepreneurship involves, by definition, innovation, and by stimulating the base infrastructure on which industries are built instead of existing "high potential" industries, more of this might come into being. From an evolutionary standpoint, the knowledge intensity of the firm is idiosyncratic: A unique combination of resources of capabilities driving firm performance. We need to recognize how complex inter-relationships between sectors and firms bring about societal progress and change from within the business system, and that new knowledge may find its end application in an entirely different context that within which it was devised.

References

Andrews, D., Criscuolo, C. and Gal, P. (2015). 'Frontier firms, technology diffusion and public policy: Micro-evidence from OECD countries'. *OECD Productivity Working Papers*, ISSN 2413-9424.

Autio, E. and Acs, Z.J. (2007). 'Individual and country-level determinants of growth aspiration in new ventures'. In A. Zacharakis (ed.), *Frontiers of Entrepreneurship Research* 2007. Babson Park, MA: Babson College.

Block, J. H., Fisch, C.O. and van Praag, M. (2016). 'The Schumpeterian entrepreneur: a review of the empirical evidence on the antecendents, behaviour, and consequences of innovative entrepreneurship'. *Industry and Innovation*, advance view.

Cantner, U., Goethner, M. and Stuetzer, M. (2010). Disentangling the effects of new venture team functional heterogeneity on new venture performance. Jena economic research papers, N 2010, 029, Max Planck Institute of Economics.

Delmar, F. and Wennberg, K. (2010). *Knowledge Intensive Entrepreneurship: The Birth, Growth and Demise of Entrepreneurial Firms*, Cheltenham, UK: Edward Elgar Publishing.

Hirsch-Kreinsen, H. and Jacobson, D. (eds.) (2008) *Innovation in Low-Tech Firms and Industries*, Cheltenham, UK; Northampton, MA, USA: Edward Elgar.

Holmén, M., Magnusson, M. and McKelvey, M. (2007). 'What are innovative opportunities?' *Industry and Innovation*, 14(1), pp. 27-45.

Kuznets, S. (1954). *Economic Change*, Heinermann: London.

Laursen, K. and Salter, A. (2006). 'Open for innovation: the role of openness in explaining innovation performance among UK manufacturing firms'. *Strategic Management Journal*, 27(2), pp. 131-150.

Laursen, K. (2012).' Keep searching and you'll find: what do we know about variety creation through firms' search activities for innovation?' *Industrial and Corporate Change*, 21(5), pp. 1181-1220.

Malerba, F. (2010). 'Knowledge-intensive entrepreneurship and innovation systems in Europe', in Malerba, F. (ed.) *Knowledge-Intensive Entrepreneurship and Innovation Systems: Evidence from Europe*, Abington, New York: Routledge.

Malerba, F., Caloghirou, Y., McKelvey, M. and Radosevic, S. (Eds.) (2015). *Dynamics of knowledge intensive entrepreneurship: Business strategy and public policy*. UK: Routledge.

March, J. G. (1991).' Exploration and exploitation in organizational learning'. *Organization Science*, 2(1), pp. 71-87.

Metcalfe, J.S. (2002).' Knowledge of growth and the growth of knowledge'. *Journal of Evolutionary Economics*, 12, pp. 3-15.

Nelson, R. R. and Winter, S. (1982). *An Evolutionary Theory of Economic Change*, Cambridge, MA: Harvard University Press.

OECD (2015). *The Future of Productivity*, OECD Publishing: Paris.

Romer, P.M. (1990). 'Endogenous Technical Change'. *The Journal of Political Economy*, 98(5): pp. S71-S110.

Schumpeter, J. (1934). *The Theory of Economic Development*, Cambridge, MA: Harvard University Press.

Schumpeter, J.A. (1939). *Business Cycles*, Volumes 1 and 2, New York: McGraw-Hill.

Schumpeter, J. (1942). *Capitalism, Socialism, and Democracy*, New York, NY: Harper & Row.

Smith, K.H. (2002). What is the 'Knowledge Economy'? Knowledge intensity and distributed knowledge bases. *Discussion Paper. United Nations University*, Institute for New Technologies, Maastricht, The Netherlands.

Smith, K. (2005). 'Changing economic landscapes: liberalisation and knowledge infrastructure's. *Changing environments*, 32(5), pp. 339-347.

Solow, R. M. (1957). 'Technical Change and the Aggregate Production Function'. *The Review of Economics and Statistics*, 39(3), pp. 312-320.

Tether, B. S. and Tajar, A. (2008). 'Beyond industry–university links: Sourcing knowledge for innovation from consultants, private research organisations and the public science-base'. *Research Policy*, 37(6), pp. 1079-1095.

Young, A. A. (1928). 'Increasing returns and economic progress'. *Economic Journal*, 38, pp. 527-542.

Acronyms

ABM	Architectural BM
AMO	Ability-Motivation-Opportunity
AUTM	Association of University Technology Managers
BTF	Behavioral Theory of the Firm
BM	Business Model
BMC	Business Model Canvas
BMF	Business Model for a flourishing future
CEO	Chief Executive Officer
CFAT	Carnegie Foundation for the Advancement of Teaching
CPD	Collaborative Product Development
CSN	Corporate Social Network
CSR	Corporate Social Responsibility
CVC	Corporate Venture Capital
DS	Design Science
DSRM	Design Science Research Methodology
FDI	Foreign Direct Investment
FEI	Front End of Innovation
FP	Financial Performance
fsQCA	fuzzy set Qualitative Comparative Analysis
GDP	Gross domestic product
GEE	Generalized Estimating Equations
HRM	Human Resource Management
HRO	High Reliability Organisations
IAOIP	International Association of Innovation Professionals
IB	International Business
ICT	Information and Communication Technology
IMS	Ideas and Innovation Management Systems
IP	Innovation Performance
IPO	Intellectual Property Office
IR	Investor Relations
IRB	Innovation Resilient Behavior
IWB	Innovative Work Behaviors
KET	Key Enabling Technology
KIE	Knowledge Intensive Entrepreneurship
KM	Knowledge Management
LDA	Latent Dirichlet Allocation
LDC	Least Developed Countries

LGT   Local Growth Teams
LLL   Linkage-Leverage-Learning
MBA   Master of Business Administration
MIT   Massachusetts Institute of Technology
MNC   Multinational corporation
MNE   Multinational Enterprises
NACE   Nomenclature of Economic Activities
NPD   New Product Development
OECD   The Organisation for Economic Co-operation and Development
OI   Open Innovation
OIPT   Organizational Information Processing Theory
PhD   Philosophiae doctor, Doctor of Philosophy
PKT   Procedural Knowledge Transparency
QCA   Qualitative Content Analysis
R&D   Research and Development
RIO   Research Innovation Office
ROI   Return Of Investment
RRBV   Relational Resource-Based View
SAIMM   Southern African Institute of Mining and Metallurgy
SHP   Small Hydro Power
SDT   Self-Determination Theory
SDU   Sustainable Development Unit
SEM   Structural Equation Modelling
SLR   Systematic Literature Review
SSM   Soft Systems Methodology
TRL   Technological Readiness Levels
TTO   Technology Transfer Office
UIC   University Industry collaboration
UTTO   University Technology Transfer Officer
VBM   Value Business Model

Index

A

Absorptive Capacity, 37, 273
Accelerated Product Innovation, 175
Action Research, 235
active resistance, 365
Adoption, 205
Africa, 435
Ambidexterity, 391
anger, 365
Applied Research, 403
Appropriability, 37
assembly, 435
Austrian economics, 379
awareness-motivation-capability framework, 163

B

Basic Research, 403
Bayesian Estimation, 273
Behavioral Theory of the Firm, 391
Big Data, 175
Brazil, 273
bridging features, 19
Business Model, 219, 235

C

Case Study, 175
Case study research, 115
chains, 19
champion of innovation, 129
China, 303
Chinese Companies, 175
Cognition, 235

Collaboration, xi, 205
Collaboration Capability, 37
collaboration performance, 191
Collaborative product development, 191
commercialization, 417
Compatibility, 37
Complementarity, 37
Complexity Theory, 323
consumer emotion, 365
consumer resistance, 365
context and innovation, 129
Continuous Performance Improvement, 323
coopetition, 163
Corporate Foresight, 149
Corporate Governance, 391
Corporate Social Networks, 205
Corporate Venture Capital, 391
CPD performance, 191
creativity, xi, 379
Creativity-based Experience, 323
Criteria, 349

D

Data Analytics, 175
Decision-making, 349
Design, 235
Design Science Research, 149
digital innovation, 163
Digitalization, xii
Discoveries, 403
disruptive innovation, 163

E

Early Stages of Product
  Innovation, 149
ecosystem, 55
Electric Vehicle, 219
Electric Vehicle Charging, 219
Emergence, 323
Emerging Economies, 115
Employee creativity, 97
Employment, 303
Enterprise Social Networks, 205
entrepreneurial beliefs, 379
entrepreneurial communities, 435
entrepreneurial ecosystems, 435
Entrepreneurial Firms, 455
entrepreneurial networking, 435
Entrepreneurial opportunity, 379
entrepreneurship, 455
Europe, 273
Exploitation, 391
Exploration, 391
External R&D, 273

F

FDI, 303
fear, 365
Federal Funding, 403
Financial Performance, 273
firm growth, 455
firm performance, 455
Flourishing Business Models, 235
Framework Development, 175
frequency, 191
Front End of Innovation, 149
Front-End Innovation, 349
frugal innovation, 69

G

Game storming, 235

Globalization, xii
Grid Modernization, 219

H

Healthcare, 417
Hierarchical Decision Modeling,
  37
HRM practices, 97
HRO, 1
human capital, 455

I

ICT impact, 191
Idea Assessment, 349
Idea Evaluation, 349
Idea Management, 323, 349
Idea Screening, 349
incentives, 249
inclusive globalization, 249
incubation, 435
indirect relationships, 19
Industrial Funding, 403
innovation, 1, 19, 205, 303, 349,
  379, 455
innovation adoption, 365
innovation champion, 129
innovation diffusion, 365
innovation hubs, 435
innovation intermediaries, 435
Innovation Interoperability, 323
Innovation Management, 115,
  149, 205, 287, 379, 417
Innovation Performance, 273, 323
Innovation Phases, 175
Innovation Process Model, 149
innovation resistance, 365
Innovation Structuration, 323
innovation teams, 379
innovative work behavior, 97
Intellectual Property, 303

intensity, 191
Interaction Effect, 403
Internal R&D, 273
inter-organizational
   collaboration, 55
Intuition, 349
Investing, 391

J

job characteristics, 97

K

KETs, 417
Knowledge Dynamics, 323
Knowledge intensive
   entrepreneurship, 455
Knowledge Management, 323
Knowledge Sharing, 205

L

leadership and supervisory
   behaviors, 97
learning asymmetry, 379
learning style, 379
Licences, 403
locations, 249

M

Macrocognition, 235
Management, xii
manufacturing, 191
Manufacturing Firms, 191, 273
Matching Quality, 37
Materiality, 235
mindfulness, 1
mixed method, 163
Mobile Learning, 235
Modern Organization, 323
Multinationals, 287

music industry, 163

N

Nanotechnologies, 303
nanotechnology, 417
negative emotion, 365
networks, 249
New Capability Creation, 115
New Product Development, 175
nonprofit innovation, 129
nonprofit sector, 129

O

Ontology, 323
open innovation, 19, 37, 55
opportunity perception, 379
opportunity recognition, 163
Organizational Communication,
   205
organizational identity, 163
organizational information
   processing theory, 191
organizational responses, 163

P

Partnership, 37
Patents, 303, 403
Procedural Knowledge
   Transparency, 205
Process Model Development, 149
proficiency, 191
project management, 1
psychological attributes, 97
Public and Private Investments,
   303

R

R&D, 403
R&D "going out" strategy, 249

R&D globalization, 249
R&D investment, 303
R&D organizational
    configurations, 249
Rationality, 349
Regional Development, 303
regional ecosystem, 55
Regional Innovation System, 303
Regional Policies, 303
relational resource-based view,
    191
resilience, 1
resistance leader, 365
resource-based view, 455
Resource-scarce environments,
    115
Reverse Innovation, 287

S

search, 455
Semantic Web, 323
Sensemaking, 205
Smart Grid, 219
SMEs, 55
social capital, 19
social enterprises, 69
social innovation, 69
social sustainability, 69
socially driven business, 69
socially driven innovation, 69
Strategic Alliances, 273
Strategic Innovation
    Management, 149

Strategic Issue Management, 149
Structural Equation Modelling,
    273
supporting features, 19
sustainability, 69, 235
sustainable business, 69
sustainable development, 69

T

team creativity, 97
teams, 1
technological diversity, 417
technology & innovation
    management, 163
technology entrepreneurs, 435
Technology Planning, 219
Technology Roadmapping, 219
technology transfer, xiii, 417
Transactive Energy, 219
Transformational Leadership, 37
Transparency, 205
Transportation Electrification, 219
trusted bridging chains, 19

U

University Technology Transfer,
    403
University-Industry Collaboration,
    37
Utility Planning, 219

Lightning Source UK Ltd.
Milton Keynes UK
UKHW020644260722
406393UK00009B/1014